WINSTON CHURCHILL

STUDIES
IN
STATESMANSHIP

WINSTON CHURCHILL

STUDIES IN STATESMANSHIP

Edited by
RAC PARKER

in association with
CORRELLI BARNETT

and
CHURCHILL COLLEGE, CAMBRIDGE

BRASSEY'S

First published in 1995
This expanded paperback edition 2002

UK editorial offices:
Brassey's, 9 Blenheim Court, Brewery Road, London, N7 9NT
UK orders:
Littlehampton Book Services,
10–14 Eldon Way, Littlehampton BN17 7HE
North American Orders:
Brassey's Inc, PO Box 960, Herndon, VA 22070, USA

A member of **Chrysalis** Books plc

RAC Parker has asserted his moral right to be identified as
editor of this work.

Library of Congress Cataloguing in Publication Data
available

British Library Cataloguing in Publication Data
A catalogue record for this book is available
from the British Library

ISBN 1 85753 351 8

Printed in Great Britain by Bookcraft Ltd

Contents

List of Plates

Acknowledgements

The contributors to this book presented their essays to a conference in Cambridge. Correlli Barnett, the Keeper of the Churchill Archives Centre at Churchill College, Cambridge, invited them and other experts from Europe and America. Josephine Sykes of the Archives Centre played an essential part in the organisation of this international meeting. Subsequently her help was indispensible in making this book. Janette Swaine, secretary at Queen's College, Oxford, contributed invaluable assistance. Brassey's did the rest under the skilled supervision of Jenny Shaw and Sharon Van Der Merwe. I am grateful to them all.

ALISTAIR PARKER
Oxford

Contributors to this book

(RAC) Alastair Parker is a Fellow of The Queen's College, Oxford. He has written *Struggle for Survival. The History of the Second World War* (Oxford University Press, 1989) and *Chamberlain and Appeasement* (Macmillan, 1993). He hopes to write a book on *Churchill and Appeasement*.

Mary Soames is the youngest daughter of Sir Winston Churchill. She was on active service in the Second World War. She has written *Clementine Churchill* (Cassell, 1979; Penguin Books, 1981) and *Winston Churchill: His Life as a Painter* (Collins, 1990).

Jon Sumida is a Professor at the University of Maryland. He is the author of *In Defence of Naval Supremacy: Finance, Technology and British Naval Policy 1889–1914* (Unwin Hyman, 1989; paperback Routledge, 1993). He is writing *The Neptune Factor: Navies and Naval Power, 1889–1989*, to be published by Routledge.

Phillips O'Brien is a Fellow of Pembroke College, Cambridge. He is writing a book studying the politics and perceptions that shaped American and British naval policy between 1900 and 1939. This will be published in 1996.

Brian McKercher is a Professor of History at the Royal Military College of Canada. His recent publications include *Esme Howard. A Diplomatic Biography* (Cambridge University Press, 1989) and, with AH Ion, *Military Heretics. The Unorthodox in Policy and Strategy* (Praeger, 1993).

Paolo Pombeni is a Professor at Bologna University. His most recent books are *Partiti e sistemi politici nella storia contemporanea (1830–1968)* (1994) and *Il costituente. Un problema storico-politico* (1995) published by Il Mulino.

Bernd Martin is a Professor of Modern History at the University of Freiburg im Breisgau. He has published *Friedensinitiativen und Machtpolitik im Zweiten Weltkrieg* (Düsseldorf, Droste Verlag, 2nd ed., 1976), *Weltmacht oder Niedergang? Deutsche Großmachtpolitik im 20 Jahrhundert* (Darmstadt, Wissenschaftliche Buchgesellschaft, 1989) and *Japan and Germany in the Modern World. A Collection of Essays* (Oxford, Berg Publishers, 1995).

Tage Kaarsted was a Professor of Modern History at Odense University until his death in 1994. His publications included *Storbritannien og Danmark 1914–20* (1974) translated as *Great Britain and Denmark* (1979), and two volumes on *De Danske Ministerier 1929–53* and *1953–72* (1977 and 1992). These books were published by Odense University Press.

Anita Prażmowska is a Lecturer in East European history at the London School of Economics. Cambridge University Press has published her two latest books, *Britain, Poland and the Eastern Front* (1987) and *Britain and Poland 1939–43. The Betrayed Ally* (1955). Her next book will be on *The 'Polish Question' in the Twentieth Century*.

François Kersaudy is a Professor at the University of Paris I, Panthéon-Sorbonne. He has published *Churchill and de Gaulle* (Collins, 1981; Fontana, 1990) and *Norway 1940* (Collins, 1990).

Warren Kimball is a Professor at Rutgers University. He has written *The Juggler: Franklin Roosevelt as Wartime Statesman* (Princeton University Press, 1991) and edited, with David Reynolds and AO Chubarian, *Allies at War: The Soviet, American and British Experience, 1939–45* (St Martin's Press, New York, 1994).

Ritchie Ovendale is a Professor at the University of Wales, Aberystwyth. He has published *The Longman Companion to the Middle East Since 1914* (Longman, 1992) and edited *British Defence Policy Since 1945* (Manchester University Press, 1994). He is writing a book on *Britain, The United States and the Transfer of Power in the Middle East, 1945–62* to be published by Leicester University Press.

Maurice Vaïsse is a Professor at the University of Reims and Director of the Centre d'Etudes d'Histoire de la Défense. He has published *Diplomatie et Outil Militaire* (Seuil, Paris, 1992) *Les Relations Internationales Depuis 1945* (3rd edn, Armand Colin, Paris, 1994) and *La Victoire en Europe, le 8 mai 1945* (Complexe, Paris, 1995).

Hans-Peter Schwarz is a Professor at Bonn University. He is the author of the two-volume life of Adenauer, *Adenauer. Der Aufsteig 1876–1952* (1986) and *Adenauer. Der Staatsmann 1952–1967* (1991) published by Deutsche Verlags-Anstalt in Stuttgart.

Wolfgang Krieger is a Professor at Munich University. He has edited, with Simon Duke, *US Military Forces in Europe: The Early Years 1945–70* (Western Press, Boulder, CO, 1993) and written on 'Germany' in David Reynolds (ed) *The Origins of Cold War Europe* (Yale University Press, 1994).

Martin Gilbert is a Fellow of Merton College, Oxford. He is the author of six volumes of the Churchill biography and ten ancillary volumes of documents, the most recent of which are *At the Admiralty, September 1939 to May 1940* (Heinemann UK, Norton USA, 1993) and *Never Surrender, May–December 1940* (Heinemann UK, Norton USA, 1995). He is at present working on the 1941 volume, *The Ever-Widening War.*

Correlli Barnett was keeper of the Churchill Archives Centre from 1977 to 1995 and remains a Fellow of Churchill College. His works of history include *The Audit of War* (1986), *Engage the Enemy More Closely: the Royal Navy in the Second World War* (1991), and most recently, *The Verdict of Peace: Britain Between Her Yesterday and the Future.* He was appointed a CBE in 1997.

Foreword to the New Edition

CORRELLI BARNETT

This volume is now even more essential to our full understanding of Winston Churchill than when first published in 1995. For as the tragic conflicts of the twentieth century recede further into history they paradoxically exert a growing fascination, evidenced by the spate of new books, feature films, and television documentaries. The focus of this fascination lies in the four national leaders who shaped the outcome of the Second World War: Hitler, Stalin, Roosevelt — and Churchill, the Englishman who in the heroic summer of 1940 saved the cause of liberty by his sheer fighting spirit.

Today the War Rooms under 'the Citadel' in Whitehall whence Churchill conducted Britain's eventually victorious struggle have become a major tourist attraction. His vast collection of papers in the Churchill Archives Centre in Cambridge are studied by more and more scholars and interested members of the public. New histories of the Second World War continue to appear, each necessarily involving a re-evaluation of Churchill's central role both in allied grand strategy and in specific campaigns such as the Bomber Offensive and the Battle of the Atlantic. Meanwhile Winston Churchill himself remains the subject of biography after biography, some judicious and insightful, some glibly hostile (revealing more about their authors than about Churchill).

Yet for the most part the war histories and the Churchillian biographies share a common characteristic in being written by English-speaking authors and from a primarily Anglo-American viewpoint. It is therefore the strength of *Winston Churchill: Studies in Statesmanship* that its ranges of topic and authorship alike reflects a wide international perspective. While the British, American, and Canadian contributors re-assess Churchill's approach to such questions as seapower or the 'Special Relationship', distinguished historians from France, Germany, Poland, Denmark, and Italy cast new light on Churchill's policies towards their own countries before, during, and after the Second World War.

And because British opinion today is still deeply divided over the closer integration of the European Union, the analyses in this book of Churchill's evolving attitudes to the future development of European political institutions remain of particular relevance.

CORRELLI BARNETT
Churchill College, Cambridge
January 2002

Introduction

ALASTAIR PARKER

This book begins and ends with two specially valuable essays. The first is from Churchill's daughter; the second from Churchill's biographer. From her father, Lady Soames inherits personal charm and literary skill. In her essay she signals, as no-one else can do, the power and vigour of Sir Winston, qualities enduring to the end of his last period as Prime Minister.

In 1954, one year after a severe stroke, Churchill contributed to stifling a crisis with an elegantly expressed display of perceptive understanding, which, at the end of the century, like many of the records of Churchill, is even more impressive with hindsight. France, facing catastrophic defeat in Vietnam at Dien Bien Phu, asked the United States to attack their Vietminh opponents. Air strikes should be enough, if the Chinese air force helped the Vietminh's bases could be destroyed. The United States service chiefs thought the West had a military superiority in the Far East which would go after a few years. Better to risk war with China and its then ally, the USSR, now than later. This was a moment to roll back the tide of Communist advance. President Eisenhower declared that Congress would insist on allied support, which, in practice, meant the British. British ministers had two emergency meetings on Sunday 25 April 1954 to contemplate the Third World War. Next day, Admiral Radford, the chairman of the US Joint Chiefs of Staff, spoke to the British heads of the armed forces and dined that evening with Sir Winston.

It was a small party: the Prime Minister, Admiral Radford, Captain George Anderson of the US Navy, and Jock Colville, Sir Winston's trusted secretary. Churchill, as usual, dominated. He pointed out to the Admiral that US bases in East Anglia would be prime targets in nuclear war. Returning to Vietnam, he impressed on Radford 'the danger of war on the fringes' where the enemy could 'mobilise the enthusiasm of nationalist and oppressed peoples'. Eisenhower held back; how much wiser Kennedy and Lyndon Johnson would have been to do the same.

By force of personality, energy and ability, Churchill influenced every part of British political life in the first half of the twentieth century. In one of the greatest and most important undertakings in British historical publication in this century, Martin Gilbert has devoted his life to a mighty biography of Churchill, backed by a continuing series of documentary volumes. There is no parallel in Britain except the Gladstone diaries; in the United States Arthur Link's work on Woodrow Wilson is on the same magnificent scale, with, some may feel, a less enjoyable subject. Martin Gilbert's study in this book suggests Churchill's range. His great biography documents it.

Vitality and vigour backed skill in writing to pay for Churchill's extravagant, self-indulgent, generous life which helped to win political office which, in return, provided subjects for books and journalism and publicity to help sales and boost his fees. His energy made Churchill noticed whatever he did. He had that charm which can go with total self-absorption. His preoccupations and interests dominated his mind, and he took for granted that they must dominate everyone else's. The result was a communicative directness and openness in manner, which could win admiration, especially from those more inclined to self-effacement.

In August 1935, G D Birla, an Indian nationalist and a close associate of Mahatma Gandhi, visited Britain. He was a rich industrialist, the sort of Indian that Churchill claimed to oppose. Birla wrote to Gandhi:

> Curiously enough, one of my most pleasant experiences was meeting Mr Winston Churchill . . . a most remarkable man. As eloquent in private talk as he is in public speech. It is impossible to reproduce the talk in writing . . . he did 75 per cent of the talking . . . it was never boring.

Churchill, though sometimes appalling, was always fun. A back-bench MP summed it up in the House of Commons at a moment when Churchill was allegedly a 'failure' in a 'wilderness':

> Whenever he makes a speech, whenever he writes a book, and, I am told, whenever he paints a picture, he is always able to produce a work of art, and not infrequently a masterpiece.

Churchill's agreeable and talented paintings were done for love not for money or power – though they earned an income in the end.

This book draws three essential conclusions about Churchill's career. First, he worked to keep Britain independent of foreign interference; it is not true that he ever forgot this overriding purpose. He never allowed the preoccupations of the government departments he headed to obscure this aim. Second, he sought full independence for Britain: to avoid any reliance on foreigners. It is not true that an American mother, his alleged 'deep love of France', or his 'passionate concern for Empire' prevented rational calculation in practice, whatever the rhetorical requirements of the moment might demand. Third, when the relative decline of Britain's resources made full independence unattainable, he sought, flexibly and without prejudice, for allies.

In short, this book suggests Churchillian prose concealed a sharp, flexible and quick intellect unencumbered by prejudices, in practice, if not in words, or indeed by abstract principles. His 'Victorian' attitudes were standard amongst the British governing class. Neville Chamberlain, Stanley Baldwin, even that later recruit Ramsay MacDonald, all believed in naval supremacy, the Empire, British independence and the need to do something to soften the sufferings of poverty and deprivation. They all believed in British superiority.

Churchill was a minister of Cabinet rank from 1908 to 1915; from 1917 to 1922; from 1924 to 1929, and 1939 to 1940; then Prime Minister from 1940–1945 and from 1951–1955. Three interruptions broke his rise: the failure of the Dardanelles operation in 1915, though his responsibility was limited; the fall of the Lloyd George coalition in 1922, and the formation of the 'National' government under Ramsay MacDonald in 1931. Lloyd George rescued him in 1917 but in 1922 Bonar Law and Stanley Baldwin detached the Conservative Party from the Lloyd George Liberals. Churchill found the disjointed Liberal Party an unsatisfactory means for renewed power; Baldwin was delighted to separate Churchill from Lloyd George and any coalition he might try to revive. He brought Churchill into the Conservative Cabinet in 1924 as Chancellor of the Exchequer, restoring his chances of becoming a possible future Prime Minister. After Baldwin's defeat in 1929, however, Churchill soon directly challenged his leadership of the Conservative Party. From 1930 to 1935 the future of India took first place in his political activity, and he became the standard-bearer of the right wing of the Conservative Party. This revolt against the Party was a great success, with sometimes more than 80 Conservative MPs voting against Party policy. It was all rendered pointless by the unexpected phenomenon of the coalition with some Labour ministers and some Liberals under MacDonald until 1935, and under Baldwin until 1937.

MacDonald did not wish to strengthen the Conservative right, and for him Churchill's stance had no appeal; Baldwin, though concealing his feelings under his customary affectation of affability, cannot have felt Churchill to be a reliable supporter. When Baldwin again became Prime Minister he kept Churchill out, in spite of Churchill's efforts to rejoin the government, and did his best to establish Neville Chamberlain as his successor. Chamberlain, as Chancellor of the Exchequer in the 1930s, presided over a fortunate period in economic history: the devaluation of 1931 helped British exports, and low commodity prices further improved the balance of payments and kept prices down. Low interest rates stimulated investment in modern industry and encouraged cheap housing. By 1937 when Chamberlain became Prime Minister recovery had generated growing prosperity, at least in southern England. He could keep Churchill out to avoid a rival Prime Minister, who would dominate the Cabinet. Soon Chamberlain had other reasons: he kept Churchill out because they disagreed. Chamberlain believed that the Second World War could be prevented by finding out what Hitler wanted, and helping him to get it. Churchill insisted that Hitler had to be confronted by a grand alliance; Chamberlain thought that would make war certain.

In the end, Churchill was proved right. As a result, and because of his successful defiance of Hitler in 1940, the legend grew of his unique insight. The essays in this book are comments on the legend that he was always right. Jon Sumida and Phillips O'Brien make a case for Churchill as a rational and effective defender of the Royal Navy whose power was the mainstay of British independence. They reject the notion that Churchill supported the Navy only when he was its responsible minister. Sumida shows the lasting influence of Jacky Fisher who brought Churchill to believe that the line of battle was irrelevant to British needs. Flotillas, especially submarines, would prevent enemy control of the waters around the British Isles; in the rest of the world, fast, long-range vessels were needed: battlecruisers and cruisers. Phillips O'Brien shows that Churchill, as Chancellor of the Exchequer in the 1920s, strenuously objected to the renunciation of British naval supremacy. He denounced American claims to naval equality. He asserted that Britain should resist American domination. Churchill wanted independence. O'Brien explains how Churchill's open pursuit of his aims could make their attainment more difficult; he did not share the bland deviousness of Stanley Baldwin.

For Brian McKercher, Churchill's hostility to the United States grew after 1918, and was at its height in the 1920s. He believes that Churchill, whatever his rhetoric, carefully calculated his handling of the outside world. The rise of Nazi Germany in the 1930s caused Churchill to reassess the effect of the power of the United States on British interests. Those interests meant world trade and the Empire: an Empire thought of as bringing influence, power and wealth to Britain. When necessary, and only when necessary, Churchill looked for support for Britain from a European balance of power to check possible threats to British interests. Whatever his literary sentiments, Churchill was a flexible realist.

Unlike Americans, the British were never eager exporters of 'democracy'. Foreigners, after all, could be expected to be quarrelsome, impractical and inept, or corrupt or inclined to crave for order and discipline. Paolo Pombeni documents the casual approval that Churchill gave to Mussolini's unsavoury and disastrous regime; Churchill's wife Clementine, as so often, showed more sensitivity.

Denmark, Churchill hardly noticed, except as somewhere on the way to the Baltic Sea; though he took steps in 1945, successfully, to help Denmark to escape Soviet occupation. Probably Stalin had, in any case, assigned Denmark to western influence. Tage Kaarsted's article demonstrates that the Danes noticed Churchill. They thought he was the leader, the symbol, the person most responsible for effective resistance to Nazi Germany.

They did not agree with Bernd Martin, author of the most controversial essay in this book. They thought Britain's decision to fight on in 1940 mattered. It may be suggested, tentatively, that they were right. The decision made more sense militarily than Martin suggests. An opposed landing on the English coast was impossible unless the British navy could be kept away, not merely for the first days, but for whatever period was required to make the German landing-force self-sufficient. The navy was even stronger than before, compared with the German, after the Norwegian campaign . Only the German air force could even hope to counter overwhelming British supremacy at sea. The RAF had been given priority in British rearmament before the war; a small well-trained élite of fighter pilots proved its competence over Dunkirk. It should be able to deny to the Germans mastery of the air over the waters around the United Kingdom.

Of course, as Bernd Martin points out, American economic and financial support was indispensable. The military power of the Third Reich compelled Britain to choose between dependence on the United States or on Hitler's Germany. The choice of the United States was obvious. The British, and Churchill, would have much preferred total independence; dependence on an American ally was clearly the next best thing. Arguably, the threat to British interests in the 1930s, presented by the United States, was bearable, though the suggestion put forward by Bernd Martin of growing economic rivalry has been widely supported. Still, he exaggerates, it may be suspected, the expansionist impulses of Presidents Harding, Coolidge, Hoover and Roosevelt. US policy was perhaps more a matter of seeking to be left alone. Certainly, if there were an American threat it did not cause British ministers in the 1930s to accept German domination in Europe: the object of Chamberlain's appeasement was to persuade Hitler and the Third Reich to turn peaceful and disarm, so that it was a policy designed to protect British independence, not to give it up. The same applies even to the would-be appeasers Martin cites, in the summer of 1939.

American help to Britain mattered. The 50 over-age destroyers of 1940 needed refitting and repair, but were useful in the decisive battles of the Atlantic in 1941. Roosevelt, indeed, took a series of valuable measures to help the British to defeat German U-boats. President Roosevelt and his advisers thought British survival a condition of successful resistance to the Nazis in any foreseeable future. Only with the United Kingdom as a well-equipped, secure and conveniently situated base, could American power effectively be brought to bear on the other side of the Atlantic. As a result, British resistance in 1940 shortened the period of Nazi control of Europe and reduced the extent of post-war Soviet influence. The United Kingdom also made a direct and significant military contribution.

It is certainly true that British and American authors, especially Churchill himself, have been reluctant to discuss the strong influences favouring a peace attempt of some sort in 1940. Halifax, the Foreign Secretary, wanted to find out German 'terms' at the end of May 1940 – but the context was a request from the French to help to stave off an Italian declaration of war. Unlike Churchill, Halifax seems to have found it hard to understand that once a government is known to be considering surrender, it becomes impossible to rally the people to a continued war. Soundings in Sweden and Switzerland may possibly have been tolerated by Churchill: it was helpful to induce Hitler to believe that Britain need not be attacked at all. But it is much more likely that R A Butler, then Under-Secretary for Foreign Affairs and apparently responsible for peace soundings, was protected by Halifax, rather than encouraged by Churchill. The diary entry cited by Martin of Sir Alexander Cadogan, the Permanent Secretary, seems to refer to the conditions for the French armistice and not to any British proposal. Churchill's wish to have Lloyd George in the government was probably intended to broaden the coalition and to win Lloyd George's support, rather than to imply any readiness to prepare for peace-making.

Certainly, Churchill viewed the scene in the summer of 1945 without wholehearted satisfaction. But he, and the British population, took pride in what they thought to be their achievements. And during Churchill's wartime Prime Ministership the British people became a coherent community to an extent unequalled before or since.

François Kersaudy's account of Churchill's uncertain and variable relations with de Gaulle shows him torn between his desire to avoid differences with Roosevelt and the fact, stressed by Eden and the Foreign Office, that de Gaulle more and more had the support of the French people as they became disillusioned with the Vichy government and its collaboration with the Germans. He represented the most promising non-Communist leader of a country whose future vitally concerned the United Kingdom. The future of Yugoslavia mattered less and, moreover, the evidence that the Cetnik leader, Mihailovic, was avoiding conflict with the axis forces to preserve his strength for a post-war struggle with Tito may have been stronger than François Kersaudy allows in his attack on Churchill's insensitivity to foreign friends.

Anita Prażmowska and Warren Kimball, from different sides of the Atlantic, answer a fundamental question about Churchill: when, if ever, did he become a cold warrior, determined to limit or roll back the gains in influence and territory secured by Stalin. They show that Churchill hoped, and expected, well into 1945, to receive co-operation from Stalin in keeping the world peaceful after the Second World War. Churchill inclined to partition and thought that countries adjacent to the USSR should have governments amenable to Moscow. Stalin, on his side, was perhaps encouraged by the effective Anglo-American exclusion of Soviet influence in Italy to suppose that Churchill and Roosevelt would not object, in practice if not in theory, to Soviet dictation in eastern Europe.

For the British, the future of Poland counted most. The war began with the German attack on Poland which brought Britain into conflict. Polish soldiers, airmen and sailors came to Britain after the fall of France, and in London an exiled Polish government established itself with real support at home. Anita Prażmowska illustrates Sikorski's friendly relations with Churchill but describes Sikorski's realistic understanding that Poland counted for less than good relations with the Soviet Union, whether to keep Stalin in the war or win his co-operation after it. Warren Kimball makes clear that Churchill's later claims to have tried to restrain Roosevelt from concession to Stalin are unfounded. Churchill's desire to contain and confront the USSR came only intermittently in 1945 at the end of Roosevelt's life.

Four of the closing essays in this book deal with Churchill's second period as Prime Minister. A bleak farce overhung his Cabinet. From early

1952 Churchill repeatedly promised to retire soon and hand over to Anthony Eden. Repeatedly, he found cause to stay. Both Churchill and Eden succumbed to serious illnesses. Eden, racked by illness, showed impatience and dismay as Churchill remained in office. As late as 29 March 1955, with his departure fixed for 5 April, Churchill decided, for a moment, that he should not go 'just to satisfy Anthony's personal hunger for power'. Both of them suggested from time to time that the other was unfit for government. In the end, Churchill's domineering charm usually made Eden grudgingly accept his wishes. Churchill, as Prime Minister, intervened in policy-making arbitrarily and unpredictably, using his personality and prestige to overwhelm protests and objections. When he retired at last, Evelyn Shuckburgh, who worked closely with Eden, commented in his revealing diary, that everyone could now admire Churchill 'for what he has done and been, and not worry about what he is doing or will do'.

As Ritchie Ovendale shows, Churchill's view of the Middle East differed violently from those of other ministers and diplomatists. He disliked concessions to the Egyptians: he strongly favoured Israel rather than the traditional Arab friends of Britain. This made difficulties for Eden and the Foreign Office, and took up time. When Churchill tried to win American backing for British influence in the Middle East, and asked for a contribution of American armed forces, he got much less attention. Churchill seems to have supposed that his prestige and personality enabled him to give orders to America. For him, President Eisenhower was a former subordinate. Eisenhower liked and respected Churchill, but did not take orders from him. It is possible that Churchill's demands caused the United States administration to make still greater efforts to avoid complicity in British plans and even to oppose them.

Maurice Vaïsse further illustrates the dangers of Churchillian arrogance. He makes it clear that Anthony Eden nourished Anglo-French co-operation far more successfully than Churchill – repeating his greater comprehension of de Gaulle. Churchill's conduct over the European Defence Community, a scheme to secure a German contribution to Western defence by integrating the Germans into a unified army, which he both pressed on France and denounced, is an example.

Hans-Peter Schwarz, Adenauer's biographer, suggests that Churchill's greatest success in relations with important post-war personages was with the West German Chancellor, Konrad Adenauer. This essay eliminates the old belief that Adenauer was fundamentally anti-British because of his experiences as Mayor of Cologne. On the contrary, Schwarz shows that Adenauer would have liked to build a post-war Europe based on Anglo-

German co-operation. Here is the fundamental post-war issue: should Britain have joined in the early stages of the building of a united western Europe and so created a union better adapted to British interests than the EEC as it developed?

Wolfgang Krieger points out that there were good reasons in the 1950s why the UK should put the Commonwealth ahead of Europe. For Churchill, the Second World War had legitimised the British Empire, and imperial development was more energetically pursued after the war than ever before. Krieger argues that Churchill supported British involvement in NATO, not to facilitate European union, but to ensure American commitment to the defence of Britain. For him, a united Europe meant Franco-German reconciliation and perhaps a negation of French pretensions to world-power status, not a surrender of any part of British sovereignty. Above all, in his last years in office, Churchill hoped to restore good relations with the USSR. It was his personal policy, disliked by the Americans, distrusted by the Europeans, opposed by his colleagues. Here, more than anywhere else, his special influence over the USA and Eisenhower became illusory.

Suitably, from the author who has enabled us, through prodigious scholarship and research, to understand Churchill, Martin Gilbert's essay shows, as well as Churchill's range, his flexibility. He stood ready to maintain British interests with varying combinations of allies and associates. After 1945, he preached Britain's links with three circles: the Commonwealth, the United States and Europe. Churchill's Europe, Gilbert's essay suggests, was, as most Englishmen have until fairly recently supposed, on the other side of the Channel. Churchill's hope was that Britain, by influencing those three groups, could pursue its interests and security. It has not always proved easy to do this. Churchill's prestige helped to improve Britain's place in the world.

1

Memories of Winston Churchill

MARY SOAMES

Since it has fallen to my lot to be Winston Churchill's child and now, of my parents' five children, sadly the only survivor, I have a unique testimony to give about Winston Churchill as a human being. I sometimes feel that his character and personality have become embalmed in his fame and in the legend which already attaches to his heroic figure. I do not wish to stray beyond the frontiers of my daughterly knowledge, but I see my modest yet perhaps not unnecessary task as that of trying to keep focused and fresh my father's personality and image.

I know that Winston Churchill's place in history is secure and I leave that, though not necessarily without comment, to the historians. Hero or antihero is too simplistic; we can perhaps agree in the words of one of the Harrow School songs he loved so much, that he will always be one of the giants of old, 'and a cherished name wherever liberty is loved'.

I would like to dwell on some aspects of his vivid personality, that long-enduring zest for life, that warmth whose glow I still feel through the passing years. Chartwell in Kent was the home of my parents for the last 40 years of their life together and it was also the scene of my own child-hood and youth. Now it belongs to the National Trust and there you can see, in the house and garden, visual testimony to some of the many-faceted aspects of Winston's personality and his ploys.

Firstly, of course, Chartwell was a veritable factory, and the lights gleamed from his study upstairs late into the night as, padding up and down the long room with its high vaulted ceiling, he dictated his books, newspaper articles and speeches, hour after hour. But there was playtime too. He always seemed to find time for what he endearingly called 'my

1

toys'. The long, high wall around the vegetable garden, which he built largely with his bare hands, bears visible witness to his love of construction and his skill as a bricklayer – he had a union card. He loved directing outdoor works, tree clearing or channelling the meagre trickle of the Chartwell stream through various courses and cascades to fill the lake-like swimming pool, his own creation too, which gleamed like an aquamarine set in the meadows.

Happy hours were passed round the dining-room table with his family, friends and colleagues and conversation, repartee and argument flashed to and fro, or long-remembered lines of verse and prose poured forth like a torrent from the store of his prodigious memory. Sometimes mealtimes lasted hours on end and I remember so well once my mother became a little restive and moved to go and he looked at her across the table and said 'Oh, Clemmie, don't go; it is so nice – let us command the moment to remain'.

And then of course there was painting, taken up by sheer chance during the First World War when he was 40, at a moment in his life and fortunes when he was all but engulfed by anguish, frustration and despair in the wake of the traumatic debacle of the Dardanelles campaign. But from that grim summer of 1915 when Churchill was at the nadir of his whole career, for over 40 years more he was to find hours of pleasure and occupation in painting, when problems of perspective and colour gave him respite from dark worries, heavy burdens and the clatter of political strife. 'Happy are the painters', he wrote, 'for they shall never be lonely. Light and colour, peace and hope will keep them company to the end, or almost to the end, of the day'. And these were to prove prophetic words for him.

As a child, I took my father's giant programme of work and play completely for granted. I only came to appreciate later what a prodigious worker he was and how he wrung from each 24 hours half as much time's worth again. Because our image now of Winston Churchill is of the old man – the war leader, the statesman figure – it is easy to forget the sheer dash and brilliance of his younger days. The war correspondent, the soldier of fortune, the radical politician of the hustings. Winston's cavalry training had made him a good horseman. He had been a first-class polo player and indeed played his last game as late as 1923 when he was nearly 50. He was a good shot and loved a day out with the hounds, fox or boar hunting, when the rigours of political life permitted.

As I grew up I came to see my father in a different perspective. I began to understand that his whole political life had been, and was, a dramatic procession of great issues. He saw events and people as on a stage lit by his own knowledge of history and his burning sense of destiny and of the march of events. And then I came to understand increasingly my father's political role, and sensed the causes and crises which dominated his life, and which would soon engulf all of ours.

Any consideration of Winston Churchill's life must recognise the role his beloved Clementine played through the 57 years they lived together, through a period as cataclysmic and changing as any in our history, and always in the glare of public interest. I often think how different might have been the course of Winston Churchill's life and career had he married a socially eager or trivial-minded woman. Churchill would always, through his talents and thrusting nature have been at the forefront of political life, but his energies might have been distracted or, who knows, the rapier of his destiny blunted or tarnished, had the woman he loved lacked the dedication, the high principles, and the fiery courage of Clementine Hozier.

Winston and Clementine's partnership was not always equable. Both had highly mettled natures. Clementine did not hesitate at times to differ from him on political questions; they often did not agree on friends; but love and loyalty never failed. Their relationship reminds me of Shakespeare's lines: 'Let me not to the marriage of true minds admit impediments'.

On the flyleaf of each volume of his war memoirs are inscribed the words 'In war resolution, in defeat defiance, in victory magnanimity, in peace goodwill'. And these words might appropriately sum up the theme of his whole life's work. In 1946 when Europe lay prostrate and divided by hatreds, in a famous speech at Zurich University he sounded a clarion call for European unity. 'Europe Arise' was the theme. He spoke of the necessity for there to be an end to retribution. There must be an act of faith in the European family. An act of oblivion against all the crimes and follies of the past. And this same generous outlook in public affairs was very much present in his private life. My father would often quote the biblical injunction 'Let not the sun go down on your wrath', and he truly practised what he preached for he was a quick forgiver.

What of my father's philosophy of life? He certainly had faith in the indomitable spirit of man and he had a strong underlying belief in a providential God. When the call came to him in 1940 he later was to write 'I felt as if I were walking with destiny, and that all my past life had been but a preparation for this hour and this trial'. And indeed, when one looks back upon the hazards and dangers through which he passed, the illnesses and accidents he suffered in his youth, the numerous close encounters with death on fields of battle, it is hard not to see a guiding and guarding hand, and he himself felt this element increasingly.

How do I see him as I, myself now over 70, look back upon this truly extraordinary man who is still to millions a world hero and who was my father? I, too, see Winston Churchill as an heroic figure and for me, of course, are mingled feelings of devotion and pride. But I also see him as a supremely blessed and happy human being for, despite the anguish of the dramas through which he lived and which he felt in every fibre of his being and in which he played so great a part, yet for these epic times and events how magnificently he was equipped in mind and spirit.

Dowered with a stalwart constitution, his manifold talents found expression in the varied and exciting events and political conflicts of his life, and in his writing and painting and in numerous lesser ploys in which he found endless employment and enjoyment. So I believe that until his very last years he did not know the meaning of the word boredom. When at long last the pace slowed; when finally politics, pen and brush were laid aside and that seemingly unquenchable well of his zest for life ran dry, the long daylight hours did indeed hang heavy. Yet from those muted last years I treasure a precious and, to me, infinitely moving picture. As a young cavalry officer in Cuba and then in India, Winston had been fascinated and amazed by the size and beauty and variety of the butterflies he saw there, and years later he caused plants and shrubs that attract butterflies to be planted at Chartwell. I remember my father on summer days in those twilight years sitting in his chair, strategically placed before the opulently flowering shrubs, watching with rapt enjoyment the vivid quivering splendour of the butterflies as they fluttered and feasted on the purple honey-laden flowers. Remembering him thus I recall Landor's lines: 'I warmed both hands before the fire of life, it sinks and I am ready to depart'.

2

Churchill and British Sea Power, 1908–29

Jon Sumida

Upon first achieving Cabinet rank as President of the Board of Trade in 1908, Winston Churchill opposed expensive Admiralty proposals to augment Britain's navy on the grounds that they were unnecessary, and would interfere with his plans for social reform. But from 1911 to 1914, as First Lord of the Admiralty, he authorised much higher naval estimates to increase the fighting power of the fleet. Following the outbreak of war in August 1914, Churchill ordered many new warships, using enormous quantities of labour, materials and manufacturing plant. In 1917 and 1918, as Minister of Munitions, however, he attempted to restrict shipbuilding to expand production for the war on land. As Chancellor of the Exchequer from 1925 to 1929, Churchill forced the Admiralty to slow its modernisation to free revenue for lower taxes and greater expenditure on social welfare. But over the course of the next decade, while out of office, he first condemned proposals for further naval cutbacks and then campaigned for general rearmament.

Churchill's wartime turnabout took place in secret discussions, and perhaps for this reason has gone practically unnoticed by historians. His pre- and post-war reversals over naval finance, on the other hand, were public and have attracted criticism. Vice-Admiral Sir Peter Gretton, for example, noted the

inconsistency of his policies towards the Services in general and the Navy in particular . . . We have already seen the pattern. Economy in the defence departments in 1910 [*sic*] to help the scheme for social security, immediately followed in 1912 by a large expansion of ship-building. Now we have savage cuts in 1925 to be followed by demands for rearmament in the 1930s . . . Despite his previous pre-occupation with welfare services . . . he seemed totally to ignore the damage to them caused by the expansion of the Naval Votes in 1912. And in the years 1925–29 he mercilessly reduced all three Services, despite his admitted preoccupation with the dangers of a resurgent Germany.[1]

Gretton attributed such behaviour in large part to the fact that: 'Churchill became absorbed in his task, whatever it was, and fitted himself with mental blinkers which allowed him to appreciate no one else's point of view'.[2] Roskill explained Churchill's post-war cutting down of the Navy while Chancellor of the Exchequer, by his throwing 'himself whole-heartedly on the side of any department of which he became head . . .'[3] 'The departmental habit of mind', wrote Richard Ollard, 'certainly offers one explanation of the apparent gyrations of Churchill's attitude towards the financial needs of the navy.'[4] This essay suggests more comprehensive explanations; Churchill's intellectual grasp went wider than these inter-pretations allow.

In a parliamentary address at the start of his political career, Churchill in 1901 emphasised the importance of British naval supremacy.[5] His opinions about naval policy and strategy, however, were not yet formed in association with Admiral Sir John Fisher, the radical First Sea Lord, whom he first met in April 1907. Fisher's influence on Churchill has been gener-ally recognised, but great misapprehension has existed as to precisely what lessons were taught, when they were learned and how they were used. Fisher's supposed effect on Churchill's thinking about the Royal Navy was on naval technology, and the main fruit of his tutoring, the replace-ment of coal by oil propulsion and the adoption of larger calibre main battery guns in capital ships. Fisher's actual programme was far more radical and wide-ranging, and his influence on Churchill more complex and less obvious.

Fisher's fundamental goals were the maintenance of British naval secu-rity at home and abroad at a price that Britain could afford. He was furthermore convinced that these ends could only be achieved through radical technological innovation. Fisher believed that changes in matériel were necessary because the battle fleet and trade defence cruiser force were too expensive, and incapable of fighting effectively. He hoped to deal with these problems by replacing the conventional battleship and armoured cruisers with an expanded flotilla and larger, new-model armoured cruis-ers, known as battlecruisers. The function of the battlecruiser was both to destroy enemy commerce raiders and to defeat enemy battle fleets that threatened the security of distant imperial possessions. And battlecruiser squadrons would be free to deploy outside home waters because fast surface torpedo craft and submarines would prevent invasion of the British Isles. A navy made up of light units and battlecruisers, Fisher expected, would be a much cheaper proposition than one consisting of battleships with their full panoply of scouting cruisers and screening destroyers, and a separate trade defence force of armoured cruisers.[6]

What matters in Fisher's ideas for present purposes is not their validity but the fact that they were the ones communicated to Churchill. And what Churchill made of whatever he was told and when, requires careful consideration. Not long after the First World War, Churchill recalled in his memoirs that for two weeks after he had first met Fisher in April 1907, the two had 'talked all day long and far into the nights', during which time he had been told 'wonderful stories of the navy and of his plans – all about Dreadnoughts [which could mean battlecruisers as well as battleships], all about submarines' and other subjects, and that when he returned to his duties at the Colonial Office he 'could have passed an examination on the policy of the then Board of Admiralty'.[7] There is good reason to believe, however, that Fisher's explanations may then have had a speculative character, and that Churchill's response, while marked by genuine curiosity and even intellectual excitement, was thus correspondingly disengaged.

In the spring of 1907, Fisher was still uncertain as to the technical feasibility of the battlecruiser and a new model submarine capable of operating for sustained periods in the North Sea, both of which had yet to be tested. Churchill's doubts as to the practicability of Fisher's vision may be gauged from his refusal of the Admiralty in March 1908 because he believed that the post offered insufficient opportunity for constructive action.[8] By this time, however, the first of the battlecruisers was about to undergo its sea trials, highly-promising associated gunnery systems appeared to be on the brink of perfection, and the development of the improved submarine was nearly completed.[9] The brighter prospects of Fisher's radical concepts may explain his reaction to Churchill's turning down the offer of the First Lordship. 'When Winston told him that he had refused the Admiralty', Asquith's daughter has related:

Fisher exploded and overwhelmed him with reproaches. What might they not together have done at the Admiralty! What a heaven-sent opportunity he had thrown away! And he so fired Winston's imagination with his glowing picture of their joint rule of the seas that

Winston was persuaded to return to my father and tell him that he had changed his mind and that if the Admiralty was still available he would like to take it. But alas! It was not.[10]

Fisher possessed strong economical instincts, was probably sympathetic to the social reform programme of the Liberals, and personally got on not only with Churchill but with Lloyd George, the radical Chancellor of the Exchequer, as well. In addition, he was much less concerned about the magnitude of the German threat than his fellow members of the Board of Admiralty.[11] Indeed, this was so much the case that there were accusations in the press that his administration had made inadequate preparations to meet the rising German navy. Fisher's noisy anti-Germanism of late 1908 and 1909 was in part a response to these charges. But what the developing crisis over German naval expansion meant to him was not the opportunity to make good previous shortfalls in battleship construction, but a chance to implement the replacement of the battle fleet and cruiser squadrons with a navy based on battlecruisers and submarines.[12]

Fisher's hopes of large savings in the navy budget depended upon the adoption of his radical naval ideas. He could not, however, guarantee the support of the Board for such a sharp departure from convention. Although he demanded that all the Admiralty's proposed six, and ultimately eight, dreadnoughts under the 1909 estimates be battlecruisers,[13] he was forced after protracted discussion to compromise, and secured only two such units. Churchill was almost certainly aware of what Fisher was trying to accomplish and how. But he, like Fisher, thought that the German threat had been exaggerated, was deeply committed to his social reform programme for both moral and pragmatic reasons,[14] and was probably sceptical about the First Sea Lord's capacity to deliver his revolutionary changes in naval force structure. However much he might have approved of Fisher's attempt to achieve a naval new order and been tempted by the potentially large economies that it offered, the risks of playing that game were too high.

The conflict between Fisher and Churchill that arose during the public controversy over the navy estimates in the late winter and early spring of 1909, therefore, was not what it seemed. The difference between the two men was not really over the magnitude of the German danger or Fisher's ideas on capital ship design – areas where there was in fact substantial agreement – but about Churchill's trepidation with regard to the devious and hazardous course being pursued by the First Sea Lord. Fisher at first seems to have been appreciative of his erstwhile protégé's predicament, berating him in February 1909 for his 'turn against the navy' after all he had 'said in public and in private', and then chaffing him with good humour the next week with the observation that 'the tongue is the very devil! (NB, Yours is slung amidships and wags at both ends!)'[15] But Fisher was infuriated by Churchill's continued spirited opposition to the increases in the size of the 1909 capital ship programme proposed by the Admiralty, which he believed threatened the realisation of an important part of his radical vision of naval force structure.

The ordering of eight battlecruisers, in addition to the four completed or under way, would have given a total of 12, against the seven all-big-gun battleships at that time built or building. With the addition of the two battlecruisers authorised by the Pacific dominions in March and June 1909, the Royal Navy in effect could have had no fewer than 14 such units in service by 1912. With two-thirds of the British Empire's first-line capital ship strength made up of battlecruisers, Fisher would have achieved the surface-ship half of his naval revolution. He thus rejoiced in the defeat of Churchill and Lloyd George within the Cabinet and the approval of what amounted to an eight-ship programme. Fisher, however, subsequently failed to carry within the Admiralty his proposals for building only battlecruisers, and by the end of the year his political unpopularity had compelled him to tender his resignation, which became effective early in 1910.

The year 1909 was, therefore, a naval policy debacle for both Fisher and Churchill. On the one hand, the battleship to battlecruiser ratio of six to four strengthened the position of those who favoured the conventional battle fleet, and the very great increase in the number of capital ships ordered – with no countervailing effect in terms of the economies that might have been produced by Fisher's fundamental reconceptualisation of naval strategy, tactics and organisation – meant that large sums that could have been spent on social reform would for certain be required to support the Royal Navy. Fisher and Churchill had ceased communicating after March 1909. A year later, just after his retirement, Fisher reopened their correspondence with a friendly letter, to which Churchill replied that he was 'sorry that the drift of events did not enable us to work together', and observed:

> I have deeply regretted since that I did not press for the Admiralty in 1908. I think it would have been easily possible for me to obtain it. I believe it would have been better for us all.[16]

Time and chance, however, were to give the pair not one but two more opportunities to unite the twin banners of naval and social radicalism.

In late September 1911, dissatisfaction with the performance of the Admiralty during the crisis with Germany over Agadir prompted Asquith to offer Churchill leadership of the Admiralty again. Churchill accepted with alacrity, and assumed office in late October. Opposition to Fisher within and without the navy was too strong to allow his return as First Sea Lord to assist Churchill, but the new First Lord sought his old teacher's advice in secret meetings and through an extensive correspondence. Fisher initially gained Churchill's agreement to build only battlecruisers and to rely on submarines to defend Britain from invasion. On 10 November, Churchill informed Vice-Admiral Prince Louis of Battenberg, who was shortly to become Second Sea Lord, that he intended to order four battle-cruisers under the 1912 estimates.[17] On 4 November, Fisher had confided to a friend that he had put the question of submarines to Churchill and after an 'all night sitting' had 'converted him'.[18] The success of Fisher's intensive propagandising, however, was short-lived.

Churchill's official advisers at the Admiralty were adamantly opposed to the replacement of the battleship by the battlecruiser. By the end of November 1911, Churchill had been persuaded that both types were nec-essary, and in May 1912 he finally decided upon a type intermediate between the battlecruiser and the battleship. The result was the ordering of a programme of fast battleships, the famous *Queen Elizabeth* class, which were to be equipped with the big guns and oil propulsion that Fisher wanted, but also heavy armour and strong secondary armament, which he did not.[19] And while Churchill appears to have been convinced that submarines were capable of controlling the narrow seas between Britain and the Continent, though not the open waters of the Mediterranean, he also believed that the Royal Navy needed a high-speed submarine to work with the battle fleet. Efforts to develop such a vessel between 1912 and 1914, which ultimately proved to be unsuccessful, were so costly that they disrupted the production of the patrol submarines that were needed to implement Fisher's radical flotilla strategy for the defence of home waters.[20]

Fisher had expected that an improved battlecruiser would be much less expensive than the battleships of the 1911 programme.[21] But the addition of heavy armour to produce a fast battleship and the decision not to reduce the gun calibre of the secondary armament increased the costs of each unit by 20 per cent. Fisher had believed that the implementation of his scheme would have made the construction of destroyers unnecessary. The continued adherence to the battle fleet concept meant that the build-ing of destroyers was continued, resulting in expenditure in 1912 and 1913 that in each of those years amounted to some three-quarters of the total cost of a fast battleship. Thus, while the adoption of larger calibre heavy guns and oil propulsion improved the performance of British capital ships, the failure to implement Fisher's grand scheme as a whole meant that there were no economies to offset higher costs.[22]

Churchill had called for naval economy until as late as February 1911. He was then deeply disturbed, however, by Germany's aggressiveness during the Agadir crisis of that July. And within three months of taking over the Admiralty, he was confronted by news that Germany intended to increase both the strength of the fleet and its state of readiness.[23] In April 1912, he proposed that Britain and Germany agree to mutual reductions in their building programmes,[24] but when this initiative failed, and with Germany's Mediterranean allies embarked on large naval programmes as well, Churchill must have believed that he had no other choice – given the impossibility of implementing Fisher's radical alternative – but to expand and otherwise improve Britain's battle fleet in order to prevent the issue of inadequate naval security from being used by the Conservatives to bring down the Liberal administration,[25] to say nothing of deterring and if necessary defeating a German attack.

Churchill's pursuit of what was essentially the old British strategy of numerically out-building her rivals caused him difficulties with both Fisher and his radical political associates. To a degree, Fisher understood that Churchill's temporising could not be helped, given the strength of the opposition at the Admiralty. The new First Lord, he confided to a friend in February 1912, was 'Napoleonic in audacity, Cromwellian in thoroughness', but could not 'go quite so far as I urge him' because 'his instruments [by which Fisher meant the service members of the Board] are inadequate'.[26] But he was clearly disappointed in the particulars of the *Queen Elizabeth* class, and then outraged by Churchill's appointments of Service enemies to important posts,[27] which resulted in a break that was not repaired until Churchill placed him in charge of the commission on oil fuel. Churchill's radical Cabinet colleagues and party following, on the other hand, were angered by the sharp increases in the navy estimates, which were the result in part of his technical initiatives. Serious opposition to Churchill from the left wing of the Liberal party was delayed, however, because of financial circumstances that made an expensive naval policy politically practicable.

New taxes introduced by Lloyd George in 1909 and an upturn in the economy resulted in a 10 per cent expansion in the central government's revenue in 1909 and 1910. Continued growth in Britain's prosperity over the next three years produced further large increments in income without recourse to additional taxes. As a consequence, although the navy estimates of 1913 were some 50 per cent above those of 1908, annual spending on social welfare over the same period rose nearly tenfold.[28] In late 1913, however, Churchill's proposals for naval spending, when combined with anticipated higher outlays in other areas, increased prospective aggregate government expenditure for the next fiscal year beyond the existing income boundaries of the state. This precipitated a bitter battle between Churchill and Lloyd George that for a time seemed destined to split the Liberal party and bring down the government.[29] The crisis ended when Lloyd George reputedly acceded to Churchill's demands on a frivolous pretext in February 1914.[30] What actually appears to have happened was more complicated and much more interesting.

By late 1913, the strong performance of submarines in the manoeuvres of that year and the year before, and continued lobbying by Fisher, had convinced Churchill that the new craft were capable of inflicting heavy losses on any battle fleet that attempted to maintain active control of the North Sea for the purposes of either close blockade or covering an invasion. And although Churchill had favoured the construction of heavy surface ships in numbers large enough to discourage German expansion, and in the process cover the Liberal Party with a fig-leaf of naval respectability, the budget crisis that materialised in late 1913 made the continuation of this policy politically difficult, if not impossible. For these reasons, the First Lord, with the full backing of his Service colleagues at the Admiralty, in December 1913 decided in secret to abandon the battleship standard. This enabled him in a meeting of the Cabinet in January 1914 to promise Lloyd George that two out of the four battleships authorised under the 1914-15 estimates would be replaced by increased submarine construction, with substantial savings. The Admiralty–Treasury agreement of 1914 was therefore, in effect, secured by the adoption of one of the principal aspects of Fisher's radical programme.[31]

The issue was still in doubt when Fisher suggested to Churchill that he be made First Sea Lord in order to put through his naval agenda and secure its attendant economies. 'I would guarantee to save four million sterling on your next year's Estimates', the Admiral wrote on 10 December 1913,

> ... *if I were First Sea Lord, but then I must be there as First Sea Lord to do it*. The First Lord *can't* do it. (Not even *you!*) It wants the *sea* responsibility and the *fighting* responsibility of your chief naval adviser to see a job of that sort through under the aegis of the First Lord's political responsibility.[32]

Fisher's economic argument was weakened by the decision to reduce prospective battleship building, but his remarks on the importance of the First Lords being supported by a First Sea Lord of like mind when making innovations may have affected Churchill's thinking nonetheless. 'A strong First Sea Lord', Churchill wrote not long after the First World War,

. . . to carry out a vigorous policy, needs the assistance of a Minister, who alone can support him and defend him. The authority of both is more than doubled by their union. Each can render the other Services of supreme importance when they are both effective factors. Working in harmony, they multiply each other. By the resultant concentration of combined power, no room or chance is given to faction. For good or for ill what they decide together in the interests of the Service must be loyally accepted.[33]

This was the *post facto* justification, in any case, for Churchill's selection of Fisher as First Sea Lord not long after the outbreak of the First World War, following the resignation of Prince Louis of Battenberg, whose German origins and other difficulties made his occupation of the post untenable.[34]

There can be little doubt that Fisher resumed the First Sea Lordship in October 1914 with the implementation of his radical pre-war agenda in mind. Within days of taking office, he had ordered no fewer than 63 new submarines, with grudging authorisation for the construction of a smaller number of destroyers.[35] In late December, Fisher suggested that an additional 42 submarines be built, and won permission to build two battlecruisers of unprecedented speed and fire power. This victory was followed by a campaign to build first two, and then four, light battlecruisers, and by the spring of 1915 Fisher was contemplating the possibility of building a battlecruiser that was even larger, faster and more heavily armed than the two approved in December.[36] In December 1914, the First Sea Lord had advised Admiral Sir John Jellicoe, the Commander of the Grand Fleet, that '"Battle cruisers and more battle cruisers" is the watchword! . . . That way lies the path to glory. Cumbersome battleships are rotten. Slow men and slow ships mean failure . . .'[37]

Churchill, for his part, strongly opposed the demands for additional battlecruisers and the second instalment of submarine orders. He won his point on the submarines, and his approval of five battlecruisers was achieved, it seems, only because they were justified as necessary for a planned amphibious operation in the Baltic that Churchill wanted but

Fisher did not, and because the First Sea Lord may have threatened to resign in the event of a refusal.[38] There can be little doubt that Churchill understood that Fisher was using the exigencies of war to obtain the revolution in naval force structure that he had been unable to get previously, and may have been sympathetic if sceptical. A sense of emergency, in addition, had opened the coffers of the nation, snapping financial restraint, and Britain's industrial assets seemed more than sufficient to meet any demands. In the first year of hostilities, Churchill later recollected:

> . . . the resources of Britain far exceeded any organisation which could employ them. Whatever was needed for the fleets and armies had only to be ordered in good time and on a large enough scale. The chief difficulty was to stretch the mind to a hitherto unimagined size of events. Megalomania was a positive virtue. Indeed, to add a nought, or a couple of noughts, to almost any requisition or plan for producing war supplies would have constituted an act of merit.[39]

But Fisher's resignation over the Dardenelles in May 1915 resulted in Churchill's ouster as First Lord – ending both their association at the Admiralty and, for a time, the latter's serious involvement in the direction of the war – and the replacement of the Liberal by a Coalition government. In March 1916, Churchill spoke against the new regime in the House of Commons, criticising what he believed was inadequate production to meet the navy's necessities in ships and equipment.[40] Churchill's speech was a political failure, and in addition manifestly wrong in light of the fact that manufacturing for the navy after his leaving office had expanded to the point that it had begun to interfere with equally important work for the merchant marine and army. The disruption of merchant shipbuilding and repair for two years by the Admiralty's takeover of practically the whole of Britain's maritime industrial establishment from early in the war was, in particular, the main reason for the serious weakening of the merchant marine by 1917. This became a major contributor to the making of the submarine crisis in the spring of that year.

In July 1917, Lloyd George, who had replaced Asquith as Prime Minister in December 1916, recalled Churchill to high office as Minister of Munitions. Although the adoption of the convoy system had by this time begun to reduce sinkings of merchant vessels by submarines, monthly losses yet remained very high. But in spite of the need for more resources for the maintenance and new construction of merchant ships, the Admiralty continued to build large numbers of warships, including many that were not required for the anti-submarine effort. This tied up labour, steel and plant, reducing the output of merchant vessels and jeopardising the supply of aircraft and tanks to the army.[41] In July and August, Churchill's questioning of some naval demands[42] provoked a strong protest from the Admiralty. In reply, he complained to Lloyd George that

> . . . at present the Admiralty claim a super priority upon all supplies; not only as respects the most urgent and vital parts of that immense business, but even in regard to comparatively commonplace needs. They assert the doctrine that the least important Admiralty needs should rank before the most urgent claims of the Army or of Aeronautics. In my view there should be a frank and free discussion on the merits in each case and a loyal and friendly effort by departments – even after a little plain-speaking – to do the best they can by the public cause . . . .[43]

But although Churchill's administrative case was strong, his political position was weak. His demand for what amounted to the imposition of sharper restrictions in navy procurement, however justified in light of the circumstances created by the protracted war of attrition on the Western Front, was diametrically opposed to the spirit that had animated his earlier approval of Fisher's large battlecruiser and submarine programmes and later call for the further expansion of production for the navy. Churchill was also highly unpopular in many Liberal and Conservative circles, and enjoyed office only because of Lloyd George's favour, which could be withdrawn at any time. He was as a consequence unable to press his views, and naval consumption of armaments output, in the absence of effective opposition from the Ministry of Munitions, continued to expand.[44] Thus Churchill later observed that 'the Grand Fleet absorbed in the final phases of the war a larger share of our resources than was its due, and our war effort in the field was unwarrantably diminished to that extent'.[45]

Over the course of the four years of the First World War, Britain built more warship and naval auxiliary tonnage than she had in the preceding quarter-century, and this included capital ships, cruisers and large fleet destroyers.[46] In May 1919, Churchill, who had by this time taken the post of Secretary of State for War and Air, was convinced in light of these facts that

> . . . there ought to be no need for naval new construction except of a minor character, for many years to come. The dockyards are choked with war vessels and I cannot conceive that any new construction is

required. In the year before the war my new construction vote was over £20 millions, which at present day prices is considerably over £30 millions. It is from this source alone that in the present circumstances a saving can be made which will enable us to reconcile imperial defence and national economy.[47]

Churchill's hopes for easy naval reductions were dashed, however, by the Admiralty's demands for major new construction, which it argued were needed to maintain naval supremacy in the face of American proposals to build 'a navy second to none', and to deter Japanese aggression against imperial possessions and the dominions in the Far East.

Churchill agreed with the principles underlying the Navy's case. In 1919, he had made it clear to Lloyd George that he believed in the vital importance of maintaining Britain's naval position and that she would be compelled to build if the Americans did so.[48] In 1921, he strongly opposed the renewal of the Anglo-Japanese alliance on the grounds that the Japanese constituted the main threat to Britain's position in the orient.[49] By this time, moreover, Churchill's pre-war conviction that surface ship strength was of diminished importance because of the ability of submarines to control at least narrow seas had been reversed by the wartime development of asdic, which he, like many others, believed greatly reduced the efficacy of underwater craft.[50] Thus, although the provisions of the Washington Naval Conference Treaty signed in early 1922 ended the threat of an open-ended, three-way naval race between Britain, the United States and Japan, Churchill strongly resisted efforts to cut naval spending below the levels that were required to build the capital ships and cruisers allowed by the naval arms control agreement.[51]

In November 1922, the bipartisan coalition that had governed since 1916 was dissolved; the Conservative government, in turn, was replaced for 10 months by the first Labour government in 1924. Churchill, who lost his seat in November 1922, was out of Parliament until November 1924. During this period, the support of the Liberal party for Labour rule, whose ideology he claimed to abhor, drove him to the Conservatives, and in 1924, following the Conservative electoral victory in the general election, he was rewarded for his change of party by being given the office of Chancellor of the Exchequer. From the beginning, Churchill was determined to 'liberalise' Conservative administration with a dose of social reform, not only because it conformed to his own long-held views on the subject, but because it would counter the appeal of the Labour party which, since holding office, was more threatening than ever before. In addition, he believed that tax reductions and a return to the gold standard would signal a return to peacetime normality that would strengthen middle-class support.[52]

Churchill's plan to cut taxes while increasing domestic spending forced economies in defence. He was also convinced that outlays on the Air Force should be increased; the Army had already suffered substantial losses. This left the Navy. In late November 1924, Churchill informed Stanley Baldwin, the Prime Minister, that there were good grounds for placing limits on the expansion of naval spending. In December, he then learned of the Admiralty's proposals for the coming estimates of 1925–26, which were some 17 per cent higher than those of the previous year. Such an increase, even considering the fact that the estimates of 1924–25 had been depressed to the lowest level since the war by the actions of the Labour government, was not only large, but was to be only the starting point for further major increases over the next several years. The Navy's leadership justified much higher spending on the grounds that imperial security demanded the construction of a fleet capable of defeating that of Japan in a full-scale war in the Far East by 1929.[53]

Churchill objected adamantly to such a build-up. Its adoption, he maintained to Baldwin on 15 December 1924, would 'sterilise and paralyse the whole policy of the government. There will be nothing for the taxpayer and nothing for social reform. We shall be a Naval Parliament busily preparing our navy for some great imminent shock.' The result, Churchill went on, would be political disaster for the Conservative party, the return of Labour rule, and the cancellation of the Navy increases. In any case, Churchill argued, the Admiralty's preparations were unnecessary because Japan, unlike pre-war Germany, did not pose a threat to vital interests, by which he meant the security of British home territory, and war with Japan was highly unlikely. The proper alternative course to that put forward by the Admiralty was a smaller naval programme that would enable the Conservative party, through a popular appeal to the electorate on a platform of domestic achievement, to gain a second term that would prevent the far more drastic naval cutbacks that were sure to come under a Labour government.[54]

Churchill's offer to the Admiralty, though less than it asked, was nonetheless considerable. He proposed, in particular, to finance completion, at a more gradual pace, of the Singapore base and the build-up of oil reserves. These provisions were much more generous than those desired by his Treasury subordinates, who had called for the elimination or delay of the entire naval programme. After contentious discussion between Churchill and representatives of the Admiralty,[55] the Cabinet voted a compromise in February 1925, which produced a naval budget for the next fiscal year that split the difference. In addition, the Cabinet created a committee, of which Churchill was to be a member, to consider the Admiralty's plans for the replacement of old warships by new over the next six years.[56]

The Cabinet's Naval Programme Committee met from March to July 1925.[57] The Admiralty's initial request was for enormous construction that would raise the Navy Estimates from the coming year's £60 million to what the navy itself conceded would be in the range of £80-85 million. Churchill observed that the cost of maintaining such a force on a war footing as intended by the Admiralty would drive the estimates upward into the range of £90–100 million. These were preposterous figures, and the Admiralty's reduction of its building plans by a third was not enough to satisfy even its staunchest supporters on the Committee and in the Cabinet. Churchill offered to guarantee Navy Estimates of £65 million starting in 1926–27, and made important concessions that would have allowed the navy more discretion in how it spent the funds allocated by Parliament. Churchill's reasonable package, however, was rejected. In July, the Admiralty won the Committee's approval for the cruiser building it wanted and recommendation for estimates of £68,873,000, but in the process had expended political capital that left it vulnerable to Treasury counterattack.[58]

In April 1925, the Cabinet had formed the Standing Committee on Expenditure. Although it was chaired by the Prime Minister, Churchill, who as Chancellor of the Exchequer was also a member, played a leading role. In August 1925, the work of the Cabinet Committee was assisted by the formation of the Treasury's own Fighting Services Economy Committee under the chairmanship of Lord Colwyn. While this committee was collecting evidence, the Locarno Treaty was signed in October 1925, which greatly improved prospects for a long-lasting peace. In November, as a consequence, Churchill called for deep cuts in defence spending, and these became the established financial guidelines for the coming 1926–27 estimates in both the Cabinet and Treasury Committees. In December, the Colwyn Committee, as instructed, recommended naval expenditure of no more than £57,500,000, which was adopted by the Cabinet Committee. Although this represented a 16 per cent reduction in the figure established in July, discussions between Churchill and the First Lord appear to have been amicable, and the recommended spending level was accepted by the Admiralty in February 1926.[59]

The Admiralty's willingness to economise was probably attributable to a combination of three factors: recognition that the Locarno accords had sharply undercut the force of their previous demands for naval preparedness; the unexpected success of their own efforts at retrenchment, which enabled them to finance the construction of the next year's authorised cruisers out of internal savings; and the expectations that the balance of the cruiser programme would be completed in the future because of substantial increases in the Navy Estimates after the famine year of 1926–27.[60] Over the three fiscal years from 1927–28 to 1929–30, however, Churchill, with the full support of the Cabinet, demanded further reductions in the Navy Estimates, albeit smaller than the drastic cut of 1926–27, which compelled the Admiralty to cancel two of the three cruisers scheduled for 1927–28, four out of five cruisers for 1928–29 and two out of three cruisers for 1929–30.[61]

These cancellations were later to form the basis of accusations against Churchill for having critically and unnecessarily reduced the strength of the Royal Navy because of his infatuation with economy.[62] Churchill's motives, however, were complex and by no means hostile to the interests of British naval power. He was determined to maintain a navy superior to that of the United States by means of either judicious concession or ill-advised intransigence.[63] Churchill's excessive denigration of the Japanese danger was in large part a reaction to the no less extreme prognostications of the Admiralty. His views were widely shared in the Cabinet, and when later proved wrong in the Second World War, it was under international circumstances – namely the rapid defeat of France – that were practically unthinkable in the 1920s.[64] And his support of restraint when it came to cruiser construction was founded on fears that going forward rapidly risked provoking building on the part of foreign navies that would leave Britain in no better and possibly an even worse condition than before.[65]

The critical issue for Churchill, however, was finance and the political implications of financial policy. Under the first Labour government, the Navy Estimates had been cut to well below the levels authorised by its Conservative predecessor. Churchill had good reason to believe, therefore, that the maintenance of adequate naval strength depended upon the continuation of Conservative government. The naval reductions he imposed while Chancellor of the Exchequer in order to underwrite the costs of limited social reform, tax reduction and at least the appearance of a pacific disposition desired by the majority of voters, thus constituted the premium that had to be paid for the insurance of victory in the next general election, upon which, in his mind, the moderate yet steady support of the Navy depended.[66]

In 1926, the heavy losses in government revenue caused by the General Strike had forced Churchill to seek three per cent cuts in the Service estimates for 1927–28.[67] And recognising that the strike had heightened awareness of Britain's social problems and thus strengthened the case of the Labour party, Churchill over the next two years redoubled his efforts to shore up electoral support for the Conservative government. The reduction in naval spending imposed on the Navy in fiscal year 1928–29 was less than Churchill wanted, but enough to enable him to initiate an ambitious scheme of local tax relief.[68] In the summer of 1928, the government was buffeted by strong agitation for disarmament, which Churchill bitterly opposed. In what was probably a response, he proposed and won approval of the practice of continuously extending the famous 'Ten Year Rule', which in effect put off the date at which Britain's defences were to be fully prepared for a major war into the indefinite future.[69] Such action was needed to provide the justification for further cuts in the Service estimates for 1929–30, including, of course, the Navy, which were offered as an attractive alternative peace policy to disarmament on the eve of the general election.[70]

As it turned out, the electoral victory of the Labour party in May 1929 meant that Churchill's political efforts were for nought. His achievements for the navy, on the other hand, were considerable. For all the complaints of the Admiralty, British naval expenditure while Churchill was Chancellor of the Exchequer was significantly higher than under the Labour governments that preceded and succeeded it. While American naval spending nominally surpassed that of Britain, British new construction, especially in cruisers, was far greater. And a comparison of British, American and Japanese naval strength in January 1932 – a good measure of the degree to which the strength of the Royal Navy was supported during the late 1920s, even allowing for the age of many of the British warships – indicates that Churchill's policies had not compromised naval supremacy.[71] The critical shortfalls were to come later, when for four years economic disaster, another naval arms reduction agreement, and the MacDonald and MacDonald-Baldwin governments combined to drive British naval expenditure to its lowest levels of the inter-war period.[72]

Churchill cherished Britain's greatness; for centuries naval supremacy had been its foundation. He was a romantic nationalist but combined that emotion with intelligent, informed, imaginative insight. He worked to harmonise British greatness with the constraints of finance, foreign relations, domestic politics and technical innovation. In 1909–29 Churchill adapted to dramatic changes as circumstances required. In 1908–9 government finance was weak, the naval balance sound, social reform urgently needed and Fisher's radical ideas fitted in. Then German dreadnought building imposed prudent reinsurance and expanded revenue permitted higher spending on the Navy.

In 1914 and 1915, plentiful financial and industrial resources and the threat from German surface ships required and enabled Churchill to press for the highest imaginable naval production. In 1917 and 1918, he gave priority to merchant ships and land warfare. After the war, especially as Chancellor, he tried to impose sensible limits both on the inflated ambitions of the Admiralty and civilian zeal for arms limitation. In the 1930s much sharper reductions in naval spending than Churchill had imposed and the ominous international situation prompted him to call for stronger defence forces, including the Navy.

Churchill's concerns were not only departmental, but responded to the changing national and international scene. He grappled with the central problem of twentieth-century statecraft; the balance between domestic amelioration and external power. His interest in both, his grandiloquence, his obvious ambition aroused mistrust. Yet, between 1908 and 1929, Churchill, to a far greater degree than any other British politician, found a succession of solutions to that problem and achieved notable success. His claims to everlasting fame and glory as Prime Minister in war lay in the future. These may overshadow, but should not obscure his previous accomplishments.

3

Churchill and the US Navy, 1919–29

PHILLIPS O'BRIEN

At the end of the First World War, the Royal Navy had achieved a measure of naval dominance unmatched since Trafalgar. With the German High Seas Fleet removed from the balance, the Royal Navy was as powerful as the rest of the world's fleets combined. The fact that the British, thereupon, had formally to renounce their right to superiority through the auspices of the inter-war naval arms-control process, was undoubtedly a heavy blow. Those responsible for making British policy pointed out that parity was only conceded to the United States. This, it was hoped, would cushion the blow. They spoke of the overriding need for Anglo-American friendship and the supposed kinship of the peoples of Great Britain and the United States. As Austen Chamberlain would write in his memoirs, published in 1935:

> No Englishman in common parlance would speak of an American as a foreigner. It comes to us naturally to think of Americans as kinsmen . . . men who shared all but a small fraction of our history, who speak the same language, who read the same Bible, who are co-heirs with us of the glories of English literature . . . It is . . . without jealousy that we have watched the phenomenal growth of the United States since the close of the Civil War, and we could give no greater proof of it than in accepting the doctrine of naval parity. To no other nation should we have made that sacrifice, to no other nation are we now prepared to make it . . . That the readiness and unanimity with which the principle of parity with the United States has been accepted in Great Britain is part due to the sentiment of which I have already spoken . . .[1]

It might seem that Chamberlain was being slightly disingenuous in his description of Anglo-American friendship, but his greatest mistake is his claim that the decision to accept parity was one of 'readiness and unanimity'. For, as he well knew, one of his Cabinet colleagues fought strenuously against accepting parity with the Americans between the end of the First World War until the close of the second Baldwin government. This colleague was Winston Churchill.

Churchill was the only member of the various governments of the period consistently to argue for the maintenance of British naval superiority. Serving first as War and then as Colonial Secretary under Lloyd George and later as Chancellor of the Exchequer, in the second Baldwin government, he almost always claimed that the British should attempt to maintain their supremacy. Churchill's plan, however, was unorthodox. His policy, as it was eventually developed, was to forego building large numbers of capital ships or spending great amounts of money on the Navy and, instead, to ensure British dominance through a lead in auxiliary ship strength (at first cruisers, destroyers and submarines but later just cruisers). He developed this scheme independently of, and often at odds with, official Admiralty policy. He fought almost every attempt by the Royal Navy either to lay down new ships or increase its funding. On the surface his actions seem contradictory. He pushed the Cabinet to fight for naval supremacy at the same time that he fought against increasing the strength of the Royal Navy. An uncharitable observer might imply that he was more interested in protecting or improving his political position, for it is true that Churchill never abandoned his hope of eventually becoming Prime Minister. It should be remarked in his favour, however, that he developed the key elements of his policy almost immediately after the First World War and, while everyone else changed position regularly between 1919 and 1927, he was alone in having a consistent, if eventually misguided, plan.

British naval policy during these years was generally determined in debates and discussions surrounding the famous naval arms control or disarmament conferences, specifically the Washington Conference of 1921–22, the Geneva Conference of 1927, the First London Conference of 1930 and the Second London Conference of 1935–36. They are events, naturally, of particular interest to historians concerned with the evolution of British naval power. One group, the largest, has dismissed British policy choices during this era as at best counterproductive and at worst disastrous. Stephen Roskill, still the greatest historian of British naval policy in the inter-war years, strikes a tone which is best characterised as 'more in sorrow than in anger'. Yet, for most, his air of resignation is probably too charitable.[2] Correlli Barnett has described the Washington Conference, the most famous of the arms control agreements as 'one of the major catastrophes of English history . . . which was to exercise a cumulative and decisive effect on the future of English power'.[3]

In the last few years, however, this view has been challenged. Two historians in particular have tried to reinterpret British policy. John Ferris has argued that the decision to accept parity in capital ship strength during the Washington Conference did not represent a real diminution of British strength while both he and Brian McKercher have argued that Britain maintained her supremacy much longer than most have assumed.[4] The critics assume Britain should have done more to protect her naval superiority, while Ferris and McKercher imply, conversely, that British policy was actually responsible for maintaining it.

To begin with, however, British policy-makers were not so much concerned with the reality of sea-power as with the perception of naval strength. One of the most pressing questions was whether Britain could afford to recognise another power as a naval equal, even if there was little or no prospect of an actual war. This question was made even more difficult by the fact that the power in question was the United States. The challenge posed by the United States was radically different from that posed by any other nation. Britain's best hope of seeing off an American challenge lay not in the inherent strengths of the British Empire, but in the lack of political will of American politicians and the American public. The industrial capacity of the United States was so large that if she ever fully entered into a naval building race with Great Britain, she was bound to win.

British politicians of every party had demonstrated an awareness of America's potential strength years before the First World War.[5] In 1905 the Committee of Imperial Defence (CID) decided to cancel all further planning for a conflict between Britain and the United States, and with a few notable exceptions the United States was thereupon removed from Two-Power Standard calculations. The question remained, however, about what policy Britain would pursue if the United States ever attempted to challenge the Royal Navy directly. President Theodore Roosevelt's build-up had made the United States the second naval power in the world by 1907, but the relative indifference of the Taft and early Wilson administrations meant that the American challenge soon faltered. The situation then changed dramatically for the worse, in British terms, during the First World War. While Britain had slowed the construction of capital ships dramatically during the war, the United States Congress went on to pass, what was up until that time, the largest naval bill in American history; the famous '1916 programme'. The reasons for this move were complicated, but stemmed mostly from President Wilson's desire to have the force necessary to confront whoever won the on-going European war. Regardless of the motivation, however, the 10 battleships and six battlecruisers called for by the bill, all to be built with the benefit of wartime technical advances, would have left the American capital ship force 'qualitatively superior' to the Royal Navy's.[6] The Royal Navy would still have had a greater number of capital ships, but the larger size, more powerful guns and technical specifications of the American ships would have provided the Americans with at least parity in fighting strength.

The question of how to respond to this challenge, and with it America's nascent naval strength, was thus brought to the fore and would remain to bedevil different British governments until 1930. It was during discussion of this question that Winston Churchill first developed, and then saw implemented, his somewhat unorthodox views on the maintenance of British naval supremacy. To begin with, he had little luck in persuading his colleagues to adopt his proposals, but during the height of the Geneva Conference the rest of the Cabinet agreed to pursue his policy to retain supremacy for the Royal Navy. What was most impressive about his performance was the political tenacity and skill that he demonstrated in implementing it. What was less impressive was the impact of policy itself, which was disastrously self-defeating and succeeded in plunging Anglo-American relations into their worst crisis of the twentieth century.

Winston Churchill, throughout his career, always demonstrated an acute interest in naval affairs. It was the Admiralty, more than any other branch of government, that he influenced most consistently throughout the decades of his public service. He served as First Lord of the Admiralty during the opening of both world wars, having already presided over the greatest build-up of British naval strength in the twentieth century. In the immediate post-war period, however, Churchill's influence over British naval policy was muted; he certainly contributed to the debate over it, but his voice was just one of many. While Walter Long and Arthur Lee, the First Lords of the Admiralty between 1919 and 1922, were not particularly effective advocates, there were other more opinionated and forceful personalities in the Cabinet. In one instance, a fascinating December 1920 meeting of the Committee of Imperial Defence, naval policy was discussed by Lloyd George, Curzon, Bonar Law, Hankey, Eric Geddes, Austen Chamberlain and Churchill, to say nothing of Admirals David Beatty and Ernle Chatfield.

The question that these men had first to reckon with was whether Britain could or should try to maintain the superiority of the Royal Navy, especially if that meant entering into competition with the United States. At the immediate conclusion of the First World War the answer seemed to be in the affirmative. The Royal Navy's predominance had been considered crucial to the defeat of Germany, and the British entered the Paris Peace Conference fully determined to fight for an American agreement recognising the maintenance of the naval *status quo*. Unfortunately for them, President Wilson planned to use American naval power to compel the Europeans to accept his vision of a new order. He refused to budge, and the result was an unhappy compromise that gave neither the British nor the Americans what they really desired.[7] Regardless, the deal reached at Paris soon became inoperable once the United States Senate rejected the Versailles Treaty. However, an important change had occurred. The hope that British naval superiority might easily be maintained had been dealt a heavy blow.

At first the British were most concerned about the future balance in capital ships (battleships and battlecruisers), in particular whether America would complete the 1916 programme. When the United States entered the First World War the First Lord of the Admiralty, Eric Geddes, even appealed to them to halt all construction on these large ships, calling them surplus to the war effort.[8] At first he was largely successful but when peace came the Americans began, somewhat hesitantly, to resume work. If the United States completed these ships their firepower and design specifications would have meant that the American Navy, while still marginally outnumbered, would almost certainly have become the strongest in the world. The question that British policy-makers had to wrestle with between 1919 and 1921, therefore, was whether they should build their own ships to match this armada or whether they should try to reach an agreement limiting American construction. This second option would almost certainly have entailed the acceptance of parity in capital ship strength, which at the time almost everyone would have agreed meant abandoning Britain's naval supremacy.

Churchill was as exercised by this question as any member of Cabinet. He was by disposition, as well as position, naturally sympathetic to the continuation of British supremacy. As Colonial Secretary he feared the impact that accepting the Americans as equals would have had upon Britain's outlying possessions, especially those in the Pacific. As he said in a letter to Arthur Balfour: 'I do not see how the foreign or colonial policy of our Empire can be carried out on the basis that we have ceased to be the leading naval power.'[9] Yet this desire was tempered by two other factors. Churchill's first foray into naval politics in 1908-9, had been as an advocate of economy in naval expenditures, and for much of the rest of his career he remained sceptical of Admiralty policy. Second, he considered excessive military spending harmful to Britain's general economic health, the protection of which was a Government's greatest responsibility.

> The Great War was not peculiar in showing once more the supreme importance of financial power as the basis of economic power, and of economic power as the basis of military power . . . the effect of any additional burden placed upon the country's finances is itself cumulative and prolongs the period of recovery to an extent disproportionate to the amount of money involved.[10]

Indeed, Churchill upheld these principles in 1919, just months after the acrimonious naval discussions in Paris, when he made a plea to halt all construction on vessels less than 80 per cent complete.[11]

The other concern that troubled Churchill was the possibility of antagonising the United States. While never as solicitous of American feelings as, say, Balfour or Lord Robert Cecil, he saw no benefit in offending the United States. He took the lead, for instance, in fighting for the modification or abandonment of the Anglo-Japanese Alliance.[12] As Colonial Secretary he saw the strategic advantages that Britain gained from the pact, but to him they were not nearly as valuable as friendship with America.

These different impulses, the yearning for superiority coupled with a desire to save money and a wish not to anger the Americans, combined in Winston Churchill to create the policy that he would fight for, in one guise or the other, until the fall of the second Baldwin government. The first real inkling of this policy came out of the 14 December 1920 meeting of the CID. The Committee, called to debate the naval impasse between the United States and Great Britain, had to consider what was, in Lloyd George's words, 'the most important and the most difficult' question it had ever discussed.[13] Almost all of the participants accepted, however grudgingly, that the British would have to appease the United States, and spent their time discussing the logistics of any such agreement. The one exception was Churchill. Like the rest he spoke of the need for friendship with the Americans and the need to reassure them about the Japanese Alliance, but unlike anyone else he made an impassioned plea for the continuation of British naval supremacy:

> . . . Great Britain must remain the strongest naval power. It would be a terrible day for the country when she ceased to be this. Great Britain, since the most remote times, had always been supreme at sea. The life of the nation, its culture, its prosperity, had rested on that basis.[14]

It was here that Churchill unveiled his unusual twist. He would accept parity with the Americans in capital ships while trying to maintain supremacy through 'a proper proportion of other units – cruisers, destroyers, and particularly submarines'.[15] It seemed a very seductive policy – one might call it naval supremacy at 'bargain basement' prices. The one problem was that in 1920 Churchill was alone in believing it was possible. The Admiralty had firmly concluded that the capital ship, or 'the strongest engine of war that the knowledge of the human race is capable of producing' was the foundation of a nation's naval strength. Beatty, for one, thought the issue beyond doubt and was dismissive of Churchill's pining for supremacy based on auxiliary vessels.[16]

The Admiralty, in fact, was less concerned with maintaining predominance than with staying level with the United States. Their eyes were fixed on the Americans' 1916 programme and they were after a firm commitment from the Cabinet to approve eight new British super-dreadnoughts. These vessels, which the Admiralty thought necessary only to supply the Royal Navy with parity, would alone have cost £75 million.[17] Such a sum would have severely taxed the financial resources of any government, let alone one like Lloyd George's which was pledged to increased social spending and smaller budgets for the armed forces.

Eventually, the Lloyd George government was freed from having to choose one policy by the agreements reached at the famous Washington Conference of 1921–22. Britain and America agreed to capital ship parity and a 10-year holiday in their construction, though the British were given the option of building two new vessels in lieu of their older force. To placate the Americans, the Anglo-Japanese Alliance was gutted and replaced with the Four-Power Treaty, which included the United States and France. This treaty, far from an alliance, merely pledged the powers to respect each others' possessions and forbade the construction of new fortifications in the Pacific. Taken together the agreements were almost universally hailed, and the British government was certainly no exception. While the Admiralty had some technical objections to the Americans' proposals on capital ships, the Cabinet swiftly accepted them. Indeed, the Cabinet seemed less suspicious of the Americans than members of their own delegation, whom they thought might be trying to sabotage an agreement.[18]

Churchill's reaction to the treaties was mixed. On the one hand he wrote a report that mourned the end of an era of dominance. 'We have abandoned all idea of naval supremacy, hitherto the foundation of our greatness, and have consented to a position of bare equality with the United States.' On the other hand he never raised objections to the agreements in Cabinet and he took advantage of this 'melancholy' turn of events to press for a 25 per cent cut in the naval budget. Yet Churchill had not given up all hope of Britain maintaining naval supremacy. In a small aside he mentioned the possibility that a long period of peace might dull the Americans' appetite for a large 'naval effort'.[19] This hope was the final piece in the Churchillian naval policy that would be adopted in July 1927. The British should try to maintain their supremacy through predominance in auxiliary ships, but in doing so they should avoid spending much money and hope that American indifference would preclude any naval build-up by the United States.

This last point was not as far-fetched as one might think. The American Congress had historically shown little interest in appropriating large sums for naval construction and at this time there existed a vocal group that was already campaigning for a massive reduction in American naval spending.[20] The agreements reached at Washington also provided Churchill with some reason for optimism. One area in which there was no agreement, specifically because of British objections, was a relative ratio for auxiliary ships. No quantitative limits were placed on a nation's cruisers, destroyers and submarines, though cruisers were subject to a weight allowance of 10,000 tons and could carry nothing larger than an 8-inch gun. This area of indecision, which was almost forgotten in the general rejoicing, would return in just a few years to plague Anglo-American relations.

Churchill, for his part, would soon lose his ability to influence British naval policy. He was jettisoned with Lloyd George just a few months after the signing of the Washington treaties. Yet when he did return, in 1924, with the exalted position of Chancellor of the Exchequer in the second Baldwin government, events and personalities had changed to create a situation more to Churchill's liking. In the first place the new government was composed of men less willing to parry his thrusts into strategic policy.[21] Baldwin, the new Prime Minister, a man of Asquithian fortitude, cared little and knew less about naval issues. The Foreign Secretary, Austen Chamberlain, was, for the first few years at least, absorbed in European matters. Gone were such men as Curzon and Bonar Law, and instead the Cabinet contained both more allies of Churchill, such as Lord Birkenhead and William Joynson-Hicks, and less assertive personalities such as the 4th Marquess of Salisbury and Baron Cushendun. The First Lord of the Admiralty, William Bridgeman, while well-meaning and stubborn, was not a star performer. Only two people, Lord Robert Cecil and the First Sea Lord, Admiral Beatty, were really equipped to withstand Churchill's various forays into naval policy. Cecil, a firm believer in the League of Nations and extremely solicitous of the United States, stood ready to oppose any attempt to regain supremacy for the Royal Navy. Beatty, on the other hand, had the stature necessary to fight for increased funding from the parsimonious Chancellor.

Another important reason for the increase in Churchill's influence was that his preconceived notions about how to restore British naval supremacy dovetailed exquisitely with the naval balance of the period, specifically the world balance in cruiser strength. Cruisers were fast, relatively lightly armed vessels of between 5,000 and 10,000 tons. Most British cruisers carried 6-inch guns, though the Washington Treaty allowed for guns of up to eight inches. Cruisers were used for two purposes; scouting and trade warfare. In the first role cruisers, during the years before the development of naval air power, were the eyes of the main battle fleet. Their high speed was used to scan the area in front of the main force and protect against a variety of threats. In their second role cruisers were sent out singly, or in small units, to protect a nation's seaborne trade or to destroy enemy commerce.

By 1924 it seemed possible that the British might be able to maintain a form of predominance because of their large lead in cruiser construction. Churchill had earlier referred to the need for the Royal Navy to maintain its lead in all auxiliary ships, but this general proviso was soon forgotten as attention became riveted on the cruiser balance.[22] Indeed, Britain's lead in this area was numerically impressive. Large wartime building, coupled with the generous programme of construction approved by the Labour government in 1924, meant that by 1925 the Royal Navy had 49 frontline cruisers either built or building. The Americans, on the other hand, had only 10 such ships, the *Omaha* Class laid down as part of the 1916 programme. In fact, Britain's closest competitor was Japan, which had 28 cruisers. Yet, while the Japanese trailed in the total number of cruisers, they had out-built the British since the end of the war. Between 1919 and 1924 they had laid down 18 such vessels to Britain's five. Since the Admiralty had concluded that the Japanese were now Britain's most likely enemy, they decided that they had to respond to this increase in Japanese construction and in 1925 they decided to push for a British programme of five new cruisers.[23] This set the stage for Churchill's first new foray into naval policy.

Traditionally any Chancellor of the Exchequer, regardless of his strategic proclivities, stood ready to resist Admiralty demands on the public purse; Winston Churchill was no exception. When the Admiralty first broached the idea of laying down five new cruisers in 1925, it was estimated that their plan would have increased the naval budget from £55.8 million to £65.5 million. Churchill had no intention of parting with so much money, and he set out to discredit the idea that underlay the

Admiralty proposals; the idea that a war might break out between Britain and Japan. In a series of Cabinet memoranda he ridiculed the notion of an Anglo-Japanese war.[24] In a direct appeal to the Prime Minister he declared: '. . . why should there be a war with Japan? I do not believe there is the slightest chance of it in our lifetime. The Japanese are our allies.'[25]

Yet, while Churchill was fighting against an increase in the fleet this should not be seen as a repudiation of his earlier views. Churchill had always maintained that naval supremacy should be maintained without excessive expenditure. Instead his obstinacy was an indication of his continued confidence in the global naval balance. He believed that Britain had maintained its naval superiority. Even though the Washington Treaty had ostensibly established capital-ship parity between the United States and Britain, Churchill, because of certain technical questions, believed there was 'absolutely no doubt' that the Royal Navy was stronger in this class. America was also 'astonishingly weak' in cruisers and trailed Britain in aircraft carriers.[26] He even dismissed Japanese cruiser construction, claiming that, while Japan had recently laid down more ships, Britain had built more than twice as much during the last 10 years.[27] The upshot of the whole controversy was that the Admiralty was given four smaller cruisers, instead of the five larger ones they had requested, and a budget increase of only £5 million. But Churchill had begun to use his influence on naval affairs and in doing so he set the stage for some extraordinary political moves during the summer of 1927.

In 1922, when Churchill reported on the need for cuts in the budgets of the Army and Navy, he mentioned the hope that the United States might lose interest in maintaining its naval strength. By 1927 it seemed that this hope had been realised. Between 1922 and 1926 the British had laid down two battleships, 12 cruisers, two destroyers and six submarines.[28] American construction, on the other hand, was distinctly nonchalant. In 1924 Congress had authorised the construction of eight large cruisers, but this was far from a guarantee that the ships would be built. Congressional authorisations were not appropriations or even commitments to appropriate. They should be seen as Congressional notices of intent, ones that could take years to be complied with and ones that Congress could revoke at its discretion. Congress had no intention of starting eight cruisers in 1924, but instead stipulated that they would all have to be begun if no agreement on limitation was reached by 1927. By 1926 only one of the eight ships authorised in 1924 had been laid down and, along with one submarine and six gunboats, constituted all of America's naval construction between 1922 and 1926.[29] It certainly seemed as if the United States was reverting to its pre-1916 tendencies.

One of the great differences between America and Britain was that naval power was vital to the latter's and not the former's existence. Naval issues did not loom large in the mind of either the American public or Congress. Before the First World War American naval construction had been spasmodic, with occasional periods of fervour followed by longer spells of apathy. The 1916 programme had run counter to the whole tradition of American naval policy, and was only made possible by the spectre of a massive European war. Even after the war there had remained a group of important Americans, of various views, who opposed the spirit of the 1916 programme. Former President Roosevelt and Henry Cabot Lodge, both supporters of a strong navy before the First World War, saw no reason for America to build a fleet to rival Great Britain's.[30] However, as long as the 1916 programme ships remained on the building slips, enough support could be gathered to see them through to completion. The real question was not so much America's particular need for these ships, but America's claim to parity. Once that need was recognised the Harding administration, as it demonstrated at Washington, did its utmost to establish parity at as low a level as possible. This being accomplished, naval issues in the United States subsided into the background.

The Coolidge administration, preferring arms control to naval construction, hoped to redress America's cruiser deficiency by applying the lessons learned at Washington and persuading the British to agree to parity at a relatively low level. Coolidge, besides being personally opposed to increased government spending, realised that there was little sympathy in Congress for a large American naval programme. With this in mind, the President invited the British and the Japanese to a disarmament conference to be held at Geneva during the summer of 1927. The British, needless to say, were wary. They had earlier agreed to American proposals at Washington because the United States had already begun the 1916 programme. By 1927 there was no sign that America had the will to lay down a large number of cruisers, and the British had no desire to scrap a large number of their own vessels simply to suit American purposes. Also, the British believed that their exposed trade routes and far-flung possessions entitled them to the world's largest cruiser force.[31] To the British, America was a happily self-contained economy, while they needed to protect their trade routes to survive. Since cruisers were considered the most effective means of trade protection, the British naturally believed they always had to have a considerable number at hand. The Admiralty's preparations for the upcoming conference thus proceeded on the assumption that their special need for cruisers should be protected.[32] The real question was how to protect it. It would clearly be very difficult to convince the Americans to acknowledge publicly Britain's right to superiority. Antagonising the Americans was also thought to be counter-productive because the British had one area where they wanted to see limitation, the building of the powerful *Washington* Class cruisers.

These vessels, weighing 10,000 tons and sporting 8-inch guns, were considerably larger and stronger than all but the biggest cruisers laid down during the First World War. Most British cruisers weighed between 3,500 and 5,000 tons and carried 6-inch guns.[33] If America or Japan proceeded to build a large number of these bigger cruisers, Britain's numerically larger force would quickly become obsolete. British proposals reflected these different concerns. They called for a continuation of the 5-5-3 ratio, but only for *Washington* Class Cruisers, hoping to limit themselves and America to 15. At the same time they wanted as few restrictions as possible on smaller cruisers, those weighing less than 7,500 tons with 6-inch guns. The British planned to maintain their cruiser supremacy by proposing such a high total tonnage allowance that the Americans would never build up to it.

These proposals, especially regarding tonnage, were bound to bring the British into confrontation with the United States. The Americans had two objectives for the Conference. They wanted a public acceptance of their right to parity in auxiliary ships, and the extension of the Washington 5-5-3 ratio to all classes at as low a level as possible. Their proposed tonnage allowances were 250,000–300,000 for cruisers, 200,000–250,000 for destroyers and 60,000–90,000 for submarines. The figure proposed by the Americans for cruisers was, in their minds, relatively generous. By 1927, the United States had completed only 75,000 tons and had a further 80,000 authorised. They would therefore need another 95,000 tons just to reach their proposed minimum. The British, on the other hand, were thinking in terms of a much greater figure. The Admiralty believed that eventually they would need 70 cruisers to both protect their trade and work with the main battle fleet. Such a force would comprise almost 600,000 tons. This was the amount they would first propose when the Geneva Conference began.

There have been a number of works that describe the personalities and proceedings of the disarmament conference held in Geneva during the summer of 1927.[34] The range of issues discussed makes it impossible here to describe anything except the particular subject of cruisers and naval superiority, but these were the crucial issues that decided the fate of the meeting. The delegates began assembling in Geneva during the second half of June. The British were led by Robert Cecil and William Bridgeman and the Americans by Hugh Gibson, the Ambassador to Switzerland, who had participated in the League of Nations discussions on arms limitation. In picking Cecil, the Cabinet chose to send the most pro-American man in the Cabinet, as well as someone who was committed to the disarmament process. He had opposed the Admiralty's requests for extra ships in 1925, and when news of the Americans' proposals for the Geneva Conference were first received he called them attractive.[35]

Cecil was a not a man ready to fight for the maintenance of British naval superiority. He had a great respect for American power and was determined not to do anything that would see the conference fail.[36] When the Americans expressed their shock at the British proposals for a cruiser limit of 600,000 tons he tried to dampen their apprehensions. He and Bridgeman called on Hugh Gibson during the morning of 29 June and categorically stated that the British recognised America's right to parity for all classes of naval vessels. This statement was quickly relayed to the State Department in Washington and from there directly to President Coolidge.[37] For the next two days it seemed that Cecil and Bridgeman did nothing but assure Americans that their right to parity was not being questioned. Bridgeman kept a diary during the conference and on 29 June he described two separate interviews with American reporters where he publicly denied any attempt by Britain to maintain naval superiority.[38] These reports were also passed on to Coolidge.[39]

In making these statements Cecil and Bridgeman were at first supported by the Foreign Office and the Cabinet. As Austen Chamberlain told Cecil after a Cabinet meeting on 4 July: 'The Cabinet were . . . quite clear that they must support Bridgeman and yourself, and that to use any other language in Washington than that which you had used in Geneva was unthinkable.'[40] Another member of the Cabinet, in his copy of the minutes, admitted that 'the principle of cruiser parity had been conceded'.[41] With all these assurances the Americans began to rest easier, and the two sides settled down to try to reach a cruiser tonnage limitation acceptable to each side.[42]

It was at this point that Winston Churchill stepped back into the fray. In late June, Churchill had submitted a paper to the Cabinet outlining his fears.:

> There can really be no parity between a power whose navy is its life and a power whose navy is only for prestige . . . It always seems to be assumed that it is our duty to humour the United States and minister to their vanity. They do nothing for us in return, but exact their last pound of flesh.[43]

To begin with, he seems to have had little impact on the Cabinet and was overruled in the general stampede to guarantee America's right to parity. Soon, however, a more concerted effort would be made to reverse this position. Beatty tried to convince Baldwin not to issue a public communiqué to the Americans about parity. Other Cabinet members, including Lord Birkenhead, began to agitate.[44] In the end, however, it was up to Churchill to organise and command the opposition to parity, a job he did with consummate skill. During a meeting of the CID on 7 July, Churchill, aided admirably by Beatty, succeeded in dominating discussion of the cruiser question.[45] Churchill made it known that he was not in the least concerned with the prospect of a breakdown at Geneva. He even mentioned the prospect of reinvigorating the Anglo-Japanese Alliance in an attempt to rein in American power. Only Austen Chamberlain attempted to combat the rambunctious Chancellor of the Exchequer, but he was never at his best when discussing naval issues. On 20 July, Churchill circulated an even more aggressive memorandum, calling parity with the United States 'fatal to British naval security', and even mentioned the possibility of an Anglo-American war.

> No doubt it is quite right in the interests of peace to go on talking about war with the United States being 'unthinkable'. Everyone knows that this is not true . . . We do not wish to put ourselves in the power of the United States. We cannot tell what they might do if at some future date they were in a position to give us orders about our policy, say, in India, or Egypt, or Canada . . . tonnage parity means that Britain can be starved into obedience to any American decree. I would neither trust America to command, nor England to submit. Evidently on the basis of American naval superiority speciously disguised as parity immense dangers overhang the future of the world.'[46]

Churchill saw the Geneva Conference as a chance for Britain to reassert her strategic independence from the United States. The rather alarming nature of his arguments began to win over converts in the Cabinet. Even Stanley Baldwin, who generally avoided discussion of naval issues, adopted much of Churchill's rhetoric when he argued that cruiser parity with America would make Britain 'vassals of the United States . . . In my opinion the moment has quite definitely come when we must stand up to them.'[47] Yet when Baldwin recorded these ideas he was not in London but on a steamship bound for Canada. His departure on 21 July was crucial.

On 19 July it had been announced that Cecil and Bridgeman were returning to London for consultations. By the time they arrived the Prime

Minister had departed and Churchill had much greater freedom in the Cabinet. He used this freedom to make sure the Geneva Conference would fail. Churchill would have liked Bridgeman to return to Geneva and claim that he had exceeded his instructions, and state that he had had no right to say what he had about parity. This the First Lord wisely declined to do.[48] But Churchill had other ideas and he decided to wreck the conference by refusing to compromise on the question of 8-inch guns. The Americans wanted the right to arm all their new cruisers with these guns, as allowed by the Washington Treaty. Churchill, however, pressed for a proposal to limit all of America's new cruisers of less than 10,000 tons, to 6-inch guns, at least until 1936. Cecil was appalled at Churchill's manoeuvrings and attacked him directly stating: 'You believe that future war is practically certain . . .'[49] Cecil's opposition would prove futile. When Churchill brought the issue up before the Cabinet he was supported by a vote of 10 to six, and his policy became the official negotiating position of the British government.

It was widely known that these proposals were unacceptable to the Americans. As Maurice Hankey described the situation to Baldwin: 'I think most people in their hearts think the Conference will now break down . . . I would mention some people who rather hope it will.'[50] As Churchill remarked a few weeks later: 'It is not true that a concession on the 8-inch gun would have turned the scale at Geneva. The basis of agreement never existed.'[51]

Cecil and Bridgeman returned to Geneva but no agreement could be reached. They then returned to Britain, and Cecil succeeded in resigning from the government. The original draft of his letter of resignation was a polemic against elements in the Cabinet.

> . . . it seemed that we were well on the road to an agreement . . . But it was just the prospect of success which was agitating those of our colleagues who had come to believe that what is now called mathematical parity between us and the Americans in smaller cruisers was a danger to the Empire, and accordingly, notwithstanding our protests, the Cabinet sent us a peremptory summons to come home.[52]

Eventually Cecil toned down the more hostile comments in his official letter, but it took little imagination to see that his anger was directed at the Chancellor of the Exchequer.

There is no doubt that Churchill had orchestrated events masterfully and demonstrated great political skill in getting the government to reverse direction almost completely in just a few weeks on the question of naval superiority. He had become the single most influential maker of British naval policy, a position he maintained for almost a year.

What Churchill did with his influence was striking. He fought against the idea of any concessions to the Americans to bring them back to the negotiating table, while at the same time continuing his crusade against any new British cruiser construction. At the same moment that he was leading the Cabinet charge to scupper the hopes of an agreement at Geneva, he began a fresh campaign against the Royal Navy's cruiser plans.[53] It would have been difficult to devise a more passive cruiser policy than the one he proposed. Churchill wanted no new construction for at least the next two years and fought on throughout the autumn and winter against Admiralty plans to lay down three cruisers in each of the next two years.[54] He was particularly successful in this fight. The Admiralty would get only one new cruiser in 1927 and no new cruisers in 1928.[55]

With the benefit of hindsight, Churchill's actions seem more than slightly contradictory. He was, however, involved in a high stakes gamble, one that he believed would maintain Britain's naval superiority. Churchill seems to have become more and more distrustful of the Americans, and even began to suggest pulling out of the whole Washington system of disarmament. Cecil claimed that Churchill first mentioned this to him in August of 1927.[56] By early 1928, after his successful fight against the Admiralty cruiser proposals, Churchill gave a fuller exposition of his plans to his Private Secretary at the Treasury, P J Grigg. Grigg made a note of Churchill's ideas which he passed on to Hankey. They provide a fascinating glimpse of Churchill's thoughts.

> The most we can hope to do in the 20 or 30 years lying before us is to have the best and strongest Navy . . . Even now we have only just escaped binding ourselves to a mathematical parity with the United States, which would in fact make it impossible for us to protect our vital overseas supplies in any war with them . . . A sound good British fleet operating through a well-conceived and well-maintained system of fuelling bases ought to be able to keep us going at heavy expense until our unique resources in ship-building and ship-manning power gave us decisive preponderance . . . These hideous and remote and improbable wars must be considered for they affect the foundations of the state . . . We should reject all proposals for a treaty of mathematical parity with the United States . . . that apart from any agreement that may be possible about the age or size of battleships, we should preserve entire liberty in numbers and design; and lastly,

we should do our utmost to keep a Navy which as a whole is stronger and better than that of the United States.[57]

Churchill, in his early years, was never as fond of the United States as his behaviour during the Second World War might indicate. As this passage demonstrates, his antipathy towards America was at its apex near the end of the second Baldwin government. There are a number of possible reasons for this. First, he saw no strategic justification for America's demands for cruiser parity. He grew more and more irritated at America's inability to recognise Britain's special cruiser needs. Second, his experience while Chancellor of the Exchequer had not served to endear him to Americans, nor they to him. Squabbling over the payment of Britain's war-time debt and other financial issues had led to friction. Churchill thought the Americans were excessively domineering in their negotiating, and wanted Britain to have the power to resist American dictation.[58] In his view American policy was 'selfish', 'extortionate' and the result of 'avarice'.[59] Likewise, the American people were 'sunk in selfishness'.[60]

Churchill's antipathy to the United States was combined with a growing scepticism about their ability to challenge Britain's position. The Americans were still 'hopelessly' behind, and he estimated that the Royal Navy was four times as strong in cruisers. Moreover, American apathy, or so Churchill reasoned, meant that they would not try to match Britain's lead, at least in the foreseeable future. He thought American cruiser programmes would be limited to just two or three ships annually, so that the British could delay any new building for a number of years. In a sense he believed the Royal Navy could have its cake and eat it too. '. . . Winston talked very freely about the USA. He thinks they are arrogant, fundamentally hostile to us, and that they wish to dominate world politics. He thinks their "Big Navy" talk is bluff which we ought to call.'[61]

The great problem with Churchill's whole analysis was this last belief about American behaviour. British manoeuvring during the conference was considered so antagonistic and offensive that it achieved the spectacular and, most would have thought, extremely unlikely result of enraging and energising both the American Congress and President Coolidge.[62] American reaction to the Geneva Conference exposed the real weakness in Churchill's plan as well as the one flaw in Britain's cruiser position. Churchill had based the success of his policy on the hope that the United States would lack the will to build a large number of cruisers, but the effect of his actions had achieved the opposite. Not since 1916 had a President and Congress been so determined to support the growth of the United States Navy.

In his Annual Message to Congress, delivered on 6 December 1927, Coolidge explicitly stated his intention to build more cruisers.[63] His specific plan, which he revealed a few days later to the Chairman of the House Naval Affairs Committee, was to build a total of 71 new vessels of all types, including 25 more *Washington* Class cruisers.[64] With these ships added to the eight already authorised in 1924 and the 10 of the *Omaha* Class, America's cruiser force would, in a matter of years, be the most modern and powerful in the world. During the conference, the British had wanted to limit the Americans, and themselves, to 15 or even 12 *Washington* Class cruisers. This was done both to save money and to prolong the viability of the Royal Navy's older fleet of smaller, less heavily armed vessels. The prospect, therefore, of the United States possessing 33 10,000-ton, 8-inch gun cruisers meant that the British, who had only 14 such vessels either built, building or authorised, would have had to stretch their resources just to stay equal.

Fortunately the American Congress, while also angered by British actions, only approved the construction of 15 new *Washington* Class cruisers. The British would still have to increase production considerably, however, to match this smaller programme. When the Admiralty first got wind of this possibility, they pressed for a complete re-evaluation of British policy.[65] More importantly, other members of the Cabinet, who had been operating under the assumption that Churchill's scenario would come to pass, began to press for a negotiated settlement of the cruiser question.

The first move by the British was the very ill-considered Anglo-French Compromise of 1928, which would have allowed a nation to build as many 10,000-ton cruisers as it wanted, but would have limited the number of these vessels that could carry 8-inch guns.[66] As a negotiating ploy it proved to be a disaster, and served only to further antagonise the Americans, who saw it simply as a way for the British to weaken their proposed force of *Washington* Class cruisers. President Coolidge became so embittered by what he saw as British deceit that he made a call for American cruiser superiority.[67]

Even though this move failed disastrously, it was symptomatic of the growing unrest in the Cabinet about the souring of Anglo-American relations brought on by the collapse of the Geneva Conference and Churchill's policy. Two members in particular, Lord Salisbury, the Lord Privy Seal, and Baron Cushendun, Cecil's successor, began to call openly for a change in British policy.[68] This move gathered impetus when Cushendun filled in as Foreign Secretary between August and November of 1927, during Austen Chamberlain's illness. A positive attempt was made to placate the Americans through concessions on the question of neutral rights, long an area of contention between the two powers. However, no agreement on this issue was going to stop American cruiser construction. That could not happen until the Americans were convinced that the British did not wish to deny them naval parity.

It soon became apparent that the British would have to make a concession on this point to appease the Americans. Robert Craigie, the head of the Foreign Office's American Department, argued precisely this in November of 1928 when he drafted a memorandum on Anglo-American relations. He dismissed the idea that the Americans would be happy with anything less than full parity.[69] This memorandum was circulated on the eve of Coolidge's bitter speech calling for American cruiser superiority, and thus provided powerful ammunition for those seeking to improve Anglo-American relations. The one great exception, naturally, was Churchill. He was so completely associated with the attempt to maintain naval superiority that he could not possibly support a concession on the American right to parity. His response came in the form of a rather sulky attack on both Craigie and President Coolidge.

> If the essay by Mr Craigie on Anglo-American relations . . . has no other object than to inculcate meekness and caution it need not be dealt with in detail . . . it would be most unwise to renew negotiations with Mr Coolidge. He has just explained to the world the view-point of a New England backwoodsman . . . Mr Coolidge will soon sink into the obscurity from which only accident extracted him.[70]

While Churchill was too committed to back down, most of the other members of the Cabinet continued to try to find a way to relax tensions with the Americans. With a British election looming in 1929, and a new administration in the White House, the Cabinet, and Baldwin in particular, wanted to do everything possible to convince the Americans that they wished to negotiate an end to the stalemate. The Prime Minister took time to talk to the American Ambassador, visiting American diplomats, and even American journalists about the need for agreement and his willingness to travel to Washington to negotiate a compromise.[71] In such an atmosphere Churchill became more and more isolated. By March Baldwin was contemplating transferring the Chancellor of the Exchequer to the India Office if the Conservatives won re-election.[72]

Fortunately for Churchill, as well as the Conservative party, Ramsay MacDonald was able to form a government after the May 1929 elections. Not only was Churchill saved from having to be part of an administration that seemed determined to repudiate the naval policy he had devised over the last 10 years, but the Conservative Party would be out of office when the Great Depression hit Great Britain. Though Churchill was spared for the moment, his actions during the previous two years deserved criticism. It still seems somewhat perplexing why he chose to assert authority so dramatically over British naval policy and, ultimately, Anglo-American relations. It might have been based on a desire to exercise political power and increase his authority in the Cabinet. If so it proved a very risky strategy that backfired and most probably would have resulted in his demotion.

In all probability it was because Churchill desperately clung to the notion that Great Britain, as a great power, had the ability to choose whether to retain naval supremacy or not. He was the only member of the Cabinet consistently to argue for the maintenance of British naval supremacy between 1919 and 1929, but for the first eight years had done nothing active to promote his policy. In 1927, however, he saw an opportunity. America seemed reluctant to build more ships while Britain already had superiority in cruisers. It seems likely that Churchill saw this as his, and the British Empire's, last chance to press for a policy of naval supremacy. In doing so he let his emotions about the Royal Navy overrun his rational ability to analyse Anglo-American relations.

Churchill had no desire to see the Empire exist on the sufferance of another power, a situation he believed was likely if the United States ever attained full parity with the Royal Navy. The paradox of his policy was that the desire to avoid sufferance was itself based on the sufferance of the United States. The British could only hope to maintain cruiser supremacy if the United States lost interest in building ships, but in following a policy designed to protect their supremacy, the Baldwin government, manipulated so superbly by Churchill, chose to adopt a position that almost guaranteed that the United States would not lose interest in building ships. This was the downfall of Churchill's policy. It was not based on Britain's inherent strength but America's inherent weakness.

In the end, Churchill's gambit represented the end of an era. Never again would a British government, either publicly or confidentially, claim naval supremacy as a right. This move was not as traumatic an event as some might have claimed, as accepting parity with America did not automatically mean that the Royal Navy would be unable to protect the Empire. It did, however, represent the end of a particular aspect of British power – the ability to determine its own naval strength. Churchill, for reasons of prestige, politics and conviction, could not bring himself to admit this era was at an end.

4

Churchill, the European Balance of Power and the USA

Brian McKercher

In reflecting on the origins of the Second World War, Sir Winston Churchill observed: 'The British people do not, as is sometimes thought, go to war for calculation, but for sentiment'.[1] His comment says much about the way in which he approached British defence policy in the inter-war period. During the Second World War and after, Churchill emerged as one of the leading exponents of the Anglo-American 'special relationship'.[2] The strategic threats to Britain posed, first by the Axis Powers and, afterwards, the USSR, required the United States' support for the defence of Europe and of Western interests, especially Britain's, in the wider world. This attitude did not suffuse Churchill's thinking in the 1920s. However, in the 1930s, his views about the United States changed. This transformation reflected his desire to use American resources to bolster Britain's European and imperial strategic position.

Churchill's conception of the Empire and the European balance formed before the First World War. It permeated his ideas between 1919 and 1939 about how Britain should defend its global interests, the *raison d'être* of Britain's position as the greatest of the Great Powers, and strive towards ensuring the equilibrium in Europe where the chief threat to Britain's security resided. He saw the Empire as a static entity in which reform should occur at a slow and steady pace determined by London. This ran counter to the views of dominion and colonial politicians such as Mackenzie King, the Canadian Prime Minister, Eamon De Valera, the Irish republican, and Mahatma Gandhi, the Indian nationalist leader;

hence, Churchill resisted these leaders. Still, he had a fixed vision of the Empire; he looked to ensure the strength of British armed forces to defend it and to expand imperial trade to make it viable economically. In these calculations, the United States could not be ignored. In the first years of peace after the First World War, when the Americans sought a 'navy second to none' and embarked on aggressive economic diplomacy, he saw the United States as a threat to Britain's leading position in the world. Ten years later, the emerging threats of Nazi Germany and Fascist Italy to the European balance of power and militaristic Japan to the white empires in the Far East, altered his outlook. By September 1939, when he joined Neville Chamberlain's War Cabinet as First Lord of the Admiralty, he had undergone an intellectual odyssey concerning the United States that lay at the base of his subsequent embrace of 'the special relationship'. When war broke out in 1939, it was cold calculation that dominated his thinking about American power and its relationship to British security.

Churchill's attachment to the Empire was sincere and profound. In 1876 his father, Lord Randolph Churchill, began service as secretary to his grandfather, the Duke of Marlborough, the Lord Lieutenant of Ireland. In his book, *My Early Life*, Churchill related that his first childhood memories were of viceregal Dublin: 'A great black crowd, scarlet soldiers on horseback, strings pulling away a brown shiny sheet [over a statue of Lord Gough], the old Duke, the formidable grandpapa, talking loudly to the crowd.' The panoply of the Empire always appealed to him, confirming his sense of Great Britain's position as a leading power and his conviction about the inherent superiority of the civilising forces of 'English' cultural and political institutions:

> I was a child of the Victorian era, when the structure of our country seemed firmly set, when its position in trade and on the seas was unrivalled, and when the realisation of the greatness of our Empire and our duty to preserve it was ever growing stronger. In those days the dominant forces in Great Britain were very sure of themselves and of their doctrines. They thought they could teach the world the art of government and the science of economics . . . They rested very sedately under the convictions of power and security.[3]

Such sentiments survived despite Churchill's view of the Empire being tempered by high office and its responsibilities. In March 1931, for instance, in a speech criticising the intention of the 'National Government' to give home rule to India, he spoke passionately about Britain's continuing Imperial mission:

Here you have nearly three hundred and fifty millions of people, lifted to a civilisation and to a level of peace, order, sanitation, and progress far above anything they could have possibly have achieved themselves or could maintain.[4]

Of course, by the post-First World War period, if not before, such sentiments ran counter to the desires of a range of dominion and colonial leaders for greater control over their own affairs. With the exception of terrorist-politicians like De Valera, many of these men shared with Churchill an emotional tie to the Empire. Mackenzie King, the most independently-minded of all inter-war dominion leaders, never disguised his attachment to the Empire rather than the 'Commonwealth', a word he disliked.[5] Yet, in 1922, during the Chanak crisis, Mackenzie King had been at the fore in dominion opposition to the government of Lloyd George, in which Churchill was the Colonial Secretary, because London decided unilaterally to commit the Empire as a whole to war against Turkey.[6] Ottawa had no desire to involve Canadian troops in hostilities designed to shore up Britain's strategic position in the eastern Mediterranean. If Turkish actions had imperilled Canadian interests that would have been different. But they did not; and, besides, the power base of Mackenzie King's government lay in Quebec. French-Canadians had little desire to fight and die for Britain anywhere, let alone half way around the world. The result of Chanak was the rejection by Ottawa and Cape Town of an 'Imperial foreign policy'. At the 1926 Imperial Conference, it led to the Balfour declaration, which allowed that Britain and the dominions were 'autonomous communities within the British Empire, equal in status, in no way subordinate to one another in any aspect of their domestic or external affairs'.[7]

Churchill was not blind to the determination of the senior dominions to follow their own diplomatic paths in the 1920s and 1930s. As Chancellor of the Exchequer in 1926, he put on public record his opposition to 'constitutional arrangements for the British Empire of a rigid character'.[8] Yet, in the same breath, he sought to unlock emotional ties buried in the breasts of dominion representatives:

The British Empire grows great and strong by the unseen, increasing heart-beats of a strong powerful people, separated from one another by immense distance of continent and seas, but united and associated for the purpose of mutual security and advancement; united also by a growing and broadening conception of corporate life and duty; and united most of all by the romance of history symbolised and enshrined in the Imperial Crown.

A child of the Victorian era appealed to other Victorian children: a strong and powerful people; a common heritage; a better future; duty; and the symbol of the Crown. The glories of the Empire experienced by the young subaltern shone through in the public utterances of a senior states-man at a time when Britain's international position differed markedly from that before 1914. But this does not mean that Churchill was not aware that the Empire underpinned Britain's position as the greatest of the Great Powers. In tandem with Britain's strengths – the Royal Navy, a sound economy, and the financial sinews of the City – the Empire's com-bined population, food and raw materials, and markets, gave those responsible for British foreign and defence policy considerable resources by which the country's national security could be safeguarded.

Despite Churchill's suggestion that the British were not calculating in their decisions for war and peace – the nub of foreign and defence policy – he and other politicians in the inter-war period determined that policy by careful design. This translated into simultaneously shielding the Empire and maintaining the balance of power in Europe because, crucially, these broad strands of foreign and defence policy were intertwined. Churchill's reputation as a strategic thinker has lately been questioned: that he was not opportunistic; that he lacked an appreciation of modern social, eco-nomic and scientific trends, as well as those touching politics and philosophy; that he shunned deep enquiry and contemplation; and that he possessed a stubborn streak that saw him adhere to particular lines of thought made hollow by changed circumstances.[9] While much of this is probably true – and no inter-war British leader was without fault con-cerning grand strategy – it remains that Churchill's strategic ideas reflected those of his generation of British leaders that rose to prominence in the decade and a half before 1914. As a perceptive recent study argues, the men who gained control of British foreign and defence policy at this junc-ture came to share a belief that Britain had to combine with other powers, at the price of pledging future military support, to maintain the balances of power in the world integral to safeguarding British interests.[10] These 'Edwardians' replaced the 'Victorians' such as the third Marquess of Salisbury, who had commanded policy after the Crimean war and evaded formal political and mutual defence commitments to other powers. This does not suggest that the 'Edwardians' and their predecessors had dissim-ilar notions about the nature of external policy. Both groups, and especially Churchill, supported Palmerston's maxim that Britain had no eternal friends or enemies, only eternal interests. Nor is it to argue that they disagreed about the ends of policy: maintaining the balances of power in Europe and elsewhere to ensure peace and security. Rather, they disagreed on the means by which those interests could best be protected and enhanced: whether there should be active British involvement in Great Power politics on the continent and the wider world, underpinned by alliances and *ententes* to preserve international stability and with the understanding that these commitments might lead to war.

Churchill then believed it best to pursue British security by defending the Empire and ensuring the European balance of power. Like his sentimental conception of Britain and its Empire, these beliefs were formed before the First World War. They did not devolve simply into two spheres: imperial defence and 'a continental commitment'. Rather, Churchill and other British leaders, whether 'Victorians' or 'Edwardians', saw the world as composed of several balances of power. Though they did not use such terminology – they thought in terms of questions needing answers, such as the 'Eastern question', the 'Indian question', the 'Chinese question', and so on – they tended to look at specific threats to national security in particular parts of the world. Grand strategy, thus, entailed pursuing foreign and defence policies that considered a series of interlocking questions on a global scale.[11]

Churchill's military service on the Indian frontier, in the Sudan, and in southern Africa shaped his perception of how and why particular policies should be pursued. In the *Malakand Field Force*, his experiences in military operations in northern India led him to deprecate the so-called 'Forward Policy' which had sought to find 'a definite and defensible frontier' between the British colony and Afghanistan. But, with a douche of realism, he observed: '. . . it is futile to engage in the controversies of the past. There are sufficient in the present and it is with the present we are concerned'.[12] British strategic thinking had to deal with the existing situation, and to this end it had to be determined so as to prevent British adversaries, at that time the Russians, the Emir of Afghanistan and border tribes, from weakening London's hold over India. Likewise, in assessing the reconquest of the Sudan, Churchill opined: 'The advantage to Great Britain is no less clear to those who believe that our connection with Egypt, as with India, is in itself a source of strength.'[13] To his mind, British control of the Sudan guaranteed control of the Nile River and 'completely destroyed' French influence in Egypt. In this context, protecting the Suez Canal, the lifeline to the eastern reaches of the Empire, remained the paramount strategic consideration.

The same considerations permeate his on-the-spot assessments of the South African war: 'how strategically powerful the Boer position . . . the Imperial Government has been in the unpleasant position of watching its adversaries grow continually stronger'. Britain could not allow a region containing substantial British investment and vital naval bases to fall from its grasp. Moreover, in this struggle, Churchill came to the realisation that a 'democratic government cannot go to war unless the country is behind it'. He placed the blame for the exposed British position in Southern Africa at the beginning of the war on both Boer enthusiasms and the 'Peace Party' in London. The latter received especial censure because in opposing early resolute action, they only produced greater casualties and a struggle costly to the Exchequer.[14]

Churchill's subsequent political career before the First World War, especially his time as First Lord of the Admiralty after October 1911, underscored the validity of his earlier assessments. It is true that he did not perceive Wilhelmine Germany as a threat to Britain until after his visit there in late 1909. Part of the reason stemmed from his ministerial responsibilities: he held office beginning in December 1905 as the Liberal Under-Secretary for Colonies and, in April 1908, entered the Cabinet as President of the Board of Trade. His time in the Colonial Office largely involved preparations to give South Africa independence – it came in 1910 – whereby Churchill undertook to entrench 'British' influence in the new constitution.[15] As President of the Board of Trade, although he looked to preserve 'free trade', his focus came to rest on alleviating social distress within the country, chiefly unemployment. With Lloyd George he promoted labour exchanges and a national insurance programme. In the debate over Naval Estimates in March 1909, Lloyd George and Churchill led the 'economists' within the Cabinet.

But after his visit to Germany in August 1909, he became convinced of the German threat.[16] Over the next five years, he worked to ensure that Britain was strong enough to deter German ambitions and, should this fail, to defeat Germany in war. In this way, he oversaw the continued improvement of the navy, the guardian of the Empire; he sided with efforts by the War Secretary, Richard Haldane, to improve the army; and he supported the *ententes* with France and Tsarist Russia as means by which the British government could have a say in continental affairs. Certainly, by 1911, Churchill understood the connection between strong armed forces and the ability of the Cabinet, diplomatically, to protect British interests in Europe and the wider world. Thus, during the second Moroccan crisis, just before he became First Lord, he supported a strong public stand against the Germans, a line of reasoning already taking hold in the Cabinet, the Foreign Office and the Admiralty. 'It is not for Morocco, nor indeed Belgium, that I would take part in this terrible business', he wrote. 'One cause alone could justify our participation – to prevent France from being trampled down and looted by the Prussian junkers – a disaster ruinous to the world, and fatal to our country.'[17] As First Lord, he made his arguments with greater force:

> The safety of New Zealand and Australia is secured by the naval power and the alliances based on the naval power of Great Britain. No European State would or could invade or conquer New Zealand unless the British Navy had been destroyed. The same naval power of Great Britain in European waters also protects New Zealand and Australia from any present danger by Japan.[18]

Thus, by the 'July crisis' of 1914, Churchill had set ideas about national strategy that arose from his military service and his political career. It might be that in his strategic thinking he was not opportunistic, lacked an appreciation of trends in modern thought, evaded deep enquiry and contemplation, and was tenacious to the point of stubbornness in promoting his beliefs. On the other hand, he understood the difficulties and dangers inherent in defending British national and imperial interests – he was one of a very few pre-war Cabinet ministers who had been willing to lay down his life for his beliefs. He comprehended the connection between strong armed forces and an effective foreign and defence policy. And, even though he might not have appreciated the value of contemporary thinkers, he understood the essence of national defence: assessing situations as they existed to prevent adversaries from becoming 'strategically powerful' so as to threaten British security. His record in this regard during the First World War is the subject of decided controversy, a result of the failed Allied landings at Gallipoli in 1915. Nonetheless, when peace returned, Churchill had firm opinions about how after 1911 Britain had defended its global interests and met Germany's zeal to upset the European equilibrium in its favour – and, of course, his central place in this story.[19] No doubt exists that these were the same views he would pursue after 1919. The war had simply changed the constellation of Great Powers, the configuration of friends and adversaries to consider when formulating national security policy; British external interests, the focus of that policy, were precisely the same.

International relations in the 15 years before 1914 had been essentially Eurocentric. Accordingly, although defending the Empire by diplomatic means had never been neglected – the Anglo-Japanese alliance of 1902 and the *ententes* with France and Russia are indicative – British foreign and defence policy had largely centred on continental Europe and the Mediterranean. By the time the Paris Peace Conference convened, however, two pre-war Powers, Austria-Hungary and the Ottoman Empire, had vanished; Germany and Russia were enfeebled; 'successor states' had arisen in central and eastern Europe; and Britain's wartime allies, France and Italy, were resolved on enhancing and expanding their interests in Europe and abroad. Moreover, although Britain was not weakened to the extent suggested by some historians,[20] the country's economic strength had decreased relative to that of two new extra-European rivals: Japan and the United States. Possessing adequate financial resources and industrial capacity, both of these emerging powers seemed willing to challenge Britain's naval mastery and its trading empire. Initially, the United States presented the more immediate threat to Britain's pre-eminent global position.

Before 1914, Churchill possessed mixed views about the United States. His mother, for whom he cared very much, was a New York heiress: 'She shone for me like the Evening Star. I loved her dearly – but at a distance'.[21] Thus, by birth half-American and exposed to his mother's reminiscences of her past, he had an appreciation of the world inhabited by his American relations, that of the so-called 'eastern establishment' and new money. Although this appreciation was certainly fuller than that of his political colleagues before 1914, such as Lloyd George or Haldane, who had not ventured across the Atlantic, he shared general upper-class British views about the United States as a place of adventure, less civilisation, more equality and ostentatious wealth.[22] 'I think mind you that vulgarity is a sign of strength', he observed on his first trip the United States in 1895. 'A great, crude, strong, young people are the Americans – like a boisterous healthy boy among enervated but well-bred ladies and gentlemen.'[23] Such attitudes changed little before 1914, seemingly enhanced by an American speaking tour he undertook in late 1900 to publicise his books on the Boer War.[24]

The First World War and its immediate aftermath produced in Churchill an animus towards the United States. He saw American strength as a potential threat to Britain's leading economic and financial position and, at the Paris Peace Conference, he deplored the inability of Woodrow Wilson to deliver on his ideas about post-war security. Initially, after American entry into the war on the British side in April 1917, Churchill was sanguine about the strength that a million fresh American soldiers would give the allied armies on the continent.[25] He also understood the value of the material support provided by the United States before and after April 1917 – for which, of course, Britain and its allies paid.[26] American economic and financial strength presaged a challenge of significant proportions to Britain as peace returned, especially as the British would have to repay war loans raised on the New York money market.

But once the Central Powers collapsed, whether or not the Americans played a decisive role in this collapse, Wilson looked to arrogate for the United States a leading role in determining the peace settlement. A week after the armistice on the Western Front came into effect, Churchill told the Cabinet:

> The British Empire and the United States have come across the seas and oceans to rescue Europe from the oppression of militarism; they cannot leave her in a welter of anarchy . . . We might abandon Europe but Europe will not abandon us.[27]

Seeing European security as an essential interest for London and Washington, he surmised that the Anglo-Americans would have to combine to ensure that a post-war balance there was established and maintained. Unfortunately, Wilson had a different conception of how to maintain peace and security that dwelt in his advocacy of the collective security provisions of the new League of Nations.[28] Moreover, on one crucial question – the emergence of Bolshevik Russia and how to meet the peril it portended via the export of revolution – Churchill found himself at odds with the American President. Supported by Lloyd George, Wilson would not countenance an Allied-sponsored military commitment to destroy the emerging Bolshevik regime.[29] While this situation created tensions between Lloyd George and Churchill, who was appointed Secretary of State for War and Air in January 1919,[30] it filled Churchill with misgivings about the purpose of American foreign policy. Such misgivings were enhanced when Wilson's political enemies in the American Congress began to question whether the United States should join the League:

> There were from the very beginning serious doubts about the credentials of President Wilson. The supreme efficacy of the League of Nations depended upon the accession of the United States. Here was the great new eternal balancing factor. Was it at the command of President Wilson?[31]

The answer was 'no'. In October 1919, the American Senate failed to ratify the Treaty of Versailles, the peace settlement with Germany, because its preamble contained the Covenant of the League. Wilson's supposed internationalist diplomacy evaporated as the United States returned to its traditional isolation from Great Power politics. In Churchill's view, Wilson's foreign policy brought 'false hopes' that 'aggravated' Europe's readjustment to peace:

Europe was left to scramble out of the world disaster as best she could; and the United States . . . was to settle down upon the basis of receiving through one channel or another four-fifths of the reparations paid by Germany to the countries she had devastated or whose manhood she had slain.[32]

In the post-1919 world essential British interests had not altered: no single state or group of states should dominate on the continent; and the defence of the Empire, with expanded holdings in the Middle East after Anglo-French partition of Ottoman domains, still involved finding answers to questions in China, India and other places. In this context American policies represented a significant challenge to Britain's continued pre-eminence as the greatest of the Great Powers. Britain had become a net debtor to the United States, although former British allies owed more to Britain than the British owed American lenders.[33] On top of this, because the British maritime blockade of the Central Powers during the three years of American neutrality offended American self-esteem and reduced the profits of American industrialists and other traders, there had arisen a body of opinion advocating that the United States build 'a navy second to none'. This group, the so-called 'Big Navy' party, influenced American politicians, especially in the Republican administrations of Warren Harding and Calvin Coolidge which succeeded that of Wilson after the 1920 presidential election.[34] In the new world order, shaped by the war and defined by the peace settlement, the American question required an answer.

Churchill's post-war concentration on policy towards the United States began when he became Chancellor of the Exchequer in Stanley Baldwin's second Conservative government in November 1924. Since the Peace Conference, his political career had taken twists that forced his attention on other matters. As the Secretary of State for War and Air until February 1921, he pushed for adequate Army and Air Force budgets at a time of significant retrenchment; and he helped co-ordinate the military response to the rebellion in Ireland.[35] Then as Colonial Secretary until October 1922, his ministerial responsibilities centred largely on bringing stability to the Middle East; the Treaty of Sèvres, the Turkish treaty hammered out of the Paris Peace Conference, collapsed because of the opposition of republican nationalists who rose in rebellion against the Sultan. Churchill's principal achievement occurred at the Cairo Conference in March 1921 which, by February 1922, produced the Anglo-Egyptian Treaty (giving Egypt nominal independence while ensuring British control of the Suez Canal) and maintained British dominance in Iraq and Transjordan.[36] In October

1922, when Lloyd George fell over the Chanak incident, Churchill fell with him. Over the next two years, Churchill rebuilt his career. He left the Liberal Party – earlier, in 1903, he had abandoned the Unionist Party to join the Liberals – and tried to find a new political home. This bore fruit with Baldwin's unexpected offer of the Exchequer in November 1924; Baldwin preferred to have Churchill in the government, supporting its policies, rather than outside, criticising them.[37]

For the life of the second Baldwin government, Anglo-American relations were dominated by the naval question. In early 1921, Washington and Ottawa pressed London to abrogate the Anglo-Japanese alliance. As Japanese policies in China during the First World War had antagonised both the Chinese and Americans, Lloyd George's ministry realised that the old compact could not continue. Therefore, at the Washington conference of November 1921-February 1922, Britain and Japan abandoned their alliance and signed three new agreements with the United States and other Far Eastern powers.[38] Two of these were designed to maintain the existing balance of power in the Far East: a nine-power treaty by which those powers with interests in China guaranteed that country's sovereignty, independence and territorial integrity; and a four-power treaty whereby Britain, the United States, Japan and France each agreed to respect the rights of the others in their 'insular possessions and insular dominions in the region of the Pacific Ocean'. The third, naval, agreement was one with wider implications. Britain, the United States, Japan, France and Italy agreed to limit their capital ships and aircraft carriers in a ratio, respectively, of 5:5:3:1.75:1.75. This meant that Lloyd George's government abandoned the two-power standard of 1889, by which the Royal Navy was to equal those of the next two naval powers combined, and accepted formal equality with the United States Navy.[39]

But the Washington naval treaty did not limit warships displacing less than 10,000 tons, especially cruisers, the main weapon for attacking and defending seaborne lines of communication. Cruiser limitation drove a diplomatic wedge between Britain and the United States in the last two years of the second Baldwin government and, in this process, Churchill simultaneously promoted two contradictory policies: enforcing Treasury parsimony on the British armed forces, including the Navy; and attempting to preserve British naval preponderance by resisting pressures from the Coolidge administration for cruiser equality. In the late 1920s, despite the Washington treaty, the British had the largest navy in the world. They had 46 cruisers and six building; the US Navy had 31. After Coolidge's election in November 1924, the Americans urged extension of the Washington treaty capital ship ratio to vessels below 10,000 tons, particularly cruisers.

Washington's determination to wrest full naval equality from the British represented the symptom of a deeper political issue in Anglo-American relations: an attempt to make impossible any future British blockade of neutral American commerce in wartime. In the summer of 1927, at Coolidge's invitation, delegates from Britain, the United States and Japan met at Geneva to limit auxiliary warships: cruisers, destroyers, submarines, and smaller vessels such as minesweepers.

Although Churchill had warmly endorsed the results of the Washington conference – 'The Pacific Agreement removes the great obstacles of the Anglo-Japanese Alliance from the path of American friendship, without subjecting Japan to anything like desertion or ill-usage at our hands. The battleship agreement is all right'[40] – the goal of the 1927 talks rankled. The Coolidge administration wanted full naval equality with Britain.[41] Churchill felt Britain would gain nothing by conceding to Washington's demands. Part of the reason stemmed from Anglo-American economic rivalry, in which he reckoned the war debt retarded Britain's full economic recovery. As Chancellor of the Exchequer, he had twice yearly to arrange British war debt payments in gold to the United States under Baldwin's Anglo-American debt settlement of 1923. The result of this transfer was that the 'United States has accumulated the greater part of the gold in the world and is suffering from a serious plethora'.[42] In early 1925, in spite of Keynes's arguments, the Bank of England and the Treasury convinced him that the pound should be tied to the dollar to prevent currency fluctuations. He then won Cabinet support to put the pound on the gold standard.[43] Notwithstanding controversy about the impact of this decision on Britain's economic performance in the 1920s, Churchill saw this policy as having as much a political as an economic dimension in augmenting the strength of both Britain and the Empire.

But where Britain had a weak hand over war debts – it had borrowed the money; the Americans wanted payment – this was not the case over naval limitation. The British had a decided advantage in auxiliary vessels, notably cruisers, and, with the wartime blockade in mind, the Americans wanted the British to reduce their numbers to a figure convenient to Washington. Just as the conference opened, Churchill placed before the Cabinet his opposition to appeasing the Coolidge administration over this issue.[44] British imperial and trade defence required a minimum number of auxiliary craft. It would be folly to imperil the Navy's ability to guard sea routes, the lifelines of both Britain and the Empire, because American legislators would not appropriate money for a large American fleet. His concern increased after the Coolidge conference began deliberating. Although the three delegations quickly agreed on limiting the displacement and numbers of destroyers, submarines and smaller craft, cruisers proved an insurmountable problem. The British wanted 70 vessels: 55 light (6,000 tons with six-inch guns) and fifteen heavy (10,000 tons with eight-inch guns); the Americans just 45: 25 heavy and 20 light. While not opposing the Americans' building to the British level, Baldwin's government made clear that the Royal Navy had an 'absolute need' for imperial and trade defence. The Americans retorted that their needs were 'relative', that the US Navy could be smaller or larger depending on British and Japanese strength. On orders from Washington, the American delegation resisted endorsing a cruiser fleet of more than 45 vessels.

Churchill played the pivotal role in recalling the British delegation to London in the midst of the conference.[45] He opposed ton-for-ton equality with the United States because Britain's national security had to be determined by British rather than American needs. If the Coolidge administration wanted to build as many ships as the British, Britain would agree. Joined by other hardliners, like Lord Birkenhead, the Secretary for India, he opposed limiting cruisers to a number convenient to the United States. Accordingly, the conference broke down. Lord Robert Cecil, the minister responsible for disarmament and a senior delegate to the conference, resigned at the action of his colleagues. He told his friend, Lord Irwin, the Viceroy of India: 'But what really moved me more than aught else was the fact that it became clear that in any definite controversy between Winston and myself on a disarmament question, the Cabinet would decide in favour of Winston . . .'[46]

Churchill's firm posture towards the United States reflected his established views about British defence policy: Britain had permanent interests rather than permanent friends or enemies; the Empire had to be preserved and protected at all costs; and Britain had to be strong enough to influence the balances of power in Europe and other regions of the globe. But, as noted above, as Baldwin's Chancellor of the Exchequer, he seemingly pursued two discrepant policies concurrently: cutting arms spending while promoting naval supremacy. Indeed, under his administration of the Treasury, arms spending decreased from £119 million to £110 million, while naval expenditure fluctuated between £56 million and £60 million.[47] In 1919, Lloyd George's government decided that defence estimates should be made on the assumption that 'the British Empire will not be engaged in any great war for the next 10 years, and that no expeditionary force is required for this purpose'.[48] Successive governments renewed the 'Ten-Year Rule' annually until, in July 1928, Churchill took the initiative of getting the Committee of Imperial Defence (CID), the senior Cabinet advisory body on foreign and defence policy, to make the Rule permanent, 'advancing henceforth "from day to day", but reviewed every year'.[49] His reasoning was sound given the temper of the times. The Baldwin government's signature to the Locarno Treaty in December 1925, whereby Britain joined with Italy in guaranteeing the Franco-German border, had brought stability to western Europe.[50] Despite cries of 'a navy second to none', the Coolidge administration fell behind the British in naval construction.[51] The Chiefs of Staff Committee (COS) saw no major threats to the Empire.[52] And, domestically, a balanced budget and less taxation might reduce unemployment and alleviate social unrest, as seen in the General Strike of 1926. With a General Election anticipated in 1929, Conservative appeal in the country would be amplified by sensible government economies in defence spending.[53]

It was at this juncture that Anglo-American relations fell to their inter-war nadir. By early 1928, on-going League of Nations preparatory discussions for a World Disarmament Conference had reached stalemate because of competing British and French draft treaties.[54] When London and Paris reached a compromise in July – which was not hard and fast but, rather, designed to revive the Preparatory Commission – its cruiser provisions antagonised official circles in Washington. On 11 November, five days after another Republican, Herbert Hoover, was elected to succeed Coolidge, the departing President called for American naval superiority over Britain; he swung his support behind a 'Big Navy' bill in Congress calling for the construction of 15 cruisers. At the base of this crisis lay the blockade question, the incompatibility of British maritime belligerent rights with the American theory of the freedom of the seas. The resolution of this crisis has been related elsewhere.[55] Within the British government, Sir Austen Chamberlain, Baldwin's Foreign Secretary, overcame Admiralty resistance to pursue an Anglo-American belligerent rights agreement should an international conference be called to codify maritime law. This was mirrored by Hoover and Baldwin who found diplomatic means to bury their differences: by Hoover suggesting, first, that a 'yardstick' was possible to equate the RN requirement for a large number of light cruisers with that of the USN for a smaller number of heavy ones and, then, by choosing an anglophile, Charles Dawes, as the new American ambassador at London; Baldwin agreed to travel to Washington for face to face discussions with the new President after the 1929 British General Election.

Although the final settlement of Anglo-American naval differences fell to Ramsay MacDonald, Baldwin's Labour successor – the Conservatives lost the May 1929 General Election – Churchill exhibited decided anti-American sentiments over the winter of 1929–30. Within the Cabinet, he called Coolidge 'a New England backwoodsman'; publicly, he allegedly disparaged Hoover as a 'son of a bitch' – a charge Churchill denied.[56] Beyond these demonstrations of personal pique, he joined other hardliners such as the First Lord of the Admiralty, Sir William Bridgeman, to block both an Anglo-American belligerent rights agreement and any reduction in British cruiser requirements. While their remonstrations were unsuccessful, Churchill's position in this debate shows his distrust of American policies because of what they portended for British national security. He argued forcefully that Britain had made repeated concessions to the Americans since 1918 in a vain attempt to keep their friendship; but concessions over Ireland, the war debt and the Anglo-Japanese alliance had been for nought. Now, reducing the cruiser fleet to appease the United States would strike at the heart of imperial defence and, assuredly, be followed by fresh American efforts to constrict Britain's ability to protect its interests.

> We shall never agree among ourselves either to abandon our belligerent rights at sea or to cut the British Navy down by treaty to the limits which the United States considers suitable to herself. . . . Whatever may have been done at enormous cost and sacrifice to keep up friendship is apparently swept away by the smallest little tiff or misunderstanding, and you have to start again and placate the Americans by another batch of substantial or even vital concessions.

At the London Naval Conference of January-April 1930, MacDonald succeeded in ameliorating Anglo-American differences; he dropped British overall cruiser demands by 20.5 per cent and got Hoover to reduce those for American heavy cruisers by 33.[57] Churchill's anti-Americanism had not dampened. When the London Naval Treaty came to the House of Commons for ratification in May 1930, he told Baldwin that he would vote against it: '. . . this [treaty] is not to end the naval controversies between Great Britain and the United States; it merely gives the United States an almost limitless right to criticise and interfere in our vital affairs.'[58]

Churchill's opposition to the London naval treaty proved to be one of his last major forays into the realm of foreign and defence policy for several years. The defeat of the second Baldwin government inaugurated in 1929 a painful phase in his political career, much of the pain being self-inflicted. He joined dissident Conservatives in looking for a scapegoat for their defeat. They picked on Baldwin who, in a difficult intra-party dispute that lasted two years, held on to his leadership.[59] Not surprisingly, Churchill found himself excluded from the Cabinet when the

Conservatives returned to office in August 1931 in a coalition government – the 'National Government' – formed by pro-MacDonald Labour members and some Liberals in a bid to give Britain firm political direction in the midst of the Great Depression. In addition, when the National Government decided to meet the demands of Indian nationalists for self-government, Churchill emerged as one of the leading critics of the process that produced the Government of India Act of 1935.[60] This, too, estranged him from the Conservative leadership and many rank-and-file MPs. Finally, in 1936, when King Edward VIII wanted to marry a twice-married American divorcée, anathema to straightlaced men like Baldwin and contrary to the doctrines of the Church of England, Churchill supported the King.[61] By December 1936, when Edward VIII abdicated to marry his paramour, Churchill's career seemed irreparably broken. Coupled with his political infidelity that had led him twice to cross the floor of the House of Commons, he had Conservative enemies aplenty. When Baldwin's chief lieutenant, Neville Chamberlain, succeeded to the premiership in May 1937, it seemed as if Churchill's chance to occupy 10 Downing Street had passed.

As is well-known, however, he again rebuilt his career in the late 1930s, as he had done after both the Gallipoli fiasco in 1915 and the fall of Lloyd George in 1922. His third political rehabilitation occurred because of his criticism of the foreign and defence policies of the Chamberlain government. Churchill's criticisms were designed to discredit the Prime Minister so as to enhance Churchill's slim chances of seizing the premiership for himself; he had had this aspiration since he entered Parliament in 1900. Still, it is just as true to say that his critique of 'appeasement', as well as his support for British rearmament to strengthen the country's foreign policy and deter potential threats to the Empire, was founded on honestly-held beliefs that Chamberlain's diplomacy was not only wrong, but dangerous. The mixture of sentiment and calculation that had formed within him before 1914 and exhibited before, during, and after the First World War informed his arguments as the international horizon darkened in the 1930s.

Churchill's sentimental conception of the Empire suffused all his actions after he lost office in 1929. In criticising Baldwin's leadership in 1929–31 the Conservative dissidents, including Churchill, argued that the time had come to strengthen Britain and the Empire from within by encouraging increased imperial trade and co-operation. Such policies would breathe vitality into their collective economies and political structures left lethargic by the onset of the Great Depression in October 1929. 'Although trade is important', he told a Canadian audience in August 1929, 'there are other and stronger bonds of Empire, and since the Conference of 1926, nothing but common interests and traditions have held the Empire together.'[62] Similarly, in his mind, any attempt to dismantle the imperial edifice smacked of treason because it undermined Britain's world power:

> The loss of India would destroy all that we have built up. Surely our generation which sent its brothers and sons and watched its fathers march to France and Flanders should be the last to be guilty of such a failure.[63]

Churchill surmised that the failure of the Empire lay at hand unless something was done quickly to meet the problems of the present with the certainties of the past. In his writings of this period, notably his study of his soldier-ancestor, the Duke of Marlborough, he sought to demonstrate how the power and purpose of 'English' foreign policy had succeeded in restricting the ambit of powers that sought to dominate the continent and limit the ideals and benefits of an 'English' presence.[64] In the assessment of a recent observer, '[Churchill] was stirred by British armies on the continent of Europe and constitutional freedoms which he believed they had left behind them. The interplay between past and present was inescapable.'[65] When he told his reading audience in 1930 that he was 'a child of the Victorian era', that British subjects of that time rested 'sedately under the convictions of power and security', he added the telling remark that 'very different is the aspect of these anxious and dubious times'.[66] If the British and their imperial kinsmen were to continue enjoying the benefits of 'English' civilisation and all that it brought in its train, the convictions of power and security had to be reasserted. In tandem with his efforts to capture high office in the 1930s, these sentiments girded his calculations about how Britain's leading position could be protected from the inroads of its adversaries who were growing 'continually stronger'.

Churchill's unfavourable view of Britain's position in the early 1930s derived from the Great Depression's deleterious impact on trade and industry: unemployment, social tension and a questioning of heretofore accepted values of normal human intercourse. In essence, he looked inward, probably a result of the political issues that confronted him in his attacks on Baldwin and Indian self-government. He did not ignore foreign policy or defence questions.[67] But on several matters which can be broadly defined as relating to foreign policy, for instance war debts, his concentration fixed on their impact on domestic reconstruction.[68] By the time Neville Chamberlain rose to the premiership, the constellation of international power that had emerged from the First World War had metamorphosed again, but in a way inimical to British and imperial security. Providing systems of security in their respective regions, no matter how tenuous they might have been, the Washington and the Locarno Treaty had broken down. The World Disarmament Conference had proved barren. The war debts and reparations regimes had collapsed. Japan had conquered northern China. Germany was reawakening under Adolf Hitler and had begun rearming. Fascist Italy was estranged from Britain and France after the Ethiopian crisis. The United States, now guided by the Democrat, Franklin Roosevelt, had receded further into isolation. Beyond the desire of Indian nationalists to separate from Britain, Canada seemed unlikely to come to British assistance in a moment of national crisis. And, above all else, although efforts were finally being made to rectify British defence deficiencies, the legacy of more than a decade of international arms limitation conferences and domestic retrenchment – for which Churchill was partly to blame – meant that Britain was in an exposed position *vis-à-vis* Germany, Italy, and Japan.

Churchill's attacks on Chamberlain's foreign policy after May 1937 came to rest on the need to speed up British rearmament, and he coupled this with the construction of a group of anti-totalitarian powers to contain Germany and Italy.[69] Before this, Churchill's perception of threat had not necessarily focused on Germany. In May 1932 he thought Bolshevik Russia, 'with its enormous armies and with its schools of ardent students of chemical warfare, poison gas, its tanks, and all its appliances', presented the chief danger.[70] But over the next few years, Nazi Germany loomed larger and larger as Britain's emerging adversary in Europe through Churchill's belief that German air rearmament was fully underway.[71] It is now known that he unknowingly exaggerated the level of German building;[72] nonetheless, his vision of how to meet the problem remained clear. He put the matter plainly to a radio audience in November 1934:

> There are those who say 'Let us ignore the continent of Europe. Let us leave it with its hatreds and its armaments to stew in its own juice' . . . I have come to the conclusion – reluctantly I admit – that we cannot get away. Here we are and here we must make the best of it.[73]

The lessons of his past, those involving cold calculation, shine through here: British strategic thinking had to deal with the existing situation; and it had to be determined so as to prevent British adversaries from weakening British security.

This was where Churchill saw problems with Chamberlain's policies. In contradistinction to fashioning balances of power in Europe, the

Mediterranean and the Far East to contain the ambitions of Germany, Italy and Japan, the Prime Minister believed that the conclusion of bilateral agreements with Britain's potential enemies could remove points of friction. He entertained uncertainty about the willingness of possible British allies, the French and Americans especially, to work with Britain to maintain international peace and security. The former, he felt, though perhaps wanting to do something, were weakened by the constant changes of government that marked the Third Republic.[74] The latter were simply unreliable. In July 1934, just after Britain's default on the war loan agreement which came about when Roosevelt refused to negotiate, he told his sister: 'we had been trying to produce amity and collaboration for 12 years without any response from them'.[75] Although Churchill understood the less than favourable COS assessments of the military situation confronting Britain after mid-1937 – three first-class powers threatened the British position in three crucial regions of the globe – and recognised that Chamberlain's foreign policy was constrained to a degree by the counsel of his military advisers, his approach differed, conforming to the 'Edwardian' notion about the balances of power and the military means to support them. His hagiographical portrayal of Marlborough's campaigns, completed between 1933 and 1938, hammered home the tradition in British foreign policy of preventing a hegemonical power on the continent.[76] Admitting that British rearmament had not yet been completed, Churchill argued that Britain, working with France, should establish a 'Grand Alliance' of other continental powers willing to deter German aggression. Perhaps, his most eloquent expression of this came within days of the German occupation of Austria in March 1938:

> If a number of states were assembled around Great Britain and France in a solemn treaty for mutual defence against aggression; if they had their forces marshalled in what you may call a Grand Alliance; if they had their staff arrangements concerted; if all this rested, as it can honourably rest, upon the Covenant of the League of Nations . . . then I say that you might even now arrest this approaching war.[77]

His arguments were consistent with British policies before 1914, during the First World War, and even in respect to the Locarno and the Washington Treaty in the 1920s. Although Chamberlain and Lord Halifax, the Foreign Secretary after February 1938, disparaged any notion of a 'grand alliance' because they felt that such a development would antagonise Hitler,[78] Churchill continued to argue his case for deterrence –

and war if need be – for the next 12 months. Only when the Germans occupied Prague in March 1939 was Chamberlain converted to drawing a line in the sand for Hitler (the Polish guarantee) and beginning rather late to build an anti-German alliance to deter further German expansion.

By the late 1930s the Americans were crucial in Churchill's strategic vision of deterring the totalitarian powers, primarily Germany and Japan. In this respect, he was no different from a range of senior British leaders whose general view of the United States was transformed after the end of naval rivalry in 1929–30 and the ill-favour engendered by the ragged end of the debt settlement.[79] Even Chamberlain joined this group – but after Prague; this showed that the changes in attitude towards the United States simply occurred at different times and for different reasons. British leaders were not blind to the persistence of American isolationism or Roosevelt's tendency to be inconsistent in pursuing his foreign policies. In Churchill's case, he had a range of American correspondents, some, such as the New York financier, Bernard Baruch, with access to the White House. From them, he learnt that American support for Britain would be more forthcoming if 'we could find some way of getting the debt question settled'.[80] Such reports only galvanised Churchill to double his efforts, through his pen, to help remove the residue of American mistrust of Britain by appealing to the sentiment of 'English-speaking' peoples. If Britain found herself at war, it would only benefit her war effort to have access to American industrial, agricultural and financial resources. In June 1937, he wrote: 'The great theories of government which the British race devised and which the English-speaking peoples have adopted and made their systems are the foundation upon which civilisation rests and without which it will fall.'[81] Not surprisingly, he began work on his history of the English-speaking peoples after he finished his study of Marlborough.

Because Germany and Italy posed the immediate threat to Britain in the late 1930s, Churchill's focus, like that of Chamberlain, the COS and the Foreign Office, rested on Europe and the Mediterranean. This does not mean that he ignored the importance of maintaining a British presence in the Empire east of Suez. He never hid his belief that if Britain either left India of its own volition or was forced out, the sub-continent would 'continuously become the prey of the Fascist dictator nations, Italy, Germany or Japan'.[82] However, the main threat existed closer to the home islands. On 27 March 1939, two weeks after the occupation of Prague and just as the British and French guaranteed Polish sovereignty, Churchill committed his grand strategic ideas to paper and circulated them to a small circle of influential men, including Chamberlain.[83] Based on 'Edwardian' conceptions about re-establishing balances of power in Europe, the

Mediterranean, and the Far East by emasculating the strategic threats posed by Britain's adversaries in these regions, it comprised the coldest calculation of gain and loss. Given the limited numbers of British ground forces – conscription was still days away – and the commitment of a large portion of these to garrisoning the Empire, he discussed the Royal Navy's disposition and tasks should war with Germany and Italy break out. He posited that the waters adjacent to Britain and Germany, as well as the Mediterranean, should be the principal theatre of operations. In the north, the Navy could keep open the sea lanes across the Atlantic while bottling up the German Navy in the Baltic Sea; air attacks on the Kiel Canal would make 'that side door useless'. Augmented by French naval units and bases, command of the Mediterranean would cut off Italian forces in Libya and Ethiopia. The impact of this action on what would be concurrent military operations against Germany to uphold the continental balance would be significant:

> A series of swift and striking victories in this theatre, which might be obtainable in the early weeks of the war, would have a most healthy and helpful bearing upon the main struggle with Germany. Nothing should stand between us and these results, both naval and military.

The main difficulty foreseen by Churchill lay in the Far East. Since the bulk of the fleet would be concentrated west of Suez, he argued that the 'farthest point we can hold in the conditions imagined is Singapore'. Nonetheless, he believed that a number of factors reinforced the security of the Empire in the East. In the first place, Japan did not have a free hand in the region; Bolshevik Russia and Japan were engaged in a border war in northern Manchuria. Even if peace returned, Tokyo would do nothing until knowing the outcome of the European conflict. But should the Japanese decide to take advantage of Britain's commitment to Europe, they could only 'take Hong Kong and Shanghai; and clean us out of all our interests there'. Churchill had every confidence that Singapore could resist any Japanese assault:

> Over these 2,000 miles of salt water, Japan would have to send the bulk of her fleet, escort at least 60,000 men in transports in order to effect a landing, and begin a siege which would end only in disaster if the Japanese sea-communications were cut at any stage.

Finally, Britain could probably count on the United States not to stand idly by if Japan moved to restructure the balance of power in the western

Pacific. The British global position was far from hopeless in Churchill's estimation, but its protection required the resolute implementation of national security policies that tied together the European balance of power with the defence of the Empire. In all of this, the United States had a leading position. It would be essential to ensure the safety of trade routes across the Atlantic to guarantee access to the material resources of the United States; and, as a bonus, should the United States decide to thwart Japanese ambitions south of the equator in the Pacific, a rough balance of power could be maintained until Britain could direct its energies eastward.

It is clear that in the inter-war period, Winston Churchill's vision of national security wedded his sentimental attachment to the Empire with careful calculation to preserve and enhance Britain's position as a global power. His childhood and military service embedded in him 'the realisation of the greatness of our Empire and our duty to preserve it'. His military service and political career before 1914 exposed him to the generational beliefs of the Edwardians about how best to pursue British security interests – both foreign and defence policy – through defending the Empire and ensuring the European balance of power. In the post-First World War period, the American question increasingly impinged on Churchill's thinking in a way that showed Churchill to be a disciple of Palmerston. British interests were eternal – maintaining the European balance and the others which comprised imperial defence, along with the perpetuation of adequate armed forces; British friends and enemies were transitory. In the inter-war period, in Churchill's mind and those of other British statesmen, the United States changed from an adversary into a potential ally. In this sense, the element of calculation played a major role. When the British had to make concessions to the Americans over war debts, for instance, where they were in an exposed position, they did so. However, when the British had no need to appease Washington, as over the cruiser question, they did not. The promotion of the concept of 'the special relationship' of English-speaking peoples, of which Churchill was a progenitor, did not emerge in his mind until it was politically expedient.

None of this means that Churchill's record as a strategist was unsullied. Clearly, it was not. Gallipoli and the retrenchment of British armed forces between 1924 and 1929 – which, by the way, included reduced spending on the Singapore naval base – are stunning examples of tarnish on his record. And if one considers the uneven course of his political career, his success rate is even poorer. Nor is it to suggest that leaders such as Churchill, who calculated carefully, were successful; or that their sentimental views of institutions such as the Empire were accurate reflections of reality. In his career, Churchill blundered, despite giving much thought to his political goals and the means to achieve them. But so, too, did men as diverse as David Lloyd George, Neville Chamberlain and even Adolf Hitler. What it does say, on the other hand, is that in the inter-war period, Churchill had particular views about the universe he inhabited; he had others about the nature of the Empire, the balances of power in the world, and the United States; and these views, wedded to sentiment and calculation in his thinking, affected the evolution of Britain as a Great Power for good and ill in the inter-war period.

5

Churchill and Italy, 1922–40

PAOLO POMBENI

The history of politics, as the history of great men, has a long and honourable tradition in European historiography. We can apply this process to the relationship between Britain and Fascist Italy. First we need to fill in the background, starting perhaps with Churchill's general approach to Italy before Mussolini appeared on the stage.

Lord Randolph's son planned in his youth (1898) to write a biography of Garibaldi: his interest in a romantic and legendary figure first attracted him to an Italian subject.[1] When G M Trevelyan's books on Garibaldi came out, Churchill's interests turned to other, more 'British' topics.

Like many other Englishmen, Churchill considered Italy mainly as a holiday destination and he spent holidays in Italy between 1906 and 1908 and visited Venice during his honeymoon, but no record of these visits has survived to prove any special interest in Italian politics or any remarks on contemporary Italy.[2] The first time he came across Italian politics in a professional capacity was in 1911, at the time of the Italian-Turkish war over Libya, and the first note regarding Italy is not a friendly one. 'We must ask ourselves', he wrote in a letter to Sir Edward Grey on 4 November 1911, 'whether we have not more to gain from Turkish friendship than from Italian policy; and still more whether we have not more to apprehend from the consequence of throwing T[urkey] than of throwing Italy in the arms of Germany.'[3]

At that time Churchill had just become First Lord of the Admiralty and was serving in a Liberal government, but he was expressing opinions which he maintained over the years: a poor opinion of the role of Italy in world affairs and a strong belief that British interest lay, at least to a certain extent, on the opposite side. The Italian venture in Tripoli was unpopular in Europe where progressives were attracted by the myth of the Young Turks' revolution. Churchill, in any case, seems to have retained from that episode a negative view of Italy.

However, Churchill's first entrance on the Italian scene was dramatic. At the outbreak of the First World War, Italy remained neutral, and France and Great Britain (as well as Germany) did their best to win her over. Churchill made a personal contribution by agreeing to an interview with the London correspondent of the Italian newspaper, *Il Giornale d'Italia*, during his visit to British troops in Antwerp. The interview was published on 23 September 1914, and was declared 'historical' by the Italian newspaper which claimed that British Cabinet Ministers seldom granted interviews. Churchill, of course, spoke in very general terms, simply stressing a general mood of friendship towards Italy and making it clear that she had nothing to fear from the *Entente* regarding her interests in the Balkans and the Mediterranean. The publication of the interview was followed by an article stressing both Churchill's tact in abstaining from a direct invitation to enter the war and the need for the Italian government to consider the new landscape sketched by the British Minister. The following day *Il Giornale d'Italia* reported the response to this interview in the Italian press (quoting *Il Secolo*, *La Perseveranza* and *La Stampa*) and noted that 'it would have been impossible to make an invitation to walk along with Britain in more attractive terms' and even dared say that '[Churchill's] words show that an agreement between Italy and the *Entente* is likely to be negotiated between Rome and London'.[4]

It would be wrong to imagine that Churchill had become sympathetic to Italy. According to Margot Asquith's diary, he spoke of Italy early in 1915 as 'the harlot of Europe'. Contempt towards Italy was widely shared inside the government: Lord Fisher, a close associate of Churchill at that time, referred to the Italians as 'mere organ-grinders! No use whatever',[5] and Asquith, describing a Cabinet meeting (23 March 1915) labelled Italy as 'the most voracious, slippery and perfidious Power'.[6] Nonetheless, negotiations went on and Churchill took part with Sir Henry Jackson in their last phase (5–10 May), discussing details of naval assistance to be offered by the British fleet to the Italian navy (irritating for him, since he already had in mind his plan for Gallipoli and saw no reason for the Italian claims). The course of the war did not seem to have suggested a substantial rethinking of the Italian political and military situation. After the Italians were defeated at Caporetto in November 1917, Churchill became once more involved with the Italian government (namely with

General Alfredo Dallolio) in his new capacity as Minister of Munitions, but this time he found the Italian requests perfectly reasonable.[7]

So far Churchill had had no dealings with prominent Italian politicians. After the end of the war, he occasionally met two of them. One was Sidney Sonnino, the Foreign Minister whom he met in Paris on 14 February 1919, in the context of establishing an anti-Bolshevik policy (finding that Sonnino supported 'very effectively' his proposal of military action against them); the other was Francesco Saverio Nitti, the Prime Minister, whom he met on 19 January 1920 at the 'allied Supreme Council' to discuss the same subject (but this time the Colonial Secretary's opinion of the Italian is unknown).[8] What we can guess from a general view of the immediate post-war period is that Italy did not improve her reputation in British governmental quarters. The Italians withdrew from Russia, and in the Turkish question played what the British judged an unpleasant role. On 23 September 1922, Lloyd George confessed to Lord Curzon his worry about the Balkan situation and said he was anxious to neutralise 'French and Italian intrigue'. On resolving the Chanak crisis (11 October 1922) Churchill himself showed 'once more his bitterness against France and Italy'.[9]

One month later another episode occurred which had, in my opinion, some importance in this account. During the electoral campaign and, to be precise, on 8 November 1922, the radical socialist and prohibitionist, Scrymgeour, attacked Churchill, directly associating him with the Fascist movement: he claimed that he was 'against any thought of civil war, but it would not surprise him, if there were one, if Mr Churchill were at the head of the Fascisti party'.[10] This was the first time that the recent buyer of Chartwell Manor had found himself identified with Fascism, and maybe such an ardent nature as his was in a certain sense pleased to be regarded as a champion of a successful anti-socialist group. Indeed, anti-socialism was becoming a permanent feature of Churchill's politics, and anti-Bolshevism deeply affected his thought in post-war years. During this period he spent a short time in Italy, a fact which went unnoticed. On 31 March 1921, he disembarked in Genoa from the *Esperia* (which he had boarded at Alexandria in Egypt after trying to settle the future of the Middle East in conferences in Cairo and Haifa) in the hope of more quickly reaching London and putting himself up as a candidate for the Chancellorship of the Exchequer. Something must have struck him, for in a letter to his wife, Clementine, written nearly six years later (at the time of his most famous Italian journey) he cites this episode in order to stress the changes brought about by the victory of Fascism.[11] We lack any direct reference, but the date is eloquent: between the winter and spring 1921 the political conflict in Italy reached its climax, with the last real attempt at confrontation between the declining left and the rising right (and Genoa, with its strong opposing factions facing each other in the port, was a hot bed of conflict).

No documentary proof of sympathy for Fascism is available to us until 1926. In a letter to Clementine written on 5 September 1923 in France, where he was on holiday, Churchill spoke of his severe disapproval of Mussolini's occupation of Fiume, against the decision of the League of Nations: 'What a swine this Mussolini is', he wrote, adding, 'I see Rothermere is supporting him'. [12] This was not a happy time in Churchill's life, no longer in power nor in Parliament since November 1922. By-elections brought no better results: in December 1923 he failed to win West Leicester as a Liberal, and in March 1924 he stood without success as an independent Anti-Socialist in the Abbey Division. But the dissolution of Parliament in October gave him a new chance: adopted as a 'constitutionalist' candidate (with Conservative support) by the constituency of Epping, he was returned to Parliament, entered government and became Chancellor of the Exchequer.

It was in this position that he found himself once more involved in Italian politics. On 14 January 1926 he began negotiations in London with the Italian Minister of Finance, Count Giuseppe Volpi, to reach a final settlement of the Italian war debt. Volpi was an important figure in Italian politics: Mussolini called him 'the last *Doge* of Venice' and considered him a fine statesman whom he could count on.[13] It is possible that Volpi made a good impression on Churchill and was able to reinforce a more positive view of Italian Fascism, which his growing fear of Socialism had undoubtedly strengthened. We lack evidence. The speech at the positive outcome of the negotiations, when Churchill 'spoke warmly of the fact that Italy possessed a government "under the commanding leadership of Signor Mussolini, which does not shrink from the logical consequences of economic facts"',[14] perhaps owed more to the ordinary emphasis of diplomatic language than to ideological sympathy for a political regime, but was certainly friendly. Churchill had relied very much on the settlement of war debts as a key issue in Conservative politics: reaching his aim with Italy was an important step in a more general game (the settlement with France was already under discussion). He certainly made some concessions to Italy, and in a letter dated 30 January 1926, P J Grigg warned him that Briand could be disappointed because 'you are treating Italy with great generosity', but it is perfectly possible that he did so in order to put pressure on France, who would make 'a disagreeable impression' if she refused to sign the kind of agreement already reached with Italy (as

Churchill made known in a letter to Paul Doumer on 1 February 1926).[15]

Certainly British views on Italian current affairs were sympathetic: for instance, the British Ambassador in Rome, Ronald Graham, was a more than benevolent observer who sent reports praising Italian political stability. He thought that in Italy 'all governments were either dictatorships or inefficient'.[16] Notable, too, was the changing attitude of the Conservative leadership toward the Italian role in post-war politics. According to a sensitive Italian observer, Alberto Pirelli, a big industrialist who served as informal adviser and who was in charge of special missions in Italian foreign policy, by November 1923 the general secretary of the Foreign Ministry, Salvatore Contarini, had detected a rapprochement with London. This improved the following year when Austen Chamberlain, in Rome for a meeting of the League of Nations, spoke with Contarini about the necessity of a united anti-Bolshevik front, to which Italy should contribute. According to Contarini's account to Pirelli, the British Foreign Minister made no reference to war debts, commenting: 'Why should you bark if you have a dog?' (the phrase is reported in English: as an explanation Pirelli adds: 'this is Churchill'.)[17] Chamberlain's enthusiasm for Mussolini increased after Locarno, and he had five private meetings with the Duce during his time as Foreign Secretary.[18] Chamberlain's words are reported: 'If I ever had to choose in my own country between anarchy and dictatorship, I expect I should be on the side of the dictators.' In May 1925, even Churchill thought that friendship with Italy was more useful than a pro-Turkish policy, reversing his old attitude.[19]

By January 1926, therefore, Churchill had diplomatic and political reasons to be sympathetic in his approach to Italy and to its chief, leaving aside any ideological sympathy. Some time after the conclusion of the Italian war debt negotiations, Clementine Churchill spent a holiday in Rome. She was alone; perhaps her husband was forced to remain in London by governmental affairs and the onset of the crisis which ended in the General Strike. But in the previous year Churchill had paid another visit to Italy. Not much is known about it, except for the fact that he stayed in Florence, probably as a guest of Marquis Bufalini. In Churchill's papers there is still a letter from the head official of the Railways Service of Florence offering the British Minister a special carriage for his journey from Florence to Paris.[20]

On 20 March 1926, Clementine sent a letter to Winston describing her staying in Rome at the Embassy. 'To begin with modern Rome: I have seen Mussolini – he came very privately to tea with Sybil [Graham's wife] the day after we arrived.' The letter shows great excitement. 'He is most impressive – quite simple and natural, very dignified, has a charming smile and the most beautiful golden brown piercing eyes which you see but can't look at . . . he fills you with a sort of pleasurable awe . . . He loves music and plays the violin himself.' And immediately afterwards: 'I had a few minutes talk with him – he sent you friendly messages and said he would like to meet you. I am sure he is a very great person.' To complete this ecstatic account, on 25 March Clementine made known to her husband that she had 'just received a beautiful signed photograph from Mussolini! . . . All the Embassy ladies are dying of jealousy!'[21] Mrs Churchill was a clever and shrewd woman and her husband respected her opinions, but in this case he was cautious. According to their youngest daughter, he replied on 28 March: 'What a picture you draw of Mussolini! I feel sure you are right in regarding him as a prodigy. But as old Birrell says "It is better to read about a world figure than to live under his rule."'[22]

Some unexpected events reinforced the romantic myth of Mussolini after that date: the three attempts on the Duce's life. In November 1925, the police had already discovered a plot to assassinate Mussolini, but it was between April and October 1926 that the Duce survived three real attempts on his life. On 7 April an aged Irish woman, Violet Gibson, shot at Mussolini; on 11 September an anarchist, Gino Lucetti, threw a bomb at the car of the head of the government; in Bologna on 31 October he was fired at from a crowd. Immediately a young student, Anteo Zamboni, was held responsible and was lynched by the Fascists. It seems that after each of these unsuccessful attempts Churchill sent a congratulatory message.[23] In any case when the Chancellor of the Exchequer planned his 1927 New Year holiday in the Mediterranean he had two good reasons to include Mussolini in the sights worth seeing: first the romantic legend of the Duce, and secondly the new political attitude of the British government toward Italy, supported both by Austen Chamberlain and by the British Ambassador in Rome.

On 15 November 1926, a letter was sent to Sir Roger Keyes, a friend then commanding the Mediterranean Fleet, to arrange the stay of Churchill, with his brother Jack and his young son Randolph. 'On leaving you', it was added, 'I am going to stay in Rome for a few days to see Mussolini (while he lasts)'. (A remark to be read in the context of the attempts on his life.)[24] A meeting between Mussolini and Churchill was recommended by Sir Ronald Graham: 'You will be interested in meeting Mussolini and I think you will both like and be impressed by him', he wrote on 2 December.[25]

This visit was planned as a magnificent holiday. The three Churchills left London on 4 January travelling overland to Genoa where they embarked on the *Esperia*. From here Churchill sent Clementine a letter painting a bright picture:

> We are just off and I send you this line by the Fascisti. They have been saluting in their impressive manner all over the place . . . This country gives the impression of discipline, order, good will, smiling faces. A happy strict school – or no talking among the pupils. Great changes have taken place since you and I disembarked from this ship nearly six years ago.[26]

They went to Naples, saw Pompeii, landed in Messina and were put in the care of Admiral Keyes. They then stayed in Malta, were spectators of the manoeuvres of the Fleet, visited Athens, and on 13 January landed in Brindisi, where they caught the night-train to Rome.[27]

Some rumour of all this must have spread in Italian quarters, since a journalist, a certain A N Cantalamessa, caught the night-train at Frosinone in a vain attempt to interview Churchill. The Chancellor did not intend to do any political work: on 16 January his private secretary made known to the Rome correspondent of the London *Central News* who had asked to do just that that: 'Mr Churchill . . . does not desire to discuss public questions of any kind, or give interviews, during his short holidays in Rome.'[28] He had two informal meetings with Mussolini, one at a ball, one after dinner.[29] Later, on 19 January he met the Pope, and had a formal conversation with him until, according to his son Randolph, they 'got on to the subject of the Bolsheviks and had a jolly half-hour saying what they thought of them'.[30]

No publicity was planned and in Churchill's correspondence with Baldwin from Rome there is no hint of a possible public statement. Baldwin told Churchill he was anxious 'to hear your account of your talk with Mussolini, tempered only with a natural regret that I shall never hear his impressions. The picture will be vivid but incomplete'.[31] However, journalists had their way. In a 'private and personal' letter to Austen Chamberlain,[32] the Ambassador explains that 'in order to get rid [of the journalists] Churchill said he would see them collectively,' because 'the press were a perfect nuisance and simply besieged the Embassy'. The Chancellor 'thought it best not to answer questions but to write out a sort of statement of the answers he would have given if questioned and to hand it to them. We translated it into Italian'. Between 50 and 60 journalists (Italians, British and foreign) received copies of what Sir Ronald judged 'extremely good as well as striking an original note'. Of course, 'Mussolini was delighted with it, but I cannot say the same as regards the Russian press representative!' That it was flattery towards a dictator in order to get a favourable return in foreign policy is suggested by the conclusion of the message: 'I am doing my best to rope the Italians into our Chinese policy, but they are a little sticky over it.'

Churchill's text[33] reveals how carefully it was planned. It started with a declaration of the general purpose of the interview: 'Although my visit is purely private, the Ambassador has suggested to me that I might make a short statement to you gentlemen of the Press who can do so much, and have done so much, to create goodwill between our two countries.' The flattery becomes immediately evident when Churchill recalls the Anglo-Italian friendship from the Risorgimento onwards (nothing more than a cliché) and speaks of 'the emotion with which in the Spring of 1915 I learned of the secret clause in the Treaty of the Triple Alliance, by which Italy stipulated that in no circumstances should she ever be brought through that Alliance into a war with England'. We know what a poor opinion of Italy Churchill had at that time!

In order to stress that the talks with Mussolini and Volpi were not politically decisive, Churchill pointed out that 'those interviews were purely private and of a general character', part of the useful habit of direct talk among the modern European 'public men'. It follows a panegyric of the Duce:

> I could not help being charmed, like so many other people have been, by his gentle and simple bearing and by his calm, detached poise in spite of so many burdens and dangers. Secondly anyone could see that he thought of nothing but the lasting good, as he understood it, of the Italian people, and that no lesser interest was of the slightest consequence to him.

A certain space was given of course to economic problems, in which Churchill pleaded in favour of 'strict and stable finance and firm national credit'. He then went on to consider the corporative system ('I have heard a great deal about your new law of the Corporations'), simply interpreted as a signal of consent:

> But at any rate in the face of such a system so ardently accepted, it is quite absurd to suggest that the Italian Government does not stand upon a popular basis or that it is not upheld by the active and practical assent of the great masses.

What is worth noting at this stage is that the text, which, it should be stressed, was prepared by Churchill alone, continues:

Mr Churchill declined to discuss Fascism in its national aspect. He said: 'Different countries have different ways of doing the same thing. Terms and words are often very misleading. The valuations and the meanings attached to terms are so different in different countries. No political issue can be judged apart from its atmosphere and environment. If I had been an Italian, I am sure I should have been wholeheartedly with you from start to finish in your triumphant struggle against the bestial appetites and passions of Leninism. But in England we have not yet had to face this danger in the same deadly form. We have our own way of doing things. But that we shall succeed in grapplings with Communism and choking the life out of it – of that I am absolutely sure.'

This is the core of the interview. Fascism was important in a world fighting against Communism, but it remains linked to a very peculiar and in any case very different 'environment' from that of Britain. 'Italy has shown that there is a way of fighting the subversive forces which can rally the mass of the people to loyal co-operation with the honour and interests of the state. She has shown that the mass of the people, properly led, value and wish to defend the honour and stability of civilised society.' This is 'the necessary antidote to the Russian poison', but it is also 'an ultimate means of protection against cancerous growth'. The end of the interview shows the real goal of Churchill's statement: 'Our policy is that England, France, Italy and Germany should work together for the revival of Europe and to heal the wounds of the war.' Locarno has been the great example of this co-operation.

Of course, the interview generated a furore. Immediately Churchill confirmed that his plan was simply to support British foreign policy. The letter, written two days after the interview, to Baldwin is about the Chinese situation and the reference to the interview seems related to it: 'You will see I had to give an interview in Rome to the journalists, but I daresay it will be found helpful.' Only a few days later did he realise the impact of it when he had luncheon in Paris with 'Briand, Peret, Vincent Auriol, about 15 MPs representing leading elements in all parties', and he reported to Clementine that he had 'conducted a general conversation in my best French and defended Debt demands and Mussolini interview with some spirit'.[34]

On his return home, too, he paid for his pro-Mussolini enthusiasm. But the subject was soon abandoned. In the 1927 autumn campaign he made several speeches against Socialism,[35] but he never mentioned Fascism. For instance, at Nottingham on 21 October, he made an indirect, but unsympathetic reference: 'The Conservative Party . . . are the only remaining bulwark at this moment against new forms of reaction and revolution, which over a large part of Europe have already reduced to impotence or destroyed the free Parliamentary institutions.' In general he defended the parliamentary constitution against socialism: 'The genius of the British race has always taught us to try and divide the powers among our rulers [. . .] Socialism means the concentration of political and economic power in the hands of the Government at the same time.' (Woodford Bridge, 31 October.)

We can confirm that Churchill considered Italy as distinctly alien from what we read in Clementine's letter to her husband that same 31 October, written in Florence, where she was on holiday.[36] She attended a celebration of the fifth anniversary of the March on Rome in the Piazza del Palazzo Vecchio and observed:

> It is wonderful how Mussolini holds not only his power, but the public imagination and interest. And he never seems to play to popularity. He always does the hard cruel thing. I do hope he lasts and does not get killed.

In addition to this consideration, an intellectual distance from Italian political methods once again emerges: 'They had two armoured cars bristling with machine guns in the middle of the Square! Imagine doing that in England to keep order at a public meeting!' And that is not all. Clementine finds 'great excitement, speculation, dismay and alarm' for new laws, one 'against motorists', the second for moralising purposes. 'The gossip is that Mussolini wants to keep in with the Pope, that he has just been obliged to offend him by telling him that he can't have any temporal power'; but the law can also please 'the Duce's drastic nature'. The content of this, 'so ridiculous' law was as follows: 'love is forbidden except between husband and wife; love is permitted only in order to make children; the sale of contraceptives is forbidden'. Clementine had already shown doubts about Mussolini during this Italian visit. Writing from the Venice Lido to her husband she confessed:

> I must say that my culte for Mussolini is somewhat diminished by the almost ferocious poster Campaign which goes on everywhere. You might think there was an Election on, tho' that is the last thing which he would allow. His photograph is everywhere, sometimes in very ludicrous attitudes. That sinister stencilled face appears in the most unexpected places – on the walls of lavatories and on the porphyry pillars of the most ancient churches . . .[37]

All this showed an unfavourable opinion of Italy and Mussolini himself. Churchill was aware that public connection with the Italian dictator could not be good for him. He refused an offer from Beaverbrook to get him filmed with Coolidge, Poincaré and Mussolini.[38] Even on the subject of the corporativist system, which was the most successful export produce of Fascism, Churchill never showed any form of interest. On the contrary, when he prepared a 'preliminary statement' for the Select Committee on Procedure on Public Business (5 June 1931) proposing an 'Economic Sub-Parliament', he quoted the German constitution as a model, but made no reference to Italian experiments.[39] The reverse was true on the Fascist side. Mussolini was delighted by the interview of such a prominent English politician and believed from the attention paid to him by the British government, that he had real power. This cannot be fully understood without knowing that Great Britain was a sort of founding myth in Italian politics: if the times when reference to the English model was considered compulsory for a statesman had gone, Italian politicians still perceived Britain as being the top international power, the guardian of the most exclusive club for international political figures. Churchill was the only member of the Cabinet to have shown such a positive attitude so soon, and it is no wonder Mussolini chose him as his ideal counterpart.

In any case, until 1933 nothing relevant happened in the relationship between Churchill and Mussolini or Italy. In October 1928, Churchill informed the Cabinet 'he had sent a telegram to Signor Mussolini and had suggested that he should send Signor Alberto Pirelli to discuss the question' of the war debt; Mussolini accepted.[40] Nothing more than ordinary affairs were to be discussed. In 1932 a leading figure of the intellectual wing of the Fascist party, Francesco Coppola, invited Churchill to a congress to be held in Rome about the future of Europe, but Churchill, now in opposition not only in Parliament but also in his own party, declined the invitation (as did other Englishmen: Keynes, Kipling, Lloyd George and Trevelyan).[41]

Finding himself in a political wilderness, Churchill showed once more a talent for scandal in using 'dark colours' in his speech. Addressing a meeting of the Anti-Socialist and Anti-Communist Union on 17 February 1933, he chose as a controversial target the resolution passed by the Oxford Union, to refuse to fight for King and country (which was simply an outburst of pacifistic spirit). 'I think of Germany with its splendid clear-eyed youth marching forward . . . I think of Italy with her ardent Fascisti, her renowned Chief, and stern sense of National duty . . .' Rhetorical statements, but impressive ones. Churchill also praised 'the Roman genius' of Mussolini, whom he described as 'the greatest law-giver among living men'. The reason for this admiration was as always the success of Fascism in its anti-Communist fight, but Fascism was rejected as a model for Britain, 'for I firmly believe that our long experienced democracy will be able to preserve a parliamentary system of government with whatever modifications may be necessary from both extremes of arbitrary rule'.[42] This conclusion was nearly unnoticed while much was made of the renewed praise of Mussolini.

Misinterpretation of the English situation was reinforced and accelerated in those years by the appointment of Dino Grandi as Italian Ambassador in London in August 1932. He was, no doubt, an intelligent man, but also a typical courtier and always ready to seize opportunities. Grandi served in London not as an objective eye of the Italian government, but as a professional flatterer of Mussolini and as an amateur diplomat who dreamed of planning a new course of history. He switched continuously from showing contempt toward the English environment (his first recorded impression of Englishmen was that they were 'frigid, ignorant, very big like the Romans': this in 1929) to a blind enthusiasm for what he thought was the English upper-class style of political life.[43] For many years Mussolini received flattering reports from Grandi, directly addressed to him as a person much more than as the Head of Government, full of supposed praise of Mussolini's genius coming from all quarters of the English ruling class. Of course there was some sympathy for the Italian dictator, who was disposed to be friendly to English politicians. To quote some episodes, in January 1934 he sent a congratulatory telegram to Brendan Bracken on the 50th anniversary of the *Financial News*; over Easter 1934 the Duce was visited by Duff Cooper who was favourably impressed, even charmed.[44] I quote only two people among Churchill's friends, it being well known that many others publicly expressed agreement on several aspects of Italian policies. Of course, the worry which ensued after Hitler's seizure of power led to an even more benevolent attitude as it was hoped that Mussolini could be useful in tempering the German dictator, who claimed to be something a pupil of his.

All this ended when it became clear that Mussolini was planning the invasion of Abyssinia. Already in the spring of 1935 Austen Chamberlain wrote to his friend Grandi informally representing British concern.[45] British opinion, even the side that was more favourable to Italian Fascism, received this aggressive policy badly. Lord Rothermere, who was considered by Grandi himself as a pillar of pro-Fascist attitudes, wrote on 13 May 1935: 'Mussolini has allowed himself to be trapped by Abyssinia'.[46] Later, on 21 August, Churchill was interviewed by Sir Samuel Hoare and Anthony Eden about the new Italian situation. According to Hoare's own secret record of the conversation he 'showed himself deeply incensed at the Italian action and more than once pressed strongly for the rein-forcement of the Mediterranean Fleet'.[47] This statement signalled a turning point. In a sense Churchill now realised that Mussolini was a dif-ficult man to manage and that this lack of trust in him would lead to a reconsideration of British policies. In a meeting at Chartwell with a group of supporters, the leader of the Conservative inner opposition spoke quite clearly.[48] On the one hand 'he thought the British public had no idea of the gravity of the situation'; on the other 'he is sorry for "poor little Italy" which has with such great exertion raised herself to the status of "a poor sort of first-class power" and is now to face an opposition against which she has no hope at all'. What in any case remained to be carefully considered was that 'of course Germany is the real trouble' (20 September 1935).

The situation was ambiguous. Churchill thought that the defence of the principles of the League of Nations was the main duty for Britain, also tak-ing into due account her relations with France, but he was at the same time anxious to find a solution with Italy in the hope of using Mussolini against German pressure – the problem of Austria was about to come on to the scene. The politics of the Italian dictator were difficult to interpret and per-haps Churchill shared the opinion of his wife that 'Mussolini must be mad – he clearly wants war for the sake of war'.[49] But he was also in an increasingly difficult position in the political arena. He was not able to return to power and the crisis did not help him in reaching this goal. Thus he stressed the peculiarity of his position: not to be in the crowd of every-day sponsors of the League, but to point to the German danger, minimising Italian colonial appetites as being 'a very small matter'.[50] In this he gained sympathy both in his own country (see, for instance, the positions of Desmond Morton and Roy Harrod[51]) and in Europe (espe-cially in Belgium and France).

In order to maintain good relations with Italy Churchill carefully avoided any contact with the Italian opposition in exile. On 18 November 1935, the former editor of *The Times*, Wickham Steed, addressed a letter to Churchill introducing Count Antonini 'who represents in England the moderate left wing of Italian opposition to Mussolini', a man 'recom-mended to me by Professor Rosselli, the head of the movement, who lives chiefly in France'. The Italian anti-Fascists were worried about a possible negative reaction of Italian public opinion to sanctions which might ben-efit Mussolini, but in any case 'in agreement with eminent moderate Italians like Count Sforza and Don Luigi Sturzo', they would prepare 'the ground so that the eventual collapse of Fascism may not be followed by a wave of sterile and violent Communism'. Churchill refused to see

Antonini: 'I am quite sure I ought not to meddle in Italian internal politics', he replied to Wickham Steed.[52]

Once more Mussolini misunderstood the whole matter. Grandi was sending him reports which evoked a true spirit of old England which allegedly was much more benevolent to Italy than official words. The Ambassador led him to believe that there was a lot of barking but no real intention of biting. Things were less simple and a real connoisseur of British life and politics such as Alberto Pirelli put a very different complexion on them,[53] but this was not enough to change the course of events.

Churchill continued with his own policies, in spite of the Hoare-Laval peace plan and the appointment of Eden to the Foreign Office. He had now to deal with two extremes at the same time: to maintain that the German threat to Europe was 'a graver matter still' (as he told the Commons on 6 April 1936, speaking critically of sanctions); and to make it clear that conciliatory politics toward Mussolini must be read as a pledge to act in international politics in the context of the old Great Powers. We will see that Churchill openly confessed these policies in his 1940 message to Italy. For the moment we should remember that Mussolini read it in a totally different way.

From Alberto Pirelli's note we know at least partially how things developed. On 3 March 1936 Pirelli had lunch with Churchill in London (face to face, he remarked). Churchill said that 'he admired Mussolini very much, but wondered if in this enterprise he had not chosen the wrong method'. In any case, Churchill suggested that the Duce could have a complete victory in time by localising the war and remaining in the League. This and other extracts of English conversation were reported to Mussolini on 10 March. From London Grandi sent a reassuring picture of 'real' British attitudes towards the Abyssinian crisis and praised Churchill for not supporting the sanctions.[54] Mussolini had the firm belief that a declining nation, as he believed Britain to be, was slowly surrendering to the idea of his own grandeur. He was also convinced that Churchill was a most open-minded politician and had perceived this new trend in history.[55] The favourable conclusion of the Abyssinian episode confirmed Mussolini's faith in himself and he started both to deal with Britain as 'first among equals' and to drive Italy into an active and imperial foreign policy (as the Spanish Civil War was to show). In addition to the facts mentioned already, in May 1937 Neville Chamberlain took office and the Duce saw this as an important improvement in his political plans. 'Chamberlain is a true gentleman [English in the original]. I had a lot of sympathy for him. I always found understanding with his brother (Albania, etc)', he told Pirelli.[56]

Between 1937 and 1939 the future appeared very uncertain for Churchill. Chamberlain's appointment robbed him of the role of a moderate friend to Italy with a view to keeping her away from Germany. The new Prime Minister was carrying on his old policies without any restraint, and indeed he extended them to Germany. Churchill had realised that things had changed: after the Spanish episode and in the context of the Rome–Berlin axis, Mussolini was no longer the 'moderate, reasonably benign and useful anti-Communist Italian leader'[57] but had become a threat to European stability. Mussolini's agreement with Germany was increasingly worrying. It is true that Churchill did not immediately take a firm and stable line on the Italian question. On 10 October 1937 he wrote in the *News of the World* that 'it would be a dangerous folly for the British people to underrate the enduring position in world history which Mussolini will hold; or the amazing qualities of courage, comprehension, self-control and perseverance which he exemplifies'.[58] But this was a revival of his old hope of transforming the ambition of a second-class power into support for British policies. It may also have been that Churchill, being a great political gambler, had true admiration for Mussolini's good fortune.

The Foreign Office at this time had a much less friendly view of Mussolini: Eden, who had already met Mussolini in Rome in February 1934, had a negative impression of the man whom he later shrewdly described as having 'the mentality of a gangster'.[59] Despite his early negative attitude toward Baldwin's protégé, Churchill began to appreciate Eden's resoluteness in dealing with the dictators, and Mussolini especially. On 20 September 1937, after the famous submarine affair, he wrote to Eden that 'Mussolini only understands superior force, such as he is now confronted with in the Mediterranean'.[60]

The resignation of Eden in February 1938 was a new turning point in the misunderstanding of the British situation on the part of Mussolini and also Grandi. Both had the impression that Italy was powerful enough to defeat a Foreign Minister of His Britannic Majesty, and Churchill, saying precisely this in the Commons ('Signor Mussolini has got his scalp'[61]), confirmed it with his authority.

From then on Churchill had to consider carefully the development of a situation that was highly unfavourable to him. Chamberlain marched forward in the direction of appeasement and his direct link with Grandi led him into believing that he had found the key to Mussolini's heart. In fact the wind was changing: Mussolini's allowing Hitler to have a free hand in Austria led many politicians on all sides of the Commons to regard future developments with concern. Anti-Nazi opinion was strong and becoming ever stronger in many intellectual and left-wing quarters. Churchill was aware of this, but there seemed to be no practical way in which to gain by it.

The strange encounter of two such naive and amateur politicians as Chamberlain and Grandi, mutually incapable of making a deep analysis of their own history and politics, led to the disaster known as Munich. Grandi, as is evident from his diary,[62] seemed to believe that Munich had changed the course of history. He wrote about the moment of Chamberlain's dramatic announcement in the Commons of Hitler's invitation to Munich. Eden was 'perhaps for ever, put in the shadow of defeat'. 'Old Churchill', Grandi claimed, had to put on 'a mask' to hide his sense of failure.[63] A similar sensation must have existed in Rome, where Mussolini interpreted Munich as another step in his ascent of the peaks of history.

Churchill failed in an attempt to use the invasion of Albania in April 1939 to obtain a re-examination of British policies toward Mussolini. Chamberlain had lamented that he was pressed by 'the two oppositions and Winston who is the worst of the lot, telephoning almost every hour of the day. I suppose he has prepared a terrific oration which he wants to let off'.[64] Nonetheless the leader of the opposition to appeasement never stopped in his pressure for rearmament, and his opposition to the dictators. These policies now began to reap their rewards. On 3 July 1939, an article in *The Daily Telegraph* asked that Churchill should be brought into government (about which Chamberlain complained to Lord Camrose, the proprietor of the newspaper). Churchill saw war approaching. Speaking to the American columnist Walter Lippmann, he ventured that he would prefer Turks to Italians as allies: 'Italy a prey, Turkey a falcon' (his old 1911 assumption). Talking at Chartwell with General Ironside he prophesied the German 'employment of Italy to create diversions. Mussolini had sold his country for his job'.[65]

Finally, in September 1939, Churchill entered into government as First Lord of the Admiralty, and on 10 May 1940 became Prime Minister. The event was commented on by Mussolini, according to Ciano's Diaries, 'with irony'.[66] Churchill in the War Cabinet of 16 April 1940, had news from the Vatican that Mussolini was 'in an abnormal condition of excitability' and 'capable of any folly'.[67] Nevertheless the old game of trying to use the weapon of exploiting Mussolini's vanity was enacted for the last time: on 16 May, Churchill sent a message to the Duce 'looking back to our meetings in Rome'. The essence remained the reasonable diplomatic message he had stressed during the past years: 'I declare that I have never been the enemy of Italian greatness, nor ever at heart the foe of the Italian law-giver'. Mussolini, who according to Ciano had at first 'appreciated the tone of it', replied two days later with a message that Ciano judged 'brief and needlessly harsh in tone'.[68]

The bilateral misunderstanding was at its climax. Churchill had always believed he was dealing with a dictator interested in making gains from his actions; a political gambler, but one interested in victory; a man who used rhetoric, as he himself did, to put a certain complexion on things, to create an atmosphere, not to say anything politically decisive. He was a professional politician, coming from a family of political professionals, having relations with a ruling class who had a tradition in this field. The Duce was just the opposite. The reasoning governing his political gambling was ideological; he lacked any form of political culture (even a practical one such as that of his British adversary); and he was alone and mistrustful both of his professional advisers and his friends, coming as he did from a background of political agitation. Mussolini bound himself to the image of 'the man of Providence' and assumed a line of action, not having in mind results, but what he supposed to be the duty of a man of providence arriving at a historical turning point. So he spoke of 'honour' and obligation to act as Britain did at the top of the international game.

When, on 23 December 1940, Churchill made his broadcast to Italy,[69] he made a sort of summary of his approach to Italy. He started by remembering that 'we were all the champions of the Italian Risorgimento. We were the partisans of Garibaldi, the admirers of Mazzini and Cavour. All that great movement towards the unity of the Italian nation, which lighted the nineteenth century, was aided and was hailed by the British Parliament and public.' He recalled the alliance in the First World War and the fact that for 15 years after that war 'we were your friends. Although the institutions which you adopted after that war were not akin to ours, and diverged, as we think, from the sovereign impulses which had commanded the unity of Italy, we could still walk together in peace and goodwill.' Churchill put all the responsibility of what he later defined 'the tragedy of Italian history' on Mussolini. 'Italians, I will tell you the truth. It is all because of one man . . . That he is a great man I do not deny, but that after 18 years of unbridled power he has led your country to the horrid verge of ruin, can be denied by none.' He was the man who 'arrayed the trustees and inheritors of ancient Rome upon the side of the ferocious pagan barbarians'.

This was highly rhetorical, but it was blended with a great deal of political realism.

> Where was the need for Italy to intervene? . . . During the first eight months of the war we paid great deference to Italian interests. But

this was all put down to fear. We were told we were effete, worn out, an old chatterbox people mouthing out-worn shibboleths of 19th Century Liberalism.

Churchill was unable to cope with the problem of a man who, like Mussolini, thought in naive terms about historical destiny. An analysis of Mussolini's speeches on the eve of the war and during its course clearly shows this *weltgeschichtliche* approach (like that of Oswald Spengler, one of his favourite authors). Thus Mussolini remained convinced that Churchill, a staunch anti-Communist, would never accept an alliance with Russia, which he desired to destroy.[70]

Churchill helped to build up the image of Mussolini as a 'great man'. He encouraged the Duce's illusion that he could win a place in history as a legislator and law-giver in a time of trouble. Mussolini and Churchill spoke different languages. Mutual misunderstanding was complete.

6

Churchill and Hitler, 1940: Peace or War?

BERND MARTIN

Nazi aims were radical; their pursuit ruthlessly cruel. Sometimes, there-fore, we exaggerate the singularity of the Third Reich and ignore the long-term causes of the Second World War. Nazism was not an accident, but the outcome of German history with its belated national unification and precipitate modernisation. In the last war the liberal capitalism of the Western democracies opposed the authoritarian systems of Germany, Italy and Japan. Like the Third Reich, but by very different methods, the United States laid claim to world political leadership.[1] At the beginning of the Second World War Britain and France, as well as the Axis powers opposed this American claim. After the German defeat of France, Churchill's gov-ernment could only acquiesce in American superiority and accept the role of a junior partner.

The confrontation between the United States and Germany which cul-minated in the Second World War began before 1914. It resulted from an antagonism between two different societies. The American declaration of the policy of the 'open door' in China was the first sign of an economic foreign policy of equal opportunity to counter the traditional imperialist spheres of influence. In 1898 and 1901 the 'open door' was directed against Imperial Germany over the German seizure of a leasehold (Tsingtao) and its defence during the Boxer rising. It was in China that the latecomer Germany and the newcomer America confronted each other. As early as 1913, the political leader of the world, Great Britain, was already in third place in industrial output. The First World War accelerated British decline. In 1917, as in 1941, with the weakening of Russia and Britain, the temptation for the USA of directly challenging the momentarily victorious competitor, Germany, was too great to resist. Germany should be converted to American ideals of an open liberal-democratic capitalist society either by military intervention as in the two world wars or by peaceful penetration of a defeated country, as happened after both wars.

American capital helped to modernise the industries of Weimar Germany and for the first time opened this market to mass-produced goods, such as automobiles and electrical equipment.[2] But democracy and the superficial imitation of the American way of life ended with the world economic crisis after 1929. Unemployed millions began to support strong, even dictatorial government, together with economic plans for a self-sustaining national market. Roosevelt and Hitler faced similar problems. Their solutions in order to mobilise the means to overcome depression were not completely different.[3] Both established a kind of personal rule by directly addressing the people. Both expanded credit and public works. But while Hitler's government favoured economic autarchy as a first step towards political domination over the European continent, the Americans believed in a free and open world. Hitler's minister of commerce and industry, Hjalmar Schacht, in his 'New Plan' advocated restricted foreign trade based on barter agreements and tight economic controls.[4] At the same time, Cordell Hull, the new US Secretary of State, hoped to open closed national markets and to lower foreign tariff-barriers: hence the powers given to the administration by the Reciprocal Trade Act. The opening up of foreign markets to American industry and to surplus agrarian products would help to overcome the economic crisis.[5]

Incompatible trade policies caused the German–American trade agreement to be allowed to expire in October 1935. Four years later, in July 1939, the US abrogated the trade agreement with Japan.[6] The Fascist countries formally united in the anti-Comintern pact in 1936; they could boast prosperous economies with an ever-decreasing number of unemployed. The American depression of 1937 suggested that the New Deal had failed.[7] In Great Britain, despite Imperial Preference, the slump persisted and forced upon the government a foreign policy of political and economic appeasement. Japan and Germany gained access to new markets in Latin America, Southern Asia and in the Balkans: their barter trade suited primary producing countries better than free trade based on market prices in hard currencies. Germany and Japan challenged the dominance of the Anglo-Americans in trade as much as in politics. More and more, the world market seemed to be closed to American products, a challenge taken up by the Roosevelt administration.

In the 'Quarantine' speech (5 October 1937) Roosevelt began a strategy of encouraging the Western democracies to resist the Fascist powers but without offering any concrete assistance. The rhetoric of democratic ideas announced America's renewed claim to international influence. The propaganda approach to domestic problems, presidential statements rather than political solutions, was transferred to the international scene. New Deal rhetoric obscured the real intentions of the President and his advisers. The veil was lifted, at least for a moment, when Britain and the United States signed the commercial agreement on 17 November 1938, soon after Munich. This treaty, embodying Cordell Hull's principle of reciprocity, made Britain the European outpost of American economic, political and military interests in Europe, a role assigned to China in Asia about two years later. They were to provide a counterweight to Germany and Japan.[8]

Hitler's handling of the crisis over the Sudeten Germans and the atrocities against the Jews during the *Kristallnacht* of 9 November 1938 gave substance to Roosevelt's denunciations of Nazi Germany. Officially, he supported 'appeasement'; unofficially, however, he criticised the hesitations of Britain and France while refusing any substantial help or any firm commitments. While the American public, thinking in isolationist terms, were surprised by the President's concern for foreign affairs, it reassured the British and French people and gave them a sense of security.[9]

Hitler did not underestimate the power of the United States. Although he wrote in his second book, unpublished in his lifetime, about a final battle of the continents, he expected later generations to settle the dispute for world dominion between a German Europe and the United States. Hitler wanted meanwhile to keep the United States out of European affairs and confined to the western hemisphere. Though the German air force gave thought to possible air raids on American east-coast towns (a base in the Azores was required) and the navy dreamed of a German fleet to surpass the British and American navies, no detailed plans for direct attack on the USA were worked out. Hitler's life's work was to eliminate the Jewish-Bolshevist 'subhuman' race in Eastern Europe as a prerequisite for winning living space for the German race. Hitler always hoped for alliance with the British, a 'Nordic' race, and after 1933 suggested to British visitors that a German continental zone of influence was compatible with the British overseas Empire.[10]

In London the ruling Conservative government, led by Neville Chamberlain after 1937, moved to and fro between German and American visions of a future world. British politicians viewed with suspicion both Nazi ideology and America's belief in her 'manifest destiny' clad in Wilsonian phrases. Chamberlain who met Hitler three times to save the peace, lost confidence in the Führer after the German seizure of Prague in March 1939. At the same time, he distrusted Roosevelt and the Americans because of their empty verbosity. Chamberlain wrote 'it is always best and safest to expect nothing from the Americans except words'.[11] Britain, even before the war, was obliged to take sides either with the Germans or Americans. With her ailing industries and her backward educational system Britain could in no way compete with either Germany or the United States. Instead, in order to survive, the crumbling Empire needed all the resources and energy that were left. Great Britain alone could not resist either the totalitarian German peril or Roosevelt's threat to the Imperial structure.

Disappointed by America's policy, especially by Roosevelt's peace appeal of 14 April 1939, the British consented to a final attempt at a general settlement with Germany. In June and July 1939 talks took place between Göring's emissary, Helmut Wohlthat, and high-ranking Conservatives, including Sir Horace Wilson, Joseph Ball and Robert Hudson. British negotiators tentatively agreed to the long-cherished German idea of a partition of the world in economic matters. Britain and Germany together would push America back to her own continent and force upon Japan the inferior status of a small power. Central Africa would be ruled by a condominium dominated by Britain and Germany. Even Communist Russia would be forced into economic co-operation with the two leading nations of the world. British spokesmen suggested a non-aggression treaty to the Germans and promised to abstain from any interference in continental affairs. The balance of power would be given up and Nazi Germany would dominate continental Europe. How much support there was in Britain for these ideas is still a matter for debate. Hitler in any case was suspicious. He firmly declined any suggestion of a British loan, telling Lord Kemsley that he was not interested in money.[12] After the outbreak of war, when Hitler himself made proposals for a partition of the world, he was even more distrusted. It was becoming obvious that he wanted more than equal partnership between the two powers.

After war broke out, the United States was for everyone – the Western democracies, the Axis Powers and the neutrals, the great unknown. Hence all of them tried to involve the US in mediation, applying their own ideas. Roosevelt disliked American mediation. He was thinking in terms of a military and political stalemate, which would have allowed the United States to impose its economic concepts of international free trade as a basis for peace. However, pressure was brought on him to make some attempt at mediating, to sound out the conditions of the warring parties, and perhaps to provide some breathing space for the Western powers to strengthen their forces. So the Under Secretary of State, Sumner Welles, came to

Europe in the spring of 1940. The Daladier and the Chamberlain governments appeared to be willing to talk to Hitler again. If America would guarantee it, both sides were prepared for a peace settlement which included territorial changes in eastern Europe, i.e., recognition of the new boundaries established by force. Many Western statesmen seemed willing to accept Hitler's demands for a central Europe dominated by the German Reich, provided a practicable security plan was established. However, when Welles, in Rome, wanted to start real talks and speculation arose about a possible peace, culminating in demands for a limited truce, Roosevelt, on Hull's advice, spoke on the radio, opposed appeasement and denied that his government would enter detailed discussion of peace questions. When Welles telephoned for Roosevelt's approval to approach Mussolini as mediator, the President refused.

German intransigence did as much to frustrate Welles's mission as Roosevelt's deliberately reserved position. The United States thus lost the last chance before the German attack in the West to frustrate the offensive by serious mediation – something Hitler had dreaded. If American policy aimed for peace in Europe, it could have used the constraints on Hitler's position to provide Britain and France with a respite lasting beyond May 1940. Moreover, an unsuccessful peace initiative by the United States would have marked Hitler as the warmonger in the eyes of the isolationist American public and would have strengthened the coalition against Hitler. Roosevelt's hesitations exposed France and Britain to Hitler's aggression. Then, after his nomination as Democratic presidential candidate, Roosevelt, on 18 July 1940, announced support for the fight against a dictatorship. Next day he signed the Act for the 'Two-Ocean Navy'. Roosevelt was immunising the American public against peace overtures and strengthening Great Britain in resistance to peace proposals. Hitler's Reichstag speech of 19 July 1940, with his 'last appeal to reason' on the part of the British had no effect in view of America's openly declared support for Great Britain. Roosevelt thus predetermined Britain's negative answer to Hitler, which was broadcast two hours after Hitler's speech.[13]

Germany's decision to enter into an alliance with Japan was made in August 1940 as a response to the American challenge. Germany hoped to throw the United States back to its own hemisphere or to neutralise it until Germany had gained complete control of the European continent. The Tripartite Pact, signed on 27 September 1940, enabled Roosevelt to denounce a global conspiracy of 'have-not-nations', to escalate its confrontation with the Japanese and to support China as a stronghold of American defence. Secretary of State Hull refused to mediate between the Kuomintang government of China and the Japanese oligarchy, although both sides had repeatedly expressed their interest in American mediation. The American strategy of non-commitment towards peace proposals included the Far East; the national security interests of the United States thus brought similar consequences in Asia to those in Europe. When the German army seemed to be winning in Eastern Europe, in 1941, Roosevelt did everything possible to enter into the war with Germany. German success, and renewed signs of the military weakness of Great Britain, gave rise to the gravest apprehensions in Washington about a future territorial reorganisation of Europe under the swastika. Only America's entry into the war seemed to provide any chance of retaining some outposts in Europe and North Africa.

Although the German High Command deliberately pursued a policy of not provoking the USA until the war against the Soviet Union was won, Roosevelt came to regard an American declaration of war as inevitable. The surest way to this end seemed a confrontation with Japanese.[14] Washington made the decision for war or peace in the Pacific when it declared a total economic embargo on Japan on 26 July 1941 – as a response to the Japanese invasion of Indo-China. The unremitting attitude of the Roosevelt administration – at the end of November 1941 it precluded even a minimum of concessions – has to be understood in terms of the global strategy of the internationalists: entry into the war against the Axis Powers was deemed necessary before they had a chance to make secure their newly-conquered *Lebensraum*. The Japanese surprise attack on Pearl Harbor provided the United States with a way out of this dilemma – that could not be solved in the Atlantic. The German declaration of war on 11 December solved another dilemma for the Roosevelt administration. The United States was not forced to go to war only against Japan, which had been designated a second-priority enemy in the 'Germany-first strategy'.[15]

In British politics, the question of a negotiated peace with Hitler was the most crucial one during the first year of the war. It remains a highly controversial, emotionally debated issue even today. Until the opening in 1971 of most war records (some still remain classified), no one questioned the official governmental attitude convincingly described in his heroic history of the war by the Prime Minister himself. According to Churchill there never were any talks within the government or even with 'That Man' (Hitler). In 1940 the new Prime Minister succeeded in blocking all peace attempts and obscuring all their traces, and after the war he created a myth most British people found comfortable. Victory in the war seemed to be linked with the total refusal in 1940 even to think of or consider any peace plans. The semi-official history of Britain's Foreign Policy during the Second World War takes that view.[16] According to Woodward it was only the Germans who put out minor peace feelers which were neglected by His Majesty's Government. Even when the relevant documents on discussions in the War Cabinet were opened, British historians did not care to tell the whole story. Foreign historians researching into this problem were resented as intruders and their studies were completely ignored. A recent study, Charmley's fascinating biography of Churchill, stirred up strong emotions when the author dared to hint at the narrow margin by which Britain stayed in the war. It sounded like treason when Charmley insisted 'that there was a good deal of support for the idea of at least opening talks to find out what Hitler's peace terms might be'.[17]

These myths seem to have become a creed, as they were bequeathed like a national treasure to the post-war generation. But many British historians as well as the general public have overlooked the fact that Britain played only a minor role in the struggle for a new world order. The real duel in the peace issue did not take place between Churchill and Hitler, but between the American President and the German Führer. The British were confined to the part of bystanders. Churchill must have at least sensed the junior role he and Britain were playing in the emerging and widening confrontation between the United States and the Fascist powers. But for Churchill, half-American and very different from the typical English Tory country squire, the choice was clear from the onset of war. Never did he waver in his political belief that only an alliance with the United States would give the help urgently needed to destroy Hitler's Germany and confront the threat of Fascism. But when the Americans provided no real help until their own entry into the war in December 1941, Churchill sometimes entertained doubts about his strategy. On 2 December 1940 he complained 'we have not had anything from the United States that we have not paid for, and what we have had has not played an essential part in our resistance'. In 1941 Britain received only 100 planes and 786 tanks without payment from the United States under lease-lend.[18] Churchill was by no means the 'die-hard' he presented to the public at the time of Britain's most dangerous hour nor the strong-minded saviour of the nation he portrayed in his history of the war. Even Churchill did not completely exclude the possibility of peace negotiations or capitulation.

Appointed as First Lord of the Admiralty at the outbreak of war, Churchill began a private correspondence with President Roosevelt in September 1939,[19] while Chamberlain remained unchanged in his suspicion of the Americans. This outlook seems to have been widely shared. In the opening months of the war the comment could often be heard 'God protect us from a German victory and an American peace. Britain and her allies propose to win this one alone'.[20] Even after the overwhelming victory of the German army in Poland, the Prime Minister wanted to keep the Americans out of the conflict: 'Heaven knows I don't want the Americans to fight for us. We should have to pay for that too dearly if they had a right to be in on the peace terms'.[21] Obviously, for reasons of military weakness, Chamberlain tried to avoid a direct confrontation with German forces. He therefore, together with Foreign Secretary Halifax, worked out a political strategy against the National Socialist threat of separating the German people from their government. The British hoped for a coup in Berlin to be staged by Göring or some prominent general. By means of economic blockade and military actions on the periphery, as planned for Scandinavia or the Middle East, their overstretched war economy would be brought to the attention of the German people. The rather naïve assumption, never shared by Churchill, was that the Germans would get weary of the war and turn their backs on Hitler. Several of the peace-feelers in the first months of the war, initiated by both sides and often supported by the neutral countries, aimed at this internal revolution in Germany. They all came to no effect when the generals and Göring remained loyal to Hitler. Therefore, by the beginning of December 1939, the British Foreign Office put an end to all informal talks with the German side.

However, the main and most dangerous offensive to be resisted in France and in Britain was the peace offensive. There was a widespread fear in French government circles and, though less markedly, in Whitehall, that Hitler might come up with a generous peace offer. Especially in France with her conflict-ridden class society, expectations ran high after the surrender of Warsaw that the war was practically over and would be finally ended by a general peace settlement. But Hitler did not make any genuine offer which might have resulted in a collapse of the defence efforts in both Western democracies. In Berlin not only Hitler but all his close advisers, such as Foreign Minister Ribbentrop, waited for the other side to give in and humbly propose peace terms to the victorious German nation. High-ranking German officials, therefore, only gave hints that Germany would be prepared to consider any such proposals. These diplomatic actions were designed to induce the French, and especially the British, to make such a proposal and thereby disclose their war aims.

How dangerous a real and realistic offer might have been is reflected by Churchill's response to the two peace speeches Hitler gave at the end of the military campaigns in Poland. Even Churchill did not want completely to close the door. When the German leader confirmed the existing borders in the West and stated that he had no war aims against the French or the British, Churchill considered taking up these proposals at least to achieve an armistice in order to gain time for the still insufficiently prepared British military. After Hitler's second vague offer, made in a Reichstag speech on 6 October, Churchill in a memorandum to the Prime Minister warned of a Super-Munich and proposed a clear-cut brief answer in the negative, without definitely closing the door to peace talks.

It was only after his first radio broadcast (12 November 1939) that Churchill took a firmer stand against the lure of peace. He then seems for the first time to have spoken in private of Germany's unconditional surrender, which evoked criticism in the Foreign Office. There the Parliamentary Under-Secretary, R A Butler, remarked that the majority of the government were not war-minded. Foreign Secretary Halifax shared this opinion, pointing out the possibility of a French surrender. Thereafter, 'we should not be able to carry on the war by ourselves'.[24] Meanwhile, the political hero of the First World War, Lloyd George, openly agitated in the press for a negotiated peace. By the end of 1939 a split ran through the British political establishment: the die-hards centering around Churchill, probably for reasons of his popularity with the public, and the majority of the Conservatives who more or less clung to the ideas of their party leader and Prime Minister, Chamberlain.

The American announcement of the Welles mission caused a panic reaction within the ranks of the governments he was sent to visit. Hitler as well as Chamberlain suspected Roosevelt wanted to play a dirty trick on them by interfering in European affairs and terminating the war on the basis of the *status quo*. The real intention of the President, to calm isolationist peace-seekers, was unknown in Berlin and London. The die-hards in the British Government like Vansittart 'were horrified at Mr Welles's idea of making peace with Hitler', while Chamberlain reluctantly consented to renewed peace talks provided American guarantees were given. Churchill, on the other hand, used the opportunity to convince the high-ranking American visitor that only total victory over Nazi-Germany meant real peace. The First Lord of the Admiralty wanted to break up German hegemony over the continent once and for all.[25] But teaching Germany a lesson or forcing her to give up her newly-acquired eastern possessions and to restore even Austria's independence was either wishful thinking or a means to get rid of the troublesome peace issue which could only weaken British fighting morale.

After becoming Prime Minister on the first day of the German assault in the West (10 May 1940) Churchill clung to his political strategy of winning over the Americans and of rejecting any thoughts of peace, at least in public. His staunch determination, as expressed in his speeches, to fight Hitler to the very end must have sounded like whistling in the dark to more realistic men in the government or military, but this rhetoric suited ordinary people in a time of crisis. When he took over, the new Prime Minister was very much distrusted and even detested within the ranks of his own party. The King and the Conservative party would have preferred Halifax to Churchill, but the Foreign Secretary hesitated.[26] It was Churchill's hour, but he first had to gain control of the government. Any generous peace offensive was feared in London much more than the German tanks pushing the British Expeditionary Force (BEF) back towards Dunkirk. Winning a political victory in the crucial peace issue meant for Churchill uniting the government and strengthening his position as Prime Minister. The opportunity came after only five days in his new office when the French Premier Reynaud started talking about France being defeated and about the possibility of a political solution. The scenario of a total French collapse had never been considered in London. The firm rock, on which, according to Halifax, all British hopes and expectations were based, crumbled overnight.[27]

Hitler, in conversation with his staff, outlined his ideas of a peace with Britain on the basis of a partition of the world, but he carefully avoided making any public statement until it was too late. On 19 July Churchill, with Roosevelt's backing, settled the issue in America's favour. Had there been a realistic German offer up to the time British forces were evacuated from Dunkirk, discussions in the War Cabinet would almost certainly have resulted in taking up negotiations with Germany, using the help of Mussolini, then still an onlooker in the struggle. On 26 May 1940 Halifax and Churchill for the first time clashed openly on the peace issue. In the War Cabinet they opened up a fierce debate which lasted three days. The Foreign Secretary favoured Italian mediation to ascertain Hitler's terms, and in the end 'to reach a settlement which would not conflict with issues', 'which were essential to us'. When the Chiefs of Staff were asked by Churchill whether Britain could defend herself, they pointed to unlimited American help and Germany's economic weakness as essential. But hoping for American help was in vain, as Churchill rightly pointed out in the Cabinet: the US 'has given us practically no help in the war'. Furthermore, the German war economy, because of the huge Russian resources it could draw on was not as weak as pictured by the British. Finding himself at a loss for rational arguments the Prime Minister had to exaggerate conceivable German peace terms nobody actually knew about, in order to keep the Cabinet on the battle line.[28]

Churchill's emotional refusal almost drove the Foreign Secretary to despair and to resignation, as Halifax did not believe that Hitler's terms would necessarily be as outrageous as the Prime Minister suggested.

Churchill spoke of the 'slippery slope' on which the French and the appeasers in the Cabinet wanted to stand. But even Churchill did not totally exclude the possibility of peace, and seems to have been prepared to make greater concessions to Hitler after the fall of France than he had contemplated before: 'If Herr Hitler was prepared to make peace on the terms of the restoration of German colonies and the overlordship of Central Europe, that was one thing'. The other thing, however, was that Churchill simply did not believe such a rational offer would come from Hitler – an assumption that proved to be right. In the end, Churchill provided clear leadership in the Cabinet with his eloquent predictions of a Carthaginian peace and a future slave state with Mosley in power. The arguments the Prime Minister presented in support of his line 'added up to an optimistic picture of apparently disastrous events by a selective interpretation of the reliable value of allies'.[30]

Despite this selective approach to a worsening war situation, Churchill showed himself a realist when offering Lloyd George a seat in the War Cabinet. The very same day he had won over the Cabinet he approached this senior politician, the advocate of peace with Hitler, in case the country had to surrender. The Prime Minister's insistence on having the former Liberal leader in the Cabinet is evidence for the belief that Churchill followed a dual strategy. The future British Pétain was first to be sworn to the cause of national integrity, and then taken into the Cabinet to prepare for a smooth transfer of power should worse come to worst. Lloyd George, however, refused to serve under Churchill whom he accused of playing for all or nothing. 'I shall wait until Winston is bust', was his answer to his friends' requests that he join the Churchill government. The old man, however, should not be labelled a senile pacifist, as Churchill did in his response to Lloyd George's last speech in the Commons when the latter openly criticised the Prime Minister. Lloyd George wanted to enter into negotiations with Germany only after the German attempt at invading the British Isles had failed. In a private memorandum he favoured an early peace since a reconquest of the continent seemed impossible. He warned of a protracted war which would in the end see Britain bankrupt and her Empire in other hands. Both Churchill and Lloyd George were proved right by history: the Prime Minister with his trust in American help and his former Liberal colleague with his vision of Britain's decline.

The successful evacuation of Dunkirk was a deliverance for the government. It stabilised Churchill's position and isolated those favouring peace negotiations, at least for the moment. But Roosevelt's support for the case of democracy in his Charlottesville speech (10 June 1940) did not stiffen French resistance. Therefore, in one of his personal messages to

Roosevelt (15 June) the Prime Minister warned that a new British government might sue for peace if no effective aid came from the United States. Two days later France asked for an armistice and Britain stood alone. Roosevelt did not answer any requests for greater help for over six weeks, a chilling time for the British.

In the summer of 1940 the American President, like his administration, felt uncertain whether or not Britain could fight on. They waited for a final decision in London either to succumb to Hitler's – not yet offered – terms or submit to America's Western leadership. Churchill provided the proof of British intention desired by the Americans when he gave orders to shell the French fleet at Oran. Britain proved her will to go on fighting, and in the eyes of Roosevelt could now be trusted. Britain was given a few antiquated, First World War American destroyers, all in need of repair, in exchange for bases in British possessions in the western hemisphere. From the very beginning of the war it was the Americans who dictated the terms of partnership to the British.[32]

On the very day of the fall of France there seems to have been a final attempt by the supporters of peace within the British government to enquire about precise German peace terms. There is no evidence at all that the talk between the Swedish envoy Prytz and the Parliamentary Under-secretary for Foreign Affairs, R A Butler, on 17 June took place at German request. On the contrary, the whole procedure looks rather like a semi-official British feeler originating from the Foreign Office and put forth probably with Churchill's tacit approval. As some key documents are still classified in the Public Record Office, final evidence, of course, is missing. But the fact remains that Butler's statement 'Common sense and not bravado would dictate the British government's policy. This would be of interest to the Swedish Minister but could not be interpreted as peace at any price' was immediately communicated in Stockholm to the Italians as a genuine British offer. The subsequent rebuke by Churchill, several days later, suggests that he may have wished to detach himself from all responsibility for this peace-feeler. If Butler had acted against the Prime Minister's wishes on so important a matter, surely he would have been dismissed. Furthermore, there is the mysterious entry in the diary of the official head of the Foreign Office, Cadogan, 'no reply from the Germans'. This formulation by the senior diplomat in the Foreign Office implies that somebody must have asked the Germans something. (Though it may have been the French.) When this attempt failed, because Hitler and Ribbentrop refused to treat the British on equal terms, Churchill delivered his most famous war speech ('This was their finest hour') in the Commons and ordered military sanctions against Sweden. The peace channel was blocked and the whole issue settled; Britain would fight the decisive battle for the sake of Christian civilisation and the British way of life.

When Hitler, after weeks of waiting for the British to give in, finally made his speech in the Reichstag on 19 July, the Führer's 'appeal to reason' fell on deaf ears in Britain. Roosevelt had already given the answer the day before when, on the occasion of accepting the candidature for a third presidential term, he openly attacked the totalitarian nations as the enemies of civilised mankind. The Presidential vocabulary sounded very similar to that used by Churchill in his last speech. While Churchill wanted to unite the British people in the common war effort, Roosevelt intended by all means to prevent any new agreement between the victorious Germans and the almost beaten British. Once elected for a third term, which was quite sure to happen in November 1940, he would take up the fight with Nazi Germany. This at least was the impression the British must have received from the Presidential address. There was no necessity for further concern about Hitler's statements and offers. Churchill won the political battle with American backing before the Battle of Britain turned out to be the first British military victory over the Germans, a victory obtained without any substantial help from the 'arsenal of democracy'.[34]

Any counterfactual approach to the peace issue requires speculative assertions. But the question may be asked what course the war might have taken if Halifax had taken over the government in May 1940. Would any alternative to Churchill really have meant the end of Britain? It can be argued that the British public would have followed a Prime Minister who sought and concluded peace with Germany. 'With Lloyd George coming out in favour of such a line, and no one of stature to oppose it, the "realists" would surely have had their way.'[35] However, it may be asked whether Halifax or Lloyd George would really have concluded a peace agreement with a vainglorious dictator like Hitler on the basis of submission. There is good reason to believe that they would have followed the same political course as Churchill, maybe less pompously and with different phraseology. Their methods would have been different but they probably would have acted more or less the same way. If, however, the British had surrendered in 1940, this would not have changed the final outcome of the last war. The United States under President Roosevelt was determined to crush not only National Socialist aggression but Japanese military imperialism as well. They would have fought the war until Germany and Japan surrendered and no longer posed a threat to America's world leadership. Britain was regarded as America's outpost in the Old World and Churchill as a kind of deputy of the American President. The Prime Minister, who often declared himself 'the first Lieutenant of the

President' really was 'holding the place' for the Americans to come. But, in any case, the margin by which Britain survived as an independent nation in the last war was very thin.

Churchill's reputation is based on his ability to speak to the British people in the summer of 1940 as no one ever has before or since. Contemporary polls prove this statement, with as many as 85 per cent approving Churchill's leadership. Churchill's real motives for taking up the fight against Hitler-Germany and his final political aims are still controversial. Winston Churchill did not understand Germany and German culture in general, let alone National Socialism in particular. He once admired German state-sponsored social legislation without realising that this was the other face of the coin he seems to have detested: Prussian militarism. Maybe he was guided, at least partly, by his personal ambition not only to write about history but to shape it. Maybe he sincerely believed in those Christian-Protestant values he proclaimed in public. The puritan outlook of 'Onward Christian Soldiers', a hymn Roosevelt and Churchill sang at a church service during their first meeting, indeed served as a common bond between the motherland and her former colony. In his political outlook Churchill was a Victorian Conservative. His ideas were deeply rooted in the nineteenth century, the heyday of British imperial power. Self-confidently Churchill never doubted his decisions and never wavered. As a war leader he thought of himself as Cromwell, the Duke of Marlborough and Nelson rolled into one, thus personifying all the military virtues of the English. Churchill covered the dark sides of British life and the disastrous war situation with language of Elizabethan grandeur.

Churchill, Roosevelt, and also Hitler and Stalin, were very popular war leaders. While Roosevelt, and Stalin, too, gained real victories, Churchill only avoided defeat. His battle for British independence, the Empire and his conservative, anti-socialist vision of Britain came to nothing. In 1945 at the end of the war Britain was totally dependent on the United States, the Empire began to disintegrate and Labour, in the search for a 'New Jerusalem', took over the government. Although the glory of Britain and Churchill ended in 1945, the myths about Churchill and his time will linger on in a world much more out of order than Britain seems to have been in her 'finest hour'.

7

Churchill and the Small States of Europe: the Danish Case

Tage Kaarsted

In 1934 a widely-published Danish encyclopaedia summarised the political career of Winston Churchill – then 60 years old – in these words:

> The verdicts on Winston Churchill's many changes and whole character may differ. However, there is general agreement that his inexhaustible energy and vividness of mind has made his career brilliant. He has managed big and varied ministries with honour although he was a rather unqualified dilettante.[1]

Ten years later he was thought to have qualified.

As a young man Winston Churchill was already well known in the Danish press. His adventures during the Boer War were much reported, and his political career before 1914 was covered at some length. In the same period, Denmark went from a rather loose two-party system into the era of a rigid four-party system, and Churchill's changing political affiliations made him slightly suspect; he was considered unpredictable. It was, however, only when Churchill took over the Admiralty in 1911 that his politics became of prime importance to Denmark.

In the early twentieth century, the Danish picture of Britain as *Perfide Albion*, dating from the Napoleonic Wars, had faded. Politically, Britain was now generally looked upon with sympathy – a sympathy strengthened by Britain's position as the dominant market for Danish exports, particularly bacon and butter. Moreover, Denmark was possessed by fear of Germany, which, in 1864, had robbed the Danish King of the Duchies of Schleswig and Holstein. Ever since, a hidden issue on the Danish political

97

agenda had been to repossess at least the Danish parts of Schleswig. In 1905–6 the Danish Prime Minister negotiated secretly with Germany, aiming at a defensive alliance in order to regain Schleswig. The Danish West Indies were discreetly offered in exchange. Luckily this came to nothing, but few Danes realised that Schleswig could only be reunited with Denmark after Germany was defeated in a European war, and nobody dared say so publicly.[2] On the contrary, changing Danish Cabinets took great pains to reassure Germany. The Danish Defence Bill of 1909 – particularly the part concerning the navy – provided Denmark with defence against a British attack on Germany through the Danish straits. The First Sea Lord, Admiral Fisher, was considered the chief advocate of such an operation, which would bring war to Denmark. But by that time Britain had given up this strategy and adopted a policy of distant blockade. Moreover Fisher retired in 1910. Still the Baltic Sea might again become a British target.[3]

In 1911 Winston Churchill was appointed First Lord of the Admiralty; he thought in an aggressive way. In *The World Crisis* (1923) he wrote:

> The policy of distant blockade was not adopted from choice, but from necessity. It implied no repudiation on the part of the Admiralty of their fundamental principle of aggressive naval strategy, but only a temporary abandonment of it in the face of unsolved practical difficulties; and it was intended that every effort should be made, both before and after a declaration of war, to overcome those difficulties.[4]

In 1913 Admiral Lewis Bayly was instructed to 'investigate and report on the question of seizing a base on the Dutch, German, Danish or Scandinavian coasts for operations of Flotillas on the outbreak of war with Germany'. Of course this might be dangerous for Denmark, but it is important to stress that such an operation did not cover the Baltic Sea. Bayly recommended Esbjerg and the Laesoe Channel (the Skaw area), and the idea was only to provoke the German fleet into action.[5]

These considerations were not known in Denmark, and Erik Scavenius, the Danish Foreign Minister, was slightly puzzled after a conversation with Sir Edward Grey, the British Foreign Secretary. Scavenius accompanied King Christian X, first cousin of King George V, on a state visit to England in January 1914. Sir Edward was spreading cloud rather than light on the intentions of the British Navy around the Baltic Sea.[6] When war became imminent, Churchill took up Bayly's plans, and in July 1914 sent them to Asquith, the Prime Minister. However, they were shelved.[7]

A few days later, on 3 August 1914, the Danish government explained its intentions to Germany when, in answer to the German envoy's enquiry, it stated that even if naval operations took place in Danish waters, this would not lead to any change in Denmark's neutral attitude. The declaration ended: 'Denmark will in no circumstances join the opponents of Germany'. At the outbreak of war between Great Britain and Germany on 4 August the Germans immediately asked whether Denmark would mine the Great Belt. Even though the Germans added, 'against both belligerent parties', this was clearly a measure of great significance to the Germans. After some hesitation and many deliberations and negotiations, the government decided to lay mines in the Belt. The decisive influence here lay with Admiral Kofoed-Hansen, who with the help of Admiral Prince Valdemar persuaded King Christian to change his views. Late in the afternoon, the British Minister in Copenhagen, Sir Henry Lowther, was informed of the State Council's decision in a statement declaring that the mine-laying operation was because of the desire of the Danes to remain neutral. Lowther naturally knew quite well what was behind all this and when, later the same day, he told the Foreign Ministry that he found the mine-laying quite reasonable, this was a result of British anxiety to avoid German action against Denmark.

On 8 August 1914, the Danish government was informed by the Danish Minister in London that Sir William Tyrell, Private Secretary to the Foreign Secretary, had said the British accepted Denmark's attitude and understood her very difficult position, and for that reason would not press Denmark. To this evidence of British understanding can be added Lowther's report of 25 August 1914. In this he wrote that Denmark 'can hardly be blamed if she be inclined to stretch a point to avoid giving offence to Germany at the present time'. There can be little doubt that the British government in August 1914 was prepared to accept a Danish policy of pro-German neutrality.[8] This was not only in harmony with British ideas before the war, but also with British ideas and actions all through it. Hankey's book on *The Supreme Command*, based on contemporary notes, explains that Great Britain did not wish to give Germany any excuse for occupying Denmark.[9] Sir Edward Grey, in his post-war memoirs, classified Denmark, Spain, Norway and Holland as countries which had decided to stay out of the war, whatever their sympathies were. 'These were the real neutrals.' Mutual concessions or promises were unnecessary, and for the British it was a question of refraining from pressing them so hard (by the blockade) that they became anti-British.[10]

In September 1914 both Grey and Churchill gave assurances to a private representative of King Christian that Britain would do nothing which could make Denmark's situation worse. Nevertheless, the Danish government was anxious about the intentions of the British Admiralty.[11] Churchill went on pondering plans to win mastery over the Baltic, either by a regular naval battle, or by seizing the Kiel Canal, possibly by invasion of Schleswig-Holstein, or by an effective blockade of Heligoland Bay. On 17 September 1914, he discussed plans for an attack with leading naval Officers, and Admiral Bayly came out in favour of sending destroyers to the Elbe to destroy the locks at Brunsbüttel simultaneously with an attack by destroyers, cruisers and submarines on Kiel.[12]

Churchill was also behind an even more ambitious plan – to take Borkum, and from there occupy Schleswig and Holstein and seize the Kiel Canal. When the British Army had consolidated itself in Schleswig and Holstein, Denmark should be urged to join the Allies, to recover Schleswig and Holstein. British troops should then land on Fünen, to ensure passage through the Great Belt, after which the British fleet would enter the Baltic and cut off supplies to Germany from the north. Finally, Russian troops would land in several places along the North German coast.

The Borkum plan was one of Churchill's favourites. The Chief of the Admiralty War Staff, Vice-Admiral H.F. Oliver, has related how Churchill often dropped in at his office to tell him how he would take Borkum (or Sylt). Oliver remembered that if he did not interrupt him or put any questions, Churchill could take Borkum in 20 minutes. On 3 January 1915, Churchill gave orders to have all the plans ready for an attack on Sylt on 1 March or 15 April. On 7 January 1915, the War Council agreed to the Borkum plan, but only in favourable circumstances – which, as we know, never occurred. After the middle of January 1915, both Borkum and Sylt faded into the background, and the loss of HMS *Formidable* destroyed Bayly's influence. The other Sea Lords considered the Borkum plan too dangerous.[13]

Lord Fisher, who was recalled soon after the outbreak of war to resume the post of First Sea Lord, like Churchill considered an offensive in the Baltic. He agreed with Churchill that in such an event, the allies should attack the German flank with large land forces in Schleswig and Holstein, and then either violate Danish neutrality or obtain active Danish support. The climax should then be to force the Belts while the Russian Army landed in Pomerania. In a colourful memorandum, Fisher vividly described how Frederick the Great had been horrified by the possibility of such an operation during the Seven Years' War. Fisher's idea was to mine the North Sea heavily to make naval engagements there impossible. Fisher himself was well aware of the weaknesses in the plan, such as the long, vulnerable lines of communication. In addition, like the Germans the British would have to disregard the legal and moral rights of neutrals.

On the other hand, Fisher opposed Churchill's plan to occupy Borkum and use the island as a base from which to close the Kiel Canal. Churchill has asserted, on his side, that Fisher did not believe in his own plan, which was never passed on for detailed planning.[14] This is correct; moreover Fisher received no support for his plan, either in the government or in the War Office. For instance, Admiral Sir J S Corbett asked whether the Germans would not mine the whole of the Baltic, and critics also declared that the enemy held all the cards: the British fleet and Expeditionary Corps would be far from reinforcement, docks and industrial centres. They believed that it would be impossible to block the Kiel Canal, and considered that there were too few mines available. They also described the passage through the Great Belt as extremely dangerous, since the Kiel Canal was only 30 miles away. Aversion to actions of this kind can also be seen from the fact that when Churchill, on 1 December 1914, put the problem of an 'advanced base' before the War Council, the Army refused to make troops available. The two leading admirals under Fisher, Jellicoe and Oliver, were also against all these projects – which they considered unrealistic – for Heligoland, Borkum and the Baltic.

Fisher apparently did not give up. The building programme which he had initiated in November 1914 could be used for a Baltic action as it included cruisers with a moderate draught, mine-layers and landing craft (in all about 600), all of it matériel which could naturally be used elsewhere. On 25 January 1915 Fisher gave his 'Baltic project' to Asquith, but the latter did not have it circulated among the members of the War Council. It is likely that Asquith, who had supported another of Churchill's plans – Gallipoli – did not wish to create uncertainty by bringing up a different project.[15] It is difficult to get to the bottom of Fisher's real intentions. The biographer of Fisher, Ruddock F Mackay, is inclined to think that Churchill was right, and that in 1914–15 Fisher was not as convinced of the advisability of a Baltic action as he later claimed, and that his shipbuilding programme was not intended especially for such an action. After the tragic campaign in the Dardanelles, and when the commission of enquiry set to work to investigate the circumstances of its failure, Fisher over emphasised his Baltic aims from 1914–15 in order to shift the blame for the Gallipoli catastrophe to Churchill. This makes a British operation in the Baltic seem even less likely.[16]

In addition to this, the Cabinet was not prepared to violate Danish neutrality in such a blatant manner. Edward Grey had already told the Danish Minister in London on 24 November 1914, that he knew 'that the attitude of the Danish government was friendly'. He had also said that he 'did not wish to cause them embarrassment'.[17] This attitude also emerges clearly in Maurice Hankey's 'Boxing Day Memorandum' of 26 December 1914. This completely ruled out the possibility of any attack on Germany which would involve the violation of Denmark's or Holland's neutrality, since it would be incompatible with Great Britain's denunciation of Germany's violation of Belgium's neutrality.[18] Asquith and Grey certainly agreed. Fisher did not and Churchill was less inhibited. In May 1915 both Churchill and Fisher retired, and there were sighs of relief in the Danish government. It believed that they both wanted a Baltic offensive, and that the consequences could be extremely dangerous for Denmark.[19]

What actually took place in the Baltic, on British initiative, was little more than symbolic. In October 1914, the Admiralty decided to send three submarines, and later two more, into the Baltic. What is interesting from the Danish point of view is that in the operational orders of 10 October 1914, it is emphasised that Denmark's neutrality must not be compromised. These submarine operations proved difficult and troublesome. The submarines operated under very difficult circumstances based in Russian harbours, but nevertheless carried out several successful operations and made the German Navy believe that there were a dozen or more British submarines in the Baltic.[20] Winston Churchill, then, was not hostile towards Denmark, but if the war demanded it he was ready to infringe Danish neutrality.

The Allied victory in 1918 gave Denmark the Danish part of Schleswig after a referendum. The League of Nations was established and Denmark happily joined it. In the 1930s, though, the Danish attitude to the League became ambivalent, on the one hand hoping that it would offer some protection against Germany's taking back Schleswig by force; on the other hand fearing that obligations towards the League could bring Denmark into war.[21] In order not to provoke Hitler and because of the basic assumption that it was impossible for Denmark to defend herself, Danish defence was cut down, and the Defence Bill of 1937 left Denmark practically unarmed. Furthermore she had no alliances. Nordic military co-operation was not possible. In 1937 the Danish Prime Minister, Thorvald Stauning, paid a visit to England and during a conversation with British Foreign Secretary Anthony Eden, (and against the advice of his Foreign Minister, P Munch), hinted at a possible German assault upon Denmark, not to regain North Schleswig, but to acquire bases on the coast of the Danish North Sea. He did not ask for a promise of British military help, but Eden interrupted anyway to say that he was glad he had not asked for any pledges.[22] In spring 1939, the Danish situation was discussed at ministerial level in the Foreign Policy Committee. At that time Britain seems to have been willing to take on a commitment, but it came too late.

A British promise of aid to Denmark never materialised because of a series of misunderstandings which led to a vicious circle of excuses. Denmark would not defend herself because there was no prospect of outside support, but the Danish failure to rearm gave the British an excuse not to add Denmark to the list of countries for whom she would be willing to fight.[23]

In the 1930s most Danish newspapers considered Winston Churchill to be an alarmist and an outsider. He was called 'an adventurer, an irresponsible rowdy, and somewhat of an artist, highly gifted, but dangerous if he is let loose'. Erik Scavenius, the former Danish Minister of Foreign Affairs, called him 'a war-crazy Tory politician'. The Danish government and the vast majority in Parliament were satisfied with Chamberlain's policy of appeasement.[24] When war broke out in 1939, Churchill again became First Lord of the Admiralty. In a radio broadcast on 20 January 1940 he appealed to the neutral countries – in a threatening manner – to join the Allies. '. . . what would happen if all these neutral nations I have mentioned were in one spontaneous impulse to do their duty in accordance with the Covenant of the League, and stand together with the British and French Empires against aggression and wrong?', Churchill asked. 'They bow humbly and in fear to German threats of violence, comforting themselves meanwhile with the thought that the Allies will win . . . Each one hopes that if he feeds the crocodile enough, the crocodile will eat him last.'[25]

Churchill's speech frightened the Danes. The British Minister in Copenhagen, C Howard-Smith, reported that the speech 'has been criticised violently to me by all classes of Danes, who absolutely refuse to see that Churchill was not inviting them to come into the war, but merely pointing out that Germany is by nature a bully and should therefore be stood up to'. On the other hand, the Danish Minister in London told his government that Churchill's impatience was generally shared in Britain. It would unfortunately weaken 'the already remarkably limited understanding among the British public of the care which naturally ought to be taken by a belligerent to avoid exposing the neutral states to the other party to the war'.[26]

Churchill's speech also worried the Danish Foreign Minister to a very high degree. He tried to make Norway and Sweden join Denmark in a peace appeal, but mainly due to Norwegian reluctance it came to nothing.[27] Churchill, however, was out of step with the policy of his government, and Lord Halifax reproved him in a letter of 26 January 1940 saying: 'It puts me in an impossible situation if a member of the Gov.

like yourself takes a line in public which differs from that taken by the PM or myself: and I think, as I have to be in daily touch with these tiresome neutrals, I ought to be able to predict how their minds will work'.[28] Churchill apologised the same day, and during a lunch with Scandinavian journalists, on 2 February 1940, he said:

> I cannot blame Denmark . . . They [the other Scandinavian countries] at least have a ditch, over which they can feed the tiger, but Denmark is so terribly near Germany that it will be impossible to bring help . . . Denmark must balance. We will get some bacon and butter, and the Germans some . . . perhaps it is best like that. Denmark does have a [non-aggression] pact with Germany, but I have no doubt that the Germans will overrun Denmark when it suits them.[29]

A few weeks later Churchill, without the metaphor about the tiger, repeated this statement in a conversation with the Danish minister in London. Thus he gave the Danish politicians an alibi to justify the fact that Denmark, on 9 April 1940 surrendered and did not go down fighting, as Churchill had hoped she would.[30]

Among those who were opposed to the general pacifist attitude was the important Danish shipowner, A P Møller who, before the war, had argued at public meetings, and in booklets distributed to all Danes, in favour of a stronger defence. He feared a German occupation and at the beginning of 1940 asked Churchill, through an intermediary, how Britain would react in such a case. Churchill answered that 'in such a situation Britain would regard Danish ships as lawful prizes, and the only advice he could give was to issue every single master with sealed orders that, should the occasion arise, they should follow the directives of a British company which had been previously mandated'. Møller did not dare take up this suggestion, since it might cause serious consequences for the Maersk ships and for Danish shipping, should the Germans learn about any such order.[31]

On 8 April 1940 Møller was convinced that a German attack against Norway and Denmark was imminent. Consequently he issued orders to all his ships to seek neutral harbours and not to obey orders from Denmark if she was occupied, but to make contact with A P Møller's American partner. In June 1940 his son, who has given his name to 'the Maersk McKinney Møller Centre for Continuing Education', at Churchill College, Cambridge, managed to get to the US in order to run the company. At that time 20 of A P Møller's 36 ships abroad were under Allied control. Soon all but two of his ships had joined the Allies. Nineteen were lost during their participation in the war against Hitler. In all, 230 Danish merchant ships worked for the Allies; 136 vessels were lost with more than 1,000 seamen's lives.[32]

Two days after the occupation of Denmark and Norway, Churchill claimed that the Germans had made a mistake: 'Herr Hitler has committed a grave strategic error in spreading the war so far to the North and in forcing the Scandinavian people, or peoples, out of their attitude of neutrality.' And on 8 May he said that Hitler had 'condemned a large part of the Scandinavian peninsula and Denmark to enter the Nazi empire of Hungryland'.[33] This was true for Norway, but not for Denmark. During the war the Danish population was in a physically better condition than before the war (less sugar), and at the end of the war the food consumption of the average Dane, measured in calorific value, was among the highest in the world. Churchill can, however, hardly be blamed for not foreseeing this in the spring of 1940. Even today, Danish popular memory considers the years of occupation as an era of physical deprivation, and Danish social historians have done little to correct that impression.[34]

On 9 April 1940 it was evident that the Danish policy of benevolent neutrality towards Germany had failed. Denmark lost her independence although the government stayed in office till August 1943 to conduct what is called a policy of negotiation, i.e., a continuation of benevolent neutrality. This had been possible in 1914-18, but it soon proved impossible after 1940 – with a German army of occupation in the country.

In Danish official circles Winston Churchill was considered responsible for the ill-fate of Denmark. This attitude was reflected in the newspaper *Politiken*, the largest circulation newspaper in Denmark which had backed the social democratic-radical coalition Cabinet in power since 1929. The appeasement line of the *Politiken* was influenced by Erik Scavenius, chairman of the Board of Shareholders. During the *Altmark* episode, when HMS *Cossack* entered a Norwegian fjord to free British prisoners, *Politiken*'s leading articles criticised Churchill, and during the Norwegian campaign it declared on 28 April: 'If . . . the English landing [in Norway] proves to be the Gallipoli adventure over again England will for the second time during a Great War learn that Winston Churchill is a dangerous man.' The reaction was dramatic. The circulation of *Politiken* fell by 31 per cent or 49,000 copies per day. A flood of protesting letters was sent to the editor. Public opinion in Denmark had all the time considered Germany the enemy, Britain a friend.[35] However, the political establishment, which had a firm hold of the Danish parliament (elected in 1939), made Erik Scavenius Foreign Minister in July 1940 and Prime Minister in 1942. The Danish people saw only one end of the German occupation, i.e., an Allied victory. In 1940 some considered this unlikely, but most people hoped for it in spite of Hitler's apparent success as a warlord.

So the Danes bowed their heads, and the first organised sabotage group was not formed till the spring of 1942. It consisted of a dozen grammar school boys between the ages of 15 and 18, who named their group 'The Churchill Club'. They succeeded in 25 operations (burning German goods wagons etc.) before they were arrested. However, they managed to get out of jail in the classical way (hacksaw and rope) and continue their sabotage by night, returning to their cells in the morning. Of course this was eventually revealed, and they were sentenced to several years of strict imprisonment. The actions of 'The Churchill-Club' had little military effect, but they were of psychological and political importance. They created goodwill for resistance at a time when there was little understanding of sabotage.[36] It was not a coincidence that the boys named their club after Winston Churchill. Danish opinion no longer considered him irresponsible, but regarded him as the statesman who would free them. The growing clandestine press proved this.[37]

Of great importance for the Danish resistance movement was the British Special Operations Executive (SOE). This was established in July 1940 based on a memorandum by Hugh Dalton, Minister for Economic Warfare, followed by the intervention of Churchill who endorsed the plan with the words 'Set Europe ablaze'. From December 1941 SOE sent agents to Denmark by parachute, in April 1942 radio contact was established, and from March 1943 a continuous stream of arms and explosives was dropped by the Royal Air Force and picked up by the increasing number of resistance groups.[38]

In August 1943 the Danish people launched a series of strikes and sabotage attacks and the government resigned rather than meet German demands to fight the resistance movement. Winston Churchill, of course, was pleased that Denmark at last had been set ablaze. As soon as the government had officially broken with the Germans, Churchill wanted Denmark to become a member of the United Nations, i.e., the Allied powers, arguing that the sabotage and the fact of the Danish merchant navy sailing for the Allies (under the Danish flag from December 1943) constituted 'a certain definite contribution' to Allied warfare. The USSR would only recognize 'the fighting Denmark' represented by the Freedom Council (with its powerful Communist representation), so Denmark did not obtain formal recognition as an ally till the war was over. She was invited to take part in the San Francisco Conference from June 1945 and thus participate in the official foundation of the UN.[39]

In London the free Danes had worked hard for the Allied cause, and

At home in the study at Chartwell, 1939.

General Election, 1935.

Winston Churchill and his daughter Mary outside Number 10 Downing Street, July 1942.

Churchill enters the garden at No. 10 with General Sikorski, Polish Prime Minister and Commander-in-Chief, 5 August 1940.

Churchill and Lloyd George at the Chinese Embassy in London, 1941.

Churchill in academic robes after receiving his honorary degree at Harvard University, 14 September 1943.

Temporarily replacing his famous 'John Bull' hat with a steel helmet, 28 August 1940.

*Roosevelt and Churchill with War Correspondents at the President's Villa,
1 February 1943.*

*Taken on the occasion of Churchill's 69th birthday which he celebrated in
Tehran. With Roosevelt and Stalin.*

During the Three-Power Conference, Yalta. Churchill, Roosevelt and Stalin in the grounds of Livadia Palace.

Churchill greets General Dwight D Eisenhower at Grosvenor House, London, 4 July 1951.

Churchill was sympathetic towards them. On 31 December 1944 they persuaded him to issue a message to the Danish resistance movement praising it for its efforts to fight the Nazis as part of the 'Grand Alliance' which included the European resistance movements. The message was written by Terkel Terkelsen, the Danish journalist then working for the BBC.[40] At that time the policy of the British government was to persuade the Danish resistance movement led by the Freedom Council to co-operate with the politicians who were more or less underground expecting to resume office as soon as the war was over. The underlying idea was to make the Danes look to Britain for security and for commercial advantages after the war.[41]

There was no agreement between the Allies as to who was going to liberate Denmark, although in the West everyone regarded Denmark as in the British sphere of influence. Nevertheless the Soviet attitude was uncertain, and Britain could not assume that the USSR would not seize control of Denmark if they were first on the spot. In April 1945 this seemed possible. In a telegram to Eden on 19 April 1945 Churchill emphasised that the British army must arrive at Lübeck first to prevent the Russians from capturing Holstein and from there going on to Denmark. In reply, Eden agreed that a Russian occupation of Denmark would be highly inconvenient. Churchill was still concerned about Denmark. On 3 May he asked the Foreign Office: 'What are the facts about Denmark?' Next day false rumours came to London that the Russians were dropping troops by parachute near Copenhagen. Churchill immediately telephoned to General Eisenhower, telling him about the importance of getting to Denmark first, and making sure that 'if any Russian parties arrived, they would arrive as our guests . . . They would be shown the greatest civility but, of course, it would be made quite clear to them that the perch was ours'. In response to this danger the Supreme Allied Headquarters prepared to land parachute troops in Denmark.[42]

Meanwhile the British 21st Army Group, under the command of Field Marshal Montgomery, was already hurrying to meet the Russians before they reached Holstein. They managed to do this on 2 May, so there could be no doubt that at least part of Denmark was cut off from the Russians. Fortunately the 287,000 German soldiers in Denmark surrendered without fighting on 5 May, and it was sufficient for Britain to send a few soldiers by air to Copenhagen, while Montgomery's tanks hastened up from Holstein to Jutland. The perch had fallen to Britain at a very low cost. The plans of the USSR are still obscure, but I think the general opinion of historians is that the Russians had no intention of occupying and/or liberating Denmark. They did, for a few months, occupy Bornholm, but this Danish island is located so far to the east in the Baltic that the British in May 1945 considered it to be in the Russian sphere of influence.[43]

Contrary to what was the case in other occupied countries such as Norway, the Germans never prohibited radio listening in what they wanted to be their model protectorate. So all Danes became familiar with Winston Churchill's voice through the broadcasts of the BBC.[44] It was extremely encouraging, and at the end of the war there is no doubt that public opinion regarded Churchill as both an eminent statesman and a hero. In 1945, as soon as the *Rigsdag* (Parliament) convened Prime Minister Vilhelm Buhl, resuming the post after an interval of two years, sent Churchill a telegram expressing the gratitude of the Danish people.

Very soon the tension between East and West came to the surface. Churchill, now leader of the Opposition, was among the first to warn publicly against the Communist menace. In March 1946 he made his famous speech in Fulton, Missouri, about the Iron Curtain in Europe, urging Britain and the USA to unite to stop the USSR from forcing Communist regimes on more countries.

This was contrary to official Danish foreign policy although Denmark had given up neutrality. Denmark considered herself as a 'bridge-builder' between East and West. Churchill's speech made politicians and newspapers divide, as in the US, on predictable lines: widespread approval on the right, slight hesitation in the centre, criticism on the democratic left and bitter resentment among the Communists.[45] On 19 September 1946 Churchill made another famous speech in Zürich. In this he urged France and Germany to be reconciled and take the lead in creating 'a kind of United States of Europe', however without Great Britain. His speech was fully reported in the Danish newspapers, but the reaction in Denmark was rather hesitant, the general opinion being against federalism, but in favour of less formal European co-operation. Consequently Denmark joined the Council of Europe in May 1949. The truth is that, until 1949, Danish foreign and defence policy was characterised by confusion. The coup in Czechoslovakia in February 1948, and the suicide or killing of Masaryk a few weeks later, made the Danish Social-Democratic government try to give the policy of non-aligned neutrality some substance. It initiated negotiations between Sweden, Norway and Denmark in order to form a Scandinavian defence league. This proved impossible as Sweden wanted it to be neutral, and Norway thought that it should lean towards Britain and America. Reluctantly, but backed by an overwhelming majority of the *Rigsdag*, Denmark signed the North Atlantic Treaty in April 1949.[46]

Denmark had placed herself on the right side of the Iron Curtain, and in October 1950 the Danes were able to pay their homage to Clementine and Winston Churchill who were the guests of the King. Winston

Churchill was decorated with the Order of the Elephant and met the members of 'The Churchill Club', who all survived the war. The streets were crowded with hundreds of thousands of grateful Danes.

Denmark is a small state and played only a minor part in Winston Churchill's concept of British interests. He was ready to infringe Danish neutrality during both wars if he considered this necessary to prosecute the war against Germany. But he had no desire to force British hegemony upon Denmark and during the Second World War he wanted only to help Denmark to restore its independence and democracy as soon as the enemy was beaten. When this was done he hoped to see Denmark in the Western Alliance.

The Danish attitude to Winston Churchill began in anxiety if not fear, but ended in esteem and admiration. Nothing has changed this view. When he died, *Politiken* praised him over 10 full pages and, in a leading article, wrote that the signal of hope, when catastrophe was looming, was 'Winston is back'. The article concluded: 'Through some of the darkest years in the history of the world Churchill's actions lend lustre to all he was'.[47]

8

Churchill and Poland

Anita Prażmowska

To start with the simple question of whether Winston Churchill liked the Poles, the answer is that he most certainly did. There is no shortage of evidence to suggest that he was impressed by General Sikorski and went to great lengths to make himself available to the Polish wartime leader. When Churchill become the British Prime Minister on 10 May 1940, British military leaders and the Foreign Office were forcefully jolted out of their hitherto complacent neglect of the Polish government-in-exile. Churchill's leadership meant that the Polish request for assistance in the evacuation of troops from defeated France was treated as a priority, and the re-equipping and training of the Poles became a matter of direct concern to the British. Churchill liked the Poles for their style, their military demeanour and the halo of martyrdom which always surrounded them during the war.

What is more difficult to ascertain is the degree to which Churchill allowed this personal enthusiasm to interfere with the realities of war. One of the biggest problems in this attempt to disentangle the Polish issue from what the British leader and his advisers thought of the Poles in Britain is the fact that Poland figured as a major topic of debate in a great number of wartime allied negotiations. At least superficially, the Polish question was a bone of contention between Britain and the Soviet Union until the Teheran Conference, and subsequently became an issue which, while no longer contended by Britain, was a source of anxiety to both. Looked at more closely, it is apparent that Poland was no more than an obstacle to Britain's pursuit of her wartime relations with the Soviet Union, but an obstacle which both sides were determined to get out of the way, precisely in order to avoid souring British–Soviet relations. This image of the Polish government-in-exile as Banquo's ghost at the British–Soviet banquet suggests that the espousal of Polish interests was, notwithstanding Churchill's personal feelings, neither advisable nor advantageous to Britain.

In order to understand fully the complexity of British–Polish relations one has to accept that these were both complex and multifaceted. Diplomatic exchanges were tied up with military collaboration, and military co-operation was pursued by the Poles in order to secure political advantages. The true nature of Churchill's relations with the Poles in London is not comprehensible unless one takes into account the interrelationship of these issues.

In July 1940 the British government was offered all the manpower resources which the Sikorski government was able to bring together as a fighting force in exile. Initially this was approximately 20,000 men rescued from France. They were mainly stationed in Scotland and commenced training in preparation for continental action. A Polish Brigade was already attached to British command in the Middle East, where it had crossed from the French Levant command of General Mittelhausser to the British side in Palestine in June 1940. But in 1942, the arrival in Iran of the Polish troops from the Soviet Union, led by General Anders, replenished with approximately 76,000 men the British Iran–Iraq front, which was under severe strain. Throughout the war the Poles continued to give proof of their determination to continue fighting Germany and provided the British with units which distinguished themselves in battle. The Polish fighter squadrons performed well in the Battle of Britain; General Kopański's brigade participated in the defence of Tobruk and in military confrontations near Gazala. Subsequently the Polish Independent Parachute Brigade, which the Poles had trained in Britain so that it could capture key strategic points at the time of entry into Poland, was used instead by the British in the effort to establish a bridgehead in Arnhem. In May 1944 the Polish Second Corps entered into battle in Italy.

This impressive roll call of Polish participation in the British battle zones gives a totally erroneous impression of great Polish importance and influence in the joint effort of the allies. The reality was much more prosaic. By the time of the Teheran Conference the British military leadership had distanced itself from the Polish government-in-exile in order to secure Soviet co-operation and assistance. For the Poles the decision to continue fighting on increasingly distant fronts which only took them further away from Poland was a desperate attempt to elicit British commitments to the defence of their cause against the Soviet Union. As the Soviet troops stood poised to enter Central Europe, in the autumn of 1943, it was a foregone conclusion that Poland was going to be in the Soviet sphere of influence. The diplomatic battles that Churchill subsequently fought on behalf of the Poles were aimed merely at ironing out details of Soviet domination of the region. Churchill neither would nor could have affected the course of developments in that region. His involvement in Polish matters was consciously confined to a mediating role and making provisions for the Polish soldiers who had fought with the British.

The Polish government-in-exile's willingness to continue the fight against Germany in spite of the September defeat was not an act of heroic altruism. It was a clearly calculated bid to secure for Poland a major role in post-war decision-making. To the members of the exile government it was also a means of ensuring that power did not slip into the hands of a more committed national leadership which could be socialist, if not outright revolutionary, in its aims. The transfer of authority to an exile government, so carefully enacted in Paris in the closing days of September 1939, and that government's assumption of a high profile in foreign affairs which was to be backed by a military contribution commensurate with future Polish territorial and political aspirations, was planned beforehand. When General Sikorski's government sought sanctuary in Britain in June 1940 it arrived with clearly formulated aims which it proceeded to implement in its relations with its new host country. But first they had to persuade the British leadership of their usefulness to the British cause. The difficulties of their task were apparent from the beginning. While the Poles had been in Paris they were viewed as a French problem. The Chamberlain government took little direct interest in their objectives and policies. When the Polish government-in-exile arrived in London it laid claim to a special status as a fighting ally and stated clear war aims. The incompatibility of British and Polish objectives was a clearly recognised problem. Notwithstanding the military collaboration backed by detailed legal agreements, which evolved over the course of the next two years, the limit of Polish usefulness to the British was highlighted by the extent of the Poles' demands and their post-war aspirations. The Churchill administration was always aware that political commitments to the Poles would have meant a devolution of British decision-making concerning the conduct of the war and post-war spheres of power. This very fact limited Churchill's willingness to reward the Poles for their military collaboration.

On arrival in Britain the Polish government perceived that the British were isolated in their fight against Germany. Sikorski and his government proceeded to try to extract commitments that Britain would, in return for military collaboration during the war, use the full weight of her power to establish Poland as a major European state after the war. The British

Foreign Office was most forcefully alerted to the extent of Polish aspirations by a memorandum which was submitted to them by the Polish Ambassador in London, Edward Raczyński.[1] Behind this initiative was Polish frustration at not being able to force the British to discuss war aims and hence an anxiety lest Poland once more become the object of Great Power politics. The views expressed in the memorandum had been approved by Sikorski and bore the hallmark of the highest Polish authority. The underlying premise of the Poles was that, after the war, Britain would recognise the need for Poland to assume a direct interest in European politics. Germany and the Soviet Union were both likely to be weakened by the war. Therefore, according to Sikorski, Britain and the United States were going to have a decisive say in the politics of Europe. According to the memorandum, an independent and strong Poland, would be an essential partner in any future stabilisation in Europe. Poland would also act as a linchpin in a central European federation. Whereas Britain was expected to be a counterweight to the political power of Germany, Poland would guarantee that Soviet interests remained Asian.[2] Polish territories were to be enhanced by the incorporation of East Prussia and territories east of the river Oder.

For the Foreign Office heads of department the air of unreality which hovered around this memorandum was accentuated by the clearly stated expectation that British forces and military capacity would be visible on the continent from the Danish Straits and the Kiel Canal to the Scandinavian countries, Poland and Czechoslovakia.[3] The general response to the Polish initiative was that it highlighted the need to avoid making incautious promises. Frank Roberts, head of the Central Department, advised 'we shall clearly have to be guided to a large extent by whatever *fait accompli* confronts us after the war'.[4] If British freedom of action was not to be curtailed by allied demands and expectations, discussions on post-war spheres of influence had to be confined to generalities. This pragmatic point of view guided Churchill and his advisers through the labyrinth of demands made by exile governments based in London.

The Poles were not put off by such tactics. They identified avenues for the exercise of influence, and organisations and military committees which they felt were likely to become forums for decision-making over the conduct and aims of the war. One of the most consistently pressed demands was for Polish representation on all joint military staff organisations. This initially took the form of a Polish claim to membership of the Supreme War Council. In the spring of 1941, when Sikorski agreed with Churchill's suggestion that the Polish Brigade in the Middle East be used by General

Wavell, a request was made that a Polish Military Mission join the British GHQ Middle East.[5] The Poles considered that the North African campaign was a prelude to the opening of a Balkan front and they wanted to establish control over military decisions there. Their aspiration to become a dominant force in central and south-eastern Europe was well known to Churchill. Wavell and Churchill did not want Polish officers to interfere with military decisions in the Middle East. In particular, they did not want to be pushed towards the Balkan front, which was a matter of considerable contention between Churchill and his military leaders.[6] The Polish demand that they should be represented on joint allied staffs was finally conceded for the Combined Chiefs of Staff membership in 1943. This victory was illusory. The Polish representative, Colonel Leon Mitkiewicz, was not permitted to participate in discussions on subjects other than those relating to Polish troops.[7]

The Poles would not accept that they did not have a say in military planning. They fought hard for the status of an allied government and that meant that they wanted to have a say in all matters concerning European and Mediterranean battle zones. In October 1942, anticipating the imminent defeat of General Rommel's forces in North Africa, Sikorski took the opportunity to press on Churchill a military plan aimed at launching Polish troops into the Balkans and establishing there and in central Europe a dominant position for Poland.[8]

Sikorski's suggestion was that the Allies should assume the military initiative in 1943. He advocated that their thrust against Germany should aim at dividing the enemy forces along the North–South line. From the North the allies should move from the North Sea into Hamburg and on to Berlin. In the south they should either enter Italy or, preferably, go into the Balkans. The Poles believed that the latter thrust would be least demanding on resources for it would supposedly capitalise on anti-German feelings in that region. Allied progress through the Balkans into Bulgaria, Romania and Hungary, combined with a national insurrection in Poland, would effectively, according to the Polish plan, make full use of Polish expertise, Polish plans for joint action with the Yugoslav government, and good Polish–Hungarian relations.[9] It was not stated so explicitly that this military plan would also establish Polish military and hence political authority in the Balkans and central Europe on the back of a British war of liberation. More importantly, it would guarantee that the Soviet thrust into Europe would be halted on the Soviet borders so that the Red Army would not penetrate further. By playing down the staying power of the Soviet military offensive the Poles were continuing to suggest that the Soviet Union had no role to play in a future Europe. In effect they were trying to manoeuvre the British into the role of guardians of European stability not merely against Germany but also against the Soviet Union. The Polish plan received little consideration although it was widely circulated. To the British at the end of 1943, the Balkan front was not a realistic proposition. But, more importantly, on the basis of military developments it had already been decided to avoid confronting the Soviet Union and accept the extension of its power to regions which Soviet troops would enter.

The Poles were demanding partners and difficult guests. The government-in-exile rejected British suggestions that Polish issues should be looked at from the perspective of the war as a whole. They took for granted that Britain would champion and support the Polish cause in return for their direct participation in that joint effort. They emphatically refused to accept that they were merely one among other allied governments in London. Sikorski frequently used his access to Churchill to press the Polish point of view. Some of his interventions were weighty, others emphatically were not. On 23 August 1941 Sikorski visited Churchill to explain that in a forthcoming radio broadcast he should not refer to the Polish government-in-exile as one of many resident in London. He wanted Churchill to make a special reference to Poland as 'Britain's first fighting ally'.[10]

Nevertheless the biggest difference of opinion, and the one with potentially the most serious implications for Britain, was on the subject of the Soviet Union. The divergence of views on all other matters paled into insignificance and confirmed the worst Polish suspicions when the two allies tried to arrive at a joint approach to the question of the Soviet Union.

From its inception the Polish government-in-exile had as one of its objectives to persuade the British and French that they should view the Soviet Union as a key enemy.[11] The Polish Ambassador in Washington was instructed to use the media to arouse public outrage at the Soviet Union's unjust treatment of the Poles and to persuade American public opinion of the unfairness of the Riga Peace Treaty decisions of 1921.[12] In Britain the Poles tried to convince the Foreign Office that Poles had a unique insight into the Soviet mentality. Generally they endeavoured to undermine any trust in the willingness and ability of the Soviet Red Army to fight the German forces.

In July 1940 Sikorski took a major political risk when he decided not only to open negotiations with the Soviet Union but also to set aside the contentious issue of the Polish eastern borders. That particular initiative came to nothing as the Soviet Union did not take up his indirect approach.

The consequences of this crisis and Sikorski's subsequent decision to sign an agreement with the Soviet Union on 30 July 1941 exposed the limits of his power within his government. The ensuing quarrels with his own generals and the rifts which emerged among the Polish exile community were to haunt him until his death. In trying to resolve these he became increasingly dependent on British support and was repeatedly challenged to prove that the Sikorski–Maisky agreement had indeed safeguarded Polish interests.[13] His own government remained dubious about the need to reach any accommodation with the Soviet Union. Sikorski had to fight against his own ministers, while struggling to resist British government attempts to marginalise the Poles. Uniquely among the Poles who were in Britain, Sikorski perceived how the course of military developments could cause his government to lose its influence. He therefore tried to minimise the divisions between the Polish government-in-exile and the British government, reasoning that if the Poles were to become an obstacle to Britain they would lose the little support they had secured as a result of military co-operation.

After Sikorski's death the Polish government lost its one remaining means of influencing the British. The personal relationship which had existed between Churchill and the Polish leader had been useful to the Poles. It had enabled them to plead their case and to obtain consideration for their grievances. Stanislaw Mikolajczyk, the leader of the Peasant Party who became the Polish Prime Minister after Sikorski's death, rarely saw Churchill and communications between the Poles and the British were now routed through the usual Foreign Office and military channels. Furthermore, the hostility which surfaced between the Polish Prime Minister and the Commander in Chief General Kazimierz Sosnkowski meant that political and military decisions were badly co-ordinated. Whereas Sikorski was always able to link military co-operation with demands for political considerations, his successors were not able to make a case for the British to support their war aims, even at the height of Polish assistance to the British war effort in Italy.

In January 1944 Soviet troops entered Polish territory. Any attempts to commit the British forces to act as a buffer against the incoming Red Army were bluntly rejected. During a meeting with Churchill, Mikolajczyk was told bluntly that the Poles were expected to reach an accommodation with the Soviet Union and the Poles in Russia.[14]

The Polish troops, which had been so useful in the British campaign in Italy in 1944, soon became a problem. In August the Chiefs of Staff received a request from the Polish High Command. The Poles sought approval (and presumably also finance) for a three-year expansion programme as a result of which the Polish army would double in size.[15] Since it was well known that the Commander of the Polish army, General Wladyslaw Anders, was pinning his hopes on a war against the Soviet Union after the defeat of Germany, the proposal was considered unfavourably. In addition Churchill's personal plans for using the Poles as a foreign legion in policing Germany had to be abandoned because of fears that Poles would not make a good occupation force. It was noted that in areas of Italy which came under Polish military control Italian Communists and Socialists were treated very badly even when they had taken part in fighting the Fascist regime. By 1945 the subject of discussions about Polish soldiers, which had hitherto been their contribution to the fighting, changed. Since they were unlikely to want to return to Poland which was, their exiled government believed, slipping under Communist control, they would become the responsibility of the British.

As Prime Minister, Churchill took a lively interest in the conduct of foreign relations. His comments on Foreign Office memoranda were incisive and frequent. He was nevertheless just as capable of paying attention to a given subject one day as he was of neglecting it a few days later. The Poles in London were liable to misinterpret a sudden concern for them, in particular since it contrasted with the relative lack of interest of the Chamberlain government. This concern was not only due to the change of British leadership. The fall of France concentrated the minds of the British military men on the question of manpower resources and the Poles represented a readily available and trained supply of soldiers. Churchill's coming to power was therefore associated with the moment in the war when the Polish government-in-exile acquired importance and was given facilities to continue recruitment and prepare for the continuation of the war.[16] Sikorski and Churchill were at one in their determination to fight. The result of this unity of purpose was immediately apparent. Courtesies were henceforth observed by both sides and official consideration was shown to the Poles. In March 1941 Sikorski agreed to allow the British to use the Polish Brigade in the Middle East even though he had been personally criticised by some of his generals for allowing the use of Polish troops on fronts which had nothing to do with Poland. In return, Churchill made clear to Eden, then in the Middle East, that he agreed with Sikorski's view that these men were 'one of the last embodiments of Polish nationality'.[17] Touchingly Churchill added: 'I hope you appreciate what we are asking of these valiant strangers and that General Wavell will have this in his mind always'.[18]

The German attack on the Soviet Union and the conclusion of British–Soviet agreements inevitably removed the Poles into the background. While Churchill's relationship with Sikorski remained as warm as before, the significance of the Poles in British wartime diplomacy inevitably diminished. Sikorski made things much easier for the British by proving himself at that tricky moment to be a statesman of unusual calibre. Although he realised that the Soviet issue was likely to threaten his position within the Polish government-in-exile, he entered into direct negotiations with the Soviet Ambassador. Churchill offered Sikorski support and the Foreign Office was willing to assist him during embarrassing moments when the Polish President and the Minister for Foreign Affairs would not go along with Sikorski.[19] The signing of the Maisky–Sikorski agreement appeared a necessary precondition for the continuation of good Polish–British relations. Sikorski had sufficient political acumen to note this. He nevertheless hoped that Britain would become the champion of Polish interests and that he would receive the support of the British leadership in his negotiations with the Soviet Union. This was clearly not how Churchill saw the matter. The British refusal to make public statements concerning post-war territorial changes left the Poles increasingly anxious that the Soviet occupation of eastern Poland was being tacitly endorsed by the British government. Sikorski's bitter disappointment was communicated to the British when the substance of the eight-point Anglo-American declaration was made public a few weeks later. The Poles felt that a reference to the rights of nations to make their own choices was likely to weaken their claim to the Polish areas which had been occupied by the Soviet Union in September 1939. An urgent request to Churchill to make a special reference to the unique character of the Polish–British relationship remained unheeded.[20]

In the autumn of 1941 British military leaders were preoccupied with the question of manpower shortages. In addition the occupation of Iran and anxiety about Iraq focused attention on the Middle East. In spite of strong opposition from his military leaders, Churchill wanted to explore the possibility of moving troops to the Middle East in order to reinforce the Caucasus front. In these deliberations Polish troops, which were being built up in the Soviet Union as a result of the Maisky–Sikorski agreement, became the object of complex diplomatic manoeuvres. Since the German attack on the Soviet Union, all subjects relating to the Poles and the future of Poland, were analysed by the British government as aspects of Britain's policy towards the Soviet Union. The need to continue the Soviet war with Germany, rather than the objective merits of the Polish case, henceforth dictated policy choices. Churchill and the Foreign Office were never free from an anxiety that British use of Polish manpower, while a necessity to the British, could cause diplomatic difficulties with the

Soviet Union. In particular, because of the British decision to postpone the opening of the Second Front, the need to have the Soviet Union continue to hold down the bulk of the German troops dictated the choice of East European allies. A friendly and militarily supportive Polish government-in-exile was no substitute for the full might and potential of the Soviet Union. The public acknowledgement of their importance that the Poles were demanding only made this infinitely delicate situation worse for Churchill. It became necessary to manoeuvre in such a way that Polish military collaboration was secured without paying a political price in the form of promises of extensive support in the future.

In September 1941 the British War Office discussed extensively the use which could be make of the Polish troops in the Soviet Union. Sikorski's desire that they should be used as part of a joint allied war effort, rather than in aiding the Soviet Union, was well known. Sikorski's instruction that General Wladyslaw Anders, the Commander in Chief of the Polish Army in the Soviet Union, gravitate south, had also been communicated to the British. Sikorski had let it be known that he wanted the Polish troops to be part of the Anglo–Polish effort to aid the Soviet Union. He did not want the Poles simply to collaborate with the Soviet Union. The War Office therefore felt confident that it was free to plan for the use of the Polish troops. Indeed, it was generally recognised that this could be an extremely advantageous situation. It was widely accepted that the Poles would be more successful than the Red Army at defending the Caucasus oil-fields. By October 1941 British military leaders were openly discussing how they could fully utilise the Polish troops then in the Soviet Union.[21]

Notwithstanding the decision to make full use of the Poles, the British consistently refused to concede political commitments to the Polish government. This was clearly evident when Lord Beaverbrook went to Moscow in October 1941. Churchill had given him full authority to offer all possible aid to the Soviet Union.[22] This meant that neither Beaverbrook nor Averell Harriman, head of the United States supplies delegation, felt that they should haggle. As far as both they were concerned, the aim of their mission was to secure Soviet military co-operation at all costs.[23] Polish hopes that their negotiating position in the Soviet Union would be strengthened by having supplies for their troops in the Soviet Union earmarked out of the pool of equipment from the United States and Britain were thus thwarted. Had Beaverbrook gone along with the Polish request, the expansion of the Polish army in the Soviet Union could have proceeded without the need to depend on Soviet supplies and this in turn would have strengthened the Poles' political position there.

Churchill's determination to benefit from the availability of Polish soldiers, while at the same time making sure that the Soviet leadership's distrust was not increased, continued even when direct requests were made to the Poles to aid the British war effort. In October the question of British aid to Soviet defence of the Caucasus was linked to the dawning realisation that the British would prefer to hold Iran on their own. On 24 October, when discussing Sikorski's forthcoming visit to meet Stalin, Churchill prompted Sikorski to make a suggestion that the Polish troops should be moved south where they could be granted an independent sector in the Soviet front against Germany.[24] The fact that Churchill wanted Sikorski to make this suggestion, leaves no doubt that he preferred that Stalin, if he disagreed with it, should have doubts about the Polish willingness to fight rather than about British motives in Iran.

By November Stalin permitted the Poles to expand their units in excess of the earlier approved quota of 30,000, provided that Britain and the United States assumed responsibility for supplies to them. At the same time by November 1941 plans for the deployment of Polish soldiers in North Africa and the Middle East became clearer. In March 1942, the earlier agreement on the expansion of Polish troops in the Soviet Union was rescinded by Stalin, who claimed that British supplies were not getting through. As a result of this crisis an agreement was reached between Anders and Stalin that all troops in excess of 44,000 men would be evacuated to Iran. For Anders this was an victory. He had retained an unshaken conviction that the Soviet Union would soon fall. By obtaining Stalin's permission to send some of the Polish soldiers to Iran, Anders was realising his ambition of fighting with the British.

In March the first stage of the evacuation took place. The second and final removal of Polish units from the Soviet Union was completed in August 1942. As a result British Middle East Command gained approximately 80,000 fully-trained men. But the British also became responsible for the civilian population which, on Anders's insistence, had accompanied the men evacuated from the Soviet Union. The brief history of military collaboration between the Polish government-in-exile and the Soviet Union was thus ended. In the Middle East the British had to commence a programme of re-equipping and training to prepare the Poles for action in Italy. The expansion of Polish units, which was halted by the ending of recruitment in the Soviet Union, was restarted in earnest when the south and west European fronts were reopened. The Poles continued to build up their forces by incorporating into their army Polish ex-POWs and displaced persons. By the end of the war the British had under their command approximately 120,000 Polish soldiers.

The commitment of all the Polish government's military resources to

Britain coincided with the British decision not to oppose Soviet demands for frontier revisions in eastern Poland. But in London the British had to contend with an increasingly angry allied government which would endeavour to undermine British policies. From 1943 onwards the Foreign Office had to cope with the damage caused by Polish intrigues among the exile governments in London. The Belgian and Greek royal governments agreed with the Polish suggestion that the British should be pushed to make commitments to post-war arrangements. They were nevertheless irritated by the Polish presumption in raising the issue, and were unwilling to be drawn into a Polish anti-Soviet crusade. The British government kept a wary eye on these initiatives and exploited fully differences between the various exile governments. Polish–Czechoslovak talks aimed at establishing a Central European Federation briefly received the blessing of the British government. They were nevertheless abandoned when Soviet indifference to these plans crystallised into opposition.

In spite of military victories in North Africa at the beginning of 1943, Britain's continuing weak negotiating position in relation to the Soviet Union was confirmed by a further postponement of the cross-Channel landing. Churchill therefore remained impressed with the need not to antagonise the Soviet leader. At the beginning of 1943 Polish–Soviet relations deteriorated beyond repair. The discovery of the Katyń graves was the obvious reason for the break in diplomatic relations between the Polish government-in-exile and Stalin. In reality differences had advanced too far and the Soviet leadership was clearly proceeding with its own plans for an alternative Polish authority in the Soviet Union. Churchill followed his previous policy, refused to be drawn into the conflict and merely offered a mediating role.[25]

On 4 July 1943 Sikorski died in an air accident off Gibraltar. The influence of the Polish government-in-exile, already on the wane and in effect confined to Churchill's support for Sikorski, collapsed. Churchill did not seek to establish anything other than strictly formal relations with Mikolajczyk. General Sosnkowski, who took over military leadership and was known for his strongly held anti-Soviet view, was shunned by the British.

Towards the end of 1943 the situation seemed to reverse itself. Hitherto Churchill had given the appearance of seeking to dissociate his government from direct involvement in Soviet–Polish relations. Now Churchill and Eden undertook to press the Poles to accept Soviet conditions. At the Teheran Conference in November 1943 Churchill opened the discussion on Poland and assured Stalin that the Poles would be made to accept the Curzon Line and the extension of the western border to the Oder line.[26]

The Mikolajczyk government's earlier demands, that Britain and America station troops in Poland to exercise control over the incoming Red Army, were rejected. Instead Churchill and Eden pressed the London government to accept the Curzon Line. The task was a thankless one for the Poles were totally unrealistic about their own and the Anglo-Americans' ability to reverse the progress of the Soviet Union in eastern and central Europe. At the same time the Soviet leadership was increasingly hinting at the need to reconstruct the Polish government-in-exile.[27] By the time of the October 1944 conference in Moscow between Churchill, Stalin and Mikolajczyk, the British position had hardened sufficiently for Churchill to state bluntly to the Polish Prime Minister that he considered the Soviet territorial changes in Poland to be fair.

Mikolajczyk had to accept that there was little that could be expected from the British government. Until August 1944 the Polish government-in-exile had pinned its hopes on a great national uprising in Poland. At least initially this was supposed to be co-ordinated with the allied forces and mark the final dramatic moment of the liberation of Polish territories. Neither the British nor the United States attached any importance to these plans. In 1943 when detailed discussions of co-ordinated Anglo-American plans in Europe commenced the Polish plan received no attention. When the uprising took place in August 1944, it was without the agreement of the London government and was confined to Warsaw. Its aim was no longer to liberate Poland but to assert control over the capital in advance of the entry of the Soviet troops.[28]

The defeat of the uprising and Soviet impassivity in the face of the German victory marked the end of the illusion that the Polish government-in-exile would control Polish territory. The Home Army could no longer even consider establishing such control. The only organised and equipped units owing allegiance to the London government were fighting in Italy. The Polish government-in-exile's claim to represent the will of the Polish people could now be ignored with impunity. In a desperate bid to assert some influence, Mikolajczyk was forced to accede to Soviet demands that the Lublin Committee, established by the Soviet troops in the liberated territories, represent the Poles in Poland. Churchill and Eden were clear as to why it was essential for the Poles in London and Lublin to be seen to be talking together. Eden telegraphed the Foreign Office from Moscow:

> The Prime Minister and I then sought to impress on Marshal Stalin how essential it was in the interests of Anglo–Soviet relations that the Polish question should now be settled on a basis which would seem reasonable to the British people.[29]

In the remaining months of the war the Polish issue lingered on in the minds of the British politicians. Anxiety lest the troops in Italy succumb to despair was a point taken up by Churchill. The British military situation in Europe was far from easy and the forthcoming Pacific confrontation preyed on the minds of political and military leaders. Churchill, as always appreciative of Polish manpower, reassured Anders at the height of the Warsaw uprising 'that neither Great Britain nor the United States would abandon Poland'.[30]

Churchill's attitude towards the Poles was straightforward. The primacy of British objectives at a time of great military difficulties dictated policies which at times appeared inconsistent and affected by Churchill's personal preferences. In reality it was a policy of seeking to minimise discontent and distrust that might mar British–Soviet relations. In that respect Churchill was unsentimental about the Polish issue. He sought to reduce and remove possible Polish–Soviet disagreements. In pursuit of that policy he was capable of being wily, bullying and encouraging. The Polish government-in-exile was not allowed to come between Britain and her interests.

The difficulty in understanding Churchill's attitude towards the Poles stems from the fact that the British Prime Minister had no compunction about making full use of Polish manpower, while clearly holding back from making commitments to the Polish government that might have damaging implications. In any case the British military situation was never such as to permit the government to be scrupulous about its manpower sources. Churchill had sympathy for the Polish soldiers. He frequently expressed support for them and at the end of the war made sure that they were neither returned to Poland forcibly, nor left unprovided for in Britain. The personal debt incurred by Britain towards the Polish soldiers was honoured by the creation of a resettlement programme which was to guarantee them employment and integration into Britain. This was nevertheless quite distinct from his policy towards the issue of the future of Poland.

9

Churchill and de Gaulle

FRANÇOIS KERSAUDY

Many of Winston Churchill's Cabinet colleagues in 1940 – and some historians since then – have wondered why the Prime Minister suddenly decided in June 1940 to back a little-known, 49-year-old, French brigadier general. Why indeed would Churchill want to support this 'relatively junior'[1] General de Gaulle, who for only 10 days had been Under Secretary of State for War in a vacillating French government, and who, after the demise of that government, had rebelled against the new authorities of his country – for which they sentenced him to death shortly thereafter?

There were three good reasons why Churchill supported Charles de Gaulle. For one thing, by the time the two men had their first meetings – in London on 9 June, in Briare on the 11th, in Tours two days later and in London again on the 16th – Churchill had lost faith in the French army, and had developed doubts about its leaders. Both the commander-in-chief, General Gamelin, and his successor, Weygand, had declared themselves unable to contain the German invaders who had overrun most of northeastern France and were directly threatening Paris. The octogenarian Marshal Pétain appeared the very picture of defeatism, as did Churchill's old and trusted friend General Georges and even the formerly resolute Premier, Paul Reynaud, who was openly contemplating the prospect of an armistice. But in shining contrast to all these men, General de Gaulle, seemingly calm, had talked of only one thing: continuing the struggle by all possible means, in France if possible, abroad if necessary. Churchill hoped that de Gaulle would persuade Paul Reynaud and his government to carry on the struggle. The declaration of Franco–British Union to which

Churchill agreed on 16 June can only be seen as a means of strengthening de Gaulle's hand. (It is noteworthy that Churchill did not believe in the feasibility of the plan, any more than did de Gaulle.)

By 17 June, after Reynaud's government had resigned and Marshal Pétain had undertaken to form a new one willing to sign an armistice with the Germans, that first reason ceased to exist. But a second one was just as compelling: at a time of mortal peril, the British people had to be told that France, their only ally, had deserted the alliance and left them all alone in the fight for survival. A greater blow to the British people's morale could hardly be imagined. Churchill, as a propagandist of genius, knew this better than anyone, and in his own words, he was casting about for some means to 'lessen the shock of the impending French surrender'[2] De Gaulle, who had made his way to Britain on 17 June, was clearly a trump card in this respect – a unique way of denying the apparently inescapable realities of the moment. Had France capitulated? Not at all: in the person of General de Gaulle, 'a fine fighting soldier with a good reputation and a strong personality'.[3] France remained allied with Britain against the common enemy.

It did require some stretch of the imagination to view the solitary French general and his handful of followers as an embodiment of France, but no one has accused Churchill of lacking imagination. After having ascertained in the latter part of June that no prominent French politicians were prepared to take on the burden, Churchill, overcoming the objections of the British military, the Foreign Office and most of his Cabinet colleagues, officially recognised de Gaulle as 'leader of all Free Frenchmen, wherever they may be, who rally to him in support of the allied cause'.[4] On this initial – and highly personal – recognition were to be based all the subsequent agreements between Free France and the United Kingdom. To which one must add that if de Gaulle was able to make himself known, recruit a few men and collect some equipment in the summer of 1940, this was almost entirely due to Churchill's merciless prodding of his highly reluctant ministers, diplomats, generals and admirals.[5]

The third reason was a purely strategic one: by the end of June 1940, the British Army had been compelled to abandon the whole European continent from Narvik to Dunkirk, and even though Churchill hated to admit it, there was simply no reasonable prospect of regaining a foothold there in the foreseeable future. This being so, Africa remained as the only promising theatre of operations, which could in due time serve as a springboard for the reconquest of Europe. Most important in this respect were North and West Africa, which were French possessions. No doubt de Gaulle, with his prestige, eloquence and forceful personality – not to mention British backing – would be able and willing to rally his compatriots there to the Allied side.

This was to prove entirely correct in Equatorial Africa (Chad, Cameroons and the Congo rallied at the end of August) and there was every prospect that it would prove true at Dakar as well. In fact, joint planning for the expedition against the latter port (first code-named SCIPIO, then MENACE) involved a degree of Anglo-French co-operation that was a model of its kind. Relations between de Gaulle and Churchill at the time were extremely cordial, with the Free French leader being received regularly at Chequers on week-ends. Granted, de Gaulle could never entirely hide his suspicions of the British, and Churchill was somewhat taken aback when, even in the relaxed setting of Chequers, his guest insisted on behaving as if he brought France with him and proved himself no easier to deal with than at Downing Street. But de Gaulle expressed a connoisseur's admiration for the Prime Minister's unflinching resolve and remarkable grasp of history, and that admiration was fully reciprocated, especially after de Gaulle's statesmanlike reaction to the tragic episode of Mers El Kebir, where British ships fired on the French fleet, [6] and his willingness to pursue the Dakar expedition even against formidable odds.

The two great men, however, were motivated less by mutual understanding and admiration than by an obvious community of interest at that juncture of the war. Hence our second question: given the community of interest – not to mention the mutual understanding and admiration – why did grave difficulties develop in the wartime relations between Churchill and de Gaulle, which at times brought them perilously close to total rupture? There is more than one answer to this question.

The failure of the Dakar expedition – for which, as Churchill well knew, de Gaulle bore no responsibility and for which the Royal Navy's inability to prevent the passage of a Vichy naval force through the Straits of Gibraltar was to blame – had the unfortunate effect of convincing everyone in London, including the Prime Minister, that the presence of Free French troops in any future expeditions against Vichy-held territories would provoke resolute opposition among the Vichy defenders, just as had happened at Dakar. Hence efforts on the part of the British military in May 1941, to exclude the Free French as much as possible from military operations in Syria – and even more from the ensuing armistice negotiations with the local Vichy commander. Hence also the total exclusion of Free French forces from the Madagascar operation a year later,[7] and of course, from the Anglo-American landing in North Africa in November 1942. The fact that all these operations encountered ferocious Vichy resistance should have shown the British that they were hopelessly deluded in this respect, but the myth endured, and their exclusion from operations in French territories had disastrous effects on British relations with the Free French, and with one French general in particular.

Even after Free French administrations were installed in French territories like Syria, Lebanon or North Africa, relations with the British authorities and armed forces were less than cordial. This was not only because local would-be Lawrences harboured secret designs of supplanting the French, or even because the British military on the spot never quite understood de Gaulle's political importance for the Allied cause; it was above all because, as Eden wrote to Duff Cooper about the French, 'there were limits to the extent to which we were prepared to incur mistrust and hostility or, still more, endanger our position in the Middle East on their behalf'.[8] In other words, it could well be necessary to thwart the French in order to propitiate the natives. That de Gaulle viewed such behaviour with distaste is a gross understatement.

Whatever the superficial appearances, Churchill was not entirely taken in by the fiction that he had so decisively helped to create. For all his personal valour, de Gaulle could not claim to represent all of France in 1940 – or even later – which is why Churchill was always trying to open new channels of communication to Vichy through intermediaries like Rougier or Dupuy, or to approach such men as Generals Georges, Weygand or Noguès in order to persuade them to 'raise the standard of revolt' and join the Allies. De Gaulle, who deemed these efforts hopeless, saw in them an obvious danger to his movement, as evidenced by the following telegram he sent to Churchill on 2 November 1940:

> General de Gaulle and the French Empire Defence Council believe it their duty to point out to the British Government that their policy and attitude towards Vichy, being inspired by specifically French considerations, differ quite appreciably from the present policy and attitude of the British government.[9]

It goes without saying that later contacts between the British and men tainted by Vichy collaboration such as Darlan, Giraud, Peyrouton or Flandin did nothing at all to allay the General's suspicions of Churchill's motives.

The fact that Churchill's attitude towards de Gaulle considerably stiffened after December 1941 is not a coincidence. After Pearl Harbor, Churchill, who valued relations with the United States above all else, was soon influenced by Roosevelt's acute Gaullophobia. On Christmas Eve 1941, a small Free French flotilla seized control of the islands of St Pierre and Miquelon from the Vichy authorities. These islands, off Newfoundland, at the entrance to the St Lawrence river, close to where Churchill and Roosevelt had met earlier that year and signed the Atlantic Charter, were not far from American home waters. De Gaulle went ahead in spite of a categorical American prohibition. Roosevelt wished to maintain good relations with Vichy. He was annoyed by de Gaulle's presumption and Hull, the Secretary of State, referred contemptuously to the 'so-called Free French'. After this affair until the Normandy landings in 1944, Churchill's outbursts against de Gaulle were overwhelmingly a reflection of Roosevelt's distaste for the Free French leader. At times, the Prime Minister borrowed from Roosevelt's vocabulary to denounce de Gaulle, and telegrams such as the following, sent from Washington by Churchill, leave little doubt as to the Prime Minister's source of inspiration:

> I must now warn you solemnly of a very stern situation developing here about de Gaulle. Hardly a day passes that the President does not mention it to me . . . When we consider the absolutely vital interest which we have in preserving good relations with the United States, it seems to me questionable that we should allow this marplot [FDR's word] and mischief-maker to continue the harm he is doing . . . I ask my colleagues to consider urgently whether we should not now eliminate de Gaulle as a political force and face Parliament and France upon the issues.[10]

That there was no break with de Gaulle after this is something of a miracle.

De Gaulle's intransigence naturally also played a part in worsening the disagreements. His habit of publicly denouncing British or American encroachments – preferably from abroad – was indeed effective in curbing some of the worst anti-French excesses, but it also drove the British government – and especially its leader – into fits of rage, with dire consequences for Anglo-French relations. It is a fact that many of de Gaulle's driving motivations either escaped Churchill or remained inexplicable to him: de Gaulle's obsession with maintaining the integrity of the French Empire throughout the war, in order to deliver it intact to a liberated France after the war; the Free French leader's adamant refusal to make any political concessions to the British, even though he was entirely dependent on them for the survival of his movement ('I am too weak to make concessions' is probably the Gaullian statement that caused Churchill the greatest perplexity); de Gaulle's eternal suspicion of British motives, which Churchill considered to be almost pathological; de Gaulle's fixation on France and the future struggle for power there, that appeared to make him oblivious of Churchill's heavy burden in trying to lead a coalition conducting crucial military operations on four continents and two oceans. (To which de Gaulle could of course point out that he was himself single-handedly leading a struggle against Vichy, foiling the plots of anti-Gaullist immigrants in the UK and the US, outsmarting Communist elements in the French resistance, thwarting Roosevelt's attempts to unseat him and conducting a war against the Axis in France, Italy, Africa, the Middle East and Indochina.)

Churchill's efforts to control the Free French authorities, meddle in the numerous plots within the movement, modify its composition or otherwise 'put the General in commission' were of course a permanent bone of contention. From Churchill's suggestion to Catroux in September 1940 that he 'ought to assume the leadership of the Free French movement'[11] to his 'secret' backing of Muselier, Darlan, Giraud, Georges, Noguès, Peyrouton, Flandin *et al*, the Free French in London were under the impression (perfectly justified) that the Prime Minister was out to 'divide and rule'. Indeed, Churchill's lifelong love of France made it almost impossible for him to tolerate a French movement on British soil that did not in one way or another respond to his conception of how France should be liberated and administered. It is a fact that Churchill and de Gaulle were united by their love of France; yet it was probably not the same love, and certainly not the same France. For Churchill, France was the refined, cultured, patrician and hopelessly romantic country he had known in the 1920s and 1930s, with excellent food and wine, witty and harmless politicians and the charming, and mostly British and American-owned villas he had grown used to during his frequent cross-Channel journeys. Proletarian France was something unknown to him, and the radical resistance movement that emerged in France during the war seems to have struck him as a strange and disquieting phenomenon – as did de Gaulle himself, who was as different as could be from the nice, old, easy-going French generals of First World War vintage who were his lifelong friends. '*Je cherche la France que j'aime*', he had confided to General Georges, '*et je ne la trouve pas dans le Général de Gaulle!*' He was to find it nowhere else either: the sweet, romantic France he loved had been swept away by the great storm of war. To General de Gaulle, on the other hand, France was something of a mystical abstraction: an eternal, merciful, but formidable, all-powerful mother whose historical mission was to illuminate the world, and for whom enslavement or even mediocrity were monstrous and unbearable anomalies. The sacred mission of her sons – all her sons – was to help her recover her past splendour, '*la Grandeur*', and though foreigners could help in an auxiliary role, there was no question of their taking control of the undertaking; hence de Gaulle's indignation at Churchill's perpetual meddling in French affairs, and his violent outbursts that eventually induced the Prime Minister to meddle somewhat more cautiously.

Given all these disagreements, it is astonishing that the de Gaulle–Churchill partnership was able to endure until the end of the war without a decisive split. The partnership probably would have collapsed but for some outside influences. The most important were a few British personalities who exercised an influence over Winston Churchill: Major Morton, Harold Macmillan, Duff Cooper and above all, Anthony Eden. The Foreign Secretary was instrumental in preventing at least five major ruptures between the two temperamental leaders, by convincing Churchill that there was no real alternative to de Gaulle, that breaking with him was a political impossibility, and that blindly following Roosevelt's entreaties would backfire badly and weaken the Prime Minister's own position in Britain. As a typical example, the following War Cabinet telegram, clearly inspired by Anthony Eden, was sent to Churchill as a reply to the Churchill telegram from Washington proposing a break with de Gaulle, quoted earlier:

> Apart from the political objections to the course which the President advocates, a precipitate break with de Gaulle would have far-reaching consequences in a number of spheres which the Americans have probably never thought about. We are sorry not to be more helpful, but we are convinced that the Americans are wrong in this and advocate a line which would not be understood here, with possible evil consequences to Anglo-American relations.[12]

King George VI helped, as evidenced for instance by the following extract from the King's diary for 9 February 1943:

> Prime Minister to lunch. He is furious with de Gaulle over his refusal to accept FDR's invitation to meet with him and Giraud . . . I warned Winston not to be too hasty with de Gaulle and the Free French National Committee . . . I told Winston I could well understand de Gaulle's attitude, and that of our own people here, who do not like the idea of making friends of those Frenchmen who have collaborated with the Germans.[13]

So, too, did several of de Gaulle's commissioners, ministers and diplomats, above all Dejean, Viénot, Catroux and, later on, Massigli and Bidault.

These men did their best to allay some of de Gaulle's worst suspicions of the British, and dissuade him from some of his anti-British initiatives.

Increasingly, the British Parliament supported de Gaulle, though only a few MPs at first, eventually it provided massive support for the Free French cause after the Darlan affair of November 1942. When the American and British invaded French North Africa in November 1942, French forces resisted. The allies needed speedy success and the easiest way of ending opposition and gaining immediate help from French soldiers and officials for the allied command turned out to be to make a bargain with Admiral Darlan. He had been prominently associated with Marshal Pétain in the French government at Vichy dedicated to collaboration in Hitler's 'New Order', and was Pétain's designated successor. The 'Darlan deal' suggested an allied preference for turncoat collaborators over de Gaulle's resistance fighters. Until his assasination on Christmas Eve, Darlan became the effective ruler of Morocco and Algeria. Generous support by the British press and public opinion also dates from that period, all this giving Anthony Eden an excellent argument against breaking with de Gaulle by pointing to the likely political consequences at home. The London-based governments-in-exile, discreetly at first, but far more vocally after the announcement of the 'temporary expedient' of Admiral Darlan in Algiers, supported General de Gaulle. These governments clearly feared that after the liberation of their own countries, the Anglo-Americans would likewise co-operate with local collaborators like Degrelle, Mussert, Nedić and other quislings.[14]

Most important was the support for de Gaulle of the whole French CNR (*Conseil National de la Résistance*), in whose name Jean Moulin addressed a message to de Gaulle in mid-May 1943, at the height of the de Gaulle—Giraud confrontation, demanding 'the immediate installation of a provisional government in Algiers under the presidency of General de Gaulle', and insisting that the latter 'remain the sole leader of French resistance whatever the outcome of negotiations'.[15] After that, it was all but impossible to break with de Gaulle without breaking with France as well – an impossibility for Churchill.

Apart from these influences, there remained something else, that owed nothing to outside pressures: Churchill's grudging admiration for the man. Indeed, that admiration does not seem to have faded appreciably after the summer of 1940; by October of that year, Sir Alexander Cadogan, Permanent Under-Secretary at the Foreign office, reading the Declaration of Brazzaville, had concluded that de Gaulle was 'a loser'. But Churchill clearly disagreed, as evidenced by his minute to Eden: 'A very remarkable document. It shows de Gaulle in a light very different from that of an ordinary military man'.[16] Through the worst confrontations, that view appears to have endured – even at Anfa in January 1943, when after a very rough interview, Churchill said to Lord Moran: 'His country has given up fighting, he himself is a refugee, and if we turn him down he is finished. Well, just look at him! He might be Stalin, with two hundred divisions behind his words.'[17] And of course, we have this unique Churchillian comment to Harold Nicolson: 'De Gaulle, a great man? Why, he's selfish, he's arrogant, he thinks he's the centre of the universe . . . He . . . You're right, he's a great man!'[18] Yet one must also remember the words of Churchill's old friend and war-time assistant, Major Morton: 'Churchill disliked any person whose character was such that he could not avoid feeling respect for that person'. Not that this was in any way unique; Charles de Gaulle himself is known to have said: 'I only respect people who stand up to me. The trouble is, I can't stand them!' After that, one may perhaps be pardoned for thinking that the two great men thoroughly deserved one another.

An interesting question is whether things could have been different. Would relations between Churchill and de Gaulle have been more harmonious, would the General have obtained allies during the war if he had himself made more concessions, and if he had cultivated closer relations with Churchill, Eden and other members of the War Cabinet? On both sides of the Channel, several witnesses of these wartime encounters think so, and this author believes that a more friendly approach to the long-suffering Anthony Eden could have helped. But the benefit of hindsight must not make historians forget that the Gaullian policy of coldness, aloofness, intransigence, arrogance, vindictiveness and outright rudeness (this is not an exhaustive list) was quite simply a means to an end, a well-calculated weapon to make up for the inferiority of the exiled leader who was politically, militarily, financially and even personally at the mercy of his far more powerful host and ally, and whose essential preoccupation was to prevent the latter from exploiting his dominant position. As a result, we can only answer the question by looking at the alternatives – by considering what happened to other governments in exile who decided to co-operate far more closely with Churchill and his Cabinet colleagues.

The case of Norway naturally comes to mind. Starting from a much stronger position than the handful of Free French (a constitutional government in exile, complete with Prime Minister, King and Crown Prince, and a huge, modern merchant fleet of 1,000 ships that was absolutely vital to the Allied war effort), the Norwegians undertook to follow a resolutely pro-British policy, based on the privileged relations between their Foreign Minister Trygve Lie and Anthony Eden. The two men decided from the outset to meet at least every fortnight to discuss all matters of common interest. There were indeed regular consultations until the end of the war, the Norwegians proved faithful and trustworthy allies, there were no confrontations, no scenes, no blackmail, and in all matters involving foreign policy, strategy, finance, and of course the disposition of the Norwegian fleet, Mr Nygaardsvold's government dutifully followed the British lead.

The results proved less than satisfactory. From the simple request of a regular air liaison between Stockholm and the UK to the Norwegian wish to appoint Prince Olav Commander-in-chief of allied forces in the event of an invasion of Norway, most Norwegian requests were met with procrastination, evasions or blank refusals. Negotiations on an agreement concerning the civil administration in liberated Norwegian territories dragged on for almost two years, and detailed Norwegian proposals for landings in Norway were simply ignored.[19] Worst of all, from the autumn of 1941 to the spring of 1944, Churchill had his Chiefs of Staff prepare half a dozen strategic plans for a large-scale invasion of Norway, and he did his utmost to have them implemented – without the Norwegians ever being told a word about them.[20] And by the spring of 1944, when Churchill had finally lost his (almost obsessive) interest in an invasion of Norway, the joint planners considered that, were the Soviets to enter Norway from the north, the British ought not to intervene, in order to remove all risk of an Anglo-Soviet confrontation.[21] Only Stalin's lack of interest in Norway at the time – he had much to do elsewhere – would appear to have saved Norway from an extensive Soviet occupation. Finally, British sabotage and intelligence activities in Norway took precious little account of Norwegian interests and suggestions – at least until they were compelled to do so by the sheer pressure of events inside Norway. To which must be added that if there was no meddling at all by British authorities in the Norwegian government set up during the war, this was only because King Haakon would have viewed such interference with the greatest disfavour – and, as the Foreign Office well knew, the old Norwegian monarch would have promptly brought the matter to the attention of his nephew, King George VI.

The Yugoslav government in exile was even less fortunate. Few governments can have been more faithful and forthcoming in their relations with the British than that of young King Peter, his Prime Minister Purić and his embattled Minister of War, Draža Mihailović. Yet as a result of a truly amazing combination of naïvety, wishful thinking, ignorance as to the real situation in Yugoslavia, an overwhelming preponderance of Communist elements within the SOE's Cairo headquarters dealing with Yugoslavia, very clever handling of British emissaries by Titoist partisans on the spot,[22] Eden's anxiety to propitiate the Soviets[23] and the comforting thought that he would not have to live in Yugoslavia after the war, Churchill eventually became convinced that the only man worthy of being backed in Yugoslavia was Tito, while all the others, including Mihailović and the whole of King Peter's government, ought to be dumped unceremoniously. All this, of course, in the superior interest of the Allied war effort. This explains the following note by Churchill to Eden on 1 April 1944:

> My idea throughout has been that the King should dissociate himself from Mihailović, that he should accept the resignation of the Puric government, or dismiss them, and that it would not do any great harm if he remained without a government for a few weeks. I hope therefore you will act most promptly now, draft the King a good declaration, make him dismiss Puric and Co., repudiate all contact with Mihailović, and make him form a stop-gap government not obnoxious to Tito.[24]

Clearly lacking the royal connections of King Haakon of Norway, as well as the forceful independence of mind and the bad temper of Charles de Gaulle of France, King Peter reluctantly complied: a new government was formed under the Ban of Croatia, Ivan Subacic, who, under British auspices, proceeded to negotiate with – and submit to – Marshal Tito; Mihailović and his gallant fighters were abandoned by the Anglo-Americans, and most of them died a cruel death at the hands of Tito's men; Tito received massive Allied assistance, personally assured Churchill in the summer of 1944 that he had no intention of introducing the Communist system in Yugoslavia,[25] and, after briefly submitting to the comedy of a coalition government whose ministers never met, promptly proceeded to establish a Communist dictatorship in Yugoslavia.

General de Gaulle – who had publicly awarded the *Croix de Guerre* to General Mihailović at the exact moment when the British were letting him down,[26] would probably have answered our last question with another one: rather than de Gaulle being more forthcoming in his wartime relations with Churchill, what would have happened if the Norwegians, the Yugoslavs and all the other exiled governments had been more intransigent? Fortunately for both Churchill and Eden, that question at least remains purely academic.

10

Churchill, Roosevelt and Post-war Europe

WARREN KIMBALL

> *He lamented that . . . he could not tell the story of how the United States gave away, to please Russia, vast tracts of Europe . . . If FDR had lived, and had been in good health, he would have seen the red light in time to check American policy.*
>
> (Churchill in conversation with John Colville)[1]

Some writers have recently asserted that Churchill, like Roosevelt, was an ineffective, befuddled politician; that they were successful neither as realists nor as idealists. They are castigated for failing to make practical decisions based on power politics and, by the same historians, for failing to stand on principle. These authors concentrate on the failures of peacemaking, and often forget that the Second World War created new relationships and dynamics. They demand that Britain and the United States should have defeated Hitler's Germany without letting the Soviet Union become a major power in Europe – thus making an omelette without breaking eggs. For conservative-idealist writers, Roosevelt was initially the great betrayer. The Yalta collection of documents in the *Foreign Relations of the United States*[2] series was released unusually early in 1955, a mere 10 years after the events, because Republican politicians hoped to stain their Democratic opponents with the Yalta tar-brush. Then Chester Wilmot, using arguments from American critics of Roosevelt and from the early volumes in Churchill's wartime memoirs, popularised the view that, because of Roosevelt, the Western allies missed opportunities to restrain Soviet expansion.[3] That theme of Roosevelt's 'sell-out' of Eastern Europe has had a long life.[4] In the last two volumes of Churchill's memoirs, Roosevelt's image became increasingly ambiguous as Churchill struggled to explain how he could argue so strongly for an Anglo-American entente, and still escape blame for the failure to prevent the Soviet take-over of Eastern Europe. By the early 1950s, Churchill depicted himself as the prescient statesman who had fought against Soviet expansion whenever he could, but to no avail. British influence, weakened by two world wars, was not enough to stop Roosevelt from, Churchill explained, giving 'away, to please Russia, vast tracts of Europe'.[5]

Perlmutter's recent *FDR and Stalin* is one of the latest books to bemoan yet again the alleged betrayal of Eastern Europe. Perlmutter begins by dismissing the validity of archival research (no one, he claims, can actually have read all those documents historians cite), then, with self-serving ease, claims to have uncovered 'new' Soviet documents that prove his case. That those Soviet documents are unimportant (one, for instance, shows that the USSR assessed Wendell Willkie as an internationalist!) and that they are cited only over the course of seven unsensational pages does not prevent the author from claiming they justified what he calls a fundamental rethinking of the history of the Second World War.

Nothing Roosevelt did escapes condemnation. He could and should have made deals with Stalin in the more favourable bargaining atmosphere that existed before the tide of war turned on the Russian front; an argument that ignores the reality that the only 'deal' the Soviets would consider was either an immediate Second Front or recognition of their Nazi–Soviet Pact frontiers. Moreover, any such arrangements would have relied on Stalin's good faith, the very thing Roosevelt is chastised for doing later in the war. Churchill is the 'realist' foil for a naive FDR. The Prime Minister accepted the Curzon Line for the Soviet–Polish boundary as a matter of *realpolitik*. But Roosevelt adopted a 'utopian vision' that brought in the United Nations to handle such frontier issues. In fact Roosevelt endorsed the Curzon Line during talks with Stalin at Teheran, and instructed his diplomats to insist that the London Poles accept that frontier; but evidence does not affect Perlmutter.[6] The Yalta agreements were, according to this interpretation, 'Old World *realpolitik*, as practised by Churchill and Stalin, winning over a sick and weakened Roosevelt who was preoccupied with pursuing the vestiges of Wilsonian idealism'. We are presented then, with what historian Mark Stoler calls a 'hard core' critique of Roosevelt, and an extraordinarily simplistic view of international relations during the Second World War.[7]

Books about Churchill continue to pour out and Churchill's associates have put out a steady stream of memoirs and diaries, almost all following the line of Churchill's memoirs.[8] The Churchill legend has come in for increasing scrutiny since 1972 when the British and American governments opened the bulk of their Second World War records. Churchill's Anglocentric perspective needed correcting. Three of the six volumes in his war memoirs dealt disproportionately with the pre-Pearl Harbor period. The Russian front and the war in the Pacific play secondary roles. His tendency to place himself at the centre of events needed revision. As Churchill later noted to President Eisenhower, the Prime Minister's war memoirs were written to promote good Anglo-American relations, so the tensions of the Second World War almost disappeared from his reconstruction of events. Wartime strategic arguments over Greece, Burma, Norway and the Second Front are all downplayed. Only Churchill's opposition to the invasion of southern France has a hint of anger in his memoirs. Disagreements over post-war policy – such things as decolonisation of the Empire, free (or at least 'freer' trade), post-war civil aviation, and the dominance of the dollar – make only cameo appearances.[9]

Increasing scepticism about the 'Good War' image of the Second World War is a reaction to ahistorical Churchill-worship. Confusing Churchill's image and words with the actions he took can result in sweeping statements that do not fit the evidence. To offer but one example, the author of a recent study, *Winston Churchill: Architect of Peace*, admiringly concluded that:

> Throughout the war, Churchill demonstrated his attachment to the principles of liberty, political sovereignty, honour, and safety . . . The sovereignty of Poland and the eventual lifting of the oppression from the remaining occupied countries of Eastern and Central Europe were first upon his mind.[10]

The 'oppression' referred to is, quite clearly from the context, a reference to Soviet domination, not to the problem that remained at hand – the defeat of Germany.

Even a cursory glance at the British minutes of the TOLSTOY talks between Churchill and Stalin in October 1944 illustrates that the Prime Minister's attachment to such 'principles' was subordinated to the requirements of power politics and British interests.[11] In return for meaningless percentages of influence in Bulgaria and Romania, Churchill received guarantees of British predominance in Greece and the eastern Mediterranean. Precisely what was decided regarding Poland is uncertain, but the thrust of the agreements was to recognise the Soviet Union's predominant interests in that nation.

Churchill's compromises at those discussions have often been explained as 'a mixture of preference and pragmatism'. Confronted by the growing reality of Soviet influence in Eastern Europe, David Reynolds suggests 'the British tried to ameliorate it as best they could'.[12] But that may well confuse Churchill's appearances with his motives. Amelioration of Soviet power was not what he tried to achieve. He sought rather to limit that power by establishing a new *cordon sanitaire* (in a somewhat less obvious form) along with the protection and even expansion of British interests in the eastern Mediterranean, especially in Greece.

The most frequently cited examples of Churchill's prescience about the Soviet threat – his proposals for military action in south-east Europe – were not seriously aimed at stopping the Red Army, but at the control of Greece and the propping up of British interests.[13] He expressed concern about 'the rapid encroachment of the Russians into the Balkans', called for more resources to be sent to Italy, a British-commanded theatre by 1944, and for an attack on the German 'armpit' (towards Vienna from the Adriatic). But the night before making that last suggestion, Churchill had learned that the Russians had advanced more quickly into Bulgaria than expected. The reaction of both the Prime Minister and Foreign Secretary Eden was not concern for Bulgaria, but for British interests, with Eden proposing the immediate launching of operation MANNA – a landing in Greece. Churchill's desire to move into the Balkans should, perhaps, be seen in the light of his comment to General Ismay about the war in the Pacific: 'Rangoon and Singapore are great names in the British eastern world, and it will be an ill day for Britain if the war ends without our having made a stroke to regain these places . . .'[14] What mattered was not liberation, but who did the liberating. Moreover, one wonders what the Russians might have done if Churchill's Mediterranean strategy had been accepted – perhaps they would have 'liberated' Denmark, the Netherlands, and Belgium! Would a swap of Antwerp for Prague have improved Anglo-American security?[15]

Whatever those arguments, the debate is made more complex by the appearance of studies of a Churchill-without-context. A new generation of historians, raised in the cynical atmosphere of the late Cold War era, has begun to extend the long standing condemnations of Roosevelt's wisdom and even intentions regarding the settlement in Eastern Europe to include Churchill. Their fundamental argument is deceptively simple: if the Second World War was the 'Good War', why did Eastern and Central Europe end up under the ruthless hegemony of the Soviet Union? The ever-popular habit of placing all the blame on Stalin – whether as madman, as implacable ideologue, or as relentless expansionist – is too mechanistic to provide a satisfying answer.[16] Better a scrupulous search for the explanation of how the betrayal of Eastern Europe could have been prevented, rather than why it happened. Instead of absolving Churchill of the 'Yalta sin', some historians now bitterly denounce the Prime Minister as part and parcel of an unsavoury spheres-of-influence settlement that condemned half of Europe to the tender mercies of the Kremlin's rule.[17]

In such studies the plight of Eastern Europe resulted from an unholy collaboration of Roosevelt and Churchill, willing to consign Eastern Europe to slavery in order to enhance their own national interests. The argument is simple: Eastern Europe was 'lost' because the Anglo-Americans never really addressed the issue of preventing it from happening. In other cases, particularly in John Charmley's *Churchill: The End of Glory*, it is a foolish and weak Prime Minister whose over-commitment to an Anglo-American alliance in the post-war world made him blind to opportunities to confront the Russians and, at the same time, promoted the loss of the British Empire. It is difficult to understand how Roosevelt can play both the roles set for him in the pages of Charmley's recent book: an exploitative imperialist, and, at the same time, naive fool. But it does not matter, for Roosevelt is not the focus, or the villain, of the piece. Charmley's Churchill is a conscious collaborator (appeaser is the loaded word Charmley prefers), not the well-intentioned and far-sighted leader of a weakened Britain, as Sir Winston himself would have had us believe.[18]

This is a variation on what Arthur Schlesinger has called 'the perfectionist clamour'. That was a dismissal of those partisan politicians who condemned the Yalta agreements for failing to live up to the Atlantic Charter principles. Seeking a small, Cold War public-relations victory for Roosevelt, Schlesinger labelled the 1945 Declaration on Liberated Europe, with its reaffirmation of 'faith in the principles of the Atlantic Charter' and promises of free elections, a blunder on the part of Soviet diplomacy because it laid down standards that Stalin obviously failed to keep.[19] But the new 'perfectionists' instead present the Declaration as a standard that the Anglo-Americans did not meet. These scrupulous idealists, viewing the past from the present, demand that leaders should have been prescient, complain that power and politics were ignored, and insist that 'Good' should have been achieved immediately.

In fact Churchill, Roosevelt and Stalin used their reading of history to construct their foreign policies. For the British Prime Minister, history taught that his nation's past was the most desirable future. No matter how he spoke of ideals and fairness, he ended up espousing the solutions that had made Britain a great and prosperous power. Balances of power upheld by coalitions (federations in the parlance of the 1940s), limited continental commitments, the maintenance of Empire – all held an irresistible attraction for Churchill. What had worked before made so much sense for the future. Charmley is, of course, right when he depicts Churchill as fascinated by the Anglo-American connection. But that connection was not to be on American terms. Throughout the war the Prime Minister sought to define the relationship with the Americans in ways that fitted Britain's traditions: a Mediterranean and peripheral military strategy, creation of European federations, a European Council seated in London, restoration of colonial empire, a strong France (albeit, if possible, not led by de Gaulle), a spheres-of-influence/*cordon sanitaire* settlement in Eastern Europe. Churchill tried to persuade Roosevelt to join in these and other approaches, sometimes with success, sometimes not – but he always tried.

For Stalin, history suggested a different lesson. The *status quo* powers, be they France, Great Britain or the United States, feared and distrusted a movement that called for change in their social order. Stalin seems to have entertained the thought that those fears could be calmed through the workings of some sort of international co-operation.[20] But the short history of the Soviet Union had given him and his advisers little reason to look with confidence on the promises of the capitalist nations. The wartime alliance against Hitler had proved remarkably successful. But there were still enough unsettling wartime disagreements to suggest that permanent 'contradictions' (as Soviet jargon labelled fundamental ideological differences) forced the USSR to look to its own interests. The delay in opening a Second Front, cancellation of supply convoys, American negotiations with the Germans in Berne, and the ever-present Polish 'question', all worked to confirm that reading of history. The Soviet Union had been invaded three times in only 25 years – physical security had to precede co-operation.

There is little evidence that Roosevelt consciously compared himself and his set of choices with those of Woodrow Wilson at the end of the First World War.[21] But the historical parallels are too strong and frequent to dismiss. Wilson initially offered the world (that is, Europe) a choice between the old order, which bred violent revolution and war, and a different way – a choice between what he called Reaction, and liberalism. Given the realities of life in the industrialised world, that seemed an easy choice for the great mass of people in Europe. By the end of the war, the three great symbols of the old order, the emperors of Russia, Germany and Austria-Hungary, were gone from the scene, leaving only America's erstwhile allies, Britain and France, to occupy the right.

But the Bolshevik Revolution of November 1917 presented a third and seductive option. Instead of moderate, progressive change that permitted the ruling class to retain some if not all of the fruits of its works, instead of progressive change that did not throw the baby out with the bath water, instead of reasonable reform that harnessed the benefits of modern industrialism to serve the majority (phrasing reminiscent of the 1912 US presidential campaign), why not, asked the Bolsheviks, turn society upside down? Why not have change from the bottom up? Hoping to forestall both extremes, Wilson's Fourteen Points were aimed as much at Lenin as they were at Clemenceau.[22]

It was not the last time an American president would perceive those alternatives. By late 1943, Roosevelt faced a similar trio of choices, though they appeared in somewhat camouflaged form. Hitler was *sui generis*, neither Reaction nor Revolution – or perhaps a mix of both. Anyway, he seemed destined to disappear. For the post-war world, Reaction took the form of Britain, its Empire and the remains of European colonialism. Eden's private secretary, Oliver Harvey, caught the image:

With Roosevelt straining to put the British Empire into liquidation and Winston pulling in the opposite direction to put it back to pre-Boer War, we are in danger of losing both the Old and the New World.[23]

Liberalism – the middle way, the golden mean – remained seated (at least in FDR's mind) in the United States.[24] Like Wilson, Roosevelt viewed war as an opportunity for change; like Wilson, Roosevelt believed great power harmony essential to avoiding war; unlike Wilson, Roosevelt chose to treat the Soviet Union as a major power. The trio of choices seemed clear to US State Department officials in 1945. A briefing paper prepared for FDR before the Yalta Conference discussed the problems of reconstructing politics in Europe, in the process laying out the dilemma of finding a middle ground between Reaction and Revolution:

These governments must be sufficiently to the left to satisfy the prevailing mood in Europe and to allay Soviet suspicions. Conversely, they should be sufficiently representative of the centre and *petit bourgeois* elements of the population so that they would not be regarded as mere preludes to a Communist dictatorship.[25]

As for revolution, it still resided in Moscow, even if the Soviet regime was deeply soiled by brutality. The presence of revolution became increasingly important and evident during the war as the Soviet Union first survived and then turned back the German onslaught. The threat of revolution was, for Churchill and Roosevelt, more than just the likelihood that the Soviet Union would impose its system on occupied and/or liberated societies in the wake of the Red Army. (Churchill, Roosevelt and Stalin all, at one time or another, indicated that they expected each other to take advantage of such situations.)[26]

For the Anglo-Americans, the problem was that revolution could also spread by the very political means they professed to support – free elections. A recurring fear among British and American policy-makers was that the initial round of elections in liberated and occupied nations after the war would bring to power the 'Communists' (which included, for most Americans, the 'Socialists'). As the American High Commissioner in Germany, General Lucius Clay, put it in March 1946: '. . . there is no choice between becoming a Communist on 1500 calories and a believer in democracy on 1000 calories'.[27] Churchill and, occasionally, Roosevelt expressed concern that those on the left might use wartime nationalism to political advantage. Tito seemed to be doing that in Yugoslavia, the Communist ELAS/EAM in Greece had offered the most effective resistance to Hitler's occupying forces, and the Socialists and Communists in France and Italy both managed to associate anti-Fascism with themselves. Hitler had not only upset the balance of politics in Europe; he had unleashed a virulent nationalism. When Churchill proposed federations in Eastern Europe, Stalin and Soviet Foreign Minister V M Molotov warned that:

> . . . the immediate point was that after this war all states would be very nationalistic . . . The feeling to live independently would be the strongest. Later, economic feelings would prevail, but in the first period they would be purely nationalistic and therefore groupings would be unwelcome. The fact that Hitler's regime had developed nationalism could be seen in the example of Yugoslavia where Croats, Montenegrins, Slovenes, etc. all wanted something of their own. It was a symptom.[28]

The Soviet leaders may have been primarily concerned with expunging any thoughts of establishing another *cordon sanitaire*, but lurking in the background is the ghostly image of Tsar Alexander and his fellow monarchs bemoaning the virulent epidemic set loose by Napoleon.

The tenets of liberalism ensured that at least the appearance of free choice among the three options presented itself in the states liberated and occupied by the Anglo-Americans, although a good deal of effort went into preventing those peoples from choosing either Communism or Socialism. But throughout most of Soviet-liberated Eastern Europe, only one choice was available, with only desultory protests from either London or Washington. Churchill and Roosevelt clearly expected little else.

But Poland was different. As the end of war in Europe drew near, Poland became the test for those who would become the cold warriors on both sides of the Iron Curtain. It became Stalin's gauge for Western intentions. It became the touchstone in the West of the Soviet Union's willingness to co-operate in the post-war world. It was too high a hurdle for those who still sought a continuation of the wartime co-operation between the great powers. The Polish question illuminates the outlines of the post-war structure that Roosevelt had in mind, one that Churchill supported and then helped undermine. Poland, like the future of European empires, the creation of a post-war international organisation, future economic institutions and practices was subordinated by Roosevelt to his broader goal of creating a long-term, co-operative relationship between the great powers; a fellowship characterised by a general atmosphere of trust along with careful concern for the interests of each. That overarching goal animated Roosevelt's policies from the beginning of the war. Just as Wilson at Paris compromised to save the League of Nations, the keystone in his plan, so Roosevelt time and again chose political and military strategies that would foster his concept of great power collaboration.[29] Poland is the place where that scheme unravelled, even if FDR refused to abandon his idea. How did the Polish issue become one of absolute and immovable principle? Why not the Baltic states, Romania, Bulgaria or even Ukraine? A cultural affinity between the Anglo-Americans and Western-oriented Poland may have played a role, although if that was the case why did the same dynamic not operate in Czechoslovakia? Poland was not geopolitically or economically crucial to either Great Britain or the United States, nor was it as important in American domestic politics as FDR and others claimed. In fact, Roosevelt grossly exaggerated 'the Polish vote' in his statements to Stalin. The claim of six to seven million Polish-Americans – 'a genial Rooseveltian exaggeration evidently plucked from the air' in Arthur Schlesinger's phrase – actually translated into less than half that number, many of whom were not voters.[30] That hyperbole was, perhaps, a bit more calculated than it appeared, for it allowed FDR to escape public responsibility for the political fact that he, Churchill and Stalin's Red Army together ensured that, in the short-run, Poland's independence would depend on Moscow's self-restraint, not Anglo-American guarantees.

Nevertheless, Harry Hopkins, Roosevelt's closest adviser, was right to label Poland 'political dynamite' for the US elections scheduled for the autumn of 1944. But that was not because of the Polish vote.[31] What Roosevelt feared was what historians claimed had doomed Woodrow Wilson's efforts at Paris, 30 years earlier. The great powers had disagreed, and compromise seemed the only way to avoid disharmony. But those compromises were too unsavoury and selfish for American tastes, and had helped convince them that the United States should take the moral high ground and go-it-alone rather than sully itself by working with the European powers in a League of Nations. Poland threatened to play the same role after the Second World War. Roosevelt had already agreed at the Teheran Conference to the Curzon Line as the Soviet–Polish boundary – a concession Poles were sure to denounce. But for the President openly to associate himself with the compromise settlement that had been emerging ever since mid-way through the war would jeopardise his goal of preventing a retreat into isolationism, without helping the Poles.[32] For the majority of Americans, however, Poland was just another East European country. Nevertheless, Poland became the measurement of success for Roosevelt's inchoate scheme of great power collaboration. As Harry Hopkins told Stalin, shortly after Roosevelt's death, Americans viewed the Polish settlement as 'a symbol of our ability to work out problems with the Soviet Union'.[33]

Defining Poland in the post-war world was no easy task. Poles themselves seemed to have a remarkably flexible definition, as illustrated by their territorial wars with the Russian Bolsheviks almost before the ink had dried on the Versailles Treaty. What Poles claimed to be Poland was as much image and dream as reality. This was, after all, a state that had, in the 1930s, embraced colonial ambitions less than a decade after it had emerged from more than a century of foreign rule.[34] Sporadically, and never in a way that would threaten British interests in places like Greece, the British Prime Minister tried to get the London Poles to accept compromises that would enable them to survive as a viable political element in a post-war Polish state. His were always the short-term solutions of geopolitical accommodation – 10 per cent here, an additional government ministry post there – but he kept trying.

However reality reared its ugly head. The trips by Eden to Moscow in 1941, and Molotov to London in 1942, almost ended with Britain committed to the Polish–Soviet boundary settlement demanded by Stalin. Churchill's warning in January 1942 that he would resign rather than lead a British government that recognised Soviet expansion proved, like all his frequent threats to resign, an empty, childish gesture.[35] Whatever his proclaimed reluctance to accept Eden's advice and let the Soviet Union keep what it had gained in the pact with Hitler, the Prime Minister readily turned to spheres of influence. Early in March 1942 he cabled President Roosevelt that the Atlantic Charter should not be interpreted 'so as to deny Russia the frontiers she occupied when Germany attacked her'.[36] But the compromise Churchill sought failed to materialise. Poles, in London and the United States, rejected any settlement that did not retain their 'historic' frontiers – even if no one knew what they were.

The compromise the British proposed aimed at securing the independence of post-war Poland, albeit at the risk of sacrificing the Baltic states.

Whatever Churchill's rhetoric, he permanently abandoned the Poles to the harsh reality of having to live with the Russian bear, and fundamentally on the bear's terms. For the rest of the war, his excursions in defence of the Poles were restricted to trying to get the exiled Polish leaders to accept the compromise offered in 1942. The steadfast rejection by the London Poles of that boundary agreement only gave further evidence to Stalin that they were his implacable opponents. It is hard to escape the conclusion that Churchill's anger at the London Poles in the aftermath of the 1944 TOLSTOY talks was conscience-salving romanticism carefully subordinated to immediate British interests. He did speak out, and speak out clearly, for something other than a Soviet-dominated puppet government in Poland, but those sentiments were never accompanied by consistent action – until March 1945, when Churchill finally took an unyielding though not public stand.[37]

Roosevelt, on the other hand, assumed that the Soviet Union would be the major player in Central and Eastern Europe after the war and avoided quixotic crusades aimed at the forlorn hope of instantaneously transforming the Bolsheviks into practitioners of liberal democracy (or free-market democracy, in today's political jargon). He paid lip-service to Polish freedom, but steadfastly refused to do anything more – no matter how Polish representatives who talked to him interpreted his remarks.[38] Stalin, for his part, kept his eye on the prize and his troops marching westward. The Soviet leader steadily rejected any separation of the issues of boundaries and governance, making the point that any settlement of the Soviet–Polish frontier would be only as good as the intentions of the Polish government in power. A 'friendly' government in Warsaw (or Lublin) was a function of the frontier issue. Moreover, what was Stalin to think of the TOLSTOY meetings, with Churchill suggesting that Central and Eastern Europe be divided up into numerically calculated spheres of influence? (And calculated they were, as the subsequent talks between Molotov and Eden demonstrate.) What else could he conclude but that Churchill and possibly Roosevelt (after all, Roosevelt's ambassador, Averell Harriman was there) had decided to drop their commitment to an interactive, co-operative post-war working relationship and opt instead for a clear, old-fashioned delineation of what belonged to whom. As historian Lloyd Gardner ruefully concludes, the percentages arrangement negotiated at TOLSTOY made the task of getting the Soviet Union 'to play a "decent role" . . . vastly more complicated'.[39]

During the Yalta talks, Churchill dismissed the Americans as 'profoundly ignorant of the Polish situation'.[40] Nothing could have been further from the truth. In reality Roosevelt and his advisers wanted to put the Polish question aside or behind them as a no-win situation that could only poison the well. Whatever happened, Poland could not be a winner. The Soviet Union would dominate any compromise; the Red Army would dominate any confrontation. Moreover, Churchill himself had been the sponsor, if not the author, of many of the concessions on Poland. When, late in the evening of the first day of the Teheran Conference, he took matchsticks and demonstrated to Stalin how the Poles and Russians could each move westward at Germany's expense by executing the parade ground manoeuvre 'left close', he had, as in 1942, accepted Stalin's solution. Details such as the fate of Lvov, or which river boundary to follow, were just that – details. A few weeks later the Prime Minister told Roosevelt that Soviet proposals for their frontier with Poland gave 'the Poles a fine place to live', with ample space and a coastline on the Baltic. Poland's responsibility to the great powers was, Churchill insisted, to accept the 'duty' of guarding 'against further German aggression upon Russia . . .'[41] Roosevelt had gone to bed before Churchill's manoeuvre with matchsticks, but there is little question that he agreed.

British domestic politics played a role in Churchill's decision in March 1945 to align his policy with his rhetoric and oppose the way the Soviet Union imposed its will on Poland. But until Churchill made that permanent shift, his conduct is best characterised by his attempt to dissuade the Poles from making a public outcry over the Katyn Forest killings. The Prime Minister soon came to suspect that the accusations against the Soviets of killing Polish officers in the USSR were correct, but argued that being right would not help Poland, while alienating the Soviet Union would harm Poland. Churchill thought the Polish reaction ill-timed and impolitic; the Poles thought a public outcry would immediately swing the British and American governments in their favour.[42] Churchill told the House of Commons that he could not 'conceive that it is not possible to make a good solution whereby Russia gets the security she is entitled to have . . . and, at the same time, the Polish nation have restored to them that national sovereignty and independence, for which . . . they have never ceased to strive'. But in practically the next breath he set the stage for the TOLSTOY talks. Sounding like FDR, the Prime Minister stated that:

> . . . the future of the whole world and certainly the future of Europe, perhaps for several generations, depends on the cordial, trustful and comprehending association of the British Empire, the United States and Soviet Russia, and no pains must be spared and no patience grudged which are necessary to bring that supreme hope to fruition.

A day later he told the President that he was planning a trip to Moscow – partly to discuss Soviet entry into the war against Japan (he left Moscow convinced that Stalin would fulfil his promise to go to war against Japan), partly 'to try to effect a friendly settlement with Poland'.[43] The percentages agreement that came from that trip, and the demands put on the Polish leader, Stanislaw Mikolajczyk, when he came to Moscow during the conference, demonstrate the gap between Churchill's rhetoric and actions.[44]

The Prime Minister warned the Poles that they would not be permitted to destroy 'agreement between the Allies'. A few months later, during the Yalta talks, Stalin reminded Churchill and Roosevelt that the USSR was *de facto* in control of Poland. Adding those two statements together suggests, very strongly, that Churchill's decision to take a hard line on Poland was for show, not a commitment to freedom.[45] That appearances might be difficult to maintain should have become clear to Churchill, and Roosevelt as well, when the Soviets refused to co-operate with the Anglo-American public relations charade of air-dropping supplies to the Polish Underground during its Warsaw uprising in September-October 1944. But the Prime Minister and the President both persisted. By the time of the Yalta meeting, they could only ask Stalin for the kind of concessions that might make the entire settlement palatable to their constituents at home: a non-Communist minister added to the provisional Polish government, a boundary adjustment that kept a few hundred square miles more as part of Poland. US Assistant Secretary of State, Archibald MacLeish – the liberals' liberal – sensed the need for good public relations in the wake of the Yalta agreements:

The wave of disillusionment which has distressed us in the last several weeks will be increased if the impression is permitted to get abroad that potentially totalitarian provisional governments are to be set up without adequate safeguards as to the holding of free elections and the realisation of the principles of the Atlantic Charter.[46]

The same pressures had developed in Britain, as Lord Beaverbrook reported to Harry Hopkins:

But over Poland the opposition is strong. It is led by a powerful Tory group who are the erstwhile champions of Munich. These followers of Chamberlain make the undercover case that Churchill beat them up in 1938 for selling the Czechs down the river, and now has done to the Poles at Yalta exactly what Chamberlain did to the Czechs at Munich.[47]

The Declaration on Liberated Europe, signed by the Big Three at Yalta, called for free elections, yet the consistent Soviet demand for a 'friendly' government in Warsaw demonstrated that none of the anti-Soviet Poles in London would be acceptable in a new Polish government, elected or not. The Declaration came together with a minimum of time and bargaining, suggesting that all three leaders understood full well what it meant. When Churchill returned to Britain after the Yalta Conference, he expressed strong faith in his work: 'Poor Neville Chamberlain believed he could trust Hitler. He was wrong. But I don't think I'm wrong about Stalin.'[48]

Perhaps Roosevelt 'felt the need for high moral purpose and a statement of American liberal political ideals'. Perhaps domestic public opinion in the United States lay behind his endorsement of the Declaration. But how could he, or Churchill, have any realistic expectation that those ideals would immediately be implemented anywhere in Europe, particularly those areas occupied by the Soviet Union? Roosevelt certainly did not believe they could work in post-war France.[49] Even Churchill pulled back from provisions in the Declaration calling for the Allies to 'establish machinery', lest that provide a lever for interference in the British Empire. He and Eden took out the teeth by changing the wording to call for the allies to 'consult together'. Roosevelt may have sincerely wanted to secure for Poland 'democratic guarantees through the promise of elections'. But, as with much of his post-war policy, liberal goals could be met only in the long term. The Declaration on Liberated Europe, and its broader forebear the Atlantic Charter, were, as Winston Churchill once remarked, 'not a law, but a star'.[50]

At times, Churchill and Roosevelt read from the same page in the book. After the Prime Minister proposed the percentages arrangement, he told Stalin that others might find the agreement 'cynical', and later drafted an (unsent) letter to Stalin warning that the terms 'would be considered crude, even callous'. But he went on to suggest that 'they might however be a good guide for the conduct of our affairs'. Moreover, Churchill observed:

> . . . viewed from afar and on a grand scale, the differences between our systems will tend to get smaller, and the great common ground which we share of making life richer and happier for the mass of the people is growing every year. Probably if there were peace for 50 years the differences which now might cause such grave troubles to the world would become matters for academic discussion.

What he and Roosevelt wanted to do, wrote Churchill, was 'to keep the world engine on the rails'.[51]

Churchill's analysis had striking parallels with the scale of social change that Roosevelt suggested that the United States and the Soviet Union would follow. American democracy and Soviet communism would move toward each other. Starting from zero and 100, the two societies would never reach the middle, he told Sumner Welles, but they might close the distance to the point of 60 for one and 40 for the other.[52]

How far apart were Roosevelt and Churchill? We can understand Wheeler-Bennett's complaint that 'Roosevelt's ambition was to establish the United Nations but to superimpose upon it an American-Soviet alliance which should dominate world affairs to the detriment of Britain and France, and to this end he made copious concessions to Marshal Stalin'.[53] He ignores the reality that FDR counted on Britain to be a major player. In fact, it was the British argument that the United Kingdom needed France in order to play the role of a major power in Europe that finally prompted Roosevelt to mitigate his anti-de Gaulle stance. Moreover, as David Dilks has put it: 'The great fear of the British was not that the Americans would dominate everything in the post-war world, but that they would go away'.[54] Rightly or wrongly, wisely or unwisely, Franklin Roosevelt had a long-term, worldwide scheme in mind. Flawed as it was, that concept can be understood only in that long-term, worldwide context. Rightly or wrongly, wisely or unwisely, Winston Churchill had his own variation on that scheme – one that played to British history, tradition and weaknesses. Whatever the chances of Roosevelt's ideas being implemented, those chances were diminished when Churchill finally concluded, a few weeks after Yalta, that the time had come to confront the Soviets over the Polish question. Great Britain did not drag the United States into the Cold War. But Churchill's March manoeuvre created an atmosphere that made it that much easier for Truman and his advisers to begin, just a few weeks after Roosevelt's death on 12 April 1945, the shift away from FDR's policies.

And all these things mattered, whatever Churchill's musing that a 50-year peace would make all their disputes subjects 'for academic discussion'. Fifty years of a dangerous armed truce followed in Europe, while tens of thousands died elsewhere in what was Cold War by proxy. Perhaps history made that conflict inevitable. But a less intense confrontation in Europe might have let the great powers live a bit more peacefully elsewhere in the world. That said, avoidance of war between the West and the Soviet Union was the prerequisite to the liberation of Eastern Europe that came after those 50 years. A Rhineland devastated in the Thirty Years War benefited no one, least of all the Rhinelanders.

11

Churchill and the Middle East, 1945–55

RITCHIE OVENDALE

At the end of the Second World War, the Middle East, to the British military mind, came second in importance only to the United Kingdom. Mons and Dunkirk were remembered. British armies should not again fight on the European continent. That was a job for Europeans. Air and naval support was possible, but that was all. Britain could not stop the advance of Soviet armies across the continent. Only the United States could do that. The security of the British Commonwealth depended on protecting the United Kingdom, maintaining vital sea communications and securing the Middle East as a defensive striking base against the Soviet Union. In September 1945 the Cabinet was informed that:

> The Middle East is a region of vital consequence for Britain and the British Empire. It forms the nodal point in the system of communications, by land, sea and air, which links Great Britain with India, Australia and the Far East; it is also the Empire's main reservoir of mineral oil. It contains the area of the Suez Canal and its terminal ports; our main naval base in the Eastern Mediterranean at Alexandria; the oilfields in Iraq and Southern Persia, the port and installations at Abadan, the pipe-line from Northern Iraq to Haifa and the port and installations at Haifa itself; and the whole line of communications by land and air running from the Mediterranean sea-board through Palestine, Transjordan and Iraq to the Persian Gulf.[1]

With the Americans moving towards joining their first peace-time 'entangling alliance' (the North Atlantic Treaty) the Chiefs of Staff disagreed as to whether British troops could be committed to the European continent again. The defence of the Middle East was critical, and Commonwealth assistance was essential. In the Chiefs of Staff papers of 1950 and 1951 the line was extended from the Middle East and the United Kingdom to part of the European continent.[2]

When the Chiefs of Staff revised Britain's global strategy in 1952 it was decided that in the Cold War Europe had to be given top priority, with the Far East next and after that the Middle East. In hot war Europe should remain a top priority, but the Middle East should be given priority over the Far East owing to the importance of communications through the Middle East, its oil and the 'necessity to prevent Communism from spreading throughout Africa'.[3] The new Conservative government reassessed British policy in the Middle East. On 4 December 1952 Anthony Eden, the Foreign Secretary, told a meeting of the Cabinet, attended by Commonwealth Prime Ministers, that the accession of Turkey to NATO had changed the whole problem. Eden hoped that Britain would conclude a treaty with Libya which would give Britain strategic facilities. It might be possible 'to devise a successful form of defence for the Middle East, based on Turkey, Cyprus and Libya'. Eden explained that it was proposed to move the British military headquarters from the Canal Zone, and that plans were being contemplated which envisaged the stationing of an armoured brigade in Libya, a brigade in Cyprus and possibly a brigade in Jordan.[4]

The problems of the Middle East changed with the development of the hydrogen bomb. Sir William Dickson, the Chief of the Air Staff, told the Cabinet on 2 June 1954:

> In view of the weight of atomic attack to which they would be subjected in the opening stages of a major war, the Russians were now less likely to be able to develop a substantial offensive through the Caucasus, and we had a better chance of holding them to the northeast of Iraq, possibly in the passes leading from Persia.[5]

The advent of thermonuclear weapons increased the vulnerability of concentrated base areas such as the Canal base. With the formation of its military alliance in the Middle East, the Baghdad Pact, British defence policy moved towards a global strategy based upon the nuclear deterrent alongside conventional forces stationed in Europe. British forces in the Middle East were reduced. This policy was outlined in the February 1955 Statement on Defence.[6]

It was Winston Churchill's peacetime administration (1951–55) which saw the passing of British paramountcy in the Middle East, an area which had been added to the British Empire between 1917 and 1921, through absence of mind, and as a result of strategic campaigns during the First World War. Afterwards, during three decades, Britain retained suzerainty over the Middle East.[7] Indeed, by January 1947 defence of the Middle East was considered as important as defence of the United Kingdom itself.[8] Churchill had distinct views on the Middle East. It was Churchill, as Colonial Secretary, who established the Middle East Department, persuaded T E Lawrence to join as an adviser on Arab affairs, effectively established Feisal as King of Iraq in August 1921, and secured the agreement of the League of Nations to the provision of a local administration for Transjordan, separating it from Palestine. When Churchill visited Palestine in 1921 he rejected demands from the Arabs for the abolition of the principle of a Jewish national home and the creation of a government elected by those resident in Palestine before the war.

As Colonial Secretary Churchill argued that the national home would be good for the Jews, the British Empire, and the Arabs who dwelt in Palestine. Planting a tree on the site of the Hebrew University on Mount Scopus, Churchill said that his heart was full of sympathy for Zionism. The 1922 White Paper on Palestine, which Churchill later referred to as *his* paper was a shrewd compromise: while suggesting continued support for Zionism it sought to reassure the Arabs and stated that Palestine would not constitute *the* national home, but merely *a* national home for the Jews with no subordination of the Arab population.[9]

Churchill frequently described himself as a Zionist. During the Second World War he fought the Foreign Office to reverse the May 1939 White Paper which effectively promised that Palestine would be controlled by the Arabs, and to secure a return to the policy of partition which would mean a separate Zionist state. Then, on 6 November 1944, Lord Moyne, the Minister Resident in the Middle East, was murdered in Cairo by the underground Zionist terrorist group, the Stern gang. Churchill told the House of Commons on 17 November that 'if our dreams for Zionism are to end in the smoke of assassins' pistols and our labours for its future to produce only a new set of gangsters worthy of Nazi Germany, many like myself will have to reconsider the position we have maintained so consistently in the past'. Plans for the future of Palestine could not be considered in such a climate: Churchill suspended British policy.[10] On 6 July 1945 Churchill suggested that the United States should be invited to take over the Palestine mandate:

I do not think we should take the responsibility upon ourselves of managing this very difficult place while the Americans sit back and criticise. . . . I am not aware of the slightest advantage which has ever accrued to Great Britain from this painful and thankless task. Somebody else should have their turn now.

Indeed Ernest Bevin, as Foreign Secretary, in December 1946, wanted to pursue Churchill's suggestion and offer the mandate of Palestine to the United States rather than surrender it to the United Nations.[11] In March 1946 Churchill told Rabbi Abba Hillel Silver of the American Zionist Emergency Council that the only solution was for the United States to join Britain in maintaining a joint trusteeship over Palestine, in which both countries would share 'common responsibility'.

Churchill, however, did agree to support the Labour government's emergency measures in Palestine in the middle of 1946. This stand was again dictated by his dislike of terrorism. He wrote to the Prime Minister, Clement Attlee, that yielding to terrorism would be a disaster. But Churchill emphasised that he still felt bound by Britain's 'national pledges' to establish a Jewish national home in Palestine with immigration up to a limit of absorptive capacity of which the mandatory power would be the judge. It should be remembered that Churchill had wryly pointed out to President Roosevelt in August 1942 that an application of the Atlantic Charter to Asia and Africa could lead to claims by the Arab majority that they could expel the Jews from Palestine, and forbid further Jewish immigration.[12]

Following the blowing up of the King David Hotel on 22 July 1946, and Truman's prevarications over the provincial autonomy solution for Palestine, prevarications dictated by the Zionist lobby operating through the American Christian Palestine Committee and using the threat of punishment in the forthcoming congressional elections in November, Churchill thundered from the floor of the House of Commons on 1 August 1946:

I think that the government should say that if the United States will not come and share the burden of the Zionist cause, as defined or agreed, we should now give notice that we will return our Mandate to UNO and that we will evacuate Palestine within a specified period.

Churchill said that the Zionists' claims now went beyond anything that had been agreed upon by Britain.[13] But by the end of January 1947 he was questioning the value of keeping 100,000 men in Palestine when they could be at home strengthening British industry; in August of that year he also criticised throwing away £30–40 million a year there.[14]

At the end of the first Arab–Israeli War Churchill was unimpressed with Bevin's warning in the House of Commons on 26 January 1949 that with over half a million Arabs being 'turned by the Jewish immigrants into homeless refugees without employment or resources', the tide of Arab nationalism was 'running high' and had bitten deep into the ordinary young Arab. Bevin commented: 'They consider that for the Arab population, which has been occupying Palestine for more than 20 centuries, to be turned out of their land and homes to make way for another race is a profound injustice', and wondered how the British people would feel if they had been asked to give up a slice of Scotland, Wales or Cornwall to another race. Churchill, in reply, argued that the coming into being of a Jewish state had to be seen in the perspective of 2,000 or even 3,000 years.[15]

As Prime Minister in the 1950s Churchill very obviously preferred the Zionists and Israel to the Arabs. He was particularly scornful of the Egyptians who with the rise of the revolutionary Free Officers Movement had only recently discovered their Arab identity. Churchill regarded the British presence in Egypt as a benevolent one. In the debate in the House of Commons on the 7 May 1946, following Attlee's statement that Britain was to withdraw all forces from Egyptian territory, Churchill accused Attlee of giving away the bargaining point at the outset. Rather than being suspicious he thought that the Egyptians should be grateful. Britain was throwing something away that had been built up with 'great labour'. The only way of ensuring that the Suez Canal was kept open was to keep troops there.[16]

Churchill thought it 'of the utmost importance to get America in' to the Middle East. At the outset of his premiership he wrote to his friend, Lord Cherwell, that he found many unpleasant truths in the latter's observations that with India and Burma gone the Suez Canal was an international rather than a specifically British interest; with Middle Eastern oil falling into American hands was it not for the United States to defend it; with the only reason for the defence of the Middle East being the need to prevent the Communists from gaining another large territory, did this not fall under the Truman doctrine and hence should it not be for the United States rather than Britain to defend the Middle East?[17]

Churchill was scornful of the supposed Russian threat. In April 1952 he wrote to Lord Alexander, his Minister of Defence, that he did 'not understand how and when the anticipated Russian threat against the Middle East would eventuate'. Churchill thought that in any global war in 1952 and 1953 the Soviet armies would move swiftly to the ocean, and subjugate the capitals of Western Europe within six weeks. But at the same time

American atomic bombs would at least paralyse communications, apart from wireless messages, between the advancing Soviet armies and the central government. The Americans had explained to Churchill the effects of atomic bombing on Soviet industry, communications and oil fields. After all this, Britain, if it still survived, could take a new view of the matter. But Churchill could not see how an anticipated Soviet invasion of the Middle East and possibly North Africa fitted in:

> If Soviet Russia is shattered as an organic military force in the first three months of the war she will certainly not be in a position to cross the Sinai Peninsula and play about in the Western Desert.

Churchill argued that if the American atomic attack succeeded, it would be possible with conventional bombing to destroy the railway and other communications through Persia and Syria. It would not be easy for the Soviet Union to cross Turkey quickly. He concluded:

> It is of course important to prevent infiltration into the Middle East in time of peace and to preserve the semblance at least of military power. But the idea of a heavy Russian invasion of the Middle East and across the Suez Canal into Egypt, Libya, Cyrenaica and Tripoli is to my mind absurd. The best defence of the Middle East would be an overwhelming air force in Cyprus sustained by the necessary anti-submarine and air carrier forces. No surface fleet exists, even in imagination, for the American, British, French and Italian navies to fight.[18]

The Defence Policy and Global Strategy Paper of June 1952 emphasised that Britain could not afford to maintain its present forces in the Middle East.[19] The Americans were interested to know whether Britain intended to reduce forces only after a settlement with Egypt, or had to do so anyway. The British avoided giving any time limit.[20]

Churchill did not regard the Middle East as a British prerogative. Indeed he consistently wanted to lessen Britain's role there, and get the Americans involved. When in January 1954 the Cabinet considered a suggestion of the American government that Washington's offer of military aid to Pakistan should be linked to the initiation of military collaboration between Pakistan and Turkey which could eventually be developed into a system of collective defence in the Middle East, Churchill favoured the building of a military association between Turkey and Pakistan as being to Britain's advantage. If Britain failed to reach a defence agreement with

Egypt its forces in the Middle East would be redeployed northwards, and the proposed defence arrangement would fit in with that. Churchill's worry was over the timing of the announcement. He did not want it made before the meeting of the four powers in Berlin: the proposal could, for the moment do nothing to increase the military strength of the West, and could be regarded by the Soviets as provocative.[21]

Churchill continued to question vigorously the nature of any British military presence in the Middle East and when, on 12 January 1954, the Foreign Secretary, Anthony Eden, suggested that, given the state of the defence negotiations with Egypt, it might be opportune to pursue the suggestion of the Turkish government that Britain stock military equipment at Mardi, on the frontier between Turkey and Syria, and that if Britain could make satisfactory arrangements with Turkey for joint defence of the area, and they include Iraq, Egypt would be strategically less important, Churchill demanded to know what forces the Chiefs of Staff proposed to operate from Mardi, how many British troops would be needed there in peacetime, and what aid the Turks would give.[22] In June 1954 it became clear that Britain's defence problem in the Middle East had been changed by the development of the hydrogen bomb. In view of the extent of the nuclear attack to which they would be subjected in the opening stages of the war the Russians were less likely to attack through the Caucasus, and Britain had a better chance of holding them to the north-east of Iraq, possibly in the passes leading from Iran. The Chiefs of Staff wanted a defence agreement with Iran which meant that Britain had to ensure that Iraq maintained in peacetime the air bases at Habbaniya and Shaiba, and made them available to Britain in war. Churchill demanded to know Britain's minimum strategic requirements in Iraq, and insisted that any indication to the Crown Prince of Iraq that Britain was willing to renegotiate the Anglo-Iraqi treaty be cleared through him.[23]

For Churchill the United States was central to any handling of the situation in Iran where Dr Muhammad Mossadeq, the Prime Minister, challenged British paramountcy in the Middle East by nationalising the Iranian oil industry, including the Anglo-Iranian Oil Company, on 2 May 1951. As officials of the Anglo-Iranian Oil Company prepared to evacuate the mainland fields and Abadan Island, Churchill told the then Prime Minister, Clement Attlee, that although he 'had never thought that the Persian oil-fields could be held by force . . . Abadan Island was quite another matter'.[24] Early in his career Churchill had helped to secure the change in the Royal Navy from coal to oil-fired ships. In the summer of 1914 he personally had secured the largest share for the British government of the company operating the Persian (Iranian) concession so that the Royal Navy could be independent of Dutch and American firms which had control over the production and marketing of oil.[25] Churchill did not want the Americans to take over. Rather he envisaged common Anglo-American action in the face of the danger of a Soviet threat to the region between the Caspian Sea and the Persian Gulf.[26] As the Americans pursued an independent policy Churchill continued to insist in September 1952 that Britain 'must do all in our power to maintain a joint Anglo-American pressure on the Persian government, though in the last resort we had no means of preventing the United States Government from financing Dr. Mossadeq in the hope of preventing Persia from going Communist'.[27]

Although it was Herbert Morrison, the Labour Foreign Secretary, who initiated the overthrow of Mossadeq by covert means, an operation in which the Americans became involved through arguments about the threat of a possible Communist take-over, it was Churchill who overrode the Foreign Office's attempts to curtail the conspiracy in February 1953, and authorised the operation to overthrow Mossadeq.[28]

After the overthrow of Mossadeq and the return of the Shah, Churchill, on 25 August 1953, warned the Cabinet about his fears of an American take-over in the area and supported the arguments of Lord Salisbury, the Lord President, that Britain needed to give financial aid to the new Iranian government along with the United States, and find a solution to the oil dispute, or 'sacrifice all prospect of re-establishing British influence in Persia'. He hoped that support of the new government would be undertaken on an Anglo-American basis. The Prime Minister warned: 'In present circumstances it would be easy for the Americans by the expenditure of a relatively small sum of money to reap all the benefit of many years of British work in Persia.'[29]

Churchill's approach to the Middle East during his final premiership was influenced by his conviction that the Americans had to be involved, and by an overriding wish to help Israel, which he described as 'the great experiment', 'one of the most hopeful and encouraging adventures of the twentieth century'.[30] Churchill did not have the same regard for the Arab states as his predecessors, and his conviction that Israel was likely to be the most reliable ally in the area and his emotional support for Zionism, combined with his friendship with David Ben-Gurion, at times led him to try to blunt the enthusiasm of his Foreign Secretary and the Chiefs of Staff for the protection of Jordan against Israel.

Above all Churchill wanted to prevent a war between Jordan and Israel in which Britain might have to honour the Anglo-Jordanian Treaty of 1948 and go to Jordan's assistance. An Israeli attack on a frontier village, with heavy loss of life among Arab women and children, though it shocked Churchill, still found him urging care that British troops should not get involved in support of Jordan against Israel.[31] Churchill even welcomed attempts to integrate Israel in an overall Middle East defence strategy.[32] The Chiefs of Staff on their side insisted that Arab goodwill was more important than that of Israel, including Egyptian co-operation in running the base in the Suez Canal Zone.[33] Churchill argued on the other hand that fear of stronger Israeli forces 'would constitute a useful deterrent against Egyptian aggressive aspirations'. In the Cabinet, Lord Salisbury, as often in these last years of Churchillian government, restrained the Prime Minister's impulses: in August 1953 he warned ministers that British help in arming Israel, if it became known to Arabs, could prejudice British negotiations with Egypt for a new treaty and lose Britain the goodwill of the Arab states.[34]

Churchill preferred Israeli support to Egyptian or Arab goodwill, which he viewed with distrust and even disdain. He complained that 'the late Mr Bevin, who had a strain of anti-Semitism in his thought, put the Foreign Office in on the wrong side when Israel was attacked by all the Arab states'. He insisted that 'Israel could come in very handy in dealing with Egypt if Neguib [then the Egyptian military ruler] attacks us'.[35] He declared:

> I do not mind it being known here or in Cairo that I am on the side of Israel and against her ill-treatment by the Egyptians. The idea of selling Israel down the drain in order to persuade the Egyptians to kick us out of the Canal Zone more gently is not one which attracts me.

He assured the Israeli Ambassador in London that 'Her Majesty's Government will always be mindful of Israel's interests.'[36]

Churchill interfered with Middle East policy. He doubted the strategic value of the area. He thought Bevin had backed the wrong side in the First Arab-Israeli War. The Prime Minister described himself as a Zionist and questioned any policy unfavourable towards Israel. But it was policy towards Egypt which particularly interested him, and which he was determined to control. He had his own ideas and he fought his Foreign Secretary, Eden, and was suspicious of the advice of the Chiefs of Staff.[37]

When he became Prime Minister, Churchill told the Cabinet on 30 October 1951 that it was the duty of the British government to keep the Suez Canal open to the shipping of the world, using force if necessary.[38] Churchill scorned the Egyptians. He resented their 'cheek', and in private told Eden to let them know, if they continued in that vein, 'we shall set the Jews on them and drive them into the gutter, from which they should never have emerged'.[39] When Egyptian crowds ran riot in Cairo on 26 January 1952, burning Shepheards Hotel and the BOAC offices, symbols of British imperialism, Churchill wrote to Eden that the 'horrible behaviour of the mob puts them lower than the most degraded savages now known'. Churchill did not approve of the Foreign Office's attempts to negotiate with the new Egyptian government about the defence of the Canal Zone. The Prime Minister was in no hurry. He felt that Britain could negotiate from strength: Egypt had almost lost its place among civilised states; whereas Britain had remained firm, cool, resolute and immovable.[40]

While in the United States in January 1953 Churchill discussed the Middle East with the new American President, Dwight Eisenhower. It was Eisenhower who demoted Britain from being the special ally to just one among a number of allies and the President hinted at this revision of the special relationship: while Britain and the United States should work together in the Middle East, there should be 'no collusion'.[41] Churchill returned 'passionately interested' in the Egyptian situation. Furious at Eden's policy, he commented that he had 'not known that Munich was situated on the Nile', and John Colville, his private secretary, was left with the impression that Churchill would never give way over Egypt.[42] The Prime Minister explained the tactics he envisaged to his Foreign Secretary:

> This military dictator is under the impression that he has only to kick us to make us run. I would like him to kick us and show him that we did not run. . . .[43]

Opposed by Eden, the Foreign Office and the military, Churchill would not give up Egypt. Early in April 1954 he reminded Eden of his 'constant interest' in the problem.[44] Churchill wanted American involvement, and approaches from Washington over the possibility of a collective defence organisation for South-East Asia, led the Prime Minister to hope that the Americans might be persuaded to join the British in a similar assurance about the security of the Middle East and the Suez Canal. Eden, however, doubted whether the Americans could be persuaded.[45] The Cabinet debated the whole approach on 22 June 1954. It was emphasised that Britain's strategic needs had been radically changed by the development of thermo-nuclear weapons. It was no longer expedient to maintain so large a concentration of stores, equipment and men within the narrow confines

of the Canal Zone. Churchill accepted the military argument for rede-
ploying the British forces in the Middle East. But he remained impressed
by the political disadvantages of abandoning the position Britain had held
in Egypt since 1882.[46]

Yet it was Churchill's peacetime administration which made the dramatic change in British defence policy, the move away from considering
the Middle East as one of the three cardinal pillars of British strategy
towards the conclusion that it was an area of more limited significance in
the age of thermo-nuclear weapons, especially at a time when Britain's
financial strictures meant a limitation of her world role. Churchill, privately, questioned the strategic significance of the Middle East for Britain,
and when he became Prime Minister actively criticised the validity of a
defence policy which gave the area priority. Churchill was unable to see
why such an emphasis should be placed on protecting the area from a
Soviet invasion, an invasion which the Prime Minister felt could not be
mounted.

Churchill felt in any case that the Americans should become involved in
an area for which Britain had undertaken responsibility in the agreement
made between their two countries at the end of 1947. In this respect
Churchill's Middle East policy was radically different from that of Attlee's
first Labour government which had decided that the Middle East was a
British preserve, and one from which the Americans should be excluded.[47]
Churchill hoped for a partnership, dominated by Britain. The Americans
did not agree; Dulles on his visit to the Middle East in 1953 concluded that
Britain could no longer meet its responsibility for the defence of the
Middle East on behalf of the West. In July the National Security Council
advocated 'greater independence and greater responsibility in the area by
the United States *vis-à-vis* Britain'.[48] Churchill's last government was associated with the beginnings of the transfer of power in the Middle East from
Britain to the United States.

Churchill, however, still had imperial leanings in the 1950s. He was
reluctant to give up Egypt and abandon a considerable British presence in
an area in which Britain had exercised influence for over half a century.
His personal predilections influenced his policy. During his final premiership he dominated policy-making towards Egypt. He would not leave
Eden alone. From the outset the approach of the two men diverged radically on this subject. Eden's absences through illness or at conferences
enabled Churchill to play a decisive role. When Eden was present, the
Prime Minister fought against the policy of 'scuttle' being proposed by his
Foreign Secretary.[49] In the end Eden's conciliatory policy prevailed.
Churchill finally gave way to the military arguments: ideas of a Middle

East Command and of a Middle East Defence Organisation based on the Canal Zone had little relevance with the development of the hydrogen bomb. Eden is often seen as Churchill's pupil, the man groomed as heir apparent. He acquired many of Churchill's habits including working from bed. Within a few months of becoming Prime Minister he had also acquired his master's views of the Egyptians. After the Suez crisis, Eden shared Churchill's emotional support for Israel.[50]

12

Churchill and France, 1951–55

MAURICE VAISSE

The main evidence for the impact on France of British foreign policy during Churchill's period as Prime Minister comes from the reports and telegrams to the Quai d'Orsay of René Massigli, French Ambassador in London from 1944 to 1954. His great experience of England, his long service there and his friendly disposition towards the English all rendered him a first-class intermediary between France and the United Kingdom.[1] In addition, René Massigli cultivated close and frequent contacts with the French President, Vincent Auriol, whose outlook was similar to his own. Both men were opposed in principle to the notion of supranationalism and in practice to the idea of creating a European army.[2] The French Ambassador was not just a simple observer of British policy. As early as 1930, Massigli had been portrayed as 'a determined partisan of the Franco-British entente'[3] and he readily acted as spokesman and defender of British policies.

Saddened by the lack of contact that characterised relations between the French and British governments, Massigli remarked during the Franco-British meetings of February 1953: 'It is more than two years since a French Prime Minister has visited London'.[4] He unhesitatingly criticised French officials both for giving insufficient attention to British concerns and for relying more on the Americans than on the British. He found the British 'offended by the lack of confidence we show in them'.[5] Massigli's view of Franco-British relations took for granted fundamental differences between the French and the British: 'We think differently; and to come to the same conclusions we take different routes. The health of Franco-British relations requires frequent airing of our differences in which no problem should be left out . . .'[6] Massigli's attitude was shared by the staff of the Quai d'Orsay who were unable to hide their irritation with the 'Europeans', those more concerned with building a Europe of the Six than 'to preserve the Franco-British entente . . . which remains one of the principal elements of our foreign policy'.[7] Indeed, Massigli's perception was not shared by all Frenchmen.

In these four years we move from frigid Cold War to a period of détente, the process of decolonisation becomes both more widespread and vigorous, European integration begins but with much difficulty and the Fourth Republic struggles in vain to resolve the problems of Indochina and the EDC. If successive French governments from Pleven to Laniel developed a policy towards Europe revolving around a Franco-German axis, such was not the case under the government of Pierre Mendès-France, whose orientation was clearly pro-British. Indeed, Massigli felt much more in tune with the government led by Mendès-France, precisely because he sought in Great Britain a privileged partner and was dedicated to a policy of collaboration with London.[8]

Winston Churchill's rise to power in 1951 was perceived in France as 'the return of the old lion'. While a member of the opposition, he was regarded as a man of impressive powers. With the prestige he had won during the war, his return to power created across the globe the most profound impression. It was as if the past had swelled up, transporting people 11 years back in time.[9] Churchill's return to power marks the restoration in Britain of a foreign policy of grandeur. Churchill applied himself more to the problems of high international and imperial politics than to the common and daily affairs of his country.[10] On certain occasions, his public messages could still inspire and stir up the emotions of his countrymen. His speech of 11 May 1953, Massigli noted, won 'the spontaneous and heartfelt support of public and parliamentary opinion. Great Britain has undergone an almost physical sensation of reawakening and renewed confidence in herself'.[11]

Yet, who directed British foreign policy: the Prime Minister or the Foreign Secretary? During the illness and recovery of Anthony Eden (April–May 1952 to May 1953), Churchill did not, according to Massigli, hide his satisfaction at having full control over foreign policy and at this time no one at the Foreign Office dared stand up to him.[12] Following a series of Franco–British meetings, Churchill asked Massigli 'Don't you think Anthony is looking older?', a remark not without malice towards the great man's expected successor. At other times, the situation at the Foreign Office was less clear, thus making it more difficult to discern who really directed the Foreign Office. René Massigli, unable to hide his preference for Anthony Eden – 'Although he had always shown reserve towards the question of Europe . . . his sympathy for France was known and his desire to co-operate with French diplomacy was incontestable'[13] – took note of every indication of the Secretary of State's growing independence of the Prime Minister and domination over the Foreign Office.[14] Following the parliamentary debates of April 1952, Massigli stated: 'Eden has demonstrated his international experience'.[15] During the summer of 1954, Eden, Mendès-France and Massigli developed important channels of communications, including Gladwyn Jebb's appointment to Paris, that became the human foundation of the Franco-British axis.

Churchill was less conciliatory. Vincent Auriol, for example, openly revealed to French ministers his concern over Churchill's impulsive character: 'Of a person such as this, I openly admit my fear . . . He has a volcanic temperament and we must beware of his impulsiveness'.[16] This was all the more worrisome at a time when Churchill was, for some, a political disappointment. During a speech of his in August 1952, 'we heard nothing but vague generalisations and contradictory statements; once again we are forced to recognise that Churchill no longer masters his brief as he once did'.[17] Was Churchill really directing British foreign policy? His failing memory, his tiredness and his penchant for good wine sometimes raised in the minds of his French colleagues doubts about his ability to meet and resolve great problems. Vincent Auriol had but a small opinion of Churchill: 'I found a man whose hearing is poor and who often repeats himself'.[18] Massigli attributed to Churchill 'the indecision and the impotence' of the British government. 'In fact, he is still active only in appearance. He gives fewer and fewer speeches.' And in September 1954, Massigli stated once again: 'At the moment, there is no British government.'[19]

In the course of his reign, Churchill acted on the one hand like a hesitant European and on the other like a 'Rule Britannia' Englishman obsessed by imperial traditions. He was a hesitant European. Churchill's policies appeared to be closer to those of France and Europe than were Labour policies. Yet, he still sought to keep a certain distance from the European movement. Churchill's attitude to his cross-Channel neighbour revealed a man deeply attached to France 'whose past is dear to him and whose future preoccupies him'.[20] It was a relationship of unrequited love, perhaps somewhat condescending. Massigli noted on numerous occasions 'the importance that the British government attaches to maintaining a complete harmony of policy between the two countries'.

Churchill often spoke as an advocate of France, explaining to the Americans the importance of France's role in Europe and the necessity of supporting her.[21] He portrayed the French Army as essential to the defence of the West. As for colonial policy, British attitudes conformed to all French expectations. To the great satisfaction of Paris, Churchill's government gave the fullest support to French positions at the UN. In order to oppose the 'anti-colonialist bloc of New York' and to counter the problem of Islamic expansion in black Africa, Massigli laboured fully to concert French and British policy at the UN. The fruit of this labour came at the end of 1954. And British attitudes concerning Tunisian and Moroccan affairs were much appreciated in Paris.[22] That being said, Churchill's critical attitude towards both French governmental instability and the indecisiveness of the leadership of the Fourth Republic was hardly to the taste of the French. Churchill went so far as publicly to counsel the French government, advising Paris during her war in Indochina, for example, to extend French military service to two years. Massigli reproached the Foreign Office:

All French respect and venerate Sir Winston; if he has some advice to give us, let him do it confidentially . . . But unsolicited advice given publicly is not appreciated.

French officials often feared that France's position would be compromised by other such unsolicited and inopportune remarks.[23] Particularly sensitive to Churchill's pretensions was the French President, Vincent Auriol, who, in a conversation with the Education Minister, André Marie, agreed that France really must escape from the 'heavy paternalism of *père* Churchill'.[24] Despite the spirit of the Entente Cordiale, whose 50th anniversary celebrations were then taking place, Churchill refused to take part in a Franco-American action to save Dien Bien Phu.

Conservative party politics brought Britain closer to Europe. Had not Churchill himself criticised the Labour party for their indifference to the question of Europe? In this area, wrote Massigli, 'new opportunities present themselves'.[25] In fact, the evaluation of the ambassador to London was similar to that of Henri Bonnet, Ambassador to Washington. In the triangular relations with Europe, the United States and the United Kingdom, the Conservatives hoped to find across the Channel enough diplomatic support to enable them to 'avoid becoming the 49th State'.[26] In fact, the British tried to tighten relations with the continent, particularly through the indirect means of the Eden plan for the revitalisation of the Council of Europe. The French quickly concluded, however, that the Conservative government's growing support for Europe did not go so far as to imply actual participation, and that a certain distance from Europe would be the rule. 'With them, not of them' seemed to be the motto of Churchill. Massigli warned French government officials to have no illusions on this score: British participation in a European federation was incompatible with the Commonwealth system.[27]

Although originally a simple observer of events, the French Ambassador in London soon evolved into an active participant in the formulation of Anglo-French relations. He often emphasised the special European character of England, and laboured to instruct Paris that British policy towards European integration would be linked to the nature of integration that evolved. Massigli concluded that Britain 'would either bow to changed circumstances or fall back upon the Commonwealth and the United States'.[28] Explaining that Great Britain's national interests imposed upon her particular and permanent continental responsibilities, Massigli sought to show that 'it is in our interest to help them to reach a clear policy' which would enable the British to retain full sovereignty and yet to co-operate fully in Europe.[29] He hinted that 'certain European structures . . . would hinder the British government from associating herself with Europe as much as she would like'.[30] In short, Massigli advised the French government against being drawn into a programme of federalism, recommending rather a European structure organised as a confederation.

With the arrival into power of Pierre Mendès-France, Massigli went even further in his defence of British policy, striving now to justify Britain's reserved attitude towards Europe. According to Massigli, Churchill (who had just launched in Strasbourg the idea of an European army that would include British forces) now found himself in a new situation, changed 'by the progressive formation, aided by the Americans, of a Europe of the Six, that is already tightly integrated'.[31]

No single problem was more typical of Great Britain's attitude towards Europe than that of the European Defence Community. The French played the game of reminding Churchill of his Strasbourg speech, as well as those he had made when still a member of the opposition, all calling for the creation of a European army in which Britain would take part.[32] Had Churchill forgotten his declarations? Massigli offered this interpretation of Churchill's position:

> The Prime Minister concealed his retreat in a smokescreen . . . He nevertheless made one point quite clear: however much England wished to collaborate as fully and as effectively as possible with the European army, she would not see herself diluted in this denationalised amalgam.[33]

The Conservative government would give its full benediction to a European defence organisation, as long as British participation remained limited. And, indeed, the government did state its decided support for the European army project. At regular intervals, Massigli reported to Paris the tremors in British foreign policy and suggested new efforts be made to persuade the British to widen their participation.[34] Yet, the British government carefully spelled out the limits of its involvement.[35] As Massigli reported of the British attitude to the proposed European Defence Community: 'We must in no way expect that the United Kingdom will be persuaded to become a member of the EDC.'[36] And he emphasised that any 'new request that she join the Community would be inopportune and embarrassing'.

Robert Schuman urged Massigli to cultivate the favourable attitudes towards a closer British co-operation with the EDC that emerged in some British circles.[37] In order to ease the work of the French government Schuman wanted from the British government 'new evidence of her determination' and urged Massigli 'to secure more boldness from the British side', particularly concerning the plan for the integration of European defence. The Quai d'Orsay's European Director, François Seydoux, went even further, seeking to 'push England to the limit in order that she adopt a position very close to our own', hoping that Britain would pledge herself 'to go in as far as France'.[38] Considering what was known about the British attitude, the French government, at the least, expected that Great Britain would maintain a sufficient level of military forces in Europe.[39]

During the Bermuda Conference, Churchill vigorously criticised France's delay in ratifying the EDC treaties. To limit the counter-productive effect of such remarks in France, French diplomacy sought support from the Foreign Office throughout the important debate on the question during the summer of 1954.[40] The London embassy staff spelled-out to the Foreign Office 'the inopportune and intolerable effects of the numerous initiatives which multiply in the various capitals',[41] all of which were provoking French opinion, as evidenced by the editorial of Claude Bourdet in the *France-Observateur* entitled '*C'est Cambronne qu'il nous faut!*' ('We need Cambronne!' – Cambronne was a French general who refused to surrender to British soldiers at the battle of Waterloo and he is famous for the word '*merde*' he flung at the British army.) At the same time, however, Massigli understood the attitude of the British: 'Our slowness [in deciding on EDC] irritates the British and it would not aggrieve them to force our hand.'[42]

René Massigli played to the fullest his role as both diplomatic counsel and argumentative arm-twister: lunching with Anthony Eden *en tête-à-*

tête; travelling to see Mendès-France over a weekend; penning personal letters to the Secretary General of the Quai d'Orsay, Alexandre Parodi, to
keep the ministry up-to-date. It is true, of course, that not everyone at the
Foreign Office and at the Quai d'Orsay was affected by Massigli's flattery.
Prime Minister Churchill, for one, was impatient towards France. The
publication of Churchill's telegram to Chancellor Adenauer illustrated
'the pressure which is growing' upon France,[43] pressure that rendered
France's eventual decision more difficult – and the failure of the EDC
more likely. Massigli also reported upon the stormy discussions that
allegedly preceded Eden's statement of 29 September: 'Every ounce of the
Secretary of State's tenaciousness seems to have been needed to overcome
the obstinate resistance of the Prime Minister.'[44]

In fact, in his hope for a Franco-British entente, Massigli made every
attempt to shape policy and lead events from the London embassy. His
telegrams addressed to the Quai d'Orsay reveal a man both formulating
policy and persuading Paris to act upon his ideas. Such efforts by Massigli
were neutralised however by Mendès-France whose policies caused
Churchill to brandish the spectre of France's imminent isolation while
Eden took on the role of arbiter between France and Germany.
'Disappointed at seeing his efforts sabotaged . . .he adopted the superior
tone of the policeman.'[45]

The other impression that Churchill leaves us with during this period is
that of an Englishman obsessed with imperial tradition. He simultaneously
sought to resuscitate the Anglo-American 'special relationship' and play
the role of intermediary between East and West. Anglo-American relations
had been strained under the Labour government, particularly after the outbreak of the Korean war. Churchill's desire to re-establish friendly relations
with Washington predate his return to power. While the House of
Commons debated the question of selecting an American officer for North
Atlantic Supreme Commander,[46] Massigli concluded that 'the basis of
Churchill's foreign policy is a strong Anglo-American entente'.[47]
Everything reveals his belief that a special sort of co-operation could still
exist between the two Anglo-Saxon countries. Massigli's analysis is striking: 'We can be sure that Churchill intends to do everything to resuscitate
the wartime entente.'[48]

This was particularly true once Eisenhower had become President.[49]
Churchill wanted to recreate the atmosphere of Anglo-American confidence so familiar to him during the Second World War. But changed times
and attitudes fostered in Churchill disappointment and bitterness, now
that he was unable to find the America he had known during the desperate days of world war. Massigli pointed out, for example, the absence in

Churchill's speech of 11 May 1953, of any reference to the United States, an absence he attributed to the Prime Minister's heartfelt dismay over the behaviour of the new American administration. The French ambassador also reported that the photograph showing Secretary of State Dulles offering, in the name of President Eisenhower, a revolver to General Neguib – at the very moment that terrorist attacks began anew against British soldiers – was little appreciated by London. In short, Churchill painfully measured 'the drop in British prestige'. This being said, we must not over-emphasise the point: the Anglo-American entente always remained the basic rule of British diplomacy.

Massigli warned against theories suggesting that radical changes in British attitudes towards America might take place, particularly 'when we see one of those periods of mutual irritation and bad feelings that, at regular intervals, come to trouble this indestructible marriage'. Churchill seemed especially anxious to improve Britain's nuclear weapons, an issue he hoped would see Anglo-American parity restored to its wartime status.[50] Massigli noted as significant Lord Cherwell's participation in the Washington conversations. The allusions Churchill made in his public speeches that British air bases would be conceded to the United States, revealed his plans to increase Great Britain's role in Atlantic nuclear policy-making.[51] In questions of formulating allied strategy, Great Britain wanted her voice clearly heard. The publication in April 1954 of the Quebec accords (29 September 1943) on Anglo-American nuclear co-operation simply reinforced previous policies: it was a question of making the MacMahon law, which limited US nuclear co-operation with foreign powers, less strict.[52] The strengthened links forged at the Bermuda Conference had first to be tested in the realm of nuclear policy.[53]

Haunted by the possibility of nuclear war, Churchill wanted to foster a climate of world peace. In the very midst of the Cold War, Churchill sought to convince the Americans that he should try to restore contact with Moscow. In his speech, Churchill's reference to the Locarno Treaties of 1925 which guaranteed France against Germany and Germany against France was interpreted as an effort to offer the Kremlin similar moral and political guarantees, if not territorial concessions. And after the death of Stalin, Churchill impatiently sought out issues that might lead to positive negotiations.[54] He said as much in his speech of 11 May 1953.[55] As for Massigli, he saw in all this Churchill's final effort, before he retired, to restore, at the highest level, a dialogue between East and West, an achievement that would make him the people's guide to peace, just as in 1940 when he had been the needed guide to war.[56] Churchill's efforts however worried many. Men like Vincent Auriol feared that the Prime Minister would make 'excessive concessions'.[57]

Yet when it was a question of France's taking steps towards international detente – when, for example, Pierre Mendès-France informed the British and American governments on 5 January 1955 of France's move toward Moscow – the British reacted angrily.[58] The French suggestion of organising a conference with the Russians did not, in the minds of her allies, even merit discussion. Winston Churchill added:

> It would be very bad for France if Pierre Mendès-France persists in his plans . . . I would feel compelled . . . to support the policy of the empty chair [leaving France unrepresented] . . . It would greatly pain me to see her hand forced this way, and [France] losing her influence in the rest of the world.[59]

As Jean Lacouture, Mendès-France's biographer, remarked: 'Never had the Americans made such precise threats, even blackmail.'[60]

The Entente Cordiale was, at this moment, entirely one-sided. It seemed, in fact, that British foreign policy had never entirely abandoned its role as honest broker. When France and Germany were once again at odds, this time over the Saar affair, the Germans hoped for Anglo-Saxon mediation, an idea Mendès-France challenged immediately. Great Britain's abstention on the UN resolution concerning the Moroccan problem angered the French representative, Henri Hoppenot, who labelled it an 'act of casual vanity'.[61] At the end of 1954 and the beginning of 1955, France found herself alone and isolated, the Anglo-Saxons having restored good relations that even saw Dulles and Anthony Eden once again on good terms.[62]

The year 1954 saw the 50th anniversary of the Entente Cordiale. Had it been up to the French Ambassador in London, the event would have been celebrated much less modestly than it was. Had he not already made numerous and positive references to the Entente Cordiale in his many telegrams to Paris?[63] In truth, Great Britain was in no way resolved to consolidate a new Franco-British alliance. From London's point of view, the German threat was no longer a question of German rearmament, but of how to integrate a rearmed Germany into the Western security framework. As far as Great Britain was concerned, the Entente Cordiale therefore no longer had a *raison d'être*. France, on the other hand, could have every reason to expect benefits from a renewed Entente Cordiale; she opposed both German rearmament and German admission to NATO. But in 1954, France was faced with both. British help could provide some return, in particular: that the Treaty of Brussels, combining Britain, France and the Benelux countries, be brought into full force.

The Franco-British rapprochement was for the most part an illusion. It was based primarily upon the convictions of but a handful of men; it was threatened by the very real and serious crisis over the EDC; and in the end, it was conditioned by the fact that French foreign policy was heavily dependent upon Great Britain. In conclusion, Churchill's return to power did not signify the renewal of Franco-British understanding and co-operation: instead it began a period of multiplied and heightened misunderstandings. It was only with the accession to power of Guy Mollet and Anthony Eden that a Paris–London axis would begin to take shape.[64]

13

Churchill and Adenauer

HANS-PETER SCHWARZ

Churchill's interest in Adenauer began only with his resumption of the prime ministership in October 1951. The two men met in May 1948 but it is unlikely that Churchill remembered their encounter. Adenauer, of course, had been acutely interested in Churchill since May 1940.

Adenauer's first recorded remark on Churchill was in May 1945, when he told a visitor, Churchill is a 'hater of Germans', Truman 'a politician of the second rank', but Stalin is 'a friend of Germany' – surprising words, soon revised.[1] Churchill's famous Zurich speech made a lasting impression on him, though a mixed one. Now leader of the Christian Democrats in the British Zone, Adenauer commented in public 'In war Churchill was our most bitter foe. But it cannot be denied that he is a man of vision in foreign policy'. Obviously he referred to Churchill's appeal for Franco-German reconciliation in 'a kind of United States of Europe'.[2] In a letter of 12 October 1946, he commented:

> I have read Churchill's speech in full in the Swiss newspapers. We cannot agree with everything, especially if he demands that every individual German state in a future federation should have its own foreign representation. In principle, however, I welcome his remarks as I have already done in speeches.[3]

When they first met, Adenauer told a friend 'Churchill made a good impression on me. He is, however, very old'. (Churchill was then 74, Adenauer 72.) Churchill told the 'group of seven Germans' that 'in his heart there was no hate or enmity towards Germans, that they should

172

unite for federalism and that a European federation would be the only sal-
vation for Germany and Europe.' When Adenauer reported to the CDU
executive he added: 'With this sentence we Germans could all completely
agree'.[4] Indeed, a 'United States of Europe' was Adenauer's own idea for
the European continent and for German recovery.

On Adenauer's first visit to England, in 1951, Churchill and the British
government pleased him by dignified ceremonial and personal warmth.[5]
Churchill continued to appeal to Adenauer's vanity especially when he told
the House of Commons on 11 May 1953: 'Dr Adenauer may well be
deemed the wisest German statesman since Bismarck'. Years later in 1959
President Heuss commented that 'Adenauer is in danger of hubris' after
Churchill had called him 'the greatest German statesman since Bismarck'.[6]
In the early 1950s the public support of Adenauer by this living legend
strengthened his position in West German politics.

In May 1956 Adenauer responded by giving Churchill the fullest honours
in Bonn when he came to receive the *Karlspreis* in Aachen. Later, Adenauer
twice visited the ailing Churchill, at Roquebrune on 13 February 1958 and
at Hyde Park Gate on 18 November 1959. In January 1965 when Churchill
died Adenauer closed his respectful tribute by saying 'I speak for the
German people, but I must also speak for myself because through all these
years Churchill showed me only friendship and amiability'. Their mutual
gifts were valued: Churchill gave Adenauer one of his own paintings;
Adenauer secured for Churchill an engraving of Bonn besieged by
Churchill's ancestor Marlborough. Even Adenauer's funeral was modelled
on Churchill's: the last farewell of the old Germany and the old Empire.[7]

Churchill's ill-health sometimes worried his German contacts. A note of
Blankenhorn, then Adenauer's closest aide, shows that in December 1951
Churchill was still lively:

Churchill is still the man known from innumerable pictures. It is true
that he has become smaller and he carries his 77 years less lightly than
the Chancellor his 75. His manner of speaking is jerky, sometimes
stuttering, hesitating, undecided, then suddenly four or five sentences
come together in an impressive construction. A strong man, an artist
in oratory, a natural person, not at all smooth, but a personality that
for all his passion and energy, never loses balance and common sense.
Quick as lightning in understanding, sometimes hasty in his reactions
to pressure.'[8]

More worrying was Churchill's condition when Adenauer, again with
Blankenhorn, visited him in May 1953. On 11 May Churchill spoke

superbly in the Commons. On the evening of 14 May he gave an excellent impression especially in a brilliant after-dinner speech. But when Adenauer met him again the next morning, his spirit seemed gone. Blankenhorn noted in his diary:

> Churchill sometimes gives an uninformed, absent-minded impression and when he wakes from his dreams and poses questions they are often off the point. The old man sits heavily in his chair, his left eye waters and if he tries to give a connected opinion – such as on the British desire for peace – he seems, as often with old men, on the edge of tears. It is hardly credible that this man, despite his physical condition, should lead the British Empire. The Chancellor sometimes gets a poor impression from his interlocutor's mistakes and makes notes of his concern on a piece of paper which he pushes over to me.[9]

Next morning, at breakfast, Sir Ivone Kirkpatrick, acting as interpreter for Sir Winston and Lady Churchill, made it clear to Adenauer that the Foreign Office constantly kept an eye on the Prime Minister.[10]

Adenauer's belief that it was essential to keep in close contact with the Foreign Office grew stronger. When Eden fell ill at that time and Blankenhorn discussed the situation with him, Walter O'Neill explained that 'the Prime Minister alone worked on foreign policy without close contact with the Foreign Office'. The fact that Eden, at a critical time, was absent, O'Neill regarded as tragic.

> He alone had much influence on the Prime Minister, he alone could overcome his self-willed effervescent nature and his refusal to accept any contradiction. Today no-one from the Foreign Office could do much. Selwyn Lloyd and the others had extremely limited influence.[11]

After Churchill suffered a severe stroke, the situation changed. With Lord Salisbury and then Eden again in charge of the Foreign Office normality returned. Adenauer became even more sceptical towards Churchill's plan for a three-power 'summit' meeting.

Churchill and Adenauer met only once again during Churchill's prime ministership in autumn 1954. Adenauer now devoted as much attention to Eden, the designated successor. For Adenauer, Britain signified a great past but also a meaningful present. He told the CDU executive on 22 May 1953: 'If you see the power of the United States and the far-reaching connections of Great Britain in every part of the world, we Germans are not in the same class'.[12] Both Adenauer and Churchill thought of themselves, and of each other, as being representative of the destiny of their countries. From Churchill's point of view Adenauer was the type of a decent, balanced German. Adenauer encouraged him in that view: 'The German tends to extremes. He is often too given to theories. We have however paid a heavy price. Germans are no longer confused by their own mentality'. 'Germany', he suggested to Churchill, 'is a mass, to be shaped. All depends on whether it is shaped by good or bad hands'. Obviously the 'good' hands would be Adenauer's.[13]

Churchill did not know much about Germans or Germany. When Adenauer brought him two boxes of cigars in May 1953, Churchill explained that the last German to give him cigars had been Kaiser Wilhelm II. Adenauer and de Gaulle learned fast to modify their stereotypes of foreign countries; Adenauer suspected that Churchill did not. Blankenhorn told O'Neill in June 1953 that Adenauer

> had the firm conviction that the Prime Minister really knew very little about the German problem or, for that matter, the problems of European unity, of which he was himself the father, as they had developed since 1945. In fact, Dr Adenauer's fear was that the Prime Minister simply did not know enough about present-day problems in Germany and the world to be able to form a wise and reliable judgement.[14]

By that time Adenauer was worried by Churchill's pressure for a summit conference and by his evident lack of interest in European problems. Blankenhorn reported of a conversation between Adenauer and Churchill that 'the Prime Minister paid no attention to what he was saying, did not seem to understand anything about the European problems involved and was obviously buried away in a world with which Dr Adenauer and others had to deal'.[15]

Adenauer therefore admired Churchill but was forced increasingly to conclude that he was not a 'European'. He trusted him and remembered his words from their first meeting in 1951: 'We will keep our word. You can trust England, we will not do any business behind your back'.[16] In a way, this first meeting was their best moment of mutual understanding. Between 1945 and 1951 Churchill had proclaimed mistrust of the USSR at Fulton on 5 March 1946, called for a united Europe in Zurich on 16 September 1946, suggested a European army in Strasbourg on 11 August 1950 and agreed to a German defence contribution. All this fitted Adenauer's hopes and dreams.

After Churchill regained office, disappointment followed. Churchill's scepticism towards a European Defence Community and, even more alarmingly, his eagerness for détente with the USSR did not fit Adenauer's aspirations. It is often alleged that Adenauer always sought intimate co-operation with France in a Carolingian Europe without Britain. He is supposed to have harboured lasting resentment at his dismissal from the mayoralty of Cologne by the British Brigadier Barraclough in October 1945. The evidence does not support this view. When he talked about the dismissal he did so because he wanted to make the British feel a sense of guilt, not from bitterness. No doubt he felt reservations towards the Attlee government, partly because it favoured the SPD, but it is wrong to believe Adenauer to be anti-British, while he certainly admired Churchill. Even in 1960 when his relations with de Gaulle had strengthened and those with Macmillan become chilly, he told Theodor Heuss:

> I will tell you what I think about the English. I had a lot to do with them as Oberburgermeister [of Cologne] during the years after 1918. I got on with them very well, between General Sir Sidney Clive and me a trusting friendship developed that lasted until his death a few months ago. With Mr Piggott, the delegate for Cologne, a similar friendship grew up, which still survives. My relationship with Kirkpatrick was, and is, full of mutual confidence. My relations with Churchill are excellent as with Eden. I have always put a high value on good relations with Great Britain and still do so. It is true I have little faith in Macmillan . . .[17]

If Adenauer had had the choice, he would have preferred to pursue European integration with Britain as his closest partner rather than with France.[18] He could not choose. A federal republic still under military occupation had to accept more or less unquestioned all relevant proposals of the Western allies in order to reach its objectives: sovereignty, no restoration of four-power control, rearmament, economic recovery based on access to Western markets, a stable democracy and the recovery of Germany's international reputation.

As it was, Adenauer had to take what he could get: membership in the Council of Europe, the European Coal and Steel Community launched by Jean Monnet and Robert Schuman, the French idea of a European Defence Community and in that context the plan for a European Political Union. Moreover, Adenauer wanted US approval before going ahead. While Britain made increasing reservations about any steps towards European integration that went beyond co-operation between the governments of sovereign states, Paris wanted to integrate an increasingly powerful

Germany into a close web of western European controls, with a maximum of French influence. Adenauer's policy towards Britain between 1951 and 1955 sought to convince the British on the one hand of the political advantages of close European integration and, on the other, to show them the disadvantages and perils of British absence.

At first he hoped that Churchill might be more receptive of the idea of European integration than Attlee, Bevin and Morrison. His first conversation with Churchill proved discouraging. Adenauer took up the subject cautiously by complaining of Morrison's remark that Britain would be a 'good neighbour' of Europe. When he spoke of his consternation at these words Churchill commented '*With* Europe, but *not in* Europe'. Adenauer still tried to convince the Prime Minister that supranational projects at least promoted Franco-German co-operation. Churchill's speech at Zurich on 19 September 1946 made it seem that Churchill shared this ambition. Churchill, however, insisted that Britain must maintain a balance. To him, Germany was stronger than France, and in case of a German attack, Britain would support France. He hoped that it would never happen and favoured Franco-German friendship, but Britain must act from outside to preserve a balance. Churchill warned that it was an illusion to believe that 'you can completely eradicate national sentiments'. Referring to the European Defence Community he suggested that it would produce the absurd situation that German and French troops 'must march together to the sound of the *Marseillaise* and the *Wacht am Rhein*'.[19]

During Adenauer's visit to London in May 1953 he was further disillusioned. Churchill did not listen when Adenauer told him about the latest negotiations for a European Political Union. He woke up again only when the Chancellor referred to the détente speech of 11 May.[20] Churchill went on to illustrate his famous theory of three over-lapping circles by a sketch on a menu card. Britain lay at the intersection of the North Atlantic community, the British Commonwealth and Europe. Within each circle Britain, Churchill assumed, would have special influence. Adenauer printed the drawing in his memoirs and added – in 1965 – 'the British position has not changed at all'. It was not that Adenauer preferred to work with France; after this meeting he told the CDU executive that 'the relationship of the Federal Republic with the US and England is incomparably better than our relationship with the French Republic'.[21]

Adenauer did not like the French-inspired project for the European Defence Community: he thought it the only way to gain French approval for German rearmament and a recovery of sovereignty. Churchill equally disliked this 'sludgy amalgam'. Adenauer was close to Churchill's point of view. After eventual French rejection of the EDC, Churchill wrote to Eisenhower on 18 September 1954:

> When I came to power again I swallowed my prejudices because I was led to believe that it was the only way in which the French could be persuaded to accept a limited German army which was my desire. I do not blame the French for rejecting EDC but only for inventing it. Their harshness to Adenauer in wasting three years of his life and much of his power is a tragedy. Also I accepted the American wish to show all possible patience and not compromise the chances of EDC by running NATO as confusing rival.[22]

Eden then succeeded in creating a flexible solution for a German contribution to European defence which lasted until the 1990s. He achieved the policies Churchill had instinctively pursued without having concrete plans to bring them about. Churchill, however, helped in Eden's success. He sent Adenauer a personal message on 1 September 1954. He suggested that Germany should not seek a stronger military force than had been suggested by the EDC treaty. He ended in his typical manner: 'I beg you to think this over as coming from one who, after so many years of strife, has few stronger wishes than to see the German nation take her true place in the world-family of free nations'. Adenauer replied:

> The idea of a link with the allocation of forces in the EDC plan had already occurred to me as well. But above all I share your view that the solution must consist in a voluntary act of self-limitation, if it is to give Germany moral dignity and respect. I therefore note with gratitude that you too consider that the solution should have a form which in no way prejudices the equal and honourable status of the German Federal Republic.

Adenauer ended his message to Churchill 'with admiration for the historic task which you are accomplishing for Europe and the peace of the world'.[23] Such compliments helped the London negotiations which led, among other points, to Adenauer's renunciation of the production of nuclear weapons in Germany. When Churchill resigned in April 1955 it could be said that he had been at Adenauer's side in Germany's comeback to the great states of the world. Adenauer wanted, in response, to arrange a state visit by Churchill to Germany in the spring of 1955 to combine it with Churchill's receipt of the *Karlspreis* at Aachen, but Churchill's departure from office spoiled his plan.

The years in which Churchill and Adenauer were both heads of government offered, it seems, the chance of building an Anglo-German understanding as the means of a new, co-operative, western Europe. The initiatives for the '*relance européene*' which led to the Messina conference in summer 1955 and to the EEC of the Six, without the British, two years later, had not been developed and the Saar still divided Germany and France. However, Churchill rejected such opportunities or never seriously considered them. In full agreement with Eden, with nearly all British politicians and the mass of British opinion, he steered British policy in those crucial years towards the old objective of independent British power linked with Empire and Commonwealth. In 1951–55 a network of international and transnational co-operation within the Community of the Six developed. Adenauer could have stayed out only if London had given some strong creative impulse. Churchill had only rhetoric to offer. In that sense the period of amiability between Churchill and Adenauer between 1951 and 1955 is a period of lost opportunities.

Moreover, Churchill's readiness to conduct a foreign policy independent of Western Europe showed itself in another way which alarmed both Adenauer and the French: his eagerness to settle the Cold War between Britain, the USA and the USSR, the 'Big Three' of the war years. Alarming, too, for Adenauer was Churchill's readiness, if driven to it, to ease the way to a 'summit meeting' by including the French. On 6 November 1951 Churchill told the Commons:

> Our great hope in foreign affairs is, of course, to bring about an abatement of what is called the cold war by negotiation at the highest level from strength and not from weakness.[24]

Two weeks later Adenauer asked Acheson, in Paris, for an assurance that the Western powers would not seek an agreement with the Soviet Union at Germany's expense.[25] In England Churchill reassured him 'We will not betray you'.[26] Adenauer had raised the question of the Polish-German frontier. Churchill told him that in 1945 the British and Americans had thought of the wrong Neisse and Churchill promised that that would be part of any future agreement. Diplomatically, Adenauer promised not to talk about it publicly and to wait until the time was 'ripe'.[27] Fortunately, Churchill's initiatives faded in 1952.

It was different after Stalin's death on 5 March 1953. Churchill again put the idea of a summit to President Eisenhower on 11 March. He stuck to it despite all objections. On 21 April he told Eisenhower: 'In my opinion the best would be that the three victorious powers, who separated at

Potsdam in 1945, should come together again'. He even suggested he might go to Moscow alone; Eisenhower and his advisers reacted with cold hostility. Until Churchill spoke to the Commons on 11 May, Adenauer, whose personal political future as well as that of his country was intimately involved, seems not to have known what was happening. Blankenhorn recommended to Chancellor Adenauer that he should not criticise this speech: that could be left to the Americans. The conversations between Adenauer and Churchill were undramatic. But Blankenhorn made clear to Sir Frank Roberts, British Ambassador in Bonn,

> that the Chancellor had been more disturbed by the Prime Minister's speech than his public comments on it would suggest . . . the Prime Minister's speech had of course been seized upon by the Socialist opposition in Germany who were now arguing very strongly that they had the high authority of Sir Winston Churchill behind the policy they had always favoured of delaying the association of the Federal Republic with the West until after four-power talks had taken place and an attempt made to achieve German unity.[28]

When Adenauer talked to Churchill he reminded him of his promise in December 1951 that 'England will never make any arrangements behind Germany's back'. Churchill repeated his pledge; Adenauer trusted him. In 1966 he wrote in his memoirs 'I came back to Bonn from London with the certainty that England would not negotiate over Germany's head'.[29] His trust is shown again in his letter to his daughter, Ria Reiners, in June 1953.

> I still worry about France. It will become the sick man of Europe. With England I get along very well and I do not believe that any disturbances are to be expected from London.[30]

Perhaps Adenauer was naive. Sir Pierson Dixon wrote to his Permanent Under-Secretary Sir William Strang:

> I think I should record that in the course of a general conversation on 16 May the Prime Minister said that he had not closed his mind to the possibility of a unified and neutralised Germany. The Prime Minister made this remark in the context of a possible high-level discussion with the Russians, and his meaning, I think, was that it might be desirable to agree to such a solution for Germany as part of a settlement with the Russians.

Strang commented 'The Prime Minister let drop a similar remark to the Minister of State and myself yesterday. He said that he would be willing to consider the unification and neutralisation of Germany if the Germans wished, but only if they wished for this'.[31] Thus Churchill apparently sometimes hoped to persuade Adenauer to reverse his policies.

Frank Roberts set out the objections in a paper written in the same month entitled 'A Unified, *Neutralised* Germany'. It would 'mean a fundamental change in allied policy pursued since 1947. It would in effect be a return to Potsdam'. It would break allied promises and give up the common objective of a closer association of West Germany 'and eventually of a reunited Germany' with the Western world

> and more especially with the Six-Power communities in Western Europe. Dr Adenauer and his Government are entirely dedicated to such a policy. Any change to the opposite policy of Four-Power unity to maintain a unified, neutralised Germany (in subjection) would certainly mean the fall of Dr Adenauer and probably the emergence from the German elections this autumn of at first no doubt a weak neutralist and Socialist government, followed sooner or later by a swing to extreme nationalism with a view to a deal with the Soviet Union. A neutralised Germany must either be disarmed or Germany must be given a national army . . . A reunited Germany with a national army would sooner or later be tempted to use its economic and military power as a bargaining factor between East and West. As the Russians would have Germany's former Eastern territories to offer and the West would have nothing, except perhaps the Saar, such a Germany would inevitably become associated with the Soviet Bloc . . . A disarmed Germany would be so weak that, American troops having departed, she would be at the mercy of the most powerful, ruthless and determined power in Europe, i.e. the Soviet Union. We should thus have created by our own action the most deadly danger to our own security and to that of the world.

A forward strategy of setting obstacles to the Red Army to the east would become impossible for NATO. This could mean an early withdrawal of American troops. Then 'NATO would no longer be an effective shield for Western Europe and the United Kingdom. We should then be dependent for our security upon Soviet goodwill'. 'The building-up of a United Europe, whether of the Fifteen or the Six . . .' which provides 'the only means of ending the Franco-German feud' would end, because 'the neutralisation of Germany would mean the withdrawal of Germany from the Council of Europe, from the Coal and Steel Community, from the European Defence Community and from the projected European Political Community. This would mean the collapse of all these bodies and sooner or later a return to German nationalism and a revival of the German quarrel with France and Western Europe'. Like Chamberlain – this is how a leading article and a cartoonist of the German paper *Die Welt* saw it – 'the old Churchill' longs for 'peace in our time'. Even if an armistice might be possible in Europe for an unspecified period, the article points out, the necessary sacrifices would be made 'mainly at German expense' The objections Adenauer had always put forward against the concept of neutralisation are the same as those fears put forward by Sir Frank Roberts. The Chancellor emphasised above all that it would be the end of another attempt to build a liberal democracy in Germany .[32]

The unease created by Churchill's search for peace was reduced by his stroke on 23 June. Adenauer throughout avoided direct criticism of Churchill, but instructed Blankenhorn to tell the Foreign Office that he was 'scared stiff by the Prime Minister's policies'.[33]

Above all, Adenauer tried to check Churchill's vagaries through the Americans.[34] Eden and Salisbury in London opposed Churchill, but Eisenhower and Dulles most effectively checked his initiative. It created one of the most difficult situations for Adenauer in his 14 years as West German Chancellor. He never harboured a grudge against Churchill and probably blamed his conduct on bad health. However, these attitudes, on the part of someone he admired and respected, compelled Adenauer to rely on the USA. They would understand the German position. 'Churchill does not have this understanding', he told the CDU party executive on 15 July 1953, and he concluded:

France does not understand our position either. Only the US have shown this understanding. For this reason, I believe that, for our own sake, our place is next to the US. We need the closest possible relationship with the US. It is the only way to bring safety to Europe, a Europe, I most emphatically repeat, that is still in the greatest danger.[35]

14

Churchill and the Defence of the West, 1951–55

Wolfgang Krieger

In the late 1950s Denis Healey, a sharp but not impartial observer, wrote that Winston Churchill '. . . always believed that Western Europe's immunity depended on the American atomic umbrella. More than the Labour leaders, he saw NATO as a political instrument for tying SAC [US Strategic Air Command] to automatic retaliation if Europe were attacked, rather than as a military instrument for the defence of Europe if the deterrent failed'.[1] Many historians agree and portray post-1945 European security policy as strongly focused on the political rather than the military side of the story. In this way the political relations between the Western powers are given more prominence than the Western alliance's military efforts to balance the Soviet military threat and to prepare for a defensive war.[2]

How is this emphasis to be explained? And how has it shaped our view of Churchill's policies on Western security? After 'the long peace', the urgent danger of a third world war in the 1950s and 1960s seems remote, even in retrospect, although such a contingency was then taken seriously by many military people as well as by some politicians and by large sections of the general public. Today Churchill's name is frequently invoked for new purposes. Among them are the efforts to construct 'a new European security architecture' and to overcome the division between the former Communist bloc countries and what is now called the European Union. All too often Churchill's support for a united Europe is brought into the argument. His Zurich speech of September 1946 is quoted by those who wish to see Britain committed to an integrated 'Europe'. In historical terms, British policies on Western integration seem to have been contradictory because on the one hand Britain stayed out of the economic-political side of European integration for two decades and became a 'difficult' member thereafter (in the eyes of some, at least), while on the other hand she has always been regarded as a staunch supporter of NATO and particularly of a large role for the United States within it. On the latter point appropriate Churchill quotations are particularly easy to find.

The availability of certain types of documents has biased research on the history of the Western alliance towards Western political interaction. Most of the documents available in Western archives concern this side of the story while military files are often withheld by the authorities beyond the 30-year rule. While much can be discovered in Canadian and US archives, other NATO countries and of course NATO itself keep their archives more or less tightly closed. Most intelligence records are still not available, including assessments of Soviet military capabilities, Western intelligence-gathering and so on. Finally, despite frequent newspaper 'revelations' about the Soviet side, most of the Eastern archives are still tightly held, too. However, a fairly clear picture can be drawn of Winston Churchill's policies on Western defence and their wider context. The starting point is his Zurich speech of 19 September 1946, exactly because it has become so familiar. It would be wrong to read into it a call for European integration in the sense which became predominant some years later, under the spell of the Rome treaties of 1957 and today's European Union.[3] Churchill had in mind above all a lasting reconciliation between France and Germany. He wanted an end to struggles to dominate one other and to quarrels over the share of the Carolingian lands they had inherited. That was what he said again and again, with a clear message that France should henceforth concentrate her energies on her own reconstruction and on Western Europe rather than seeking to return to the kind of global status which, in Churchill's eyes, only Britain, the United States and the Soviet Union could rightfully claim.

His familiar image of the three circles in which Britain's foreign relations were placed – Europe, the Commonwealth and the Atlantic hemisphere – indicates clearly that he had in mind a loosely configured Europe which consisted of nation states which were to be 'united' in purpose rather than a Europe tied together in any formal constitutional ways along the lines of a federal superstate. This was only logical, as seen from a wider historical perspective, because Britain could hardly play her traditional role of balancing the powers of continental Europe if she entered into any tight, long-term commitments with certain European nations or groupings. It was the special circumstances of the overbearing Soviet military threat which led Churchill to accept such an alliance as NATO became under his second premiership. In fact there are indications that he thought of that arrangement as temporary. While it is difficult to tell how much faith he actually had in NATO's temporary nature, his overall view of global affairs clearly led him to believe that the United States would not keep large military forces stationed in Europe for a long time and that the Soviet leaders might agree to a general European settlement in the not too distant future.

From Churchill's writings, speeches and private remarks during this period, we can identify four basic beliefs which formed the background to his policies on Western security issues. The Empire was uppermost in his mind. This is a point which tends to be forgotten when looking at things from a present-day perspective. But the Empire was the symbol of Britain's global role which distinguished it from European powers of comparable population such as Germany, France, Italy and Spain. In Churchill's view the Empire's legitimacy had been enhanced rather than diminished by the Second World War. The practical effect of this imperial priority was momentous. Among other things it kept Britain from entering into close economic integration along the lines of the Schuman Plan. Thus Britain refused to accept the notion promoted by what became the Europe of the Six, that the European co-operation brought about by the Marshall Plan should form the basis of permanent integration. As it happened, Britain's imperial economic ties, both in investment and in trade, reached their all-time peak only in the 1950s: about 65 per cent of her overseas investment and more than half of British trade.[4]

Churchill's second fundamental belief was in the uniqueness of British relations with the United States. With respect to the post-1945 period, as distinct from the war, it cannot be too strongly emphasised that no American president ever believed in it in the way Churchill and several of his successors did. Yet, for a variety of reasons, most US presidents found it useful to pretend. To Churchill's great surprise, his old wartime associate, Dwight D Eisenhower, did not share this belief although no president had ever known Europe better. This is even true in the nuclear field, where no president was to be more strongly in favour of sharing nuclear weapons with America's European allies. To make things worse for the British, this American disbelief in the special relationship was not a sign of lack of interest in European affairs as such. Indeed most Washington policy-makers who took a keen interest in Europe wished to see an integrated Europe in which Britain played a full part, whereas the British proponents of the special relationship – Churchill above all – argued they could be most helpful to the Americans if they stayed outside 'Europe'.

Third we need to realise that Churchill believed that a final European settlement, perhaps as grandiose as that of the Vienna Congress, could and should be pursued. While Stalin was alive, Churchill argued he had some kind of special magic if only a way could be found for the two to get together. His idea was to pick up where things had been left at Potsdam in the summer of 1945. He had boundless faith in his summit skills, and as an example he often quoted his 'percentage agreement' with Stalin in October 1944. Although it is not clear what concessions he might have been willing to make in the 1950s to the USSR, the idea must have crossed his mind. At a dinner with Jean Monnet and other French leaders, on 10 September 1951, he said he would 'give the Russians access to warm waters by instituting international control of the exits of the Baltic and the Dardanelles'.[5] Here, too, it is important to note the transitory nature Churchill attributed to both the UN and NATO. He still had not completely given up his notion of three zones of influence, each headed by what he acknowledged as truly great powers – i.e., the permanent members of the UN Security Council minus France and China. At the end of the war, under American pressure, this concept of separate spheres had been scrapped in favour of a one-world security area under the UN Charter, in which the possibility of regional arrangements such as NATO was, however, explicitly encouraged. But Churchill had not fully reconciled himself to this single framework and he regarded the Soviet Union as a legitimate great power for whose benefit the world map of security arrangements might well be redrawn, provided the Soviets were willing to yield at least some control over some of their wartime and post-war gains.

It was this readiness on Churchill's part for a general settlement that neither Washington nor the other West Europeans were prepared to share. Sharp differences arose between the Western powers on that account, but even more significantly, the fear of a great power sell-out to the Soviets stuck in the minds of many leaders, particularly the Germans and others who were geographically close to the Iron Curtain. In a larger historical perspective, the Soviet threat always was both a unifying and a dividing factor in Western security. But Churchill's notion of a grand reshuffling of cards, a notion which was incidentally to remain active in the minds of his two successors, Eden and Macmillan, was particularly divisive to the Western camp. Amazingly, as in the Marshall Plan in the summer of 1947, the Kremlin did relatively little to exploit this situation.

Finally, in Churchill's basic foreign policy creed, there was the conviction that the chief unit in all international relations was the nation state. He was not, however, a champion of the right to national self-determination for each and every national or ethnic group. In a conversation in December 1940 he spoke of Europe's five great powers: England, France,

Italy, Spain and Prussia (*sic!*). They would be joined by four confedera-
tions – Northern, Middle European, Danubian and Balkan – to make up
a European security system in the future.[6] The idea of a confederation in
south-eastern Europe went back to his search after 1918 for a structure
which could replace the collapsed Habsburg empire. Another aspect of it
was his, temporary, desire for a territorial rearrangement of Germany
along pre-Bismarckian lines. But the central point in the present context is
Churchill's apparent notion that nation states without the weight of the
great powers should organise themselves into a confederation of some
sort. Thus his belief in the European nation state was not unqualified
even before the onset of the Soviet threat and the consequent need for a
new balance with the help of American military forces deployed on
European soil.

It seems likely therefore that his idea of a United Europe was a combination of three elements: first, a unity of purpose, including a system of
interstate arbitration to replace the old rivalries which had led to the disaster of 1914; secondly, the reconciliation of France and Germany which
would put France in charge of the detailed management of Germany for
the benefit of all Europeans, while the general management would of
course be left to the higher levels of the world order; and, thirdly, a need
to organise the smaller European states and ethnic groupings into one or
more federal structures.

As nearly always with politicians, such beliefs or even convictions must
not be taken too literally. Churchill often got carried away by his historical imagination and his love of grandiose phraseology. There is no strict
consistency in his notions of 'Europe' and there is no telling how much he
might have been willing to join in European integration if the circumstances and personalities he was dealing with had been different. It can be
shown, however, that his policies on Western security were more coherent
and more concrete. One of them was his advocacy of German rearmament, the subject which was to dominate the internal Western debates for
the four years of Churchill's second premiership.[7] In his Zurich speech and
on subsequent occasions he urged the continental Europeans to accept
Germany back into the family of nations. As he put it: 'There can be no
revival of Europe without a spiritually great France and a spiritually great
Germany'.[8] In parliamentary speeches on 16 and 28 March 1950, he
explicitly demanded a German defence contribution.[9] The day after the
North Korean attack, Churchill spoke to the House of Commons of the
need to speed up that process and to involve Britain more directly because
France was too weak to shoulder the burden alone.[10] Seven weeks later, on
11 August 1950, he addressed the Assembly of the Council of Europe,

making his famous proposal for a 'European army' to which Germany should be invited to contribute. It was this move which led Chancellor Adenauer to address formally the three Western victorious powers proposing a German defence contribution.

'The only alternative', as Churchill wrote to President Truman, was 'a kind of neutrality arrangement by Germany, France and the smaller countries with the Soviets'. In that letter he also added a point not publicly made at Strasbourg, which concerned the need to extend American, and later presumably NATO's, nuclear deterrence, in order to bring all member states of the European army, including Germany, under the Western umbrella.[11] In a private outline of the European army scheme Churchill spelt out further details. National components would be supplied at the division level, not below, as the soon-to-be-announced French plan by Premier Pleven envisaged. '. . . the military organization would follow the model of SHAEF. It would seem that about 60 divisions should be formed and stationed in Europe with another 40 earmarked as reinforcements . . .' A unified military command would operate under 'a civilian Defence Chief responsible to the existing national governments acting together and/or through the United Nations . . .'[12]

Roughly similar figures would eventually reappear in NATO's Lisbon force goals of 1952. Although Churchill purposely refrained from committing himself precisely, the civilian defence chief was presumably conceived along the lines of the future NATO Secretary General rather than the defence minister of the European Defence Community (EDC) plan. He did, however, drive home two points again and again. First, Britain could not become part of such a European army. And second, '. . . no effective defence of Europe was possible without the armed strength of Germany', as he told the House of Commons on 14 December 1950.[13] That demand was made just at the moment when the Labour government, amid great pains, decided in favour of German rearmament and when the arrival of General Eisenhower as NATO's commander-in-chief began to transform the original North Atlantic Treaty of April 1949 into a military pact with its own forces, command structures and supporting organisations.[14]

As to the plan put forward by French Premier René Pleven, Churchill disagreed particularly with the idea that German rearmament could only be made acceptable if national military forces were to be more or less abolished by keeping national military units well below the level of the division. As a logical by-product the French national army would also be sacrificed. But in Churchill's view, a 'European army which did not preserve national contingents would have no fighting spirit'.[15] A more colourful description of how Churchill often ridiculed the EDC proposal is reported in Dean Acheson's memoirs: Churchill '. . . pictured a bewildered French drill sergeant sweating over a platoon made up of a few Greeks, Italians, Germans, Turks and Dutchmen, all in utter confusion over the simplest orders'.[16] Significantly, Churchill only made this type of argument in private rather than publicly. On 6 December 1951, a few weeks after becoming Prime Minister, he told Parliament that Chancellor Adenauer, during his first visit to London, had promised that the Germans would not press for a national army. Yet in Cabinet, five days later, he approvingly quoted Field Marshal Montgomery's suggestion that a European army should be made up of units which retained their national character and were 'integrated under one United Nations Command'.[17]

How the UN was to figure in an arrangement which was meant to come under NATO command is not entirely clear, given that the Soviets rather than some arbitrary international lawbreaker were the reason for having such an army in the first place. At any rate, it is blatantly obvious that Churchill did not think much of the French-dominated EDC scheme. There remains only the question, why he did not seek more actively to topple it, and here the answer is presumably that the Americans were not prepared to put pressure on France along Churchill's lines. What can be documented is Churchill's cautious criticism of the EDC during his first visit to the Truman White House as Prime Minister in January 1952. He called it 'the only method of integrating German forces in the defence of Western Europe ...' His fear was that 'the "sacrifice of nationality" . . . would damage the loyalty of the soldiers'.[18]

In fact, his objections were much broader. Already the Attlee government had disagreed with the way in which the Pleven plan made German rearmament a vehicle for European integration French-style – i.e., in parallel with the European Coal and Steel Community (ECSC) which would exclude Britain both in Europe and at the NATO level. Of course Jean Monnet, the author of both plans, emphasised that the linkage between them served to make it impossible for Germany to use rearmament as leverage against the economic controls in the ECSC structure.[19] But in practice, the exclusion of Britain from major aspects of allied policy *vis-à-vis* Germany was just as real. Germany would not be a NATO member and NATO would only deal with the European army at a relatively superficial level, concerned only with organisation, equipment and training. No wonder the British Defence Secretary, Emmanuel Shinwell, called the French plan 'disgusting and nauseous, military folly and political madness'.[20] Put simply, the task appeared to be: how can a rearmed Germany be locked into a cage without also imprisoning Britain?

During and after the NATO Council meeting in Rome in late November 1951, the British would only promise 'to co-operate to the maximum degree possible' with the European army. Secretary of State Dean Acheson put considerable pressure on the British not to hold up the deliberations on the EDC but to think in concrete terms how such a co-operation could work.[21] On 18 December 1951, after conferring with the French government in Paris, Churchill issued a communiqué expressing British support for the EDC and affirmed that Britain saw no prospect of joining. The explanation given to his Cabinet at home was that he wished to 'forestall any further suggestion that the delay in securing agreement to the creation of a European army was due to the unhelpful attitude of the United Kingdom government'.[22] In other words, he refused to accept any blame in case the EDC were to fail which, quite clearly, he hoped it would. Incidentally, there seems to have been a difference of opinion between Churchill and his Foreign Secretary, Anthony Eden, on that point. While Eden hoped that the EDC would succeed because it would forestall the need to accept Germany into NATO and to accept a German 'national army', the Prime Minister told his Cabinet that 'he would not be unduly disturbed if the present plans for a European Defence Community were not carried into effect'.[23]

The most difficult, and for Churchill perhaps the most disappointing, results of the EDC negotiations was the response of the United States. The Americans accepted the French plan practically wholesale. They sent Eisenhower as NATO's Supreme Commander and they massively reinforced their military presence in Europe, without ever using any of these moves as leverage on France to make German rearmament a swift reality rather than a subject of endless negotiations. Washington fulfilled its side of the bargain and allowed France to put off German rearmament indefinitely. This policy had considerably weakened the British position before Churchill came into office. Arguably it weakened it after Churchill's return to office because Churchill's strongly pro-American stance made it unnecessary for Washington to make concessions on any of those issues.

A rare incident when the Americans refused to follow the French lead occurred shortly before the NATO Council meeting in Lisbon at the end of February 1952. This was the gathering at which NATO's force goals, including the German defence contribution, were to be formally approved. At issue was a resolution passed in the French parliament which demanded a joint British–American guarantee to provide for the eventuality of an EDC signatory breaking out of its membership obligations. Needless to say it was Germany which was on the parliament's mind. The document envisaged would have been roughly similar to the 1919 British–American guarantee treaty which had come to naught because the US Senate refused to ratify it. Surprisingly, in early 1952 Churchill declared himself in favour of such a guarantee while the Americans refused to go beyond their existing commitments and declarations of support for the EDC. Eventually public language was found to soothe the French parliament.[24] What remains unclear is the degree of sincerity on the part of the British. How could they honestly hold Germany or anyone to a 50-year membership guarantee in a body which they themselves thought ill-conceived and given that NATO allowed its signatories to withdraw after 20 years?

Perhaps Churchill hoped Eisenhower would be helpful to Britain's position on the EDC. Indeed there were some grounds to expect such help, for at least some of the American military leadership were as sceptical of the EDC as the British. In early 1953, when Churchill came to see Eisenhower before he was sworn into office as President, the American military leadership, notably Omar Bradley, considered alternative policies of obtaining a German defence contribution.[25] But Eisenhower and Dulles blocked them. Both were enthusiastic supporters of European integration, including France's EDC policy.[26] Churchill never seems to have admitted to himself that there was no common ground with Eisenhower on those issues. Right from the start of his conferences with Eisenhower it is clear from the transcripts how deep was the gap was between them on European questions. At times the Prime Minister found it convenient to believe that the President was a mere mouthpiece of his foreign minister. Churchill's hatred of Dulles may well have been aggravated by the latter's views on West European matters.[27] It is therefore ironic that finally it was to be not the Americans but a French parliamentary revolt against the EDC which got Britain out of her corner.

Churchill's quiet hope for a failure of the EDC by no means faded with the actual signing of the treaty on 27 May 1952. He may have calculated that the unpopular provisions for German rearmament could well prevent ratification on the part of at least some of the signatory states. But there was another prospect which excited him even more: the possibility of a grand European settlement in a summit meeting of the wartime 'big three'. If the summit succeeded the EDC could very well become superfluous. In August 1950, Malcolm Muggeridge observed about Churchill: 'He obviously still has a great affection for Stalin'.[28] 'Affection' may have been the wrong word, but Churchill certainly seems to have believed in his own ability to convince Stalin of the benefits of a grand post-war peace settlement. On 14 December in his speech in support of German rearmament, he told the House of Commons: 'I am strongly in favour of every effort made by every means, to secure a fair and reasonable settlement with

Russia.' Clearly, he regarded German rearmament as a bargaining chip to that end. But he also linked it to the American nuclear deterrent, which he called 'at the present time almost our sole defence', and which he proclaimed the key to any negotiations with the Soviet Union. 'Its potential use is the only lever by which we can hope to obtain reasonable consideration in an attempt to make a peaceful settlement with Russia.'[29]

An American-led peace based on nuclear deterrence, was this what Churchill had in mind? Or did he expect that Britain could match the United States and the Soviet Union in terms of nuclear weapons? One clue might be his fear

> that the USA could not be counted upon to continue indefinitely with their present scale of rearmament and aid to Europe. In two or three years they would insist on having a show-down, and Russia would then have to withdraw from her present forward positions in Poland and Czechoslovakia, or there would be war.[30]

Would Washington risk such a threat of war against a nuclear-armed Moscow and on the basis of a still militarily weak Western Europe? There is a danger of taking Churchill's remarks too literally. The first statement was made in Parliament with the clear intention of embarrassing the left wing of the still governing Labour Party, while the second one is taken from his talks with French leaders just after the outbreak of the Korean War.

In June 1952, while working with his trusted helpers on the last volume of his Second World War memoirs, he said '. . . if Eisenhower were elected President, he would have another shot at making peace by means of a meeting of the Big Three. For that alone it would perhaps be worth remaining in office'.[31] Here is another confirmation of his hope for comradeship with Eisenhower, his wish to exclude France and others and his repeated claim, over the next three years, that only he personally could conduct such negotiations! In early January 1953, before Eisenhower was sworn into office, Churchill paid him a visit to discuss such an initiative. As it turned out the new President was interested, but said he might prefer to meet Stalin first on a one-to-one basis, which was not a pleasing thought for Churchill.[32] Stalin's death on 5 March 1953 seemed to open up new hopes for a European realignment. Now Churchill wished to exploit those hopes for himself rather than leaving the initiative to the Americans. On 11 March 1953, he proposed a summit. There followed a curious exchange of messages in which Eisenhower pleaded caution while Churchill seems to have been apprehensive lest Washington attempt to freeze him out. To his Cabinet he reiterated that a meeting of the great powers 'should be limited to the Soviet Union, the United States and the United Kingdom, who could take up the discussion at the point at which it had been left at the end of the Potsdam Conference in 1945'.[33]

Eisenhower's 'chance for peace' speech of 16 April 1953, which linked better East-West relations to a list of concrete points for discussion, was followed by Churchill's public offer for negotiations, made in the House of Commons on 11 May 1953.[34] In a lengthy reference to the Locarno Treaty of 1925, Churchill suggested: 'Russia has a right to be assured that . . . the terrible events of the Hitler invasion will never be repeated, and that Poland will remain a friendly Power and a buffer, though not, I trust, a puppet State'. He then went on to propose a conference 'confined to the smallest number of Powers and persons possible' which 'should meet with a measure of informality and a still greater measure of privacy and seclusion'. Apart from this dubious reference to Poland, one could hardly be surprised that Western leaders, particularly in Paris and Bonn, were shocked. 'It probably cost us the EDC in France', Eden noted in his diary. Upon the urging of Eisenhower, Churchill had to admit France into that 'smallest number of powers' if such a conference ever were to materialise.[35]

The following month, the uprising in East Germany and his stroke kept Churchill from pursuing his initiative, yet he frequently came back to it in private conversations. He considered Moscow's reactions in East Germany 'surprisingly patient', talked about 'a real UNO with Russia working with the rest for the good of Europe' and the abolition of nuclear weapons. Indeed the 'hope of attending a Four Power Conference in, say, September' – France was now accepted by him – became strong medicine for his physical recovery. From his sick bed he fought the idea of a foreign ministers' conference to precede such a summit. And he spoke out strongly against any objections which the sceptical Eisenhower might have against his holding a separate meeting with Malenkov. He even called Eisenhower 'weak and stupid' and expressed his regret that the Democrat Stevenson had not become President instead.[36] After Churchill recovered he made the possibility of a summit a central argument for staying on as Prime Minister. Eden, who was strongly opposed to Churchill's summit, would have to wait his turn for another two years.

To Churchill's disappointment, the British summit proposal did not go well. The new Soviet leadership was unhelpful, demanding among other things that Communist China be included, which they knew was totally unacceptable to Washington. At the December 1953 Bermuda meeting of the British, the French and the Americans, Eisenhower did his best to support the French on the EDC and to throw cold water on the summit idea.

The final communiqué did not even mention the Locarno proposal or make any friendly noises in the direction of Moscow. From an American point of view, the Korean armistice of July had removed the most important urge for a summit. Eisenhower hoped to strengthen NATO first, particularly by seeing the EDC ratified. Moreover he prepared his 'atoms for peace' initiative in which he sought to open new avenues for diplomacy and trade which were very different in style and substance from the old follow-up to Potsdam idea.[37] In February 1954 the Berlin conference of the foreign ministers showed that the Soviets were hardly eager to solve even the smaller items of a grand European settlement. At a further meeting with Eisenhower in July 1954, Churchill came back again to his idea of getting together with the Soviet leadership and received the same cold shower. Finally, at a Cabinet meeting on 26 July 1954, he buried his proposal.[38] The eventual summit at Geneva a year later was to take place, without Britain, three months after Churchill handed over the premiership to Eden.

As Churchill's hopes for a summit soured, two aspects of Western security became prominent. One was the struggle over EDC ratification and related issues of NATO policy. The other was nuclear diplomacy and the impact of the H-bomb, for the H-bomb had a fundamental effect on the way in which he came to see post-war international relations. Whether or not Churchill may have hoped for a collapse of the EDC, the Eisenhower administration did everything it could to keep the EDC alive and Churchill's own heavy emphasis on the closest possible relations with Washington left him no choice but to go along with them, however reluctantly. But he would not yield easily. During the Bermuda conference in December 1953, he told the French that he would not support them in their effort to keep the Saar territory under French control.[39] In private conversation with Eisenhower Churchill suggested accepting Germany directly into NATO if France failed to ratify the EDC treaty. Both statements were a clear indication that he might associate himself more closely with Chancellor Adenauer who had won a remarkable election victory in September and whom he increasingly trusted. Needless to say, the Germans would have been only too happy to get help from London.[40] But Eisenhower refused to discuss any such contingencies.[41]

In plenary session at the Bermuda conference, Churchill used strong language against the French: 'Three years had been completely wasted in getting what was absolutely necessary for a good strong German army . . . We could not go on for three more years without a German army.' He threatened 'to make a new version of NATO achieving the same hope as EDC, with controls over the German army by the NATO organisation so as to make it quite clear that this army could not be used against France or to precipitate war to regain the Eastern lost territories'.[42] He made the same point again later in the discussions, this time invoking the fear that the USA might withdraw its forces from Europe which, in turn, would force the British to withdraw from the continent as well. In the next sentence, however, he admitted indirectly how little leverage Britain had on this issue: 'If US troops were withdrawn from France, it would expose Britain to mortal danger.'[43] No doubt this was a hidden reference to France's defeat in 1940. But Eisenhower hit back by telling the British that he disagreed on the need to bring Germany into NATO and that if the EDC were obstructed the United States might fall back on a strategy of peripheral defence.[44] Whatever the exact meaning of this term might have been, the message to Churchill was clearly that the United States was backing France up to the hilt.

Given this 'correlation of forces' at the negotiating table, France even managed to get a number of concessions from the British. Eden suggested to the Cabinet that an assurance should be given to Paris regarding the continued deployment of British forces on the continent. Further he proposed that a British armoured division might be 'under command of an EDC corps, if the Supreme Allied Commander, Europe, agreed on operational grounds, and [kept] there as long as he wanted'.[45] Among the further concessions offered was an assurance that France would remain a member of the NATO Standing Group despite the fact that she was scheduled to merge into the EDC structures. More and more the French government demanded what became a whole series of assurances from the Americans and British and from the Germans before they were willing to submit the EDC treaty to the French parliament. At the same time Paris could not even give a fixed date for a vote on EDC ratification. There was only one point, in late June 1954, where a response to a possible non-ratification was agreed between the British and the Americans. It envisaged an end to the linkage between the EDC and the transfer of sovereignty to the Federal Republic of Germany.

In a follow-up telegram to Dulles on 19 August Churchill again proposed 'some variant of NATO' and in a memorandum to his defence minister, Lord Alexander, he added that such a NATO might have to be one without France.[46] Alexander, however, vehemently opposed such a proposal because Britain would lose the Channel ports, a whole range of supply assets, the protection of the American air forces stationed on the continent, a wide range of Mediterranean facilities, and of course the weight of the French armed forces which could not be replaced by either the British or the Americans or, indeed, the Germans.[47] On 23 August

1954, Churchill received the French premier at Chartwell. He assured him that he continued to support the EDC but was considering a NATO solution as a second-best choice. He also mentioned the possibility of an 'empty chair' being reserved for France and, worst of all, a withdrawal of British and American forces from the continent to positions of a 'peripheral defence'. Mendès-France indicated a willingness to bestow sovereignty on Western Germany in a separate act but complained that he had not been fully informed of the British-American talks on that issue. His response to the NATO option was vague, but it led Churchill to telegraph Dulles that his French opposite number 'was much keener about NATO' than expected. He concluded that Mendès-France was pessimistic about finding a majority for the EDC in the French parliament.[48]

After the EDC was defeated in the French parliamentary vote, Churchill told his Cabinet that the decision 'had put the German government into a strong tactical position *vis-à-vis* Germany's Western Allies'. To tone down Bonn's advantage he sent a message to Adenauer asking him not to demand a higher level of German military forces in the forthcoming negotiations. He added: 'This might well be expressed in terms in no way derogating from the equal and honourable status of the German Federal Republic.'[49] He then sent Eden on a tour around the chief European NATO capitals plus Bonn and Rome, the latter to discuss Eden's proposal for bringing both into a modified Brussels Pact. The eventual NATO-cum-Western Union solution was largely worked out by Eden. As an inveterate opponent of the EDC, Churchill felt vindicated. He telegraphed to Eisenhower: 'I do not blame the French for rejecting EDC but only for inventing it. Their harshness to Adenauer in wasting three years of his life and much of his power is a tragedy.'[50] Little did the Prime Minister appreciate, or could he know at the time, that Bonn had many a reason to be pleased with this outcome and of course that Adenauer would carry on in office for another nine years.

In part the French rejection of EDC was associated with resentment towards Britain. Many in France attributed the French defeat in Indochina to the lack of help from the United States and Britain. There were suspicions of an Anglo-American nuclear partnership with the arrival of American nuclear weapons in Europe from early 1954. At heart was France's status within the alliance which was expected to be critically altered by the envisaged nuclearisation of NATO. In March 1954 Churchill had informed Parliament about the basing right related to US nuclear weapons which he had given to the Americans two months earlier.[51] In reaction the French government wanted to be sure to be on the same footing with the British and to be able to offer bases in France and in French North Africa for the same purpose. Simultaneously, however, a national French nuclear force was also discussed. Either way, the EDC more and more came to be considered as an obstacle, though French nuclear thinking throughout most of the 1950s was carried on with an alliance context in mind.[52] At any rate it was in the summer of 1954 that the French military leadership proposed to accomplish German rearmament by modifying the Brussels Treaty.[53] This solution would leave France eventually to play a role as a nuclear weapons state within the alliance and would put Germany at a safe distance from France in terms of NATO membership status.

Next to the EDC débâcle and Churchill's interest in a grand European settlement via summit diplomacy with the Soviets, his policies and views with respect to nuclear weapons deserve particular attention.[54] To a large extent the issue was of course an aspect of British–American relations and of the conflict with the Soviets. After the end of the war Churchill had hoped to make his Quebec agreement of 19 September 1944 a key platform from which to tackle the broad structures of international security. This is what he told Attlee who sought his advice in October 1945:

> I should greatly regret . . . if we pressed them [the Americans] to melt our dual agreement down into a general international arrangement consisting, I fear, of pious empty phrases and undertakings which will not be carried out.[55]

This is not to say Churchill rejected international control out of hand, but he certainly was aware how such a step would dissolve the special nuclear relationship. At Fulton in March 1946 he spoke out against entrusting 'the secret know-how or experience of the atomic bomb . . . to the world organisation [the UN] while it is still in its infancy'.[56] In August 1946, the American MacMahon Act put an end to the nuclear partnership, which Churchill deeply regretted. But he still hoped that something positive would come from the American initiative for international nuclear controls in the UN. After all, the US delegation was headed by his old friend Bernard Baruch.

Churchill often spoke about a 'breathing space' which existed before the Soviets would have the bomb, too, which he considered likely within a few years. In September 1948, while the Berlin crisis was under way, he wrote to Eden that once the Soviets have the bomb 'nothing can stop the greatest of all world catastrophes'. In the next sentence, however, he pointed out the fast-growing strength of the US Strategic Air Command and that he had been informed that the Soviets were unlikely to have the bomb within a year's time.[57] Somehow he seems to have hoped the Soviets could be forced back behind their own borders during the interim when they did not have the bomb. On 3 December 1950, the day before he flew to Washington to discuss with Truman any possible use of atomic weapons in the Korean war, Attlee explained to Churchill the circumstances under which the Quebec agreement had been allowed to lapse. Among the reasons was the US Congress's refusal to grant the President the kinds of powers over nuclear matters which the agreement had encompassed. A *modus vivendi* understanding had been made in January 1948 to allow for the continued exchange of technical information and of raw materials.[58] Lord Cherwell informed him along the same lines but Churchill's immediate response is not recorded. In February he did, however, ask President Truman to publish the original agreement and to agree 'that the atomic bomb shall not be used from British bases without our prior consent'.[59] Truman asked not to be embarrassed in this way and remained silent on the point of 'prior consent'.

Four years later, in January 1955, Churchill still complained to President Eisenhower that the West would be in a stronger position had it not been for the scrapping of the Quebec agreement.[60] But by that time the advent of the hydrogen bomb had dramatically changed the world – or so it seemed to Churchill. Apart from his awe at its vast destructive power, he made two observations about it when he first had a full briefing in March 1954 – i.e., after the second American H-bomb test. The first observation was that 'after a certain quantity had been produced on either side the factor of "over-taking", "superiority", etc. loses much of its meaning'. The other was: 'A powerful incentive to achieve surprise would be given to the weaker – what about Pearl Harbor?'[61] Both observations seemed to point in the same direction of giving a possible new advantage to Britain as much the smallest great power among the three.

On 5 April 1954, Churchill spoke in the House of Commons about the H-bomb. On that occasion, with Eisenhower's consent, he read out the text of the Quebec agreement, blaming the Attlee government for having lost the privilege of being told about the American nuclear weapons programme.[62] In July 1954 the Cabinet considered British H-bomb development. Churchill argued that '. . . we could not expect to maintain our influence as a world power unless we possessed the most up-to-date weapons'. The purpose was 'to prevent major war' and to have these weapons as 'the main deterrent'. The net additional cost, he assured his colleagues, 'would not be very substantial' because the H-bombs would be made in place of fission bombs already planned for. Interestingly, for all the differences Churchill saw between the two kinds of nuclear weapons, he now argued that from a moral standpoint there was no difference in producing one or the other or indeed in accepting the protection of the United States with the H-bomb deterrent. In addition the H-bomb would give Britain more influence with the Americans in case they were thinking of using that weapon irresponsibly, for example against China or preventively against the Soviet Union.[63] On 1 March 1955, Churchill told the House of Commons about the British H-bomb programme. His key argument was of the H-bomb as an equaliser between states with 'enormous spaces and scattered population', such as the Soviet Union, and a smaller country like Britain. The result was, in his view, 'an equality or near equality of vulnerability'. Then came his famous phrase that 'safety will be the sturdy shield of terror, and survival the twin brother of annihilation'.[64] A month later he resigned as Prime Minister.

Finally, we return to a basic question asked at the outset: how does the absence of many key military and intelligence records on the Western side and of most archival sources from the Eastern side shape our understanding of Churchill's policies with regard to Western security? The precise answer is of course impossible to know, but certain rough guesses may be permitted. It is clear, for example, that President Eisenhower pursued a more open policy with regard to nuclear co-operation. The new US Atomic Energy Act of 1954 and the subsequent British-American agreement of June 1955 are markers along this path. However, the precise substance, timing and usefulness of those exchanges is far from clear. The same is true for the follow-up of Churchill's request at the December 1953 Bermuda meeting for data on US nuclear bombs. This information would allow the British to configure some of their bombers to nuclear use before Britain had her own atomic bombs.[65] Another gap in our knowledge concerns the process by which the nuclearisation of NATO took place. Apparently the Eisenhower administration wished to integrate a good deal of the British-American relationship in nuclear matters into NATO channels. This process started in the autumn of 1953 with the American 'New Look' strategy and the 'New Approach' studies in NATO. Yet, without much fuller access to British military documents and to NATO archives, it is still difficult to trace those developments with any precision.[66]

In the field of intelligence, guesses are even harder to make though the CIA's new initiative to declassify groups of records for the early Cold War period may eventually give some indication about the information value and the character of the intelligence side of the 'special relationship'. A comparison between the historiography of the Second World War before and after the opening of the files on deciphering (ENIGMA, MAGIC, etc.) may or may not be appropriate. Some important work has been done or is under way, but it must be assumed that the picture is still very incomplete. Given Churchill's avid interest in intelligence matters during the war, it would be surprising indeed if he had not closely followed and used this tool during his second term as Prime Minister.[67]

Perhaps those hitherto unavailable documents will only confirm the present image we have of Churchill's Western security policies. But they may not, and it is well worthwhile to pursue the subject further as access to archives improves.

15

Churchill and the European Idea

MARTIN GILBERT

The theme of 'Churchill and Britain's Place in the World' and my topic, 'Churchill and the European Idea' were brought together by Churchill himself in a speech at Llandudno in 1948. It was there that he spoke, not of Europe alone, but of what he called the 'three great circles among the free nations and democracies', with Britain as a central and linking factor. The three circles were Britain and the Empire, the United States, and a United Europe.

Describing these as 'three interlinked circles', Churchill told his Conservative Party audience: 'You will see that we are the only country which has a great part in every one of them. We stand, in fact, at the very point of junction.' Standing at the 'centre of the seaways and perhaps of the airways also', Britain had the opportunity of joining the three circles together. Churchill hoped that she would 'rise to the occasion in the years that are to come'.[1]

What part did each of the three circles have in Churchill's mind and experience? As a young man he held high hopes of the beneficent nature of Britain and the British Empire. When he was in his seventies he was able to transfer those hopes to the British Commonwealth. First Empire and then Commonwealth were for him capable both of being benevolent and constructive entities in themselves, and of serving as an indispensable counterweight to the imperial ambitions of Russia, first under the Romanovs and then, since 1917, under what he called, in 1947, 'another family . . . much more powerful, and much more despotic'.[2]

For Churchill, India in the days of the British officers on the North-West Frontier, with whom he served in 1897, was the forerunner of 'the Light of Asia' which he encouraged his fellow Harrovian, Nehru, to lead, upholding, as Churchill wrote to Nehru in 1955, 'the freedom and dignity of the individual as the ideal rather than the Communist Party drill book'.[3]

Between 1897 and 1945, while fighting politically to maintain Britain's presence in India, Churchill was emphatic that British rule must not rest on force of arms. It was this conviction that underlay his strong parliamentary condemnation of General Dyer in 1920, after the Amritsar Massacre, which Churchill called 'a monstrous event', telling the House of Commons, whose Conservative majority was far from uniformly critical of General Dyer:

> Frightfulness is not a remedy known to the British pharmacopoeia . . . Our reign in India, or anywhere else, has never stood on the basis of physical force alone, and it would be fatal to the British Empire if we were to try to base ourselves only upon it.[4]

The material and moral welfare of the Indian people had been asserted by Churchill in myriad speeches in the early 1930s, not as rhetoric, but as a reality to be desired and achieved. Hence his advice to Gandhi, sent through G D Birla, when the India Bill, against which he had fought tooth and nail, was passed by Parliament:

> It is now on the Statute book . . . You have got immense powers . . . So make it a success . . . I do not care whether you are more or less loyal to Great Britain . . . Tell Mr Gandhi to use the powers that are offered and make the thing a success.[5]

The second of Churchill's 'three great circles' was the United States. His span of experience of that country, his mother's country, though she only lived there as a child, was unusual for any British politician. It began with his first eager encounter with New York in 1895 and culminated in his persistent efforts during his second premiership to persuade the United States to join Britain in seeking some form of accommodation, or at least amelioration, of relations with the Soviet Union. Churchill had many disagreements with the Americans over policy in virtually each decade of his public life, and some extreme disagreements, culminating in December 1940 when America's exceptionally tough position on Britain's war debt led him to telegraph to Roosevelt: 'It is not fitting that any nation should put itself wholly in the hands of another, least of all a nation which is fighting under increasingly severe conditions.'[6] Despite the disagreements, Churchill felt a bond with this largest of all the 'English-Speaking Peoples', as he termed them, devoted substantial sections of his history of that name to the story of the United States, and was often restrained, and urged others to be restrained, in their public criticisms at times of crisis.

His pro-American enthusiasms were real: at the turn of the century he suggested to his mother that her literary journal, in which British and American writers would appear, should be called *The Anglo-Saxon Review* and he devised a symbol for it, the British and American flags lying against each other. In 1933, at a dinner at Chartwell with Franklin Roosevelt's son James, he responded to a favourite parlour game about each participant's 'fondest wish' with the words: 'I wish to be Prime Minister and in close and daily communication by telephone with the President of the United States. There is nothing we could not do if we were together.' Then he called for a piece of paper on which he drew the pound and dollar signs intertwined, handing the paper to James Roosevelt and asking him to take it to his father. 'Tell him this must be the currency of the future.'[7]

In a discussion of Churchill and the European idea, his attachment to Empire and Commonwealth on one hand, and to the American connection on the other, are intertwined. In the long ebb and flow of change in Europe, often dramatic change, Churchill had experience enough, spanning more than 50 years of public life, to recognise Britain's strengths and limitations, whether military or financial. He knew that to maintain Britain's interests, varying combinations of allies and associates were needed. When one failed, as did the United States in 1920 or, through no fault of her own, France in 1940 or the Soviet Union in 1945, others had to be tried.

Perhaps the most remarkable alliance that Churchill ever proposed was with Bolshevik Russia. In order to bring the Bolsheviks back into the war in the early months of 1917, and take the military pressure off the British, French and American troops then facing a massive and successful German offensive on the Western Front, he proposed that Britain and the United States should offer the Bolsheviks a formula such as 'safeguarding the permanent fruits of the Revolution' in return for Russia's re-entering the war. 'Let us never forget', he explained, 'that Lenin and Trotsky are fighting with ropes round their necks . . . Show them any real chance of consolidating their power, of getting some kind of protection against the vengeance of a counter-revolution, and they would be non-human not to embrace it.'[8]

This wartime expedient was never tried. Later, Churchill's approaches to the Soviet Union between 1941 and 1945 recognised the need to create and preserve a wartime alliance, in the national, and also international, interest of defeating Hitler, or, in its earliest phase, of not being defeated by Hitler. The defeat of Hitler was not, however, an end in itself, but an essential step for the much-declared restoration of the independence of the states which Hitler had overrun, and the maintenance of their future independence. According to the recollection of Charles Bohlen, when at the first Yalta plenary session Roosevelt agreed with Stalin that peace should be made by the Great Powers and not by the small ones, it was Churchill who interjected: 'The eagle should permit the small birds to sing and care not whereof they sang.'[9] For 'Eagle' read also 'Bear'.

Churchill's intervention was unsuccessful. Confronted by Stalin's intransigence and the advance of his army, he could not be the effective champion of small states. His rhetoric was genuine, but his powers were limited, almost non-existent. He had tried to hold the Yalta summit earlier, before the Red Army was so far forward. As Roosevelt could only go by sea and Stalin by land, he had suggested Jerusalem as the venue. But neither Great Power agreed to this proposal.

With regard to Poland, the future independence of which was regarded by many in Britain as the litmus test of victory over Hitler, Churchill devoted several hundred wartime hours, in London and in Moscow, as well as at Yalta and later at Potsdam, to trying to effect an accommodation between the London Poles and Stalin, with a view to rescuing what could be rescued of Polish independence. In its wording, the Yalta Declaration on Liberated Europe was a powerful instrument, upholding in theme, and in specific content, Polish democratic rights, and the democratic rights of all central and eastern European States.

Under the Yalta Declaration, Poland secured 'free and unfettered elections as soon as possible on the basis of universal suffrage and secret ballot'.[10] It was not, however, the Declaration, which Stalin was willing to sign, but the Soviet Union's subsequent violations of it, that destroyed the ideal of a Europe of democratic and independent sovereign states. That ideal was limited to the areas west of the Red Army stopping line.

It is as a war leader that Churchill is most remembered. But for him, the coming of war in 1939 was not a cause for rejoicing but for distress. He understood the effect war would have on Europe's stability, unity and political evolution, and had spent five years trying to persuade first Baldwin and then Chamberlain to follow policies that, in his view, might be able to avert war. In the years leading up to 1914 his had also been the voice, and the advocacy of practical measures, to avert war. Deterring the Kaiser at Agadir in 1911, and Hitler 25 years later, were aspects of his attempt to use British power to prevent a European war, and to protect those in Europe who might be threatened by the instability of aggression.

The European idea by which Churchill was animated was not a Europe in arms, but a Europe able to avoid the destruction which the use of arms would create. His knowledge of the destructive power of war did not come from books. By 1900 he had already experienced fighting on the North-West Frontier of India, in the Sudan and in South Africa. During the South African conflict, which he saw at close quarters, he expressed an opinion others have voiced after him: 'Ah, horrible war, amazing medley of the glorious and the squalid, the pitiful and the sublime, if modern men of light and leading saw your face more often, simple folk would see it hardly ever.'[11]

A year and a half after this assertion that first-hand knowledge of the horrors of war could, and ought to, influence political leaders, Churchill listened in London to calls for the creation of an army capable of fighting a European enemy. 'I have frequently been astonished to hear with what composure and how glibly Members, and even Ministers, talk of a European war', he told the House of Commons three months after entering it, and went on to make the point that whereas, in the past, wars had been fought 'by small regular armies of professional soldiers', in future, when 'mighty populations are impelled on each other', a European war could only end 'in the ruin of the vanquished and the scarcely less fatal commercial dislocation and exhaustion of the conquerors'.[12]

Despite his own sense of excitement on several occasions when he had been in action, Churchill had no illusions about the true nature of war, as seen on the battlefield. A year after his marriage to Clementine he wrote to her from the German army manoeuvres, to which he had been invited as a guest of the Kaiser: 'Much as war attracts me and fascinates my mind with its tremendous situations, I feel more deeply every year, and can measure the feeling here in the midst of arms, what vile and wicked folly and barbarism it all is.'[13]

Churchill's foreboding at the possibility of a European war, and his recognition of the nature of warfare, led him to seek various measures of amelioration before 1914, aimed at averting a European conflict. Just as in industrial relations he advocated and put into practice arbitration procedures, including the setting up in 1908 of a Compulsory Court of Arbitration, the forerunner of ACAS, so he worked behind the scenes on several crucial occasions before 1914 to find means of reducing Anglo-German friction. One of these was the mission of his friend Sir Ernest Cassel to see the Kaiser in 1912. Another was his proposal later that year, and again in 1913, for a Naval Holiday to halt and eventually reduce the competitive naval arms race. There was also his proposal to visit Tirpitz in May 1914 in order, face to face, to use his skills of persuasion and compromise to avert the imminent European conflict, and to come to an agreement on a wide range of outstanding naval issues, including what in recent years had proved a crucial factor in détente with Russia, the mutual inspection of defence installations.

As late as 29 July 1914 Churchill was proposing to the Cabinet what we would now call (as a result of his Edinburgh speech of 1950) a 'European Summit' to pull back from the brink of war. His idea was that the European rulers should 'be brought together for the sake of peace'.[14]

In the inter-war years, Churchill continued to advocate various schemes designed to avert a second European war. In 1920 he urged on Lloyd George 'early revision of the Peace Treaty by a conference to which the New Germany shall be invited as an equal partner in the rebuilding of Europe'. This would rally 'all that is good and stable in the German nation'.[15] In a Cabinet memorandum that year he proposed, following the withdrawal of all American guarantees to France, that Britain negotiate a 'binding alliance' between Britain, France and Germany. France would have the security that she did not have in 1914. But to win Germany to this alliance, he wrote, 'implies a profound revision of the Treaty of Versailles, and the acceptance of Germany as an equal partner in the future guidance of Europe'.[16]

Again the phrase 'equal partner' at a time when there was a climate of anti-Germanism, making that concept of 'an equal partner' almost outrageous. These proposals were made, also, when the immediate danger of Communism was receding, and the focus of Churchill's attention, which a year earlier had been Russo-centric, was on the emergence of a Europe that would have a strength, and ideological cohesion of its own, essentially democratic, in which the Weimar Republic would be welcome. Not only the Communist danger, but the nature of war itself, influenced Churchill's search for amelioration. In 1928, in his introduction to the third edition of A P Herbert's book about Gallipoli, *The Secret Battle*, in which a brave man is shot for cowardice, Churchill wrote:

> It was one of those cries of pain wrung from the fighting troops by the prolonged and measureless torment through which they passed; and like the poems of Siegfried Sassoon should be read in each generation, so that men and women may rest under no illusion about what war means.[17]

In 1932, shortly after seeing Nazi youth on the march in Munich, Churchill proposed a conference that would seek to redress the grievances created by the Treaty of Versailles and its associated treaties, and do so before the powers that had been defeated in 1918 themselves felt strong enough to redress that balance by force. He specifically mentioned, in this context, the German grievance of the Danzig corridor and the Hungarian grievance of Transylvania. The only way to revive what he called 'the lights and reconciliation' in Europe was the 'removal of the just grievance of the vanquished'.[18]

When Churchill suggested making use of international conferences to effect an amelioration of tension, as he did in 1914 and in 1932, and almost a quarter of a century later in trying to bring Eisenhower with him to Moscow, or at least to a neutral European capital, to open talks with the Soviet Union, he did so as someone with considerable experience as a conciliator. As early as 1906, his Treaty negotiations with the defeated Boers marked him out among his older Liberal colleagues of that time as someone who had the skills, and the will, needed to reconcile heightened animosities, and not to humiliate the defeated.

Churchill's negotiating ability was connected with his belief that almost nothing was too complex to be susceptible to amelioration (he did give up, for a day or two after 8 May 1945, with regard to Stalin and the bitter dispute over the arrested Polish emissaries, informing Frank Roberts: 'It is no longer desired by us to maintain detailed arguments with the Soviet Government about their views and actions.')[19]

The destructiveness of the 1914-18 war, and the emergence of Communism in Russia, led Churchill, in the aftermath of the Versailles Treaty, to seek what he called, in 1921, an 'appeasement' of hatreds in Europe. The secret records of his ministerial activities confirm his recurring involvement in several different contexts, and with practical results. That same year, 1921, in search of a viable 'appeasement' in Ireland, he took a central part, at Lloyd George's request, in the Irish Treaty negotiations. Four years later he conducted, under Baldwin, the complex European and American war-debt negotiations, in 1926 the coal negotiations, and subsequently the Irish boundary and debt negotiations. In each of these instances he sought workable compromises. Even after the Conservative defeat in 1945, Clement Attlee used him, in a private capacity, to seek a compromise on the vexed and vexatious question of Britain's post-war American debt.

The 1921 European 'appeasement' example is illuminating. Churchill was being questioned, one might almost say cross-questioned, by the imperial prime ministers as to why he was in favour of developing trade relations with Germany, and at the same time giving France the sort of guarantees that America's withdrawal from Europe had denied them. He went out on a fairly precarious limb, for 1921, to explain to them that a commitment to France 'will give you greater freedom, in my humble opinion, to establish new relations, new co-operation with Germany in the further reconstruction and rebuilding of Europe . . .'

This was the same attitude Churchill was to take after 1945. In 1921 he expressed it with an urgency that was to be borne out by events: 'It might well be,' he explained, 'that being at once the ally of France and the friend of Germany, we might be in a position to mitigate the frightful rancour and fear and hatred which exist between Germany and France at the present time and which, if left unchecked, will most certainly in a generation or so bring about a renewal of the struggle of which we have just witnessed the conclusion.'

Churchill summed up his European policy of 1921 in the words: 'The aim is to get an appeasement of the fearful hatreds and antagonisms which exist in Europe and to enable the world to settle down.'[20] In this sense, Europe was the world in Churchill's perspective: the land from France on the Atlantic to Poland on the Baltic. This had been the Europe of his youth, and was to remain his 'Europe' even after its second devastation and political eclipse in 1945. In his 1948 'three great circles' speech, he still envisaged a future for Europe that was more than a mere appendage to the Great Powers. 'What should be the majestic centre of world security and later on of world co-operation, and finally of world government', he said, 'has been reduced to a mere cockpit in which the representatives of mighty nations and ancient states hurl reproaches, taunts and recrimination at one another . . .'[21]

In the appeasement debate after Hitler's rise to power, Churchill's arguments centred around how to avert war. He looked to the deterrent power of the unity, if it could be achieved, of the threatened states, as he was to do, again, after 1945. In the years before 1939 Churchill did not believe that Hitler would challenge a European order that was united in its determination not to be overthrown, and had the means to assert itself. He wanted a combination of the rearmament of the threatened states, and the upholding of the covenant of the League of Nations against unprovoked aggression: Arms and the Covenant.

Where did the Soviet Union, with 'terrorism on an unprecedented scale...the denial of the most elementary rights of citizenship and freedom' as he told the Cabinet in 1920,[22] come in to this perspective? Regarding Nazism as the immediate threat, he did not endorse, either publicly or privately, Baldwin's assertion in 1936 to a delegation of senior Conservatives (of which he was one) that: 'If there is any fighting in Europe to be done, I should like to see the Bolshies and the Nazis doing it.'[23] Despite his hatred of Bolshevism, Churchill recognised after 1919 that it could not be overthrown by force, even by the armed force of the anti-Bolshevik Russians themselves. In the mid-1930s, when the twin successes of Soviet Communism and German Nazism were, for the time at least, assured, he put the case for a European middle ground, and did so with the strong encouragement of two senior officials at the Foreign Office, Robert Vansittart and Rex Leeper. As he told an audience in Paris in 1936: 'Between the doctrines of Comrade Trotsky and those of Dr Goebbels there ought to be room for you and me, and a few others, to cultivate opinions of our own.'[24]

Although as a young man Churchill had opposed any Tsarist expansion into the Aegean, and in 1915 rejected Russia's claim to Constantinople, even Bolshevik Russia was not beyond the pale of his search for a *modus vivendi*. In 1919 he had proposed a compromise between Lenin and Denikin which was in line with his search for ways other than war to reach equable solutions. Seeking, between 1935 and 1939, a gathering together of the threatened states of Europe, Churchill was prepared to involve Russia in Europe, and through his personal contacts with the Russian Ambassador, Ivan Maisky, encouraged Russia to seek a role in a European defensive arrangement. He also wanted the United States to be brought in to balance the weight of Axis and pro-Axis states that had emerged by 1938. Presaging his 'three great circles' of 1948, he was critical a decade earlier of British hostility to the involvement of the United States in European affairs.

Churchill's attitude and policies with regard to the United States had a pragmatic base: British national interest, and on two occasions at least, in 1918 and 1940, survival. He knew as much as anyone, as a result of his work at the Ministry of Munitions in 1917 and 1918, how the United States' contribution to the Great War would have been decisive had the war gone on into 1919 or even 1920, as was widely assumed as late as September 1918. He was aware of the dangers that came to European stability as a result of America's withdrawal from the post-Versailles settlement. He wanted the United States to act as a democratic ally for the European democracies, and could be as critical, though almost always in private, about the extent of American neutrality, as he could be about the refusal of his former Conservative Cabinet colleagues to welcome America's tentative willingness to become involved in Europe; and he was both publicly and privately enthusiastic when, after 1945, the Labour government welcomed the return of the United States to Europe.

Regarding the 1939-45 war as the unnecessary war, Churchill could be bitter at times that his ideas on how to avert it had been dismissed. He devoted the first 313 pages of Volume I of his war memoirs to the pre-war years, determined, in 1948, to point out the failure of Europe to protect itself other than by war. One example of how Churchill not only thought peace could be preserved, but tried actively to foster it, dates from 1925, when the Foreign Office under Austen Chamberlain was seeking an Anglo-French Treaty to give France a guarantee of its borders, and of Belgium's borders, that would make clear to Germany that any repetition of 1914 would mean an Anglo-German war, whether the aggression was against Belgium or, and this had been a crucial lack of clarity in 1914, against France.

Churchill, who had favoured an Anglo-French agreement in 1921, but in the hope that once France was contented Germany could be brought back in to the European circle, now proposed something different, designed to create a new concept, not a continuation of confrontation and immolation (what he called the 'black accounts of Teuton and Gaul'[25]) but a way forward to harmony. Churchill wanted to bring Germany into the equation as an equal, and as a beneficiary of British and French concessions. It was for Britain, he told the Committee of Imperial Defence, to take the initiative to bring about 'a real peace' between France and Germany, first satisfying Germany's post-Versailles grievances, and then offering security guarantees simultaneously to Germany and France.[26] The latter, as far as borders were concerned, was what emerged – in the Locarno Treaties – though his proposal to satisfy Germany's territorial, and other grievances, was not accepted by his colleagues.

After 1946 Churchill worked for a similar European arrangement, whereby Germany would be brought back as an equal partner. As Professor Schwarz has documented, he even had in mind, in 1953, the possibility of a united, though disarmed, Germany.[27] It is interesting to see that a year later he explained to Eisenhower that the plan then being put forward by Eden that would create a variant of NATO, with Germany included in it, 'may lead as time passes to United Europe and also gain for us both what we have tried for so hard, namely, the German comrade-ship'.[28]

When Churchill tried to peer into the future as far as post-1945 was concerned, he had the guidance of his own experience of what had happened in 1919. Then he had been an opponent of harsh peace, to the anger of his constituents. In supporting Roosevelt's concept of unconditional surrender, he had specifically laid down that this was not to be a punitive measure. His words to the House of Commons in 1945 are as striking now, in their essential humanity, as they were when he spoke them:

I read somewhere that when the ancient Athenians, on one occasion, overpowered a tribe in the Peloponnesus which had wrought them great injury by base, treacherous means, and when they had the hostile army herded on a beach naked for slaughter, they forgave them and set them free, and they said: 'This was not done because they were men; it was done because of the nature of Man.' Similarly, in this temper we may now say to our foes, 'We demand unconditional surrender, but you well know how strict are the moral limits within which our action is confined. We are no extirpators of nations, or butchers of peoples. We make no bargain with you. We accord you nothing as a right. Abandon your resistance unconditionally. We remain bound by our customs and our nature.'

Between 1918 and 1990 the European idea had been forced to submit to a number of cruel distortions (of which I was made very aware in Berlin and Warsaw in 1957, in Budapest in 1961 and in Moscow in 1983). For Churchill in freedom, as for many of those living under successive tyrannies, whether Nazi, Fascist or Communist, there was an ideal, a moral scheme, that was central to the European idea: the ideal of parliamentary democracy and personal liberty. In 1944 Churchill set out for the Italian government, then in the process of formation, what he considered that ideal to be: the ideal of every European state emerging from tyranny, whether of the right or the left:

Is there the right to free expression of opinion and of opposition and criticism of the government of the day?

Have the people the right to turn out a government of which they disapprove, and are constitutional means provided by which they can make their will apparent?

Are their courts of justice free from violence by the Executive and from threats of mob violence, and free of all association with particular political parties?

Will these courts administer open and well-established laws which are associated in the human mind with the broad principles of decency and justice?

Will there be fair play for poor as well as for rich, for private persons as well as government officials?

Will the rights of the individual, subject to his duties to the state, be maintained and asserted and exalted?

Is the ordinary peasant or workman who is earning a living by daily toil and striving to bring up a family free from the fear that some grim policy organisation under the control of a single party, like the Gestapo, started by the Nazi and Fascist parties, will tap him on the shoulder and pack him off without fair or open trial to bondage or ill-treatment?

'These simple, practical tests', Churchill commented, 'are some of the title-deeds on which a new Italy could be founded.'[29] Much as the imposition of Communist regimes in 1945 was a source of distress to him, it did not deflect from his belief that all of Europe would eventually be able to participate in, and benefit from, the ideals set out in his message to the Italian people. Indeed, the Italian people's own narrow escape from a Communist future in 1945 was a source of encouragement to him. In Greece he had actively intervened at Christmas 1944 to prevent a Communist seizure of power. In contrast to Poland, Greece was a country where he was able to take effective action, albeit with great physical as well as political difficulty, and did manage to influence the course of events by his personal intervention on the spot.

Following the acquisition of nuclear weapons by the Soviet Union after 1945, Churchill knew that there could be no military defeat of Communism without the mutual destruction of both sides. In seeking areas and avenues of compromise with the Soviet Union, on one occasion he advised the President of the Board of Trade, on the eve of an official visit to Moscow: 'What we want, you tell them, is easement. We may not settle all our problems: we want easement.'[30] The President of the Board of Trade was the Labour politician, Harold Wilson.

How did Churchill envisage the end of Communism in Europe, and the return of the Eastern European states, and perhaps even of Russia itself, to the European idea: to the independence of the democratic individual nation state? In a speech to the Massachusetts Institute of Technology at the height of the Cold War, he spoke as follows:

> Laws, just or unjust, may govern men's actions. Tyrannies may restrain or regulate their words. The machinery of propaganda may pack their minds with falsehood and deny them truth for many generations of time. But the soul of man thus held in trance or frozen in a long night can be awakened by a spark coming from God knows where and in a moment the whole structure of lies and oppression is on trial for its life.[31]

When Churchill spoke these words, he had already, at Fulton, Missouri, spoken of a 'new unity of Europe . . . from which no nation should be permanently outcast'.[32] Within six months, speaking in Zurich, he elaborated this, speaking of how France and Germany ought to take the lead in creating what he called a United States of Europe, whose right 'to live and shine' would be championed by Britain, the British Commonwealth, the United States 'and, I trust, Soviet Russia – for then indeed all would be well'.[33] To put forward in 1946 the concept of Russia championing a United Europe, and to do so in a speech which he knew would be closely studied, was not the work of a cold warrior or a man of confrontation, but of someone for whom the cataclysms of two world wars were a vivid reality.

In 1917 Churchill had opposed what became the Passchendaele offensive: what he described in the Commons as 'those dismal processes of waste and slaughter which are called attrition'.[34] In 1943, after watching a Royal Air Force film of the bombing of a German city, he had exclaimed: 'Are we beasts? Are we taking this too far?'[35] His postulation in his Zurich speech of an eventual Russian participation in a democratic Europe was derived from this knowledge of the destructive power of war. That Russian participation took almost half a century to become reality. In 1994, during John Major's visit to Moscow, two important Anglo-Russian agreements were reached, aimed at reducing areas of potential military conflict. 'It has taken a long time and a lot of effort to try and change the way we think', was John Major's comment, and he added: 'We want the European Union to build a closer relationship with Russia.'[36] This was the very development that, even at the height of the Cold War, Churchill had wanted.

Three years after his Zurich speech, Churchill proposed at Strasbourg the next step in the path of European reconciliation and unity. The forum was the first meeting of the Council of Europe, when Churchill, as Leader of the Opposition, led the Conservative delegation. His dramatic question, 'Where are the Germans?' was followed by the suggestion that the arrival of a German delegation, not in a year's time, but much sooner, would be 'highly beneficial' for European security.[37] This was not a sudden aberation but a long-thought-out progression. In the Commons he had spoken 10 months earlier of the part Britain should play in the bringing in of Germany. 'My hope is that free, liberal civilisation and democratic parliamentary processes will win the soul of Germany for Europe', he said, 'and that the great underlying harmonies of the European families will predominate over the feuds that have hitherto rent our famous parent Continent and brought upon it miseries and humiliations beyond the power of statistics to measure or language to describe.'[38]

This theme was elaborated on six weeks later during a Foreign Affairs debate in the House of Commons, when Churchill welcomed one recent development, and suggested another. His welcome was to the fact that, as the Labour Foreign Secretary Ernest Bevin, had indicated on the previous day, the United States 'may now be willing to do what they have never done before, or dreamed of doing before, namely, to give a guarantee to

Western Europe against aggression, coupled with practical measures of military co-operation'. This, Churchill said, should be followed, he believed, by further progress in 'bringing Germany back into Western Europe'. This might be assisted, he suggested, by the United Europe Movement, of which he was co-President, with Leon Blum and Paul-Henri Spaak.

The main thrust of Churchill's thought in regard to Germany's relationship with those she had conquered in the West in 1940 was not organisational but psychological. The relationship between Germany, which in 1948 he still envisaged as being divided up into several separate states, and France, Belgium, Holland and Luxembourg, should, he said, be 'a continuous confluence of ideas and goodwill between them all'. The movement toward European unity, he believed, could 'only achieve success through the reconciliation and goodwill of whole peoples, irrespective of their internal political or party bias, divisions or labels'. It was for governments to plan for the constitutions, economic settlements and military arrangements of European unity, but he believed that the existing structure of the European Movement had a part to play before that stage. 'We hope that sentiment and culture, the forgetting of old feuds, the lowering and melting down of barriers of all kinds between countries, the growing sense of being a "good European" – we hope that all these will be the final, eventual and irresistible solvents of the difficulties which now condemn Europe to misery.'[39]

This was Churchill's prescription, and prognosis, in December 1948, at a time when the concept of the 'good European' might seem utopian. A decade earlier, when Nazism was the immediate enemy, he had set out the same prescription. 'The conception of a "United States of Europe" is right', he wrote in the mass-circulation *News of the World* in 1938, five months before Munich. Every step was right 'which appeases the obsolete hatreds'. Every 'stride towards European cohesion' was not only 'beneficial to the general welfare' but would make Britain 'a partner'.[40]

Churchill's views in 1938, as in 1948, make it clear that security against the current threat of Communism was only one aspect of his concept of a united Europe, a concept which in 1948 focused on bringing Germany into the West European alignment. The wider harmony of interests played its part, as did human rights. When he spoke in Brussels in 1949, to the Council of the European Movement, he gave his support to a European Court of Human Rights, and explained: 'We have a Charter of Human Rights, and we must have a European means of defending and enforcing it.' It must not be possible, he argued, 'within the boundaries of a United Europe', for abuses of human rights to take place such as the arrest and imprisonment two months earlier of Cardinal Mindszenty in Hungary.

Having myself attended for two consecutive years, and spoken at, the United Nations Human Rights Commission in Geneva, I know the importance not only of mechanisms to uphold the Charter of Human Rights to which Churchill referred, but the positive part that the European states, in my day the West European states, play in that process. There were many at Geneva in 1985 and 1986 who regarded the East-West divide as immutable, and the concept of a 'good European' as limited, for as far as the eye could see, to the working together of the democratic institutions of Western Europe. I was certainly one of them. It is therefore all the more remarkable when discussing the subject of Churchill and the European idea to find that it was during his speech in Brussels in 1949 that he stated that the supporters of a United Europe could not 'rest content' with the division of Europe in two parts, 'the free and the unfree'. And he gave, as the slogan to follow: 'The Europe we seek to unite is *all* Europe.'[41]

Churchill was confident, despite a few lapses into pessimism which were not entirely surprising given the intensification of confrontation at the time, for example, of the Berlin blockade, that the threats to Western Europe would not turn to war if a policy of deterrence were followed. Hence his support for the Truman Doctrine, which he encouraged before it was enunciated by the President, and his support for NATO, where he both encouraged and supported Ernest Bevin. Here, again, was the recognition, which in Churchill's case dated back to 1917, of the essential American part in the shield. Stalin's actions in Eastern Europe and elsewhere in 1945 and 1946, and in Czechoslovakia in 1948, made it essential, in Churchill's view, for the European idea, then temporarily at least confined to Western Europe, to have an outside protector.

The reconstruction of ruined Europe after 1945 was an important concern of Churchill's. Both in 1919 and again in 1945 he had been a leading advocate of putting Germany back on its feet on both occasions to ensure that Communism did not spread further westward, and also as a humanitarian act. His desire in 1945 to find some way to tackle the poverty of the post-war years, and to prevent despair leading, as it had done briefly in 1918 and 1919, to anarchy and revolution outside Russia, was a source of direct inspiration to George Marshall in the evolution of the Marshall Plan. At the press conference in which he launched his Plan, Marshall said that it was Churchill's call for a United Europe that had influenced his own belief that, with American financial help, the European states could work out their own economic recovery.[42]

If one can indeed draw up Leviathan with a hook, one might sum up Churchill's European idea as a Europe in which West and East were united in a single multinational structure, with Britain, the United States and, if possible, a non-confrontational Russia, as sponsors and guarantors of European security. The continental European nation states, retaining their individual characteristics, would sustain their development within democratic systems. Human rights would prevail. In his 1938 *News of the World* article he used the words, writing of Britain: 'We are with Europe but not of it. We are linked but not comprised. We are interested and associated, but not absorbed.' As early as 1938, it was a union of states 'with a tradition of liberty': looking forward to the eventual revival of democracy in those European states which had turned their backs on it.

Today the question of the European Union and sovereignty is very much on our British national agenda. Forty-eight years ago, in his capacity as a co-President of the United Europe Movement, Churchill said this about European federation, the European Union of today:

> It is said with truth that this involves some sacrifice or merger of national sovereignty. But it is also possible and not less agreeable to regard it as the gradual assumption by all the nations concerned of that larger sovereignty which can also protect their diverse and distinctive customs and characteristics and their national traditions all of which under totalitarian systems, whether Nazi, Fascist, or Communist, would certainly be blotted out forever.

In the statement of aims which he drafted in 1946 for the United Europe Movement he envisaged what he called 'an effective European Union' to restore prosperity and to maintain freedom the aim of which, geographically, was to unite all Europe 'from the Atlantic to the Black Sea'. If, however, the countries of Western Europe would, as he put it, 'make a start on their own', it could be left open to the other states 'to join later as and when they can'.[43]

It would seem that 'as and when they can' is almost now. As we focus in our discussions today on Churchill and the European idea, Britain is engaged in negotiations with the Vysegrad Four – Poland, Hungary, the Czech Republic and Slovakia – for them to enter the European Union: of which Britain is a part.

Afterword:
Churchill – Achievement and Legacy

CORRELLI BARNETT

As the historical perspective lengthens, it becomes easier to place Winston Churchill's career and its lasting legacy in the true context of an era of global transformation – political, military, and technological – that was revolutionary not only in scope but also in sheer rapidity. When Churchill became First Lord of the Admiralty in 1911, the Royal Navy was the most powerful in the world, superior in battleship strength to France and Germany put together.[1] This maritime supremacy served as both the expression and the guarantee of Britain's hegemony as the Mother Country of the most populous and extensive empire in history; as the greatest and wealthiest of trading nations; and as the centre of a world financial system based on gold-standard sterling. Yet barely 30 years later Churchill found himself Prime Minister of a Britain reduced to terrifying military and economic weakness, with a vulnerable Empire to protect against two existing enemies and a potential third, and herself in present mortal peril of defeat at the hands of Nazi Germany.[2]

Indeed, barely *two* decades had elapsed since Churchill as Minister of Munitions in the final year of the Great War had presided over the largest military-industrial complex in the world at that time, capable not only of lavishly equipping all the armed forces of the British Empire, but also of supplying the American Expeditionary Forces in France with much of their equipment, including their medium artillery and ammunition. Now, in summer 1940, and in the bleakest contrast, Britain was having to buy large quantities of military supplies from North America, as well as advanced machine-tools to equip her own new armaments and aircraft factories.

Yet in August 1940 the Chancellor of the Exchequer warned Churchill that these and other overseas purchases would exhaust Britain's remaining gold and dollar reserves by the end of the year. She would then be unable either to wage war or even to sustain the life of her people, dependent as this was on imported foodstuffs and raw materials.[3] It was a mere quarter of a century, a blink of an eye in historical terms, since Britain had been the world's largest creditor nation.

Joseph Conrad in a memorable metaphor once likened Britain to a mighty ship starred with lights. It could be said therefore that Churchill began his political voyage as an officer of the watch in this proud, richly freighted, and seemingly invulnerable vessel, only to find himself promoted captain at the very moment when disaster threatened to capsize and sink her.

Does the very speed of these transformations in Britain's fortunes account for a fundamental dissonance in Churchill's behaviour as war leader, especially in 1940 and 1941, those years of peril? On the one hand, he was all too realistically aware, detail by detail, of the strategic vulnerability of the British Empire and of Britain's own desperate military and economic weakness. On the other hand, his responses remained instinctively still those of the leader of that world and imperial power which Britain had so recently been in fact as well as facade. He brought to the dire plight of 1940–41 the inner psychological assurance of an Edwardian imperial upper-class Englishman. For him, Adolf Hitler even in the hour of German triumph over France remained just a ghastly foreign upstart, faintly comic. And although Britain's terrifying weakness compelled Churchill to wheedle Franklin Roosevelt for future economic aid and politico-military support, the style of his dealings with the President was always that of one leader of a great nation negotiating with another on a basis of equality – and, for that matter, also that of an upper-class Englishman comfortably conducting business with an upper-class American.

It was surely this inner assurance – as well as sheer pugilistic spirit – which inspired Churchill in the summer of 1940 to gamble Britain's future on fighting on, even though the money was going to run out by the beginning of 1941, even though there was no certainty whatsoever that the United States, then deep in neutrality, would ride to the rescue in time either with dollars or soldiers.

Had Churchill instead simply accepted the bleak logic of Britain's truly appalling predicament in summer 1940, he might well have decided to explore the possibilities of a deal with Hitler, as wished by defeatist members of his Cabinet like Lord Halifax. Yet it surely can be seen from the perspective of 2002 that such a deal must have left a militarily and economically enfeebled Britain dependent on Hitler's continued goodwill:

the off-shore island of a Nazi Europe. If in Britain's plight a degree of dependence on a superpower there had to be, then English-speaking and democratic America seemed to Churchill then, and must seem to us in retrospect today, the only choice. In the United States he therefore placed Britain's hopes first of longterm wartime survival and then of ultimate victory. In truth, the 'Special Relationship' which British politicians still celebrate in the 21st century was from the beginning founded on one-sided need.

Yet if Churchill were successfully to woo the support of the President, the Congress, and the American people, he had to give continuing proof that Britain really was resolved, and able, to fight on: that she was a runner worth backing. Churchill's keen awareness of this surely influenced even his purely operational decisions in 1940–41, whetting the edge of his own natural eagerness to strike a blow wherever he could. Thus he ordered the sinking of the French battleships in Mers-el-Kebir, Algeria, in June 1940 even though the British admiral on the spot believed, as have naval historians since, that given more time a peaceful surrender could have been negotiated. Yet this act of violence against a recent ally served the political purpose of demonstrating to the world – and especially America – that Britain, far from being on the way out after France's capitulation, had reverted to her old ruthless fighting self.

Historians have also generally agreed that Churchill made a disastrous strategic mistake in February 1941 when he halted Major-General Richard O'Connor's pursuit of the wreckage of the Italian Army in Libya in order that O'Connor's best troops could be sent to Greece in readiness to meet an expected German invasion. Thereby was forfeited the chance of occupying Tripolitania and ending the campaign in North Africa before German troops under Rommel could even arrive. Moreover, by the end of February, when the final decision had to be taken about despatching an expeditionary force to Greece, it had become clear that the prospects of a successful defence were poor indeed. Nevertheless, on 4 March the expeditionary force was duly despatched, only to be evacuated in April with heavy loss in men and matériel after the collapse of the Greek front.

But what would have been the effect on American opinion if Britain had passively left the gallant Greeks (already exhausted by their long campaign against the Italians) to their fate? This was, after all, the critical time when the Lend-Lease Bill, on which depended Britain's future ability to wage war or even feed her people, was going through Congress (introduced on 10 January and passed into law on 11 March). Moreover, from the end of January 1941 until the end of March important Anglo-American staff talks were taking place in Washington about future grand strategy. Was, then, the expedition to Greece a case where a wrong decision on the level of theatre strategy was right on the higher level of statesmanship?

Churchill's resolve in 1940 that Britain would fight on – a resolve made almost by default – must stand as his supreme stroke of statesmanship, for what eventually followed from it was the saving of western Europe from a future of barbaric dictatorship, and the inauguration instead of an era of unparalleled democratic progress and prosperity.

In the short term, however, the British refusal to make peace had no effect on Hitler's decision to attack the Soviet Union in 1941. It is also true that all Churchill's patient diplomacy vis-a-vis the American President from the summer of 1940 up to December 1941 failed to inveigle the United States into the final step of declaring war on Germany. Nonetheless, Roosevelt gradually gave Britain all possible help short of that. By the Lend-Lease Act America committed herself to underwriting the British war effort just when the exhaustion of Britain's own resources of gold and dollars would have made it impossible for Britain to carry on the conflict very much longer. In August 1941 Roosevelt, though President of a still-neutral country, joined Churchill in publishing common war aims in the form of the Atlantic Charter.

These were notable developments which could never have occurred if Britain had lapsed into neutrality. Yet the truly world-shaping consequences of Churchill's 1940 resolve to fight on only came later – after America had been pitchforked into the conflict by the Japanese attack on the US Pacific Fleet in Pearl Harbor on 7 December 1941 and Hitler's subsequent declaration of war. For now Britain was joined by America in a fully fledged alliance against common enemies.

The way was open for further strokes of Churchillian diplomacy in Washington by which the swelling military and industrial power of the United States could be pulled behind a British grand strategy focussed on defeating Britain's own mortal enemy, Nazi Germany. At the first wartime 'summit' conference in Washington in December 1941 ('Arcadia'), Churchill by sheer power of argument and personality (but brilliantly backed by his highly professional and experienced Chiefs of Staff) persuaded President Roosevelt and his military advisers to endorse a broad statement of allied global strategy ('WW1'] largely drafted by the British. This proclaimed that 'nothwithstanding the entry of Japan into the war, our view remains that Germany is the prime enemy and her defeat is the key to victory.'[4]

Despite subsequent slippage of American resources towards the struggle in the Pacific against Japan, this fundamental choice henceforward shaped Anglo-American strategy. It led to the commitment of ever more powerful American forces to fight alongside British-Commonwealth forces in North Africa, Sicily, Italy and eventually (with the British Isles themselves acting as the essential advanced American base) from the beaches of Normandy in 1944 to the heart of Germany in 1945.

The liberation of Western Europe marked the fulfilment of the patient endeavours of Churchill's statesmanship since the mortal danger of 1940. More, it constituted the essential preliminary to European economic reconstruction under the Marshall Plan in 1948–51, that launch-pad for the soaring prosperity of the second half of the 20th century.

All this might be deemed legacy enough. Yet in 1946 Churchill, now out of office, became the first statesman to alert the peoples of the West to the new threat to liberty and democracy from Stalin's Soviet Union. It was his speech at Fulton, Missouri, which made the words 'Iron Curtain' the long-standing shorthand for the division of Europe between the democracies of the West and the dismal communist tyrannies installed in the East by the Soviet Union. Today the impact of this speech on world opinion, its lasting resonance during the Cold War, can hardly be doubted, even though at the time it was the task of statesmen actually in government to consolidate the security of free Europe under American protection by the North Atlantic Treaty of 1949 and the creation of Nato in 1950.

Yet the essential instrument of this consolidation lay in the Anglo-American 'Special Relationship' so carefully fostered by Churchill in wartime, and represented in the late 1940s by President Harry Truman and Secretary of State George Marshall for America, and Prime Minister Clement Attlee and Foreign Secretary Ernest Bevin for Britain. In fact, the 'Special Relationship' stands to this day as a Churchillian legacy with continuing influence on world affairs, its essential cohesion proven again and again from the Korean War in 1950 to the aftermath of the destruction of the World Trade Centre in New York City on 11 September 2001.

The closeness of wartime trans-Atlantic comradeship, to say nothing of Churchill's romantic notion of the civilising destiny of all the English-speaking peoples, served to colour his postwar views on the future political relationship between Great Britain and the nations of Continental Europe. It could almost be said that these views simply updated the foreign policy of his old Liberal Cabinet colleague, Sir Edward Grey, back in the 1900s: the concert of Europe (including Germany) restored, but a concert in which Great Britain would once again play a semi-detached role, as befitted a world and imperial power. This was indeed the broad policy towards European development embraced by Labour and Conservative cabinets alike from 1945 until 1963, when Harold Macmillan made his abortive attempt to get Britain into the Common Market created by the 1957 Treaty of Rome. Even after Edward Heath did finally sign the United Kingdom up to the Treaty of Rome in 1973, British public opinion continued to manifest a Churchillian ambivalence about 'Europe'; and still does so in the 21st century.

A fundamental reason for this ambivalence lies in the belief that Britain differs from Continental European countries in having global connections and responsibilities, or, in short, the belief that she remains a world power. The belief, which has shaped British policy towards both Europe and the United States ever since the Second World War, is really a by-product of Churchill's own successful statesmanship during that war. For this enabled Britain to emerge from the conflict as one of the 'Big Three' victorious powers, ranking with the United States and the Soviet Union. Understandably enough, the British people at the time and afterwards succumbed to the illusion that Britain (with the Commonwealth) was a victor in her own right, whereas in truth her whole war effort at home and on the field of battle had depended on American subsidies through Lend-Lease. From this illusion therefore sprang another, common to both the Labour and the Conservative parties in the postwar era: that Britain was still, and would remain, a first-class world power.

In wartime it unquestionably fulfilled urgent political and strategic needs vis-a-vis powerful allies that Churchill's personality had enabled Britain to 'punch above her weight' (to borrow the words of Douglas Hurd, Foreign Secretary in 1989-1995). However, the British attempt for the sake of 'status' and 'prestige' to play this role in peacetime from the resources of a second-class industrial economy led to half a century of financial and military overstretch. This in turn ranged foreign secretaries and ministers of defence against chancellors of the exchequer – not least during Churchill's own second administration in 1951-55. It remains a live issue today.

It may help us to appreciate how much the world of today owes to the legacy of Churchill's statesmanship if we try to imagine the longterm consequences of a British government led after 10 May 1940 by Lord Halifax, the Conservative Party's preferred successor to Neville Chamberlain. In the first place, there would have been in all probability no combatant Britain in 1941 for America to join as an ally after Pearl Harbor: no advanced base on the edge of Europe ready for future deployment of American armies and air forces. In such a case, American strategy would have focussed entirely on the Pacific. Secondly, the Soviet Union might, it is true, have eventually succeeded on its own in defeating Nazi Germany, without the supplies in fact shipped by the Arctic convoys, without the Anglo-American bomber offensive against German industry and cities, and without the allied land campaigns in Italy and north-west Europe. But had the Red Army been victorious in such circumstances, its advance into Europe would not have stopped at the Elbe, as it did in May 1945 face to face with General Eisenhower's Anglo-American armies, but on the Channel and North-Sea coasts. Western Europe would have exchanged one appalling tyranny for another, and without hope of rescue. For in such a situation the United States would surely have chosen to consolidate her own spheres of influence: the Americas, Japan, and the Pacific rim. There would have been no 'Iron Curtain', no 'Cold War', no eventual defeat of Soviet Communism, and no consequent liberation of all Europe.

From all such dread probabilities Winston Churchill delivered us.

Afterword: Churchill – Achievement and Legacy

1   C.f. Marder, A. J., *From the Dreadnought to Scapa Flow: the Royal Navy in the Fisher Era, 1904–1919*, Volume I, *The Road to War, 1904–1914*, (London, Oxford University Press, 1961) pp. 124–130.

2   See Correlli Barnett, *The Collapse of British Power*, (London, Eyre and Spottiswoode, 1972, and London, Pan Books, 2002, Part I.

3   Barnett, *The Collapse of British Power*, p.14, citing CAB 66/11, WP40(40)324, 21 August 1940.

4   J.M.A. Gwyer, *Grand Strategy*, Vol III, Part I, *June 1941–August 1942*, HMSO, London, 1964, p.359.

Notes

Chapter 2 Churchill and British Sea Power, 1908–29

1   P Gretton, *Winston Churchill and the Royal Navy* (New York 1969), pp 244–5.
2   *Ibid.*, p 245.
3   S Roskill, *Churchill and the Admirals* (London 1977), p 77.
4   R Ollard in *Churchill*, eds R Blake and Wm R Louis (Oxford 1977), p 279.
5   Gretton, *Churchill and the Royal Navy*, p 13.
6   J Sumida, *In Defence of Naval Supremacy* and N Lambert, 'Fisher and the Concept of Flotilla Defence'. I am grateful to Nicholas Lambert for permission to use his revolutionary, unpublished article.
7   W S Churchill, *The World Crisis* 5 vols in 6 (New York 1923–31) Vol 1, p 71.
8   Gretton, *Churchill and the Royal Navy*, p 17.
9   Sumida, *In Defence of Naval Supremacy*, pp 135, 158–9, Lambert, 'Fisher and the Concept of Flotilla Defence', p 200.
10 V Bonham Carter, *Winston Churchill: An Intimate Portrait* (New York 1965), p 123.
11 Fisher 'Economy is Victory', *Memories* (New York 1920), pp 55–61; Sumida, *In Defence of Naval Supremacy*, pp 27–8, 57, 330; *Fear God and Dread Nought: The Correspondence of Admiral of the Fleet Lord Fisher of Kilverstone* 3 vols, ed A J Marder (London 1952–9)

Vol 2, pp 329, 335, 503; R F Mackay, *Fisher of Kilverstone* (Oxford 1973), pp 387–91, 409.

12 Marder, *From Dreadnought to Scapa Flow: The Royal Navy in the Fisher Era, 1904–19* 5 vols (London 1961–70) Vol 1, pp 112–13; Marder, *Fear God and Dread Nought* Vol 2, pp 234–5; Mackay, *Fisher of Kilverstone*, pp 371–2, 382–4, 387–91, 408–9.

13 Lambert, 'Fisher and the Concept of Flotilla Defence'.

14 R S Churchill, *Winston S Churchill.* Vol 2: *1901–14. Young Statesman* (Boston 1967), pp 29–31, 254–5, 269; G L Bernstein, *Liberalism and Liberal Politics in Edwardian England* (Boston 1986), pp 96–104, 114–15, 125–8.

15 Marder, *Fear God and Dread Nought* vol 2, p 226.

16 R Churchill, *Companion* Vol 2, pp 988–9.

17 Sumida, *In Defence of Naval Supremacy*, p 258.

18 Mackay, *Fisher of Kilverstone*, p 434.

19 Sumida, *In Defence of Naval Supremacy*, pp 258–60.

20 Lambert, 'Influence of the Submarine on Naval Strategy' (Oxford DPhil thesis 1992), pp 221–6.

21 Marder, *Fear God and Dread Nought* Vol 2, p 420; Sumida, *In Defence of Naval Supremacy* appendix, table 16.

22 *Ibid.*, appendix, tables 8–10, 16.

23 R Churchill, *Winston S Churchill* Vol 2, pp 500–17.

24 J H Maurer, 'Churchill's Naval Holiday: Arms Control and the Anglo-German Naval Race, 1912–14', *Journal of Strategic Studies* no 15 (March 1992), pp 102–27.

25 R Churchill, *Winston S Churchill* Vol 2, p 670.

26 Marder, *Fear God and Dread Nought* Vol 2, p 430.

27 *Ibid.*, vol 2, pp 434–40, 457–8.

28 Sumida, *In Defence of Naval Supremacy*, p 189.

29 F W Wiemann, 'Lloyd George and the Struggle for the Navy Estimates of 1914', *Lloyd George: Twelve Essays,* ed A J P Taylor (New York 1971), pp 69–91; B K Murray, '"Battered and Shattered" Lloyd George and the 1914 Budget Fiasco', *Albion* no 23 (Autumn 1991), pp 481–507.

30 R Churchill, *Winston S Churchill* Vol 2, pp 661–2.

31 Lambert, 'British Naval Policy, 1913–14: Financial Limitation and Strategic Revolution' (draft article).

32 R Churchill, *Companion* Vol 2 part iii (1960), italics in the original.

33 W Churchill, *World Crisis* Vol 1, p 74.

34 Sumida, *In Defence of Naval Supremacy*, pp 254–5.

35 Mackay, *Fisher of Kilverstone*, pp 465–7.

36 Sumida, *In Defence of Naval Supremacy*, pp 291–5.
37 Marder, *Fear God and Dread Nought* Vol 3, p 106.
38 Mackay, *Fisher of Kilverstone*, pp 462–4; Sumida, *In Defence of Naval Supremacy*, pp 290–2.
39 W Churchill, *World Crisis* Vol 4, p 2.
40 M Gilbert, *Winston Churchill* Vol 3, pp 716–28.
41 Sumida, 'Forging the Trident: British Naval Industrial Logistics, 1914–18', *Feeding Mars, Logistics in Western Warfare from the Middle Ages to the Present*, ed J A Lynn (Boulder 1993)
42 Gilbert, *Companion* Vol 4 part i, pp 113–14, 134–5.
43 Gilbert, *Churchill* Vol 4, p 42.
44 Sumida, 'Forging the Trident'.
45 W Churchill, *World Crisis* Vol 4, p 4.
46 D K Brown, *A Century of Naval Construction: The History of the Royal Corps of Naval Constructors, 1883–1983* (London 1983), pp 122–3.
47 Churchill to Lloyd George, 1 May 1919, in B M Ranft, *The Beatty Papers: Selections from the Private and Official Correspondence and Papers of Admiral of the Fleet Earl Beatty* 2 vols (Aldershot 1989–93) Vol 2, p 38.
48 *Ibid.*
49 Gilbert, *Winston Churchill* Vol 4, p 607.
50 Ranft, *Beatty Papers* Vol 2, p 157; W Hackmann, *Seek and Strike: Sonar, Anti-Submarine Warfare and the Royal Navy, 1914–54* (London 1984).
51 Roskill, *Naval Policy Between the Wars* Vol 1, pp 338–40; Gilbert, *Winston Churchill* Vol 4, pp 768–70, 909.
52 Gilbert, *Winston Churchill* Vol 5, pp 62, 65, 92–100.
53 *Ibid.*, pp 68–75; Ferris, *Men, Money and Diplomacy*, pp 158–9.
54 Gilbert, *Companion* Vol 5 part i, pp 303–7; Ferris, *Men, Money and Diplomacy: The Evolution of British Strategic Policy 1919–26* (Ithaca 1989), p 162.
55 Gilbert, *Companion* Vol 5, part i, pp 349–51, 357–8, 359–68, 373–6, 378–9, 383–8, 397–400.
56 Gilbert, *Winston Churchill* Vol 5, p 86; Ferris, *Men, Money and Diplomacy*, pp 161–3.
57 *Ibid.*, pp 101–5, 128–30; *Companion* Vol 5 part i, pp 426–8, 503, 508–18.
58 Ferris, *Men, Money and Diplomacy*, pp 165–9.
59 Roskill, *Naval Policy Between the Wars* Vol 1, p 478; Gilbert, *Winston Churchill* Vol 5, pp 138–43; *Companion* Vol 5 part i, pp

641–2; Ferris, *Men, Money and Diplomacy*, pp 170–4; Ranft, *Beatty Papers* Vol 2, pp 310–1.

60 Ferris, *Men, Money and Diplomacy*, p 174; Ranft, *Beatty Papers* Vol 2, pp 310–1.

61 H T Lenton and J J Colledge, *Warships of World War II* (London 1964), p 12; B Mallet and C O George, *British Budgets, Third Series, 1921–2 to 1932–3* (London 1933), pp 187–277.

62 Gretton, *Churchill and the Royal Navy*, p 2; W D McIntyre, *The Rise and Fall of the Singapore Naval Base* (Hamden 1979), pp 48–52, 66–8; R O'Neill, 'Churchill, Japan and British Security in the Pacific: 1904–42', *Churchill*, eds Blake and Louis, pp 275–89.

63 Gilbert, *Winston Churchill* Vol 5, p 301; *Companion* Vol 5, part i, pp 1030–6, 1340–3, 1380–2; Ferris, *Men, Money and Diplomacy*, p 162.

64 *Ibid.*, pp 79, 85, 88, 101–2.

65 *Ibid.*, pp 83–5, 102, 248.

66 Gilbert, *Winston Churchill* pp 76–7; A J P Taylor, *English History, 1914–45* (Oxford 1985), pp 236–7; A F Havinghurst, *Britain in Transition: The Twentieth Century* (Chicago 1985), pp 202–6.

67 Gilbert, *Companion* Vol 5, part i, pp 897–902, 935–7, 943–6.

68 Gilbert, *Winston Churchill* Vol 5, pp 237–84; *Companion* Vol 5, part i, pp 1062–3, 1072–8, 1088–1100, 1106–9, 1114–6, 1122–3, 1182–5, 1199–1200.

69 Gilbert, *Winston Churchill* Vol 5, p 290.

70 *Ibid.*, pp 250, 288, 310; *Companion* Vol 5 part i, pp 1388–9, 1400–1, 1413–4, 1421–4.

71 Roskill, *Naval Policy Between the Wars* Vol 1, pp 575, 580–3, 586–8.

72 Ferris, *Men, Money and Diplomacy*, pp 188–9; G C Peden, *British Rearmament and the Treasury: 1932–9* (Edinburgh 2979), p 8.

Chapter 3 Churchill and the US Navy, 1919–29

1 A Chamberlain, *Down the Years* (London 1935), pp 232–36.

2 S Roskill, *Naval Policy Between the Wars: Volume I* (London 1968), pp 300–54, 498–516, and *Volume II* (London 1976), pp 37–70; Roskill, *The Strategy of Seapower* (London 1986), p 148; C Hall, *Britain America and Arms Control 1921–37* (Basingstoke 1987), p 193; A Marder, *Old Friends, New Enemies Vol I* (Oxford 1981), p 6; FH Hinsley, *Command of the Sea: The Naval Side of British History 1918–45* (London 1950), p 22.

3 C Barnett, *The Collapse of British Power* (London 1972), p 272.

4 J Ferris, 'The Symbol and the Substance of Seapower: Great Britain and the United States, and the One-Power Standard, 1919–21, *Anglo-*

American Relations in the 1920s ed B J C McKercher (London 1991), pp 55–80; McKercher 'Wealth, Power and the New International Order: Britain and the American Challenge in the 1920s', *Diplomatic History* vol 12/4 (1988), p 411.

5 'Naval Estimates', 1901–2, 17 January 1901, Selborne Mss, Bodleian Library, Oxford; 'The Two-Power Standard' Memorandum, 1919, Asquith Mss 21, Bodleian Library, Oxford.

6 Marder, *From the Dreadnought to Scapa Flow*, Vol 5 (Oxford 1970), p 220.

7 *Ibid*, pp 224–37.

8 Geddes Mss A/426/1, Public Record Office.

9 M Gilbert, *Winston S Churchill, Companion* part ii, Vol 4, p 1379.

10 Churchill to Baldwin, 25 March, 1925, Baldwin Mss 232, Cambridge University Library.

11 Gilbert, *Winston S Churchill, Companion* part ii, Vol 4, p 780.

12 PRO, CAB 23/25, May 30, 1921; Gilbert, *Winston S Churchill, Companion* part iii, Vol 4, p 1539.

13 Lloyd George Mss F 192/1/5, House of Lords.

14 *Ibid*.

15 Beatty Mss 13/28/14, National Maritime Museum.

16 'Battleship vs Submarine', 16 December 1920, PRO ADM 116/3442; Beatty Mss, 13/28/14.

17 Memorandum, 22 November 1920, ADM 116/1776.

18 Lloyd George to Balfour, 15 November 1921, ADM 116/3445.

19 Report of Committee on Part I of the Geddes Report, Beatty Mss 8/11/4.

20 H and M Sprout, *Towards a New Order of Sea Power: American Naval Policy and the World Scene 1918–22* (Princeton 1943), chap 7; W Braisted, *The United States Navy in the Pacific 1909–22* (Austin 1971), pp 477–81, 499–502; R Kaufman, *Arms Control in the Pre-Nuclear Era: The United States and Naval Limitation Between the Two World Wars* (New York 1990), pp 23–32.

21 McKercher, *The Second Baldwin Government and the United States, 1924–29* (Cambridge 1984), pp 5–19.

22 Memorandum by Sea Lords, 4 August 1925, Baldwin Mss 2.

23 'Navy Estimates', 5 February 1925, CAB 24/171.

24 Memorandum, 7 February 1925, CAB 24/171. Churchill to Baldwin, 15 December, 1924, Baldwin Mss 2; Gilbert, *Winston S Churchill, Companion* part i, Vol 5, pp 259–68, 426–8, 443–4.

25 Churchill to Baldwin, 15 December 1924, Baldwin Mss 2.

26 Gilbert, *Winston S Churchill, Companion* part i, Vol 5, p 364.

27 'Navy Estimates', 7 February 1925, CAB 24/171.
28 Roskill, *Naval Policy Between the Wars: Volume I* (London 1968), Appendix C.
29 'Ships Laid Down Each Year by the Five Principal Naval Powers', 1934, SCCCNO, National Archives, Washington DC.
30 Roskill, *Naval Policy Between the Wars: Volume I*, p 214.
31 'Empire Naval Policy and Co–operation', April 1926, ADM 116/2311.
32 'Papers Prepared for the British Empire Delegation to the 1927 Geneva Conference', ADM 116/2609; 'Plan for the Naval Limitation and Disarmament Conference at Geneva', 17 March 1927, ADM 116/3371.
33 *Jane's Fighting Ships of World War I* (London 1990), pp 55–62.
34 Roskill, *Naval Policy Between the Wars: Volume I*, pp 498–516; McKercher, *The Second Baldwin Government and the United States 1924–29*, pp 65–76.
35 Cecil to Churchill, 24 July 1925, Cecil Mss 51073, British Museum; Cecil to Baldwin, 9 March 1927, Baldwin Mss 130.
36 Cecil to Tyrell, 24 June 1927, Cecil Mss 51118.
37 Gibson to Secretary of State, 29 June 1927, Coolidge Mss Series 20, Library of Congress, Washington DC.
38 Bridgeman diary, 29 June 1927, Bridgeman Mss 1, Churchill College, Cambridge.
39 Gibson to Secretary of State, 30 June 1927, Coolidge Mss Series 20.
40 Chamberlain to Cecil, 5 July 1927, Cecil Mss 51078.
41 Cabinet Minutes, 4 July 1927, Templewood Mss C IV, Cambridge University Library.
42 Royal Institute of International Affairs, *Survey of International Affairs – 1927* (Oxford 1929), p 51.
43 Churchill, 29 June 1927, CAB 24/187.
44 Beatty to Baldwin, 30 June 1927, Birkenhead to Baldwin, July 1927, Baldwin Mss 130.
45 CID, 7 July 1927, CAB 24/187.
46 Gilbert, *Winston S Churchill, Companion* Vol 5, pp 1030–5.
47 Baldwin memorandum, 21 July 1927, CAB 24/188.
48 Gilbert, *Winston S Churchill, Companion* Vol 5, pp 1037–8.
49 Cecil to Churchill, 26 July 1927, Cecil Mss 51073.
50 Hankey to Baldwin, 28 July 1927, Baldwin Mss 230.
51 Gilbert, *Winston S Churchill, Companion* Vol 5, p 1049.
52 Draft Cecil to Baldwin, 9 August 1927, Baldwin Mss 131; Cecil to Chamberlain, 10 August 1927 and 18 August 1927, Cecil Mss 51078–9.

53 Gilbert, *Winston S Churchill, Companion* Vol 5, p 1035; Churchill to Baldwin, August 18, 1927, Baldwin Mss 2.
54 Gilbert, *Winston S Churchill*, Vol V, Companion, pp 1075–7, 1088–95, 1106–9, 1114–6.
55 Roskill, *Naval Policy Between the Wars: Volume I*, pp 555–9.
56 Cecil to Chamberlain, 18 August 1927, Cecil Mss 51078/9.
57 Churchill recorded by P J Grigg, 10 February 1928, Hankey Mss 5/1, Churchill College, Cambridge.
58 Gilbert, *Winston S Churchill*, Vol V, Companion, pp 1348–9, 1352.
59 *Ibid*, pp 329, 340–1, 683.
60 *Ibid*, p 536.
61 *Ibid*, pp 1088–95, 1098–1103, 1342.
62 G Davis, *A Navy Second to None* (New York 1940), pp 322–33.
63 *Message of the President of the United States* (Washington DC 1927), pp 2–4.
64 Davis, *A Navy Second to None*, p 326.
65 Memorandum, 11 May 1928, ADM 116/2578.
66 Memorandum, 26 June 1928, ADM 116/2578; 28 August 1928, CAB 24/197.
67 'Address of President Coolidge', 11 November 1928, Hoover Mss Box 214, Herbert Hoover Presidential Library, West Branch, Iowa.
68 Salisbury to Baldwin, 22 May 1928, Baldwin Mss 2; Cushendun, 16 June 1928, Baldwin Mss 230.
69 Memorandum, 12 November 1928, Baldwin Mss 109.
70 Memorandum, 19 July 1928, CAB 24/199.
71 Bell to Hoover, 2 May 1929, Castle to Kellogg, 21 November 1928, Hoover Mss; Houghton to Castle, 17 December 1928, Castle Mss, Herbert Hoover Presidential Library.
72 Gilbert, *Winston S Churchill, Companion* Vol 5, p 1452.

Chapter 4 Churchill, the European Balance of Power and the USA

1 C R Coote and P D Bunyan, eds, *Sir Winston Churchill. A Self–Portrait* (London, 1954), p 214.
2 W S Churchill, *The History of the English-Speaking Peoples*, 4 vols. (Toronto, 1956–58). Max Beloff, 'The Special Relationship: An Anglo-American Myth', in M Gilbert, ed, *A Century of Conflict, 1850–1950: Essays for A J P Taylor* (London, 1966), pp 149–71; D Reynolds, 'A "Special Relationship"?: America, Britain and International Order since World War Two', *International Affairs*, 62(1985/86), pp 1–20; H B Ryan, 'A New Look at Churchill's "Iron

Curtain" Speech', *Historical Journal*, 22(1979), pp 895–920. R H Ferrell, ed, *The Eisenhower Diaries* (New York, 1981), p 223.

3   W S Churchill, *My Early Life. A Roving Commission* (1930), 15, pp 9–10.

4   R Rhodes James, ed, *Winston S Churchill. His Complete Speeches, 1897–1963*, Vol 5 [hereafter *Complete Speeches*] (London, New York, 1974), 5006.

5   Mackenzie King diary, 12 September 1923, Mackenzie King MSS [National Archives of Canada, Ottawa] MG 26 J13 1923.

6   C P Stacey, *Canada and the Age of Conflict*, Vol II: *1921–1948. The Mackenzie King Era* (Toronto, 1981), pp 17–27; D Walder, *The Chanak Affair* (London, 1969).

7   Cmd.2768: *Summary of the Proceedings of the Imperial Conference, 1926*, p 9.

8   *Complete Speeches*, Vol 4, 4103–04.

9   Tuvia Ben-Moshe, *Churchill, Strategy and History* (Hemel Hempstead, Boulder; Co, 1992), esp pp 317–33. Cf. D Jablonsky, *Churchill: The Making of a Grand Strategist* (Carlisle Barracks, PA, 1990).

10 K E Neilson, *Britain and the Last Tsar: Anglo-Russian Relations, 1894–1917* (Oxford, forthcoming). Cf. K E Neilson, '"Greatly Exaggerated": The Myth of the Decline of Great Britain before 1914', *International History Review*, 13(1991), pp 695–725.

11 Cf. Simon Bourette-Knolwes, 'The Global Micawber: Sir Robert Vansittart, the Treasury, and the Global Balance of Power, 1933–35', *Diplomacy and Statecraft* (forthcoming); B J C McKercher, 'Diplomatic Equipoise: The Lansdowne Foreign Office, the Russo-Japanese War of 1905–05, and the Global Balance of Power', *Canadian Journal of History*, 24(1989), pp 299–339.

12 Churchill, *Malakand Field Force*, pp 307–12.

13 Churchill, *The River War* (London 1989 reprint) pp 360–4.

14 Churchill, *London to Ladysmith via Pretoria* (London 1989 reprint), p 10.

15 R Hyman, *Elgin and Churchill at the Colonial Office 1905–08: The Watershed of the Empire-Commonwealth* (London, 1968). Cf. Churchill minute for Elgin [colonial secretary], 15 March 1906, in R S Churchill [later Martin Gilbert], *Winston S Churchill, Companion* Vol 2 part i [hereafter *Churchill*; the companion volumes in the style *Churchill Companion* Vol 2 part ii, pp 528–30.

16 Churchill memorandum, 3 November 1909, *Churchill Companion* Vol 2 part ii, pp 961–62.

17 Churchill to Lloyd George, 31 August 1911, *ibid.*, p 1119.

18 Churchill memorandum, undated [but February 1912], *ibid.*, *Companion* Vol 2 part iii, pp 1511–14.

19 Cf. W S Churchill, *The World Crisis 1911–1918*, 4 vols. (London, 1923–1927); R Prior, *Churchill's 'World Crisis' as History* (London, 1981).

20 See F C Costigliola, 'Anglo–American Financial Rivalry in the 1920s', *Journal of Economic History*, 37(1977), pp 911–34; P M Kennedy, *The Rise and Fall of the Great Powers. Economic Change and Military Conflict from 1500 to 2000* (New York, 1987), pp 275–343; C P Parinni, *Heir to Empire: United States Economic Diplomacy, 1916–1923* (Pittsburgh, 1969). For studies that disagree, see David French, *The British Way in Warfare, 1688–2000* (London, 1990), pp 175–201; and the special issue of the *International History Review*, 13(1991) on 'The Decline of Great Britain', which includes Gordon Martel, 'The Meaning of Power: Rethinking the Decline and Fall of Great Britain', J R Ferris, '"The Greatest Power on Earth": Great Britain in the 1920s', B J C McKercher, '"Our Most Dangerous Enemy": Great Britain Pre-eminent in the 1930s'.

21 Churchill, *Early Life*, p 19.

22 Cf. R L Rapson, *Britons View America: Travel Commentary, 1860–1935* (Seattle, 1971); S Strauss, 'The American Myth in Britain', *South Atlantic Quarterly*, 72(1973), pp 66–81; M Weidhorn, 'America Through Churchill's Eyes', *Thought*, 50(March 1975), pp 5–34.

23 Churchill to his brother, 15 November [1895], *Churchill Companion* Vol 1 part i, pp 599–600. Cf. W S Churchill, *Thoughts and Adventures* (London, 1932), pp 52–3.

24 R H Pilpel, *Churchill and America* (New York, London, 1976), pp 34–56.

25 Amery diary, 10 May 1917, Esher to Haig, 30 May 1917, *Churchill Companion* Vol 4 part i, pp 60, 64–65.

26 Churchill, *World Crisis*, III, pp 226–27.

27 Cabinet paper, 19 November 1918, *Churchill Companion* Vol 4 part i, pp 417–21.

28 G W Egerton, 'Ideology, Diplomacy and International Organisation: Wilsonism and the League of Nations in Anglo–American Relations, 1918–1920', in B J C McKercher, ed, *Anglo–American Relations in the 1920s. The Struggle for Supremacy* (London, Edmonton, Alta., 1990), pp 17–54.

29 Churchill, *World Crisis*, IV, 173–74; Council of Ten Minutes, 14

February 1919, Department of State, *Papers Relating to the Foreign Relations of the United States, 1919. The Paris Peace Conference*, Vol 3 (Washington, DC), pp 1041–4. Cf. L Killen, *The Russian Bureau: A Case Study of Wilsonian Diplomacy* (Lexington, KY, 1983).

30 Churchill (2) to Lloyd George, 16 February 1919, Lloyd George to Churchill, 16 February 1919, *Churchill Companion* Vol 4 part i, pp 535–7, 538–9.

31 Churchill, *World Crisis*, IV, p 149.

32 *Ibid.*, 127.

33 Treasury memorandum, 'The British Case on War Debts', nd [but March 1933 from internal evidence], T172/1512 [Public Record Office, Kew].

34 Admiralty memoranda, 'Freedom of the Seas' [CID 239B], 6 March 1920, 'Naval Commitments', 19 July 1920, both CAB 4/7 [Public Record Office, Kew]. Cf. D C Allard, 'Anglo–American Naval Differences During World War I', *Military Affairs*, 44(1980); A J Marder, 'The Influence of History on Sea Power: The Royal Navy and the Lessons of 1914–1918', *Pacific Historical Review*, 41(1972), pp 413–43; S W Roskill, *Naval Policy Between the Wars*, Vol 1: *The Period of Anglo-American Antagonism, 1919–1929* (London, 1968), pp 71–130.

35 K Jeffrey, *The British Army and the Crisis of Empire, 1918–1922* (Manchester, 1984); C. Townsend, *The British Campaign in Ireland, 1919–1921: The Development of Political and Military Policies* (Oxford, 1975).

36. J Darwin, *Britain, Egypt, and the Middle East: Imperial Policy in the Aftermath of War, 1918–1922* (London, 1981); A S Klieman, *Foundations of British Policy in the Arab World: The Cairo Conference of 1921* (London, 1970).

37 K Middlemas and J Barnes, *Baldwin. A Biography* (London, 1969), pp 279–83.

38 R Dingman, *Power in the Pacific: The Origins of Naval Arms Limitation, 1914–1922* (London, 1976); M G Fry, *Illusions of Security: North Atlantic Diplomacy, 1918–1922* (Toronto, 1972); I Nish, 'Britain and the Ending of the Anglo-Japanese Alliance, *Bulletin of the Japan Society of London*, 53(1967), pp 2–5.

39 M Murfett, 'Look Back in Anger: The Western Powers and the Washington Conference of 1921–1922', in B J C McKercher, ed, *Arms Limitation and Disarmament, 1899–1939: Restraints on War* (Westport, CT, 1992), pp 83–103.

40 Churchill to the Prince of Wales, 2 January 1922, *Churchill Companion* Vol 4 part iii, 1709–10.

41 D Carlton, 'Great Britain and the Coolidge Naval Disarmament Conference', *Political Science Quarterly*, 83(1968), pp 573–98; R W Fanning, 'The Coolidge Conference of 1927: Disarmament in Disarray', in McKercher, *Arms Limitation*, pp 105–27; B J C McKercher, *The Second Baldwin Government and the United States, 1924–1929: Attitudes and Diplomacy* (Cambridge, 1984), pp 55–76.

42 Churchill to Niemeyer, 2 January 1925, T171/245.

43 Gilbert, *Churchill*, Vol 5, pp 92–100.

44 CAB 24/187, [CP 189(27)], 29 June 1927.

45 McKercher, *Baldwin Government*, 73–76. Cf. CC 43(27)1, and Appendices, CAB 23/55.

46 Cecil to Irwin, 29 September 1927, BL [British Library, London] Add MSS 51084.

47 'Government Expenditure and Tariffs', in D Butler and A Sloman, *British Political Facts, 1900–1975*, 4th ed (London, 1975), p 314. 'British Navy Estimates and Actual Expenditure 1919–39', in Roskill, *Naval Policy*, II, p 489.

48 J R Ferris, 'Treasury Control, the Ten Year Rule, and British Service Policies, 1919–1924', *Historical Journal*, 30(1987), pp 859–83.

49 Gilbert, *Churchill*, Vol 5, pp 290–2.

50 J Jacobson, *Locarno Diplomacy. Germany and the West, 1925–1929* (Princeton, 1972), 3–67. Cf. Gilbert, *Churchill*, Vol 5, pp 124–25.

51 'Naval Building Programmes as Finally Implemented 1919–1939', in Roskill, *Naval Policy*, I, pp 580–2.

52 CAB 53/12, COS 28, CAB 53/13, COS 100, CAB 53/14, COS 141.

53 Churchill to Baldwin, 6 June 1927, Baldwin MSS [University Library, Cambridge] p 5; 10 April 1929, *ibid.*, pp 164.

54 D Carlton, 'The Anglo–French Compromise on Arms Limitation, 1928', *Journal of British Studies*, 8(1969), pp 141–62; McKercher, *Baldwin Government*, pp 142–7.

55 B J C McKercher, 'Belligerent Rights in 1927–1929: Foreign Policy Versus Naval Policy in the Second Baldwin Government', *Historical Journal*, 29(1986), pp 963–74; *idem.*, 'From Enmity to Cooperation: The Second Baldwin Government and the Improvement of Anglo-American Relations, November 1928–June 1929', *Albion*, 24(1992), pp 65–88.

56 On Coolidge, see Churchill memorandum 19 November 1928, *Documents on British Foreign Policy*, Series *IA*, V, 883–85; FO 371/12839/6071/6071.

57 Greg Kennedy, 'The 1930 London Naval Conference and Anglo-American Maritime Strength, 1927–1930', in McKercher, *Arms*

Limitation, pp 149–71; R G O'Connor, *Perilous Equilibrium. The United States and the London Naval Conference of 1930* (Lawrence, 1962).

58 Churchill to Baldwin, 17 May 1930, Baldwin MSS 117; 'Naval Disarmament Treaty', 2 June 1930, *Complete Speeches*, V, pp 4814–22.

59 S Ball, *Baldwin and the Conservative Party. The Crisis of 1929–1931* (New Haven, 1988).

60 Rhodes James, *Study in Failure*, pp 181–215. Cf. W S Churchill, *India. Speeches and an Introduction* (London, 1931).

61 Gilbert, *Churchill*, Vol 5, pp 809–31.

62 *Complete Speeches*, Vol 5, pp 4670–71.

63 Churchill, *India*, p 141.

64 W S Churchill, *Marlborough: His Life and Times*, 4 vols. (London, 1933–1938).

65 K Robbins, *Churchill*, (London, 1992), p 107.

66 Churchill, *Early Life*, p 10.

67 Churchill, *Complete Speeches*, Vol 5, 5170–75, 5543–51.

68 *Ibid.*, pp 5052–53.

69 *Ibid.*, Vol 6, 5869–70, 6004–13, 6071–72.

70 *Ibid.*, Vol 5, 5170–75.

71 Churchill speeches, 'Defence', 7 February 1934, 'The Need for Air Parity', 8 March 1934, 'Air Estimates', 19 March 1935, all *Complete Speeches*, Vol 5, pp 5321–26, 5338–44, 5543–51.

72 N Gibbs, *Grand Strategy*, Vol 1: *Rearmament Policy* (London, 1976), pp 135–40; Gilbert, *Churchill*, Vol 5, pp 568–78.

73 Churchill, *Complete Speeches*, Vol 5, 5433–36.

74 Cf. Chamberlain diary, 5 July, 19 October 1935, and Chamberlain to Prince, 16 January 1938, quoted in K Feiling, *The Life of Neville Chamberlain* (London, 1946), pp 265, 268, 322–24.

75 University of Birmingham, NC 18/1/879.

76 Ben-Moshe, *Churchill*, pp 100–07; Jablonsky, *Churchill*, pp 41–44.

77 Churchill, *Complete Speeches*, VI, 5923–27.

78 Halifax memorandum, 21 March 1938, CAB 27/627, FP(36)56.

79 B J C McKercher, "No Eternal Friends or Enemies': British Defence Policy and the Problem of the United States, 1919–1939', *Canadian Journal of History*, 28(1993), pp 257–93; D Reynolds, *The Creation of the Anglo–American Alliance, 1937–1941. A Study in Competitive Co–operation* (Chapel Hill, 1981), pp 7–62.

80 *Churchill Companion* Vol 5 part iii, p 628.

81 *Ibid.*, pp 704–05.

82 *Ibid.*, pp 658–59.
83 *Ibid.*, pp 1414–17.

Chapter 5 Churchill and Italy, 1922–40

1   Martin Gilbert, *Churchill. A Life* (London 1992), p 87.
2   Gilbert, *Churchill. A Life*, pp 181, 185, 200; Mary Soames, *Clementine Churchill* (London 1979), p 45.
3   Gilbert, *Winston S Churchill*, Vol 3 (London 1971), p 189.
4   Gilbert, *Churchill*, Vol 3, p 115.
5   Gilbert, *Churchill*, Vol 2, p 426.
6   H H Asquith, *Letters to Venetia Stanley* (Oxford 1982), p 501.
7   Gilbert, *Churchill* Vol 4 1916–22 (London 1975), pp 53–9.
8   *Ibid*, pp 243–8, 372.
9   *Ibid*, pp 825, 861.
10 *Ibid*, p 879.
11 Gilbert, *Winston S Churchill, Companion* Vol 5 part i. *Documents* (London 1979), pp 907–9.
12 *Ibid*, pp 59–60.
13 I de Begnac, *Taccuini Mussoliniani* (Bologna 1990), pp 506–48.
14 Gilbert, *Churchill* Vol 5, p 142.
15 Gilbert, *Churchill. Companion* Vol 1, pp 636–7.
16 A Berselli, *L'Opinione Pubblica Inglese e il Fascismo* (Milan 1971), p 204.
17 A Pirelli, *Taccuini. 1922–43* (Bologna 1984), pp 56–9, 66.
18 D Dutton, *Austen Chamberlain. Gentleman in Politics* (London 1985), pp 248, 262, 293n.
19 Gilbert, *Churchill. Companion* Vol 1, pp 722–3.
20 Churchill Archives Centre, Churchill College, Chartwell Papers, 1/178, f. 50.
21 Gilbert, *Churchill. Companion* Vol 1, pp 675–6, 677n.
22 Soames, *Clementine Churchill*, p 212.
23 R Churchill, *Twenty-One Years* (London 1964), p 49.
24 Gilbert, *Churchill. Companion* Vol 1, p. 878.
25 Chartwell Papers, 1/188, f. 71.
26 Gilbert, *Churchill. Companion* Vol 1, pp 907–8 (6 January 1926).
27 Churchill, *Twenty-One Years*, pp 48–50.
28 Chartwell Papers, 2/151, ff 24–5, 27–31.
29 Gilbert, *Churchill* Vol 5, p 225.
30 Churchill, *Twenty-One Years*, p 50.
31 Gilbert, *Churchill. Companion* Vol 1, p 914.
32 Gilbert, *Churchill. Companion* Vol 1, pp 917–8.

33 Chartwell Papers, 9/82A, ff 137–47.
34 Gilbert, *Churchill. Companion* Vol 1, pp 918, 927–8.
35 Press cuttings in Chartwell papers, 9/82 A.
36 Chartwell Papers, 1/179, f 52–3.
37 Gilbert, *Churchill. Companion* Vol 1, p 1058.
38 *Ibid.*, pp 1051–2.
39 Chartwell Papers, 2/177, ff 45–7.
40 Gilbert, *Churchill. Companion* Vol 1, p 1366.
41 D Mack Smith, *Mussolini's Roman Empire* (London 1977), p 46.
42 Gilbert, *Churchill*, Vol 5, pp 456–7.
43 P Nello, *Un Fedele Disubbidiente, Dino Grandi* (Bologna 1993), pp 215–345.
44 C E Lysaght, *Brendan Bracken* (London 1979), p 120; D Cooper, *Old Men Forget. Autobiography* (London 1953), p 183.
45 D Dutton, *Austen Chamberlain*, p 314.
46 Gilbert, *Churchill. Companion* Vol 2, p 1171.
47 Gilbert, *Churchill* Vol 5, p 662.
48 Gilbert, *Churchill. Companion* Vol 2, pp 1262–4.
49 *Ibid*, p 1256 (5 September 1935).
50 Gilbert, *Churchill* Vol 5, p 677.
51 Gilbert, *Churchill. Companion* Vol 2, pp 1300–1; 1305–7.
52 Chartwell Papers, 2/238, ff 49–51.
52 Nello, *Un Fedele Disubbidiente*, pp 243–59; Pirelli, *Taccuini*, pp 129–34.
54 Pirelli, *Taccuini*, pp 170–6.
55 *Ibid.*, p 177.
56 *Ibid.*, p 194.
57 R Rhodes James, *Anthony Eden* (London 1987), p 115.
58 R Rhodes James, *Churchill. A Study in Failure* (London 1970), p 28.
59 A R Peters, *Anthony Eden at the Foreign Office 1931–38* (London 1986), p 381n.
60 Gilbert, *Churchill* Vol 5, p 869.
61 *Ibid.*, p 905.
62 R De Felice, *Mussolini il Duce. Lo Stato Totalitario 1936–40* (Torino 1981), pp 507–27; Nello, *Un Fedele Disubbidiente*, pp 329–45.
63 De Felice, *Mussolini il Duce. Lo Stato Totalitario*, p 526.
64 Gilbert, *Churchill* Vol 5, p 1056.
65 *Ibid*, pp 1074–5, 1093.
66 G Ciano, *Diario 1937–43* (Milan 1990), p 429.
67 Gilbert, *Finest Hour. Winston S Churchill 1939–41* (London 1983), p 241.

68 *Ibid.*, p 340; Ciano, *Diario*, pp 432–3.
69 Chartwell Papers, 9/145, ff 76–87.
70 I de Begnac, *Taccuini Mussoliniani*, pp 566, 574.

Chapter 6 Churchill and Hitler, 1940: Peace or War?

1 Bernd Martin, 'Amerikas Durchbruch zur politischen Weltmacht', *Militärgeschichtliche Mitteilungen* 57 (1981), pp 57–98.
2 Clemens Verenkotte, *Das brüchige Bündnis: Amerikanische Anleihen und deutsche Industrie 1924–1934* (Bern 1992).
3 John A Garraty, 'The New Deal, National Socialism and the Great Depression', *American Historical Review*, Vol 78 (1973), pp 907–44.
4 Doerte Doering, *Deutsche Außenwirtschaftspolitik 1933–1935* (Berlin, PhD thesis, 1969).
5 Detlef Junker, *Der unteilbare Weltmarkt. Das ökonomische Interesse in der Außenpolitik der USA 1933–1941* (Stuttgart 1975); Lloyd C Gardner, *Economic Aspects of New Deal Diplomacy* (Madison 1964); Joachim Bengelsdorf, *Die Landwirtschaft der Vereinigten Staaten im Zweiten Weltkrieg* (Freiburg, PhD thesis, 1994).
6 Hans–Joachim Schroeder, *Deutschland und die Vereinigten Staaten 1933–1939. Wirtschaft und Politik in der Entwicklung des deutsch–amerikanischen Gegensatzes* (Wiesbaden 1970), p 150f. Martin, 'Die Auswirkungen der Weltwirtschaftskrise in Japan', *Die Peripherie in der Weltwirtschaftskrise: Afrika, Asien und Lateinamerika 1929–1939*, ed Dietmar Rothermund (Paderborn 1982).
7 Richard Polenberg, 'The Decline of the New Deal 1937–1940' and David Brody, 'The New Deal and World War II', *The New Deal. The National Level*, eds John Braeman *et al* (Ohio 1975).
8 Richard Kottman, *Reciprocity and the North Atlantic Triangle, 1932–1938* (New York 1968).
9 Klaus Schwabe, *Der amerikanische Isolationismus im 20.Jahrhundert. Legende und Wirklichkeit* (Wiesbaden 1975); Wayne S Cole, *Roosevelt and the Isolationists 1932–1945* (Lincoln 1983).
10 *Hitlers zweites Buch*, ed Gerhard L Weinberg (Stuttgart 1961); Alton Frye, *Nazi Germany and the American Hemisphere 1933–1941* (New Haven 1967); Andreas Hillgruber, 'Der Faktor Amerika in Hitlers Strategie 1938–1941', *Nationalsozialistische Außenpolitik*, ed Wolfgang Michalka (Darmstadt 1978), pp 493–525; Jochen Thies, *Architekt der Weltherrschaft. Die 'Endziele' Hitlers* (Düsseldorf 1976).
11 Keith Feiling, *Neville Chamberlain* (London 1946), p 325

12 *Documents on British Foreign Policy* 3 Series Vol VI, ed E L Woodward (London 1953) No 354; Martin 'Friedensplanungen der multinationalen Großindustrie, 1932–40, als politische Krisenstrategie', *Geschichte und Gesellschaft*, 2, (1976), pp 66–88.

13 Martin, *Friedensinitiativen und Machtpolitik im Zweiten Weltkrieg 1939–42* (Dusseldorf 1976), pp 135–53, 207–33, 301–36.

14 Theo Sommer, *Deutschland und Japan zwischen den Mächten 1935–1940. Vom Antikominternpakt zum Dreimächtepakt* (Tübingen 1962); Paul Walter Schroeder, *The Axis Alliance and Japanese-American Relations* (New York 1958). Martin, *Friedensinitiativen*, pp 407–24.

15 Martin, 'Germany and Pearl Harbor. The German-Japanese Alliance and the Outbreak of War in the Pacific', *Fifty Years After. The Pacific War Re-examined*, eds Chihoro Hosoya and Akira Iriye (Tokyo 1994, in Japanese). *Kriegswende Dezember 1941*, eds Jürgen Rohwer and Eberhard Jäckel (Koblenz 1984).

16 E L Woodward, *British Foreign Policy in the Second World War*, 5 vols (1970–76). Vol 2 (London 1971), ch 25 'The Refusal to Consider German Suggestions for a "Compromise" Peace'.

17 John Charmley, *Churchill: The End of Glory. A Political Biography* (London 1993), p 400.

18 David Reynolds, 'Churchill and the British "Decision" to Fight on in 1940: Right Policy, Wrong Reasons', *Diplomacy and Intelligence during the Second World War*, ed R Langhorne (Cambridge 1985). D Reynolds, *The Creation of the Anglo–American Alliance 1937–41. A Study in Competitive Co-operation* (London 1981), p 167.

19 *Churchill and Roosevelt: the Complete Correspondence*, 3 vols, ed Warren F Kimball, (Princeton 1984).

20 Reynolds, *The Creation*, p 79.

21 Quoted by Donald C Watt, *Succeeding John Bull. America in Britain's Place. 1900–1975* (Cambridge 1984), p 87.

22 Martin, *Friedensinitiativen*, pp 82ff, 154ff; Christopher Hill, *Cabinet Decisions on Foreign Policy. The British Experience October 1938 – June 1941* (Cambridge 1991), pp 100–45.

23 Hans–Jürgen Heimsoeth, *Der Zusammenbruch der Dritten Französischen Republik. Frankreich während der 'Drôle de Guerre' 1939/1940* (Bonn 1990); Martin, *Friedensinitiativen*, pp 58–9, 65, 67–8, 73, 127.

24 Reynolds, 'Churchill and the British Decision', p 149.

25 Martin, *Friedensinitiativen* pp 77, 207–33.

26 Kevin Jefferys, *The Churchill Coalition and Wartime Politics*

1940–1945 (Manchester, 1991), pp 35–40; Charmley, *Churchill*, p 396; Lord Birkenhead, *Halifax. The Life of Lord Halifax* (London 1965), p 453.

27 Reynolds, 'Churchill and the British Decision', p 149
28 Martin, *Friedensinitiativen*, pp 243, 250f; C Hill, *Cabinet Decisions*, pp 146–87; D Reynolds, *The Creation*, pp 103–4; J Charmley, *Churchill*, p 404.
29 Martin, *Friedensinitiativen*, pp 250–1.
30 Reynolds, 'Churchill and the British Decision', pp 151–2.
31 Martin, *Friedensinitiativen*, pp 251, 254; Reynolds, 'Churchill and the British Decision', pp 151, 154; Charmley, *Churchill*, p 449.
32 Charmley, *Churchill*, p 449; Martin, *Friedensinitiativen*, p 290; Reynolds, *The Creation*, p 131; E L Woodward, *British Foreign Policy*, Vol 1, pp 355–71.
33 *Ibid.*, Vol 1, p 204; Martin, *Friedensinitiativen*, pp 270–74; Charmley, *Churchill*, p 423; *The Diaries of Sir Alexander Cadogan 1938–1945* ed D Dilks (London 1971), 18 June 1940.
34 Martin, *Friedensinitiativen*, pp 301–36.
35 Charmley, *Churchill*, p 400.
36 Gordon A Craig, 'Churchill and Germany', *Churchill – A Major New Assessment of his Life in Peace and War*, eds R Blake and W R Louis (Oxford 1993), pp 21–40; Paul A Addison, *Churchill on the Home Front 1900–1955* (London 1992); Roy Hay and Peter Hennock, *Die Entstehung des Wohlfahrtsstaates in Großbritannien und Deutschland 1850–1950*, ed W Mommsen (Stuttgart 1982).

Chapter 7 Churchill and the Small States of Europe: the Danish Case

1 *Illustreret Dansk Konversationsleksikon* vol 5, 1934, p 208.
2 Troels Fink, *Spillet om dansk neutralitet 1905–1909* (Aarhus 1959). Carsten Holbraad, *Danish Neutrality. A Study in the Foreign Policy of a Small State* (Oxford 1991) p 41.
3 Arthur J. Marder, *From Dreadnought to Scapa Flow. The Royal Navy in the Fisher Era, 1914–19* Vol 1–2 (London 1961-65), II p 23. Hans Branner, *Småstat mellem stormagter. Beslutningen om mineudlægningen august 1914* (Copenhagen 1972), pp 108–13.
4 Winston Churchill, *The World Crisis I-II* (London 1923), Vol 1, p 152.
5 Branner, *op cit* p 215.
6 Viggo Sjøqvist, *Erik Scavenius. En biografi* I-II (Copenhagen 1973) Vol 1, pp 73–76.

7 Tage Kaarsted, *Great Britain and Denmark 1914–20* (Odense 1979), p 49.
8 Kaarsted *op cit*, p 42-43. P Munch, *Erindringer I-VIII* (Copenhagen 1959-67), Vol 2, p 213–21.
9 Lord Hankey, *The Supreme Command 1914-1918 I-II* (London 1961), Vol 1, p 182.
10 Viscount Grey, *Twenty-five Years 1892-1916 I-II* (London, 1925), Vol 1, p 162.
11 Kaarsted, *op cit*, p 85.
12 Churchill, *op cit*, II pp 19-32. Marder, *op cit*, II pp 176–78.
13 Marder, *op cit*, II pp 185–90.
14 Kaarsted, *op cit*, p 51.
15 Marder, *op cit*, II pp 191-98. Paul Guinn, *British Strategy and Politics 1914 to 1918* (Oxford 1965), p 71. Martin Gilbert, *Winston S. Churchill* Vol 3 1914–16, pp 225–26.
16 R F Mackay, *Fisher of Kilverstone* (Oxford 1973), p 459. Kaarsted, *op cit*, p 52.
17 Kaarsted, *op cit*, p 52.
18 Hankey, *op cit*, Vol 1, p 247.
19 *Ove Rodes dagbøger 1914–18* (Aarhus 1972), p 92.
20 Marder, *op cit*, Vol 2, p 178. Kaarsted, *op cit*, p 55.
21 Susan Seymour, *Anglo Danish Relations and Germany 1933–45* (Odense 1982), p 60.
22 Seymour, *op cit*, p 63. Viggo Sjøqvist, *Danmarks udenrigspolitik 1933–1940* (Copenhagen 1966), pp 190–4.
23 Seymour, *op cit*, p 94. S. Newmann, *March 1939* (1976), pp 209–10, 212.
24 Peter P Rohde, *Den danske Arbejderbevægelses Historie* (Copenhagen 1983), p 119. Sjøqvist, *Scavenius* II p 54.
25 *The Churchill War Papers, Vol. I, At The Admiralty September 1939–May 1940* ed Martin Gilbert, (London 1993), pp 673–4.
26 Seymour, *op cit*, pp 146–7.
27 Sjøqvist, *Danmarks udenrigspolitik*, p 347.
28 War Papers, pp 689–90.
29 Sjøqvist, *op cit*, p 349. Terkel M Terkelsen, *Fra pålidelige kilde* (Copenhagen 1977), pp 36–41.
30 Seymour, *op cit*, pp 143, 158. For a general view vide, *Scandinavia during the Second World War* ed Henrik S Nissen (Minnesota 1983).
31 Ove Hornby, *'With Constant Care'. A.P. Møller: Shipowner 1876–1965* (Copenhagen 1988), p 156.

32 Hornby, *op cit*, pp 177, 313. Jørgen Hæstrup *et al*, *Besættelsen 1940–45* (1979), pp 32, 133.
33 War Papers, pp 1023–4, 1249.
34 Sigurd Jensen, *Levevilkår under besættelsen* (Copenhagen 1971).
35 Sjøqvist, *Scavenius II*, pp 64–69. Niels Thomsen & Jette D. Søllinge, *De danske aviser 1918–1991* (Odense 1991), p 174.
36 Jørgen Hæstrup *et al*, *op cit*, pp 96–97.
37 Erik Lund, *A Girdle of Truth. The Underground News Service Information 1943–45* (Copenhagen 1970).
38 Jørgen Hæstrup, *Europe Ablaze. An Analysis of the History of the European Resistance Movements 1939–45* (Odense 1978), p 262. Vide Jørgen Hæstrup, *Secret Alliance. A Study of the Danish Resistance Movements I-III* (Odense 1976–77).
39 Aage Trommer, *Myte og sandhed i besættelseshistorien* (Copenhagen 1974), p 95.
40 Terkelsen, *op cit*, pp 114–15.
41 Seymour, *op cit*, p 212.
42 Seymour, *op cit*, p 215. Erik Thostrup Jacobsen, *Foden i døren. Danmark mellem Sovjetunionen og England 1944–45* (Odense 1984), pp 102–3.
43 Trommer, *op cit*, pp 90–2.
44 Jeremy Bennett, *British Broadcasting and the Danish Resitance Movement 1940–45* (Cambridge 1966).
45 Fraser J. Harbutt, *The Iron Curtain. Churchill, America and the Origins of the Cold War* (Oxford 1986), p 197. *Vide Social-Demokraten, Politiken* and *Berlingske Tidende* (Conservative) 6 March 1946.
46 Kjersti Blidberg, '"Just Good Friend". Nordic Social Democracy and Security Policy 1945–1950', *Forsvarsstudier 5*, (Oslo 1987). Holbraad, *op cit*, p 86–107. Eric Einhorn, *National Security and Domestic Politics in Post-War Denmark 1945–1961* (Odense 1975), pp 8–23. Max Beloff, 'Churchill and Europe', in *Churchill* ed. Robert Blake and William Roger Louis, (Oxford 1993), p 450.
47 *Politiken*, 25 January 1965.

Chapter 8 Churchill and Poland

1 Public Records Office (henceforth PRO) FO 371, 26419, C14/14/62 20 November 1940.
2 *Ibid.*
3 *Ibid.*
4 *Ibid.*

5   PRO FO 371 26751, C3977/2784/55, 24 March 1941.

6   M Howard, *The Mediterranean Strategy in the Second World War* (London 1993), pp 10–4.

7   L Mitkiewicz, *W najwyzszym sztabie zachodnich aliantow 1943–1945* (London 1971), pp 28–9.

8   Polish Institute and Sikorski Museum (henceforth PISM) A.XII. 4/80 17 November 1942.

9   *Ibid.*

10 PISM Kol 1/DCNW, September 1941.

11 PISM AIV 1/2, 7 March 1940.

12 PISM PRM 21/4 December 1940.

13 M Pestkowska, *Uchodzcze Pasje* (Paris 1991), pp 96–8.

14 PRO FO 371 39402, C8477/8/G55 31 May 1944.

15 AJ Prazmowska 'Polish refugees as military potential', *Refugees in the Age of Total War*, ed AC Bramwell (London 1988), pp 229–30.

16 PRO PREM 3/351/1, 20 June 1940.

17 PRO PREM 2/357, 14 March 1941.

18 *Ibid.*

19 PRO FO 371 26756, C8373/3226/55, 26 July 1941; E Raczynski, *W Sojuszniczym Londynie. Dziennik ambasadora Raczynskiego 1939–1945* (London 1960), p 119.

20 PRO FO 371 26758, C9279/3226/55, 18 August 1941.

21 PRO WO 193/661 18 September 1941 and CAB 79/14 COS(41)340 Meeting, 2 October 1941.

22 M Gilbert, *Finest Hour. Winston S. Churchill 1939–1941* (London 1983), pp 1204–5.

23 A J P Taylor, *Beaverbrook* (London 1972), p 488; E M Bennett, *Franklin Roosevelt and the Search for Victory. Soviet–American Relations 1939–1945* (Wilmington 1990), pp 32–3.

24 *Documents on Polish–Soviet Relations* General Sikorski Instytut (London 1961) No.132, pp 182–4, 24 October 1941.

25 Gilbert, *Road to Victory. Winston S. Churchill 1941–1945* (London 1986), pp 389–90.

26 PRO PREM 3/136/8, 1 December 1943.

27 M Kitchen, *British Policy towards the Soviet Union During the Second World War* (London 1989), pp 180–1.

28 J Ciechanowski, *The Warsaw Rising of 1944* (Cambridge 1974), p 243.

29 PRO FO 371 39414, C14115/8/G55, 12 October 1944.

30 PRO FO 371 39411, C244/8/G5, 26 August 1944.

Chapter 9 Churchill and de Gaulle

1   W S Churchill, *Second World War* Vol 2, p 136.
2   *Ibid*, p 172.
3   PRO CAB 65/7, WC 188 (40), 23 June 1940.
4   CAB 65/8, 28 June 1940.
5   François Kersaudy, *Churchill and de Gaulle* (London 1990), pp 89–91.
6   *Ibid*, pp 86–8.
7   Churchill, *The Second World War* Vol 4, p 199.
8   St Antony's College, Oxford, MEC Shone Papers, British Legation to FO no 69, 30 April 1945.
9   C de Gaulle, *The Call to Honour* (London 1955) docts, pp 52–3.
10 FO 371/36047, Prime Minister to Deputy Prime Minister and Foreign Secretary, pencil no 166, 21 May 1943.
11 G Catroux, *Dans la bataille de Méditerranée* (Paris 1949), p 20.
12 CAB 65/38, to Prime Minister from Deputy Prime Minister and Foreign Secretary, 23 May 1943.
13 J W Wheeler-Bennett, *King George VI* (London 1958), p 560.
14 FO 371/36887, Collier to Eden, no 21; FDR Library, PSF/34, D Biddle to FDR, 23 November 1942.
15 De Gaulle, *L'Unité* (Paris 1958), p 101.
16 M Gilbert, *W S Churchill* vol 6, p 867.
17 Lord Moran, *Struggle for Survival* (London 1966), p 81.
18 A Gillois, *Histoire secrète des Français à Londres* (Paris 1973), p 251.
19 O Riste, *London Regjeringa* vol II (Oslo 1974), pp 135–6, 162–3.
20 Kersaudy, *Vi stoler på England* (Oslo 1991).
21 FO 371/43250: WC (JP) (44) 164, 11 July 1944, p 3.
22 N Beloff, *Tito's Flawed Legacy* (London 1985), pp 87, 94–105.
23 E Barker, *Churchill and Eden at War* (London 1978), pp 273–4.
24 Churchill, *Second World War* Vol 5, pp 421–2.
25 Churchill, *Second World War* Vol 6, p 81.
26 De Gaulle, *L'Unité*, p 203.

Chapter 10 Churchill, Roosevelt and Post-war Europe

1   *The Fringes of Power* (New York & London, 1985), diary entry of 1 January 1953, p 658.
2   US Dept. of State, *Foreign Relations of the United States* (Washington, 1862–) [hereafter *FRUS* plus volume title].
3   Chester Wilmot, *The Struggle for Europe* (New York, 1952).
4   Robert Nisbet, *Roosevelt and Stalin: The Failed Courtship* (Washington, 1988); Amos Perlmutter, *FDR and Stalin: A Not so*

Grand Alliance, 1943–1945 (Columbia and London, 1933). William Larsh, 'W Averell Harriman and the Polish Question, December 1943–August 1944', *Eastern European Politics and Societies*, 7: 3 (Fall 1993), pp 513ff.

5 Colville, *op cit*, p 658.

6 Perlmutter, *Roosevelt and Stalin*, pp 7, 21, 87–94, 162, and *passim*.

7 Perlmutter, *Roosevelt and Stalin*, p. 167; cf Kimball, *Churchill & Roosevelt*, III, pp 521–30.

8 Kimball 'By Inspiration and Instinct: Seven Authors in Search of the genuine Churchill', *Times Literary Supplement* (London), 9 August 1991, pp 21–22.

9 Kimball, 'Wheel within a Wheel: Churchill, Roosevelt, and the Special Relationship', in *Churchill*, eds Robert Blake and Wm. Roger Louis, (Oxford, 1993), pp 291–307.

10 Steven J Lambakis, *Winston Churchill: Architect of Peace* (Westport and London, 1993), p 167.

11 PREM 3/434/7, Public Record Office. Gilbert, *Road to Victory* (London and Boston, 1986), ch. 53.

12 Reynolds, 'Great Britain: Imperial Democracy', *Allies At War: The Soviet, American, and British Experience, 1939–1945*, D. Reynolds, W F Kimball, A O Chubarian, eds. (New York, 1994), p. 341; Kimball, *The Juggler: Franklin Roosevelt as Wartime Statesman* (Princeton, 1991), ch. 8.

13 TM Barker, 'The Ljubljana Gap Strategy: Alternative to Anvil/Dragoon or Fantasy?' *Journal of Military History*, 56 (January 1992), pp. 57–85.

14 Churchill to Ismay, 24 June 1944, in Martin Gilbert, *Road to Victory*, p. 834. *FRUS, Quebec, 1944*, p 314; Gilbert, *Road to Victory*, pp 959, 963–66.

15 See Tage Kaarsted in this volume.

16 John L Gaddis, 'The Tragedy of Cold War History', *Diplomatic History*, 17:1 (Winter 1993), pp 1–16.

17 Remi Nadeau, *Stalin, Churchill, and Roosevelt Divide Europe* (Westport, 1990); R. C. Raack, *World Affairs*, 155:1 (Summer 1992), pp. 13–21; 'Stalin Plans his Post-War Germany', *Journal of Contemporary History*, 28:1 (January 1993), pp 53–73; 'Stalin's Plans for World War II', *Journal of Contemporary History*, 26:2 (April 1991), pp 215–28.

18 John Charmley, *Churchill: The End of Glory* (London, 1993).

19 *FRUS, Yalta Conf.*, pp. 848–49, 972. Arthur M. Schlesinger Jr., 'Roosevelt's Diplomacy at Yalta', *Yalta: Un Mito che Resiste*, ed Paola

Brundu Olla (Roma, n.d. [1987]), pp 146, 152.

20 D S Clemens, 'Yalta: Conference of Victory and Peace', *Yalta: Un Mito Che Resiste*, pp 7–38.

21 See *The Public Papers and Addresses of Franklin Delano Roosevelt*, Samuel I. Rosenman, ed. (13 vols.; New York, 1938–50), 12: 368–69; 13: 442. cf Gardner, *Spheres of Influence*, p. 248 and Kimball, *The Juggler*, note 9 to ch 9, pp 271–72.

22 Lloyd C Gardner, *Safe for Democracy: The Anglo-American Response to Revolution, 1913–1923* (New York and Oxford, 1984).

23 *War Diary of Oliver Harvey*, John Harvey, ed (London, 1978), 23 October 1942, p 171.

24 See Kimball, *The Juggler*, ch 9.

25 Gardner, *Spheres of Influence*, p 222.

26 E.g., *FRUS, 1943*, I, p542.

27 Jean Edward Smith, ed, *The Papers of General Lucius D. Clay: Germany, 1945–1949* (2 vols; Bloomington, 1974), I, p 184, letter to Echols and Peterson, 27 March 1946. cf Gabriel Kolko, *The Politics of War* (New York, 1969).

28 Gilbert, *Road to Victory*, p 1026. cf Keith Sainsbury, *The Turning Point* (New York and Oxford, 1985).

29 Kimball, *The Juggler*, esp. chapters 5 and 9. cf '"Dr. New Deal": Franklin D. Roosevelt as Commander in Chief,' *Commanders in Chief: Presidential Leadership in Modern Wars*, ed, J. Dawson (Lawrence and Kansas, 1993), pp 87–105.

30 Schlesinger, 'Yalta', p 145; *FRUS, Tehran Conference*, p 594.

31 Lord Avon (Anthony Eden), *The Reckoning* (London and Boston, 1965), p 495.

32 Cf. Robert A Divine, *Second Chance* (New York, 1967), and Robert C Hilderbrand, *Dumbarton Oaks* (Chapel Hill and London, 1990). Arthur Schlesinger, 'Roosevelt's Diplomacy at Yalta', *Yalta: Un Mito Che Resiste*.

33 Robin Edmonds, *Setting the Mould: The United States and Britain, 1945–1950* (New York, 1986), pp 47–8.

34 Taras Hunczak, 'Polish Colonial Ambitions in the Interwar Period', *Slavic Review*, 26:4 (December 1967), pp 648–56.

35 Martin Kitchen, *British Foreign Policy towards the Soviet Union during the Second World War* (New York, 1986). Steven Miner, 'Stalin's "Minimum Conditions" and the Military Balance, 1941–1942', *Soviet–U.S. Relations, 1933–1942*, eds, G N Sevost'ianov & W F Kimball (Moscow, 1989), p 82. cf. Miner, *Between Churchill and Stalin* (Chapel Hill, 1988).

36 Gardner, *Spheres of Influence*, p 174; Churchill to Roosevelt (C-40), 7 March 1942, Kimball, *Churchill & Roosevelt*, I: 394.

37 Kimball, *The Juggler*, pp 173–81.

38 Jan Ciechanowski, *Defeat in Victory* (Garden City, NY, 1947).

39 Gardner, *Spheres of Influence*, p 206.

40 Lord Moran [Charles Wilson], *Churchill: Taken from the Diaries of Lord Moran* (Boston, 1966), pp 235–36.

41 *FRUS, Teheran Conference*, p 512.

42 Clemens, 'Yalta: Conference of Victory and Peace', *Yalta: Un Mito Che Resiste*, p 25.

43 Churchill to Roosevelt, 29 September 1944 (C–789), Kimball, *Churchill & Roosevelt*, III, pp 340–41; Gilbert, *Road to Victory*, p 978.

44 PREM 3/434/7; E L Woodward, *British Foreign Policy during the Second World War* (5 vols; London, HMSO, 1970–76), 3: pp 146–53 and 5: pp 229–31.

45 Clemens, 'Yalta: Conference of Victory and Peace', *Yalta: Un Mito Che Resiste*, p. 26; Gilbert, *Road to Victory*, p 1015.

46 MacLeish to Undersecretary Grew, 24 January 1945, *FRUS, Yalta Conference*, pp 101–2.

47 Harry L Hopkins personal letters (FDR Library), microfilm roll 20, Beaverbrook to Hopkins, 1 March 1945.

48 Ben Pimlott, *The Second World War Diary of Hugh Dalton, 1940–45*. (London, 1986), p 836n.

49 Julian G Hurstfield, *America and the French Nation, 1939–1945* (Chapel Hill, 1986).

50 The quotations are from Clemens, 'Yalta: Conference of Victory and Peace', *Yalta: Un Mito Che Resiste*, p. 28, 34–35. Churchill's comment is in his *The Second World War*, VI, p. 393.

51 Churchill, *The Second World War*, VI, pp 227, 231–33.

52 Sumner Welles, *Where Are We Heading?* (London, Hamish Hamilton, 1965), pp 31–2.

53 John Wheeler-Bennett, *The Semblance of Peace* (London, 1972), as quoted in Nisbet, *Roosevelt and Stalin*, p 95.

54 David N Dilks, 'Churchill as Negotiator at Yalta', *Yalta: Un Mito Che Resiste*, p 97.

Chapter 11 Churchill and the Middle East, 1945–55

Part of the research for this paper was made possible by a research grant from the Small Grants Scheme in the Social Sciences of the Nuffield Foundation.

1   Public Record Office, London, CAB 129/2, f 20, CP(45)156.
2   CAB 131/9, DO(50)45, *Documents on British Policy Overseas*, series II, Vol 4 (London 1991), pp 411–34.
3   CAB 131/12, Annex 1, D(52)26, 17 June 1952.
4   CAB 128/25, ff 344–5, CC102(52).
5   CAB 128/27, part 1, f 284, CC37(54)3.
6   *Cmd. 9391, Statement on Defence 1955*, (London February 1955).
7   R Ovendale, *The Origins of the Arab–Israeli Wars* 2nd edition (London 1992), pp 17–144.
8   CAB 128/11, ff 7–8, CM6(47)3, Confidential Annex, 15 January 1947.
9   Ovendale, *The Origins of the Arab–Israeli Wars*, pp 53–8.
10 Ovendale, *Britain, the United States, and the End of the Palestine Mandate, 1942–1948* (Woodbridge 1989), p 32; M Cohen, *Churchill and the Jews* (London 1985), p 329.
11 *Ibid*, pp 64–5, 183.
12 *Ibid*, pp 128, 40.
13 *Ibid*, p 153.
14 W R Louis, *The British Empire in the Middle East 1945–51* (Oxford 1985), pp 467, 11.
15 Ovendale, *The Origins of the Arab–Israeli Wars*, pp 139–40.
16 T H A Owen, *Britain and the Revision of the Anglo–Egyptian Treaty, 1949–1954* (Ph. D. thesis, Aberystwyth 1991), pp 18–20; Louis, *The British Empire in the Middle East*, pp 238–41; Louis, 'Churchill and Egypt', *Churchill* eds R Blake and Louis, (Oxford 1993), pp 473–8.
17 PRO, PREM 11/208, M16(C)/51, ff 6–7.
18 PREM 11/49, ff 180–3, M190/52.
19 CAB 131/12, D(52)26, para 80.
20 PREM 11/49, ff 21–5, Franks to Foreign Office, 1 August 1952, and reply 3 August, 1952.
21 CAB 128/27, part 1, ff 31–2, CC1(54)2.
22 CAB 128/27, part 1, ff 43–4, CC2(54)6.
23 CAB 128/27, part 1, ff 283–4, CC37(54)3.
24 Louis, *The British Empire in the Middle East*, p 672.
25 Martin Gilbert, *Winston S. Churchill 'Never Despair' 1945–1965* (London 1988), p 617.

26 *Ibid.*, pp 617–8.

27 CAB 128/25, ff 213, CC82(52)5.

28 JA Bill, 'America, Iran, and the Politics of Intervention, 1951–1953', p 286; Louis, 'Mussadiq and the Dilemmas of British Imperialism', *Mussadiq, Iranian Nationalism, and Oil*, eds Bill and Louis (London 1988), pp 252–6.

29 CAB 128/26, part 2, ff 388, CC50(53)4.

30 PREM 11/941, f 51, Churchill to Sharett, 23 April 1954. These words were drafted by Churchill, see f 53, draft by J R Colville, 23 April 1954.

31 B Morris, *Israel's Border Wars 1949–56* (Oxford 1993), pp 244–62; Ovendale, *The Origins of the Arab–Israeli Wars*, p 150; CAB 128/26, part 2, f 512, CC68(53)6, 19 November 1953.

32 PREM 11/489, ff 18–20, PM/51/153, Eden to Churchill, 22 December 1951.

33 PREM 11/489, ff 13–16, NCDB/PM/15, NCD Brownjohn to Churchill, March 1953, enclosing D(53)21, 26 March 1953.

34 PREM 11/489, D(53)8th meeting, 7 May 1953; ff 4–7, C(53)228, draft despatch to the British Ambassador at Washington, 7 August, 1953; CAB 128/26, part 2, ff 366–7, CC48(53)5, 10 August 1953.

35 PREM 11/465, f 18, PM/MS/53/48; f 16, M94/53; Ovendale, *Britain, the United States and the End of the Palestine Mandate*, p 133.

36 PREM 11/465, f 8, M103/53, Churchill to Strang; f 2, Foreign Office to Cairo, telegram no 857; f 5, Foreign Office to Tel Aviv, telegram no 154; f 4, Foreign Office to Tel Aviv, telegram no 155.

37 Ovendale, 'Egypt and the Suez Base Agreement', *The Foreign Policy of Churchill's Peacetime Administration 1951–1955*, ed JW Young (Leicester 1988), pp 137–55; Louis, 'The Tragedy of the Anglo–Egyptian Settlement of 1954', *Suez 1956: the Crisis and its Consequences* eds Louis and R Owen (Oxford 1989), pp 43–71; W S Lucas, 'The Path to Suez: Britain and the Struggle for the Middle East, 1953–56', *Britain and the First Cold War*, ed A Deighton (London 1990), pp 253–72; Louis, 'Churchill and Egypt', pp 480–90; Owen, *Britain and the Revision of the Anglo–Egyptian Treaty 1949–1954*, pp 234–493.

38 CAB 128/23, f 4, CC1(51)7.

39 E Shuckburgh, *Descent to Suez. Diaries 1951–56* (London 1986), p 29.

40 PREM 11/91, M21/52.

41 PREM 11/392, Churchill to Eden, 6 January 1953.

42 Shuckburgh, *Descent to Suez*, pp 74–5, Diary 20 January 1953.

43 PREM 11/392, Churchill to Eden, 20 February 1953.
44 PREM 11/702, Colville to Shuckburgh, 7 April 1954.
45 CAB 128/27, part 1, ff 227–8, CC29(54)2, 15 April 1954.
46 CAB 127/27, part 1, ff 320–2, CC43(54)1, 22 June 1954.
47 Ovendale, *Britain, the United States, and the End of the Palestine Mandate*, pp 220–1, 88–91.
48 *Foreign Relations of the United States*, 1952–4(9) (Washington 1986), pp 394–8.
49 R Rhodes James, *Anthony Eden* (London 1986), pp 345, 358.
50 V Rothwell, *Anthony Eden. A Political Biography 1931–57* (Manchester 1992), p 182.

Chapter 12 Churchill and France, 1951–55

1   Ministry of Foreign Affairs Archives, Paris: Archives diplomatiques (ARD), Série Z, Europe 1949–55, Grande-Bretagne, Vols 76–91; Série Secrétariat des conférences, Vol 74; série Papiers d'Agent, Archives Privées (PAAP), Sous-série 217, Massigli, Vols 47–58.
2   Vincent Auriol, *Journal du Septennat* (Paris 1970–4), 20 October 1953, p 470.
3   Maurice Vaïsse, *Sécurité d'Abord* (Paris 1981), p 42.
4   ARD, Série Z, Europe, Vol 84, telegram Massigli/Bidault, 18 February 1955.
5   ARD, Série Z, Europe, Vol 84, telegram Massigli/Laniel, 6 May 1954.
6   BBC interview (9 February 1959), PAAP 217, Massigli, vol 54.
7   Note François Seydoux, 26 January 1953, Vol 80.
8   Vaïsse, 'La Grande-Bretagne, une partenaire privilégiée', *Pierre Mendès-France et le mendésisme* eds F Bédarida and J-P Rioux (Paris 1985), pp 279–86). René Massigli, *Une Comédie des Erreurs* (Paris 1978), p 475.
9   ARD, Papiers d'Agent, Archives privées, PAAP 217, Massigli, vol 47, Grande-Bretagne, Massigli/Schuman, 6 January 1951.
10 ARD, PAAP 217, Massigli, Vol 47, Massigli/Schuman, 19 December 1951.
11 ARD, Série Z, Europe, Vol 91, Massigli/Bidault, 18 June 1953.
12 ARD, Série Z, Europe, Vol 91, Etienne de Crouÿ–Chanel/Bidault, 7 September 1953.
13 René Massigli, *op cit*, pp 293, 361.
14 ARD, Série Z, Europe, Vol 90, Massigli/Schuman, 19 January 1952.
15 ARD, PAAP 217, Massigli, Vol 47, Massigli/Schuman, 10 April 1952.
16 Auriol, *op cit*, 30 October 1951, p 519.
17 ARD, PAAP 217, Massigli, Vol 47, Massigli/Schuman, 1 August 1952.

18 Auriol, *op cit*, 17 December 1951, p 598.

19 ARD, PAAP 217, Massigli, Vol 47, Massigli/Laniel, 8 June 1954; Vol 101, Massigli/Parodi, 10 September 1954.

20 *Ibid.*, Vol 80, note following conversation Churchill/Bidault, 13 February 1953.

21 ÀRD, Série Z, Europe, Vol 90, telegram de Crouÿ–Chanel/MAE, 7 December 1951; Vol 91, telegram Daridan (Washington)/Bidault, 7 January 1953.

22 ARD, Série Z, Europe, Vol 90, telegram Bonnet/Schuman, 14 January 1952; Vol 79, telegram Parodi/Ambassade du Caire, 7 October 1952; PAAP, 217, Massigli, vol 54, Massigli/MAE, 22 September 1953; telegrams Massigli/Schuman, 22 September 1953, 5 February and 21 December 1954, 17 April and 28 October 1952.

23 *Ibidem*, telegram Massigli/Bidault, 15 May 1953; Massigli, *op cit*, pp 375–378.

24 Auriol, *op cit*, 22 May 1953, p 178.

25 Massigli, *op cit*, p 292.

26 ARD, Série Z, Europe, vol 79, Bonnet/Schuman, 13 December 1951; Vol 90, Bonnet/Schuman, 15 January 1952; ARD, PAAP 217, Massigli, Vol 52, Massigli/Schuman, 2 October 1952.

27 ARD, Série Z, Europe, vol 90, telegram Massigli/Schuman, 28 December 1951.

28 ARD, Série Z, Europe, telegram Massigli/Schuman, 30 November 1951.

29 ARD, Série Z, Europe, telegram Massigli/Schuman, 12 June 1952.

30 *Ibidem*, Vol 79, telegram Massigli/Schuman, 30 June 1952.

31 Massigli/Mendès-France, 25 October 1954.

32 Note François Seydoux, 'L'Angleterre et la Communauté européenne', 26 January 1953.

33 Vol 67, telegram Massigli/Schuman, 8 December 1951.

34 ARD, Série Z, Europe, Vol 79, Massigli/Schuman, 18 December 1951; vol 90, telegram Bonnet/Schuman, 9 January 1952; telegram Massigli/Schuman, 11 March 1952.

35 *Europe 1949–55*, CED, Vol 68, telegram MAE/Massigli, 9 April 1952.

36 ARD, *Europe 1949–55*, CED, Vol 69, telegram Schuman/Massigli, 5 December 1952.

37 Note François Seydoux, 26 January 1953.

38 Note, Sous-Direction d'Europe centrale, Jean Sauvagnargues, 10 February 1953. ARD, Europe 1949–55, Vol 70, memo 14 February 1953.

39 Joseph Laniel, *Jours de Gloire et Jours Cruels* (Paris 1971), p 263.
40 ARD, Série Europe, Vol 81, telegram Massigli/Mendès-France, 7 July 1954.
41 ARD, Europe 1949–55, Vol 75, telegram Massigli/Mendès-France, 28 June 1954.
42 *Ibid.*, 7 July 1954.
43 ARD, Europe 1949–55, Vol 77, Massigli/Mendès-France, 6 October 1954.
44 Jean Lacouture, *Pierre Mendès-France* (Paris 1981), pp 366–7.
45 Massigli, *op cit*, pp 490–1; telegram 5077, 23 December Massigli/Pierre Mendès-France.
46 ARD, PAAP 217, Massigli, Vol 51, Massigli/Schuman, 23 April 1951.
47 ARD, Série Z, Europe, Vol 90, Massigli/Schuman, 1 November 1951.
48 ARD, Série Z, Europe, Vol 90, telegram Massigli/Schuman, 26 November 1952.
49 *Ibid.*, Bonnet/Schuman, 14 January 1952.
50 *Ibid.*, telegram Massigli/Schuman, 26 January 1952; Vol 91, Massigli/Bidault, 18 June 1953; Vol 90, telegram Massigli/Schuman, 14 November 1951.
51 ARD, PAAP 217, Massigli, Vol 52, telegram Massigli/Schuman, 21 December 1951.
52 ARD, PAAP 217, Massigli, Vol 47, Massigli/Schuman, 31 December 1952; Vol 21, de Crouÿ-Chanel/Bidault, 20 April 1954.
53 ARD, Série Z, Europe, Vol 91, telegram Massigli/Bidault, 19 December 1953.
54 ARD, Série Z, Europe, Vol 90, telegram Massigli/Schuman, 14 November 1951; Vol 79, telegram Bonnet/Schuman, 13 December 1951; Vol 91, Massigli/Bidault, 18 June 1953; Massigli, *op cit*, p 373.
55 Massigli, *Une Comédie des Erreurs*, pp 374–5.
56 ARD, PAAP 217, Massigli, Vol 47, Massigli/Laniel, 8 June 1954.
57 *Journal*, 23 May 1953, p 191.
58 Georgette Elgey, *La République des Illusions* (Paris 1965), Vol 3, pp 293–4.
59 *Oeuvres complètes*, p 656.
60 Lacouture, *op cit*, p 371.
61 Telegram 6192–97, 13 December 1954, François-Poncet/Mendès-France, AD; telegram 17625–30, 13 December Mendès-France/Massigli; telegram 16, 17 December 1954, Hoppenot/Mendès-France; note 23 December Hoppenot/Mendès-France.
62 David Carlton, *Anthony Eden, a Biography* (London 1981), p 348.

63 ARD, Série Z, Europe, telegram 2939, 24 July; telegram 2973, 27 July.

64 Vaïsse, 'France and the Suez Crisis', *Suez 1956: The Crisis and its Consequences* (Oxford 1989), eds W R Louis and R Owen, pp 131–44.

Chapter 13 Churchill and Adenauer

1 H-P Schwarz, *Adenauer. Der Aufstieg 1876–1952* (Stuttgart 1986) and *Adenauer. Der Staatsmann 1952–1967* (Stuttgart 1991).

2 *Adenauer, Erinnerungen 1955–9* (Stuttgart 1967) p 13f; Speech in Mulheim, 9 September 1946, Stiftung Bundeskanzler-Adenauer-Haus, Rhöndorf.

3 *Adenauer, Briefe 1945–47* (Berlin 1983) p 337.

4 Adenauer-Stiftung (eds), *Konrad Adenauer und die CDU der Britischen Besatzungszone 1946–9* (Bonn 1975) p 497.

5 Adenauer, *Erinnerungen 1945–53* (Stuttgart 1965) pp 500–12; Otto Lenz, *In Zentrum der Macht* (Dusseldorf 1989) p 191f.

6 House of Commons, 11 May 1953; Theodor Heuss, *Tagebuchbriefe 1955–63* (Stuttgart 1970) p 440.

7 Stiftung Bundeskanzler-Adenauer-Haus 04.09. Gilbert, *Churchill VIII* (London 1988) pp 1306–7; Moran, *Struggle for Survival* (London 1966) p 762.

8 Blankenhorn, diary note, 4 December 1951.

9 *Ibid.,* 15 May 1953.

10 Memo by Sir F Roberts, 17 April 1953, PRO, FO371/104131.

11 Blankenhorn, Diary, 15 June 1953.

12 Adenauer, 'Es mußte alles neu gemacht werden' *Die Protolkolle des CDU-Bundesvorstandes 1950–3* (Stuttgart 1986) p 520.

13 Adenauer, *Erinnerungen 1945–52* p 507.

14 Blankenhorn, Diary, 15 May 1953; FO 371/10665.

15 *Ibid.*

16 Adenauer, *Erinnerungen 1945–53* p 508.

17 Heuss and Adenauer, *Unserem Vaterland Zugute. Der Briefwechsel 1948–63* (Berlin 1989) pp 298–301.

18 Adenauer, *Erinnerungen 1945–53*, pp 490–512. Gero von Gersdorf, *Adenauers Außenpolitik Gegenüber der Siegermächten 1954* (Munich 1994) pp 187–230.

19 Adenauer, *Erinnerungen 1945–53* pp 505–7.

20 Adenauer, *Erinnerungen 1953–55* (Stuttgart 1966) pp 205–8; FO 371/103705.

21 Adenauer, 'Es mußte alles neu gemacht werden', Die Protokolle des CDO-Bundesvorstandes 1950–3 p 520.
22 P G Boyle, The Churchill–Eisenhower Correspondence, 1953–5 (Chapel Hill 1990) p 175.
23 Ibid., pp 170, 171.
24 Hansard, 6 November 1951.
25 D Acheson, Present at the Creation (London 1969) p 584.
26 Adenauer, Erinnerungen 1945–53 p 508.
27 Blankenhorn's oral account to the author. In his memoirs Adenauer was more cautious.
28 P G Boyle, The Churchill-Eisenhower Correspondence, 1951–53 pp 31–53; Roberts and Strong, 15 May 1953, FO 371/103705.
29 Adenauer, Erinnerungen 1953–5 pp 205–9.
30 Adenauer to Ria Reiners; Briefe 1951–3 (Berlin 1987) p 384.
31 FO 371/103660, 19 May 1953.
32 FO 371/103660.
33 Roberts to Strang, 17 July 1953, FO 371/103665.
34 Foreign Relations of the United States, 1952–4, Vol VII (Washington 1986) pp 4468–4470.
35 Adenauer, 'Es mußte alles neu gemacht werden', Die Protokolle des CDU-Bundesvorstands 1950–3 (Stuttgart 1986) p 648.

Chapter 14 Churchill and the Defence of the West, 1951–55

1 Denis Healey, 'Britain and NATO', Nato and American Security, ed Klaus Knorr (Princeton 1959), p 214.
2 For example, The History of the Joint Chiefs of Staff, The History of the Office of the Secretary of Defence, Anfänge westdeutscher Sicherheitspolitik.
3 Max Beloff, 'Churchill and Europe', Churchill: A Major New Assessment of His Life in Peace and War, ed Robert Blake and Wm Roger Louis (Oxford 1993), pp 448 et passim.
4 Bernard Porter, Britain, Europe and the World, 1950–1982. Delusions of Grandeur (London 1983), p 119. David Reynolds, Britannia Overruled: British Policy and World Power in the 20th Century (London 1991), pp 173ff.
5 M Gilbert, Never Despair: Winston S Churchill 1945–65 (London), p 636. References in this section to 'Gilbert' are to this volume.
6 Beloff, loc cit, p 446.
7 Saki Dockrill, Britain's Policy for West German Rearmament, 1950–55 (Cambridge 1991).

8 Gilbert, p 266.

9 Roland G Foerster *et al*, *Von der Kapitulation bis zum Pleven-Plan, Anfänge westdeutscher Sicherheitspolitik* ed Militärgeschichtliches Forschungsamt, Freiburg, Vols 1–3, Vol 1, Munich 1982, p 328.

10 Gilbert, p 536.

11 *Ibid.*, pp 543–4.

12 *Ibid.*, p 544.

13 *Ibid.*, p 574.

14 Gregory W Pedlow, 'The Politics of NATO Command, 1950–62', *US Military Forces in Europe. The Early Years, 1945–70* ed Simon Duke and Wolfgang Krieger (Boulder 1993), pp 16–42.

15 Gilbert, p 636.

16 Dean Acheson, *Present at the Creation: My Years in the State Department* (New York 1969), p 598; Edward Fursdon, 'The Role of the European Defence Community in European Integration', *NATO and the Founding of the Atlantic Alliance* eds Francis Heller and John Gillingham (London 1992), pp 213–40. *Das Nordatlantische Bündnis 1949–56*, eds Klaus A Maier and Norbert Wiggershaus (Munich 1993).

17 Gilbert, pp 666–9.

18 *Ibid.*, p 682.

19 *Anfänge westdeutscher Sicherheitspolitik* vol II (1990) pp 14 ff. Alan S Milward, *The European Rescue of the Nation-State* (Berkeley 1992), pp 21–45, 345–433.

20 Walter S Poole, *The Joint Chiefs of Staff and National Policy, History of the Joint Chiefs of Staff* Vol 4, p 212.

21 *Anfänge* Vol 2, p 80.

22 Gilbert, p 669.

23 *Ibid.*, p 779. *Foreign Relations of the United States (FRUS)* 1951/III part 1, p 701.

24 *FRUS* 1952–4/V part 1, pp 39, 78 ff.

25 *History of the JCS* Vol 4, p 212.

26 *History of the JCS* Vol 5, p 285.

27 Gilbert, pp 792, 867. Stephen E Ambrose, *Eisenhower: The President* (New York 1984), p 21.

28 Gilbert, p 547.

29 *Ibid.*, p 575.

30 *Ibid.*, p 635.

31 *Ibid.*, p 735.

32 *Ibid.*, pp 790–1.

33 *Ibid.*, p 819.

34 Ambrose, *Eisenhower* Vol 2, pp 91 ff.

35 Gilbert, pp 829–33.

36 *Ibid.*, pp 863–8.

37 Richard G Hewlett and Jack M Holl, *Atoms for Peace and War, 1953–61: Eisenhower and the Atomic Energy Commission* (Berkeley 1989), Chapter 8.

38 Gilbert, pp 1006–7, 1036.

39 *Anfänge* Vol 2, p 165.

40 David C Large, 'Grand Illusions, The United States, the Federal Republic of Germany, and the European Defence Community, 1950–4', *American Policy and the Reconstruction of West Germany, 1945–55*, eds Jeffry M Diefendorf et al (Cambridge 1993).

41 Gilbert, p 918.

42 *Ibid.*, p 926.

43 *Ibid.*, p 931.

44 *Ibid.*, p 932; cf *Anfänge* Vol II, p 190 on that issue during the EDC ratification crisis in the summer of 1954.

45 *Anfänge* Vol 2, p 184.

46 *Ibid.*, p 199.

47 *Ibid.*, pp 206–7. Jean Doise and Maurice Vaïsse, *Diplomatie et outil militaire 1871–1969* (Paris 1987) pp 414–20, 426–32. Wolfgang Krieger, 'Die Ursprünge der langfristigen Stationierung amerikanischer Streikräfte in Europa, 1945–51', *Vom Marshallplan zur EWG. Eingliederung der Bundesrepublik in die westliche Welt*, ed Ludolf Herbst (Munich 1990). Wolfgang Krieger, 'American Security Policy in Europe before NATO', *NATO and the Founding of the Atlantic Alliance* eds Heller and Gillingham, pp 99–128.

48 *Anfänge* Vol 2, pp 218–20.

49 Gilbert, p 1056.

50 *Ibid.*, p 1057.

51 Simon Duke, 'US Basing in Britain, 1945–60', *US Military Forces in Europe* eds Duke and Krieger, pp 117–52.

52 G-H Soutou, *The French Military Program for Nuclear Energy, 1945–81*, Nuclear History Program Occasional Paper no 3 (1989). Marcel Ducal and Yves Le Baut, *L'arme nucléaire française. Pourquoi et comment?* (Paris 1992).

53 *Anfänge* Vol 2, pp 187–8.

54 Jan Melissen, *The Struggle for Nuclear Partnership: Britain, the United States and the Making of the Ambiguous Alliance, 1952–59* (Groningen 1993), pp 9–33. Margaret Gowing, *Independence and Deterrence: Britain and Atomic Energy, 1945–52* Vol 2 (London

1974). Ian Clark and Nicholas J Wheeler, *The British Origins of Nuclear Strategy, 1945–55* (Oxford 1989).
55 Gilbert, p 157.
56 *Ibid.,* p 199.
57 *Ibid.,* p 432.
58 Gilbert, p 573; Melissen, *op cit*, pp 15–16.
59 Gilbert, p 595.
60 *Ibid.,* p 1091.
61 *Ibid.,* p 595.
62 *Ibid.,* pp 965–7.
63 *Ibid.,* pp 1019–23.
64 *Ibid.,* pp 1099–1100.
65 Melissen, *op cit*, pp 14–15.
66 The 1991 Harvard dissertation by Robert Wampler, *Eisenhower and American, British and NATO Nuclear Strategies in the 1950s* (2 vols) (Oxford and New York 1995); R Wampler *NATO Strategic Planning and Nuclear Weapons, 1950–57*, NHP Occasional Paper 6 (University of Maryland 1990).
67 Christopher Andrew, *Her Majesty's Secret Service: The Making of the British Intelligence Community* (Penguin 1987), pp 448 ff.

Chapter 15 Churchill and the European Idea

1 Speech of 9 October 1948. Unless otherwise stated, all footnote references can be found in the main and document volumes of R S Churchill, *Winston S Churchill* Vols 1 and 2, and M Gilbert, *Winston S Churchill* Vols 3 to 8.
2 Private Article, November 1947.
3 Churchill to Nehru, 21 February 1955.
4 Speech of 8 July 1920.
5 Letter of 25 August 1935 from G D Birla to Gandhi.
6 Telegram of 28 December 1940.
7 Recollection communicated by Kay Halle, who was present at Chartwell on that occasion in October 1933, and who later reproduced the pound-dollar symbol in her book, *Churchill on America and Britain.*
8 Draft memorandum, 7 April 1918.
9 C E Bohlen, *Witness of History* (New York 1973), p 181.
10 Declaration on Liberated Europe, 11 February 1945.
11 *Morning Post*, 10 January 1900.
12 Speech of 13 May 1901.
13 Letter of 15 September 1909.

14 J A Pease, diary entry for 29 July 1914.
15 Letter of 24 March 1920.
16 Draft memorandum of 19 August 1920.
17 A P Herbert, *The Secret Battle* with an introduction by the Rt Hon Winston S Churchill (London, 3rd edn, 1928).
18 Speech of 23 November 1932.
19 Prime Minister's personal telegram T836/5, to Moscow, 10.05pm, 8 May 1945.
20 Imperial Conference, London, 7 July 1921.
21 Speech of 9 October 1948.
22 Cabinet memorandum of 1 May 1920.
23 Defence Deputation, 29 July 1936.
24 Speech of 24 September 1936.
25 W S Churchill, *The World Crisis* Vol 4, p 544.
26 Committee of Imperial Defence, 13 February 1925.
27 Note by Sir Pierson Dixon, 19 May 1953, quoted in Professor Hans-Peter Schwarz, 'Churchill and Adenauer'.
28 Letter of 18 September 1954.
29 Message to the Italian people, 28 August 1944.
30 Harold Wilson, *A Prime Minister on Prime Ministers* (London 1977), p 268.
31 Speech of 31 March 1949.
32 Speech of 5 March 1946.
33 Speech of 19 September 1946.
34 House of Commons, 5 March 1917.
35 Diary of Richard Casey (later Lord Casey), 27 June 1943.
36 Transcript of a briefing, Moscow, 15 February 1994, Central Office of Information.
37 Speech of 17 August 1949.
38 Speech of 28 October 1948.
39 Speech of 10 December 1948.
40 Article of 29 May 1938.
41 Speech of 26 February 1949.
42 Press Conference, 12 June 1947.
43 'United States of Europe', 'Statement of Aims', October 1946.

Index

This book makes a very special contribution to our understanding of the personality, life and work of Winston Churchill for it showcases assessments from a group of impartial historians, mainly drawn from outside Britain, whose aim it is to inform and assist the reader rather than engage in uncritical adulation or baseless denigration. The essays are framed by a personal memoir from Churchill's daughter, Lady Soames, a concluding chapter by Sir Martin Gilbert and, new for this paperback edition, an Afterword by Correlli Barnett

By examining Churchill's attitudes and policies towards the evolving challenges of the twentieth century, the book enables us to freshly view such a significant career in the context of a new millennium.

Brassey's

64 Brewery Road
London N7 9NT

£14.99

ISBN 1-85753-351-8

9 781857 533514

EL RELATO DEL
MONSTRUO

SHAUN HAMILL

EL RELATO DEL MONSTRUO

Traducción de Jeannine Emery

UMBRIEL
Argentina • Chile • Colombia • España
Estados Unidos • México • Perú • Uruguay

Título original: *A cosmology of monsters*
Editor original: Pantheon Books, a division of Penguin Random House LLC, New York
Traducción: Jeannine Emery

1.ª edición abril 2020

ISBN: 978-84-16517-33-6
E-ISBN: 978-84-17981-06-8
Depósito legal: B-3.673-2020

Fotocomposición: Ediciones Urano, S.A.U.
Impreso por Romanyà-Valls, S.A. – Verdaguer, 1 – 08786 Capellades (Barcelona)

Impreso en España – *Printed in Spain*

Este libro es para mi madre, Patrice Hamill;
mi mentora, Laura Kopchick,
y mi mujer, Rebeka H. Hamill

Era una persona que representaba nuestras psiques. Entró de algún modo en las sombras que existen en el interior de nuestros cuerpos; fue capaz de entender algunos de nuestros miedos íntimos y de llevarlos a la pantalla. La historia de Lon Chaney es la historia de amores no correspondidos. Saca a la luz esa parte oculta que todos tenemos dentro, porque tememos no ser amados, tememos que nunca nos amen, tememos que una parte nuestra sea grotesca, y que el mundo le dé la espalda.

—Ray Bradbury

Después de acostarse, tuvo un sueño sin precedentes de grandes ciudades ciclópeas formadas por bloques gigantes y monolitos que alcanzaban el cielo, todos rezumando un espeso líquido de color verde, y siniestros con horror latente. Una serie de jeroglíficos habían cubierto los muros y los pilares, y desde algún sitio indeterminado más abajo provino una voz que no era una voz, sino una sensación caótica que solo la imaginación podía convertir en sonido, pero que él intentó reproducir con la casi impronunciable mezcla de letras, «Cthulhu fhtagn».

—H. P. Lovecraft, *La llamada de Cthulhu*

Parte uno

EL GRABADO
EN LA CASA

CAPÍTULO 1

Empecé a coleccionar las notas de suicidio de mi hermana mayor Eunice cuando tenía siete años. Aún las conservo en el último cajón de mi escritorio, sujetas con un clip negro. Fue de las únicas cosas que me permitieron traer, y las he leído con frecuencia los últimos meses, buscando consuelo, sabiduría, o quizás tan solo una señal de que he tomado las decisiones correctas por todos nosotros.

Con el tiempo Eunice descubrió que estaba guardando sus cartas y empezó a dirigírmelas. En una de mis favoritas, escribe, «Noah, no hay tal cosa como un final feliz. Solo hay buenos sitios en los que parar».

A mi familia no se le da bien lidiar con los finales; jamás los sabemos sobrellevar. Pero tampoco somos buenos con los comienzos. Por ejemplo, yo desconocía el primer cuarto de esta historia hasta hace poco, y me pasé la mayor parte de mi juventud y los primeros años de la adultez esquivando, como Jervas Dudley, las tumbas selladas de nuestra historia familiar. Es exactamente la clase de dolor que quiero evitarte a ti, quienquiera que seas. Para conseguirlo, tengo que empezar por los márgenes más alejados de la sombra que se cierne sobre mi familia, con mi madre, Margaret Byrne, la mujer alta, de tez blanca y pelo rojizo, en otoño de 1968.

CAPÍTULO 2

Como yo, mi madre nació cuando sus padres ya estaban casados hacía muchos años. Pero a diferencia de mí, cosechó los beneficios de haber nacido de padres que tenían solvencia económica. Su padre, Christopher Byrne, era un comprador de prendas femeninas destinadas a los grandes almacenes de Dillard's, y tenía una relación personal con el mismísimo William T. Dillard.

Margaret no conocía bien a su padre; creía que era un guapo desconocido que olía a cigarrillos y que siempre traía obsequios a casa de sus viajes a Nueva York; en su mayoría, grabaciones de los elencos originales de Broadway a los que asistía cuando viajaba. Pero jamás le faltó de nada. Creció en una gran casa en los suburbios de Memphis, Tennessee, y siempre tenía una paga generosa, ropa bonita, coches y, cuando llegó el momento, la cuota de la matrícula en la *alma mater* de sus padres: Tilden University, una pequeña universidad cristiana y conservadora en Searcy, Arkansas.

Jamás tendrás que preocuparte por el dinero, le dijo su madre, y en 1965 parecía cierto.

Mi abuelo había tenido tanto éxito con Dillard's que en 1966, cuando mi madre se matriculó para realizar su primer año en la universidad, dejó la compañía para abrir su propia tienda. Sin embargo, para el invierno de 1967, la tienda tuvo un inicio flojo, y en el verano de 1968, cuando Margaret volvió a casa para sus vacaciones de verano, su madre le dio la noticia: la tienda había quebrado. Los Byrne pagarían su matrícula un año más, pero tendrían que quitarle su coche, su paga mensual y la residencia universitaria.

Cuando Margaret les recordó que necesitaría por lo menos dos años más para terminar su licenciatura en Inglés, por no hablar de su máster en Bibliotecomanía, su madre le dijo, «Te sugiero que te des prisa en conseguir un marido antes de preocuparte por tu licenciatura».

Apenas desalentada, Margaret hizo lo que pudo ante una situación prácticamente imposible. Cuando volvió a Searcy en otoño, consiguió un empleo en Bartleby's, la única librería del pueblo, y le alquiló una habitación a la dueña, Rita Johnson, una viuda cuya única religión era la palabra escrita, y cuya postura política se inclinaba más hacia Betty Friedan que hacia Richard Nixon. La señora Johnson vivía en una acogedora casa de dos plantas cerca del campus, cobraba un alquiler exiguo y casi no estableció normas. No le importaba a qué hora volviera a casa mientras que no llevara chicos al segundo piso, y la dejaba usar la televisión y el tocadiscos todo lo que quisiera en tanto mantuviera bajo el volumen.

Esta libertad recién adquirida fue un cambio repentino, casi desconcertante, después de las reglas estrictas que debían cumplirse en la residencia estudiantil. Margaret jamás había querido asistir a Tilden, donde era obligatorio firmar un compromiso moral, y asistir forzosamente al servicio religioso del domingo por la mañana. Se había matriculado porque era la única universidad que su padre le pagaría. Había soportado todos los rituales religiosos con la esperanza de obtener un título universitario, una profesión y una vida propia. Y ahora, viviendo con la señora Johnson, tenía su primera experiencia de lo que podía depararle la vida.

Adoraba su alojamiento nuevo, su libertad recién estrenada y, lo mejor de todo, le encantaban las penumbras y los angostos pasillos de Bartleby's. Le gustaba colocar los libros recién llegados, exhibirlos por temas, y ayudar a sus clientes, espíritus afines, a encontrar historias. La única molestia de su vida laboral era un joven llamado Harry, que acudía quizás dos veces por semana y le hacía preguntas cuyas respuestas ella sospechaba que ya conocía: *¿Quién escribió Grandes esperanzas? ¿Dónde tienen las biografías?* Siempre le agradecía a Margaret la información, pero independientemente de aquello en lo que manifestara interés, siempre terminaba instalándose sobre el suelo del sector de ciencia ficción, donde leía libros sin comprar jamás ninguno.

Parecía joven, alrededor de la edad de Margaret, y supuso que debía asistir también a Tilden. Se preguntó cómo encontraba tiempo para leer tanto *y* asistir al mismo tiempo a la universidad. Además, si asistía a Tilden, era probable que tuviera dinero suficiente para comprar libros. ¿Por qué perder el tiempo en la librería? Le molestaba, pero cada vez que le preguntaba sobre el asunto, volvía a colocar la mercadería sin comprar sobre el estante, se disculpaba y se marchaba.

Durante cierto tiempo Margaret trabajó treinta y dos horas por semana en la tienda, asistía a clases y estudiaba en su tiempo libre, pero esa rutina terminó siendo más difícil de lo que había anticipado. El trabajo, aunque fuera relativamente fácil y lo hiciera en el ambiente sereno de Bartleby's, era agotador. Después de un turno completo, le dolían los pies y sentía el cerebro exprimido. Lo único que quería era recostarse en el sofá de la señora Johnson y ver la televisión. Las noches en que se obligaba a estudiar, el proceso era lento, repetitivo y arduo. Le costaba concentrarse, y tenía que leer los párrafos o frases sueltas una y otra vez para extraer alguna aproximación del sentido de lo que leía. Se sentía todo el tiempo cansada, se quedaba dormida, faltaba a clases y entregaba los trabajos tarde o ni siquiera los hacía. Para finales de septiembre, sus notas eran peores que nunca.

Su red de salvación, hilvanada por la voz burlona y fantasmal de su madre, apareció en la forma de Pierce Lombard, un chico de su curso de Civilización Occidental. Alto y delgado, tenía un corte de pelo rapado que había pasado de moda hacía diez años y párpados caídos que resaltaban sus oscuras ojeras. Siempre parecía estar dormido y parecía tener cerca de diez años más de los que tenía (veinte), pero invitaba a Margaret a salir al menos una vez por semana y provenía de una familia adinerada de magnates del pollo. Lo más probable es que si alguien hubiera salido a comprar a mediados del siglo veinte en algún supermercado del sur de los Estados Unidos, habría terminado comprando un pollo Lombard. A veces Pierce intentaba explicarle el negocio a Margaret, pero cada vez que lo hacía, ella se distraía.

No iban con frecuencia al cine, porque Pierce desaprobaba la mayoría de las películas (era conservador y devoto incluso para los estándares de Tilden), pero cuando sí lo hacían, prestaba atención, y jamás sonreía ni soltaba una carcajada. A veces, en la oscuridad, Margaret lo miraba en lugar de prestarle atención a la película. Ahora parecía tener treinta años. ¿Qué aspecto tendría en diez o veinte años, cuando las presiones de la empresa avícola ya lo tuvieran agobiado?

Era amable, siempre le abría las puertas para que pasara y decía «por favor» y «gracias». Cuando iban con su Mercedes a algún lugar para besuquearse, sus besos parecían matemáticamente calculados para situarse en el límite entre la pasión y los buenos modales; sus manos permanecían en su cintura, el estómago o la cara. Margaret, una «buena chica», aún virgen, se imaginaba que el amor verdadero debía de ser un deporte de contacto, intenso y peligroso, algo que sucedía en las vías del ferrocarril o sobre el lecho de los bosques, dos cuerpos que intentaban expresarse pureza espiritual. Se preguntaba si Pierce, él también un «buen chico», estaba esperando a que ella manifestara una afinidad espiritual antes de demostrar ese tipo de pasión, así que una noche a comienzos de octubre, metió la mano en su entrepierna y le oprimió la ingle. Él se sobresaltó, la apartó de un empellón y se retiró al rincón más alejado del asiento del conductor.

—¿Por qué has hecho eso? —preguntó.

—Porque quería hacerlo —respondió ella.

—Eso no viene al caso —dijo—. No deberíamos hacerlo.

La llevó a casa después de eso, sin darle un beso de buenas noches.

Siempre había supuesto que la religión era algo que se hacía con gente educada, no en privado. Sin duda, nadie podía creer en ninguno de los conceptos que decían aceptar los domingos. Pierce era un chico. ¿No debía presionarla para conseguir más, intentando ver hasta dónde podía llegar? ¿Alguien creía que a Jesucristo le importaba lo que hicieran con sus partes privadas? Pierce debía de estar encantado de que ella hubiera mostrado algún interés en su pene, ¿no?

Después que Margaret intentara toquetearlo, Pierce dejó de llamarla, y se sentaba bien lejos de ella en clase y durante los servicios religiosos. El tiempo libre que Margaret recuperó no la ayudó a mejorar sus notas: suspendió tres exámenes seguidos. Cuando su profesor de Álgebra le devolvió su examen de mitad de trimestre con una gran F en la primera página, murmuró: «Póngase a estudiar, señorita Byrne».

Empezó a sentir una furia creciente y errática por lo injusto de la situación. ¿Por qué tenía que sufrir la impericia de su padre en los negocios? ¿Por qué tenía que ser responsable de convencer a un bobo dormilón de que gozara de su cuerpo? ¿Cómo se suponía que debía tener éxito alguien en aquellas circunstancias?

El día que le devolvieron el examen de Álgebra, fue furiosa a cumplir con su turno en Bartleby's. La señora Johnson percibió su estado de ánimo y la dejó sola para reponer la sección de ciencia ficción, lo que habría estado bien, salvo que Harry estaba bloqueando el pasillo, apoyando la espalda contra las estanterías y con un libro de cubierta dura en el regazo. Un letrero de «Por favor, no lea los libros» colgaba directamente encima de su cabeza.

Margaret cruzó los brazos y lo miró furiosa. El sol se colaba por la ventana que quedaba detrás de ella, y su sombra se estiró por el pasillo, alcanzándolo.

—Hola, Margaret —dijo, sonriéndole—. Quería preguntarte si tienes algo de Philip Roth. —Cuando no le devolvió la sonrisa, preguntó—: ¿Qué sucede?

—¿Sabes leer? —preguntó—. ¿Entiendes las palabras de las páginas que estás hojeando? ¿O te sientas aquí porque quieres parecer inteligente ante los que pasan?

—Sé leer.

—¿Entonces por qué no…? —Arrancó el letrero de «Por favor, no lea los libros» del estante de encima de su cabeza e intentó lanzárselo. La hoja endeble revoloteó a través del aire entre ambos y cayó indiferente al suelo. Harry la observó aterrizar antes de levantar la cabeza para mirarla.

—¿Por qué no qué? —preguntó.

—¿Por qué no lo... *lees*? ¿*Lo compras*? —Le aferró el hombro—. Levántate.

Quizás sorprendido por la intensidad de su ira, Harry hizo lo que le ordenaban, y permitió que lo arrastrara por la fuerza a donde estaba la señora Johnson en el mostrador principal, con el libro aún abierto en sus manos.

—Harry está listo para comprar el libro —dijo. Lo empujó hacia la caja registradora.

Harry le dirigió una mirada lastimera, pero apoyó el libro sobre el mostrador. Era un libro de cubierta dura, grande y lustrosa, de los que se suelen colocar sobre las mesas de café.

La señora Johnson sostuvo el libro y comprobó el precio sobre la solapa delantera.

—¿Estás seguro, Harry?

Él lo afirmó con un gruñido. La señora Johnson registró el total en la caja. Harry hizo una mueca de desazón cuando se lo leyó, pero extrajo su cartera descolorida y agrietada y le pagó. La señora Johnson puso el libro en una bolsa.

El joven le dio las gracias farfullando y se marchó.

Lo observó salir antes de dirigirse a Margaret.

—¿Qué ha sido eso?

—Nada —respondió.

—¿Nada de verdad, o no quieres hablar del tema?

—Lo que usted prefiera, señora Johnson.

—Cuida tu lengua, jovencita.

Margaret volvió a su trabajo reponiendo libros en las estanterías. A medida que transcurrió su turno, su ira se fue desvaneciendo hasta que desapareció por completo, dejándola desconcertada por la fuerza y la potencia de su arrebato. Algunos detalles acudían una y otra vez a su cabeza, aspectos que jamás había advertido de Harry: la manga harapienta de su camisa; la tela rugosa por el exceso de lavados; las rodillas descoloridas de sus vaqueros; un indefinido olor grasiento que ella no conseguía identificar, imposible de ignorar en su presencia.

Para cuando acabó su turno aquella noche, sentía una sorda vergüenza que solo se intensificó cuando encontró a Harry esperándola en el aparcamiento. Se encontraba sentado con las piernas cruzadas sobre el capó de un Chevy viejo y destartalado, con las manos en el regazo. Ella casi nunca veía coches tan viejos en el campus. Quizá estuviera estudiando con una beca. O, como ella, intentando pagarse los estudios trabajando. Con la cara sonrojada, se obligó a caminar hacia él.

—Ese libro ha sido muy caro —dijo Harry.

—Puedes devolverlo. Si tienes el recibo, te lo pueden devolver en efectivo.

Hizo una mueca.

—No podría hacerle algo así a la señora Johnson. Siempre es muy amable conmigo.

—¿Puedo pagártelo? —preguntó ella. Hurgó en la bolsa buscando su cartera.

Él sacudió la cabeza de un lado a otro como debatiendo consigo mismo.

—Iba a ir al cine esta noche. Supongo que si realmente quieres arreglar las cosas, podrías comprar las entradas.

—¿Quieres que vaya al cine contigo?

—Yo conduzco —dijo—. Tú hazte cargo de las entradas.

—¿Qué quieres ir a ver?

—*La semilla del diablo* acaba de estrenarse en Little Rock.

Margaret había oído hablar de la película. La semana anterior, el predicador la había denunciado en la capilla, empleando términos generales y excitantes: *blasfema, profana, espantosa*. Expulsarían a cualquier estudiante que fuera pillado viendo la película (o leyendo la novela de Ira Levin en la cual se basaba). Pero ni la advertencia del Dr. Landon (ni los mensajes pegados en todo el campus) describían la película en detalle. ¿Por qué era profana? ¿Por qué blasfema?

Si Margaret hubiera seguido viviendo en la residencia, ni siquiera habría contemplado la idea. Pero la señora Johnson no la delataría; la propietaria de Bartleby's consideraba que todo el mundo debía tener acceso a todas las historias, sin reparar en su moralidad inherente. Estaría orgullosa de ella por tomar su propia decisión.

Pero Little Rock era un viaje en coche de ochenta kilómetros desde Searcy, y Margaret aún tenía deberes de química sin terminar. Se lo señaló a Harry.

—Conduciré a toda velocidad hasta allí y de vuelta —dijo él.

Ella se miró el suéter y la falda sencillos que había vestido para ir a clase aquella mañana. No era justamente el mejor conjunto para una primera salida, pero se trataba de una compensación, no de un romance. La ropa ayudaría a delimitar las expectativas de Harry como correspondía.

—Entonces, vamos —dijo ella.

CAPÍTULO 3

Era una película de terror protagonizada por aquella chica de Peyton Place, acerca de una joven pareja casada que se muda a un apartamento nuevo y termina enredándose con los adorables vecinos mayores y practicantes de satanismo de la casa de al lado. Margaret compró las entradas de cine, y Harry se hizo cargo de las palomitas de maíz y los refrescos. Durante la película, sus dedos se tocaron en el cubo de palomitas un par de veces, pero Harry no intentó cogerle la mano ni pasar el brazo sobre sus hombros. Miraba absorto la pantalla.

La película no era de esas de terror que hacían saltar del asiento, pero resultó inquietante a un nivel más primario y profundo. Margaret se encontró identificándose con el personaje del título cuando el marido y los vecinos hostigaban y aislaban a Rosemary, el demonio la violaba y era incapaz de hacer nada salvo dar a luz al engendro de aquella unión impía. Mientras Rosemary acunaba a su bebé en su camita negra y empezaban a aparecer los créditos de cierre, se recostó hacia atrás en su asiento, pasmada. ¿Podían terminar así las películas? ¿Con el diablo triunfante, y la heroína derrotada?

El hechizo de la película duró hasta que Harry rompió el silencio en el aparcamiento.

—Si nos damos prisa puedo conseguir que llegues a tu casa a las diez y media.

Margaret dejó que le abriera la puerta del coche y estudió su cara. Tenía una nariz larga sobre una boca pequeña, una barbilla afilada, y ojos marrones coronados por unas gruesas cejas oscuras. Si hubiera estado en una fiesta, no se habría fijado en él desde el otro lado de una habitación, pero tenía una cara agradable, cordial. Sintió que se disipaba el efecto de la película.

—¿Tienes hambre? —preguntó ella—. Yo estoy muerta de hambre.

—Podría comer algo —dijo él.

La llevó a un McDonald's a unas manzanas, probablemente el único sitio abierto del pueblo. Al entrar en el coche de nuevo, Margaret cogió la bolsa de Bartleby's del asiento entre los dos.

—Quiero ver lo que me ha costado tanto tiempo de estudio esta noche —dijo.

—Quizá convenga que esperes hasta terminar de comer para mirarlo —dijo Harry—. Es bastante asqueroso.

Le pidió que fuera a buscar un sitio mientras pedía la comida. Ella eligió un reservado junto a una ventana, sacó el libro del bolso y lo apoyó plano sobre la mesa: *Visiones de Cthulhu: ilustraciones inspiradas en la obra de H. P. Lovecraft*. La cubierta tenía una pintura de un monstruo enorme y horrible, que se asemejaba vagamente a un ser humano. Tenía los brazos y las piernas abultadas y musculosas; sus manos y pies acababan en garras, en lugar de dedos. La cabeza de la criatura, semejante a la de un pulpo repugnante, bulboso y de múltiples ojos, se unía a una masa de tentáculos que colgaban hacia abajo sobre el pecho y el enorme vientre redondo. Un par de alas en punta pero de aspecto un tanto frágil brotaban de su espalda. Margaret se preguntó cómo podía alzar vuelo una criatura tan obesa.

—Espero que aún sigas con hambre para comer todo esto. —Harry se hallaba de pie junto a ella con una bandeja de hamburguesas, patatas fritas y refrescos.

Margaret le dio un golpecito a la cubierta del libro.

—¿Esto es Cthulhu? —Lo pronunció *kit-hulu*, y supo por la mueca de Harry que lo había pronunciado incorrectamente.

—Es la interpretación de un artista, sí —dijo—. Y se pronuncia *kuh-thu-lu*.

Tiró el libro hacia sí, haciendo lugar para que él pudiera apoyar la comida.

—No parece aterrador, solo desagradable, como la versión monstruosa de un Buda gordo en un restaurante chino.

Harry se rio e inclinó la cabeza para mirar mejor.

—Sí, supongo que guarda cierto parecido.

—¿Se supone que debe dar miedo?

Se sentó delante de ella.

—En la historia da miedo. Pero quizás sea una de esas obras que no pueden traducirse sin perder alguna parte esencial. Es como si solo funcionara en la imaginación.

Ella abrió el libro, giró a una página al azar y encontró la pintura de otro monstruo… este era más indefinido y amorfo, una única masa de carne con cuatro ojos negros. Tenía una boca brillante con forma de vulva y una hilera de dientes afilados. Una masa de tentáculos se sacudía detrás de su espalda. Flotaba entre las estrellas, eclipsando un pequeño planeta que se hallaba en primer plano.

—¿Y este tipo? —preguntó.

—Azathoth. —Levantó una hamburguesa con queso y la desenvolvió.

Margaret cerró el libro con cierta reticencia y lo colocó en el asiento de al lado. Eligió con los dedos una patata frita de una de las pequeñas bolsitas sobre la bandeja.

—Así que todos los dibujos del libro están basados en una historia de este autor, Lovecraft.

Harry asintió, masticando su comida.

—Es un libro grueso —dijo—. Debió de crear muchos monstruos.

Harry se cubrió la boca con una mano y habló mientras comía.

—Muchos, y además están todos conectados.

—¿En qué sentido? ¿Están emparentados entre sí, como una familia?

Harry tragó y bebió un sorbo de su refresco.

—Algunos, sí. Pero me refiero a que todos existen en un mundo compartido. Un poco como aquellas películas en las que Drácula se encuentra con el monstruo de Frankenstein, ¿sabes?

Ella se encogió de hombros.

—Vi una en la que Abbott y Costello se encontraban con el hombre lobo.

—Es la misma idea. Están todos en el mismo sitio, compartiendo un espacio, respirando el mismo aire. Como muchos de los cuentos de William Faulkner, que transcurren en el mismo condado.

—¿Alguna vez has hecho esa comparación en una clase de inglés?

—Hace mucho que no lo hago —dijo—. Aprendí la lección.

—¿A los profesores no les interesa?

Harry empezó a decir algo, pero se detuvo y se metió una patata frita en la boca.

CAPÍTULO 4

Volvieron a casa de la señora Johnson un poco antes de la medianoche y se quedaron sentados en el coche, sin saber qué decirse.

—Bueno —dijo Harry al fin—. Gracias por la película.

—Y a ti por comprar un libro caro —dijo Margaret—. Apreciamos tu compra. —Se rio de su propia broma, un sonido estridente y demasiado fuerte.

Él miró con fijeza hacia delante, con la boca fruncida del lado izquierdo de la cara.

—Supongo que te veré en la tienda.

—Buenas noches, Harry. —Se deslizó sobre el asiento y lo besó en la mejilla. La tenía áspera por la barba incipiente.

Salió del coche y subió por el camino de entrada. No sabía si se sentía aliviada o feliz porque él no hubiera intentado nada. Ese hilo de pensamientos colisionó rápidamente con la tensión por los deberes… aún no había empezado el ensayo para Literatura Americana, y las ecuaciones de Química seguían en el limbo de las matemáticas.

—¡Oye!

Se volvió para ver a Harry corriendo hacia ella, sujetando algo en una mano. Se detuvo a medio metro y le tendió un pequeño libro de cubierta blanda con el lomo agrietado: *La tumba y otros relatos*, de H. P. Lovecraft. La cubierta era negra con letras blancas y tenía la fotografía de la frente de un hombre dividida por la mitad. Una muchedumbre de insectos rojos brotaba del lugar donde debía estar su cerebro.

—Para que veas si te gusta —dijo Harry—. Mi madre me regaló este libro por mi decimotercer cumpleaños.

Margaret aceptó el libro.

—Está bien, parece bueno… —empezó a decir, pero él la interrumpió, cerrando la distancia entre ambos. Aferrando ambos lados de su cara, la besó.

Acabó antes que Margaret tuviera la oportunidad de pensar en lo que sucedía. Harry se alejó trotando de nuevo hacia su coche y la dejó subiendo aturdida los escalones de la casa, buscando torpemente sus llaves y deseando haber pedido una hamburguesa sin cebolla.

CAPÍTULO 5

Margaret se quedó despierta toda la noche para terminar *La tumba*, como si el elenco de genios, locos y horrores casi indescriptibles de la novela encerrara la clave para entender al joven raro que visitaba la librería y con quien había compartido un beso breve con olor a cebolla.

El libro no sirvió de mucho. Harry no parecía un loco, un monstruo ni, sin ánimo de ofender, un genio. Solo supo que le gustaba lo macabro, y que tenía una paciencia extraordinaria para la prosa áspera y retorcida. Encontró a Lovecraft casi imposible de leer. Los relatos tenían personajes, porque eran personas con un nombre que existían en una página, pero jamás se desarrollaban ni cambiaban, y nunca establecían interacciones humanas significativas. Cada vez que hablaban, parecían manuales escolares antropomórficos de otra dimensión. La mayoría de las historias parecían tratar de la suerte de un único superviviente que relataba la exploración de cierta ruina antigua y enloquecía al darse cuenta de que estaba construida (y en ocasiones aún habitada) por algún horror primordial. Tenía un lenguaje con florituras, plagado de adjetivos, muy lejos de la impresionante experiencia de terror en las pinturas de *Visiones de Cthulhu*.

Por otro lado, muchos de los relatos transmitían la sensación de que en cualquier momento se manifestaría algo oscuro. El narrador se iba dando cuenta de modo paulatino de que el «mundo real» reconfortante que habitaban los seres humanos no era, en realidad, más que una tenue gasa que podía ser descubierta en cualquier momento para revelar un abismo de terrores por detrás. Era algo así como lo contrario a Moisés y la zarza ardiente, o Pablo, de camino a Damasco. El mismo concepto básico de la religión, *el mundo no es el mundo*, pero distorsionado.

Seguía dándole vueltas a esa idea cuando entró dando tumbos a la clase de Civilización Occidental de la mañana siguiente. No notó a Pierce acercándose hasta que se sentó junto a ella.

—¿Vuelves a hablarme? —preguntó Margaret.

Pierce suspiró, y sus fosas nasales se ensancharon.

—Admito que tal vez tuve una reacción desmedida. Pero lo que hiciste…

Ella se recostó hacia atrás sobre su silla, alzando las cejas. Aquello ya podía ser bueno.

Él se llevó una mano a la frente.

—Intento disculparme. —Frunció el ceño, y por algún motivo le resultó familiar.

—Eres muy bueno haciéndolo. Espectacular.

—¿Puedo invitarte a salir esta noche? ¿Y tener una conversación adulta de verdad? ¿Por favor?

Por primera vez en casi una semana, Margaret sintió el tirón de la voz de su madre en la base del cráneo. La palabra «marido» marcaba a fuego su mente. Estaba demasiado cansada para negarse.

Pierce la llevó a Capitán Bill, el restaurante más caro de Searcy, un sitio donde se podía comer carne y pescado. Tenía viejas redes de pescador y arpones que colgaban de las paredes y los techos. La animó a pedir lo que quisiera y eligió langosta para demostrar que iba en serio. Margaret pidió una ensalada. Jamás había comido langosta. Cuando miraba a sus padres comerla, hallaba que todo el asqueroso asunto de hacerlo —los baberos, el exceso de fluidos, los caparazones rotos en los cuales se ocultaba una ínfima cantidad de carne— era repugnante. Su madre y su padre bien podían haber estado comiendo gigantescos insectos rojos. Pensarlo la hizo recordar la portada de *La tumba* y se alegró nuevamente de haber pedido una ensalada.

Terminó su plato antes de que Pierce acabara de romper el caparazón, escarbar, mojar y masticar. Su frente brillaba incluso en la tenue luz del restaurante. Margaret intentó decidir si ya estaba quedándose calvo. ¿Y estaba sudando por el esfuerzo con la langosta? Eso no podía estar bien, ¿verdad?

Cuando el camarero trajo la cuenta, Pierce la apoyó en mitad de la mesa mientras extraía su cartera de la chaqueta. Ella la miró y luego a Pierce, y lo vio mirándola, asegurándose de que hubiera visto el total. Él fingió no haberlo notado, arrojó sobre la mesa algunos billetes y le dijo al camarero que se quedara con el cambio.

Está haciendo un esfuerzo, se dijo ella, regañándose a sí misma.

Después de la cena (y un puñado de caramelos de menta de cortesía), condujeron al aparcamiento junto al parque de la ciudad. Era una noche despejada con cientos de estrellas. Las constelaciones le recordaron a Margaret a Azathoth, de *Visiones de Cthulhu*, el monstruo vagina que se impulsaba por los cielos con sus tentáculos. Se preguntó adormilada qué haría Harry en aquel momento, y deseó haberse echado una siesta antes de salir.

Estuvo a punto de dormirse cuando Pierce dijo:

—No tienes que sentarte tan lejos. —Ella se sobresaltó cuando él dio una palmadita en el sitio junto a él.

Margaret se arrimó un poco más cerca. Él le pasó un brazo alrededor, y ella se obligó a recostarse sobre su cuerpo. No era tan desagradable. Resultaba algo reconfortante, humano.

—¿Sigues enfadada conmigo? —preguntó.

—No.

—Lo entiendo si lo estás. Me comporté como un verdadero imbécil.

—No pasa nada. —Le dio una palmadita en el pecho. Advirtió que, sinceramente, le traía sin cuidado.

Él respiró hondo.

—La verdad es que me asusté cuando tú… hiciste lo que hiciste. No hemos estado saliendo durante tanto tiempo, y sucedió muy pronto. No lo manejé como un hombre. En cambio, hui como un niño y me oculté de ti. Le pregunté a Dios: «¿Por qué haría ella algo así? Es una buena chica». Y al final, Él me respondió, *Lo hizo porque te quiere*.

El cuerpo de Margaret se puso rígido.

—¿Hablas mucho con Dios? —Ella jamás rezaba fuera de la iglesia o las comidas con otros cristianos, e incluso entonces solo inclinaba la cabeza, cerraba los ojos y decía *Amén* cuando correspondía.

—Todo el día, todos los días —dijo—. Sea como sea, lo que quiere decir es que Dios me dijo que me quieres, y además, que el motivo por el cual hui era que yo también te quería y no estaba preparado para admitirlo.

—Se removió en su lugar y la escudriñó. A la luz de la luna, su frente resultaba casi cegadora. Una vena destacaba en su cuero cabelludo. ¿Estaría latiendo? ¿Se encontraba bien?—. Te quiero, Margaret. Sé que es pronto, pero mis padres dicen que cuando lo sabes, lo sabes. Si tú estás lista para tomártelo en serio, entonces yo también. Quiero que vengas a casa conmigo durante las vacaciones de Acción de Gracias. Quiero que conozcas a mi familia.

Margaret se enderezó. Pierce le sonrió con una especie de benevolencia, una expresión que ella asociaba con la cara de su padre la mañana de Navidad, la mirada de un hombre que entrega un regalo.

—Es… es un paso enorme —dijo ella.

—Te quiero, Margaret —repitió. Se inclinó y la besó. Ella dejó que la empujara sobre el asiento y trepara encima de ella. Aceptó sus besos y sus manos torpes. Mientras le mordisqueaba las orejas y el cuello, advirtió algo con el rabillo del ojo… algo en la ventanilla de Pierce. Pero cuando se movió para verlo mejor, había desaparecido. Intentó entregarse de nuevo al ritmo de los besuqueos y puso las manos sobre su cara, lo besó, dejó que empujara su lengua dentro de su boca como un gusano grueso y pegajoso. Abrió los ojos, y esta vez la vena de su frente latía de verdad mientras se entregaba a la excitación sobre el cuerpo mayormente pasivo de ella. Margaret levantó la mirada hacia un lado y vio otra cosa fuera de la ventanilla, esta vez en su propio lado del coche… una figura enorme con hombros anchos y encorvados, y dos ojos naranjas que resplandecían.

Emitió un sonido sordo de pánico y empujó los hombros de Pierce con las manos para apartarlo de encima, para que sacara su lengua de su boca y pudiera advertirle, pero él tan solo gimió y la manoseó con mayor ímpetu. La vena de su frente se había estirado sobre su ceño, dividiéndolo en dos planos separados de piel sudorosa y pálida. Ella se retorció, intentando quitárselo de encima. Algo se movió bajo la piel de su frente. La vena palpitó dos veces y luego estalló.

La cabeza de Pierce se partió, y cientos de diminutos insectos rojos salieron y se derramaron sobre la cara de Margaret, entrando en su pelo, deslizándose por entre los pliegues de su vestido y su piel, miles de piernas minúsculas retorciéndose en su afán de libertad. Propinó una patada a Pierce para apartarlo, gritó y se escabulló hacia atrás, golpeándose el cuerpo. Tenía que quitarse los insectos de encima, tenía que salir del coche, se iba a morir allí dentro si no conseguía hacerlo…

Sujetó la manilla de la puerta por detrás y tiró de ella. La puerta se abrió de golpe, y cayó sobre el suelo exterior. Pierce fue hacia ella arrastrándose sobre el asiento, y Margaret intentó ponerse en pie y moverse para alejarse antes de tener que ver su cara, ver las arañas sepultándose en sus ojos, desbordando sus fosas nasales y entrando a raudales en su boca para comérselo de adentro hacia fuera... pero estaba demasiado cansada tras pasar toda la noche leyendo, exhausta de tanto gritar, y apenas podía moverse. Cuando la cara de Pierce emergió a la luz de la luna, no pudo evitar mirarlo. Se hallaba un poco sudoroso y aturdido, la cara arrebatada por la excitación interrumpida (y posiblemente por el sobresalto), pero, por lo demás, normal. La vena se había desvanecido, y su frente cerosa estaba despejada y plana.

—¿Qué sucede? —preguntó. Salió del coche y se arrodilló delante de ella.

Margaret parpadeó un par de veces, jadeando.

—Estoy bien —dijo, dirigiéndose a sí misma tanto como a él—. No pasa nada.

CAPÍTULO 6

Explicó que no había dormido demasiado la noche anterior, y quizás estuviera sufriendo algún tipo de pesadilla. Pierce interpretó el papel del novio preocupado y no hizo demasiadas preguntas. Pero ella se encontró con hambre de nuevo y, no deseando seguir besuqueándose con él, le preguntó si podían pasar por un autoservicio.

Así fue como se encontró por segunda vez esa noche en una fila, mirando fuera de la ventana del coche de Pierce mientras él pedía patatas fritas y un batido para ella. Sentía la cara magullada, como si hubiera estado acariciando papel de lija. No quería hablar, no quería pensar. Solo quería mirar fuera de la ventana y dejarse llevar. Que Pierce lidiara con la voz incorpórea que salía del altavoz del autoservicio. De todos modos, incluso su inocua conversación, un intercambio de menos de cincuenta palabras, la inquietó. ¿Qué sucedía? ¿Por qué sentía un pánico indefinido en el pecho? Se dio la vuelta en su asiento y observó el coche, intentando discernir el origen de su malestar. No fue hasta que se acercaron a la ventanilla que lo comprendió. Harry abrió el cristal plegable para recibir su dinero.

Sus ojos se encontraron con los de Margaret al otro lado del coche, y su boca se abrió con aparente sorpresa.

—¿Estás seguro de que quieres esto? —preguntó sonriendo al ofrecer el batido—. Podría tener raíz de tannis dentro.

—¿Disculpa? —preguntó Pierce.

Margaret sacudió ligeramente la cabeza. Harry la miró y luego de nuevo a Pierce.

—Nada, lo siento —dijo.

—¿Cuánto has dicho que era? —preguntó Pierce.

Harry se lo dijo, e hicieron el intercambio. Contó el dinero, cerró la ventanilla, y Pierce condujo fuera del autoservicio. De camino a casa de la señora Johnson, Margaret sostuvo el batido con ambas manos, pero no se atrevió a darle un sorbo. Cuando llegó a casa, lo llevó a la cocina y lo arrojó por el fregadero, tras lo cual se dirigió arriba. No había duda de que era raíz de tannis.

Se quedó dormida casi de inmediato. Soñó con aullidos, como si un lobo o perro de caza estuviera sufriendo un gran dolor no lejos de allí.

CAPÍTULO 7

La madre de Margaret se alegró cuando la llamó para contarle las novedades del día de Acción de Gracias. Estaba tan emocionada que tuvo que alejar el auricular de la oreja.

—Esa es mi niña —dijo la señora Byrne.

—Tengo muy malas notas —dijo Margaret—. Voy atrasada en todas mis clases.

—Solo tienes que aguantar hasta que cerréis el trato —respondió su madre—. Puedes hacerlo, princesa.

—Mamá.

—¿Qué?

—No me parece.

—¿No te parece qué? —preguntó la señora Byrne.

No me parece bien, pensó Margaret. Lo que dijo en cambio fue:

—No me parece real todavía.

—Lo será —dijo la señora Byrne, como si pudiera leer el trasfondo en la voz de su hija—. Solo practica estar enamorada y espera a que suceda.

Mientras se preparaba para ir a clase por las mañanas, Margaret se repetía el mantra una y otra vez. *Estamos enamorados. Estamos enamorados.* Al cepillarse los dientes, intentaba imaginar a Pierce junto a ella, ambos turnándose para escupir en el lavabo. Al arreglarse el pelo y vestirse, intentaba echar de menos a Pierce, preguntarse dónde estaba, qué hacía. Intentaba echarlo de menos, esperar con impaciencia el curso de Civilización Occidental. Corría sosteniendo la cometa de su relación por encima de la cabeza, intentando que echara a volar sola. Siempre parecía necesitar una pequeña ayuda extra.

Harry dejó de ir a la tienda. Entendía por qué se alejaba... Le había ocultado dónde trabajaba, y no solo lo había descubierto, sino que lo había hecho mientras salía con otro hombre. Un hombre que conducía un Mercedes. Margaret también se habría mantenido alejada. Pobre Harry. Pero ella aún tenía su ejemplar de *La tumba*, que había sido un obsequio de su madre. Seguramente, iba a querer que se lo devolviera, y Margaret estaba ansiosa por deshacerse de él. Incluso dos semanas después de volverse loca en el coche de Pierce, siguió teniendo pesadillas sobre figuras acechantes y aullidos lejanos. Estaba casi segura de que era culpa del libro. *La tumba* incluía una historia titulada «El sabueso», acerca de un par de ladrones de tumbas que desentierran a un hechicero muerto hace cien años solo para encontrar algo inhumano dentro del ataúd, «con sus cuencas fosforescentes y afiladas fauces sanguinolentas, haciendo una mueca retorcida con la boca para mofarse de mi inevitable condena. Y cuando lanzó de aquellas fauces sonrientes un aullido profundo y sardónico como el de un sabueso gigante... tan solo grité y eché a correr...».

Tomó prestada una bicicleta del garaje de la señora Johnson y cruzó pedaleando el pueblo al McDonald's. Llegó durante la hora de almuerzo y encontró a Harry en la caja registradora, atendiendo una larga cola de clientes. No la vio cuando ella se unió a la cola; estaba completamente concentrado en quienquiera que estuviera justo delante de él. Se lo veía contento, como si cada cliente fuera precisamente la persona que estuviera esperando ver. La mirada duró hasta que Margaret llegó al inicio de la cola. En aquel momento pareció quedar absorto por la caja registradora.

—¿En qué puedo ayudarte? —preguntó.

—Quiero devolverte tu libro.

—Pues devuélvemelo.

—¿Cuándo es tu hora de descanso?

—Ya ha pasado.

—¿Cuándo acaba tu turno?

Suspiró.

—Salgo a las tres.

Ella miró su reloj. Era la 1.45.

Abrió el bolso y examinó su exiguo contenido.

—Ponme las patatas fritas más pequeñas que tengas. Para comer aquí.

Harry registró la venta en la caja y le entregó un pequeñísimo paquete de patatas fritas sobre una bandeja. Ella las llevó a una mesa en el rincón, se sentó, y comió lo más lento posible… tan lento que las últimas patatas estaban frías y blandas antes de terminarlas. Aun así le llevó solo quince minutos. Su atención se desvió a la ventana, al cielo azul brillante en el exterior, y a Harry tomando pedidos en el mostrador. ¿Cómo era posible que alguien conservara el buen humor así?

Por fin, a las tres y cinco, Harry se acercó a su mesa arrastrando los pies y se desplomó al otro lado del reservado con un gemido. Al sentarse, una oleada de aceite de cocina se desprendió de él. El estómago de Margaret emitió un rugido. Él hizo girar la pequeña gorra blanca de McDonald's entre las manos mientras hablaban.

—¿Qué puedo hacer por ti, Margaret? —preguntó.

Ella empujó *La tumba* hacia el otro lado de la mesa.

—Quería asegurarme de que recuperaras tu libro.

—Te lo agradezco, pero no hacía falta.

—Pero te lo dio tu madre. Fue un regalo de cumpleaños.

Harry se frotó la cara y miró al techo entornando los ojos.

—Oh, sí, aquello.

—¿A qué te refieres?

—A nada. Solo que… si te fijas en la fecha de publicación, fue hace apenas dos años. Las cuentas no salen. Salvo que creas que tengo quince años.

Margaret le quitó de nuevo el libro de un tirón y se fijó en la página de derechos de autor.

—¿Y por qué mentirías acerca de ello?

—Creí que mejoraría mis posibilidades de salir de nuevo contigo. —La miró de arriba abajo—. Pero ese no es el motivo por el cual estás aquí.

Margaret se retorció en el reservado e intentó decidir cómo responderle.

—No te preocupes —dijo él—. Lo entiendo. Vi la ropa y el coche de tu novio. La elección no es difícil: el chico universitario o el pueblerino que se gana la vida detrás de una caja registradora.

—No sabía que no ibas a Tilden —dice—. Creía que eras como yo… sin dinero y que trabajabas para pagarte los estudios.

—Supongo que podría haberlo aclarado —dijo—. Pero de nuevo… en la segunda cita.

—¿Así que no estás en la universidad? ¿Entonces por qué no estás en Vietnam?

—Mi padre está muerto y mi madre padece de esquizofrenia paranoica —dijo—. Tengo una prórroga. —Hizo girar su gorra sobre un dedo índice. Margaret movió la boca en círculos, pero no consiguió que saliera ninguna palabra de ella. —No pasa nada, de verdad —dijo él—. No tienes que explicarme nada.

—¿Podemos ser amigos?

La gorra salió girando de sus dedos y aterrizó en el suelo. Se inclinó para recogerla.

—¿Cómo se sentirá el Capitán Mercedes si lo fuéramos?

—Se llama Pierce —dijo ella—. Es una buena persona. Un buen cristiano.

—¿Eso es importante para ti?

—Asisto a una universidad cristiana —dijo—. ¿Acaso tú no crees en Dios?

Harry dejó caer la gorra sobre la mesa.

—Jamás lo he conocido.

Margaret emitió un sonido burlón.

—Así que tu familia tiene el dinero suficiente para enviarte a Tilden, pero no para evitar que tengas un empleo —señaló él.

—Mi padre siempre decía que pertenecíamos a la clase acomodada, pero que no éramos ricos. —Al instante, lamentó las palabras, odiaba cómo sonaban.

Harry se encogió de hombros.

—Supongo que hay ricos y ricos. Desde aquí abajo, todo parece igual.

Ella también respondió desestimando el asunto.

—Si tú lo dices. Sea como sea, hemos perdido todo el dinero. Por eso tuve que conseguir un empleo.

—Yo he trabajado desde que tenía catorce años —dijo—. Trabajé mientras asistía al instituto.

—Intenta hacerlo mientras estás en la universidad —dijo.

—¿En la universidad? ¿Te refieres a asistir a clase doce horas por semana?

—Hay más que eso —dijo ella—. Deberes, ejercicios, ensayos, exámenes parciales y finales.

—¿Qué estudias?

—Marketing —dijo, sorprendida por la espontaneidad de la mentira.

Puso los ojos en blanco.

—¿Tú y el buen cristiano planeáis conseguir empleos de marketing después de casaros? ¿Esperas que todo tu arduo trabajo resulte en grandes dividendos durante los siguientes diez años, para cuando seas un ama de casa con tres niños?

La cara de Margaret ardía.

—*Se llama Pierce* —repitió.

—Me alegro por él.

—Entonces. —Margaret tamborileó los dedos sobre el libro—. Eres un hombre adulto que sigue leyendo historias de fantasmas y monstruos.

—Eso ya lo sabías —respondió él.

—Supongo que no había pensado en ello hasta ahora —dijo—. ¿No te sientes un poco ridículo? ¿Cómo si tal vez debieras estar leyendo libros para adultos?

—Creo que el horror es el género de ficción más importante del mundo —dijo.

Ella estuvo a punto de contarle lo de la presencia que había visto al otro lado de la ventana de Pierce, los insectos rojos, las semanas de pesadillas. Casi le gritó por fomentar que su cabeza se llenara de terrores nocturnos con el estúpido libro. En cambio, decidió también ridiculizarlo.

—¿Eso? —Señaló el libro—. Es una basura ilegible y pretenciosa.

Harry volvió a levantar el libro.

—¿Qué quieres de mí, Margaret?

—Nada. Solo quería devolverte tu libro… tu *libro de mentiras*, como ha resultado ser.

Volvió a reírse, pero esta vez no sonó hostil, tan solo sorprendido.

—¿Qué? —preguntó ella.

Él alzó ambas manos como rindiéndose.

—Nada. Me gusta cómo expresas las cosas cuando estás enfadada. Ya veo por qué quieres estudiar Marketing.

—En realidad, he mentido sobre eso —admitió—. Estoy estudiando Inglés.

Harry se inclinó hacia delante, apoyó la cara entre las manos y se rio aún más fuerte.

—No hace falta que te burles de mí —dijo ella—. Ya estoy avergonzada.

Él se enjugó las lágrimas de las mejillas, intentando recomponerse.

—¿Por qué estamos tan desesperados por causar una buena impresión en el otro? Escucha, siento lo que he dicho respecto a que te convirtieras en un ama de casa con tres niños y sin empleo. Me crio una madre soltera que tenía dos empleos. Me enseñó a tener la sensatez de no pensar de ese modo. —Echó un vistazo a su reloj e hizo una mueca—. Hablando de lo cual, necesito volver a casa y ver cómo está.

Ambos se pusieron en pie. Margaret le dirigió una mirada a la bicicleta de la señora Johnson, encadenada a la verja que estaba fuera, y luego a Harry.

—¿Me llevas?

CAPÍTULO 8

Cuando llegaron a casa de la señora Johnson, Harry salió para ayudar a Margaret a descargar la bicicleta del maletero.

—¿Así que tú y el buen cristiano estáis saliendo en serio? —preguntó.

Ella le dio un puñetazo en el brazo.

—Basta. Y sí, iré a conocer a su familia el día de Acción de Gracias.

—Ni siquiera ha llegado Halloween —dijo él—. Falta mucho tiempo para el día de Acción de Gracias.

—¿Y qué? —preguntó ella.

Harry cerró el maletero y se apoyó sobre él, con los brazos cruzados.

—Mi madre nunca dejó de tener citas hasta que ella y mi padre se casaron. Tuvo una cita incluso la noche antes de la boda.

—No me lo creo —dijo Margaret.

—Lo juro por Dios…

—En quien no crees…

—Dijo que quería estar segura.

—¿A dónde quieres llegar, Harry?

—Aún no estás casada. Ni siquiera es el día de Acción de Gracias. Quizás podríamos vernos alguna vez más antes de eso.

Margaret hizo una mueca.

—No creo que a Pierce le guste.

—Entonces me alegra no preguntárselo a él —dijo Harry—. ¿A quién le importa lo que él quiera? ¿Qué es lo que tú quieres? —Cuando no respondió en seguida, dijo—: Por lo menos intentémoslo una vez más.

—No me harás cambiar de opinión.

—Es posible que no —accedió—. Pero tampoco estoy dispuesto a renunciar todavía a ti.

Estamos enamorados, se repitió Margaret para sí, intentando imaginar a Pierce en su cabeza. *Estamos enamorados*.

CAPÍTULO 9

En la segunda cita, Harry sacó a Margaret de Searcy y de nuevo siguió todos los letreros para dirigirse a Little Rock. Una vez en la ciudad, extrajo un trozo de papel del bolsillo de su camisa y lo leyó mientras conducía por el área del centro. Entraron en un vecindario residencial ruinoso, bordeado de casas antiguas en varios estadios de deterioro… ventanas rotas, porches hundidos, canalones desprendidos. Seguramente habían sido bonitas alguna vez, pero se preguntó quién podía seguir viviendo allí.

Se detuvieron en la esquina de una de aquellas calles, a la sombra de una casa de dos plantas con torretas y un letrero hundido en el jardín: ¡CASA EN-CANTADA! Una hilera de personas empezaba en la base del porche y se extendía por la acera.

—¿Qué es este lugar? —preguntó Margaret.

En 1968, un año antes que la Mansión Encantada abriera en Disneylandia, y mucho antes de que proliferaran sus copias en todo el país, Harry no podía echar mano del término *casa encantada* como una noción cultural que fuera fácilmente comprendida, y tuvo que apelar al equivalente más cercano.

—Se supone que es como la casa de la risa de un carnaval o un tren fantasma —dijo, dando la vuelta a la manzana y buscando un sitio para aparcar—. Pero es una casa de verdad. Así que replica en realidad cómo sería entrar en un sitio embrujado. —Estiró el cuerpo delante de ella para abrir la guantera y extraer un periódico doblado. Margaret alcanzó a ver un titular (NIÑO LOCAL DESAPARECIDO) antes de que él se lo pasara, señalando un pequeño anuncio en una esquina.

Inclinó el papel para poder leerlo a la luz de la farola mientras él retrocedía para entrar en un espacio libre delante de la atracción. El anuncio era un pequeño cuadrado negro, en el que aparecía la caricatura de un fantasma genérico encima de una leyenda en negrita blanca: «¡Venga a la Casa Encantada y ¡EXPERIMENTE UNA PESADILLA DE LA VIDA REAL!».

—¿Esto te parece divertido? —le preguntó ella.

—Si no quieres entrar, no hay problema —respondió—. Podemos ver una película o puedo llevarte a casa. —La tensión se filtró en su voz. Estaba muy empeñado en entrar, pero también quería ser considerado.

—No, hagámoslo —dijo ella—. ¿Cómo de a menudo tengo la oportunidad de vivir una pesadilla real?

Se unieron a la cola, avanzando lentamente hacia la puerta cada veinte minutos, mientras grupos de personas divertidas salían a través de la verja que rodeaba el lateral de la casa. Por fin estuvieron delante de la vendedora de entradas, una mujer mayor y robusta con pelo lacio y gris y un cigarrillo encajado en una esquina de la boca. Harry pagó. La mujer le dio el cambio y señaló hacia el interior.

—¿Debemos…? ¿Cómo funciona? —preguntó Harry.

—Entren y verán —respondió la mujer. Su voz era similar al sonido de dos piedras rozándose con aspereza.

La puerta principal estaba abierta, pero cintas de papel color naranja colgaban del techo ocultando lo que había detrás. Margaret y Harry se abrieron paso apartándolas y entraron en un vestíbulo tenuemente iluminado, con una bombilla parpadeante por encima y lucecillas color naranja que colgaban del pasamanos y se retorcían hasta perderse en la oscuridad del segundo piso. Margaret se inclinó hacia delante y echó un vistazo escaleras arriba. Algo se movió, una forma recortada contra la oscuridad, apartándose de la vista. Ella retrocedió y chocó contra Harry.

—¿Te encuentras bien? —le preguntó este.

—Claro —masculló. Quizás aquello había sido una mala idea.

Un grupo de cuatro adolescentes entró detrás de ellos, dos parejas riéndose y apoyándose unos en otros. Su energía era palpable y tranquilizadora. Harry y Margaret se hicieron a un lado para dejar que los chicos tomaran la delantera. Los siguieron por el pasillo, que se abría a la derecha a una sala. Cuatro personas se hallaban sentadas sobre un sofá sobrio y de aspecto incómodo, llevaban puestos disfraces raros, aunque no atemorizantes. Parecían una familia: el padre, vestido de traje, con un grueso bigote negro; la madre, con largo pelo negro y lacio y un vestido ceñido al cuerpo que moldeaba su silueta; un chico regordete con una camiseta de rayas y un corte tipo casco; y una chiquilla con un vestido negro y pelo negro trenzado a ambos lados de su carita adusta y malhumorada. Tenían la vista fija en la pantalla de una televisión que brillaba con la estática.

—¡Bienvenidos! —dijo el padre, sacudiendo la mano en el aire—. Estamos viendo la previsión del tiempo por la televisión.

—Parece que esté nevando, Gómez —le dijo la madre.

¿Gómez? ¿De dónde le sonaba el nombre a Margaret?

—Siempre parece que va a nevar —dijo la chiquilla.

—Sabes, Miércoles, es una observación excelente —concedió Gómez.

¿Miércoles? ¿Gómez?

—Oh, es como aquel programa de la televisión —dijo una de las chicas adolescentes—. La, eh… ¿cómo se llamaba?

—*La familia Addams* —dijo Harry, en voz tan baja que solo Margaret lo oyó. Cuando atrajo su atención, la miró como disculpándose. Estudió a los imitadores de los Addams. Ahora lo veía, claro, ¿pero acaso *La familia Addams* no era una comedia que se burlaba de los monstruos? ¿Acaso no era una comedia de equivocaciones y no una de terror? El anuncio del periódico no parecía anticipar un espectáculo cómico.

—Dado que nos hemos quedado atrapados por la nieve, tendrán que cenar con nosotros —dijo Gómez—. ¡Lurch!

Una figura levemente más alta que el promedio se acercó arrastrando los pies por el pasillo en dirección a los visitantes. Llevaba un esmoquin y maquillaje que lo hacía parecer como el monstruo de Frankenstein. Emitió un gruñido con tono de pregunta.

—Lurch, lleva a nuestros huéspedes al comedor, ¿sí? —dijo Gómez.

El monstruo enfundado en el esmoquin volvió a gruñir. Margaret, Harry, Gómez y los adolescentes lo siguieron por el corredor hacia un enorme comedor alumbrado con velas, donde se había dispuesto una mesa larga para doce personas. Lurch caminó alrededor de la mesa y retiró seis sillas. Cuando nadie hizo movimiento alguno para aceptar la invitación, se inclinó hacia delante y quitó la tapa de una fuente en mitad de la mesa. Hizo un gesto hacia el contenido, una masa negra que parecía retorcerse bajo la luz parpadeante.

Ni siquiera entonces se acercó ninguno. Lurch metió la mano en la fuente, cogió un puñado de lo que fuera que había dentro y lo arrojó hacia los visitantes. La masa se partió en el aire, y Margaret tuvo tiempo de distinguir miembros largos y un brillo de plástico. Los adolescentes soltaron un grito cuando la sustancia negra los golpeó y rebotó cayendo sobre el suelo. Margaret escudriñó las formas: arañas de caucho. Lurch estaba arrojándoles arañas de caucho. Por lo menos no eran rojas.

—Oh, vamos —dijo Harry.

—Lurch, ¿qué te he dicho sobre jugar con la comida? —preguntó Gómez. Estaba mucho más cerca de lo que a Margaret le hubiera gustado, y su aliento apestaba a cigarrillos—. ¡Ahora tenemos que limpiar a nuestros huéspedes! —Margaret sintió alivio cuando se abrió paso delante del grupo y los condujo a una puerta al final del pasillo. Un chorro de humo se filtraba por una rendija entre la puerta y el suelo.

Avanzaron con lentitud hasta una cocina tan llena de humo que Marga-ret no podía ver el suelo. Un hombre con gafas y una bata blanca se hallaba de pie en el centro y revolvía una cacerola humeante.

—¡Esta vivo! —gemía—. ¡Vivo!

Los hombros de Harry se desplomaron un poco, y su cara cayó en sus manos.

—¿Cómo está la sopa, Henry? —preguntó Gómez.

—Va viento en popa, señor Addams —dijo el hombre en la bata del la-boratorio. Con la cuchara de metal batió algo en la cacerola, salpicando agua sobre la estufa.

—¡Me alegro! —dijo Gómez—. ¿Tienes por casualidad toallas limpias? Hemos tenido un pequeño percance en el comedor.

—Nada limpio, lo siento —dijo Henry—. Es decir, salvo que… *san-griento* no significa lo mismo que *sucio*. —Levantó una toalla blanca empa-pada de color rojo carmesí.

Gómez se giró para dirigirse una vez más a los visitantes.

—Creo que tenemos algunas toallas en el baño de arriba si quieren diri-girse hacia allí.

—No estamos sucios —dijo Harry—. ¿Podemos volver a salir por donde hemos entrado?

—Tonterías —dijo Gómez—. Acabamos de remodelar la habitación de huéspedes de arriba. No pueden no visitarla. ¿Lurch?

Lurch reapareció en la entrada de la cocina.

—Lleva a nuestros huéspedes arriba para proporcionarles toallas limpias —dijo Gómez.

Lurch emitió un gruñido y les hizo una seña para que volvieran al pasillo.

Margaret entró primera, con Harry justo detrás.

—Es una casa pequeña —susurró, cerca de su oreja, exhalando su aliento cálido sobre su cuello—. No puede haber mucho más. —Luego, un segundo después—: Lo siento.

Margaret lideró la expedición escaleras arriba y se hizo a un lado en el rellano para dejar pasar al resto del grupo. Se hallaban de pie en un corredor estrecho, sumergido en penumbras, alineado a ambos lados con puertas ce-rradas. También había, de modo incongruente, un tiesto con una planta alta sobre la pared, delante de las escaleras. Se inclinó sobre el pasamanos y miró hacia abajo, al primer piso. Pensó en la figura que había visto mirándola desde aquel sitio al entrar. Aquella parte no había parecido falsa ni parte de una broma, sino real. Se apartó del pasamanos con un empujón y encaró al grupo apiñado.

—¿Y ahora dónde? —preguntó uno de los adolescentes.

La puerta en el extremo más lejano del corredor se abrió de golpe. Lurch se giró y descendió las escaleras, dejándolos solos.

Avanzaron por el pasillo. No aparecieron ni fantasmas ni espíritus malignos. La casa parecía aún más silenciosa que antes. Vacía.

La habitación al final del corredor estaba bañada en una luz rosada y empalagosa, y se hallaba decorada como el dormitorio de una anciana. Tenía un antiguo tocador a la izquierda, y una cama de dos plazas en la esquina opuesta. La cama se hallaba apoyada sobre una estructura de metal, y la cabecera y la piecera eran tan elevadas que parecía una cuna para adultos. Un bulto yacía bajo las mantas, sin moverse.

Fotografías antiguas en blanco y negro colgaban sobre las paredes: niños sonriendo y riendo un día de verano en la playa; el retrato de un soldado en su atuendo formal, con el sombrero inclinado en un ángulo que debió de considerarse desenfadado; una pareja recién casada huyendo de una iglesia, con las cabezas gachas y las manos alzadas para protegerse de una embestida de arroz; la foto de un accidente, en la que un coche había impactado lateralmente en otro. El lado del pasajero del primer coche estaba aplastado y derrumbado; el parachoques de detrás del segundo estaba cubierto con una pancarta que rezaba *Recién Casados* y una hilera de latas vacías. Una segunda fotografía de un accidente colgaba cerca de la primera: representaba un cuerpo bajo una sábana empapada de sangre de uno de los lados. Una mano colgaba libre y visible, el encaje blanco deteniéndose en la muñeca; una alianza matrimonial de diamantes brillaba con la luz del sol. Margaret se quedó mirándola un largo rato. ¿Era real? ¿Estaría trucada?

—No lo entiendo —dijo una de las chicas—. Da un poco de miedo. Pero ¿cuál es la broma?

—¿Y qué tiene que ver esto con *La familia Addams*? —preguntó Margaret.

—No lo sé —dijo Harry.

Una de las chicas señaló el bulto en la cama.

—¿Qué es eso?

—Ve a ver —dijo la otra.

—Ni hablar.

Discutieron otro momento más hasta que el más alto y fornido de los dos chicos se ofreció para investigar. El chico más pequeño lo siguió, un paso o dos por detrás, el torso ligeramente alejado de la mitad inferior de su cuerpo, como frenado por el propio sentido común.

El chico alto se hallaba de pie encima del bulto sobre la cama, de espaldas a la habitación. Se sacudió la rigidez de las manos y las extendió para levantar el cubrecama. Margaret se pasó la lengua por los labios resecos, pensó en la figura observándola a través de la ventanilla del coche de Pierce. Extendió la mano para sujetar la de Harry, quien la atrapó con la suya.

El chico alto cogió el cubrecama y lo apartó de un tirón. Su amigo gritó, las chicas soltaron un alarido y Margaret dio un paso hacia la puerta. El chico se quedó inmóvil, con la manta en la mano, mirando hacia abajo. Margaret aún no podía ver lo que observaba.

—¿Qué es? —preguntó Harry. Soltó a Margaret y dio un paso adelante para ver mejor. El chico alto soltó la manta y levantó el bulto de la cama. Se dio la vuelta y lo extendió para que todo el mundo pudiera ver que era un cojín con un dibujo infantil de Drácula. Las chicas se rieron, y Harry volvió junto a Margaret.

—Este sitio es oficialmente lo peor —dijo—. ¿Quieres irte?

—Sí, por favor —respondió ella.

Salieron de la habitación, dejando a los adolescentes solos. Pero cuando llegaron al tiesto con la planta sobre el rellano del segundo piso, se encontraron con que el camino para descender las escaleras estaba bloqueado por una puerta corrediza de metal.

—No me he fijado en ella cuando subíamos —dijo Harry. Le dio un tirón. Se sacudió un poco, pero no se movió.

—¿Ahora qué? —preguntó Margaret.

—Déjame ver —respondió él. Empezó a toquetear la puerta. Margaret miró hacia atrás, a la habitación rosada, y notó que la casa se había vuelto a quedar en silencio. ¿Qué hacían los chicos allí dentro?

Esforzándose por escuchar, intentó distinguir sonidos que delataran personas besuqueándose. Tan concentrada estaba que no se percató de que la planta en el tiesto se movía hasta que la tuvo agarrada.

Margaret gritó. Presa del terror, se retorció hacia un lado y otro, intentando soltarse. La planta, tal vez sorprendida por su alarma, la soltó de golpe, y ella salió despedida hacia delante golpeando a Harry, quien chocó contra la puerta. Ambos rebotaron y cayeron sobre el duro suelo de madera.

Margaret empujó a Harry para apartarlo e intentó levantarse, pero sus piernas se enredaron con las de él, y volvió a caerse. Su cabeza golpeó con fuerza contra el suelo, y un destello de dolor blanco cruzó sus párpados cerrados. Pestañeó varias veces, intentando enfocar la mirada. Era vagamente consciente de que alguien trasladaba su cuerpo y le aferraba los brazos para ponerla de pie.

—Vamos —dijo Harry. Su mano se cerró sobre la suya y la arrastró hacia una puerta recién abierta, al final del corredor, lejos de la habitación rosada, la planta, las escaleras y la puerta. Esa sala estaba vacía, iluminada por una única bombilla, y tenía un agujero negro donde debería haber estado la ventana.

Harry la soltó, caminó hacia el agujero negro y echó un vistazo dentro. Miró a Margaret de nuevo y en aquel momento se quedó boquiabierto. Su mirada se tornó repentinamente lejana y ausente. Antes de que ella pudiera preguntar lo que sucedía, una silueta pasó por la puerta a sus espaldas e interrumpió toda reflexión sensata. Alta y encorvada, envuelta en una capa carmesí, la figura tenía una cara larga y peluda y un hocico repleto de colmillos gigantes. En lugar de manos tenía patas con largas garras curvas. Sus ojos destellaban con un brillo color naranja. La criatura señaló a Margaret con una garra y bramó con un sonido inhumano y animal.

Margaret soltó un aullido. Harry la sujetó y levantó, y cuando ella le miró los ojos, él parecía haber vuelto al presente. Sonrió y dijo: «Confía en mí». Luego la arrojó dentro del agujero negro.

Chocó con un plástico negro y descendió a toda velocidad a través de la oscuridad. Su cuerpo chirrió contra la textura del tobogán. Oyó algo detrás de ella acercándose con rapidez, grande, ruidoso e imposible de ver. Al volver la cabeza e intentar echar un vistazo para ver si era Harry o el monstruo vestido de rojo, el tobogán llegó a su fin y Margaret salió estrepitosamente a la noche fría y despejada. Quedó suspendida un instante, ingrávida, y luego aterrizó con un golpe seco sobre algo grande y suave.

Se hallaba recostada sobre una alfombra mullida en lo que parecía el jardín trasero de la casa. También había una adolescente que le gritaba. El corazón le latía con fuerza y seguía intentando despejar la cabeza. Le llevó un momento comprender lo que le decía: ¡Hazte a un lado! Así que seguía en posición horizontal sobre la alfombrá cuando el tobogán escupió a Harry, que aterrizó justo encima de ella.

En aquel instante de 1968, tendidos en la postura del misionero fuera de La Casa Encantada, mi madre miró a Harry a la cara y sintió que se desvanecía la vida holgada junto a Pierce. En su lugar, vio un período de años diferentes y más duros extendiéndose ante ella: una boda pequeña, cargada de preocupaciones; demasiados hijos; la vida en un vecindario de trabajadores; una frugalidad extrema; ropa usada; compras en tiendas de segunda mano. Sintió que no tenía fuerzas para resistir ni ánimo para impedir que se hiciera realidad.

No le contó a mi padre nada de aquello. En cambio, colocó las manos sobre su cara y dijo: «Mi madre te odiará».

La secuencia Turner I: Margaret

Cuando Margaret irrumpe despierta en el sueño fluido de la
Ciudad, aquella mezcla de recuerdo y pesadilla, cree que
está en el minúsculo apartamento que compartía con Harry,
en el sector más empobrecido de Lubbock: aquel cuartucho
ruinoso de una sola habitación con la alfombra raída y las
paredes forradas de madera, aunque apenas puedan verse
detrás de las pilas de cajas que invaden la habitación,
cajas llenas de libros de bolsillo, cómics y revistas *pulp*
de Harry.

Las cosas de Harry están por todos lados. La mesa de la
pequeña cocina está cubierta bajo su máquina de escribir y
pilas de papeles escolares y garabatos de rascacielos
urbanos que ella jamás reconoce. Siempre promete que pondrá
orden, pero nunca parece encontrar el tiempo para hacerlo.
Es un modo estresante de vivir, esquivando de puntillas las
pertenencias de otra persona, no hallándose nunca a gusto
en la propia casa.

Tun.

El sonido parece provenir del dormitorio. Margaret
abandona la sala atestada de cosas para ir a investigar.
Cuando abre la puerta y entra, se encuentra a sí misma en
la cama. Harry está dormido junto a ella, con la boca
ligeramente abierta. Lleva la máscara de dormir para que
ella pueda dejar la luz encendida y leer. La máscara es de
color lavanda y está contorneada de encaje, pero Harry
nunca se queja al ponérsela, y Margaret lo quiere por
ello.

Tun.

Esta vez parece provenir de algún lugar en el interior de la habitación, pero no advierte cuál. *Tun. Tun-tun.* Como si la habitación misma estuviera dentro del sonido. Apoya el libro sobre el vientre y nota por primera vez que está embarazada. *Tun. Tun-Tun.* Su barriga está enorme y redonda como un globo demasiado inflado, a punto de estallar. ¿Viene del interior de la habitación o del interior de sí misma? Coloca las manos sobre la barriga. *Tun-Tun.* Su vientre reverbera al ritmo del sonido.

Sacude el hombro de Harry, pero él se gira sobre el costado, alejándose de ella.

Tun. Tun-Tun.

Sus entrañas se contraen con una fuerza repentina y feroz, y suelta un jadeo, acurrucándose en una bola alrededor de su barriga. Algo va mal. Cierra los ojos y succiona aire a través de sus labios secos y los dientes apretados. El dolor se retrae lentamente convirtiéndose en un sordo latido en su cintura. Tal vez sea solo una molestia digestiva. Tal vez haya comido algo que le ha sentado mal al bebé.

Se endereza y sale del dormitorio. Tiene intención de dirigirse al baño, pero debe de haberse equivocado de camino porque ya no está en el apartamento. Se encuentra de pie en un pasillo largo, oscuro y estrecho, en cuyas paredes cuelgan cuadros enmarcados. En el otro extremo hay una única puerta cerrada. *Tun. Tun-Tun.* El sonido, tan tenue que lo siente más que lo escucha, resuena a través de los antiguos suelos de madera. Apoya una mano sobre la barriga. El bulto del bebé ha desaparecido. No tiene el vientre plano de nuevo, no exactamente, pero ha desaparecido el montículo y los calambres que lo acompañaban.

Se vuelve para mirar la puerta por la que ha pasado, pero se encuentra en cambio delante de una pared vacía. *Tun-Tun.* El pasillo late, vibra. La puerta del fondo se

abre y gira hacia dentro. Un débil gimoteo sale flotando en
el aire como una brisa. Margaret no quiere ir a la
habitación, pero no puede dejar de caminar hacia ella.

La habitación está oscura. Extiende la mano hacia el
interruptor, inundándola de una suave luz rosada, del color
de la náusea. Se trata de una habitación de bebé vacía. No
hay juguetes, ni cambiador, ni móviles, ni papel pintado
alegre. Solo varias fotografías enmarcadas en blanco y
negro sobre las paredes, una mecedora y una cuna. Camina
hacia la cuna, pero los lloriqueos han cesado. La cuna está
vacía, las mantas arrojadas a un lado. ¿Cuánto tiempo hace
que está aquí?

Margaret aprieta la barandilla con las manos. *Oh,
cielos. Oh, cielos.*

Mira alrededor de la habitación, pero no ve nada fuera
de lo normal. Se agacha hasta quedar de rodillas, gimiendo,
y mira bajo la cama. No ve al bebé, pero hay una fotografía
enmarcada que acumula polvo. La levanta.

Es una fotografía de Margaret y Harry en el juzgado el
día de su boda. Harry lleva uno de los viejos trajes de su
padre, que no le queda demasiado bien: le queda holgado y
suelto sobre su cuerpo enjuto. Parece un niño jugando a
disfrazarse. Margaret lleva un vestido verde sencillo que
le compró la señora Johnson (verde, no blanco, porque la
señora Johnson quería que pudiera ponérselo más de una
vez). Los padres de Margaret no aparecen en la fotografía
porque se negaron a asistir a la ceremonia, pero la madre
de Harry, Deborah, está allí, con gesto lánguido, mirando
ceñuda algo que está fuera de cámara. Es lo más alegre que
se la puede ver, como alguien que intenta fingir felicidad
a pesar de un dolor de muelas lacerante.

El bebé emite un sonido, desviando la atención de
Margaret de la fotografía. El sonido se ha desplazado al
pasillo. Se apoya contra la cuna para ponerse en pie. Su
barriga ha vuelto a ponerse redonda y dura. El bebé llora

en el pasillo, y algo se mueve en el vientre de Margaret, agitado por el sonido. Abandona la habitación del bebé, con la fotografía en la mano y se encuentra de nuevo en el dormitorio.

Encuentra a Harry despierto, sentado en la cama. Dos pequeñas figuras se arrastran sobre su cuerpo, resoplando y dando manotazos. Guardan un cierto parecido con una figura humana, pero no tienen piel. Le recuerdan a los diagramas de su antiguo libro de texto de anatomía del instituto: la musculatura del cuerpo humano brilla y los músculos nervudos se flexionan y estiran con cada movimiento. Pero las cabezas de las pequeñas criaturas son alargadas. Parecen calaveras, con hocicos que sobresalen y ojos del color naranja intenso de los conos de tráfico. Estas criaturas suben y bajan arrastrándose sobre el cuerpo de Harry, lanzando mordiscos a su carne.

Harry, gime ella.

¿Qué tienes ahí? Señala la fotografía enmarcada. Margaret se la entrega, y ambos la examinan. El sonido de los bebés masticando palpita en su cabeza como una migraña.

Harry señala a su madre. *Es una buena persona. No es culpa suya que sea así.*

Por supuesto que no, dice Margaret. Quiere tocarlo, consolarlo, pero teme que los pequeños monstruos la muerdan.

No soy como ella. No tengo esa clase de enfermedad.

Lo sé, dice ella.

Métete en la cama, dice él.

No creo que quiera hacerlo, dice ella.

Él la mira extrañado. *No importa lo que tú quieras.*

Uno de los bebés trepa sobre su pecho y le da un mordisco a su mejilla. Él no parece advertirlo. El bebé dentro de Margaret se mueve, da patadas intentando liberarse de la prisión de su vientre. *Tun. Tun-tun.*

Harry, dice ella. *Harry, tenemos que escapar.*

¿Escapar?, pregunta él.

Su vientre se contrae de nuevo. No, no es una contracción. Es como si estuvieran arrastrando clavos oxidados por dentro. Intenta aferrarse al lateral de la cama, pero pierde el equilibrio y cae de espaldas sobre el suelo. Se gira de lado con el vientre entre las manos.

Estos no son nuestros bebés, dice, apretando los dientes.

Harry se inclina por encima de la cama para poder verla sobre el suelo. Quizás quiera dirigirle otra sonrisa extrañada, pero no le queda suficiente piel en la cara para saberlo. Jirones dentados de carne cuelgan como cortinas agitadas por la brisa. Parece imposiblemente lejos.

Margaret. Claro que son nuestros bebés.

Sus caras aparecen por encima del lateral de la cama, escudriñándola con sus ojos naranjas. Gorjean y balbucean. Se mecen de un lado a otro, cobrando impulso para lanzarse hacia delante y bajar al suelo. Vienen a ayudar, a sacar con sus minúsculos y afilados dientes al tercer bebé de su vientre para que salga al mundo.

Parte dos

LA TUMBA

CAPÍTULO 1

Para el verano de 1982, Margaret y Harry Turner llevaban casados trece años. Transitando la treintena, ambos tenían el cuerpo y la cara más blandos, aún no rollizos, pero empezaban a ensancharse y a comprar prendas nuevas en tallas más grandes e indulgentes. Vivían en una casa de ladrillo, en un buen vecindario de Vandergriff, Texas, con sus dos hijas: Eunice, que acababa de cumplir seis años, y Sydney, de diez (yo no entraría en escena hasta casi un año después). Harry trabajaba para el departamento de carreteras, y Margaret se había convertido en ama de casa desde que abandonara Tilden y se casara con Harry en la primavera de 1969. La vida no era demasiado emocionante, pero todo el mundo parecía más o menos satisfecho... hasta la mañana en la que Margaret despertó de un inquietante sueño rosado y encontró el lado de la cama de Harry vacío.

Fue un golpeteo lo que la despertó. Desorientada y confundida, se incorporó sobre un codo y miró alrededor del oscuro dormitorio. Según su reloj despertador eran las cuatro de la mañana. La puerta de la habitación, generalmente cerrada de noche, estaba abierta. Se levantó y se puso las pantuflas. Caminó por el pasillo, dejando atrás las habitaciones aún silenciosas de las chicas, y entró en la sala, donde encontró la puerta corredera de cristal que daba al jardín, abierta de par en par.

Harry se hallaba de pie sobre el césped sin cortar, descalzo, desnudo e inmóvil, de espaldas a Margaret.

—¿Harry? —lo llamó.

Pero no dio señales de haberla escuchado. Ella cruzó el jardín para pararse junto a él. Tenía los párpados caídos, medio cerrados, y dirigía su mirada vacía a la cerca de madera que delimitaba el jardín.

—Harry —volvió a decir.

Emitió un gruñido. ¿Seguía durmiendo? Jamás había sido sonámbulo, aunque la expresión de su cara le resultaba un tanto familiar. Puso la mano sobre su brazo.

—Me ha visto —dijo—. Tiene mi rastro. —Las palabras se oyeron con claridad pero sin inflexión. Margaret sintió temor.

—¿Por qué no entramos? —preguntó.

—Un laberinto —dijo.

Ella le tiró del brazo, y él no se resistió a ser guiado de vuelta al dormitorio.

—Es demasiado temprano para estar levantado un sábado —dijo, y lo empujó con suavidad sobre la cama—. Durmamos hasta tarde, ¿de acuerdo?

—Me duele la cabeza —dijo con el mismo tono apagado y monótono.

—Duerme un poco más y quizás te sientas mejor.

Harry cerró los ojos y permaneció quieto. Margaret se metió en la cama junto a él, pero a pesar de que él estuviera roncando a los pocos minutos, ella estaba completamente despierta. Se levantó, preparó una jarra de café y empezó a prepararse para el día.

No mucho después, mis hermanas se despertaron con el sonido y los aromas de Margaret en la cocina: Sydney, que tenía el pelo oscuro y casi negro de mi padre; una boca pequeña; la tez clara y los ojos marrones con párpados pesados; Eunice, que tenía el pelo pelirrojo de mi madre, ojos verdes y piel rojiza (casi cubierta de manchas). Sydney, presuntuosa y terca; a menudo, enfadada. Eunice, dócil y fácil de manejar. Hermanas a las que no se reconocería como hermanas si no se sabía que lo eran. Ahora despiertas, devoraban el desayuno y ayudaban a Margaret a repasar una lista para la celebración del cumpleaños número seis de Eunice.

Harry se despertó por segunda vez a alrededor de las ocho. Se duchó, se vistió y se sirvió una taza de café. Tras terminarla a toda velocidad en unos pocos sorbos, anunció que se iba a recoger el pastel de cumpleaños. No besó a Margaret al salir. Ella y las chicas se quedaron de pie en la cocina, oyendo el coche arrancar y salir marcha atrás del camino de entrada.

—¿Papi está bien? —preguntó Eunice.

—Lamenta que sea tu estúpido cumpleaños —dijo Sydney.

—Discúlpate —dijo Margaret.

—Siento que no le gustes a papá, Eunice.

—Sydney —dijo Margaret, con tono amenazante.

—Solo bromeaba —respondió su hija mayor. Era lo más cercano que ofrecería a una disculpa, pero pareció satisfacer a Eunice, así que Margaret lo dejó pasar.

CAPÍTULO 2

Margaret jamás habría descrito a Eunice como una chica popular, pero de todos modos fue bastante gente a su fiesta. El señor y la señora Henson, que vivían calle abajo, llevaron a su hija, Krissy, y el señor y la señora Sangalli fueron con su pequeño hijo asmático, Hubert. Un par de amigos del trabajo de Harry, Rick y Tim, trajeron a sus chicos, y Sydney también invitó a algunas amigas. Las chicas mayores se encerraron en su dormitorio para evitar lo que aquella llamó amablemente una «fiesta para bebés», pero todos llevaron regalos y se aseguraron de saludar y desearle feliz cumpleaños a Eunice antes de desaparecer.

Para sorpresa de Margaret, la pareja sin hijos que vivía al lado también se presentó. Daniel y Janet Ransom se habían mudado unas semanas atrás, y Margaret los había invitado por cortesía. Daniel era el nuevo profesor de teatro del instituto, y Janet enseñaba ballet en un estudio.

—Qué amables sois al haber venido —les dijo Margaret cuando tuvo un momento—. No creía que os interesara demasiado.

—No siempre estaremos sin hijos —dijo Janet—. Nos pareció buena idea conocer el terreno, ¿sabes? —Menuda, tenía los huesos pequeños como los de un pájaro y era esbelta como un chico. Su pelo marrón estaba recogido en un moño apretado en la nuca. Era igual que como Margaret siempre había imaginado a la Kitty de *Anna Karenina*: como una bonita estatuilla de porcelana frágil. Margaret jamás había sido tan delgada, y ahora, más ancha y gruesa que nunca, se sentía incómoda y fea junto a Janet y su guapo marido.

—No le creas —dijo Daniel—. Está a la caza de nuevos clientes.

Margaret se rio. Janet parecía avergonzada.

—Es cierto que he traído algunos folletos del estudio, por si crees que a Sydney o Eunice les puede interesar —dijo. Dirigió a Daniel una mirada hostil.

Él se frotó la nuca.

—Cuántos libros de terror tenéis —dijo, señalando el estante contra una pared cercana, provisto de Stephen King, Angela Carter, Peter Straub, Shirley Jackson, William Peter Blatty, Ira Levin, James Herbert, Ramsey Campbell, Thomas Tyron, y, por supuesto, H. P. Lovecraft.

—Deberías ver los que tenemos guardados —dijo Margaret. Tenían una unidad de almacenamiento en el U-Haul del centro, lleno de cajas de viejos libros de bolsillo, revistas *pulp* y cómics. Harry había sido reacio a separarse físicamente de su amada colección, pero convino en que, por el momento, no tenían sitio suficiente.

—Y tú, Margaret, ¿qué haces? —preguntó Janet.

—Soy madre y ama de casa —respondió—. Pero ahora que las chicas son más mayores, estoy pensando en volver a estudiar. —Había estado hablando de matricularse de nuevo desde 1969, pero nunca parecía ser el momento adecuado.

—Yo no sé si podría soportar estar todo el día en casa con niños —dijo Janet—. Creo que me daría por suicidarme.

—Te aseguro que hay días que a mí también me pasa —señaló Margaret.

Sonó menos divertido de lo que quiso y, cuando nadie se rio, se disculpó para ir a dar una vuelta. El resto de los adultos se hallaban apoyados sobre las encimeras de la cocina y sentados a la mesa del comedor, bebiendo de vasos de plástico y sacando trozos de pizza de una pila de cajas de Domino's. Los chicos se hallaban todos fuera, en el calor abrasador de agosto. Jugaban en el interior y en los alrededores del castillo inflable que habían alquilado y situado en el jardín. Harry también estaba sentado fuera, junto con Rick y Tim, supuestamente para evitar alguna travesura que pusiera en peligro la vida de algún niño.

Margaret se detuvo ante la puerta acristalada para mirar a Harry. Se hallaba con la mirada fija en una distancia intermedia mientras Rick y Tim se reían a ambos lados de él. Su botella de cerveza colgaba entre las puntas de los dedos de su mano derecha. Había permanecido retraído y silencioso incluso después de volver con el pastel. ¿Recordaba haber caminado dormido? ¿Se sentiría bien? Aquella versión de Harry era muy diferente del hombre al cual estaba habituada.

Se levantó de la silla y se dirigió hacia la puerta acristalada. Margaret lo saludó con la mano y le sonrió comprensivamente. Él pareció atravesarla con la mirada. Sus movimientos eran rígidos y espasmódicos, como si hubiera quedado maltrecho por trabajar excesivamente.

En aquel mismo instante, Eunice saltó fuera del castillo inflable, con la sonrisa de toda niña agasajada que rebosa de felicidad. Su pelo rojizo se sacudió por detrás como una llamarada de verano. Harry no la vio ni oyó, así que cuando ella se arrojó sobre su espalda, no tuvo oportunidad de prepararse. Margaret extendió la mano para sujetar la manilla de la puerta en el momento en que Harry avanzó dando tumbos y soltó su cerveza. La botella estalló contra el patio de cemento, formando una pequeña explosión de espuma y cristal verde.

Eunice lo soltó y se dejó caer sobre el pavimento. Harry se enderezó y se giró para arremeter contra ella, sujetándole los hombros.

—¿Qué narices te pasa? —Su grito quedó amortiguado por la puerta, pero de todos modos se oyó.

Tim, el más fornido de sus amigos, apartó a un lado a Eunice, que se había asustado. Rick cogió el brazo de Harry y empezó a hablar con el tono de voz calmado y bajo de un hombre que ha tenido que intervenir en múltiples peleas de puños. Harry se apartó bruscamente y le dio un puñetazo directo en la nariz. Las manos de Rick acudieron velozmente a su cara, y pisó los trozos de cristal roto, machacándolos con su calzado deportivo.

El cuerpo de Margaret por fin consiguió moverse. Abrió la puerta de un tirón, corrió hacia fuera y se situó entre Rick y Harry. Por un instante creyó que había cometido el peor error de su vida. Los ojos de Harry estaban enloquecidos, aterrados e iracundos.

Ella alzó ambas manos, murmurando:

—Oye, oye. Estás bien. Estás bien.

Harry se pasó la lengua por los labios y se meció sobre los pies, resollando, con los puños apretados. El sudor se deslizó entre los omóplatos de Margaret y se acumuló cerca de la base de su columna. El aire húmedo le provocó un escozor en la piel.

—Harry —dijo, con su tono de voz más tranquilizador—. No pasa nada. Está todo bien. Solo te has asustado.

Parpadeó, y cierta pieza esencial volvió a encajar en su sitio con un clic. Volvió a ser Harry. Miró alrededor, al castillo inflable y sus habitantes atemorizados; a Rick en la silla del patio con los dedos cubiertos de sangre, cerrados sobre la nariz y la boca; a Tim, dándole palmaditas a Eunice en la espalda, y a Sydney y sus amigas, reunidas en la puerta acristalada como visitantes de un zoo.

Margaret lo cogió del brazo y por segunda vez en el día lo llevó dentro, pasando junto a las chicas, avanzando por el pasillo, hasta llegar al dormitorio principal.

—Acuéstate —le dijo.

—No estoy cansado —respondió.

—No me importa. Por hoy has perdido tus privilegios de estar en el patio. —Cerró la puerta con fuerza al salir.

Margaret inventó excusas vagas explicando que Harry no se sentía bien y prometiendo una visita inminente al médico que respondería todas sus preguntas, todo mientras conducía a los visitantes a la puerta principal. Eunice se quedó mirando boquiabierta la disolución de su fiesta, y huyó a su habitación, con la cara enrojecida y surcada de lágrimas. Sydney se quedó sentada en el sofá, con la cara impávida, viendo una película por televisión mientras Margaret barría los cristales del porche, arrojaba los platos desechables a la papelera, vaciaba los vasos de plástico y llevaba toda la basura al garaje.

Dejó los globos y las guirnaldas colgadas, aunque ahora parecían fuera de lugar, una falsa fachada para ocultar algo horrible.

Se sentó en el sofá con Sydney y pasó el brazo alrededor de sus hombros. La chica permaneció rígida a su lado, sin apartar la vista de la televisión.

—Déjame en paz —dijo.

Margaret la soltó y se levantó para ver cómo estaba Eunice. Encontró a su hija menor en la cama, mirando hacia la pared. Se sentó y le masajeó la espalda.

—Mi fiesta —dijo, con la voz espesa.

—Lo sé, cariño. Lo siento, pero papá no se encuentra bien, y yo... —Dejó de hablar, sin saber qué decir—. No quería que papá contagiara a nadie más si lo que tiene es contagioso. Ahora está durmiendo una siesta. ¿Por qué no te tumbas un rato y luego terminamos tu celebración esta tarde?

—¿Y mi castillo inflable?

—No veo por qué no podamos conservarlo un día más. —Obligaría a Harry a conseguirlo si tenía que hacerlo. Era lo menos que podía hacer. Besó a Eunice en la mejilla y luego acudió al dormitorio principal.

Harry seguía en la cama, mirando con fijeza el techo. Se frotó la mano derecha, cuyos nudillos estaban hinchados. Margaret cerró la puerta y se apoyó contra ella.

—Lo sé —dijo él—. Lo sé.

—El término *locura* apenas sirve para describirlo —dijo Margaret.

—No sé lo que ha pasado.

—Esta mañana estabas sonámbulo. ¿Lo recuerdas?

Advirtió por su cara de sorpresa que no tenía ni idea. Habían estado alerta a que sucediera algo así durante toda su relación. A causa de su madre, lo habían sometido a pruebas muchas veces para detectar la esquizofrenia, pero los médicos siempre lo habían declarado en perfecto estado de salud. Ahora ya había pasado demasiado tiempo para que aparecieran los síntomas, pero no resultaba imposible. Margaret no podía sacudirse de encima la imagen de su cara esa mañana… la mirada distante, los ojos sin vida. ¿Por qué le resultaba tan familiar?

—Escucha… no creo que vuelva a suceder —dijo Harry—. No es… no es lo que te preocupa. No sé lo que es, pero no es eso. Si… si… algo más *sucediera*, te prometo que veré a un médico, ¿vale? —Cuando no respondió, dijo—: Margaret, por favor, déjame intentarlo a mi modo primero.

CAPÍTULO 3

A última hora de la tarde, se volvieron a reunir para acabar la celebración del cumpleaños de Eunice. Harry jugó con las chicas en el castillo inflable mientras Margaret calentaba las sobras de pizza. Ella y Harry dejaron que las chicas se comieran la pizza y el pastel al mismo tiempo, con porciones generosas de helado al lado del plato. Después de cenar, dejaron que Eunice se abalanzara encima de la pila de regalos sobre la mesa de café, arrancando las brillantes envolturas con los ojos desorbitados por el subidón de azúcar. Se sentaron en la sala, rodeados de los nuevos juguetes, juegos y ropa, y vieron una película por la televisión. Margaret se recostó sobre el sofá, y Harry se tendió en el suelo, con las chicas acurrucadas a ambos lados. Cada cierto rato, Margaret le pasaba una mano por el pelo, gozando del modo como se encrespaba entre sus dedos.

Esa noche, después que las chicas se fueron a dormir, felices y aliviadas, Harry y Margaret hicieron el amor. Las paredes de la casa eran delgadas, por lo que tenían que moverse despacio y en silencio. Le dio tiempo a Margaret para estudiar la cara de Harry, sentir cómo se reafirmaba su pilar de amabilidad y ternura. Sus besos suaves parecían insistir en que la tarde había sido una casualidad, que todo iba bien. Y después, mientras yacían uno al lado del otro, sudorosos y tersos, él le susurró las antiguas palabras:

«Te quiero hasta el final de los tiempos, y lo que venga después».

Era una frase cursi que había acuñado en su noche de bodas, una declaración tan dramática que Margaret se había reído en sus narices. Desde entonces se había convertido en una clave entre los dos, parte del lenguaje privado de un matrimonio, una frase irónica y sincera a la vez, algo que se pronunciaba con una expresión burlona en la mirada y un latido en el pecho.

—Y lo que venga después —coincidió ella, y apoyó la cabeza sobre su pecho.

CAPÍTULO 4

En las semanas que siguieron a la fiesta, Harry cubrió el pago del seguro para que le arreglaran la nariz a Rick, inscribió a Sydney para tomar lecciones de ballet en el estudio de Janet Ransom, y le compró a Eunice un ordenador Commodore 64 y una pila de disquetes para acompañarlo.

Margaret aparentó estar emocionada y se unió a la algarabía de las niñas cuando Harry entregó los regalos, pero en cuanto estuvo a solas con él, preparándose para meterse en la cama, le dijo:

—Sé que te sientes mal, y pagar las facturas médicas de Rick es lo correcto, pero me hubiera gustado que no gastaras tanto dinero comprando cosas frívolas para las niñas.

Harry la miró por encima de su ejemplar de *La zona muerta*.

—Este es el tipo de cosas que las niñas recordarán en veinte o treinta años. Eso es la niñez.

—Ese ordenador ha costado casi seiscientos dólares —dijo, frotándose crema hidratante en las manos—. Y eso sin contar siquiera todos los juegos que has comprado.

Harry dejó caer el libro sobre su pecho.

—¿Qué quieres que haga? ¿Que entre en el dormitorio de Eunice y le quite el ordenador?

—Por favor, no vuelvas a comprar nada tan caro. Aún tenemos que afrontar los gastos de Navidad.

Lo observó hacer un esfuerzo por pasar de la furia a la tranquilidad. ¿En qué momento se había enfadado tanto? ¿Por qué estaba tan encolerizado?

—Tienes razón. Debí haber hablado contigo antes de hacerlo.

Pero al día siguiente, llegó una hora tarde a casa del trabajo, y cuando Margaret se reunió con él en el garaje, encontró la parte trasera de su camioneta llena de madera y bolsas de la ferretería.

—¿Qué diablos es esto? —preguntó.

—Construiré una casa embrujada para Halloween —dijo.

Aunque Halloween era la celebración favorita de Harry y siempre la celebraba con las niñas, por lo que Margaret sabía, jamás había vuelto a otra casa embrujada desde que lo hicieran en 1968. Decir que se sorprendió por el anuncio era quedarse corto.

—Lo acordamos —dijo ella.

—Esto es genial —dijo Sydney. Empujó a Margaret para abrirse paso hacia el garaje, abrió el maletero y empezó a descargarla.

—Sydney, basta —dijo Margaret—. Papá llevará todo esto de vuelta a la tienda.

Sydney se detuvo a medio camino entre el coche y la puerta de la casa, con una bolsa de plástico en los brazos. Miró a Harry.

—No lo llevaré de vuelta a la tienda, cariño —le dijo este a Sydney—. No te preocupes.

—Chicas, id a vuestras habitaciones —dijo Margaret.

Agachando la cabeza, las chicas salieron rápidamente del garaje.

Margaret señaló la madera en la camioneta.

—Acordamos que no habría más compras grandes —dijo.

Tras un momento, él extendió la mano.

—Ven fuera conmigo.

Ella dejó que la guiara a través de la casa y al jardín. Al caminar, el césped le pinchaba los tobillos desnudos. Harry se detuvo en el centro y trazó un lento círculo, haciéndola girar a su alrededor.

—¿Qué ves? —preguntó.

—Que es hora de que cortes el césped —respondió.

—Estoy esperando a que empiece el otoño y aniquile el césped de una buena vez, pero no sucede.

El nudo de frustración en el pecho de Margaret se aflojó levemente.

—Fuiste tú quien quiso mudarse a Texas.

—No, Texas es donde encontré el empleo —dijo—. Pero dime... ¿qué más ves?

Ella cerró los ojos, respiró hondo y los volvió a abrir. Estudió el jardín, un gran cuadrado llano y ligeramente inclinado de tierra cubierta de hierba, delimitado en tres de sus lados por una cerca alta de madera. Un pequeño patio de cemento se hallaba justo fuera de la puerta trasera, con la parrilla, una mesa y algunas sillas de plástico, dispuestas alrededor. Sobre el césped había una manguera enrollada; seguía sujeta al grifo que sobresalía de la pared de la casa. Advirtió que ella y Harry estaban de pie exactamente donde lo había encontrado caminando sonámbulo un par de semanas atrás.

No lo mencionó.

—Veo un jardín normal y corriente —dijo, en cambio.

—Lo sé —dijo—. Así me sentía yo hasta el día del cumpleaños de Eunice. Pero luego, sentado en el porche mientras miraba el castillo inflable, algo se disparó en mi cabeza, y vi todo esto como los cimientos de otra cosa. De algo maravilloso. Y ahora no puedo dejar de pensar en ello. —Se tocó la sien e hizo una mueca de dolor—. Es como una molestia que jamás desaparece.

—¿Por eso perdiste la cabeza y empezaste a gritar y a golpear a la gente?

—No estoy seguro. —Dejó caer la mano y frunció el ceño—. Pero sea lo que sea, tengo que admitir que algo falta. No tiene nada que ver contigo ni con las chicas —se apresuró a añadir, y volvió a estirar el brazo para sujetarle la mano. Parecía un gesto mecánico, superficial—. No, es como si... me levantara todos los días, me pusiera la camisa y la corbata, luchara contra el tráfico para llegar a una oficina en la que paso la mayor parte de las horas en que estoy despierto, y luego volviera a casa demasiado extenuado para hacer otra cosa que no sea ver la televisión un rato y quedarme dormido. Y a veces creo que, en el mejor escenario posible, es todo lo que puedo anhelar hasta que me retire, y entonces estaré demasiado viejo y arruinado para hacer otra cosa que desperdiciar los últimos años de mi existencia delante del televisor, esperando el correo, esperando que alguna de mis hijas adultas me llame o me venga a visitar. Y luego moriré, y asunto concluido.

—Algunas personas la considerarían una vida bastante exitosa —le dijo Margaret.

—¿Y tú?

Casi mintió y le dijo que sí, que sería una gran vida, y que debía dar por terminado el asunto. Pero había desaparecido gran parte de la furia, y la fría sensación en el estómago era demasiado fuerte para ignorar.

—Tú me conoces. Tuve mi oportunidad de una vida segura y «exitosa», y te elegí a ti. Quería la aventura.

—Eres más inteligente que yo —dijo—. Ahorré mucho dinero para estudiar, pero luego me licencié en ingeniería. Quería demostrar que podía cuidarte, que no seríamos pobres. Debí ser valiente como tú.

Una casa embrujada. Margaret las asociaba con la criatura lobuna que había visto al final de la Casa Encantada… la que tenía los ojos color naranja y una capa roja. La que la señaló como eligiéndola entre el resto, inmediatamente antes de que Harry la arrojara por el tobogán. La criatura que había visto fuera de la ventanilla del coche de Pierce Lombard justo antes de alucinar con una plaga de insectos que estallaban de su frente. Jamás había hablado de ninguna de esas cosas con Harry. Ni le había contado lo de los sueños de aullidos, lobos y bebés raros. Ahora no parecía el momento para mencionarlos.

—Así que dime —dijo, apretándole la mano con la suya—. ¿Cómo piensas cambiar algo de eso construyendo una casa embrujada en el jardín?

—No estoy seguro —dijo—. Pero parece algo importante. Siento como si haciéndolo, fuera a comprender lo que tengo que hacer después.

Margaret giró la cara de Harry hacia ella.

—Te propongo un trato. Tú quieres construir algo y ser irresponsable. Yo quiero algo a cambio.

—¿Qué?

—Yo tampoco me siento feliz —dijo. Respiró hondo y luego dijo lo que había estado afligiéndola desde su primera conversación con Janet Ransom—.

Quiero terminar mi carrera. No puedo hacerlo salvo que no tengamos que preocuparnos por el dinero. Eso significa que tienes que tener un empleo, Harry, aunque sea uno que detestes. Así que este es el trato: puedes construir esto, pero tienes que seguir poniéndote la corbata y luchando contra el tráfico hasta que yo me gradúe y encuentre un empleo. ¿Puedes hacerlo?

Algo pasó fugazmente por su cara, algo difícil de descifrar a la luz menguante.

—Creo que sí —dijo, y de pronto ella advirtió por qué la expresión que llevaba mientras caminaba sonámbulo le resultaba tan familiar. Era exactamente la misma cara que había puesto en La Casa Encantada la noche que Margaret había visto la figura enfundada en la capa color carmesí. La expresión que parecía indicar una ausencia total detrás de los ojos.

CAPÍTULO 5

Dejó que Harry fuera a buscar a las chicas y les diera la noticia en la sala mientras calentaba su pastel de carne en la cocina.

—¿Construirás toda una casa? —preguntó Eunice.

—No será toda una casa, tonta —señaló Sydney—. Igual que el castillo inflable no era un castillo entero.

—Sydney, no insultes a tu hermana —dijo Margaret.

—Está siendo grosera, pero tiene razón —le dijo Harry a Eunice—. Solo es un nombre. Lo construiré todo en el garaje y la montaremos en el jardín.

—Entonces será como un jardín encantado —dijo Eunice.

—Hablando en sentido estricto, sí —dijo Harry—. Pero si lo hacemos correctamente, la gente olvidará que es nuestro jardín cuando estén dentro. Creerán que realmente están viendo monstruos y fantasmas.

—¿Por qué íbamos a querer asustar a la gente? —preguntó Eunice.

—Porque a veces es divertido que te asusten —respondió Harry—. Y creo que lo haremos bien. Yo haré la mayor parte del diseño y de la construcción, pero podéis diseñar una habitación propia y yo la construiré.

—¿Puedo inventar lo que quiera y la construirás? —preguntó Sydney.

—Siempre que sea razonable —dijo Harry.

—Yo puedo hacer los disfraces —dijo Margaret, sorprendiéndose. No había tenido intención de ofrecerse, pero ahora se hallaba luchando con el principal problema de su vida adulta. Jamás había querido tener hijos. Pero Harry sí. Había esperado que la llegada de su primer bebé la convirtiera de algún modo en una madre natural, el tipo de mujer que se henchía de orgullo por su prole. En cambio, los nacimientos de Sydney y de Eunice la habían dejado indiferente. Cumplió con su deber, amamantando, jugando, cantando, leyendo y alimentándolas, pero jamás sintió la fuente profunda de amor intenso por sus hijas que sentía por Harry. Habría sido un consuelo creer que quizás todos los padres sentían lo mismo, que en realidad llevaba años enamorarse de los hijos, pero Harry había sollozado con el nacimiento de cada niña, y parecía sinceramente emocionado de verlas todos los días después del trabajo. No parecía importar que le quitara tiempo y espacio personales, y Margaret creía que de algún modo las chicas comprendían instintivamente la diferencia entre el corazón de Harry y el suyo. Siempre se sentía en una situación desventajosa cuando estaba con ellas, deseosa de demostrar un nivel adecuado de amor.

—¿Estás segura? —preguntó Harry. Parecía sorprendido y agradecido.

—Sí —respondió Margaret.

Durante el resto de la noche, se sentaron alrededor de la mesa de la cocina, dibujando planos sobre papel milimetrado.

Mi padre el ingeniero era un coleccionista obsesivo y registraba meticulosamente todos los datos, así que la mayoría de esos diseños han sobrevivido. Los guardo en una libreta en mi escritorio, junto con los dibujos de mis hermanas de sus propias ideas: una habitación llena de cabezas de muñecas, una habitación donde una madre te perseguía, y mi favorita, una que parece normal y corriente, como si quizás hubieras llegado al final de la casa encantada, pero luego las luces se apagan y voces incorpóreas empiezan a susurrar verdades horribles. Las notas de Eunice sobre este dibujo lo describen como «La habitación de los malos secretos».

Al final de la noche, Harry llevó todas estas ideas dispares y las puso sobre la mesa de la cocina. Se frotó el mentón y frunció el ceño.

—En este momento tenemos una gran cantidad de ideas azarosas que provocan temor —dijo—. Lo que tenemos que hacer es elegir una gran idea atemorizante, y dejar que todos los pequeños sustos deriven del principal. Creo —dijo, dando golpecitos con el borrador contra sus papeles—. Creo que deberíamos hacer un cementerio. Podemos hacer lápidas falsas y una cerca puntiaguda negra delante de la casa, y luego, en el jardín trasero, construiremos un sepulcro. Cada habitación puede ser una clase de sepulcro o cripta. Quizás haremos un sarcófago egipcio con una momia. Otra podría ser como una de esas sepulturas sobre la tierra que hay en Luisiana, ¿no os parece?

—¿Por qué entierran a la gente sobre la tierra en Luisiana? —preguntó Sydney.

—Porque Luisiana es una gran ciénaga —dijo Eunice—. Cuando intentan enterrar a las personas por debajo de ella, sus cadáveres terminan saliendo a flote. No permanecen allí.

Margaret y Harry miraron a Eunice sorprendidos, quien pareció sobresaltarse por la atención repentina.

—¿Es cierto? —preguntó Sydney.

—Sí —dijo Harry. Permaneció centrado en Eunice—. ¿Cómo lo sabes?

Echó una mirada de remordimiento a la estantería de la sala, y luego miró la mesa.

—No lo recuerdo.

CAPÍTULO 6

La vida continuó. Harry iba a trabajar por las mañanas, y Margaret mandó pedir una solicitud de ingreso a la Universidad de Texas en Vandergriff. Por las noches, Harry transformaba su pila de madera en paredes modulares, techos y suelos. Sydney le hacía compañía en el garaje, llevando gafas de seguridad de tamaño infantil y haciendo sus deberes mientras él medía y cortaba.

La niña empezó clases de ballet, y Janet Ransom dijo que tenía un talento innato. Siempre que Margaret pillaba a Sydney realizando las cinco posiciones delante del espejo de su dormitorio, advertía una expresión de feroz concentración, una especie de agitación eufórica. Parecía motivada a perfeccionar sus posiciones, a ejecutarlas con gracia. Eunice se dedicó a su ordenador con un fervor similar. Todos los días después del colegio, se retiraba a su dormitorio, se instalaba delante del voluminoso teclado marrón, y no se movía salvo que se lo ordenaran. Harry había elegido bien sus regalos. A Margaret jamás se le habría ocurrido realizar ninguna de esas actividades. Le dolía darse cuenta de que, a pesar de que pasaba la semana lejos de sus hijas, él podía intuir mejor sus necesidades y deseos.

En cuanto a sus propias necesidades, Harry se quedó sin madera antes de terminar la estructura básica de la Tumba y le dio por recorrer el vecindario después del trabajo, en busca de obras de construcción desatendidas y vecinos derribando cercas. Acumuló tanta madera que se quedó sin espacio en el garaje y tuvo que dejar una enorme pila bajo una lona junto a la casa. A partir de esta nueva reserva, construyó más paredes y suelos, superficies sencillas e inofensivas que se apilaban como bloques delgados de construcción en el garaje. Harry y Margaret tenían que aparcar ahora en el camino de entrada para que el proyecto tuviera espacio para crecer.

Durante un tiempo, todo pareció marchar bien... hasta la noche en la que un grito despertó súbitamente a Margaret de su sueño.

Los bebés, pensó, flotando a través de los últimos jirones rosados de un sueño que se evaporaba. *Los bebés están gritando*. Alcanzó a Harry en el instante en que abría la puerta del dormitorio de Eunice de un tirón y encendía las luces. La niña se hallaba sentada en la cama, con el cuerpo completamente presionado contra la cabecera, emitiendo aquel sonido cristalino y terrible, el sistema de alarma que detiene el corazón de todo padre.

—¿Qué pasa? —gritó Harry por encima del estruendo—. ¿Qué tienes? —Se sentó en la cama y le sujetó la cara entre las manos. Sus ojos le recordaron a Margaret los de Harry durante su episodio en la fiesta de cumpleaños. Tenían algo salvaje, no completamente humano.

Eunice hizo un esfuerzo por abrir y cerrar la boca un par de veces, y luego señaló al otro lado de la habitación, hacia su ventana, que daba al jardín trasero.

—Había un hombre.

—¿Qué? —preguntó Margaret.

—Hijo de puta —dijo Harry. Empujó a Margaret con el hombro para pasar a su lado y salir de la habitación. Al hacerlo, Sydney salió de su propio dormitorio, atemorizada, su pelo revuelto como un nido de ratas.

—¿Qué pasa? —preguntó.

—Nada, cariño, vuelve a la cama. Harry, espera —llamó Margaret tras él. ¿Y si *realmente* había alguien en el jardín? Harry no tenía ni zapatos ni arma.

—No volveré a la cama hasta que alguien me diga lo que está pasando —dijo Sydney.

Margaret tuvo el impulso momentáneo de cruzarle la boca a su hija beligerante y desobediente de una bofetada. Es lo que hubiera hecho su propia madre. Pero la preocupación venció a la ira, y echó a correr tras Harry. Había dejado la puerta corrediza abierta y rondaba el jardín con la linterna en la mano. Movió el haz de luz de un lado a otro sobre el terreno que tenía delante.

—Vuelve dentro con las chicas —ordenó.

—¿Debemos llamar a la policía? —preguntó ella.

—¿Qué está pasando? —Sydney había seguido a Margaret y se hallaba parada detrás con los brazos cruzados.

—Ve con tu hermana —le dijo esta.

—Maldición, Margaret, ¿puedes volver dentro? —preguntó Harry.

Tenía sentido lo que pedía. Dadas las circunstancias, las chicas seguramente no debían quedarse solas. Al cruzar el patio hacia la puerta, un dolor intenso y punzante atravesó el arco de su pie derecho. Soltó un grito.

Harry le dirigió un haz de luz.

—¿Qué sucede?

—He pisado algo —dijo—. No te preocupes.

Entró renqueando a la casa, encendió la luz de la cocina y se sentó a la mesa. Apoyó el pie herido sobre la rodilla izquierda. La planta estaba tan asquerosa que desde fuera no podía ver sino mugre. Apartó la suciedad con el dorso de una mano, desencadenado otro pinchazo de dolor que atravesó sus nervios. Debía de ser una astilla.

Se dirigió saltando con un solo pie a la habitación de Eunice, con la pierna derecha colgando por detrás como un flamenco, y se apoyó del marco de la puerta. Sydney se hallaba sentada junto a ella en la cama, sujetándole la mano y susurrando. Se detuvo al verla.

—Sydney, ve a buscar las pinzas al cajón superior del baño —dijo Margaret.

—¿Qué ha pasado? —preguntó Sydney.

—*Ahora*, Sydney... —empezó a decir, pero sintiéndose culpable aña-dió—. He pisado algo fuera y no me lo puedo quitar. ¿Me ayudas?

Sydney se puso en pie para obedecer. Margaret se acercó cojeando a la cama, se sentó e hizo una mueca de dolor. Sostuvo la mano de Eunice e in-tentó sonreír.

—¿Qué ha encontrado papi? —preguntó la niña.

—Aún nada, pero está buscando.

—De verdad que he visto a un hombre —dijo ella—. Me crees, ¿no es cierto?

Sydney volvió con las pinzas, proporcionando una anhelada interrup-ción. Eunice y Margaret se sentaron en el suelo, y esta apoyó la cabeza sobre las rodillas de su hija. Sydney se sentó en la cama con el pie de su madre apoyado en su regazo. Margaret le pidió a Eunice que le sostuviera las manos, no porque necesitara consuelo sino porque quería distraer a su hija. Sydney encontró la astilla, y tras un par de intentos, la extrajo. Salió del cuerpo de Margaret con un escozor final.

—Lo tengo —dijo, la victoria convirtiéndose en amargura.

Margaret se sentó y sostuvo las pinzas que le entregó su hija. Examinó el objeto apretado entre las puntas: un largo y delgado trozo de cristal verde. Debía de ser de la botella que Harry había dejado caer en la fiesta semanas atrás. Desde entonces ella había barrido una y otra vez el patio. ¿Cómo seguía allí este trozo?

Aplicó Neosporin y una venda en el pie y llevó la esquirla a la cocina. Tenía intención de tirarla, pero por algún motivo era reacia a hacerlo. En cambio, la dejó caer en una bolsa de sándwiches de plástico y la ocultó en el fondo del cajón donde guardaba los paños de cocina y las manoplas. No supo por qué sintió el impulso de hacerlo, pero lo sintió.

Harry volvió a entrar, ceñudo, mientras cerraba el cajón. Una pregunta se formaba ya en sus labios.

—¿Has visto algo? —preguntó Margaret para distraerlo.

Apoyó la linterna sobre la mesa del comedor.

—He recorrido el jardín tres veces, pero no he visto nada. Ha debido de sufrir una pesadilla.

Después de eso intentaron que las chicas volvieran a dormirse, pero Eu-nice se negaba a creer que lo hubiera soñado todo.

—Sé lo que vi —insistió.

—A veces es difícil darse cuenta de la diferencia entre dormir y estar despierto —le dijo Margaret—. Los sueños pueden parecer muy reales. ¿Por qué no te duermes ahora y hablamos de ello por la mañana?

—¿Puedo dormir en tu cama? —preguntó la niña.

—No —dijo Margaret.

—Sí —dijo Harry al mismo tiempo.

—Yo también iré —dijo Sydney—. No seré la única que duerme sola después de esto.

Así que toda la familia Turner se amontonó en la cama matrimonial de Margaret y Harry, estos por fuera y las niñas por dentro. Ellas se durmieron casi en seguida, Harry poco después, con Sydney acurrucada a su lado. Pero Eunice siempre había lanzado patadas, desde el vientre materno en adelante, y cada vez que Margaret empezaba a dormirse, su pie o rodilla le asestaban un golpe en la cadera, el estómago, el muslo o la espalda. Cerca de las cuatro, cansada de las agresiones, salió de la cama, preparó una taza de café y se sentó delante del televisor. Encontró una vieja película en la emisora local. Era una película muda sobre un hipnotizador profesional que se valía de un sonámbulo para cometer homicidios. Para cuando salió el sol, se sentía incluso menos descansada que cuando había estado despierta en la cama, objeto de golpes ocasionales.

Harry y las chicas salieron tambaleándose del dormitorio un poco después de las seis, atraídos por los aromas a tocino y pan tostado. La conversación en la mesa se limitó a peticiones simples: pasa esto, puedes pasarme aquello, etcétera. Margaret vio a Harry marcharse al trabajo, acompañó a las chicas al colegio, y una vez que tuvo la casa para sí, llevó la escoba y un recogedor al porche y barrió de nuevo. Y de nuevo. Y luego una tercera vez. Tras cada pasada, miraba el contenido del recogedor, pero solo encontró polvo. Sabía que debería estar aliviada, pero en lugar de ello sintió una vaga decepción, como si se hubiera perdido una pista, una señal.

Apoyó la escoba contra el lateral de la casa y caminó hacia la ventana del dormitorio de Eunice. Pequeña y rectangular, parecía de aquellas que se suelen colocar al nivel del suelo para iluminar un sótano, en lugar de ocupar el sitio que tenía, bien elevado en la pared. Alguien tendría que ser bastante alto para ser visto siquiera desde el interior, mucho menos para trepar a través de ella desde el exterior. ¿Por qué lo intentaría siquiera cuando había ventanas más bajas y de tamaño normal en los otros dormitorios? ¿Porque era la única ventana que no se veía desde la calle? Se necesitaba una escalera para alcanzar la altura suficiente para abrirla… o ser lo bastante fuerte para subir con una mano y manipularla con la otra.

Entró en la casa, guardó la escoba y buscó una banqueta. La llevó al jardín, situándola sobre la tierra suave bajo la ventana. Luego se subió para ver más de cerca.

Empezó a sentir una náusea ligera en la boca del estómago. Tres hendiduras profundas recorrían el ladrillo a la derecha de la ventana, y habían doblado hacia fuera por lo menos dos centímetros del lado izquierdo del marco de la mosquitera.

Se aferró al marco de la ventana para evitar caerse, volvió la cabeza y vomitó sobre el césped. Sus dedos rozaron el duro ladrillo mientras su cuerpo se convulsionaba y sentía un ardor en el pecho.

CAPÍTULO 7

Cuando Harry llegó a casa del trabajo, Margaret lo hizo trepar y mirar por sí mismo. Recorrió con los dedos el ladrillo y tocó la ventana con una mirada iracunda.

—Lo ves, ¿verdad? —preguntó ella desde su sitio en el suelo.

Harry descendió las escaleras.

—Veo algunas imperfecciones en el ladrillo, y que la mosquitera está desencajada, pero ninguno de los dos significa necesariamente algo. Todo ladrillo tiene sus imperfecciones, ¿verdad? Puede que esté así desde que la construyeron. Y la mosquitera podría estar así por el uso prolongado. No lo sé. No he realizado el mantenimiento aquí fuera como debía haberlo hecho.

—Así que lo que dices…

—Digo que no hay motivo para entrar en pánico. —Recogió la banqueta para llevarla de nuevo dentro.

—Sé lo que parece —dijo ella, cruzando el patio detrás de él—. Pero después de lo que Eunice vio anoche, ¿no crees...?

Harry lanzó la banqueta contra la casa y se dio la vuelta a tal velocidad que Margaret retrocedió un paso.

—Cielos —dijo él—. ¿Puedes dejar de hablar del tema de una maldita vez?

Ella retrocedió otro paso.

—¿Hace falta que *inventes* problemas nuevos que yo tenga que resolver? —preguntó—. ¿Tan aburrida estás?

—¿Te has vuelto loco? —preguntó—. ¿En qué mundo es un problema inventado? Eunice vio algo, y la ventana tiene algo raro. No creo que eso me convierta en una histérica.

Harry cerró los ojos y se frotó las sienes.

—No, tienes razón —dijo. El tono belicoso fue desapareciendo—. Pero anoche no encontré nada, así que salvo que haya entrado volando, no sé cómo es posible que haya habido alguien ahí fuera. Eunice es una niña. No podemos dejar que sus pesadillas dominen las horas en que estamos despiertos. —Levantó la banqueta y la llevó dentro.

En lugar de seguirlo, Margaret se sentó en una silla del patio. Era la primera vez que le había levantado la voz sin disculparse. ¿Cómo podía decir que no había visto nada raro en la ventana? ¿Acaso estaba loco? ¿Lo estaba?

CAPÍTULO 8

Incluso trabajando todas las noches de la semana desde la hora de la cena hasta la hora de dormir y todo el día los fines de semana, Harry seguía atrasado con la Tumba.

Durante la primera semana de octubre, empezó a quedarse trabajando hasta tarde y durmiendo sobre el sofá si acaso dormía. Hizo máscaras de papel maché, fabricó monstruos de caucho, pintó las paredes modulares y discutió con las chicas acerca de las ideas que tenían para sus habitaciones hasta que se decidieron por un sepulcro de orfelinato para Eunice y un sepulcro para una bailarina vampiresa para Sydney.

Trajo a casa latas de telaraña en aerosol, pequeños paquetes de insectos de juguete y dientes de vampiro de plástico. Los accesorios de Halloween se acumularon en el garaje e invadieron la cocina, donde Margaret había instalado su máquina de coser sobre la mesa. Jamás había cosido demasiado. Su madre le había enseñado cómo hacerlo, pero también le había transmitido la idea de que se trataba de un trabajo poco digno: solo debía coser en una emergencia (por ejemplo, si una camisa se desgarraba estando de vacaciones o si se hallaba en un estado de extrema pobreza). Ahora sintió sorpresa y placer al descubrir que tenía un verdadero don para hacerlo: sus primeros disfraces le salieron tan bien o mejores que los patrones de la tienda de telas.

—Guau —dijo Harry, cuando le enseñó un traje blanco artísticamente harapiento, con largos faldones que había confeccionado para él. Aunque la tela era nueva, daba la impresión de haber estado descomponiéndose durante cien años, y las puntadas eran justo lo bastante torcidas para confundir al ojo—. Podrías ganarte la vida haciendo esto.

Pero no pudo gozar del elogio. Hacía dos semanas que vomitaba casi todas las mañanas. Había hecho el cálculo: tenía un retraso de dos semanas. Siguió cosiendo y dejó el asunto para más adelante.

Harry empezó a construir fuera de la casa. Transformó sus paredes modulares en un laberinto de habitaciones y pasillos en el jardín. Todas las noches trabajaba hasta después del ocaso, pegando dos linternas con cinta adhesiva a un casco protector para seguir viendo mientras martillaba y taladraba. Cuando su trabajo se alargó hasta después de las ocho y luego de las nueve, los vecinos empezaron a quejarse. En lugar de cambiar sus hábitos de trabajo, los reclutó para que ayudaran con la construcción, les asignaba personajes o, en el caso de Janet Ransom, la incorporó como «asesora de movimientos» de los actores. Aduló a sus nuevos coconspiradores por sus talentos recién descubiertos, y de pronto dejaron de quejarse del ruido de la construcción (e incluso se entusiasmaron con él).

Además del trabajo en el jardín, Harry empezó a construir una plataforma plana encima del tejado inclinado de la casa para alojar una señal.

—Quiero que lo vea todo el vecindario… toda la ciudad… y vengan para Halloween —dijo.

Cuando Margaret se quedaba dormida de noche, oía su voz amortiguada encima de su dormitorio, y pisadas que iban y venían encima de su cabeza, un invitado impaciente que aguardaba que le abrieran la puerta.

CAPÍTULO 9

Dos semanas antes de Halloween, Harry se tomó un día libre y condujo a la familia a Tyler para visitar a su madre, Deborah, con motivo de su cumpleaños. El viaje llevó casi toda la mañana… una distancia a la que Deborah Turner había objetado cuando Harry y Margaret le propusieron mudarla a la residencia Weirwood.

—Jamás vendríais a visitarme —había dicho—. Es demasiado lejos.

No se había equivocado. Margaret y Harry tenían suerte si podían ir cada dos meses, pero Weirwood era la residencia de salud mental con cuidados a largo plazo más bonita de Texas. Tenía habitaciones espaciosas para residentes individuales; jardines exuberantes y bien cuidados; un horario cargado de actividades, y personal para ayudar con asuntos tales como el manejo del dinero, la salud y el estado físico.

Margaret también había vacilado respecto a meter a Deborah en Weirwood. Cuando ella y Harry se mudaron a Texas, sugirió que Deborah viviera con ellos.

—¿Acaso no es una solución más caritativa? —preguntó.

Harry había envuelto ambas manos alrededor de su tazón, con la mirada fija en los posos. Le llevó un largo tiempo responder.

—Qué amable que lo ofrezcas, pero no sería como piensas. Creo que tú… —interrumpió lo que estaba diciendo y se rascó el mentón. Dio golpecitos en el panfleto de Weirwood sobre la mesa de la cocina delante de él—. Te aseguro que esto es lo mejor.

Deborah se encariñó de inmediato con el sitio. Trabó amistad con los demás, decoró su apartamento, y se metió de lleno en el tejido. Parecía contenta cuando Harry, Margaret y las chicas iban de visita. Sus únicas quejas eran respecto a cuánto crecían sus nietas durante los intervalos de las visitas.

—¡Oh, no! —decía, ahuecando sus caras—. ¡Dejad de crecer ya mismo!

Aquella visita empezó de modo parecido, con el ritual de los abrazos y exclamaciones, seguido por la barbacoa y el pastel en la mesa de picnic sobre el césped. Después del almuerzo Harry y las chicas corrieron por los alrededores con uno de los perros del centro, una golden retriever llamada Daisy. Se lanzaban pelotas de tenis, y Daisy corría entre ellos, intentando arrebatárselas en el aire. Margaret y Deborah se quedaron sentadas en la mesa y observaron, bebiendo refrescos. Margaret lanzaba miradas furtivas a Deborah hasta que la anciana tomó la palabra.

—¿Qué es lo que te preocupa, cariño?

—¿Qué? —preguntó Margaret, sorprendida.

—Soy vieja pero no estúpida —dijo Deborah—. Ni ciega. Algo ha estado preocupándote desde que has llegado.

Margaret tuvo que obligarse a decir las palabras. Por alguna razón, decirlo en voz alta le dio entidad, lo hizo real.

—¿Cuándo supo —preguntó— que estaba… que no estaba bien?

Deborah se volvió para mirarla.

—¿Sucede algo con Harry? ¿O con las chicas?

—Las chicas están bien, creo —respondió Margaret—. Pero Harry ha estado un poco… raro últimamente.

—Empecé a tener días malos cuando estaba en el instituto —dijo Deborah—. Algunas veces, las luces eran demasiado intensas, los sonidos demasiado fuertes. Era como tener una resaca, pero sin la bebida. A veces me quedaba sin dormir durante una semana, y luego dormía tres o cuatro días seguidos. No podía hacer amigos o conservarlos. Tenía cambios de humor impredecibles. No sentí absolutamente nada el día de mi boda, y me dio un ataque de risa durante el funeral de mi marido. A veces, cuando hablaba con otras personas, me señalaban que lo que decía no tenía ningún sentido. Cuando Bill vivía, me ayudaba a manejarlo y a ocultarlo. Después de que lo llamaron a prestar servicio militar, cuando solo nos teníamos Harry y yo, se volvió mucho más difícil. Empecé a sentir que todas las personas en el supermercado me miraban y hablaban de mí. Veía mensajes ocultos al leer los ingredientes en una lata de sopa o al mirar el fondo de mi tazón de café. —Bebió un sorbo de su bebida—. Tenía un álbum de recuerdos con las etiquetas de los alimentos, recortes de periódicos, una gran cantidad de notas de la oficina donde trabajaba. Estaba muy *segura* de que alguien intentaba decirme algo. Solo tenía que descubrirlo. Y luego, una noche la policía me recogió en el arcén de la carretera, a veinte kilómetros de mi casa, descalza y con el camisón puesto, sin tener ni idea de cómo había llegado allí. Harry se había despertado solo en la casa e hizo la llamada. Debía de estar sonámbula. De lo contrario, ¿quién sabe lo que podría haber sucedido? Seguramente conozcas el resto.

Los hospitales, los medicamentos, el período en el que Harry vivió con sus tíos.

—Harry nunca me ha contado nada de eso —dijo Margaret.

—No me sorprende. Fue una época terrible para ambos —respondió Deborah—. Ningún niño debería tener que lidiar solo con un padre que sufre problemas mentales.

Parpadeó mirando su regazo, y Margaret le sujetó la mano. Ahora no tenía el valor para contarle nada sobre el comportamiento reciente de Harry. Sea lo que fuera que le deparara el futuro, Margaret tendría que soportarlo sola.

—¿Ya no cree que recibe mensajes secretos? —preguntó en cambio.

Deborah le dirigió una mueca tensa y carente de humor.

—No.

—¿Qué creía que tenía que hacer? Cuando aún los escuchaba.

—Nada que tuviera algún sentido. Por eso lo llaman locura.

CAPÍTULO 10

Salieron hacia Vandergriff cerca de las cinco. Las chicas durmieron en el asiento trasero mientras Margaret y Harry escuchaban la radio delante. Margaret pensó en su conversación con Deborah. Le daba mil vueltas a sus respuestas en la cabeza. Estaba tan preocupada que no advirtió a Harry. Fruncía el ceño y se frotaba las sienes, succionando el aire a través de dientes apretados. Cuando faltaban noventa minutos para llegar a casa, soltó un jadeo y viró bruscamente hacia el arcén de la carretera, tirando del freno de un modo tan violento que Margaret salió arrojada hacia delante, contra su cinturón de seguridad.

—¿Qué...? —empezó a decir. Los brazos de Harry se alzaron rápidamente alejándose del volante. Una mano chocó contra su ventanilla y la otra golpeó a Margaret en el costado de la cabeza. Se meció hacia la derecha, más sorprendida que herida, mientras las chicas se despertaban y empezaban a gritar. Las piernas de Harry se sacudían y sus pies apretaban los pedales, acelerando el motor. Pequeños gorgoteos salían del fondo de su garganta. Parecía estar ahogándose. Arqueó la espalda, golpeándose la cabeza contra el reposacabezas.

Una *convulsión*. La mente de Margaret cogió la palabra, aferrándose a ella como un salvavidas. ¿Qué podía hacer? En las películas la gente siempre metía algo en la boca de la persona… como una cuchara de madera… para evitar que se mordiera la lengua. ¿Dónde se suponía que debía encontrar una cuchara? Mierda. Mierda. Mierda. Ahora las chicas soltaban alaridos, empeorándolo todo mucho más.

—¡Callaos! —les gritó—. Callaos para que pueda pensar.

El cuerpo de Harry quedó inerte y se desplomó hacia delante, con el mentón pegado al pecho y los ojos cerrados. Las chicas hicieron silencio. Las lágrimas se deslizaban por la cara de Sydney, cada aliento repiqueteando con sus mocos. Eunice tenía los ojos secos pero estaba pálida. Las respiraciones de Harry eran poco profundas por la boca abierta mientras se enjugaba la cara con el dorso de una manga. Margaret se dio cuenta de que ella tenía una mano contra el pecho y la otra cerca del hombro de Harry. Dejó que se apoyara encima de este.

Abriendo los ojos, Harry tomó un aliento tembloroso y la miró.

—¿Dónde estamos? —preguntó.

CAPÍTULO 11

Margaret condujo el resto del camino a casa. Dejó a Eunice y a Sydney con los Ransom y luego llevó a Harry a la sala de urgencias del Vandergriff Memorial. Estuvieron horas en la sala de espera atestada de gente antes de que fueran conducidos a una consulta. Eran las 3.00 a. m. para cuando una médica asomó la cabeza y prometió que estaría con ellos lo antes posible.

—Ve a buscar a las chicas y descansa un poco —dijo Harry—. Te llamaré cuando sea hora de que me vengas a buscar.

No quería admitirlo, pero le gustó dejarlo allí. Necesitaba espacio. Lo besó en la frente, sus labios resecos contra la frente salada de él, y se marchó para buscar a las chicas. Después de llevarlas a casa, las tranquilizó con promesas anodinas y las acostó. Puso el despertador temprano para poder llamar al colegio y tener a las chicas en casa.

No podía dormir. Buscó algo que ver en la televisión, pero no encontró nada. Sabiendo que se equivocaba, cogió una antología llamada *Grandes historias de terror americanas*, de la estantería de Harry. Echando un vistazo al índice, encontró un título que reconoció muy bien: «El sabueso», de H. P. Lovecraft. Sabía que debía devolver el libro al estante, pero no pudo evitar releer la historia por primera vez desde 1968. Esta vez, le llamó la atención un pasaje en particular:

Nuestra casa solitaria parecía viva con la presencia de algún ser maligno cuya naturaleza no podíamos intuir, y cada noche aquel aullido demoníaco se extendía sobre el páramo azotado por el viento, cada vez más fuerte. El 29 de octubre encontramos en la tierra blanda bajo la ventana de la biblioteca una serie de huellas completamente imposibles de describir.

—Tienes que ayudar a papá.

Margaret se sobresaltó, arrancada de la historia, y soltó el libro sobre el regazo. Sydney estaba de pie delante de ella. Ni siquiera la había escuchado entrar en la habitación.

—No debes acercarte así a las personas —le dijo—. Y estoy ayudándolo. Todos lo estamos haciendo. Está con los médicos, y lo mejor que podemos hacer ahora es descansar, para que cuando vuelva a casa podamos cuidarlo.

Sydney le dirigió una mirada seria e indiferente, más parecida a la de un supervisor enfadado que a la de una niña.

—No me refería a eso.

—Entonces dime a qué te referías.

Frunció el ceño, y una expresión compleja se adueñó de su cara.

—¿Por qué ya no lo quieres?

—Tienes diez años, Sydney. Ni siquiera sabes lo que es el amor.

—Eso es una gilipollez. —Salió de la habitación hecha un vendaval. Margaret estaba demasiado sorprendida para reaccionar. Pensó en la palabrota de su hija. La sala parecía diminuta y la asfixiaba por todos los lados. Su estómago se contrajo y lo presionó con las manos, haciendo un gesto de dolor, antes de coger el libro y terminar el relato de Lovecraft. Durante su primera lectura, había desdeñado el melodrama histérico, pero esta vez, las últimas oraciones quedaron grabadas en su mente y no pudo deshacerse de ellas:

> *La locura cabalga a lomos del viento… garras y dientes afilados en siglos de cadáveres… escurriendo muerte a horcajadas de una bacanal de murciélagos provenientes de las ruinas negras como la noche de los templos enterrados de Belial… Ahora, a medida que los aullidos de aquella monstruosidad muerta y descarnada se vuelven más y más fuertes, y el zumbido y aleteo sigiloso de aquellas malditas alas tegumentosas se acerca cada vez más, buscaré el olvido con mi revólver, mi único refugio contra lo innombrable.*

—¿Dónde estás? —siseó hacia el silencio de la casa—. ¿Qué quieres?

CAPÍTULO 12

El hospital hizo que Harry permaneciera allí hasta prácticamente la hora de la cena del día siguiente. Cuando Margaret y las chicas lo fueron a buscar, las estaba esperando en la acera donde se recogía y dejaba a los pacientes. Tenía un aspecto terriblemente cansado, pero por lo demás estaba bien. Caminó hasta el coche y se derrumbó sobre el asiento del acompañante con un suspiro de alivio. Apoyó la cabeza contra la ventana y cerró los ojos mientras Margaret encendía el coche.

—Y bien, ¿qué han dicho?

—Nada todavía —respondió—. Quieren que vea a un especialista. Someterme a más pruebas. —Extrajo una tarjeta de negocios del bolsillo de su camisa, pero la volvió a guardar antes de que ella pudiera echarle un buen vistazo.

—¿Eso es todo? ¿Ni siquiera han hecho conjeturas de algún diagnóstico? Harry sacudió la cabeza.

—No quieren hacer diagnósticos prematuros. Podría ser un sinfín de cosas, así que lo mejor es esperar hasta saber más.

Era como si tuvieran permiso para fingir que no había nada de qué preocuparse, y si mi madre aceptó la respuesta demasiado rápido, no puedo culparla.

Ahora, con varias semanas de retraso, llevó a casa un test de embarazo y se lo hizo durante las horas en las que tenía la casa para ella. Aquí es donde entro yo en la historia, aún fuera de escena pero presente en el color de agua de un vial, en el kit de prueba Daisy 2. Mi madre se sentó en el borde de la bañera y dejó caer la cara entre las manos. Un bebé. Qué cosa tan horrible.

Se frotó el estómago en el sitio donde imaginaba que yo me hallaba flotando, subdividiéndome, ganando masa y forma.

—Lo siento, bebé —murmuró. Ojalá hubiera podido responder, hubiera podido apoyar mi mano sobre la pared de su vientre y tranquilizarla. Pero seguí adelante, felizmente ignorante en mi pequeño mundo perfecto; existiendo, aunque sin poder acompañarla en su desesperación.

Ni tampoco era la única novedad problemática que acababa de surgir. Cinco días antes de Halloween, Margaret había recibido un llamado de Wilma Cabot, de la oficina de admisiones de UTV, informándole de que habían rechazado el cheque por su cuota de admisión.

Una piedra fría se asentó en su estómago.

—Estoy segura de que debe de haber un error.

—Claro —dijo Wilma, y su bondad sumó otra capa más de hielo a sus entrañas—. Pero la realidad sigue siendo que no ha pagado la cuota de admisión.

—¿Entonces mi solicitud queda rechazada? —¿Cómo era posible que no se hubiera podido cobrar el cheque? El saldo en el banco era alrededor de mil dólares. La cuota era de solo diez.

—No, señora —dijo Wilma—. Si puede enviarnos un cheque válido o un giro postal antes de finales de noviembre, aún podremos procesarla.

Margaret prometió pasar personalmente con el dinero en los siguientes días, le dio las gracias a Wilma y colgó. Fue al escritorio donde conservaba todos sus registros financieros y revisó los últimos meses. Por lo que podía ver, no había nada raro.

Harry llegó tarde a casa, y cuando volvió a alrededor de las seis y media, estaba en el asiento de copiloto de la camioneta de Rick mientras este daba marcha atrás en el camino de entrada. Al abrir la puerta del garaje, se encontró a los dos descargando un ataúd de plata pulida del maletero.

—¿Qué diablos es esto? —preguntó.

—Hola, Margaret —dijo Rick. Parecía avergonzado, como si lo hubieran pillado haciendo algo mal.

—Ahora, no, Rick —dijo, y volvió su mirada de furia hacia Harry—. ¿No ibas a construir el ataúd?

—Nos estamos quedando sin tiempo —dijo—. Esto es más sensato.

—¿Cuánto ha costado? —preguntó Margaret.

—Nada —respondió, pero Rick miró al suelo, incómodo, y añadió—. Me lo ha dado el teatro comunitario del centro.

—¿Simplemente han dejado que te lo llevaras?

—Por todos los cielos, sí —dijo Harry. Se rascó la nuca. Rick se dirigió a la entrada y se apoyó contra el capó de la camioneta, de espaldas a ellos—. Está bien, ha costado un poco de dinero.

—¿Cuánto?

—Cien dólares.

—¡Harry!

—¿Qué? —preguntó—. Lo donaré al departamento de teatro del instituto cuando terminemos. Daniel Ransom me ayudará con la organización de la cola. Si sigue viviendo aquí, seguramente tenga un gran peso en la vida de Sydney. Querrá estar en sus obras. —Estudió su reacción, pero no le gustó lo que vio—. ¿Cuál es el problema?

—Hoy me han llamado de la universidad —dijo—. *Han rechazado* mi cuota de admisión.

—¿En serio? —Margaret no distinguía si su sorpresa era fingida o real.

—Teníamos un trato —dijo—. Pero ahora están rechazando nuestros cheques ¿y estás gastando una pequeña fortuna en un solo objeto para convencer a nuestro vecino de que pase dos o tres horas vendiendo entradas?

—¿Puedes tranquilizarte? Me pagarán el viernes. Llama a la oficina y pregúntales si puedes llevar el cheque el lunes que viene.

—Ese no es el tema —dijo ella—. No debería tener que preocuparme por lo que gastas a mis espaldas. Jamás hemos sido esa clase de matrimonio.

Harry se pasó ambas manos por el pelo.

—El dinero ya se ha gastado, Margaret. Lamento que tras todos los años que te he mantenido y que te he animado para que volvieras a la universidad, te quedaras sentada como una inútil en casa, sin hacer nada. Lamento que después de una década de estar a tu servicio, decidiera hacer una maldita cosa por mí mismo, y lamento que justo coincidiera con tu repentino interés en tu educación. Ya te he ofrecido una solución al problema, así que dime, por favor, ¿qué más quieres de mí?

Quería que la vida volviera a ser como lo había sido tan solo seis meses atrás. Quería poder preocuparse por su marido y quería sentir un amor sin complicaciones ni ambigüedades, para que ninguna parte de ella deseara que realmente estuviera enfermo o loco. Quería no tener que preocuparse por si debía traer un bebé a aquella familia que se desintegraba o si debía liberarlo para que volviera al éter. Quería todas aquellas cosas, pero no encontraba un modo de expresar ninguna.

—Nada —dijo—. No quiero que me des ni una sola cosa.

CAPÍTULO 13

De bebé, Eunice llevó a mi madre al borde de la locura con su insomnio, y mi madre no consiguió que durmiera toda la noche hasta que cumplió dos años. Incluso entonces, no creo que mi hermana durmiera. Se volvió experta en entretenerse sola, mirando sus libros, enseñándose a leer con una linterna, y a veces escabulléndose a la sala para ver la televisión después de que todos estuvieran dormidos.

Sin embargo, después que papá le comprara la Commodore 64, ya no tuvo que correr riesgos con la televisión. Durante algunas semanas jugó a los juegos que mi padre le había llevado, pero se cansó muy rápido de las tareas simples y repetitivas... emparejar palabras con imágenes, resolver cálculos matemáticos fáciles, luchar contra dragones y naves espaciales... y decidió probar con el procesador de textos enseñándose a sí misma mecanografía. Escribía de noche, con cuidado de evitar hacer ruido con el golpeteo del teclado.

Como solo tenía seis años (aunque adelantada para su edad y con una inteligencia excepcional), no dominaba todos los pormenores del formateo y la gramática, así que su diario electrónico del año 1982 no tenía sangrías ni espacios; por eso es difícil leer toda la obra. Pero este texto de juventud es un preludio interesante de su obra tardía, un vistazo imprescindible a una época que solo podré conocer alguna vez a través de fotografías, entradas de diario, artículos periodísticos y los recuerdos fragmentados e incompletos de los miembros de nuestra familia que sobrevivieron. Menciono todo esto ahora para llamar tu atención a una nota que Eunice escribió durante la semana antes de Halloween:

Papá no se siente bien. Vomita casi todo el tiempo, pero no quiere que nadie se entere. Mami está triste, pero finge que no lo está. Mami y papi fingen todo el tiempo. Ayer le pregunté a Sydney si creía que papi era raro ahora y me dijo que soy una estúpida. Pero no sé si puedo confiar en Sydney. Una vez le pregunté con quién se quería casar y me dijo que iba a esperar hasta que mami se muriera para casarse con papi. Así que Sydney está fingiendo porque papi está fingiendo y Sydney quiere portarse bien por papi. Hoy papi se ha caído y ha temblado como aquel día en el coche. Estábamos en el jardín. Mami y Sydney estaban en la tienda, y yo no sabía qué hacer. Pero ha cabado rápido, y papi me ha hecho prometer que no se lo diría a nadie. Yo también estoy fingiendo. Espero que Halloween termine pronto para que podamos dejar todos de fingir.

Merece la pena señalar esto por dos motivos: primero, es una prueba de que mi padre le ocultaba a mi madre información sobre su salud. Segundo y quizás más importante, me recuerda que es probable que Eunice no estuviera durmiendo durante el tiempo que aseguró haber visto un hombre en su ventana. Seguramente estaba completamente despierta, golpeteando sobre su teclado en la oscuridad, cuando echó un vistazo y vio que algo la observaba.

CAPÍTULO 14

El día después de la pelea por el ataúd, Margaret fue a su ginecóloga para que lo confirmara: estaba realmente embarazada. Intentó tomarse la noticia con estoicismo, pero la médica le proporcionó la dirección y el teléfono de un centro de planificación familiar en Dallas.

—Solo por si acaso —le dijo.

Cuando llegó a casa aquella tarde, encontró a Harry en el jardín delantero, levantando una cerca endeble y torcida.

—Has llegado temprano —le dijo ella.

—Me he tomado unas vacaciones —dijo Harry, sin levantar la mirada—. ¿Dónde has estado?

—En la tienda de telas —mintió. Y luego, para explicar la falta de bolsas de compra—: No he encontrado lo que buscaba. —Harry no insistió sobre este punto, sino que siguió trabajando. Margaret dejó caer el bolso dentro y se dirigió caminando al colegio para recoger a las niñas. Cuando volvieron, Harry había terminado con la cerca y estaba colocando lápidas de poliestireno en el césped. Si habéis visto una casa embrujada como esta, conocéis la broma. Las losas sepulcrales tienen nombres graciosos: Frank N. Stein, Dr. Acula, y así sucesivamente. Pero Harry no conocía o le traían sin cuidado las formalidades de un cementerio falso. Todas sus lápidas llevaban los nombres de las personas que conocía: Daniel Ransom, de la casa de al lado; Rick y Tim, del departamento de carreteras; él mismo; Margaret, y, sobre dos pequeñas cruces cerca de la puerta principal, Eunice y Sydney. Cuando Eunice vio la cruz con su nombre impreso, empezó a llorar.

—¿Por qué has hecho eso? —preguntó.

Harry interrumpió su trabajo.

—Se supone que es una firma, como cuando le pones nombre a tus deberes. Quería que la gente supiera quién ha trabajado en la Tumba.

—¿Por qué quieres que me muera? —preguntó la niña. Por lo visto, no había comprendido la explicación de Harry.

—Me parece una gran idea —dijo Sydney—. Gracias, papi.

Eunice agachó la cabeza y embistió contra el pecho de Sydney. Esta cayó de espaldas al suelo con un graznido. Luego la pequeña saltó encima de ella, sujetándole los brazos con las rodillas y golpeándola con las manos abiertas.

—¡Cállate! —le gritó—. ¡Cállate, cállate, cállate!

Sydney, más grande y más fuerte, liberó el brazo derecho retorciéndolo y propinó una bofetada a su hermana en un lado de la cabeza. Eunice se meció a un lado, pero mantuvo el equilibrio y continuó con la descarga de tortazos.

—Harry —dijo Margaret—. ¡Ayúdame!

Harry, que había seguido colocando las lápidas en hileras pulcras sobre el césped, abandonó por fin el trabajo y cruzó el jardín, donde golpeó a Eunice en la mejilla con el dorso de la mano. La pequeña cayó derribada al suelo y aterrizó sobre el césped. Permaneció allí, hecha un ovillo, con las manos sobre la cabeza. Sydney se puso en pie y pasó corriendo por delante de Margaret para meterse en casa.

—¿Por qué cojones has hecho eso? —le gritó Margaret a Harry.

Harry parpadeó. Miró a Eunice y luego a Margaret. Un asomo de arrepentimiento apareció un instante en su mirada, pero luego se encogió de hombros.

—Me has pedido ayuda —dijo.

—No *vuelvas* a ponernos una mano encima —dijo—. O te mataré yo misma. ¿Entiendes?

Por un instante creyó que la golpearía de todos modos. Se quedó parado, respirando con fuerza y moviendo la mandíbula. Luego cruzó el césped, levantó la lápida donde la había dejado y volvió a ponerse manos a la obra.

Margaret ayudó a Eunice a levantarse y la condujo dentro para examinar el daño. Tenía el labio roto, pero salvo eso, parecía estar bien. Envolvió un poco de hielo en un trapo y lo presionó contra su cara.

—Lo siento —dijo la niña—. Me he asustado.

—Lo sé, cariño. —Margaret jamás había visto a Eunice pelear con nadie, ni siquiera en preescolar. Era la primera vez que sucedían muchas cosas, ninguna de ellas buena.

—Ahora tengo miedo todo el tiempo —dijo.

Margaret echó un vistazo al pasillo, hacia la puerta cerrada del dormitorio de Sydney. Creyó oírla llorando.

—¿Papi aún nos sigue queriendo?

Margaret se obligó a mirar de nuevo a su hija.

—Por supuesto.

Después de eso, Eunice no la volvió a mirar. Se quedó con la vista fija en la mesa y dejó que el hielo se derritiera contra su cara. Margaret pasó una mano sobre el pelo rojizo y flácido de su hija, y de pronto lo entendió todo a la vez: abandonaría a Harry. Lo haría con inteligencia, daría los pasos con sigilo... abortaría, se matricularía en la universidad, encontraría un empleo... pero huiría de aquella casa terrible y asfixiante lo más pronto posible, para alejarse de la sombra monstruosa del hombre al que una vez había amado, y para encaminarse hacia una vida mejor.

Masajeó la nuca de Eunice.

—Yo arreglaré esto —dijo—. Lo arreglaré todo. Solo tienes que resistir un poco más.

CAPÍTULO 15

Al día siguiente llamó al centro de planificación familiar mientras Harry trabajaba en el jardín. La primera cita disponible era el nueve de noviembre, y costaría $150 del propio bolsillo. La mujer del teléfono le dijo que necesitaría que alguien la llevara a casa en coche después. Margaret dijo que no sería un problema, y colgó.

Más tarde, se quedó ante la mesa de la cocina haciendo cuentas. Ciento cincuenta dólares por el aborto, más otros diez dólares por la cuota de admisión. Varios cientos para el depósito y el alquiler del primer mes de un apartamento de tres dormitorios. ¿Cómo se suponía que encontraría esa cantidad de dinero? No llamaría a sus padres para pedírsela. No podía dejar que la arpía de su madre supiera que, sí, era cierto, su matrimonio caía en picado, incendiándose de un modo espectacular. No podía pedírselo a una amiga porque en realidad no tenía ninguna. Maldita sea, ni siquiera sabía a quién pedirle que la llevara a casa de vuelta de la clínica.

Mordisqueó el extremo de su lápiz, y miró la sala al otro lado del cocina, donde se encontraba la estantería llena de novelas de terror. Todas las viejas revistas y cómics de Harry seguían en un almacén en el centro. Cajas y cajas de cosas que debían de tener algún valor. Jamás echaría de menos algunos objetos y, si ocurría, supondría que se habían perdido en alguna u otra mudanza. Margaret esperaba estar bien lejos para entonces.

Llamó a algunas tiendas de cómics de la zona, y preguntó si compraban viejas revistas *pulp*. La mayoría no lo hacía, pero una tienda le dio la información de contacto de un coleccionista local llamado Jamie White, que accedió a reunirse con ella la tarde del día siguiente en el almacén.

Por la mañana, Margaret robó la llave de repuesto del almacén del llavero que Harry tenía en el garaje y condujo al establecimiento junto a la carretera, en el otro extremo del pueblo. Cuando llegó, miró a su alrededor buscando a un hombre mayor, alguien que se correspondiera con la voz que había escuchado en el teléfono, pero la única persona en el aparcamiento era una mujer reclinada contra el costado de un coche.

Cuando Margaret aparcó y salió, la mujer se enderezó y caminó hacia ella. Parecía más joven, pero no por mucho, y su pelo marrón claro estaba sujeto en una coleta. Llevaba vaqueros y un suéter de Mickey Mouse. Mickey estaba vestido como Gene Kelly en *Cantando bajo la lluvia*, y colgaba de una farola.

—¿Margaret? —preguntó la mujer. Le ofreció la mano, y ella la estrechó—. Soy Sally, creo que teníamos una cita.

—Creía que me encontraría con Jamie White.

—Jamie es mi tío —dijo—. Quería venir él mismo pero se ha retrasado con otro cliente. A veces lo ayudo yo.

Margaret retorció la boca y cerró los puños con fuerza un par de veces. Ya se sentía nerviosa, y desviarse de su plan, aunque fuera mínimamente, la hizo sentirse peor.

—Te prometo que sé lo que estoy haciendo —dijo Sally White—. Me encargo de este tipo de cosas todo el tiempo. Pero si no te sientes cómoda, estoy segura de que puedes reprogramar la cita con mi tío…

—No —interrumpió Margaret—. No. Tiene que ser hoy.

—Está bien —dijo Sally, con un tono sorprendentemente amable—. Te sigo.

El trastero de Harry estaba en el cuarto piso de un edificio climatizado. Sally silbó cuando Margaret subió la puerta enrollable y reveló las prístinas cajas de color blanco apiladas del suelo al techo, de adelante hacia atrás.

—¿Puedo? —dijo, señalando una de las cajas.

Margaret la ayudó a bajarla de la parte superior de la pila y apoyarla en el suelo del pasiloo. Sally examinó con cuidado el contenido, manejando con cautela todo lo que tocaba. Cada cierto tiempo sacudía la cabeza o maldecía en voz baja. Le enseñó a Margaret una copia de *Weird Tales*. La fecha de la portada era febrero de 1928. Aparecía un hombre enfundado en una gabardina, empuñando un revólver en una mano, y una mujer con un traje de baile, a punto de desvanecerse, desplomada sobre él. «La mesa de fantasmas», de Elliot O'Donnell, decía.

—¿Te puedes creer que esta fuera la primera publicación de «La llamada de Cthulhu»? —preguntó Sally—. Y ni siquiera está en la *portada*. —Hizo una mueca de incredulidad—. Es como publicar un ejemplar de Action Comics sin que aparezca Superman en la cubierta. Aunque al principio también lo hacían.

—No sé mucho de cómics —confesó Margaret.

—Escucha —dijo Sally. Señaló una lista de nombres cerca de la parte inferior de la portada: H. P. Lovecraft, Ray Cummings, Seabury Quinn, Frank Owen, Wildred Taiman, John Martin Leahy—. Se trata quizás de la obra de ficción más importante de Weird y su autor es una nota al pie. Una locura.

Sally echó una mirada al almacén y las pilas de cajas que quedaban.

—¿Todo esto está lleno del mismo tipo de contenido? —preguntó.

—Revistas y cómics. Pósteres de películas. Cosas así.

Sally hizo una mueca; parecía estar discutiendo consigo misma.

—¿Qué? —preguntó Margaret—. ¿Qué sucede?

Sally suspiró.

—Mi tío me ha enviado aquí con un cheque. Me dijo que te ofreciera entre cincuenta y doscientos dólares si creía que había lo suficiente para justificarlo, y si accedieras a vendérselo todo.

—¿Todo? —Margaret miró detenidamente el trastero. Cualesquiera fueran ahora sus sentimientos hacia él, no podía olvidar los años de amor y cuidado que Harry había dedicado a reunir esa colección, y lo difícil que había sido para él sacarla de su casa y almacenarla en el otro extremo de la ciudad. Este montaje de cajas era el modo en que construía su visión de mundo, un reflejo de su personalidad. Era como lidiaba con la enfermedad de su madre y la muerte de su padre. Se odiaba por esa punzada de sentimentalismo, pero no pudo ignorarla.

—Mi tío no tenía ni idea de lo que encontraría aquí —dijo Sally—, y si hubiera venido él mismo, quizás te habría ofrecido, no lo sé, quinientos o mil dólares.

Sonaba como una fortuna para Margaret, que tenía tendencia a resolver las cosas en el acto.

—¿Puedes llamarlo y preguntárselo?

—El problema —dijo Sally— es que es probable que, si tú entendieras de esto, conseguirías quinientos dólares solo por lo que contiene esta caja. Generalmente, mi trabajo es engañar a las personas que no saben lo que tienen para que me vendan las cosas, y luego nosotros las vendemos por mucho, mucho más. En general, no tengo problemas con hacerlo porque apenas son uno o dos cómics o una caja de revistas, pero esto... —Sacudió una mano hacia el almacén—. Esto es demasiado grande. Hay que catalogarlo, averiguar lo que realmente vale, y luego o lo vendes tú misma o dejas que alguien como mi tío o yo te hagamos una oferta honesta.

En otro momento Margaret le habría agradecido a aquella mujer su franqueza, pero ahora quería gritar.

—Es increíblemente gentil que intentes ayudarme —dijo con paciencia—, pero necesito el dinero hoy mismo. ¿Por qué no te llevas esta caja, me das un cheque por doscientos dólares y estamos en paz?

—No puedo —dijo Sally.

—Por favor —dijo Margaret, la desesperación filtrándose en su voz.

Sally la estudió un momento. A Margaret no le gustó el brillo de astucia que notó en su mirada; hizo que se sintiera expuesta.

—Entonces, es algo muy serio —dijo. No era una pregunta.

Margaret asintió, en tensión. Sally rebuscó en la caja delante de ella una vez más, extrajo cerca de diez revistas y las colocó sobre el suelo. Levantó su bolso, extrajo un bolígrafo y un cheque doblado. Lo alisó sobre una rodilla, lo llenó y se lo entregó a Margaret. Tenía un valor de doscientos dólares.

—Sigo engañándote —dijo—. Pero no por tanto.

—Gracias —dijo Margaret.

Sally cogió otro trozo de papel del bolso, garabateó algo y se lo entregó.

—Este es el teléfono de mi casa. Hablaba en serio cuando he dicho lo que he dicho. Si realmente quieres vender todo esto, puedo conseguirte un precio justo. Necesito tiempo para determinar lo que tienes.

—Gracias —volvió a decir Margaret.

Sally se puso en pie, la ayudó a devolver la caja a su torre y cerró la puerta enrollable. Se dieron la mano.

—Llámame —dijo Sally—. Te cobraré un diez por ciento sobre el precio final de venta. A propósito, es una comisión baja.

CAPÍTULO 16

Margaret cobró el cheque en un Western Union y escondió el dinero en un viejo bote de aspirinas al fondo de su cartera. Condujo a la oficina de admisiones de la universidad, pagó la cuota de admisión en efectivo y guardó el resto para la segunda semana de noviembre. Se preocuparía por el coste del apartamento después de Halloween.

El ritmo de trabajo en la Tumba se volvió frenético. La familia se volvió a unir. Nadie mencionó las convulsiones o los estallidos de Harry. Margaret hizo a un lado los pensamientos sobre médicos. Era como si hubieran hecho un pacto silencioso: no más gritos, peleas de puños o confrontaciones hasta noviembre. Les daba permiso para llevarse bien y ser corteses el uno con el otro, aunque no hubiera precisamente cariño.

La casa era un caos de desorden; se parecía más al *backstage* de la atracción que se encontraba en el jardín que a una casa. Sydney, que más adelante tendría experiencia con teatro en el instituto, conoció por primera vez, en el otoño de 1982, el raro conjunto de aromas de un *backstage* en su propia casa… tela, pegamento, sudor y polvo, todos flotando en el aire viciado como fantasmas de espectáculos antiguos.

Luego, la mañana de Halloween, Harry puso un cartel en el jardín que decía ESTA NOCHE CASA EMBRUJADA GRATUITA, con letras rojas chorreantes y sangrientas. Eunice les sacó una fotografía a mis padres en cuclillas justo al lado, que yo rescaté antes de abandonar mi casa por última vez.

En la fotografía mi madre y mi padre se inclinan a ambos lados del letrero, con la casa y el falso cementerio a sus espaldas. El sol brilla demasiado fuerte, y Eunice se olvidó de apagar el flash, así que la imagen está sobreexpuesta, descolorida, como si la hubieran tomado al inicio de un invierno nuclear. Mi padre lleva vaqueros y un suéter de Texas Tech. Puedo distinguir las ojeras oscuras, incluso con la ausencia de color. Mi madre tiene puestos vaqueros y una chaqueta vaquera, y parece avergonzada, como les sucede universalmente a todas las madres delante de la lente de una cámara, pero tanto ella como mi padre están sonriendo, y en sus sonrisas no veo nada de la manía delirante ni de la falsa alegría que me describieron después. Solo veo a mis padres, felices. Veo por qué pudieron quererse en un comienzo.

Más tarde aquella mañana, el Mundo del Globo (los mismos que habían suministrado el castillo inflable para la fiesta de Eunice) llegó con un globo gigante, que ayudaron a Harry a instalar e inflar sobre la plataforma del techo. Fue adquiriendo forma por encima del vecindario, alzándose como una criatura terrorífica desde más allá de las estrellas: un enorme fantasma blanco, que se veía desde una gran distancia en la ciudad plana y aún no desarrollada de Vandergriff. En todo el pueblo, los niños soltaron sus juguetes y detuvieron sus juegos cuando la señal entró anunciándose en su campo de visión, como una llamada del mundo de los espíritus de que la víspera de Halloween había comenzado. Pronto las calles estarían sumidas en la magia oscura, y el mundo del más allá revelaría su cara.

CAPÍTULO 17

Para la mitad de la tarde, una multitud de gente se había reunido en la acera… no solo chicos y padres, sino adolescentes y estudiantes universitarios. Los amigos y vecinos que habían accedido a prestar ayuda llegaron a alrededor de la hora de la cena y encontraron una pila de pizzas esperándolos («No podemos pagarles, pero por lo menos deberíamos darles de comer», dijo Harry). Estos «Personajes de la Tumba» devoraron su comida y luego entraron en la sala para vestirse de vampiros, hombres lobo y fantasmas de muertos. El señor y la señora Ransom se ocupaban de la cola, y ya se encontraban exhaustos. Esta se extendía delante de la casa a lo largo de toda la manzana y doblaba la esquina.

Volviendo dentro, Margaret realizaba, presa del pánico, arreglos de último momento a los disfraces mientras Harry maquillaba. Cuando el disfraz de monje del señor Haggarty se desgarró (había subido algunos kilos desde la primera vez que lo midieron), a Margaret se le acabó el hilo de zurcir. Envió a Eunice a buscar más, pero la niña volvió un momento después, sin poder encontrarlo.

—Creo que se nos ha cabado —dijo.

—Agarra esto —dijo Margaret. Eunice cogió la tela rasgada y la unió por encima del estómago del señor Haggarty mientras Margaret corría a toda velocidad al dormitorio. Había una pequeña posibilidad de que hubiera dejado un costurero de emergencia sobre el tocador. Procedió a arrancar los cajones del mueble y a descargar el contenido sobre el suelo. Cuando acabó con los suyos, empezó con los de Harry. Volcó sus camisas dobladas, sin encontrar un costurero. Luego vació el cajón de los calcetines y la ropa interior. Tampoco encontró el costurero, pero sí otra cosa, un revoloteo veloz del rabillo del ojo, tan breve que casi no lo vio. Se detuvo, apoyó el cajón vacío sobre la cama junto con los otros, y luego apartó a un lado los calcetines y la ropa interior para ver lo que había encontrado.

Se trataba de un folleto satinado que había sido doblado por la mitad, como para que entrara en un bolsillo. Margaret lo levantó y lo desdobló. Impreso encima decía «Glioblastoma y Astrocitoma Maligno», encima de algunas fotografías de caras genéricas: serias pero rudas, mostrándole al espectador que no dejarían que aquella cosa (lo que fuera) las venciera. Un logo en la parte inferior informó a Margaret de que se trataba de una publicación de la Asociación Americana de Tumores Cerebrales.

Hojeó el folleto, intentando asimilarlo todo de una sola vez, concentrándose no en las oraciones, sino en los párrafos, las fotografías, los diagramas de células cerebrales que no comprendía (y le resultaba imposible hacerlo). Palabras individuales se adhirieron a su mente: *cirugía, radiación, dolores de cabeza, convulsiones, desinhibición.* En la última página, encontró una nota adhesiva con algunas otras palabras garabateadas en la letra pequeña y cuadrada de Harry: *inoperable, radiación, antipsicóticos, cambio de personalidad, 6 meses-1 año.*

Se sentó en la cama entre los cajones volcados. Harry había ido al especialista. Le habían diagnosticado. Glioblastoma. Un tumor cerebral. Un perro de caza invisible al acecho. Todo cobró sentido. La desaparición del dinero. El comportamiento errático, los gritos, los golpes, la crueldad. La casa embrujada, la fanática determinación de terminarla a cualquier precio. De seis meses a un año.

—Oh, Harry —exhaló.

—¡Mamá! —llamó Sydney, devolviéndola al momento presente.

—¡Ya voy! —respondió gritando. Dejó el folleto y cruzó la casa con piernas temblorosas. Se apoyó contra el marco de la puerta. Todo el mundo estaba de pie en un círculo alrededor de Harry—. No he podido encontrar más hilo —dijo.

—Tendremos que arreglárnoslas —dijo Harry. Miró alrededor al equipo artístico y técnico reunido allí—. Muy bien, todo el mundo. Divertíos esta noche, pero también recordad que estamos haciendo un trabajo importante. —Notando el escepticismo en algunas de las caras de su público, alzó una mano—. Escuchadme. Los seres humanos somos criaturas pequeñas e insignificantes arrojados a un universo enorme y aterrador. En una historia de terror, ya sea una película, un libro o una casa embrujada, tenemos que encarar esa realidad. Pero por atemorizantes que sean las cosas, por terrible que sea lo que el público tenga que afrontar o soportar, siempre hay un final feliz. Cuando aparecen los créditos o el lector cierra el libro, o cuando nuestros visitantes se marchen de aquí esta noche, sus vidas continuarán. Porque habrán encarado la oscuridad, el sol brillará un poco más mañana, y los monstruos de la vida real ya no serán tan atemorizantes. Durante un día, o una hora, o incluso un instante, la vida será un sitio mejor. —Parecía a punto de seguir, pero en cambio sacudió la cabeza—. Sydney, pon a cada uno en su sitio. Mamá y yo iremos a la cabaña del sepulturero.

La multitud de actores se dispersó. Margaret y Harry se abrieron paso hacia el garaje. Parecía el set de rodaje de una película antigua: paredes de madera ásperas, un viejo calendario, un fogón de cartón en mitad de la habitación con una bombilla naranja dentro para simular el fuego; un pequeño escritorio cerca de la puerta principal, con algunos papeles dispersos encima; un par de palas apoyadas en un rincón; y en mitad del recinto, el elegante ataúd plateado que Harry le había comprado al Teatro de Vandergriff. Margaret empezó a ponerse el disfraz, pero se detuvo y bajó la mirada al forro afelpado y brillante, ajado y desteñido tras años de uso.

—¿Quieres ensayar tus líneas? —preguntó Harry.

—No, ya me las sé —respondió ella.

—Pues entonces. —Se frotó las sienes.

—¿Cómo te sientes? —preguntó Margaret, subiéndose la cremallera del mono y poniéndose una gorra azul.

Harry frunció el ceño.

—Siento que no ha quedado del todo bien. Podría haber hecho más. Todo el tema debería haber quedado mejor.

—Tendrá que servir —dijo ella—. ¿Quieres que te ayude a meterte en el ataúd?

Alzó sus manos mientras él se metía dentro. Luego se inclinó para cerrar la tapa.

—Escucha, Margaret...

—Estoy embarazada —dijo. No había querido decirlo. Por lo que sabía, planeaba hacerse un aborto en poco menos de dos semanas. La confesión salió espontáneamente de su boca, lo único que se le ocurrió para demorar la verdadera conversación. Un anuncio de vida, para esquivar uno de muerte.

La reacción de mi padre a mi nacimiento inminente fue un malestar apenas disimulado.

—¿Estás segura?

—Completamente.

Abrió la boca para decir algo más, pero un fuerte golpe en la puerta del garaje lo interrumpió. Apartó la mirada hacia la puerta y luego volvió a mirar a Margaret.

—¿Qué ha sido eso?

—Quizás sea Daniel Ransom, intentando meternos prisa —respondió Margaret.

El golpe volvió a sonar, dos veces más.

—Quizás —dijo Harry—. Margaret —volvió a decir, y se le veía atemorizado.

Ella no quería escucharlo. No aquella noche. Al día siguiente lidiarían con el glioblastoma. Analizarían e intercambiarían opiniones acerca de la infinidad de tratamientos agotadores, la posibilidad de que su marido guapo, cariñoso y tierno quedara reducido bajo la fuerza de la radiación, embotado por medicaciones destinadas a detener las convulsiones y evitar que atacara a sus hijos. Al día siguiente hablarían de lo que harían conmigo, el parásito que se hallaba reuniendo masa en el vientre de Margaret. Mañana encararían la aparición en el umbral de la casa, exigiendo que la dejaran entrar. Pero no esa noche.

Se inclinó hacia delante y lo besó.

—Te quiero —dijo—. Hasta el final de los tiempos y lo que venga después.

Harry extendió una mano hacia ella, como para mantenerla cerca, pero ella se enderezó, se colocó el bigote falso sobre la cara, y caminó hacia la puerta. Los golpes se habían vuelto insistentes, continuos.

—Vamos a darles a todos un buen susto —dijo

La secuencia Turner II: Sydney

Cuando Sydney entra en la Ciudad, lo hace aterrada. Un grito
aún resuena en su corazón. Pero el temor se desvanece casi
al instante cuando se encuentra fuera de la casa en la que
vivió la primera mitad de su niñez, la casa que asocia con
amor, plenitud y seguridad. Está de pie, en una cola que se
extiende a lo largo de toda la manzana desde el garaje. Todo
el mundo está disfrazado, incluida Sydney. Lleva un tutú
rosa, sucio y arrugado, y los brazos, hombros y cara,
emplastados con maquillaje blanco. Un enorme fantasma
inflable se mece de un lado a otro sobre el tejado,
atrayendo a los visitantes. Tiene un aspecto siniestro
contra el cielo crepuscular; un estremecimiento de placer la
recorre por dentro. Es la casa embrujada que edificó con su
padre cuando tenía diez años… el último proyecto que
hicieron juntos como familia antes de que papá enfermara.

La puerta del garaje está abierta, pero se le ha
incorporado una falsa fachada. Parece la entrada de una
pequeña casucha… una pared vieja y erosionada con una
puerta del lado derecho y un ventanuco velada a la
izquierda.

El señor Ransom, de la casa vecina, se encuentra de pie
delante del garaje, contando grupos para entrar. Hay seis
personas delante de Sydney que quieren entrar juntas y
están dispuestas a esperar, así que el señor Ransom hace
que se aparten y llama a Sydney y a la persona detrás para
que vayan a la puerta.

¿No deberías estar dentro?, pregunta el señor Ransom.
Sydney anticipa una regañina, pero él guiña el ojo. *No se*

lo diré a nadie, dice. Gira el picaporte y empuja la puerta para abrirla.

Sydney y un grupo de desconocidos entran lentamente a la cabaña del sepulturero. Una pequeña mesa de trabajo y una silla se hallan a la derecha, y un enorme ataúd domina la mitad del recinto. Su madre, Margaret, está sentada a la mesa de trabajo, vestida con un mono azul y una gorra, con una peluca gris y un bigote falso. Se encuentra inclinada sobre unos documentos, con un termo de metal lleno de café a un lado. Levanta la mirada y finge sorpresa.

¡Oh, hola!, dice. Tiene la voz alterada y rasposa pero de todos modos dista de ser masculina. *No esperaba que vinieran invitados tan pronto, pero son bienvenidos de todos modos. De hecho, si quieren saber la verdad, me vendría bien que me dieran una segunda opinión acerca de un par de cuestiones. ¿Creen que podrían ayudarme?*

¡Claro!, dice un niño del grupo.

Demos una vuelta, dice la Sepulturera. Se pone en pie y señala hacia otra puerta al fondo del recinto. *Hay algo raro aquí, no sé bien…*

La tapa del ataúd se abre de golpe, y un hombre con un sombrero de copa y un esmoquin se sienta y suelta un rugido. El grupo grita, y Sydney también se sobresalta, aunque sabe que solo es su padre, maquillado. Parece inhumano.

¿Ven? Es exactamente el tipo de cosa a la que me refiero, dice la Sepulturera. Abre la puerta, la que habitualmente da a la cocina, pero que ahora se abre a un túnel oscuro de paredes modulares que conducen a través de la casa hacia el jardín trasero. El espectro de esmoquin aúlla a espaldas de Sydney y los visitantes, pero no los persigue.

Tuve que romperle ambas piernas con una pala para que permaneciera donde estaba, admite la Sepulturera, conduciendo al grupo por el corredor. En las paredes se abren paneles. Un tentáculo emerge cerca del zócalo y toquetea la pierna de Sydney. Deja una sensación fría y viscosa en sus piernas. No grita, pero se sacude quitándose el tentáculo de encima y sigue al grupo a la habitación contigua.

Al hacerlo, el grupo desaparece, y se encuentra sin el disfraz, fuera de la casa embrujada y sobre el sofá de la sala. La casa sigue desordenada tras los preparativos de Halloween de la semana anterior. Mamá ha realizado algunos intentos vanos por ordenarla, pero aún sigue habiendo rollos de tela apoyados en los rincones, y la mesa del comedor está cubierta de maquillaje y prótesis. La familia entera sigue exhausta, inmersos en un estupor soporífero.

Eunice está sentada junto a Sydney en el sofá. Su madre y su padre están en el canapé en diagonal, dándose la mano. Desde Halloween se llevan mejor, y Sydney no está segura de lo que siente al respecto. No sabe si su madre merece el perdón de su padre.

Su madre dice: *Tenemos noticias.*

¿Buenas o malas?, pregunta Eunice.

Ambas, responde. *En primer lugar, tendremos otro bebé.*

¿Esa es la buena o la mala noticia?, pregunta Sydney.

Su madre suelta una risa burlona. *La buena, sabelotodo.*

¿Cuál es la mala noticia?, pregunta Eunice.

Papá se pasa la lengua por los labios. *Tengo cáncer.*

¿Qué es cáncer?, pregunta Sydney. Ha escuchado la palabra en la televisión y sabe que es algo malo, pero no sabe por qué.

Es una enfermedad, dice Eunice. *Son muchas células anómalas que se dividen y destruyen el tejido de tu cuerpo. Es como si te comieran vivo.*

Tanto su madre como su padre le dirigen una mirada entre el asombro y el asco.

Te pondrás mejor, ¿verdad?, pregunta Sydney.

Sus padres intercambian miradas. *Tengo buenos médicos y tienen esperanzas*, dice su padre, pero es mentira. Los

adultos siempre mienten a Sydney. Le dicen que Santa Claus
es real y que los monstruos son falsos, que siguen
queriéndose cuando es falso, que están haciendo lo que
pueden cuando es evidente que no les importa. Esta es una
mentira más que se añade a todas las demás.

Eunice les dirige a sus padres una sonrisa débil. Sydney
quiere vomitar. *Con permiso*, dice. Sale corriendo por la
puerta trasera, alejándose de esos embusteros, pero se
encuentra de nuevo en la Tumba la noche de Halloween, con
un grupo de visitantes que siguen a la Sepulturera a una
habitación que está completamente oscura. El grupo se ríe
nervioso.

Las tinieblas absolutas se quiebran durante un instante
de una luz cegadora, y la sensación de algo que se mueve,
demasiado veloz para seguir, antes de que el recinto vuelva
a quedar sumergido en la oscuridad. Los demás visitantes
lanzan un grito ahogado. Una persona emite un gañido.

La luz vuelve, esta vez en dos destellos, luego en tres.
Sydney distingue una figura en el extremo más alejado de la
habitación, menuda y ágil, y se reconoce a sí misma: la
versión de sí actuando la noche de Halloween. Observa a su
doble realizar las cinco posiciones, y siente sus propios
músculos flexionándose y estirándose incluso estando
inmóvil entre los desconocidos. Se ha convertido en público
y artista a la vez, y cuando la música empieza a retumbar
desde un equipo de sonido oculto en el rincón —un popurrí
de piano ligero pero enérgico al que se unen campanas
resonantes y una suave línea de bajos— las luces
estroboscópicas segmentan sus movimientos fluidos en una
serie de imágenes fijas: los brazos en alto, la pierna
lanzada hacia arriba, la cabeza agachada hacia delante, los
brazos extendidos a los lados, de puntillas, girando por
toda la sala como le enseñó la señora Ransom.

Aquella tranquilidad particular se apodera de Sydney, la
tranquilidad que siente solo cuando baila. La versión de sí

que observa desaparece, fundiéndose con la versión que
baila. Levanta una pierna como un pájaro, *croisé derrière*.
Gira una, dos, tres veces, y al girar por tercera vez, se
encuentra sentada sobre la cama en el dormitorio de Eunice
mientras su hermana está sentada al escritorio leyendo en
voz alta de un libro de la biblioteca, cómicamente grande.

*Glioblastoma es un tumor que deriva de los
astrocitos, células con forma de estrella que
constituyen el tejido que sostiene el cerebro, el
pegamento que lo une todo. Se trata de un tumor
sumamente maligno…*

¿Qué significa maligno?, interrumpe Sydney.
Potencialmente mortal, dice Eunice. *Muy peligroso.*
Retoma la lectura. *Se trata de un tumor sumamente maligno
porque las células se reproducen a toda velocidad y
presenta una amplia red de vasos sanguíneos. Hay dos clases
de glioblastoma, el primario o «de novo», que se forma y
aparece muy rápidamente, y el instituto, que tiene un
período de crecimiento más lento y largo pero sigue siendo
muy agresivo.*
¿Cuál es el que tiene papá?, pregunta Sydney.
El primario, responde Eunice.
Sydney y Eunice permanecen en silencio, intentando
encontrar un modo de vivir con las implicaciones
apocalípticas de esta información.
Me crees, ¿verdad?, pregunta Eunice. *¿Lo del hombre que
apareció en la ventana?*
Sydney se levanta y abandona el dormitorio, pero al
pasar por la puerta, se encuentra en una sala de hospital.
Papá está en la cama, sin pelo, con el cuerpo devastado y
macilento. Mamá tiene su silla pegada a él. Parece grotesca
junto a papá, como si engordara a la misma velocidad que él
pierde peso. Como si estuviera exprimiéndolo para alimentar

al bebé nuevo. Sydney y Eunice se sientan en un sofá en el
rincón, viendo un programa de televisión con el volumen
bajo. El tema parece ser la pesca.

Mamá tiene una libreta que hace equilibrios sobre su
regazo, tomando notas y realizando bocetos basados en lo
que le dicta papá. Están trabajando en la casa embrujada
del año que viene, como si fuera algo que papá estará aquí
para hacer. La idea de papá es una ciudad entera, y ahora
él y mamá la están poblando de edificios.

Es un hotel, está diciendo papá. *No remoto como* El
Resplandor, *sino en el centro, elegante… y está abandonado.
Las ventanas están abiertas, y las cortinas ondean. La
nieve sopla dentro, y hay adornos navideños y accesorios de
payasos raros diseminados por todos lados. Como un cruce
entre una casa de la risa y un parque de atracciones
navideño.*

Mamá levanta el bloc de dibujo para enseñárselo. *¿Te
gusta?*

Papá le arranca el bloc y el lápiz. Da la vuelta a la
página y realiza trazos rápidos y violentos con el lápiz.
*Te lo juro por Dios, Margaret, prefiero morir solo que
pasar un minuto más contigo.*

Eunice esconde la cara en las manos, pero Sydney
mantiene la cabeza erguida. Está enfermo. Cuando dice cosas
terribles no sabe lo que dice, aunque en este caso ella
está secretamente de acuerdo con él. Mamá es débil. Sydney
puede ver el dolor trazado en la cara sencilla de su madre.
No es lo bastante fuerte. No merece a su padre. Está lista
para que muera.

Sydney cree que ella también se moriría si tuviera que
elegir entre eso y pasar la vida con mamá.

Y de pronto se encuentra de nuevo sobre el escenario de la
Tumba. Vueltas, vueltas y vueltas. El tintineo de las
campanillas y el golpeteo del piano con el bajo de fondo y,
cada cierto rato, una ráfaga brillante de ruido que

interrumpe la música como un sobresalto en una película de terror. Un tumor derivado de astrocitos. Células con forma de estrella que, por algún motivo, resultan preciosas en la imaginación, como malvaviscos que flotan entre cereales azucarados. Jadeos cortos y controlados. No dejes que el público vea lo duro que trabajas. Sé la Sydney que actúa. Haz que parezca fácil. Gira, gira, gira. Desinhibición, radiación, antipsicóticos, convulsiones, cambios de personalidad, inoperable. Gira, gira, gira, más rápido ahora, porque aunque Sydney es fuerte, no quiere ver el resto.

Lo hace de todos modos. A pesar del baile, pierde la calma, se transforma en la Sydney pequeña y triste, y vuelven a arrastrarla a escena.

Cuando sucede está en la habitación con papá. Hace dos semanas que nació su hermano menor, Noah. Papá estaba demasiado débil para sostenerlo, y de todos modos no parecía interesado. Sydney lo comprende. ¿Por qué molestarse en conocer a un bebé que jamás criará? Eunice está con mamá y el bebé en una habitación diferente. Sydney las visita muy rara vez. Quiere estar con papá. Siempre ha disfrutado estando a solas con él, teniéndolo todo para sí, pero por algún motivo, incluso cuando solo están ellos dos en la habitación, últimamente siente otra presencia. Algo que no puede ver, que los observa a ambos.

Como si no bastara con esta sensación espeluznante, los últimos días no han sido buenos. Aunque papá estaba escribiendo y dibujando mucho, ya no tiene la fuerza para hacerlo. Se queda mirando el vacío, con la respiración entrecortada, y Sydney se para a su lado y le sujeta la mano. No parece reconocerla, parece atrapado en su propia mente, a solas consigo mismo. Pero de pronto su mano aprieta la suya. Inhala bruscamente, como si experimentara un gran dolor.

Se vuelve para mirarla, los ojos alertas y presentes. Aterrados.

Eunice tenía razón.

¿Papi?, pregunta. Es la única palabra que consigue decir bajo su mirada intensa, más intensa que cualquier reflector.

Margaret, dice.

Sydney. Soy Sydney, papi.

Los dibujos. Los diseños. Está todo allí. Tienes que hacerlo, dice.

¿Tengo que hacer qué?, pregunta Sydney.

Nos ha visto. Tiene nuestro rastro.

Su padre cierra los ojos. Su respiración es tranquila y profunda. Sydney lo llama un par de veces más antes de advertir que su pecho ha dejado de moverse por completo.

Gira, gira, gira. Sydney está otra vez sobre el escenario de la Tumba. Ella misma está quedándose sin aliento. Se desliza más despacio para realizar el cuarto *arabesque* de Vaganova, y luego está en el funeral de su padre, con Eunice, su madre, el señor y la señora Ransom, todos los vecinos, el abuelo y la abuela Byrne, la abuela Turner, todos reunidos alrededor de una tumba abierta mientras un pastor habla encima del ataúd de papi. Noah solloza, y mamá se lo pasa a Sydney. Le pide que lo lleve lejos hasta que se calme. Sydney quiere preguntar por qué no lo puede llevar la abuela Turner, pero sabe por qué. La anciana tiene un aspecto terrible. Tiene la piel cerosa, los ojos hundidos. Dentro de seis meses, morirá por sobredosis de somníferos. Todo el mundo dirá que fue un accidente sabiendo que no lo fue.

Pero eso será más adelante. Ahora Sydney lleva a Noah al otro lado del cementerio, pronunciando todas las palabras más terribles que conoce con su voz más suave y tranquilizadora: *hijo de puta, idiota, cabrón, tu puta madre, mierda, maldito.* Estudia cada lápida que pasa. Todas parecen afiladas y duras. Qué fácil sería silenciar a Noah para siempre. Nadie lo echaría de menos, salvo quizás

Eunice, pero sea como sea a ella le gusta todo el mundo. Es probable que eche de menos sus mocos después de sonarse la nariz.

Sydney no suelta a Noah. Camina de un lado a otro llevándolo en brazos, dándole palmaditas en la espalda, lo maldice y maldice a su madre por enviarla lejos en plena despedida a su padre. Es el último de una larga serie de fracasos por su parte: está vendiendo la casa, y la familia se mudará a un apartamento como gente pobre. Lo perderán todo.

Sydney se encuentra de nuevo sobre el escenario. Gira, gira, gira. Tan rápido como pueda, más rápido todavía. La Sydney bailarina necesita ser la única Sydney. Ella descubrirá lo que su padre necesitaba. Hará lo correcto. Hará que se sienta orgulloso de ella.

Parte tres

EL SER
EN EL UMBRAL

CAPÍTULO 1

—Quítatelo, Noah.

—Deja que se divierta. ¿Cuál es el problema?

—Está ridículo.

—A nadie le importará.

—¿A dónde ha ido? Noah, ven aquí. No tenemos tiempo para esto.

Agosto de 1989 y yo tenía seis años. Me ocultaba tras las cortinas amarillentas de la sala de nuestro sórdido y ruinoso apartamento, mientras mi madre, Eunice y la socia de mi madre, Sally White, discutían sobre lo que había elegido ponerme aquel día. Se nos hacía tarde para la función de *Sonrisas y lágrimas* que presentaba el Instituto Vandergriff, pero yo quería ponerme un disfraz: una máscara ordinaria y endeble y la copia de una capa, fabricada aquel verano para sacar partido de la película de Batman. Desde que Sally me la había comprado, hacía una semana que no me la quitaba.

Apenas prestaba atención a la conversación. Las cortinas de la sala se hallaban colgando ante la puerta de cristal corrediza del pequeño patio interior de nuestro apartamento, y me volví para mirarla. Cada unidad de nuestro complejo tenía una superficie de tres por cuatro metros que estaba abierta a la intemperie, y cercada en tres de sus lados por las paredes de la unidad (en nuestro caso, la ventana de mi habitación a un lado, una pared blanca delante que limitaba el baño de mi madre y, en diagonal a ambas, la puerta de cristal corrediza que daba a la sala). La cuarta pared separaba nuestro patio del patio vecino. Piensa en ello como la versión del pobre de un porche trasero o de un balcón: un trozo de cielo que podías llamar tuyo pero sin una vista del vecindario o ni siquiera del aparcamiento. Un alma más generosa quizás habría destacado la privacidad que ofrecía tener esa clase de patio interior, pero según mi propia experiencia, era difícil sentir otra cosa que no fuera estar confinado sobre aquella pequeña extensión de cemento agrietado.

—Noah, puedo ver tu calzado deportivo —dijo mamá—. Sal ahora o tendrás que quedarte en casa y perderte la obra.

Reaparecí arrastrando los pies. Mi madre, Eunice y Sally se hallaban en mitad de la alfombra manchada de color beige; mi madre, de brazos cruzados; Eunice, con una mochila en la espalda, y Sally, ocultando una sonrisa tras la mano.

—Quítatelo —volvió a decir mi madre.

—¿Y por qué Eunice puede llevar su mochila? —pregunté.

—Eunice lleva los deberes.

—Todos los de la obra llevarán disfraces —insistí.

—Quítatelo.

Me desaté la cuerda anudada alrededor del cuello y tiré de la máscara quitándomela de la cabeza. Las prendas se deslizaron al suelo a mis espaldas.

—Tu pelo es un horror —dijo mi madre.

—Margaret —dijo Sally—. A nadie le importará si parece un poco alborotado.

Mi madre se pellizcó el puente de la nariz.

—Está bien. Vamos.

CAPÍTULO 2

El aparcamiento del instituto era un verdadero caos para cuando llegamos, y mi madre tuvo que aparcar lejos de la entrada, guiando con cuidado su viejo Ford Torino, que resollaba al avanzar entre los grupos de gente que se movía con lentitud. Jadeó y resopló furiosa conforme cruzaba el aparcamiento llevándome a rastras; tuve que correr para no caerme. El instituto tenía un aspecto monumental y sofisticado comparado con el edificio de mi colegio de primaria, y contemplé admirado las interminables taquillas y vitrinas repletas de trofeos mientras apresurábamos el paso hacia el auditorio, con sus asientos plegables de felpa y su telón negro azulado. Encontramos cuatro asientos juntos cerca del escenario.

—No te tomes personalmente el malhumor de tu madre, querido —dijo Sally, inclinándose hacia mí mientras nos acomodábamos—. Hemos tenido un día duro en la tienda.

Se refería a Monstruos al Acecho, la tienda de recuerdos y cómics que habían abierto en 1984, utilizando las ganancias por la venta de la amplia colección de terror de mi padre. Si el malhumor de mi madre era una indicación, todos los días eran días duros en la tienda.

Al otro lado, Eunice ya había sacado el contenido de su bolso. Miró el libro de texto que tenía en el regazo con el ceño fruncido y trazó números sobre un cuaderno de espiral.

—¿En qué trabajas? —pregunté.

—Álgebra —respondió.

—¿Es difícil?

—Solo cuando las personas me interrumpen. —Me guiñó el ojo para demostrar que no lo decía en serio.

Un silencio nervioso descendió sobre el público. Las luces del auditorio se atenuaron. Una serie de campanillas empezaron a sonar en el foso de la orquesta, y un coro de voces de mujer se elevó a izquierda y derecha de mi sitio. Dos hileras de monjas avanzaron deslizándose por los pasillos. Llevaban velas en las manos y cantaban una canción solemne y bella que no pude distinguir. Sus voces flotaron hacia nosotros, armoniosas y conmovedoras. Al llegar al final del auditorio, subieron al escenario, se pararon delante del público y estallaron en un cántico gozoso de «Aleluya». Se alejaron en una hilera, desapareciendo entre bambalinas al tiempo que sus voces se disipaban, dejando el escenario vacío y oscuro.

Un momento después, un proyector se deslizó sigilosamente hacia arriba, revelando una figura ante un lienzo pintado. Llevaba el vestido sencillo de una postulante y sostenía un cubo de madera con ambas manos. Sydney, de diecisiete años, en el papel de María. A diferencia de la María casta y maternal de Julie Andrews, Sydney se había dejado el pelo largo y marrón, recogido hacia atrás en una coleta, y a pesar del vestido ancho y suelto, cuando empezó a cantar resplandecía bajo la intensa luz:

Mi día en las colinas ha llegado a su fin, lo sé.
Una estrella ha salido para decirme que es hora de marcharme.

Las cuerdas de la orquesta se elevaron uniéndose a ella y acompañándola mientras giraba lentamente sobre el escenario dejando que la canción se desplegara. No era la personificación de Julie Andrews ni de Mary Martin, sino de alguien con las características singulares de Sydney: una joven herida, perpleja y en carne viva, algo privado que se había vuelto público. Presioné la palma contra la boca y las lágrimas me hicieron cosquillas en los nudillos al rodar por encima. No quería emitir ni un sonido y romper ese frágil hechizo.

—Oye —susurró Eunice, dejando caer algo sobre mi regazo. Bajé la mano y sentí la tela ordinaria y resbaladiza: mi capa y capucha de murciélago. Los apreté en las manos, deslizando los dedos sobre las puntas ligeras de las orejas flexibles de murciélago. Seguía siendo una agonía oír a Sydney cantar, pero algo se aflojó en mi pecho y lo hizo soportable.

CAPÍTULO 3

El teatro entero se puso en pie para ovacionar al elenco cuando los actores aparecieron en escena, pero deliró de verdad cuando Sydney salió y encabezó el saludo final.

Después, las familias aguardaron cerca del auditorio a que salieran sus respectivos miembros del reparto y del equipo, y también para hablar con el director del espectáculo, el señor Ransom. Para 1989, siete años después que él y su esposa se hubieran mudado a la casa contigua a la antigua residencia de mi familia, y hubiera ayudado a mi padre a organizar la Tumba, Daniel Ransom se había vuelto más robusto y su oscuro pelo raleaba. Pero aún conservaba una voz profunda y dominante y una carcajada rápida, y cuando me sonreía, no dejaba de sentir como si fuera yo mismo el que traía luz al mundo.

—Qué tipo tan pretencioso —masculló mi madre, observándolo sonreír mientras aceptaba felicitaciones y sus carcajadas resonaban en el auditorio.

—No te acerques a él y no lo mires —dijo Sally.

—Aquí viene de todos modos. Daniel —dijo mi madre, estrechando su mano.

—Ha sido un espectáculo maravilloso —dijo Sally.

El señor Ransom desestimó el elogio con una mano; se sentía tímido y satisfecho consigo mismo a la vez.

—¿Os ha contado Sydney que la primera parte con las monjas desfilando entre las hileras fue idea suya?

—No me sorprende, si te refieres a eso —señaló mi madre.

Su sonrisa quedó petrificada y se volvió falsa.

—Es una chica especial.

—Son todos especiales, ¿verdad? —preguntó mi madre—. Por lo menos, cuando llega la época de recaudar fondos.

La sonrisa se evaporó.

—No estoy pidiendo dinero, Margaret. Solo tengo una muy buena opinión de tu hija.

—Le diré que lo has dicho —dijo mi madre. Abrió el bolso y empezó a hurgar dentro.

—Y ya que estamos hablando del tema —dijo, ya fuera porque no se dio cuenta o porque ignoró la evidente despedida—. Falta muy poco para Halloween. ¿Has vuelto a considerar mi propuesta?

—Ya tienes mi respuesta —dijo mi madre.

Hice una mueca al tiempo que el señor Ransom nos dirigía rápidamente un mínimo saludo.

—Siempre es un placer, Margaret. Sally, Eunice, Noah —dijo, asintiendo a cada uno de nosotros. Se refugió en una multitud de admiradores.

—Sabes que está pasando por un momento difícil —dijo Sally.

Se refería al colapso de su matrimonio. Todos estábamos enterados, pero nos referíamos a la situación utilizando frases como *momento difícil* o *problemas*.

Mi madre dirigió una mirada de escepticismo a la espalda del señor Ransom.

—Bua bua.

Me echó un vistazo y miró ceñuda la capa que llevaba apretada en el puño.

—¿De dónde has sacado eso?

CAPÍTULO 4

Sydney fue a cenar con algunas amigas después de la obra. Solo salió para que la felicitáramos y para anunciar sus planes. Luego volvió a desaparecer en los camerinos. Mamá se lamentó sobre el tiempo perdido, pero ya no le quedaba energía para seguir enfadada. Estaba cansada.

Cuando volvimos al apartamento, Sally nos besó a todos en la mejilla y se marchó. Mi madre nos despidió y se retiró a su propia habitación, dejándonos a Eunice y a mí solos en la sala.

—Es una noche de colegio, caballero —dijo ella, dejando caer una mano sobre mi hombro—. Y hace rato que deberías estar en la cama. Ve a lavarte los dientes y a ponerte el pijama.

—¿Me lees un cuento? —pedí.

—Un ratito, pero solo si te das prisa —dijo.

Hice lo que me ordenó y, después de colgar mi capa en el armario, me metí en la cama. Cuando Eunice entró en mi habitación un rato después con un libro de tapa blanda en una mano, tuvo que hacer malabarismos para llegar a mi cama, cruzando un campo minado de juguetes y ropa sucia de puntillas, e incluso después de llegar a la cama y pedirme que me hiciera a un lado, tuvo que sacar muñecos de acción y naves espaciales de debajo de las mantas para hacerse un sitio y poder sentarse.

—¿Cómo puedes dormir con tantos trastos en la cama? —preguntó, apoyando un Cazafantasmas sobre mi mesilla de noche.

Siempre me había costado dormirme de noche, y como no era tan inteligente como Eunice a mi edad, en lugar de leer o escribir para dormir, jugaba. Me corrí hacia la pared para hacerle un sitio. Se sentó junto a mí y empujó las gafas sobre la nariz. Sentí su brazo huesudo y cubierto de pecas helado contra el mío. Abrió un ejemplar de *La búsqueda onírica de la desconocida Kadath* y empezó a leer:

> Se alzaron de inmediato por delante las sierras escarpadas de una costa de aspecto leproso, y Carter vio las sólidas y desagradables torres grises de una ciudad. Su modo de inclinarse y torcerse, el modo de apiñarse, y el hecho de no tener ventanas, turbaron en exceso al prisionero; y lamentó

amargamente el sinsentido de haber bebido el vino raro de aquel mer-
cader de turbante torcido. A medida que se acercaban a la costa, y la
terrible fetidez de aquella ciudad se intensificaba, vio sobre las colinas
quebradas una gran cantidad de bosques, algunos de cuyos árboles reco-
noció parecidos a aquel solitario árbol lunar en el bosque encantado de
la tierra, de cuya savia los pequeños y pardos zoogs elaboraban vino.

Habíamos estado leyendo *Kadath* algunas noches. Me costaba seguir la historia, con sus escuetas descripciones y la preponderancia de palabras ridículas como *zoogs*, pero me gustaba oír la voz de Eunice. Su modo de hablar lento y esmerado, el modo en que parecía manipular cada palabra como un objeto delicado, preciso, siempre me tranquilizaba. Ya había empezado a dormirme sobre su hombro cuando cerró el libro dando por terminada la lectura y se levantó para acomodarme las sábanas.

—¿A quién quiero más? —preguntó.

—A mí —dije, despertándome un poco.

—¿Y a quien quieres tú más?

—A ti —dije.

Me besó en la frente.

—Que duermas bien, principito. —Encendió mi lucecilla nocturna, apagó la luz del techo, y se dispuso a salir del dormitorio.

—Eunice —dije.

Hizo una pausa.

Moví la boca un instante, buscando las palabras. Quería comunicar mi temor, mi necesidad de que permaneciera cerca, pero también temía que si decía algo, pudiera decidir que Lovecraft era demasiado intenso para leer de noche, y dejara de leérmelo.

—Nada —dije—. Buenas noches.

—Buenas noches. —Cerró la puerta tras ella.

Los arañazos empezaron en cuanto cerró la puerta, unos arañazos rápidos e insistentes contra el cristal de la ventana de mi dormitorio. Hacía unas semanas que sucedía, y había unido las cortinas con alfileres para que nadie pudiera ver el interior de la habitación, aunque la ventana solo diera al patio cerrado y privado de nuestro apartamento. Un pequeño resquicio permanecía visible entre los paneles, y al mirar a través de él solo vi oscuridad.

Los arañazos crecieron en intensidad, una melodía pavorosa y chirriante. Deseé haber ocultado mi capa de Batman bajo mi almohada en lugar de colgarla en el armario. Con mi capa, podía sentirme valiente y seguro. Pero para ir a buscarla, tendría que pasar delante de la ventana. En cambio, hundí la cabeza en la almohada y esperé a que el sonido se detuviera. Pareció continuar durante horas.

CAPÍTULO 5

En sus mejores días, cuando las cosas transcurrían de forma agradable, mi madre y Sydney mantenían una paz precaria: cortés y respetuosa, pero jamás cálida. Pero la mayoría del tiempo discutían. Eunice y yo conseguíamos descansar de todo ello durante las semanas anteriores a un recital de baile o una obra teatral, pero una vez que Sydney tenía la oportunidad de descansar, el ciclo volvía a empezar. Un ejemplo fue la semana después de *Sonrisas y lágrimas*, cuando nos encontrábamos todos juntos en el coche después del colegio, Eunice y yo en el asiento trasero, Sydney y mi madre delante, cuando mi hermana estalló tras varios minutos de silencio:

—El señor Ransom me contó lo que dijiste de mí.

—¿Y qué fue lo que dije? —preguntó mi madre. Sonaba cansada. Incluso aburrida.

—Dijiste que no era especial —dijo Sydney.

Mi madre se encorvó sobre el volante.

—Voy a pasarle por encima a ese hombre con mi coche.

—Te deseo suerte sorprendiéndolo con esta ratonera —dijo Sydney.

—No dije que no fueras especial. Estaba de broma. Sé que no puedes entenderlo ahora, porque tienes diecisiete años, pero no es profesional que tergiverse mis palabras y te mortifique. Debería hablar con tu director. —Mamá solía amenazar con hacerlo, pero no lo decía en serio, y Sydney lo sabía.

—También me dijo que volviste a rechazarlo —dijo mi hermana.

—Siempre lo hago —dijo mi madre—. ¿Por qué iba a cambiar ahora de opinión?

—¿Cambiar de opinión acerca de qué? —pregunté.

—¿Y si no tuvieras que participar en ello? —preguntó Sydney—. Podrías darme los viejos papeles de papá y podría hacerlo yo.

El coche volvió a quedar en silencio. Nadie hablaba jamás de mi padre en mi presencia... ni siquiera Eunice. Si preguntaba por él, cada cierto tiempo me suministraba algún detalle (era alto, tenía el pelo oscuro como yo y Sydney, y había muerto de cáncer), pero generalmente cambiaba de tema o intentaba distraerme. Entiendo por qué mi madre evitaría el tema, pero no Eunice y Sydney. Quizás el dolor de su enfermedad y muerte las había dejado marcadas de un modo particular, y el silencio se había convertido en la forma que tenía la familia de seguir adelante. No estoy seguro. Vivir con una familia herida por un dolor que no recuerdas es como estar sentado detrás de una persona demasiado alta en un cine. Las personas a tu alrededor ríen, lloran y reaccionan a algo, pero tú no tienes ni idea de lo que es.

—Deberías saber que no puedes pedirme algo así —dijo mi madre en voz queda.

—Esos papeles me pertenecen a mí tanto como... —dijo Sydney, la frustración y la ira le daban a su perfil un aspecto grotesco.

—¿Qué papeles? —pregunté.

—Noah, cállate —dijo Eunice, apretándome el brazo con tanta fuerza que me dolió.

—Sydney, te aconsejo que des marcha atrás con esta conversación —dijo mi madre.

Sydney emanaba furia en forma de oleadas calientes y palpables. Parecía hacer más calor en el coche. ¿Era posible? Me incliné hacia la ventanilla abierta, intentando que la brisa me diera en la cara. El coche se estremeció y sacudió, y me golpeé la cabeza contra el marco de la ventana.

—¿Qué sucede? —dijo Eunice.

Me froté la cabeza. Mi madre quitó las manos del volante y las alzó como una delincuente rindiéndose ante la policía. Sydney la miró, y la furia se convirtió en confusión.

—No estoy segura —respondió mi madre—. Yo...

Un chorro brillante de luz naranja salió del capó del coche, ahogando el final de su oración y enviando un nuevo torrente de calor agobiante al interior del coche.

—¿Qué está pasando? —volvió a preguntar Eunice.

La luz naranja empezó a oscilar y danzar. El capó del coche estaba ardiendo.

Un hombre apareció en la ventanilla de mi madre, golpeando el cristal. Tenía las manos cubiertas con una capa grasienta, y una bandana le apartaba una masa de pelo mugriento de la cara. Creo que estábamos todos demasiado sorprendidos para gritar.

—¡Saque a esos niños de ahí! —gritó, su voz amortiguada.

Eunice se inclinó encima de mí y me desabrochó el cinturón de seguridad con un movimiento rápido. Mi madre y Sydney salieron del coche y abrieron las puertas traseras. Mi madre sacó a Eunice tironeándola del brazo, y Sydney me alzó como un bebé, sujetándome a su pecho. Retrocedió varios pasos y casi se tropezó con el bordillo mientras mi madre y Eunice corrían al otro lado de la calle.

El hombre de la ventana había detenido su Volkswagen de color azul justo detrás del Torino de mi madre. Abrió la puerta corrediza, hurgó entre una impresionante variedad de desechos de comida rápida y ropa sucia, y localizó un extintor de fuego. Leyó las instrucciones del lateral del tanque rojo brillante, murmurando para sí, y luego cruzó de nuevo delante del Torino, plantó los pies con firmeza y oprimió el gatillo. Un chorro de espuma blanca recubrió el capó del coche, sofocando el incendio.

—¡Mierda! —exclamó el hombre. Seguía apuntando el extintor hacia el coche, como si esperara que el fuego volviera a encenderse—. Uno compra una de estas cosas porque, ya sabéis, la seguridad primero y todo lo demás, pero jamás piensa que la usará realmente. —Nos echó un vistazo. Seguíamos al otro lado de la calle, mi madre y Eunice, tomadas de la mano, y yo en brazos de Sydney—. ¿Estáis todos bien?

Nos habíamos detenido en una calle residencial, completamente desierta salvo por nuestra familia y el desaliñado bombero improvisado. Sydney pareció advertir que seguía conmigo en brazos. Se inclinó hacia delante y me apoyó sobre el suelo.

—Creo que estamos bien —dijo mi madre.

El hombre volvió caminando a su camioneta, arrojó el extintor en el maletero lleno de trastos, y nos saludó con la mano.

—Que tengan un buen día —dijo. Se alejó, dejándonos en la calle con nuestro coche muerto.

CAPÍTULO 6

Mi madre hizo que remolcaran el coche de nuevo a casa y llamó a Rick, según Eunice un viejo amigo de mi padre de su época en el departamento de carreteras. Se trataba de otra tenue conexión con mis propios orígenes secretos: un chico bueno y barrigón con botas de cowboy que venía a veces a ayudar con el mantenimiento del hogar, pero que también se negaba a hablar conmigo sobre mi padre, incluso cuando conseguía llamar su atención.

Aquel día no tuve oportunidad de molestarlo. Cuando llegó en su camioneta, mi madre se reunió con él en el aparcamiento con una cerveza en la mano. Abrió el capó ennegrecido del Torino mientras mis hermanas y yo aguardábamos sentados en el porche delantero. Mamá se quedó de pie junto a él, con los brazos cruzados. Estuvo solo unos instantes fisgoneando antes de enderezarse y limpiarse las manos con un trapo. Se bebió la cerveza a toda velocidad y luego impartió su diagnóstico. La cabeza de mi madre languideció.

—Parece que son malas noticias —dijo Eunice.

—El coche *se prendió fuego* —dijo Sydney.

—¿Siempre se prenden fuego los coches? —pregunté.

—Casi nunca —dijo Eunice.

Mi madre estrechó la mano de Rick, quien, tras saludarnos, volvió a meterse en su camioneta. Aquella lo observó alejarse, pateó un trozo de gravilla suelta y luego se acercó penosamente por el camino de entrada.

—¿Y? —preguntó Sydney.

—Tengo que hacer algunas llamadas —respondió mi madre.

Llevó el teléfono a su dormitorio y permaneció dentro durante horas. Eunice preparó hamburguesas y macarrones gratinados con queso para la cena; yo me puse de pie sobre el banquillo junto a ella, pasándole lo que fuera que pidiera. Mi madre aún no había salido cuando la comida estaba lista, así que le preparamos un plato, lo pusimos en el microondas y comimos sin ella.

Apareció más tarde, no mucho antes de la hora de irme a dormir, y se sentó a la mesa mientras nos reunimos alrededor de ella. Antes de hablar se comió la mitad de la comida que tenía en el plato.

—El motor del coche está destruido. Rick tendría que reconstruirlo de cero.

—¿Qué ha pasado? —preguntó Sydney.

Mi madre bebió un largo sorbo de su vaso de agua.

—El fuego ha destruido toda prueba, así que jamás lo sabremos con seguridad.

—Pero es *capaz* de arreglarlo —dijo Eunice.

—Reconstruir un motor cuesta mucho dinero —dijo mi madre.

—¿Cuánto? —pregunté.

—Mucho más de lo que podemos pagar en este momento. —Apretó los puños—. Acababa de hacer el cambio de aceite.

—¿Qué vamos a hacer? —preguntó Eunice.

—Sally puede llevaros a ti y a Noah al colegio, y me llevará y traerá del trabajo. Sydney, tú tendrás que conseguir que una amiga te lleve al colegio y a los ensayos.

Sydney ya lo hacía la mayor parte del tiempo, pero de todos modos preguntó:

—¿Durante cuánto tiempo?

—Durante cierto tiempo —dijo mi madre—. Tenemos poco dinero, y no veo que esa situación vaya a cambiar pronto.

—No tendría que ser así —señaló Sydney.

—Sydney —dijo mi madre. Presionó el talón de las manos contra las cuencas de los ojos—, estoy teniendo un día difícil. ¿Podrías por esta vez dejar de sacarme de quicio y ponerte de mi lado?

—Lo estoy intentando —respondió mi hermana, imitando el tono frustrado de mi madre con increíble exactitud—. Ya no se trata de lo que tú sientes. Nos hemos aguantado en este apartamento de mierda, la carne picada de peor calidad y la pasta asquerosa, el coche que se sacude y se incendia… lo hemos hecho a tu modo durante años, y mira dónde estamos. ¿Podrías por favor considerar la idea de que quizás valga la pena intentar algo diferente esta única vez?

Mi madre puso los codos sobre la mesa y se aferró el mentón. Miró la comida a medio terminar sobre el plato, y luego recorrió la habitación con la mirada. Sus ojos se posaron en mí y frunció el ceño. Me encogí bajo su mirada… solo se quedaba mirándome así cuando había hecho algo malo. El resultado es que jamás me gustaba que me miraran.

Suspiró.

—Dile al señor Ransom que estamos dispuestos a hablar sobre una casa embrujada.

Sydney se puso de pie y se dirigió al teléfono.

—No estoy prometiendo nada más —dijo mi madre—. Una conversación.

Si Sydney la oyó, no dio señales de ello.

CAPÍTULO 7

El sábado por la noche, Sally nos condujo a todos a casa del señor Ransom para cenar. Seguía viviendo al lado de la antigua casa de mi familia, e insistí en sentarme junto a la ventanilla del lado del conductor para poder echar una buena mirada cuando llegáramos. Se trataba de otra pieza de historia familiar de la que había oído hablar pero que jamás había visto. A veces, cuando paseaba por el pueblo, observaba casas al azar intentando imaginar a mis hermanas jugando en el jardín, mi padre cortando el césped, mi madre leyendo junto al ventanal, todos dispersos en una abrumadora cantidad de espacio, donde se podía estar todo el día sin ver a otra persona si se deseaba.

Cuando aparcamos en la entrada del señor Ransom y Eunice señaló nuestra antigua casa, quedé decepcionado por la realidad: una casa de ladrillos con un árbol en un jardín descuidado, y una camioneta oxidada en el camino de entrada.

—¿Es esa? —pregunté.

—El jardín estaba mejor cuidado cuando era nuestra —señaló mi madre.

—Era un bonito sitio para vivir. Más bonito que donde vivimos ahora —dijo Sydney, sentada detrás del asiento del pasajero y mirando resuelta hacia el otro lado.

La casa del señor Ransom tampoco tenía demasiado buen aspecto. Cruzamos un sendero bordeado de césped descuidado, pisando periódicos empapados de agua, y nos agachamos para pasar debajo de una rama demasiado baja antes de llegar a la puerta. Cuando mi madre tocó el timbre, el señor

Ransom vino a abrir la puerta vestido con una camisa. Tenía la cara llena de trocitos de papel higiénico ensangrentados donde se había cortado afeitándose. Al invitarnos a pasar, el cuello de su camisa estaba torcido.

El interior de la casa parecía más agradable: láminas enmarcadas en las paredes, pañuelos decorativos sobre las lámparas, muebles tapizados en tela blanca inmaculada y protegidos por fundas de plástico brillantes. De todos modos, había un olor rancio y polvoriento, como a un sitio donde la gente no había vivido en cierto tiempo.

—He pedido comida —dijo, conduciéndonos a la mesa de la cocina, que tenía una pila de cajas de pizza, platos de cartón, vasos y cubiertos de plástico. Parecía la escena de la fiesta de cumpleaños de un chico triste. Lo único que le faltaba eran los sombreros de punta y el mantel decorativo.

—Vaya… qué despliegue —dijo mi madre.

—Ha llegado mucho más rápido de lo que creía —dijo—. Así que quizás se enfrió.

—Podemos calentarla enseguida —dijo Sally. Abrió una de las cajas, tocó la corteza y se internó en la cocina como si fuera dueña del sitio.

—¿Tiene un lavabo? —pregunté.

—No sería una casa de verdad si no lo tuviera, ¿verdad? —preguntó el señor Ransom, y luego sonrió para manifestar que era una broma—. Al final del pasillo a la izquierda.

Crucé la sala polvorienta y me dirigí pasillo abajo, demasiado tímido para admitir que aún no distinguía la izquierda de la derecha. Encontré tres puertas, elegí una y la abrí. En cuanto le di al interruptor de luz supe que había entrado en el dormitorio de un niño: había sábanas de Masters del universo, cortinas de Superman y un set de juego de la Baticueva instalado en mitad de la habitación. Delante de él había una figura de acción de Batman boca abajo sobre el suelo, como si lo hubieran abandonado en la mitad del juego.

Como habíamos ido tan justos de dinero aquel año, no tenía muchos juguetes nuevos. A medida que el torrente de productos de Batman inundó las estanterías de las tiendas, había podido observar varios de cerca, pero no poseía ninguno, y la Baticueva era el santo grial: un trozo de plástico moldeado de color gris al que le habían dado el efecto de piedra, con escaleras rojas y plataformas azules donde Batman podía pararse y cavilar, un batiordenador con un enorme monitor donde podía resolver sus misterios y, en la parte de atrás, una celda para delincuentes y una plataforma secreta que podía deshacerse de un villano (o de un héroe) arrojándolo a una fosa profunda.

Me incliné sobre la Baticueva. Tenía la boca reseca por el deseo, y levanté el Batman. Metí la mano libre en mi bolsillo, evaluando el espacio disponible. ¿Notaría alguien el bulto? No era robar de verdad... la familia del señor Ransom se había marchado, y ¿quién echaría de menos un solo juguete?

—¿Te has perdido?

Dejé caer el pequeño muñeco y casi suelto un grito. El señor Ransom se hallaba dentro de la habitación. Me sujeté las manos con fuerza detrás de la espalda.

—No sé distinguir la derecha de la izquierda. Y luego he visto todos los juguetes.

—Es la habitación de mi hijo Kyle —dijo.

—Creía que ya no vivía aquí.

—Estoy deseando que algún día vuelva, por lo menos de visita. Quiero que esta habitación permanezca exactamente como la recuerda.

—Qué amable, señor Ransom —dije. La cara me ardía de vergüenza.

—El lavabo está al otro lado del pasillo —dijo, guiándome fuera de la habitación y cerrando la puerta detrás de nosotros. Abrí la puerta del lavabo, y empezó a volver por el pasillo, pero antes de que pudiera entrar, me llamó.

—Tu lado izquierdo es el lado de tu corazón —dijo, poniendo la mano sobre ese sitio. Lo imité, y nos quedamos mirándonos un instante como si estuviéramos prometiendo lealtad a la bandera.

En los años transcurridos desde entonces, he pensado mucho en aquel momento. En los antiguos tiempos, el lado izquierdo era considerado el lado siniestro o malo. Ser zurdo era un indicio de que se tenía una deficiencia moral. Los profesores te pegaban con una regla si te pillaban escribiendo con la mano izquierda. Así que me parece adecuado que el corazón, el símbolo del amor, el órgano que supuestamente mueve a tomar las decisiones más importantes de nuestras vidas, lata en el lado izquierdo del cuerpo.

Cuando volví, todo el mundo se disponía a comer la pizza recalentada.

—Este es el trato —dijo el señor Ransom mientras me sentaba de un salto en una silla junto a Eunice—. El departamento de teatro se excedió en los gastos de producción de *Sonrisas y lágrimas*, y solo contamos con dinero para montar puede que un solo espectáculo más este año. El problema es que se supone que tenemos que realizar *cuatro* más.

—Así que ambos tenemos problemas de dinero.

El señor Ransom se frotó la barba de chivo.

—Tu familia ya ha demostrado tener talento para una clase particular de diseño de producción, y yo tengo un poco de dinero y un departamento lleno de chicos que se mueren por estar delante de un público. Así que… —Señaló a Sydney—. Nos pareció que el departamento podía colaborar con tu familia para realizar una casa embrujada este año. Iríamos a medias. Si funciona, mi departamento gana el dinero suficiente para poder realizar otro año de producciones teatrales, y tú puedes arreglar tu coche o quizás comprar uno nuevo.

Mi madre deslizó la yema del dedo sobre el borde de la copa de vino mientras pensaba.

—Tú tienes el dinero y los chicos. Parece que no necesitas mi ayuda.

—Necesitamos la visión que tiene tu familia; de lo contrario, será otra casa encantada mediocre más —dijo el señor Ransom.

—Esa «visión» —dijo mi madre, haciendo comillas en el aire alrededor de la palabra— era de mi difunto marido. Yo tan solo confeccioné los disfraces.

—Eunice y yo también diseñábamos algunas partes —dijo Sydney—. No fue solo papá.

—Tú hiciste unos dibujos graciosos y tu padre te alabó por ello —dijo mi madre.

—Mentira —dijo Sydney.

—Sydney —dijo Sally.

—Vete a la mierda, Sally.

—*Sydney* —dijo mi madre.

—Sea como sea —dijo el señor Ransom, levantando la voz—, tengo entendido que Harry dejó muchos diseños sin usar.

—Esos no se tocan —dijo mi madre.

—No son tuyos para que decidas qué hacer con ellos —dijo Sydney.

—Claro que lo son —dijo mi madre. Sydney parecía a punto de lanzarse encima de la mesa. Mi madre la desafió con la mirada—. Si me pones a prueba, les prenderé fuego esta misma noche.

Me metí un trozo de pizza en la boca. No tenía hambre... de hecho, sentía un poco de náuseas... pero tenía que hacer *algo*.

—Quizás esto haya sido una mala idea —dijo el señor Ransom—. No quise causaros problemas. Estoy seguro de que tenéis otro plan para recuperaros económicamente.

Mi madre dio un enorme mordisco a la pizza. Después de tragar, apuró el vino de una sola vez.

—Si tuviera otro plan, no estaría aquí. Sally, ¿tenemos dinero?

Sally vació lo que quedaba de la botella de vino en la copa de mi madre.

—Haremos que funcione.

—Costará menos de lo que creéis —dijo el señor Ransom—. Tenemos un taller de escenografías en el colegio, así que podemos aportar materiales para la construcción. Los estudiantes trabajarán para obtener créditos escolares, así que no tenéis que pagarles, y podemos vender entradas en el colegio a un público cautivo. Vosotros podéis quedaros con los decorados, el atrezo, los disfraces y la mitad de las ganancias.

—¿De verdad crees que habrá ganancias? —preguntó mi madre.

—Claro que sí —respondió él.

CAPÍTULO 8

Aquella noche me senté sobre el suelo del dormitorio de las chicas, con la espalda contra su tocador compartido y los pies presionados contra el pie de la cama de Eunice. Su dormitorio, aunque más grande que el mío, parecía mucho más pequeño con las dos camas encajadas dentro a la fuerza, las paredes decoradas con programas de los espectáculos de Sydney y un enorme poster de Paula Abdul. El único objeto decorativo de Eunice era una foto de Ursula K. Le Guin, que colgaba directamente encima de su cama, como un crucifijo o un atrapasueños. Las chicas iban y venían pasando encima de mí, un revuelo de pijamas, desmaquillantes, cremas hidratantes, cremas para la cara y cepillos de dientes.

—¿Por qué se mudó la familia del señor Ransom? —pregunté. Aunque me había enterado de la separación cuando sucedió, no había empezado a pensar en los Ransom como personas, como una familia, hasta que visité su casa silenciosa y vacía, y sentí el modo en que le afectaban las personas ausentes al señor Ransom, que se había cortado al afeitarse y no conseguía siquiera servir una pizza caliente para sus invitados.

—No es asunto tuyo —dijo Sydney. Me apartó del tocador—. Necesito el último cajón.

Me metí en la cama de Eunice, y hojeé su grueso manual de álgebra. Las series de letras y números imposiblemente complejos que se hallaban impresos dentro parecían un lenguaje alienígena. Me mareaba con solo contemplarlos. Volví a cerrar el libro.

—Sí, pero ¿por qué? —insistí.

Eunice apareció saliendo del lavabo y se metió en la cama de un salto conmigo. Cogió el reloj despertador de la mesilla de noche entre las camas y lo apoyó en su regazo para programarlo.

—A veces las personas se casan con la persona equivocada y, cuando sucede, pueden permanecer juntos y odiarse o hacer lo correcto y separarse.

—No le busques pretextos —dijo Sydney. Sacó un top del cajón.

—¿Mamá se casó con la persona equivocada cuando se casó con papá? —pregunté—. ¿Por eso no habla de él?

—Que no te vuelva a oír hablar así de papá —advirtió Sydney. Salió de la habitación dando zancadas y cerró la puerta del lavabo de un portazo.

CAPÍTULO 9

—¿Cómo es una casa embrujada? —le pregunté a Eunice más tarde, después de estar absorto en la lectura de diez páginas de *Kadath* antes de dormir.

—Jamás he estado en ninguna —dijo—. Solo en la que construimos con mamá y papá cuando tenía tu edad.

—¿Te dio miedo?

—A mí no, pero como ayudé a construirla ya sabía todo lo que sucedería. Pero creo que sí les dio miedo a las personas que vinieron a visitarla.

—¿Y mamá y papá?

—Ambos parecían enfadados y preocupados la mayor parte del tiempo —dijo—. Discutían mucho.

—Entonces, ¿por qué iba a querer mamá hacerlo de nuevo?

Eunice hizo una mueca.

—No quiere, Noah. Tiene que hacerlo. Sydney es la que quiere.

—¿Y por qué Sydney tiene tantas ganas de hacerlo? ¿Y por qué mamá no quiere usar los antiguos diseños de papá?

—No lo sé —dijo Eunice. Por primera vez en mi vida, no le creí.

CAPÍTULO 10

Aquella noche no hubo arañazos en la ventana, solo un fuerte crujido que me despertó con un sobresalto. Abrí los ojos y me incorporé. El apartamento estaba oscuro y silencioso a mi alrededor, lo cual quería decir que estaban todos en la cama. O había soñado el ruido o provenía del patio interior.

Salí de la cama, abrí las cortinas y presioné la cara contra el cristal. Algunos juguetes yacían diseminados donde los había dejado, y algo pequeño y negro reposaba sobre una silla de jardín oxidada, casi invisible en la oscuridad. Aún medio dormido, desbloqueé la ventana y deslicé el panel corredizo para abrirla lo más silenciosamente que pude.

El cemento resultaba frío y áspero contra mis pies desnudos; el aire húmedo apestaba a gases de escape. Caminé hacia la silla de jardín y levanté el objeto: una figura de acción de Batman, tan brillante y prístina como si acabara de salir de su envoltorio: el juguete que había estado a punto de robar de casa del señor Ransom. Giré en un círculo lento, pero no encontré ninguna figura acechando en las sombras.

CAPÍTULO 11

Mi madre y Sydney se instalaron en un viejo almacén en el otro extremo del pueblo. Mi madre vendió una vieja tirada de *El asombroso Spider-Man* para pagar el alquiler, y el fin de semana después de la firma, mi familia realizó un viaje en el coche de Sally a nuestro viejo trastero. El señor Ransom y un par de chicos de su curso de teatro se encontraron con nosotros allí, y juntos sacamos todo el atrezo, los disfraces y los decorados de la Tumba. Observé con una mezcla de asombro y decepción mientras volvían a ver la luz una pieza tras otra... Asombro, ante la posibilidad de ver finalmente esa pequeña parte oculta de la historia familiar, y decepción ante lo cursi que parecía todo bajo las implacables luces fluorescentes: paneles endebles de madera pintados para que parecieran los ladrillos de piedra caliza de la tumba de una momia; máscaras de monstruos de papel maché descamado; disfraces intencionalmente andrajosos con unas puntadas que podrían hacer delirar a un héroe de Lovecraft. Había erigido enormes salas de pesadilla en mi imaginación, y, como la casa antigua de mi familia, la realidad resultó decepcionante. A mi madre, Sydney y Eunice, por otro lado, se las veía afligidas y preocupadas.

Una vez que cargaron y ataron todo —el contenido entero entró en dos camionetas— condujimos al nuevo almacén, situado en los límites del pueblo, al final de un largo y estrecho camino bordeado de árboles. Sydney se bajó del coche para abrir la verja, y nos detuvimos en un enorme aparcamiento ante un edificio rectangular, tan aburrido y gris como un bloque de cemento. Mi madre nos condujo a través de la puerta de entrada acristalada hacia un área de recepción con un enorme escritorio y algunas sillas polvorientas contra la pared. Luego pasamos por un par de puertas dobles y entramos en el almacén mismo, un gran espacio abierto con suelo de cemento y vigas expuestas, un par de lavabos en un rincón, y una serie de puertas de garaje levadizas sobre la pared que daba al aparcamiento. Motas de polvo revoloteaban bajo nuestros pies, y el aire caliente y sofocante me produjo un picor en la nariz.

Abrieron dos de las puertas industriales y lo llevaron todo dentro, esparciéndolo sobre el suelo vacío. Mientras los chicos de teatro bebían refrescos en el aparcamiento, mi madre, Eunice, Sydney y el señor Ransom examinaron cada objeto, evaluando qué podía reusarse y qué descartarse. Rápidamente se dieron cuenta de que la idea original de mi madre... reconstruir la Tumba, retocar la pintura y añadir un par de salas... no funcionaría. Para empezar, gran parte de la madera que mi padre había rescatado durante la construcción se había podrido o estaba rajada, lo que la volvía inservible. Además, todo parecía pequeño y ordinario expuesto en un sitio tan grande y bien iluminado.

—Si le pedimos a la gente que venga hasta aquí por esto... —dijo el señor Ransom, señalando el decorado deslucido—... se sentirán estafados.

—Esto no funcionará en absoluto —dijo mi madre—. Así que tenemos algunas semanas para imaginar algo a partir de cero —dijo. Se pasó ambas manos por el pelo.

—No necesariamente —dijo Sydney. Abrió la cremallera de la omnipresente mochila de Eunice y extrajo una pequeña carpeta, de la cual sacó una pila de papeles y los repartió entre todos. En la hoja que me dio a mí había una imagen de un grupo de adolescentes apiñados en una habitación, con una linterna encendida bajo la cama mientras algo los escudriñaba desde su escondite en el armario. Al intercambiar dibujos, caí en la cuenta de que cada uno mostraba al mismo grupo de adolescentes en una escena diferente. En una, los chicos se desplazaban a través de una morgue mientras detrás de ellos un cadáver se incorporaba en un cajón abierto, aún amortajado con una sábana. En otra, los chicos cruzaban una pequeña charca, pisando de piedra en piedra, mientras una mano áspera y membranosa salía del agua para atrapar el tobillo de una pobre chica. En otra, en la biblioteca de un hombre rico tapizada con cabezas de animales, el monstruo había aferrado a la misma chica, llevándosela a rastras mientras el resto de los chicos se estrechaban unos a otros aterrorizados. En cada dibujo, los chicos compartían una única linterna.

—¿Los has hecho tú? —preguntó mi madre.

Sydney asintió.

—No tenía ni idea de que podías dibujar —dijo.

—¿Por qué siempre hay una linterna? —pregunté.

—Ese es el concepto —explicó Sydney, aliviada ante el cambio de tema—. Elegimos algunas de las habitaciones atemorizantes más mundanas, las que resulten fáciles de montar en un par de semanas, y añadimos un elemento de persecución. Así que además de los sustos habituales, hay un monstruo que te sigue, e intentas escapar antes que te encuentre. Solo dejamos entrar gente en grupos de cuatro, y la única luz del sitio es una linterna. Quizás incluso infiltremos cada cierto tiempo a uno de los nuestros dentro de un grupo, y el monstruo puede «atrapar» a esa persona. Sería algo barato y no tendríamos que reinventar la rueda en pocas semanas.

Todos le volvieron a entregar los dibujos a Sydney, pero mi madre retuvo el suyo. Tenía la cara tensa, como si le hubieran estirado la carne.

—¿Cómo se te ocurrió esto? —preguntó.

Sydney se ocupó afanosamente de la pila de hojas.

—El señor Ransom siempre dice que la necesidad tiene cara de hereje, ¿verdad? Solo intenté pensar en algo que fuera fácil. —Extendió la mano para recuperar su dibujo.

—Estos dibujos están bien hechos —dijo mi madre—. Más que bien hechos. —Parecía abatida por el asunto y le devolvió a Sydney el dibujo con una reticencia evidente—. ¿Esto es *realmente* lo que quieres?

Siguió un momento de silencio, que solo rompió el resoplido del señor Ransom.

—Cielos, Sydney —dijo—, odiaría ser tú cuando te vas a dormir de noche.

Nos miró a uno por uno, con una media sonrisa en la cara, que se desvaneció cuando ninguno de nosotros se rio.

—Hablando de lo cual, ¿creéis que Noah debería presenciar esta conversación? —preguntó Eunice.

—¿Qué? —pregunté— ¿Qué he hecho?

—Nada —dijo mi hermana—. Pero no quiero que tengas pesadillas.

Mi madre señaló por encima de nuestros hombros.

—Eunice, lleva a tu hermano a la oficina mientras hablamos.

—Quiero ayudar —dije.

—Ve a jugar con Eunice —dijo mi madre.

—Lo llevaré, pero volveré —dijo ella—. Yo soy parte de esto.

Mi madre se lo pensó.

—Está bien —dijo—. ¡No toques nada! —gritó mientras Eunice me alejaba a rastras.

CAPÍTULO 12

—No es justo —dije mientras Eunice me arropaba en la cama aquella noche.

—La vida no es justa, amigo.

—Mamá me habría dejado ayudar si no hubieras dicho nada.

—Mamá no está prestando la debida atención —dijo—, pero yo sí, y tienes que confiar en mí cuando digo que esto será demasiado atemorizante para ti. —Se inclinó y me besó la frente—. ¿A quién quiero más que a nadie?

Era demasiado temprano para esa pregunta.

—Espera… ¿acaso no me vas a leer un libro?

—Lo siento, pero tengo que empezar a escribir el guion esta noche. El señor Ransom quiere que trabaje con una chica de su clase de dramaturgia, así que tengo que pensar en algunas ideas antes de reunirme con ella mañana. Quizás tenga tiempo en un par de días, ¿de acuerdo? —Se dio prisa por llegar al otro lado de la habitación y apagó el interruptor—. Buenas noches, principito.

Me quedé en la cama echando chispas. ¿Por qué mi familia siempre me excluía? ¿Por qué jamás era parte de las cosas?

Cuando empezaron los arañazos en el cristal, en lugar de temor, sentí que la furia formaba una dura bola en mi estómago. Salí de la cama y abrí las cortinas de un tirón. La furia se disipó al instante, sustituida por el asombro.

Mi primera impresión fue la de una piedra oscura, alta y monolítica, que me impedía ver el patio interno, pero que se movía turbulenta, agitándose contra un fondo igualmente lóbrego, como nubes de humo alborotadas. Me acerqué un poco más, intentando calibrar el tamaño del objeto. En ese instante, se movió, la parte superior descendió, y una cara larga y peluda se situó al mismo nivel que la mía, presionando el hocico contra el cristal y exhalando ráfagas de niebla. Sus ojos eran de un naranja intenso.

Empecé a retroceder, pero luego me di cuenta de que solo lo estaba haciendo porque era lo que se suponía que debía hacer. Era lo que hacían las personas en la televisión y en las películas cuando veían un monstruo. En realidad, yo no tenía miedo. Quería ver a ese ser.

La criatura permaneció inmóvil, como comprendiendo y respetando mi deseo. Dejé que mi mirada se detuviera en el pelaje de color marrón, los ojos naranjas y el hocico protuberante mientras apoyaba las garras sobre el cristal. Su ropa era como una sombra viviente, encogiéndose y alejándose de la luz, a veces negra, a veces, roja.

Apoyé una mano sobre el frío cristal y separé los dedos. La criatura ladeó la cabeza y remedó mi movimiento, posando su pata de largas garras justo delante de la mía. Miró nuestras manos y luego me miró de nuevo. No podía sacudirme la sensación de que estaba ante un perro, y me reí un poco. Exhaló con fuerza, empañando el cristal. Sobresaltado, retrocedí un paso. Quizás fuera un perro, pero los perros aún podían morder.

Me moví para mirar a través del cristal no empañado. La criatura también se había retraído dentro de su capa, así que solo permaneció visible su hocico. Asomaba en mi dirección desde el interior, mientras que las cuencas de sus ojos lanzaban un destello color naranja.

Me incliné hacia delante, levantando un dedo.

—Espera un segundo —dije—. ¿Me entiendes?

La criatura levantó un dedo, y asintió lentamente, como ensayando el gesto por primera vez. Me llevé el dedo a los labios para señalarle que hiciera silencio. De nuevo, me imitó.

Dejé que la cortina cayera y crucé el dormitorio hacia mi cubo de juguetes. Abrí el panel delantero lo más silenciosamente posible y metí el brazo con fuerza a través de los bordes afilados de plástico hasta tocar el fondo, donde había ocultado la figura de acción de Batman. Luego cogí mi linterna de la Rana Gustavo de mi mesilla de noche.

Desbloqueé y abrí la ventana lo bastante como para escurrirme a través de ella.

Me quedé de pie sobre el cemento del patio interno, descalzo. La criatura mantuvo la distancia. Erguida hasta alcanzar toda su altura, parecía alcanzar al menos los dos metros de estatura. La mayor parte de su considerable altura estaba oculta por la capa amorfa. Encendí la linterna para verla mejor, pero alzó las garras y apartó la mirada.

—No te gusta eso —dije.

Sacudió la cabeza.

—No.

—Lo siento —dije, y la apagué.

La criatura volvió a mirarme, su respiración húmeda y jadeante. Me sentí incómodo bajo la mirada brillante e inalterable. No estaba acostumbrado a estar tan expuesto ni a llamar la atención. Levanté el Batman.

—¿Tú has traído esto? —pregunté.

Asintió.

—¿Por qué? —pregunté.

La criatura se agachó y levantó un trozo de la tiza que empleaba para dibujar sobre la acera. Realizó varios trazos lentos y temblorosos sobre el suelo. Apunté mi luz a ese sitio y leí una única palabra escrita con letras dentadas apenas legibles: AMIGO.

—Amigo —dije—. ¿Quieres ser mi amigo?

La criatura asintió.

—¿Por qué?

Permaneció agachado ante mí pero sin responder.

Volví a alzar el Batman.

—No has robado esto, ¿verdad?

La criatura sacudió la cabeza. *No.*

A espaldas de ella, la luz de la sala se encendió. ¿Nos había oído alguien? La criatura se encogió sin darse la vuelta, como si incluso esta iluminación velada la afectara.

—Ahora tengo que irme —susurré—. Adiós.

Me volví hacia mi ventana abierta y me agaché para escabullirme dentro. Una de las garras del monstruo aterrizó sobre mi hombro. Tuve la sensación de que me arrastraban, como cuando estás a punto de quedarte dormido. A mi alrededor todo se volvió suave y agradable como una manta...

Me golpeé la cabeza contra la ventana. Estaba otra vez en el patio, acuclillado fuera de mi ventana, con la pata de un monstruo sobre el hombro. Me la quité de encima, avergonzado, como si me hubieran pillado desnudo.

—¿Qué quieres? —pregunté.

La criatura escribió un nuevo mensaje con la tiza, y dirigí mi linterna al suelo para leerlo: ¿DENTRO?

Si lo hubiera pedido antes, habría consentido dejarlo entrar, pero ahora, tras despertar de la dulce neblina, decliné.

—Podría meterme en problemas —le dije. Y luego, tras debatir conmigo mismo un instante, añadí—: Puedes volver mañana si quieres.

No intentó detenerme mientras me escabullía dentro mi habitación. Se quedó mirando al tiempo que el cristal se cerraba deslizándose entre nosotros.

—Buenas noches —susurré, apoyando la mano sobre la ventana. La criatura, mi monstruo, mi Amigo, puso su pata delante de la mía y arañó el cristal, gimoteando quedamente.

CAPÍTULO 13

Una vez que decidieron el concepto, mi familia y el departamento de teatro del instituto empezaron a trabajar de veras. No volvieron a permitir que entrara en el almacén, así que no pude ver nada de ello. En cambio, pasaba mis tardes y noches en la habitación trasera de Monstruos al Acecho, haciendo los deberes y entreteniéndome. Sally me recogía del colegio y me llevaba de vuelta a casa por la noche. Revisaba mis deberes, me metía en la cama, y se quedaba hasta que mi madre, Sydney y Eunice volvieran.

Veía a mi familia solo por las mañanas cuando pasaban unas junto a otras, arrastrando los pies, somnolientas, preparándose para el día. Echaba de menos a Eunice, pero Mi Amigo me venía a visitar cada dos noches, llegando a veces entre el momento en que Sally me despedía con un buenas noches amable aunque rutinario y aquel estado raro y fluctuante entre la vigilia y el sueño. Rasguñaba el cristal tan suavemente como si estuviera sacudiéndome el hombro. Si hubiera sido mayor, o un poco más cuidadoso, o si los adultos me hubieran prestado más atención cuando era pequeño, quizás me habría preocupado ser descubierto allí fuera. Pero estaba demasiado acostumbrado a ser invisible, y fuera como fuera, era difícil preocuparse por algo una vez que llegaba Mi Amigo. Al principio, jugábamos con las figuras de acción, pero las manos fuertes y torpes de la criatura terminaban quitándoles las cabezas y los brazos. Luego lo intentamos con juegos de mesa, pero parecía costarle recordar las reglas, y me cansé de ganar todas las partidas, así que empezamos a revisar mi colección de libros. Primero, le leía yo, y luego copiábamos frases y dibujos. La caligrafía de la criatura siguió siendo deplorable, pero cuando intentamos copiar ilustraciones de *Danny y el dino-saurio*, sus reproducciones terminaron siendo bastante fieles al contenido del libro.

—Se te da bien esto —dije, frustrado al comparar nuestro trabajo sobre la acera con el libro. Mis propios dibujos eran manchas de color toscas e incomprensibles—. Me gustaría dibujar como tú.

La criatura me ofreció un grueso cilindro azul de tiza, que acepté. Se puso detrás de mí, apoyó una pata sobre mi hombro derecho y la otra alrededor de mi muñeca izquierda, y empezó a guiar mi mano sobre el suelo. De nuevo me sentí inundado por aquella sensación increíble de felicidad etérea, de calidez, y consuelo, y deseo satisfecho. Apenas era consciente del cemento delante de mí, como lo sería alguien ante el camino que se extiende al otro lado de un parabrisas manchado y mugriento.

Cuando la criatura me soltó, la sensación se esfumó, y la emprendí contra él, frustrado y desorientado, con la tiza alzada en una mano, listo para pegarle. Mi Amigo también parecía atontado; su cabeza se bamboleaba de un lado a otro. Me dirigió una mirada inquisitiva.

—Lo siento —dije—. No era mi intención.

La criatura señaló por encima de mi hombro. Levanté mi linterna y apunté la luz hacia donde había realizado mi dibujo guiado: una ciudad gigantesca y extensa en miniatura, como vista desde la cima de una colina, que se extendía en círculos concéntricos de imponentes rascacielos. En el medio, el núcleo de esta extraña célula era una torre que se elevaba hasta el cielo. Me resultó familiar, algún sitio en el que ya había estado.

—¿Yo he hecho esto? —pregunté.

La criatura me señaló a mí, luego se señaló a sí misma, y después entrelazó las garras de sus patas. Lo habíamos hecho juntos. Se inclinó hacia delante y escribió la pregunta que realizaba todas las noches sobre el pavimento: ¿DENTRO?

Le di la respuesta de todas las noches:

—Esta noche no.

No le hablé a nadie sobre la criatura, aunque en aquel momento no supe por qué. Llámalo instinto. Ahora que echo la vista atrás, no me preocupaba parecer loco; pero me encantaba tener algo que fuera solamente mío, algo que mi familia no pudiera ocultar ni arrebatarme.

CAPÍTULO 14

La construcción de la casa embrujada (a la que bautizaron con el nombre del Laberinto del Terror) terminó a mediados de septiembre, pero el señor Ransom y los chicos de teatro no se marchaban hasta después de que me hubiera ido a dormir, quedándose para ensayar. Puesto que la llegada de Sydney a casa (anunciada por la luz de la sala detrás de la cortina del patio interior) era la nueva alerta para irme a la cama, empecé a quedarme hasta más y más tarde con el monstruo. Mi rendimiento en primer año, que jamás había sido brillante, empezó a decaer. Sally se aseguraba de que terminara los deberes y los entregara, pero fallaba en los exámenes y me quedaba dormido en clase. Como no estorbaba, mi profesora, la señora Column, no dedicaba mucha energía a mantenerme despierto. Mis días adquirieron un carácter distante un tanto surreal, como si estuviera observando una película larga, aburrida, mal proyectada, que me costaba entender. En aquellas oportunidades en que veía a mi familia, todos estaban preocupados. Solo querían hablar del Laberinto del Terror, que apenas comentaban de modo oblicuo en mi presencia. Hasta Eunice estaba distante. La echaba de menos y sentía celos de ese nuevo proyecto que me la había usurpado.

Por fin, una noche, harto de que me excluyeran de todo, le pregunté al monstruo:

—¿Cómo llegas aquí todas las noches?

Inclinó la cabeza, pero no respondió.

—¿Acaso vuelas?

No lo entendió o no quiso responder.

Me pasé una mano por el pelo y suspiré.

—¿Puedes llevarme a otro sitio?

La criatura se inclinó hacia delante, sostuvo el trozo de tiza, y escribió una pregunta sobre el pavimento: ¿A DÓNDE?

—Quiero ver la casa embrujada —dije—. Llévame al Laberinto del Terror.

Mi amigo se puso en pie y retrocedió. Extendió las garras de su zarpa derecha. Parecía más la mano de un ser humano adulto que la de un horror indescriptible, y a medida que me envolvió con su abrazo, sentí tibieza y solidez.

Me ciñó con fuerza contra su torso, rodeándome con su capa, bajo la cual llevaba una túnica áspera y holgada que me raspó la cara.

Al ponerse en cuclillas, los músculos de sus piernas se endurecieron. Luego el suelo desapareció bajo mis pies, y en su lugar solo sentí un vacío. Alcancé a vislumbrar fugazmente destellos del mundo más abajo, interrumpidos por la tela ondulante de su albornoz: el patio se encogió, revelando el edificio de siete unidades donde vivíamos. Avanzamos inclinándonos de costado hasta que el ángulo cambió y no alcancé a ver más que el negro violáceo del cielo nocturno de Vandergriff contaminado de luces. Las preocupaciones quedaron muy lejos, como una débil señal de radio proveniente de otro estado. Pegado contra la criatura, me dejé llevar, con algo de frío pero sereno, reconfortado, alejado del mundo. La criatura despedía un olor particular, algo fragante y terroso, como el departamento de jardinería de Walmart. La imagen de un inmenso prado de flores bajo un cielo oscuro y cargado invadió mi mente, y, más allá, un horizonte vasto, en el que solo parecían existir las siluetas de agujas, torres y coliseos.

El sobresalto de nuestro aterrizaje me sacó de mi ensueño. Mi Amigo apartó la capa hacia atrás para liberarme. Me alejé dando tumbos, con las piernas flojas y la cabeza mareada y confusa. Tropecé hacia delante y me raspé las manos con el pavimento. El dolor me despejó la cabeza. Nos encontrábamos en el aparcamiento de delante del almacén. La camioneta del señor Ransom estaba aparcada cerca de una de las puertas del garaje, enmarcada en una calavera de poliestireno. Era inquietantemente convincente bajo las farolas del aparcamiento. La criatura se acercó, y le hice un gesto para que se alejara.

—Estoy bien —dije. Tras un momento de respirar aire puro, se me pasó el mareo. Me acerqué a la puerta de la calavera. Mi Amigo permaneció donde habíamos aterrizado.

—¿No vienes conmigo? —pregunté.

Sacudió la cabeza. Le di un tirón a la manilla de la puerta delantera, pero no se movió. Estaba a punto de volverme y decirle a Mi Amigo que lo olvidara, que debíamos volver a casa, cuando la puerta cedió. No se oyó ningún clic ni chispa mágica. Por un momento no se movía, y al siguiente se abrió de par en par.

Las luces de la oficina delantera estaban apagadas, y las dejé así. En lugar de eso, encendí mi linterna. Habían limpiado el salón desde la última vez que había estado allí, y quitado la capa de polvo que lo recubría todo. El escritorio delantero y las sillas de la sala de espera habían desaparecido, y las puertas dobles que conducían al almacén estaban ocultas tras un muro negro con una puerta blanca en el centro; el pomo de latón había perdido su brillo y estaba abollado. Se giró con facilidad en mi mano, y la puerta se abrió hacia dentro silenciosa. Caminé por el oscuro pasillo, que giraba hacia la derecha antes de abrirse a una biblioteca... una especie de sitio donde los médicos y profesores de las películas antiguas solían reunirse para buscar consejo. Una alfombra roja y dorada se extendía sobre el suelo, y un sofá de cuero agrietado se hallaba delante de un enorme escritorio de aspecto antiguo. Detrás del sofá había un falso hogar, oscuro y vacío. Las paredes de la sala estaban cubiertas de cabezas de animales embalsamados, ciervos en su mayoría, aunque de vez en cuando había un alce o un pez fijado a la pared.

Encima del hogar colgaba una tabla de montaje vacía con un hoyo en el centro. Lo escudriñé, intentando ver lo que había detrás, pero la oscuridad permaneció remota e impenetrable. Pensé en el plan inicial de Sydney para aquel sitio: un monstruo acechando a través de un oscuro laberinto y un visitante con una única linterna para abrirse camino. Sabía que era todo falso y el objetivo era divertirse, pero saberlo no me servía cuando estaba justo en mitad del laberinto o cuando había un monstruo real que me aguardaba en el aparcamiento. Un monstruo que se había negado a acompañarme dentro. ¿Quién entendía las nuevas reglas? Seguí adelante, adentrándome más y más en el Laberinto del Terror.

Después de la biblioteca seguía una larga sala rectangular bordeada a ambos lados por lo que supuse que eran archivadores. El suelo era de mosaicos azules, con desagües colocados a intervalos regulares. Dos camillas metálicas para realizar autopsias se hallaban una al lado de la otra en el centro de la sala, ambas vacías. Y en el otro extremo había una puerta de madera con un panel de cristal esmerilado y una frase que no comprendí: OFICINA DEL FORENSE. Al lado de la puerta había un tiesto con una planta enorme.

Me acerqué a uno de los enormes cajones del lado derecho de la sala. Tenía una pequeña etiqueta blanca justo en la mitad, e impresa encima en letras pequeñas y pulcras ponía RESCATE, J. Tiré de la fría manilla metálica, pero no cedió. La solté y continué proyectando mi luz sobre todos los nombres de los cajones: Vogler, Goldman, Daniels, Price. Leí cada uno en voz alta, pronunciando las palabras lo más silenciosamente posible, disfrutando de sus sonidos al vocalizarlas: Sangalli, Smith, Stephens, Turner.

Al pronunciar este último detuve mi mecánica repetición. Turner, H. ¿Sería Harry Turner? Tomé la manilla y tire de ella. Esta se abrió para mí.

Dirigí mi linterna a una caja rectangular que tenía dos metros de profundidad, y contenía un estrecho catre sobre ruedecillas. Sobre el catre yacía un bulto enorme, en líneas generales, con forma humana, bajo una sábana blanca. Extendí la mano para tocarlo.

Una carcajada estalló en el edificio, sonora y alegre. El bulto bajo la sábana se desvaneció de mi mente. Dejé el cajón abierto, pasé junto al tiesto con la planta y crucé la puerta de la OFICINA DEL FORENSE, entrando a un espacio grande y relativamente bien iluminado. Tenía el suelo de madera y un escenario atiborrado de instrumentos. Habían colocado un único micrófono bajo un foco y una pancarta que rezaba ¡BIENVENIDOS A CASA, CHICOS!, en letras blancas, rojas y azules. El suelo estaba cubierto de globos, y dos figuras se hallaban entrelazadas sobre una silla plegable en la mitad de la sala. Incluso de espaldas reconocí la forma del señor Ransom, sus brazos fornidos envueltos alrededor de la adolescente sin camiseta, sentada sobre su regazo. Ella hundió la cara de él en su escote, arrojando la cabeza hacia atrás, con los ojos cerrados y la boca abierta. También la reconocí: Sydney.

—Dilo —dijo.

El señor Ransom gimió, emitiendo gruñidos voraces como los de un cerdo ante un comedero. Ella le aferró el pelo y tiró con fuerza para que tuviera que mirarla. En una película porno, habría estado sonriendo, provocándolo. En cambio, había algo dañado y vulnerable en su cara.

—Dilo —volvió a decir.

—Te quiero —dijo él, con voz ronca y entrecortada.

Ella tiró con más fuerza del pelo del señor Ransom.

—De nuevo —insistió. Quizás intentaba que sonara como una orden, pero parecía que estaba a punto de llorar.

—Te quiero, Sydney —dijo el señor Ransom.

Con la mano libre, Sydney llevó el brazo hacia atrás y se desabrochó el sujetador. Los tirantes se deslizaron de sus hombros y descendieron a lo largo de sus brazos. El hombre realizó otro sonido ahogado y voraz contra el pecho de ella, y mi hermana soltó un grito, como si algo le doliera. El sonido me causó un sobresalto, y solté la linterna. Golpeó el suelo con un estrépito, y los ojos de Sydney se abrieron bruscamente, brillantes por el temor y la sorpresa.

Soltó la cabeza del señor Ransom y su mirada se clavó en la mía.

—¿Noah?

El señor Ransom empezó a girarse. Hui a toda velocidad. Los oí moviéndose mientras volvía corriendo por el laberinto de salas y entraba en el aparcamiento. Yo era pequeño, estaba completamente vestido y me impulsaba el terror, así que salí sin que me atraparan, ileso. Mi Amigo estaba allí donde lo había dejado, y me lancé a sus brazos.

—Llévame a casa —dije. El calor me envolvió al tiempo que la criatura cerraba la capa a mi alrededor y mis pies abandonaban el suelo.

Aterrizamos en lo que parecieron segundos después. La criatura abrió su capa, y volví a pisar el patio conocido. Me incliné hacia delante, vagamente consciente de la criatura en cuclillas junto a mí, raspando el suelo con la tiza. Mi cabeza empezó a despejarse, y estiré la mano hacia la ventana, para abrirla, pero la pata de la criatura se posó sobre mi hombro, y de inmediato todo volvió a tornarse confuso. Me quité su pata de encima.

—¿Qué? —pregunté—. ¿Qué sucede?

Señaló al suelo, y entorné los ojos para leer lo que había escrito en la oscuridad:

¿DENTRO?

—No.

La criatura resopló y garabateó dos palabras más antes de volver a mirarme:

AMIGO

AYUDA

Subrayó la segunda palabra tres veces, y la tiza se rompió con el tercer trazo. Noté su decepción en la postura encorvada y la curva rígida de su cuello.

—No —volví a decir, sacudiendo mi cabeza aún con más firmeza.

No intentó detenerme cuando empujé mi ventana para abrirla y trepar dentro, y para cuando me giré y cerré la ventana había desaparecido.

En cierto momento Sydney entró en el apartamento. Se acercó a la puerta de mi dormitorio, la sombra de sus pies visible a través de la rendija bajo la puerta. Su respiración era agitada y extrañamente fuerte. Parecía haber acabado una maratón, tomando profundas bocanadas de aire que casi sonaban como resuellos, sus exhalaciones, entrecortadas e irregulares. Finalmente, se marchó.

CAPÍTULO 15

Al día siguiente funcioné en piloto automático; estuve distraído durante y después del colegio. Me pasé la tarde en la habitación trasera de Monstruos al Acecho, leyendo una vieja revista doble de Archie con cara de sueño hasta que escuché a Sally hablando con alguien en la parte de delante de la tienda. La persona con la que hablaba se rio, y en el acto reconocí al señor Ransom. Miré alrededor buscando una salida pero permanecí petrificado en mi silla cuando la escuché decir, «Claro, pasa atrás».

El señor Ransom avanzó dando tumbos hasta la sala de descanso, llevando una enorme caja.

—¡Ahí está mi amigo! —dijo. Su voz resonó con alegre histrionismo. La caja parecía lo bastante grande como para meter a un chico dentro si se te ocurría cómo meter el cádaver. Se detuvo delante de mí, impidiéndome ver la puerta principal—. Me alegra que estés aquí. Hay algo que hace tiempo que quiero regalarte. —Apoyó la caja sobre la mesa y se alejó un poco de ella—. Vamos —dijo.

Dejé a un lado mi libro de cómics y me puse de pie sobre mi silla. Al extender las manos hacia las solapas sueltas de la caja, vacilé.

—No te morderá —dijo, la irritación filtrándose en su voz.

Me obligué a dirigir las manos hacia delante y abrí las solapas. Al ver el contenido me quedé sin aliento. Era el set de juego de la Baticueva; el juguete que había codiciado durante semanas estaba justo delante de mí.

—¿Te gusta? —preguntó el señor Ransom.

—¿No es de su hijo? —pregunté.

—Lo era —dijo—, pero sea como sea tiene demasiados juguetes, y vi que te gustó cuando tu familia vino a casa a cenar. —Alzó las cejas, esperando que dijera algo también.

Saqué las manos de la caja.

—Qué amable, señor Ransom, pero de todos modos no tengo una figura de Batman —dije. Era mentira, pero ¿qué explicación probable podía ofrecer respecto a cómo lo había obtenido?—. Solo podría contemplarlo.

Suspiró.

—También te quería traer el Batman de Kyle, pero a pesar de buscarlo por todos lados, no lo he encontrado. Sé que Kyle no se lo llevó consigo, y no he tenido ningún invitado en mi casa desde que tu familia vino de visita. ¿Así que todavía quieres quedarte ahí parado y decirme que no lo tienes?

—Yo no robé el Batman de Kyle —le dije.

—Puedo guardar el secreto si tú también lo haces. ¿Puedes guardar un secreto, Noah?

Miré el juguete nuevo y no respondí.

—Lo que viste anoche —dijo— entre Sydney y yo… era algo privado, para las personas mayores. Si se lo contaras a alguien, tanto tu familia como yo podríamos meternos en problemas. —Caminó alrededor de la mesa y me presionó el hombro con su enorme mano de oso—. No querrás causar problemas a tu familia justo antes de que abra su nuevo negocio, ¿verdad?

—No. —Habría accedido a lo que fuera con tal de que dejara de tocarme.

Empezó a dirigirse a la salida, y luego se detuvo y se giró de nuevo.

—Noah —dijo.

—¿Sí, señor Ransom?

—¿Cómo llegaste al almacén?

Mientras estuviéramos guardándonos los secretos el uno al otro, no veía motivo para mentir.

—Volé —dije.

Me escrutó con una mirada extraña y se marchó.

CAPÍTULO 16

Una vez en casa me escondí en mi habitación, haciéndome un ovillo con la manta sobre la cabeza. Le dije a Sally que no me sentía bien y me dejó solo.

Por fin llegó Eunice y vino a mi habitación. Se sentó a mi lado sobre la cama y me puso una mano sobre el hombro.

—¿Qué sucede? —preguntó.

—Nada —dije.

—Antes nunca me mentías.

Permanecí oculto bajo la manta, reflexionando acerca de los secretos que ahora guardaba: el de Sydney, el del señor Ransom, el mío. Empecé a llorar.

—Noah —murmuró, recorriendo mi espalda de arriba abajo con la mano—. Noah, Noah, Noah. Está bien. No importa lo que sea, está bien.

Aun así no me sentí más liviano. Aunque realizamos de todos modos el ritual de decirnos *te quiero*, se abrió una brecha entre nosotros. Su afecto parecía algo maquinal, y ahora yo era un mentiroso.

Tumbado en la cama, deseé que mi familia no hubiera decidido nunca construir una casa embrujada. Me traía sin cuidado que siguiéramos siendo pobres para siempre si las cosas podían volver a estar como antes. Cuando empezaron los arañazos fuera de la ventana, arrojé las mantas a un lado y levanté el Batman del suelo. Mi Amigo se hallaba fuera, arrastrando las garras contra el cristal. Le hice una seña para que retrocediera, y obedeció. Desbloqueé la ventana y salí.

Cuando me puse en pie, la criatura intentó acortar la distancia entre nosotros. Lo detuve levantando en alto la figura de Batman.

—¿Robaste esto de casa del señor Ransom?

La criatura sacudió la cabeza.

No.

—¿Estás mintiendo? —pregunté.

Bajó la cabeza.

—¿Por qué lo has hecho?

La criatura levantó un trozo de tiza, y rodeó las palabras que había garabateado la noche anterior: AMIGO. AYUDA.

—¿Ayuda? —pregunté—. ¿Ayuda? ¿En qué sentido puede resultar esto una ayuda? —Estaba furioso por la injusticia de todo ello, por el modo en que me habían pillado y abrumado con aquella carga—. Podrías meterme en muchos problemas. Vete.

La criatura se puso de pie, todavía aferrando la tiza con extraña delicadeza entre las garras. Inclinó la cabeza con aparente perplejidad.

—Sé que me entiendes. Vete —dije, ahuyentándolo con las manos. Se mantuvo inmóvil. Arrojé el Batman, y lo golpeó justo encima del ojo izquierdo. Su cabeza se sacudió hacia atrás y soltó la tiza. Sus ojos brillaron con un matiz de naranja más intenso. Un gruñido profundo brotó de su garganta. Detrás de él, la puerta corrediza de cristal se iluminó al encenderse la luz de la sala. La criatura se dio la vuelta, advirtiéndolo también. Me agaché para pasar por mi ventana y la cerré de un tirón justo cuando oí el pestillo de la puerta corrediza de cristal deslizándose por su riel con un grato murmullo. Me quedé quieto tras las cortinas, esperando gritos de susto o incluso de violencia. En cambio, oí las pisadas inconfundibles de mi madre sobre el cemento, deteniéndose por fuera de mi ventana y luego retirándose dentro. Si vio las inscripciones sobre el suelo, jamás me dijo nada acerca de ello.

Seguí despierto cuando Sydney entró en casa alrededor de la medianoche y se dirigió directo al lavabo. Cerró la puerta y abrió el grifo, pero podía oír su voz áspera y quebrada por encima del rugido del agua. Sydney, agitada, sollozando a solas en mitad de la noche.

CAPÍTULO 17

Dos días antes de que el Laberinto del Terror abriera al público, el señor Ransom volvió a invitar a mi familia a cenar a su casa, prometiendo que esta vez sí prepararía una verdadera cena hogareña. Esta vez Sally no vino con nosotros, pero le prestó a mi madre el coche para el viaje. Cuando llegamos a la casa de los Ransom, encontramos un Ford Fiesta aparcado junto a la camioneta del dueño de la casa en el camino de entrada.

—¿Quién más vendrá a cenar? —preguntó Eunice.

—A mí no me ha dicho nada —respondió mi madre.

Sydney miró hacia delante, muda en el asiento delantero, e intenté interpretar lo que sucedía mirándole la nuca. Habíamos estado evitándonos con gran éxito desde que la había pillado con el señor Ransom, y esta era la primera vez en más de una semana que estábamos juntos en el mismo sitio durante más de unos minutos.

Habían cortado el césped, retirado los periódicos y podado la rama errante, así que ya no bloqueaba el sendero. Cuando llamamos al timbre, una mujer menuda y delgada, apenas más alta que Eunice, respondió. Si no hubiera sido por las líneas de risa alrededor de la boca, podía haber confundido a Janet Ransom con una chica cuando esta enfundó a mi madre en un abrazo.

—¡Me alegro de verte, Margaret!

Mamá devolvió el abrazo un instante demasiado tarde; su sorpresa e incomodidad, aparentes en su postura. La señora Ransom la soltó y nos estrechó a Eunice y a mí en un abrazo tieso e incómodo.

—Eunice, eres toda una jovencita —dijo—. Y, Noah, pareces una versión en miniatura de tu padre. Qué asombroso.

Nadie me había señalado aquello jamás, y seguía procesándolo cuando la señora Ransom ciñó a Sydney con el abrazo más fuerte y largo.

—Oh, Sydney —dijo, aferrando la nuca de mi hermana como si fuera un bebé.

Mi hermana también tardó un poco en devolverle el abrazo.

—Oh, sí, soy yo —dijo.

El señor Ransom apareció en el umbral, limpiándose las manos en un paño de cocina.

—Sorpresa —dijo, con voz débil.

—No le echéis la culpa a él. Fue idea mía —dijo la señora Ransom—. ¡Entrad! ¡Entrad!

Habían ventilado el interior de la casa: el aire estaba fresco y fragante. Las luces centelleaban, y habían quitado el polvo de los muebles. En mitad de la sala había un chico jugando sobre el suelo con una Nintendo que no había estado antes allí.

—Kyle —dijo el señor Ransom—. ¡Modales!

El chico suspiró y se puso en pie. Estrechó la mano de todos.

—Tú eres Noah —dijo cuando le tocó el turno de estrechar la mía; el tedio se transformó en hostilidad—. Tú tienes mi Batman y mi Baticueva.

—Noah, ¿robaste los juguetes de Kyle? —preguntó mi madre. Hacía una semana que la Baticueva se hallaba dentro de su caja en mi habitación, y ella no lo había advertido.

—El señor Ransom me la regaló —dije.

—¿Ah, sí? —preguntó mi madre. Se asomó a la cocina, donde el señor Ransom iba de un lado a otro, revisando el horno, revolviendo el contenido de una enorme olla.

—Daniel se ha encariñado mucho con Noah —dijo la señora Ransom—, y supongo que un día se sintió generoso. —Su sonrisa parecía demasiado amplia, como si, a pesar de las palabras que salían de su boca, creyera con absoluta certeza que yo era culpable de haberle robado a su hijo.

La mirada que mi madre le dirigió al señor Ransom pasó a un gesto ceñudo.

—De todos modos, si Kyle quiere que le devuelvan sus juguetes, estoy seguro de que Noah no tendrá problemas en devolvérselos.

—Tonterías —dijo la señora Ransom—. No vamos a aceptar que nos devuelvan un regalo, ¿verdad, Kyle?

—No —respondió el niño, sombrío.

—¿Por qué no le enseñas a Noah tu habitación? —preguntó.

—Ven —dijo, y lo seguí por el corredor.

Su habitación tenía casi el mismo aspecto que el que tenía la última vez que había estado allí, solo que menos polvorienta y sin su Baticueva. Una infinidad de juguetes de los Cazafantasmas se hallaban diseminados sobre la alfombra.

—¿Te gustan los Cazafantasmas? —pregunté.

—Me gusta más Batman.

—Te lo devolveré.

Parecía que nada lo habría hecho más feliz, pero sabía muy bien que no debía acceder.

—Me metería en problemas. Es muy idiota. Mi madre se puso furiosa con mi padre cuando se enteró de lo de la Baticueva, pero ahora tampoco permite que me la devuelvan. Mi padre me ha comprado una Nintendo para disculparse. Mi madre también se ha enfadado por eso.

—¿Se enfurece bastante?

Sonrió un poco.

—Todo el tiempo.

En ese momento el señor Ransom nos llamó a la mesa. Kyle y yo nos sentamos uno al lado del otro; la atmósfera entre nosotros se despejó y desapareció la hostilidad. Comimos juntos en amigable silencio mientras los adultos conversaban.

—Vaya… —dijo mi madre cuando ya nos habíamos sentado todos y efectuado los comentarios de rigor acerca de lo delicioso que parecía y olía todo. Señaló hacia el señor y la señora Ransom, sentados a la cabeza y al pie de la mesa—, esto *sí* que es una sorpresa.

—¿Cuánto lleváis con esto? —exigió Sydney.

—Sydney, modales —dijo mi madre.

—Hace alrededor de un mes —respondió el señor Ransom.

—¿Un *mes*? —Sydney le dirigió una mirada feroz. Este le echó un vistazo, y luego se cruzó con mi mirada. Kyle miró alrededor de la mesa, confundido por la repentina tensión. Me atiborré la boca de comida, fingiendo haberme olvidado de todo.

—Sydney, ¿qué sucede? —preguntó mi madre.

Mi hermana presionó una servilleta hecha una bola en un puño. Con el pulgar y el dedo índice, rasgó fragmentos diminutos de papel de un extremo y los dejó caer sobre la mesa. También parecía respirar con dificultad, pero no creo que ninguno de los adultos notara esa mínima alteración en el movimiento de sus hombros, pecho y espalda. Era buena actuando. Se trataba del tipo de cambio sutil que solo un hermano puede detectar.

—Señor Ransom, nos vemos todos los días —dijo—. Jamás me había contado nada.

—No le corresponde al señor Ransom contarte su vida personal —señaló mi madre—. Es tu profesor, no tu amigo.

El señor Ransom bebió un sorbo de su copa de vino.

—No parecía apropiado, Sydney —dijo.

—Daniel me ha contado cosas increíbles sobre la coreografía que has preparado para el salón de baile de la casa embrujada —dijo la señora Ransom. Extendió la mano por encima de la mesa para coger la de ella—. Me encantaría ir a verla y quizás darte algunos consejos.

Sydney tragó con fuerza, y la vi controlar su respiración.

—Por supuesto —dijo—. Me encantaría que me diera algunos consejos.

—Una cierta vidriosidad en la comisura de sus ojos, que apenas se notó antes de que volviera a endurecer su mirada, me hizo daño en lo más profundo.

CAPÍTULO 18

Cuando llegamos a casa, Sydney permaneció en la puerta mientras el resto entramos en la sala para quitarnos las chaquetas y los zapatos. Se quedó de pie, recortada contra la puerta abierta, con los brazos apretados con fuerza alrededor de su estómago.

—¿Sydney? —preguntó mi madre, con las manos detenidas sobre los cordones del calzado deportivo.

—Todo esto es un gran error —dijo.

—¿A qué te refieres? —preguntó mi madre.

Sydney sacudió apenas la cabeza.

—Me refiero a que renuncio.

Mamá hizo una pausa al quitarse uno de sus zapatos.

—¿Renuncias a qué?

—Al Laberinto de Terror —respondió—. Renuncio. No trabajaré más. Está todo mal, y no quiero seguir participando de él.

—Inauguramos pasado mañana —dijo mi madre.

—No es mi problema —respondió mi hermana. Caminó por el pasillo hacia la habitación de las chicas.

—Por supuesto que es tu problema, jovencita —dijo mi madre. Se levantó para ir a por ella enfurecida, pero se tropezó con los cordones desatados. Evitó caerse apoyándose contra la pared del pasillo y siguió avanzando hacia la habitación de las chicas con pasos largos y precavidos. No cerró la puerta tras ella, así que Eunice y yo pudimos oír la conversación que siguió:

—Hemos hecho todo esto… todo este proyecto estúpido, sacrificado y *desquiciado*… por ti —dijo mi madre—. Es tu criatura, tu concepto, tu sueño. No tienes derecho a renunciar.

—¡Desde el principio has boicoteado todo el maldito proyecto! —gritó mi hermana—. No es mi culpa que te guardaras los diseños de papá y lo arruinaras.

—No hay *ningún* diseño —dijo mi madre—. ¡Jamás los hubo! Hay una colección de tonterías que tu padre dibujó mientras se moría de un tumor cerebral. Era algo que hicimos para pasar el tiempo mientras esperábamos el final. No hay nada allí.

Un silencio salió flotando de la habitación y recorrió el pasillo, lo bastante largo como para que Eunice y yo tuviéramos tiempo de mirarnos en lugar de dirigir la vista al corredor.

—Estás mintiendo —dijo Sydney por fin, su voz empequeñecida.

—No —dijo mi madre. Bajó también la voz, adoptando la delicadeza que se espera de una madre que consuela a su hijo. Aquella delicadeza me produjo una punzada por dentro, un ansia real: mi madre casi nunca hablaba con aquel tono de voz.

—¿Entonces por qué los guardaste para ti? ¿Por qué no dejas que nadie los vea? —preguntó Sydney.

—No tengo que responder ninguna de esas preguntas —seguía hablando con delicadeza, pero se percibió por debajo la dureza familiar.

—Y yo ya no tengo que trabajar en esta maldita casa embrujada —dijo Sydney—. Tú y el señor Ransom podéis divertiros juntos.

No sé quién dio el portazo cuando mi madre abandonó la habitación. Empezó a caminar por el pasillo hacia la sala y volvió a tropezarse con los cordones. Esta vez no pudo sujetarse a la pared, y en cambio cayó hacia delante sobre el suelo de linóleo, maldiciendo. Aterrizó sobre las manos y las rodillas, se sentó y se arrancó los zapatos, arrojándolos a la sala. Un instante después, ella misma siguió el mismo derrotero, echando chispas. Sentí un escalofrío cuando su mirada exaltada se detuvo en mí, y luego en Eunice.

—¿Alguno de vosotros tiene idea de lo que está sucediendo? —preguntó.

—No —respondió mi hermana. Parecía realmente sorprendida.

Estuve a punto de confesar y contarle lo que había visto. Anhelaba quitarme de encima el peso de lo que sabía, dejar que un adulto lidiara con ello, pero había hecho una promesa. Incluso había recibido un pago a cambio de mi silencio.

CAPÍTULO 19

Mi madre y el señor Ransom reemplazaron a Sydney con otra chica del departamento de teatro. Mi hermana pasó la mayor parte de los dos días anteriores al estreno en su habitación, en pijama. No preguntó por el Laberinto del Terror, y directamente dejó de pelear con mi madre. Si ella le decía que hiciera algo, Sydney lo hacía sin protestar.

Aunque ahora era mi niñera de facto, seguíamos evitándonos. Me mantuve alejado de la habitación de las chicas, donde parecía hablar durante horas seguidas, con un tono demasiado bajo para poder escucharla en secreto. No sabía si estaba hablando por teléfono o leyendo sus obras de teatro favoritas en voz alta, y mantuve las distancias. Cuando salía para ver la televisión, me retiraba a mi habitación. Intenté jugar con mi nuevo Batman y Baticueva un par de veces, pero la experiencia era amarga y triste. Era la primera vez que obtenía algo que deseaba pero de un modo equivocado, y esa circunstancia arruinó el regalo.

La noche del estreno mi madre y Eunice me abrazaron y me hicieron prometer que me portaría bien con Sydney. Esta les deseó suerte. Mi madre volvió a dirigirle una mirada extrañada y penetrante, como si supiera que algo iba mal, quizás incluso sospechara la naturaleza del problema, pero temiera preguntar y saberlo a ciencia cierta.

Después de que se marcharan, Sydney se sentó a mi lado sobre el sofá, donde veía la televisión. Cuando me puse de pie para marcharme, me puso una mano sobre el hombro y me pidió que me quedara. Nos quedamos sentados en silencio un rato, y me quedé tan absorto en el programa que cuando por fin habló me sobresalté.

—Hay algo que no entiendo —dijo—. ¿Cómo llegaste al almacén?

No respondí. Puso los ojos en blanco y emitió un sonido de desagrado, poniéndose de pie furiosa. Se dirigió a la habitación de las chicas en el instante en que alguien llamaba a la puerta.

—Ve y abre, ¿vale? —me dijo.

Abrí la puerta, pero encontré el porche vacío. Salí fuera y miré a mi alrededor. El aparcamiento también parecía desierto; no había otra cosa más que coches vacíos bajo las luces parpadeantes. Además, estaba más silencioso de lo que jamás lo había oído. Por lo general podía oírse el tráfico o los sonidos de los vecinos en sus porches. Ahora era como si estuviera encendida la televisión con el volumen completamente apagado.

—¿Quién es? —pregunté. Mi voz resultaba fuerte en el silencio artificial.

Dentro del apartamento, Sydney soltó un grito.

Corrí de nuevo adentro, dejando la puerta abierta a mis espaldas. Abrí la puerta de su dormitorio de par en par. La habitación era un caos: cajones abiertos, ropa en pilas desordenadas, las camas sin hacer, libros abiertos y colocados boca abajo… Pero salvo yo, no había nadie. Las cortinas se mecían ligeramente delante de una ventana abierta que daba a nuestro porche delantero. ¿Había estado abierta al acudir a abrir la puerta? No lo recordaba, pero lo dudaba.

Volví a la puerta principal y miré la ventana abierta desde fuera. Además de abierta, parecía estar en condiciones perfectamente normales. No había ni sangre, ni objetos caídos, ni cristal roto.

—¿Sydney? —llamé.

Detrás de mí se apagaron las luces de todo el apartamento. Me quedé quieto, escuchando. Empezó un nuevo sonido, tan débil que apenas podía oírlo fuera del silencioso apartamento: *crich-crich-crich*.

Me dirigí a mi habitación. *Crich-crich-crich* contra la ventana, suave y titubeante. Al acercarme, el sonido se volvió más fuerte, más excitado. Corrí las cortinas de un tirón. Mi Amigo estaba en el patio, encorvado, con las palmas extendidas sobre el cristal. Parecía asustado, de algún modo transmitiendo su preocupación con sus opacos ojos de color naranja. Apoyé la mano sobre el cristal, delante de la suya, y sentí su increíble calor a través de la barrera.

Descorrí el cerrojo de la ventana y la abrí por completo. Me hice a un lado y le señalé que entrara.

—Amigo —dije—. Ayuda.

La secuencia Turner III: Eunice

Cuando Eunice llega a la Ciudad, la ponen a trabajar
detrás de un escritorio. En su mente lo percibe como
varios escritorios. En primer lugar, lo percibe como el
que tenía en la habitación que ocupaba en la antigua casa
donde vivía mientras su padre aún estaba vivo. Se imagina
desvelada, machacando las teclas de su Commodore 64. Le
encanta el sonido de sus dedos, un suave chasquido
melódico que acompaña el discurrir de sus pensamientos. A
veces cierra los ojos porque las palabras fluyen mejor en
la más completa oscuridad, liberadas de su mirada
arbitraria. Otras veces deja los ojos abiertos pero aparta
la mirada, para darles un descanso de la intensa luz de la
pantalla. Ahora, en esta réplica de su viejo dormitorio,
vuelve la cabeza hacia la derecha, dirigiéndola a su
ventana alta y estrecha… y entonces es cuando ve la cara
escudriñándola.

En la vida real gritó y se metió en la cama, pero ahora
se incorpora y se acerca a la ventana para ver mejor. Pero
por más cerca que esté, la figura sigue siendo una mancha
negra al otro lado del cristal, una sombra incierta. Parece
parpadear, paralizada entre dos posiciones, como una imagen
en una cinta de vídeo detenida. Por algún motivo, está
atrapada. Debería sentir alivio, pero en cambio se siente
apesadumbrada, desanimada, abatida de un modo que no
consigue identificar, como si estuviera enferma pero sin
los síntomas, sin fiebre, sin dolor de cabeza, sin náuseas,
pero presa del desaliento. El sentimiento crece al mirar la
figura en la ventana.

Intranquila, camina hacia su escritorio y se sienta, pero al apoyarse, se encuentra en un área enorme y bien iluminada. En lugar de la dura silla de madera del escritorio de su niñez, está sobre una silla plegable de metal, y el escritorio y el ordenador han sido sustituidos por una mesa de juego plegable y una horrible máquina de escribir eléctrica marrón. Está sentada en mitad del almacén de su familia a finales del verano de 1989, escribiendo el guion original del Laberinto del Terror.

Si hubiera estado trabajando sola, Eunice se habría instalado en la oficina principal, donde todo está más tranquilo, pero su coguionista, Merrin Price, quiere estar allí. Después de todo, se trata de un proyecto grupal, y Merrin cree que escribirán un mejor guion teniendo a todo el equipo a su alrededor inspirándolas. Eunice no está segura de creérselo, pero Merrin es mayor, así que deja que sea ella quien lo decida.

Eunice siempre ha sido la escritora de la familia, así que se siente ofendida cuando el señor Ransom insiste en que Merrin sea su coautora. No puede quitarse de encima la sensación de que se la han endosado. La chica es un poco demasiado rolliza para desempeñar papeles principales, y tiene una voz frágil que se quiebra cuando la presionan demasiado. Cuando actúa sobre el escenario, parece abrumarse, y lo que sea que tenga de especial o singular se pierde por completo, sobre todo cuando la comparan con Sydney.

Eunice puede identificarse con ello: durante toda su vida ha observado al mundo darle el paso a su hermana como el Mar Rojo, mientras ella corre detrás, esperando no ahogarse. Aun así, no tiene ganas de tener a Merrin controlándola mientras escribe. No se queja porque jamás se queja. Estando mamá y Sydney en guerra perpetua, la responsabilidad por mantener la paz siempre recae en ella, al margen de lo que sienta.

Eunice se remueve en su asiento y ve a Merrin junto a ella. Esta sonríe, y algo se afloja en su pecho. Puede respirar mejor. La figura oscura en la ventana de su dormitorio desaparece de su mente. El recuerdo adquiere un matiz tenue y descolorido, como una mala fotocopia de una máquina cuyo tóner está a punto de acabarse.

¿Por dónde quieres empezar? pregunta Merrin.

Eunice se enfrenta a la máquina de escribir, apoya los dedos sobre las teclas de inicio. Respira profundo, cierra los ojos y empieza a teclear. Cada golpe de tecla suena como un disparo minúsculo, y el carro resuena cada vez que llega al final de una línea:

Vosotros los visitantes entraréis a un almacén conducidos por una especie de portero. Contará a los integrantes de su grupo, y, si son un número primo (tres, cinco o siete), levantará su walkie-talkie y emitirá una sola palabra: Innsmouth. Al entrar habrá una chica parada justo en el interior.

—Había demasiadas personas en mi grupo —dirá—. Espero que me permitáis acompañaros. Soy Katie —dirá. Sonreirá. Nadie pensaría en rechazar a esta chica.

Vuestro grupo entra en una sala oscura. El portero cierra la puerta detrás de vosotros, sellándoos dentro, sumiéndoos en la oscuridad más absoluta. Os dejan así el tiempo suficiente para notar una tranquilidad escalofriante. La respiración de vuestros amigos se torna fuerte. Os preguntáis si os han olvidado o si debéis seguir adelante a ciegas. Oís un clic, un único haz de luz que se enciende de golpe, dirigido directamente a vuestras caras cegándoos.

—No deberíais estar aquí —dirá la voz. Se escurrirá como un cubo de hielo que os han echado por la espalda. Esta es LA GUÍA.

La campanilla de la máquina de escribir suena, indicando
el final de otra línea. Eunice golpea la tecla de retorno y
el carro vuelve a toda velocidad a su posición inicial. Se
sacude la rigidez de las manos y mira por encima del hombro
a Merrin. Los ojos de la chica se desplazan de la hoja a la
cara de Eunice.

Me acabas de dar escalofríos, dice Merrin. Eunice nota
por primera vez que sus ojos son azules.

La habitación vuelve a cambiar, y ahora Eunice está
sentada a la mesa del desayuno de su casa, delante de su
hermano menor, Noah. Ahora solo lo ve por las mañanas. Sigue
levantándolo para ir al colegio, sigue asegurándose de que
esté vestido y alimentado, pero no tiene tiempo para leerle
o responder a su letanía de preguntas acerca del mundo. Por
el motivo que sea, ha dejado de pedirle esas cosas. Se ha
convertido en una presencia lánguida y silenciosa, con
bolsas oscuras bajo los ojos caídos. Es raro. Eunice se
siente más plena ahora que antes, como si ahora estuviera
más completa. Se pregunta por un instante si de algún modo
su ascenso se vincula con el descenso de su hermano pequeño.

No le gusta la idea. Aparta la mirada de él y se
encuentra de nuevo en el almacén, delante de la máquina de
escribir. Mientras ella y Merrin escriben, el edificio se
llena con el gemido de las sierras y los taladros, con el
estruendo de los martillos. A ellos se une el repiqueteo de
las máquinas de coser, el siseo metálico de tijeras
cortando tela. El esqueleto se forma alrededor de las
autoras de esta producción: la morgue, la biblioteca, el
salón de baile y una serie infinita de corredores. El pecho
de Eunice se llena de luz, tan intensa que debe de estar
brillándole a través de los dientes. No sabía que era
posible sentirse así. No comprendía lo apagada, y gris, y
cansada, y desganada que se sentía hasta este momento,
sentada junto a Merrin y soñando con modos de aterrorizar y
deleitar a desconocidos.

En realidad, está soñando con modos de aterrar y
deleitar a Merrin. Si la chica reacciona a una idea o una
línea, si se ríe o grita o le da una palmada a Eunice en la
espalda, ella sabe que es bueno. La primera vez que Merrin
toca a Eunice, ella se sobresalta en su silla y escribe una
tontería sobre la página.

Lo siento, dice Merrin, y se aparta.

Sin contar los empujones accidentales de los
desconocidos del público, es la primera vez en años que
alguien que no es Noah ha tocado a Eunice.

No pasa nada, dice. Un calor sube por el hombro hacia
sus mejillas y orejas. *Solo estaba concentrada, y me has
sorprendida.*

Lo siento, dice Merrin. *No volverá a pasar.*

No, en serio, no pasa nada, repite. Se reacomoda en su
silla y se encara a la máquina de escribir. *Aquí. Inténtalo
de nuevo. Finge que he escrito algo superlativo.*

Por un instante, no sucede nada, y le preocupa haber
vuelto las cosas irrevocablemente incómodas. Luego la mano
de Merrin aterriza sobre su hombro.

Tu trabajo es superlativo, Eunice, dice, acercando la
boca a su oreja. Eunice arde.

Se toman sus descansos delante de la máquina de
escribir, comiendo el almuerzo directamente de las bolsas
de papel marrón. El aire acondicionado está encendido, pero
las puertas están abiertas, y el aire está denso y quieto.
El sudor se acumula y brilla en el hueco de la garganta de
Merrin, y a Eunice le preocupa si está sentada demasiado
cerca o lejos para el gusto de esta.

¿Tienes novio?, le pregunta Merrin.

Eunice sacude la cabeza.

Aún no.

¿Cuántos años tienes?

Trece.

Merrin asiente, masticando una uva.

¿Y tú?, pregunta Eunice. *Apuesto a que has tenido miles de novios.*

Merrin se ríe, un sonido gutural y sorprendido. *No muchos chicos quieren salir con una chica gorda.*

No lo eres, dice Eunice, porque es lo que se supone que debe decir cuando alguien se menosprecia a sí mismo.

Merrin sacude la mano desestimando el comentario. *No pasa nada. Ya lo he aceptado. Pero tú... eres muy delgada, así que imagino que es solo cuestión de tiempo.*

Eunice inclina la cabeza para mirar su cuerpo. Es delgada, tiene el pecho plano, las caderas estrechas y nalgas pequeñas. Cuando Sydney tenía trece años, su figura cambió, y las curvas cambiaron los planos lisos de su cuerpo, transformándola en mujer. El cuerpo de Eunice sigue obstinándose en ser como el de un niño.

Vuelve a mirar a Merrin, observa el movimiento de su boca alrededor de la fruta. Sostiene el siguiente mordisco en una mano y cruza el otro brazo sobre el estómago como intentando ocultarse. Lleva una camiseta negra y vaqueros azules que le ciñen el cuerpo amplio y voluminoso. Las uñas de sus dedos están pintadas de rojo, pero el esmalte está saltándose. Sus ojos son de un color azul brillante, sus mejillas regordetas, rosadas y encendidas; su pelo oscuro corto y marrón enmarca su cara. Eunice observa el suave descenso de sus hombros, las nalgas anchas y redondas, y cree que el cuerpo de Merrin es lo opuesto al suyo, agresivo y explícitamente femenino.

Merrin nota su mirada y deja de masticar. *¿Qué?*, dice con la boca aún llena de comida.

Si fuera un chico me gustaría salir contigo, dice Eunice. Siente la cara acalorada e inclina la cabeza, pero la habitación ha vuelto a cambiar. Sigue sentada a la mesa, pero ahora su máquina de escribir ha desaparecido y está rodeada de otras personas. Es el día de la audición, cuando Sydney y el señor Ransom harán el reparto de los papeles que Eunice y Merrin han creado.

Eunice jamás ha tenido que escuchar a nadie más interpretar su trabajo, y se ruboriza cuando los aspirantes leen sus líneas. Realiza interminables notas sobre cómo arreglar sus múltiples defectos como escritora (y ser humano). Cuando llega el momento de elegir el papel del Guía, Eunice levanta la mirada de su libreta para ver un salón de baile lleno de personas mirándola.

¿Qué?, dice.

Merrin dice que quieres leer para el papel, dice el señor Ransom.

Cuando Eunice abre la boca para protestar, Merrin le da un pequeño empujón. Camina hacia el centro de la sala bajo el escrutinio general. Quiere huir, salir gritando, furiosa con Merrin. ¿Cómo se atreve a hacer esto? Pero luego Eunice la ve mirándola y guiñándole el ojo.

Cuando estés lista, dice el señor Ransom.

Eunice carraspea, echa un vistazo a la copia de su guion, y empieza a leer.

No deberíais estar aquí. Carraspea de nuevo, o intenta hacerlo. Tiene algo atascado que no se mueve. *¿Cómo habéis entrado? Las paredes aquí se vuelven delgadas, cada vez más desconcertantes. Hay puertas donde solía haber muros, y en lugar de luz prolifera la oscuridad. El único modo de salir es atravesarlo hasta el otro lado. No puedo acompañaros, pero puedo ofreceros ayuda.* Esto suena como una mala versión de Tolkien. ¿Quién ha escrito esto? ¿A quién se le puede pedir que diga esto en voz alta? *Un único haz de luz, para enseñaros el camino. Usadlo con discreción.* Realiza un gesto vago para simular la entrega de la linterna a un visitante. *Oh, y una advertencia. Una gran desgracia que solía estar contenida anda suelta. Deambula a sus anchas, sin importar que haya paredes o puertas. Así que debo advertiros: por mucho que escuchéis o veáis, intentad no hacer demasiado ruido. El sonido atraerá a la criatura. Que tengáis suerte.*

Eunice levanta la vista, mirando de nuevo al público de
caras que la observan. Ojalá tuviera la habilidad de
desaparecer.

Gracias, dice, esperando que le pidan que se retire.

El señor Ransom y Sydney cruzan una mirada, y luego la
vuelven a mirar.

Eunice, ¿quieres este papel?, pregunta el profesor.

Eunice dirige la mirada más allá del señor Ransom, más
allá de las caras reunidas, a Merrin. Esta le hace una
señal con el pulgar hacia arriba.

Creo que sí, dice.

El señor Ransom le dice: *es tuyo.*

Eunice vuelve caminando a la mesa. Merrin le da una
palmada en el brazo y sonríe feliz. ¿Qué haría falta, se
pregunta Eunice, para sentirse así todos los días?

Se da la vuelta para mirarla, para decir algo, pero de
nuevo vuelve a cambiar la sala. Ahora está de pie en un
espacio pequeño, encerrado, agobiante y oscuro, junto a una
mesa con linternas y botellas de agua en el suelo de debajo.
Mira hacia abajo: lleva una túnica encapuchada color blanco.
Está en la puerta principal del Laberinto del Terror, la
noche de estreno, interpretando el papel de Guía.

Han sido dos días cargados de tensión. Sydney renunció
en el último minuto, y tuvieron que buscar a otra actriz
para reemplazar su papel; ahora es Merrin la que interpreta
el gran número de jazz en el salón de baile. Noah sigue sin
tener buen aspecto, y le preocupa, pero es una preocupación
distante, porque en algún lugar, no lejos de allí, Eunice
puede oír visitas que ríen y gritan, y sabe que el
Laberinto del Terror está funcionando. La gente se está
divirtiendo. Se imagina una dramaturga, ocultándose en el
vestíbulo del teatro, escuchando sus espectáculos a través
de puertas cerradas. Realiza una reverencia en la
oscuridad, mirando al centro del edificio. Desearía que su
padre estuviera vivo para ver esto.

Mira, piensa. *Mira lo que hemos hecho para ti*. Se pregunta cómo le va a Merrin en el salón de baile.

Más tarde, cuando todo el mundo se quita el maquillaje y se vuelve a cambiar para ponerse su ropa habitual, Eunice encuentra su máquina de escribir en un rincón del camerino. Deja de cambiarse un instante para apoyar la mano encima de ella. Merrin se acerca y la abraza desde atrás.

¿Acariciando tu máquina de escribir?, pregunta.

Deberíamos hacerle un monumento, dice Eunice, inclinándose hacia el abrazo. *¿Has oído al público esta noche? ¿Es así siempre? ¿Montar una obra?*

Cuando tenemos una buena noche, dice Merrin antes de soltarla. *Oye, ¿qué harás ahora?*

Nada, dice Eunice, intentando sonar despreocupada aun cuando el corazón le galopa en el pecho. *¿Por qué? ¿Quieres hacer algo?*

Merrin se pasa la lengua por los labios. *Brian Smith y yo vamos a ir a su casa a pasar el rato. Tiene un hermano pequeño que tiene casi tu edad. He pensado que quizás podríais congeniar.*

Eunice hace lo posible por no parecer completamente abatida. *Oh, vaya, qué amable eres, Merrin.*

¿Qué sucede?, pregunta.

Le lleva a Eunice un lapso de tiempo vergonzosamente largo pensar en una respuesta. *No pasa nada. Pero le prometí a Noah que esta noche lo acostaría. Hace mucho que no lo hago, ¿sabes?*

¿Qué he hecho?, pregunta Merrin.

Eunice aún no se ha terminado de quitar toda la pintura de la cara, pero se dirige al perchero donde cuelga su ropa de calle. Merrin la sigue.

¿Me puedes decir por favor qué he hecho mal?, insiste Merrin.

En serio. Se lo prometí a Noah, dice Eunice. Se quita la túnica y la cuelga en el perchero. Luego empieza a vestirse.

Entonces, otra vez será, dice Merrin.

Claro. Eunice percibe la mirada de Merrin, esperando que se dé la vuelta, pero no lo hace. Se sitúa de espaldas a ella hasta que se marcha.

De pronto, Eunice no puede mantenerse en pie. Vuelve a la máquina de escribir y se sienta. No llora. No aquí. Cierra los ojos e intenta no ver a Merrin, intenta ni siquiera pensar en ella. No ha tenido malas intenciones. Creía que estaba haciendo algo bueno. Eunice sencillamente quería un favor diferente. Quería escucharla pronunciar las palabras prohibidas, que validara esa sensación de podredumbre que siente en lo más profundo que le provoca vergüenza y temor de sí misma.

Cuando levanta la mirada, está en una habitación diferente. Al principio, le cuesta comprender lo que ve. Da la impresión de ser una enorme sala con techos abovedados y un suelo de mármol extenso y vacío que refleja la luz de la luna. Las paredes parecen hechas de un material negro que se retuerce, como tentáculos que se deslizan unos sobre otros. Pero luego está de vuelta en el dormitorio de la casa antigua, y tiene otra vez seis años, y la máquina de escribir es la Commodore 64. Mira las palabras en la pantalla: *Una gran desgracia que solía estar contenida anda suelta. Deambula a sus anchas, sin importar que haya paredes o puertas.*

Se da la vuelta de nuevo hacia la pantalla. Sus manos permanecen en su regazo cuando aparece otra línea en el monitor:

Por mucho que escuchéis o veáis, intentad no hacer demasiado ruido. El sonido atraerá a la criatura. Que tengáis suerte.

De algún sitio cercano le llega el sonido de risas, y aquí en la Ciudad, donde existe dentro y fuera del tiempo, reconoce el sonido. Es Noah, su hermano pequeño, haciendo demasiado ruido para esta hora de la noche. Vuelve a mirar

la ventana para ver si la figura que está allí también lo
ha oído, pero la figura ha desaparecido.

Siente un dolor agudo en el pecho. La cara de Merrin
desaparece de su imaginación, sustituida por una imagen de
Noah. *Una gran desgracia que solía estar contenida anda
suelta.* Eunice se pregunta, y ella, ¿qué gran desgracia ha
soltado?

Noah vuelve a soltar una carcajada. Eunice sabe que
debería levantarse para ir a ver cómo está, para ver qué
puede haber junto a su ventana, pero una sensación de
agobio la aplasta, una enfermedad sin síntomas, el
cansancio que ningún reposo puede remediar. Siente la cara
hundiéndose hacia el escritorio. Levanta las manos para
intentar mantenerse erguida, y sus dedos caen sobre las
teclas del ordenador. Empiezan a teclear sin su
consentimiento mientras su cara se acerca más y más a la
pantalla.

Suelta.

Suelta.

Suelta.

EL QUE SUSURRA EN LA OSCURIDAD

CAPÍTULO 1

—¿Estás seguro de que sabes qué hacer? —susurré enérgicamente.

Era mediados de agosto de 1999. Yo tenía dieciséis años y estaba agazapado sobre el tejado de la casa de mi familia, empapado de sudor, el pelo pegado a la frente. Desde mi posición estratégica, alcanzaba a ver los jardines traseros de nuestros vecinos por tres de los lados: el azul intenso de una piscina a mi izquierda, un jardín sembrado de juguetes a mi derecha, y un cenador y una plataforma elegantes en el jardín delante del nuestro.

Flotando en el aire a algunos metros del borde del tejado, Mi Amigo extendió los brazos.

—Confío en ti —dije.

Chocó las patas dos veces y las volvió a extender, como un padre intentando convencer a un niño de saltar a la piscina. Retrocedí tres pasos, me enjugué el sudor de la cara con mi camisa, y tomé carrerilla. Con los brazos abiertos como un pájaro, me alcé, la tierra alejándose un instante… y luego me detuve bruscamente en pleno vuelo cuando la criatura me atrapó por debajo de las axilas.

Nos quedamos suspendidos juntos, cara a cara. La boca de la criatura se abrió en una sonrisa boba, y le rasqué detrás de la oreja. Inclinó la cabeza hacia mi mano.

—Buen trabajo —dije—. Pero ¿habrá algún modo de hacer esto sin que duela tanto? Me van a doler las axilas.

Mi Amigo se alejó flotando hacia el tejado y me volvió a apoyar. Retrocedió a su sitio anterior y palmoteó dos veces antes de extender los brazos. *Vamos.*

Sacudí los miembros, intentando olvidar el dolor en los hombros. Respiré hondo dos veces y cerré los ojos. Incluso a aquella altura lastimosamente baja, apenas dos pisos, no podía evitar que me acecharan imágenes de huesos partidos o un cuello roto. Si quería jugar a ese juego más a menudo, tendría que aprender a ser temerario.

Retrocedí subiendo a la cima del tejado y corrí pendiente abajo. Esta vez incliné las piernas un poco y me impulsé un poco más al saltar. De nuevo me levanté, con los brazos extendidos, y de nuevo empecé a descender. El pánico intentó abrirse paso, pero cerré los ojos y me imaginé una figura salida de un mito: Dédalo, huyendo de la isla-prisión de Creta, sus alas fabricadas con plumas de pájaros y cera, los brazos abiertos, la cabeza erguida, recortado contra la luna. Esta vez, en lugar de detenerme abruptamente, tuve la sensación silenciosa de que mi peso se desplazaba, como lo haría en el agua. La criatura me atrapó con cuidado y me giró en un lento círculo. Abrí los ojos con la intención de hablar, pero algo en su semblante me detuvo. Durante un momento, quizás menos de un segundo, tuve la impresión de estar mirando la cara de una persona y no la de un animal. Aquello sucedía de vez en cuando, como ver algo con el rabillo del ojo, y, como todo lo que revolotea en la periferia de la visión, esta impresión desaparecía en cuanto intentaba concentrarme en un detalle particular.

—Buen trabajo —dije ahora, y le volví a rascar detrás de las orejas—. Ya está bien por hoy.

Volvimos a entrar por la ventana de mi dormitorio. La criatura se desplomó sobre mi cama, y los resortes chirriaron bajo su peso. Bajé, me preparé un sándwich en la cocina, y lo llevé arriba para comer. Cuando volví, encontré un sobre que debió de haber sido deslizado bajo la puerta de mi dormitorio. Lo levanté y lo llevé a mi escritorio, donde me senté a leerlo mientras comía mi sándwich.

Querido Noah:
Hoy estaba en mi laboratorio de geología, mirando por la ventana, y he empezado a pensar en todas las capas de la tierra, y en cómo, mientras excavamos, perforamos, y todo lo demás, extraemos todas aquellas cosas que son nuevas para nosotros, pero que en realidad son antiguas. Me pregunto si los seres humanos no son iguales. Si cada tic de la personalidad, cada talento o defecto ya está en su sitio, esperando a ser descubierto. Mi pasión por la

escritura, por ejemplo: ¿ya existía cuando nací? ¿O
apareció después de que papá me comprara mi primer
ordenador? Me gusta pensar que ya la poseía, y que
papá solo fue lo bastante astuto para saber dónde
excavar.

   Por supuesto, no todos los exploradores son tan
amables. La mayoría de las personas en tu vida
quieren hurgar en tu interior para obtener cosas que
ellos desean: sexo, atención, una sonrisa, permiso
para cambiar el carril de la carretera. Están a la
caza para obtener cosas para ellos, no para dártelas.

   Cuando esto me sucedió, empecé a deprimirme. ¿En
cuánto tiempo conseguiría vaciarme el mundo?

   Sé que en los últimos años no me he portado muy
bien. He ido a mis médicos y tomado mi Paxil como una
buena chica y, por lo general, soy capaz de salir de
la cama y funcionar todos los días. Pero me siento
disminuida, Noah. No me entristezco tanto como antes,
pero tampoco me siento jamás realmente feliz. Quizá
ya esté vacía.

   Tuya (aunque apagada),
   Eunice.

Cada uno manejó lo que le había sucedido a Sydney a su modo. En 1989
mi madre denunció su desaparición a la policía, e incluso relató con fidelidad
mi historia de gritos, luces atenuadas y una habitación saqueada. Pronto las
furgonetas de los medios de comunicación estaban instaladas fuera de nuestro apartamento. Dejamos de mirar la televisión porque nuestras caras estaban en todos los canales de noticias locales (y, brevemente, internacionales).
Pero a medida que las semanas se transformaron en meses, sin nuevas pistas
sobre su paradero, el interés del público mermó. Las camionetas de noticias
se marcharon. La policía aún la consideraba una investigación activa, pero no
advertí mayor actividad por su parte.

Alrededor de esa época Eunice experimentó su primer episodio de
depresión. Mi madre hizo que la hospitalizaran brevemente y luego la

medicaran. Los médicos ayudaron un poco, pero por mucho que le ajustaran la medicación y las dosis, aún le costaba funcionar en el mundo. No podía permanecer en un empleo durante más de algunas semanas, y si bien seguía obteniendo extraordinarios resultados en sus exámenes, no podía concentrarse completamente en nada. Se graduó del instituto un año después de lo planeado y, tras un semestre, fracasó estrepitosamente en el cumplimiento de la beca completa que le otorgó la Universidad de Texas en Austin. Desde entonces, Eunice había estado viviendo de nuevo en su antiguo dormitorio, trabajando con ahínco en obtener un título intermedio de la universidad comunitaria de Vandergriff, tomando una o dos clases por semestre, y trabajando de vez en cuando en Monstruos al Acecho y el Laberinto del Terror cuando necesitaba dinero para sus gastos.

Fue durante este período cuando empezaron a aparecer sus «notas de suicidio». No sé por qué las conservé. Supongo que estaba desesperado por su compañía, aunque solo fuera por escrito. Cada cierto tiempo sacaba a relucir la idea del suicidio, como algo que conservaba en el bolsillo trasero, pero no podía imaginar a mi divertida y cariñosa hermana haciéndole daño a alguien, y menos a sí misma.

Leí esta última nota dos veces y la volví a meter de prisa en su sobre. La coloqué en una caja de zapatos bajo la cama, junto con las demás. Dejé que mi mano se detuviera sobre los sobres; sentí el consuelo reseco y mullido de mi escondite, y luego cerré la caja. Mi Amigo masculló cuando me subí a la cama junto a él, pero se corrió hacia un lado y me hizo un sitio.

—Un millón de gracias —dije. Como respuesta, se acercó a mi lado contoneándose hasta que tuvo la espalda apoyada contra mi pecho. Su calidez atravesó la capa y mi ropa, y no hizo sino aumentar mi estado acalorado, pero seguía habiendo cierta dulzura, un consuelo ante el contacto, una sensación de haber vuelto a casa. Me sumió rápidamente en el sueño, incluso mientras intentaba tomar nota mental de ir a ver cómo estaba Eunice por la mañana.

CAPÍTULO 2

Como un cruel premio de consuelo por nuestra pérdida, la situación financiera de mi familia experimentó una gran mejora tras la desaparición de Sydney. El Laberinto del Terror atrajo grandes multitudes durante sus primeros dos años, y Monstruos al Acecho, impulsado por el boom de los cómics a comienzos de los años noventa, resultó lucrativo por primera vez. Nos pudimos mudar del apartamento a una casa de cuatro dormitorios. Sally White permitió que su participación del éxito de la tienda la llevara aún más lejos: aunque intentó mantener la híbrida amistad y sociedad con mi madre tras la desaparición de Sydney, se terminó cansando de que mi madre la maltratara y excluyera. Vendió su mitad de Monstruos al Acecho y se mudó a Indiana con un novio en 1993. Aunque recibimos una invitación para la boda, mi familia no asistió.

No éramos felices, pero sí financieramente solventes, lo cual, tras mi niñez sumida en la pobreza, resultaba casi lo mismo. En 1999 mi madre finalmente accedió a contratarnos a Kyle Ransom y a mí como empleados a sueldo del Laberinto del Terror. Nuestra primera misión como asalariados fue ir a ver la producción de *Las brujas de Salem*, que el padre de Kyle presentaba en el instituto de Vandergriff, un sitio ideal para encontrar nuevos talentos. Mi madre nos entregó una pila de folletos, invitando a realizar audiciones, y prácticamente nos echó por la puerta la noche del estreno.

Siempre he odiado *Las brujas de Salem*. Es interminable y lúgubre, y la idea más interesante de la obra —la posibilidad de que haya brujería en Salem— se reduce a una metáfora del macartismo. Además, puede ser que sea medio delirante, pero detesto las narrativas en las que el pobre hombre inocente es acusado falsamente por una joven sexy.

El señor Ransom creó un decorado interesante: un árbol gigante que dominaba la escena, con todos los jueces sentados en las ramas. Pero los actores parecían perdidos mientras deambulaban por el escenario y se gritaban acusaciones con una expresión pétrea. La chica que interpretaba el papel de Abigail, cuyo pelo era tan rubio que parecía plateado bajo las luces del escenario, hizo una buena imitación de Sue Lyon en *Lolita*, pero para cuando el John Proctor con la cara cubierta de acné eligió ser colgado en lugar de firmar una falsa confesión, Kyle y yo estábamos sentados con las barbillas apoyadas sobre los puños, ansiando el saludo final.

Después de la obra encontramos al señor Ransom al pie del escenario, estrechando manos con admiradores. Había sufrido un paro cardiaco no mucho después de la desaparición de Sydney, y tras la operación y unos cambios de dieta severos, había perdido mucho peso, pero el cambio lo hacía tener un aspecto aún menos saludable. La piel le colgaba alrededor de la cara y se acumulaba en su cintura como una vela a medio derretir, y su tez rojiza era ahora de una palidez que le daba un aspecto más fúngico que humano. Era el único participante de la temporada inaugural del Laberinto del Terror al que habían vuelto a invitar tras 1989.

Al acercarnos ahora, con los folletos en mano, no vi a la señora Ransom por ningún lado. Cuando se lo mencioné a Kyle, parecía incómodo.

—Los jueves da una clase —dijo—. Vendrá a la función del sábado.

—Es una historia importante —dijo el señor Ransom, estrechándole la mano a un hombre que parecía el abuelo de alguien.

—Por supuesto —dijo el anciano—, pero me pregunto si los adolescentes estarían de acuerdo. —Levantó la mirada hacia un auditorio en su mayoría vacío detrás de él.

El señor Ransom sonrió, tenso.

—Muchas gracias por venir —dijo. Se volvió hacia nosotros, obligándose a cambiar el gesto amargo de la cara—. Chicos, ¿qué os ha parecido?

—Ha sido intenso —dije.

—Muy oscuro —dijo Kyle.

—Muy fiel al texto —señalé.

—Es una de las grandes obras norteamericanas —dijo el señor Ransom—. ¿Quién soy yo para recortarla?

La chica que había interpretado a Abigail emergió de la zona del backstage, sin el disfraz pero con la cara aún cubierta de maquillaje. De cerca era *muy* bonita. Tenía el pelo reluciente y unos brillantes ojos azules. Se detuvo cuando nos vio a Kyle y a mí.

—Hola, Kyle —dijo. Asintió en mi dirección—. Hola, Noah.

—¿Nos conocemos? —pregunté, desconcertado.

Me dio un puñetazo en el brazo.

—Vamos, déjalo ya.

—¿Que deje qué?

Sus ojos se abrieron con incredulidad.

—Nos sentábamos a dos filas de distancia en la clase de inglés de la señora Thurston. Durante todo el octavo curso. —Se llevó la mano al pecho—. ¿Donna Hart?

—Ah, sí —dije, pero sonó a mentira—. Disculpa, soy un poco despistado.

Nos quedamos de pie en un silencio incómodo hasta que Kyle intervino:

—La obra ha sido intensa.

—Muy oscura —dije, secundándolo.

—Hiperfiel al texto —dijo Kyle—. ¡Y has estado genial!

—Lo mejor de todo —dije, porque quería compensarla por haber herido sus sentimientos.

Me dio otro puñetazo en el brazo.

—Basta —dijo, evidentemente complacida.

—Oye, ya que estás aquí —dijo Kyle, entregándole un folleto—, deberías venir a hacer una prueba para el Laberinto del Terror en un par de semanas.

—Es la casa embrujada que dirige mi familia —dije.

—Sé lo que es —dijo—. No soy una ignorante. —Estudió el folleto.

—Siempre necesitamos actores —dije.

Kyle me tiró del brazo.

—Tenemos que irnos.

Entendí la indirecta.

—Nos vemos, Donna Hart.

—Claro —dijo—. Quién sabe, quizás la próxima vez me recuerdes.

Empezamos a subir los escalones hacia el escenario. Cuando ya no nos podía oír, Kyle me detuvo.

—¿Jamás te fijaste en esa chica? —me preguntó.

—Claro —mentí—. Es solo que no recordaba su nombre.

—¿Cómo puedes olvidar algo sobre una chica como esa?

Era una buena pregunta. Era encantadora y agradable a la vista, pero incluso ahora estaba esfumándose de mi mente.

—Estoy demasiado ocupado —dije.

—¿Qué te pasa? —No respondí de inmediato, y soltó un bufido—. No te entiendo ni un poco. Si estuviera en la misma liga que esa chica, no podría

pensar en otra cosa. De hecho, de ahora en adelante no pensaré en otra cosa.
—Cerró los ojos.

—Kyle —dije.

—Shhh —dijo. Me entregó la pila de folletos con los ojos aun cerrados—. Tú ve a meditar en lo que sea que te ocupa tanto tiempo y reparte los folletos. Yo pensaré en Donna por ambos.

CAPÍTULO 3

Cuando Kyle y yo volvimos a casa, había un Honda CR-X desconocido aparcado en la entrada detrás de la camioneta de Eunice. La puerta trasera estaba cubierta de pegatinas de grupos musicales como AFI, Bikini Kill, MxPx y los Misfits. En el parachoques había una pegatina gigante que decía LA PORNOGRAFÍA VIOLA LA MENTE. Al pasar por la puerta principal oí un sonido tan raro que, al principio, no lo reconocí: la risa de Eunice.

La encontramos en la mesa del comedor junto a una chica rechoncha y achaparrada con pelo azul de punta. Llevaba una sudadera con capucha y parches sujetos a las mangas con imperdibles. Ella y Eunice estaban inclinadas sobre un libro de texto. Ambas levantaron la vista cuando entré. La chica punk tenía una media sonrisa, pero Eunice tenía las mejillas arreboladas por la risa y los ojos llorosos.

—Noah —graznó—. ¿Cómo va todo?

—Bien —respondí—. He repartido la mayoría de los folletos. —Apoyé la pila que quedaba sobre la mesa.

Eunice señaló a la desconocida que estaba a su lado.

—Te presento a Brin. Está en mi clase de inglés.

Intercambiamos saludos y le ofrecí a Brin un folleto.

—¿Una casa embrujada? —preguntó.

—Es el negocio familiar —expliqué. Eunice parecía incómoda, como si hubiera preferido que yo no dijera nada.

—Bueno —dijo la joven, hurgando en su bolso—, si estamos intercambiando folletos… —Me entregó un cuarto de hoja arrugada. A primera vista, creí que era un anuncio para un show de rock punk: tenía el típico aspecto descolorido de una fotocopia, y el fondo era una estrella náutica gigante cruzada por una pancarta, pero esta decía IGLESIA DE LA BIBLIA REDENTORA. Y por debajo, en letra blanca casi ilegible, en lugar de una lista de grupos musicales, había un horario de servicios y eventos religiosos.

—¿Asistes a esto? —pregunté.

—Tú también puedes, si quieres —dijo, mirándome y luego a Eunice—. Quizás te haga cambiar de opinión acerca de cómo te ganas la vida.

El malestar aparente en la cara de mi hermana se hizo más visible, pero sonrió.

—Sí, tal vez.

Antes de que yo pudiera responder de algún modo (seguramente grosero) a esta invitación, mi madre entró en la sala. Tenía la boca tensa, su semblante más pálido que lo habitual.

—Mamá, ella es Brin... —empezó a decir Eunice.

—Hemos repartido la mayoría de los folletos —dije, pero mi madre nos desestimó a ambos con la mano.

—Noah, es hora de decir buenas noches. Kyle, probablemente deberías irte derecho a casa. Seguramente tu madre querrá verte. Brin, quizás no sea mala idea que tú también te vayas.

—¿Qué sucede? —preguntó Eunice.

La boca de mi madre se movió un instante, y cuando habló, su voz se quebró.

—Hoy ha desaparecido una niña.

Para la mañana siguiente, la historia sería inevitable en el canal de noticias local y nacional, pero mi madre nos relató los hechos imprescindibles a todos los que estábamos en la sala: aquella mañana, Maria Davis, de nueve años, y su hermano de cinco, Bobby, se habían dirigido en sus bicicletas a una vieja tienda Winn-Dixie, clausurada, que estaba a pocas calles de su casa. Veinte minutos después Bobby había dado la vuelta y había regresado a casa, pero para la hora de la cena, Maria aún no había vuelto. Cuando sus padres condujeron a la tienda, encontraron su bicicleta tumbada en el aparcamiento, pero ninguna señal de Maria. Llamaron a la policía, que llamó al FBI.

Mi madre se paró detrás de una silla en la cabecera de la mesa del comedor mientras nos contaba todo esto, aferrándose al respaldo con los nudillos blancos. Después de terminar, nos quedamos todos sentados en una especie de silencio pasmado… Brin y Kyle incluidos.

Yo fui la primera en hablar:

—¿No creéis que tenga nada que ver con Sydney, verdad?

—Aún no lo saben —dijo mi madre—, pero la policía no me habría llamado si no creyeran que es una posibilidad.

Kyle y Brin se despidieron de nosotros. Brin y Eunice intercambiaron una sonrisa prolongada que no supe interpretar. Tenía asuntos más urgentes de los cuales preocuparme.

Después de eso mi madre, Eunice y yo nos sentamos juntos en la sala durante casi dos horas, mirando con fijeza la televisión, sin hablar. No creo que ninguno de nosotros supiera qué decir o pensar. Jamás habíamos abandonado la esperanza de que Sydney hubiera sencillamente huido, que el grito que había lanzado al partir hubiera sido una especie de broma elaborada, exactamente el tipo de cosa que una adolescente iracunda con una tendencia por casas embrujadas podría hacer. Había albergado la secreta esperanza de que estuviera en Los Ángeles, de que quizás algún día iría al cine y la vería en la pantalla o leería su nombre en los créditos finales. Pero ahora que había desaparecido otra chica, era mucho más difícil fantasear con ello.

Cuando mi madre me envió a la cama, Eunice me siguió arriba e incluso vino a mi habitación, lo cual ya casi nunca hacía. Se sentó en mi cama y me observó mientras me quitaba los zapatos.

—¿Te encuentras bien? —preguntó.

—Supongo que sí.

Se quedó sentada un momento, recorriendo la manta de arriba abajo con la mano.

—¿Y tú? ¿Estás bien? —pregunté.

Lo pensó.

—¿Qué te parece Brin? —preguntó.

No era lo que esperaba.

—¿La chica que ha venido? No lo sé. Es agradable, supongo. Parece bastante religiosa.

—Dice que hoy en día asiste a la iglesia más que nada por diversión —señaló—. Muchas de sus amigas del instituto siguen asistiendo. Tienen un grupo musical de punk rock de alabanzas o algo así.

—¿Ahora te gusta el punk? —pregunté.

Eunice sonrió mirando el suelo, y luego se puso de pie.

—Debo dejarte descansar. Buenas noches, Noah. —Me dio un beso rápido en la mejilla y se marchó.

Esperé hasta que oí que cerraba la puerta de su dormitorio al final del pasillo antes de llamar al monstruo.

—¿Estás aquí dentro? —Por lo general, ante esta invitación, Mi Amigo emergía del armario o de debajo de la cama, pero esa noche no hubo respuesta.

A veces sucedía. Algunas noches la criatura llegaba tarde, justo antes de que me durmiera, y otras ni siquiera aparecía. Pero me hubiera venido bien la compañía aquella noche, algún consuelo de alguien que no estuviera sufriendo como mi familia. Me quedé dormido sentado junto a la ventana de mi dormitorio, esperando a que Mi Amigo volviera a casa.

CAPÍTULO 4

Durante los días que siguieron a la desaparición de Maria Davis, a medida que la prensa nacional se obsesionó cada vez más con el caso, hubo un cambio definitivo en el clima emocional de Vandergriff. Jamás había sido un pueblo idílico donde todo el mundo se sonreía, pero ahora había cierta tensión en las mandíbulas de todos, un frunce en el ceño. Había menos chicos jugando en los parques o jardines delanteros por las tardes, y la calle de fuera de nuestra casa estaba más tranquila de noche. Oía menos risas en todo el pueblo, aunque mucho más en los pasillos del instituto. Estábamos todos tensos y con las hormonas alborotadas, y éramos demasiado jóvenes para tomarnos algo en serio. Hubo una asamblea en el auditorio donde un oficial de la policía local nos explicó que habría más presencia policial en el edificio y en el aparcamiento del instituto para vigilar las cosas. El mismo oficial nos recordó que no aceptáramos comida ni invitaciones para viajar en coches de desconocidos. Nos enseñó un póster con un número de teléfono y nos imploró que llamáramos a aquel número si alguna vez veíamos algo sospechoso.

—Incluso si no estáis seguros de si vale la pena informar de ello, hacedlo. Quizás estéis salvando vuestra propia vida.

La presentación entera tuvo el tono de una mala broma contada por alguien que sabe que está contando una mala broma pero que no puede parar. Como si algo de eso fuera a ayudar a devolver a Maria a casa, o a impedir que hubiera otra desaparición. También había habido asambleas escolares y noticias en todo el país después de que Sydney desapareciera.

Mi madre, Eunice y yo tuvimos varias discusiones acerca de si debíamos abrir el Laberinto del Terror aquel año. Aunque yo quería que se inaugurara por motivos puramente egoístas, tenía que admitir que había buenas razones para considerar no hacerlo. Después de todo, la mayoría de nuestros empleados eran estudiantes del instituto, y era posible que nos resultara difícil ocupar esos papeles si los padres no se sentían seguros de que sus hijos caminaran de noche durante seis semanas seguidas. Cada vez que salía el tema, hablábamos en círculos hasta que volvíamos a posponerlo, pero me di cuenta de que la posibilidad de abrir nuestra temporada de 1999 desaparecía.

Aparte de hablar de trabajo, mi familia y yo no hablábamos mucho. Cada uno se mantenía a resguardo en su propio rincón dentro de la enorme casa: mi madre, abajo, delante del televisor; Eunice en su dormitorio, y yo en el mío. Echaba mucho de menos al monstruo. Casi había renunciado a la esperanzas de volver a verlo alguna vez cuando, una semana después de su última aparición, me desperté bruscamente con un arañazo contra la ventana de mi dormitorio. La criatura estaba en cuclillas sobre el tejado, recorriendo el cristal de arriba abajo con una garra.

Descorrí el cerrojo de la ventana y la abrí. Me hice a un lado e intenté adoptar una expresión hosca mientras la criatura entraba en mi dormitorio. Tenía la intención de gritarle, regañarlo, exigir un relato pormenorizado de su paradero durante la última semana. Lo que terminé haciendo fue desplomarme contra él y abrazarlo con fuerza. Me devolvió el abrazo, y la vieja sensación de consuelo y dicha se apoderó de mí, mezclada con el aroma de su capa mohosa y de su pelaje. Mi furia se disipó, y sentí alivio.

—Te he echado tanto de menos —dije contra su pecho—. Estaba muy preocupado. —Quería seguir, pero Mi Amigo me estrechó aún más, y mis pies abandonaron la alfombra. Estábamos en el aire, la cabeza de la criatura a centímetros del techo.

Mi Amigo realizó una maniobra para que saliéramos por la ventana hacia la cálida noche veraniega. Lo primero que pensé fue que quería jugar otra ronda de salta y atrapa; en cambio, me desplazó para que quedara pegado contra el costado de su cuerpo, y se lanzó hacia el cielo. El viento me silbaba en los oídos y me azotaba el pelo. El pueblo se encogió bajo nosotros, una constelación de luces cada vez más pequeña. El aire se volvió más y más frío y ligero, y tuve que respirar cada vez más profundamente para llenar mis pulmones.

El monstruo detuvo nuestro ascenso a una gran altura del cielo nocturno y quedó suspendido en su sitio, girando en un lento círculo. Hacia Dallas vi la Reunion Tower, y hacia Fort Worth, el sólido rectángulo de Burnett Plaza. El propio parque de atracciones de Vandergriff, Fun Mountain, estaba justo abajo; la torre de lanzamiento se encontraba iluminada, aunque el parque estuviera cerrado.

Sin advertencia alguna, la criatura me soltó. El parque vino a mi encuentro a toda velocidad como el zoom de una cámara fotográfica mientras descendía dando manotazos a través del cielo. La torre de lanzamiento se elevó como la estocada de una espada. Un grito brotó de mi garganta, y agité desesperado los brazos como si hubiera algo a qué aferrarse.

Oh, cielos, oh, cielos, había llegado el momento, me iba a morir, y lo peor era que iba a *doler*…

Pero antes de hacer añicos todos los huesos de mi cuerpo contra una atracción de un parque de atracciones, la criatura me atrapó, sujetándome del torso, y me hizo volar en círculos alrededor de la torre, con las luces de neón como una nebulosa estroboscópica en la periferia de mi visión. Mi grito de terror dejó paso a un alarido de placer. La energía me recorrió por dentro. Solté un aullido. Una carcajada. La criatura cerró su mano con más fuerza, desencadenando una oleada de calor vibrante desde nuestro punto de contacto. El mundo adquirió una tonalidad dorada, y mi corazón galopó en mi pecho. Entonces, la criatura me volvió a soltar.

Esta vez no caí en picado. Esta vez me elevé. No iba particularmente rápido, pero advertí que ascendía realizando una espiral imprecisa, solo. Mi Amigo se quedó justo atrás y debajo, manteniéndose a la par pero sin tocarme. Estaba volando bajo mi propio poder. Me giré para mirar a la criatura.

—¿Cómo lo has hecho? —pregunté—. ¡Es asombroso!

Como siempre, no respondió. Me alejé volando de la torre y hacia la carretera. Me desplazaba más lenta y torpemente que la criatura —resultó que aprender a volar no era tan diferente como aprender a nadar—, pero conseguí permanecer a flote e impulsarme en la dirección correcta por mí mismo. Súbitamente, toda la preocupación y la ansiedad de la última semana dejaron de tener importancia. Lo único que importaba era aquel ascenso, aquella sensación de poder y libertad absolutos.

Finalmente, la excitación se desvaneció, fundiéndose con un agotamiento placentero. Para cuando regresamos a la casa, mi habilidad temporal de vuelo estaba desapareciendo. Me sacudí y serpenteé por el aire como un insecto ebrio, y aterricé dando tumbos sobre el tejado, sobre las manos y las rodillas. La criatura aterrizó junto a mí, una sensación más que un golpe, un sutil cambio de aire.

—Qué calor hace aquí fuera —dije—. ¿Tienes calor?

No esperé la respuesta de la criatura. Entré en mi dormitorio y me desvestí hasta quedarme en ropa interior. Incluso desnudo, la piel me escocía con un calor antinatural. La cara me ardía al tacto, y noté que mis shorts se habían elevado con mi hinchazón. Me apoyé sobre el escritorio y tomé un par de respiraciones profundas pero inútiles. No podía aliviarme. Me giré y vi que la criatura me había seguido dentro.

—Creo que me has echado demasiado polvillo mágico —dije—. Tengo caloooo… —La cabeza me daba vueltas.

La criatura me miró preocupada. Me tocó la cara y el pecho, dejando que su pata se detuviera allí. Mi corazón seguía latiendo acelerado, y la cara me palpitaba enardecida. La criatura levantó un bolígrafo y una hoja de papel de mi escritorio y escribió:

AMIGO ¿AYUDA?

—¿Puedes ayudarme? —pregunté. Mi voz sonaba remota y deformada, como distorsionada por un sintetizador.

Apoyó el bolígrafo y el papel. Me puso una pata sobre el hombro, y con la otra guio mi mano hacia mi entrepierna. La habitación palpitaba a nuestro alrededor; mi estómago se contrajo de nuevo. El mundo se apagó, haciéndose menos presente…

—¿Estás seguro de que quieres estar aquí… para esto? —pregunté, avergonzado y excitado a la vez ante la perspectiva.

La criatura olisqueó el costado de mi cara con el morro húmedo; el pelo rozando mi mejilla ardiente. Dejé caer mi ropa interior alrededor de los tobillos, me aferré a mí mismo, y empecé a dar tirones, sintiéndome dentro y fuera del cuerpo. No tardé demasiado. Cuando me tensé preparándome para el clímax, Mi Amigo me palmeó el hombro con fuerza. Mi ojo interior se refractó en decenas de fragmentos, un caleidoscopio impregnado de luz dorada. Cada versión distorsionada de mí mismo se retorció en éxtasis hasta el infinito.

Cuando acabó me desplomé hacia delante, y habría caído al suelo si Mi Amigo no me hubiera atrapado y retenido contra el olor mustio de su capa. Me recostó en la cama y se colocó detrás de mí, cruzando uno de sus brazos por encima. Ya no sentía el calor atrapado en mi interior, sino circulando entre nosotros. La carga individual se había transformado en un consuelo compartido gracias al contacto.

—Gracias —dije. Me alejé a la deriva, llevado por el pulso de mi orgasmo que se desvanecía, conducido al océano del sueño con la impresión pasajera de haber sido besado en la mejilla por un par de cálidos labios humanos.

CAPÍTULO 5

Me desperté a la mañana siguiente con una idea para abrir el Laberinto del Terror sin que nuestros empleados corrieran ningún riesgo. Estableceríamos un sistema que requeriría que los empleados menores de edad avisaran cuándo se dirigían al establecimiento o volvían a casa. A mi madre le gustó la idea, así que el negocio volvió a ponerse en marcha. Aquella semana empezamos a trabajar con el objetivo de tener el sitio listo para la temporada de 1999.

El Laberinto del Terror había crecido considerablemente desde 1989, de seis a quince salas. Cuatro de las nuevas habitaciones estaban en un segundo «piso» que construimos en 1995. Así que incluso contando la sala de descanso de los empleados, el taller de disfraces, los camerinos, los lavabos, la sala de vigilancia y el laberinto del monstruo, seguíamos usando cerca de dos tercios de la superficie disponible. Ya había empezado a bosquejar ideas para el empleo del tercio que restaba. Trabajaba provisoriamente con la idea de un equipo que se lanzara a perseguir a sus víctimas con la sierra eléctrica, y me sentía entusiasmado porque mi madre aún no lo hubiera rechazado.

Kyle y yo pasábamos nuestras tardes y atardeceres barriendo y limpiando la atracción, verificando la condición de las luces y las piezas (como las del túnel del vértigo) para comprobar su efectividad, reparando o sustituyéndolas según fuera conveniente. Eunice, en una de sus fases más energéticas, accedió a venir a ayudarnos, siempre que Brin también pudiera hacerlo.

—Ha aceptado venir a ver el sitio si yo la acompaño a su iglesia alguna vez —dijo.

—¿Por qué ibas a querer ir a una iglesia? —pregunté—. ¿Especialmente, una iglesia de rock punk? Detestas ambas cosas.

—Estoy probando algo nuevo —respondió—. ¿Por qué no intentas ser amable?

En cuanto Brin entró al edificio por primera vez, hizo un gesto de repugnancia leve.

—¿Os parece bien que la gente os pague por esto? —preguntó.

—Nadie te obliga a estar aquí. Está claro, ¿no? —le dije.

—Ven, te enseñaré el sitio —dijo Eunice. Brin se dejó conducir al laberinto y desapareció de la vista. Mientras mi madre, Kyle y yo trabajábamos, las carcajadas resonantes de mi hermana nos interrumpieron una y otra vez, provocadas por las incesantes bromas de Brie.

—¿Qué cojones? —pregunté tras la primera hora de esa tontería.

—Vigila el lenguaje —dijo mi madre, con un tono amable mientras marcaba algo en su sujetapapeles. Estábamos en la biblioteca del profesor mientras Kyle encendía y apagaba las bombillas naranjas del hogar—. Eunice jamás ha tenido muchas amigas. Deja que disfrute de esta, aunque sea bastante grosera.

—¿Hay alguien prestándole atención a mi trabajo asombroso con las bombillas? —preguntó Kyle, en cuclillas delante del hogar.

—Sí, estás haciendo un trabajo excelente —dijo mi madre, sin mirar—. Ahora, cállaos ambos para que pueda pensar.

Las audiciones se llevaron a cabo el fin de semana después de que termináramos las reparaciones. Mi madre y yo nos sentamos ante una mesa del salón de baile mientras Kyle hacía pasar al grupo habitual de estudiantes de teatro ilusionados con participar. Donna Hart fue la primera que entró por la puerta. Interpretó el monólogo de Abigail en *Las brujas de Salem*, cuando empieza, «Ya no soporto las miradas procaces, John», y cantó un verso de «Ya no sé cómo quererlo», de *Jesucristo Superstar*. Desplegó todos sus encantos, dirigiendo su interpretación hacia los letreros de salida que estaban en el fondo del auditorio del instituto, al otro lado de la ciudad.

Mi madre mantuvo la mirada en el sujetapapeles, garabateando notas durante por lo menos diez o quince segundos después que Donna terminara de cantar. Cuando levantó la mirada, se frotó la nariz con la parte trasera de una mano y dijo:

—¿Qué tal gritas?

—Supongo que bien —respondió ella, alisándose los pliegos de su falda.

Mi madre hizo un pequeño gesto.

—Adelante, entonces.

Donna se aclaró la garganta y descargó un grito puro y cristalino.

Mi madre volvió a su tablilla.

—Gracias, Donna. Estaremos en contacto.

La joven me sonrió de camino a la salida. Le devolví la sonrisa porque supuse que era lo que correspondía, y tras comprobar que mi madre no miraba, le hice un gesto con el pulgar hacia arriba.

Cuando terminaron el resto de las audiciones, Kyle, mi madre y yo nos sentamos en un círculo, en el salón de baile, y comparamos notas.

—La primera tarea —dijo mi madre— es determinar los papeles que tendréis vosotros dos.

Kyle se apoyó sobre el respaldo.

—Vaya, hombre, hace tanto que espero esta pregunta. —Cerró los ojos—. Profesor. Quiero ser el profesor. Y quiero ser titular.

—Veremos cómo va este año —respondió—. ¿Noah?

Yo también había estado esperando esa pregunta. Hacía tiempo que sabía mi respuesta, pero parecía raro decirla en voz alta y admitir que quería ese papel, porque aunque me moría por obtenerlo, temía que no lo obtuviera. También tenía miedo de lo que pensaría mi familia por pedirlo.

—Monstruo —dije—. Quiero ser el monstruo.

Kyle me miró compasivamente.

—El pobre niño modesto… Es su única opción.

Nadie se rio. Me ardía la cara, y tenía la vista fija en el suelo.

—Entonces serás el monstruo —dijo mi madre, con tono neutro.

CAPÍTULO 6

Más tarde, volviendo a casa en el Pinto de Kyle, retomó su tema favorito: Donna Hart.

—Tienes suerte, maldito cabrón —dijo—. Le gustas.

—No le gusto —respondí.

Me miró de soslayo con seriedad.

—¿Por qué haces esto?

—¿El qué?

—Entiendo que seas tímido, pero en algún momento vas a tener que salir con *alguien*. Quiero decir, no eres gay, ¿no?

—Vete a la mierda —dije. En Vandergriff, en 1999, había pocas propuestas más atemorizantes. Menos de un año antes, habían atado a Matthew Devries, un hombre gay de veintipocos años, a la parte trasera de una furgoneta y lo habían arrastrado varios kilómetros por un tramo de una carretera de dos carriles. Había sucedido en Artemis, a unos veinte minutos de nuestro pueblo.

—Escucha —dije—, si te prometo flirtear con una chica bonita, ¿dejarás de hablar de ello?

Chocó las manos y las alzó sobre la cabeza como si se hubiera anotado un punto.

—Las manos en el volante, Super Dave —dije.

Quería hablar con Eunice acerca de ello, pero cuando llegué a casa su dormitorio estaba vacío. Era probable que hubiera salido con Brin. Sin pensar realmente en lo que hacía, pasé junto a su habitación y me dirigí a la que estaba al fondo del corredor.

El cuarto dormitorio de la casa era lo que mi madre llamaba el *home office*. Tenía un archivador, un escritorio, un ordenador y una planta artificial en un rincón. Se suponía que era para mi madre, pero podía contar con los dedos de una mano la cantidad de veces que la había encontrado allí. Era más frecuente que Eunice o yo usáramos el ordenador para hacer los deberes o para jugar. La habitación estaba casi siempre vacía, como si todos conociéramos su verdadero propósito y estuviéramos esperando una excusa para sacar los muebles y hacer lugar para su verdadera ocupante.

También era la única habitación de la casa donde teníamos una fotografía de Sydney. Estaba encima del archivador: un retrato escolar de veinte por veinticinco centímetros en un marco dorado: Sydney, en un vestido de tirantes, con la melena abultada con laca, la brillante sonrisa que empleaba sobre el escenario dirigida hacia la cámara. No estoy seguro de por qué mi madre eligió exhibir esa fotografía. La habían tomado al comienzo de su último año, apenas dos meses antes de que desapareciera, y era la fotografía que inevitablemente acompañaba todas las noticias que aparecían en el periódico o la televisión. Esa fotografía se convirtió en el pequeño avatar de su desaparición de nuestras vidas.

Levanté la foto, cuidando no dejar mis huellas sobre el cristal. Me pregunté si los padres de Maria Davis estaban pasando por algo similar en este momento; si tenían una fotografía de su hija que encapsularía a la perfección su pérdida, sus remordimientos, su dolor y los fracasos que percibían como padres.

Me dije que no debía seguir. Maria podía estar viva y en algún sitio. Y Sydney también. No sabía *nada* sobre ninguno de los dos casos. No de verdad. Apoyé la foto, pasé junto al dormitorio de Eunice y entré en el mío. Mi Amigo estaba sentado en el suelo, mirando ceñudo un cómic abierto en su regazo. Marcó su sitio con su dedo cubierto de garras cuando entré, y señaló el cielo nocturno. *¿Fuera?*

—Esta noche no —dije—. Tengo trabajo que hacer. —Me levanté y tomé mis lápices y algunas hojas de papel de mi escritorio. La criatura me miró con curiosidad—. Tengo que diseñar un nuevo disfraz de monstruo para el Laberinto del Terror. Había pensado en basar el dibujo en ti.

La mirada de la criatura se volvió turbia y momentáneamente preocupada. Dejó el cómic a un lado y extendió la mano hacia el papel y los lápices. Una vez que se los pasé, escribió: ¿QUIERES PARECERTE A MÍ?

—Pues sí —dije—. Eres increíble. ¿Por qué no habría de querer parecer-
me a ti?

Pensó en la pregunta un momento, pero no pareció que se le ocurriera
una buena respuesta. Con aspecto de estar aún perturbado, devolvió los lápices y el papel. Me senté delante de la criatura sobre el suelo, con la espalda
contra el tocador. Volvió a la lectura, y empecé mi bosquejo. Bosquejé durante varias horas, apenas consciente de otros sonidos en la casa... mi madre
yendo y viniendo arriba y abajo en la cocina, y luego instalándose delante del
televisor.

Jamás he sido un gran artista, así que me llevó varios intentos dibujar
algo que tuviera siquiera algún parecido con la criatura. Quería captar su tamaño, su pelaje apelmazado, el modo en que sus ojos relucían amenazantes y
angustiados, pero todo lo que dibujaba se parecía a un perro con una sudadera con capucha. Seguía resoplando sobre mi libreta cuando hubo un golpe
en mi puerta, y Eunice entró antes de que tuviera la ocasión de invitarla a
pasar.

—Hola —dijo, y luego hizo una mueca—, ¿estás bien?

Eché un vistazo al sitio donde había estado la criatura sobre el suelo, que
ahora estaba vacío, y luego de nuevo a Eunice. Tragué y me pasé la lengua por
los labios secos y cuarteados.

—Sí —dije—. Me has sorprendido, eso es todo.

Entró y se sentó en la cama.

—Tu cama está realmente caliente.

—Sí, por eso me he movido al suelo.

Recorrió con la mano el cubrecama, con gesto preocupado.

—¿Tienes fiebre? Parece como si hubieras dejado aquí un ladrillo ardiente.

—Estoy bien —dije.

Echó un vistazo a la ventana abierta, y por un segundo pareció a punto
de decir algo, pero luego frunció el ceño y se la vio levemente afligida.

—¿Necesitabas algo? —pregunté.

Parpadeó un par de veces y se puso en pie.

—Tienes razón. Es tarde.

—No tienes que marcharte —dije—. ¿A dónde has ido esta noche?

Se quedó inmóvil en mitad de la habitación con aquella mirada extraña
y afligida de concentración un instante más. Una media sonrisa incierta y

pequeña emergió, y lanzó una mirada a un lado como si hubiera podido encontrar una respuesta en el rincón de mi habitación.

—He ido con Brin a su iglesia —dijo, y se volvió a sentar en mi cama.

—¿Un viernes por la noche?

—Realizan un acto religioso o un evento casi todos los días o noches de la semana —dijo—. Brin dice que quieren apelar a personas con horarios no tradicionales, que quizás no tengan libre los domingos por la mañana o los miércoles por la noche.

Me volví a recostar contra el escritorio.

—¿Y cómo ha ido?

De nuevo, aquella mirada furtiva, su rechazo a mirarme.

—Ha sido… raro. Primero, la iglesia está situada en el escaparate de un horrible centro comercial, entre un salón de manicura y un local de preparación de impuestos. Los cristales delanteros están pintados de negro, así que nadie puede mirar hacia dentro ni hacia fuera, y el interior parece el escenario de un concierto de punk rock… solo un grupo de sillas plegables delante de un pequeño escenario con luces de colores y una pared al fondo de color negro.

»Todos los que han venido para el servicio eran parecidos a Brin… tenían tatuajes, el pelo de punta, parches en las chaquetas… pero todos traían Biblias. Era como algo salido del Twilight Zone. Todos querían estrecharme la mano y darme la bienvenida «al rebaño». Había un grupo musical de alabanza que ha tocado piezas de música punk rock realmente fuerte y veloz, y no entendía nada de lo que decían. Además, todo el mundo se abalanzó hacia la parte delantera del salón y ha empezado a rockanrolear…

—¿Y tú también has rockanroleado? —pregunté. Por lo huesuda y frágil que era, me imaginé que en una pista de rock Eunice se haría añicos como el cristal.

—No —respondió—. Me he sentado en mi sitio, pero Brin ha bailado. Y luego, después que todo el mundo quedara presa del frenesí, ha aparecido el pastor y se ha hecho silencio. Tenía una voz realmente tranquilizadora, como alguien que te anima a alejarte de la cornisa. Ha empezado a hablar de lo feliz que estaba de vernos a todos, y de lo bendecidos que éramos por tener ese espacio para estar juntos y alabar al Señor. Pero luego se ha vuelto raro. Ha empezado a decir que había notado que no todos se sentían impulsados a bailar por el Espíritu Santo, y te juro que me miraba *directamente a mí*. «Espero que en el futuro encuentres la fuerza para dejarte ir y dejar que el Espíritu te impulse», ha dicho. He intentado restarle importancia con una carcajada. Quizás era su modo de ser amigable, ¿sabes? Animándome a participar.

»Pero *después* ha empezado a hablar de la gente que ha abandonado la Iglesia y ha empezado a asistir a otras, y ha empezado a despotricar contra la lealtad. Ha empezado a nombrar personas, una por vez, a revocar cualquier bendición que hubieran recibido alguna vez a través de la iglesia. Algo así como, «Jane Dunlop, que conoció a su marido en esta iglesia, y cuyo bebé se bautizó aquí... revoco tu matrimonio y la salvación de tu hijo. Estás condenada». Lo ha hecho con alrededor de veinte personas diferentes. Y, Noah, a todo el mundo le ha parecido *perfecto*. Gritaban, «¡Amén!», y «¡Alabado sea Jesús!».

—¿Incluso Brin? —pregunté.

—Brin no —dijo Eunice—. Ella se ha quedado sentada. Después, le he dicho que el sermón me había parecido raro y desacertado, y me ha dicho, «Pues ya sabes lo que me parece la forma en que tu familia se gana la vida». Así que hemos hecho un trato: yo me tomaré un tiempo del Laberinto del Terror este año, y ella intentará buscar una iglesia diferente. Una que no sea tan... hostil. Y mientras tanto, ella y yo podemos salir juntas sin sentirnos raras por ello.

—Espera —dije—. ¿A qué te refieres con «tomarte un tiempo»?

—De todos modos, no es que haya estado superinvolucrada este año —dijo—. Ha sido un semestre duro, y creo que me merezco tomarme un año.

—Sí, pero ¿dejar que una fanática religiosa te intimide para que renuncies? Eunice, eso está mal.

Seguía sin mirarme a los ojos.

—No estoy renunciando. Solo estaré... tomándome un tiempo. —Se volvió a poner de pie—. De todos modos, es tarde. Buenas noches, pequeño. No te quedes despierto toda la noche. —Me besó en la mejilla y se fue.

Esperé despierto, pero Mi Amigo no volvió.

CAPÍTULO 7

Le entregué el nuevo bosquejo a mi madre al día siguiente en la mesa del desayuno, esperando que lo aprobara sin reaccionar demasiado. En cambio, su expresión pasó de la preocupación a la alarma absoluta.

—¿De dónde has sacado esto? —preguntó.

Fingí estudiar el dibujo.

—No sé. Me lo he inventado. ¿Por qué?

Parecía a punto de decir algo.

—¿Qué? —pregunté.

—Nada —dijo.

—Mamá, es obvio que no es «nada». —¿Por qué estaba volviéndose loca? Recorrió con los dedos mi bosquejo y luego me echó un vistazo.

—No has... ¿Jamás has visto a este ser?

Ahora había despertado mi propia curiosidad.

—¿Y *tú*? —pregunté.

La tensa línea de su boca adquirió diferentes formas antes de que terminara negando con la cabeza.

—No. No, por supuesto que no. Este asunto de Maria Davis me tiene muy nerviosa, es todo.

No supe cómo responder a eso. ¿Qué tenía que ver el disfraz de un monstruo con Maria Davis?

—Lo siento —dijo mi madre—. Es que me asusta.

Supe que iba a ceder y dejarme hacerlo a mi modo, así que dejé de profundizar en el tema.

—Es la idea —dije.

CAPÍTULO 8

Me negué a participar de los ensayos hasta que tuviera listo mi disfraz. Me habría sentido como un tonto intentando llevarme a la gente a la fuerza vestido con mi ropa de calle, y una vez que mis colegas hubieran visto aquella imagen ridícula, ¿cómo conseguiría que me tomaran en serio con un disfraz? Por bueno que fuera el producto final, mis víctimas siempre recordarían al Noah sudoroso que veían siempre. Cuando vieran al monstruo la primera vez, tenía que ser un monstruo.

Así que mientras mis compañeros de elenco se aprendían el texto y los movimientos que debían realizar, yo memorizaba la madriguera del monstruo, una serie de pasadizos al lado de la atracción que le permitía monitorear a los visitantes sin ser visto, y aparecer de modo fortuito para aterrorizar y/o llevarse a rastras a nuestros «infiltrados», personajes que siempre se llamaban Brad o Katie. Daba vueltas corriendo; mis pasos resonaban sobre el suelo de cemento y las escaleras de madera, sacudiendo las paredes de los decorados más endebles. Tenía que poder desplazarme por ese espacio vestido con un disfraz pesado y una máscara que limitaba mi visión, y hacerlo a oscuras. Así que corrí y corrí. Para el final de la primera semana podía navegar por él con los ojos cerrados.

En los descansos, me sentaba junto a una puerta industrial abierta, bebiendo agua a borbotones y absorbiendo cualquiera que fuera la brisa que soplara aquel día. A veces, Donna (que se incorporó al elenco como una de las Katie) y Kyle me acompañaban. Kyle interpretaba el papel del «amigo chiflado» en esas pequeñas escenas, bromeando y elogiándome delante de Donna. Yo me esmeraba por interpretar el papel del «tipo normal con cierto interés».

El nuevo disfraz estuvo listo para finales de la segunda semana, y lo presentamos en los ensayos ese mismo viernes. Sin mostrárselo a nadie de antemano, o dejando que supieran lo que hacíamos, mi madre anunció al elenco que empezaríamos a ensayar con las luces apagadas. Los Brad y las Katie, agrupados y haciendo el papel de «el público», tendrían una sola linterna para desplazarse por el almacén.

Para ese primer ensayo sin luces, mi madre me dio libertad para aparecer donde quisiera y cuando quisiera que se me ocurriera. A medida que los Brad y las Katie recorrían la atracción, me mantenía al corriente en silencio de lo que sucedía. Con las luces encendidas, se habían desplazado con arrogancia y seguridad tediosa. Ahora, entre el silencio y las sombras, sus carcajadas se volvieron nerviosas.

—Cielos —dijo uno de los Brad cuando escudriñé la biblioteca del Profesor—, sé que es falso, pero Cielos.

Donna paseó la linterna hacia un lado y hacia el otro, pero seguí conteniéndome. Los seguí a la morgue, y luego al salón de baile, donde el grupo musical empezó su gran número estridente y otros actores de reparto bailaban el vals alrededor del salón, impidiendo el paso de los Brad y las Katie, y obligándolos a abrirse paso entre un océano de bailarines. La sala, con su tenue iluminación y amplia superficie, debió de haber sido un alivio de la insoportable tensión vivida en las salas más pequeñas y oscuras que la precedían, pero mis presas habían quedado nerviosas y expuestas. Atravesaron la sala arrastrando los pies, con la linterna momentáneamente apagada, como un nudo de nerviosa energía, y alcanzaron las puertas dobles marcadas con el letrero de SALIDA en el otro extremo. Al pasar por ellas se hallaron de nuevo completamente a oscuras.

—Donna —dijo una de las Katie—. Linterna.

Donna encendió la luz y encontró su nariz a centímetros de mi hocico.

—Boo —dije.

Su grito me hizo dar las gracias por tener puesta la barrera amortiguadora de la máscara. El grupo entero gritó aterrorizado. Me agaché para pasar por una de mis salidas secretas y volví a mi laberinto.

—Noah, ¡eres un imbécil! —gritó alguien.

CAPÍTULO 9

Aquel grito, aquel momento de terror que había creado, me provocó tal emoción que, en un arrebato de frenética alegría, decidí que era hora de intentar algo con Donna. Cuando llegó Mi Amigo al atardecer aquella noche, le dije:

—Necesito la mejor flor que conozcas. Algo difícil de conseguir.

La criatura levantó el bolígrafo y la libreta de mi escritorio. ¿POR QUÉ?, escribió.

—No tiene importancia —dije—. ¿Lo harás?

Suspiró. AMIGO AYUDA, escribió. VUELVO PRONTO. Se dirigió fatigosamente a la ventana y salió volando hacia el cielo nocturno.

Caminé de un lado al otro de la habitación, esperando. Mi Amigo volvió cerca de media hora después, llevando en la mano una flor negra con un tallo largo. El corazón de la planta brillaba débilmente, como una lamparilla parpadeante. La luz estaba rodeada de espinas.

NO TOQUES LA PARTE DEL MEDIO, escribió la criatura. TAMPOCO LA MIRES CON FIJEZA. PODRÍAS CAER DENTRO. Señaló la flor. ¿PARA QUÉ?

—Para una chica —dije con desgana. Me ardía la cara, pero seguí de todos modos—. También necesito otro favor. Necesito que me hagas volar de nuevo.

La criatura me miró con fijeza.

—¿Qué sucede? —pregunté.

NADA, escribió. AMIGO AYUDA.

Un instante después, tras recibir una recarga de energía de la criatura, me lancé a volar por el cielo, con la flor negra apretada contra el pecho. El monstruo me siguió a cierta distancia para asegurarse de que no muriera estrellado. Busqué la dirección de Donna en la solicitud que había entregado para trabajar en el Laberinto del Terror, pero como yo acababa de conseguir mi carné de conducir, aún tenía una idea muy imprecisa del trazado del pueblo. Cada cierto rato debía descender y verificar los nombres de las calles. Finalmente, me encontré encima de una casa de un solo piso, sobre una calle llena de casas casi idénticas. Mientras me mantenía suspendido por encima, la criatura se detuvo a mi lado.

—Estoy intentando adivinar cuál es su ventana —dije.

La criatura se desplazó hacia el lateral izquierdo de la casa y señaló una ventana justo detrás de la cerca.

—¿Estás seguro? —pregunté.

Asintió.

Lo seguí y me dejé caer sobre el suelo.

—Quédate cerca pero fuera de la vista, ¿sí?

Se quedó suspendida en el aire sobre mi cabeza, enfadada, y luego se internó flotando en el jardín detrás de la casa. Golpeé el cristal con los nudillos, di un paso atrás y alcé la flor. Las cortinas se agitaron, apartándose apenas. Sentí que iba a vomitar. ¿Por qué había pensado que aquello sería una buena idea? ¿A qué chica le parecería romántico lo que estaba haciendo? Era lo que haría una persona loca.

La cara de Donna apareció entre las cortinas, los ojos enturbiados por el sueño, el pelo sujeto hacia atrás en un moño dorado encima de la cabeza. Llevaba una camiseta y pantalones de pijama. Movió la boca en silencio, pronunciando mi nombre como una pregunta: ¿Noah?

—Lo siento —susurré—. Me iré.

Levantó un dedo para decir, *Un minuto*, y desapareció. Cuando volvió, movía la mandíbula. Estaba masticando chicle. Descorrió el cerrojo de la ventana y la empujó lentamente para abrirla. Cuando la había alzado por la mitad, se agachó y asomó la cabeza.

—¿Qué haces aquí? —susurró.

—He venido porque… —Me detuve y carraspeé. Me hubiera venido bien un trago de agua—. Estás haciendo un gran trabajo en la obra y quería agradecértelo.

Sonrió. Por lo menos, estaba contenta de verme.

—¿En mitad de la noche?

—Después de todo, *somos* una casa embrujada, ¿verdad? —pregunté.

Señaló hacia mi pecho.

—¿Qué es eso?

Recordé la flor.

—Esto es para ti —dije, mirando su tenue resplandor en lugar de mirarla a ella—. A modo de felicitación… lo que sea.

—¿Vas a dármela o a quedarte mirándola? —preguntó. Arranqué la mirada de la hipnótica luz y se la entregué. Escudriñó los pliegues, mientras la luz le daba a su cara un tinte de color naranja. Donna era *realmente* bonita. ¿Por qué seguía olvidándome de eso? ¿Por qué no se quedaba su cara grabada en mi mente?

—Es preciosa —murmuró—. ¿Qué es?

—Una gentileza de ébano —respondí, encantado con mi propia creatividad espontánea—. La NASA la diseñó en un laboratorio; están experimentando con plantas que puedan llevar en naves espaciales, o plantar en asteroides para promover atmósferas respirables.

Pareció costarle algún esfuerzo mirarme de nuevo.

—Estás burlándote de mí.

—No lo haría jamás —dije—. Pero hablando en serio, no toques las espinas del centro: son venenosas.

—¿Les llevas flores a todos los Brad y las Katie?

—Solo a ti —respondí.

Aferró la parte delantera de mi camiseta y me dio un tirón hacia ella. Mi primer beso fue rápido y firme, terminó antes de que tuviera oportunidad de reaccionar. Donna me soltó, y retrocedí tambaleando un paso.

—¿Nos vemos en el trabajo? —preguntó.

—Sí, guay —dije, pasándome una mano por el pelo revuelto por el viento—. De todos modos, ahora tengo que volar de vuelta a casa.

Se rio.

—Eres muy raro. —Atrancó la ventana y cerró las cortinas de un tirón. Observé cómo se alejaba el brillo naranja de la gentileza de ébano. Un recuerdo raro me vino a la mente: las monjas deslizándose entre las hileras de asientos, llevando velas durante la presentación de *Sonrisas y lágrimas*, la producción del señor Ransom de 1989. Con eso en mente, la euforia del minuto anterior desapareció, y me sentí invadido de nuevo por una gran tristeza. Me abrí paso con dificultad a través del jardín lleno de hierbas hasta que estuve parado justo debajo de Mi Amigo.

—¿Me ayudas? —pregunté.

Soltando un suspiro sonoro, descendió suavemente al suelo y me sujetó los hombros. Una descarga de energía se transmitió entre nosotros. Mi estómago se contrajo y mi corazón empezó a galopar en el pecho. Cuando lo solté, doblé las piernas y me impulsé hacia arriba para volar. La criatura mantuvo las distancias en el vuelo de vuelta, apartando la mirada cada vez que le echaba un vistazo. Una vez en mi casa, volé a través de mi ventana, pero Mi Amigo permaneció fuera.

—¿Estás enfadado conmigo por algo? —pregunté.

Vaciló, luego sacudió la cabeza.

—No estás enfadado.

Sacudió la cabeza.

—¿Así que vienes dentro?

Volvió a sacudir la cabeza, y dándose la vuelta, salió volando hacia el cielo nocturno.

Cerré la ventana y caminé por el pasillo hacia la habitación de Eunice. Quería hablar con ella sobre Donna, compartir el triunfo de la noche, pero cuando llamé a la puerta, fue Brin la que abrió. Tenía la cara arrebolada, y el pelo de punta torcido.

—¿Necesitas ayuda? —preguntó.

—¿Estás de broma? —pregunté. Me incliné de lado, y se movió para impedirme ver.

—Un segundo, Noah —dijo Eunice, en algún sitio que no alcancé a ver. Parecía agitada, y comprendí lo que seguramente habían estado haciendo antes de llamar. Debió de vérmelo en la cara, porque Brin ladeó la cabeza y alzó las cejas.

—Olvídalo —dije. Caminé de vuelta a mi propia habitación, me desvestí y me fui a la cama. Reviví el beso de Donna, intentando extraer más detalles de la memoria, pero, asombrosamente, persistía en ser un recuerdo borroso. Había placer mezclado con sorpresa. Pero más que placer físico o deseo por la persona que me había besado, se trataba más bien de un placer intelectual ante el hecho de haber besado a una chica.

Risas ahogadas se oían desde el otro lado del corredor, Eunice y Brin jugando tras una puerta cerrada. Supuse que su acuerdo —olvidar la iglesia y olvidar la casa embrujada— estaba funcionando bien. Me puse la almohada sobre la cabeza para no escuchar, y después de un rato pude dormir.

Cuando me desperté a la mañana siguiente y bajé a desayunar, encontré a mi madre y Eunice en el sofá de la sala, pálidas y casi sin pestañear, delante del televisor. Estaban viendo las noticias.

—¿Qué ha pasado? —pregunté.

Eunice apartó la mirada de la pantalla lentamente.

—Ha vuelto a suceder.

CAPÍTULO 10

La segunda víctima de secuestro, en otoño de 1999, fue un chico de doce años, llamado Brandon Hawthorne. Brandon se había ido a dormir en casa la noche anterior, como lo hacía habitualmente, y sus padres habían visto la televisión hasta tarde y se habían quedado dormidos sin incidente alguno.

Alrededor de las tres de la mañana, el padre de Brandon se despertó, fue al lavabo y luego decidió comprobar cómo estaba su hijo. Encontró su ventana abierta y la cama vacía. La familia Hawthorne había llamado a la policía, pero hasta ahora la búsqueda no había arrojado ninguna pista. El chico simplemente había desaparecido.

Habría sido imposible ignorar las similitudes entre esa desaparición más reciente y la de Sydney diez años antes. El nombre y la fotografía de mi hermana empezaron a aparecer de nuevo en las noticias, y los reporteros llamaron a mi madre a casa y al trabajo para pedirle citas o entrevistas. A mí no me contó nada acerca de ello, pero oí los mensajes en nuestro contestador automático, y estuve de acuerdo con ellos. Estaba pasando algo raro.

Pasaron diez días sin que el monstruo viniera a visitarme. Hacía un mes que habían raptado a Maria Davis. No habían aparecido testigos, y si había nuevas pistas, la policía no estaba informándolo a la prensa. Soñaba con volar por encima de Vandergriff mientras el viento me alborotaba el pelo y me lo enredaba. Soñaba con una luz dorada, con el deseo de elevarme y sentirme realizado. Soñaba que Sydney gritaba una y otra vez. Soñaba con ventanas abiertas, pero jamás soñé con Donna.

En el trabajo el elenco empezó a llevar los disfraces durante los ensayos. Los Brad y las Katie se turnaron siendo mis víctimas. Me volví experto en moverme con el traje puesto, adaptándome a sus formas de defenderse y caer desplomados. Nadie se movía como Donna. Se retorcía y me golpeaba cuando la sacaba de la vista. En la oscuridad del laberinto, permanecía presionada contra mí incluso después de apoyarla sobre el suelo.

A veces intentaba hablar conmigo.

—Así que esta es la madriguera del monstruo. Para ser sincera, estoy un poco decepcionada. Creía que se parecería más a la de *Buffy* o la de *Aliens*. Otra vez: «¿Recuerdas la flor que me regalaste? Me olvidé de regarla como dos días y aún sigue viva».

Jamás cedía a la tentación de charlar con ella. Si Donna creyó que mi comportamiento era raro, no dijo nada. Comíamos juntos en el instituto y nos dábamos la mano en el pasillo antes de clase. Venía conmigo y con Kyle a los ensayos por las tardes. Desde fuera, probablemente parecíamos una pareja normal del instituto, pero todo lo que decía sonaba muy lejano, como algo que sucedía en un pasillo distante.

Quería hablar con Eunice sobre el tema, pero cada vez que pasaba por su dormitorio, la oía allí dentro con Brin, y había aprendido a no interrumpirlas. En cambio, esperé a que mi hermana viniera a verme, lo cual, por fin hizo el último viernes por la noche antes del estreno del Laberinto del Terror.

Se suponía que debía ir a casa de Donna para ver una película juntos, pero la llamé y fingí estar enfermo para no tener que ir. Eunice y yo llevamos su camioneta al instituto, donde me dejó practicar con mi carné de conducir nuevo. Después fuimos a una cafetería que estaba abierta las veinticuatro horas para beber un refresco (yo) y café (ella).

—Vaya —dijo, vertiendo crema en su taza y revolviendo el líquido de color negro hasta que se tornó un marrón claro—. Me han dicho que has empezado a salir con una Katie llamada Donna.

Esbocé una pequeña sonrisa y mordí mi pajita. Había echado de menos lo graciosa que podía ser cuando quería hacerse la cómica.

—No lo sé —dije—. Supongo.

—Está bien, no tienes que sentir vergüenza. Me alegra que por fin hayas salido al mundo y estés conociendo gente. Estaba empezando a preocuparme de estar pasándote mis tendencias antisociales.

—No es que sienta vergüenza —dije—. Me refiero a que Donna es agradable, pero… Me ha estado costando pensar en otra cosa que no sean Maria Davis y Brandon Hawthorne.

Eunice dejó de distraerse con su café para mirarme. En ese momento pareció mirarme realmente a la cara por primera vez en la noche.

—¿A causa de Sydney?

Encogí los hombros.

—Supongo que sí. ¿Crees que el que está raptando a las personas ahora es el mismo individuo?

Bebió un sorbo de café.

—No lo sé. No lo he pensado demasiado.

—¿En serio?

—Sé que es egoísta —dijo—, y espero que encuentren a esos chicos, y que estén bien. Maldita sea, espero que podamos pasar página con Sydney. Pero no son problemas que yo pueda resolver. En este momento tengo mis propios asuntos de qué ocuparme.

—¿Qué…? —vacilé, porque me preocupaba lo que significaría reconocerlo abiertamente—. ¿Te refieres a Brin?

Sus mejillas se arrebolaron y miró con fijeza su taza de café, pero asintió.

—¿Y está noche dónde está? —pregunté.

—En un retiro parroquial —respondió Eunice.

—Creía que se había tomado un respiro de ese sitio —señalé.

—Esto es una especie de gran despedida —dijo—. Ha estado asistiendo a la iglesia con algunas de esas personas durante años, y prácticamente le rogaron que fuera este fin de semana. Es una oportunidad para despedirse. —Y luego, ya fuera porque no me vio o porque prefirió ignorar mi mirada de escepticismo, siguió—: ¿Sabes? No me di cuenta de lo sola que estaba hasta que dejé de estarlo. Es gracioso. Ella me entiende. Supongo que yo también la entiendo a ella.

Reprimí mi antipatía por Brin.

—Me alegra que tengas una amiga —dije.

Irradiaba una tímida felicidad, con las manos apretadas alrededor de su taza. Empujé con suavidad mi vaso de refresco hacia el otro lado de la mesa hasta que chocó con su taza.

—Salud —dije.

CAPÍTULO 11

El Laberinto del Terror se inauguró y atrajo grandes multitudes a pesar de los toques de queda y de las pesadillas de la vida real en nuestro pueblo. Embosqué a desconocidos, golpeé paredes, sacudí puertas y coseché gritos realmente sonoros. A veces dejaba que pasara indemne algún Brad o alguna Katie, y a veces los atrapaba, aterrorizando al público. Lograba que los infiltrados se mantuvieran nerviosos y acrecentaba el terror de las visitas, haciendo que la catarsis de salir al aparcamiento, a plena vista de nuestros guardias de seguridad, fuera mucho más dulce. Era un monstruo eficaz. Me encantaba el trabajo. Cuando llevaba el disfraz puesto, separado del mundo por una barrera de pieles, tela y plástico, nada más importaba.

Era solo al final de la noche, cuando me quitaba mi segunda piel y me volvía a transformar en Noah Turner, cuando me sentía confundido y ansioso. Donna y yo continuamos dándonos la mano y cada cierto tiempo nos dábamos un beso en el trabajo, pero nada de eso me hacía sentir algo. Pensé mucho en la nota de suicidio de Eunice, en las personas excavándose unas a otras buscando cosas que querían y necesitaban. Me sentía como una cáscara vacía a la que hacían funcionar de modo remoto. Mayormente, sentía un temor vago y nebuloso. Como si algo terrible estuviera a punto de suceder, algo que yo sería incapaz de detener.

Terminó no siendo una cosa, sino una serie de ellas.

El lunes después de abrir, llegué a casa del colegio y encontré la puerta del dormitorio de Eunice cerrada. Me detuve fuera, atento por si escuchaba carcajadas apagadas o ruido de sábanas, pero solo oí silencio. Volví abajo para prepararme un bocadillo. Al pasar por el comedor con mi sándwich de mantequilla de cacahuate y mermelada, noté un sobre blanco sobre la mesa de la cocina. ¿Una nueva nota de Eunice? Me senté a leerla mientras comía. El sobre contenía varias hojas de papel, pero la página que estaba encima era una nota en una letra que no reconocí.

«Por tanto, Dios los entregó a pasiones vergonzosas, puesto que las mujeres cambiaron las relaciones naturales por las que van contra la naturaleza, y del mismo modo, los hombres abandonaron las relaciones naturales con la mujer y ardieron en pasiones lujuriosas los unos con los otros. Hombres con hombres cometieron actos indecentes, y recibieron en sí mismos el castigo que merecía su perversión. Además, como estimaron que no valía la pena tener en cuenta el conocimiento de Dios, él los entregó a una mente depravada, para que hicieran lo que no debían hacer». —Romanos 1, 26-28

Me he arrepentido de mis pecados. Si te preocupa el mundo del más allá, tú también lo harás. Por favor, no me vuelvas a llamar.
Tu hermana en Cristo,
Brin

La nota de Eunice venía en la hoja siguiente:

Querido Noah:

El amor es ridículo, ¿verdad? Un desequilibrio
químico, una enfermedad. La contraemos, enloquecemos
durante un tiempo, ¿y qué hacemos cuando pasa? Si
tenemos «suerte», tenemos que cargar con un
matrimonio imperfecto, una hipoteca, y niños
aborrecibles, necesitados y resentidos. Nuestras
ambiciones y sueños y grandeza potencial terminan
extinguiéndose por desear un poco de contacto humano
y algunos orgasmos (contracciones corporales
pasajeras que fácilmente pueden conseguirse estando a
solas). Y, sin embargo, el 99% de toda la música, la
literatura, el cine y el arte están dedicados al
amor. El mundo sigue adelante como si esto fuera lo
mejor y más natural. Cantamos interminables canciones
sobre contraer la enfermedad, y sobre las cicatrices
escabrosas que quedan cuando la enfermedad se
extingue.

Pero ¿sabes qué es peor que contagiarte del amor?
Que el objeto de tu enfermedad no corresponda a lo
que sientes. Escucharle decir «No, gracias» cuando se
lo declaras. Lo peor es saber, en lo más profundo,
que en realidad no lo dice de verdad, pero está
dejando que algún canalla la asuste para que lo diga
de todos modos. ¿Por qué tienen tanto poder los
canallas del mundo? No lo sé.

No había ninguna conclusión graciosa al final, ninguna despedida tranquilizadora. La carta simplemente se detenía. Fui al dormitorio de Eunice y
llamé a la puerta. Abrió con el pelo revuelto y la cara hinchada.

—¿Qué pasa, Noah?

Miré detrás de ella a la habitación oscura, y tuve la impresión de un espacio más profundo y amplio… el enorme salón de baile de un cuento de hadas,
con ventanas del suelo al techo llenas de luz de luna. Eché un vistazo a la cara
cansada e impaciente de mi hermana, y luego de nuevo al dormitorio. Esta vez

tenía el aspecto del dormitorio de Eunice… ordenado, atiborrado de libros, con un televisor pequeño sobre el tocador, emitiendo una pálida luz azul.

Levanté su nota.

—Quería asegurarme de que estabas bien.

—Estoy bien —dijo.

—Me da la impresión de que quizás no lo estés.

—*Estoy bien* —repitió, poniendo énfasis en cada palabra—. Creía que te gustaba leer lo que me pasa por la mente, pero si no eres lo bastante maduro para lidiar con ello… —Extendió la mano para tomar la nota.

—No, no —dije, retrocediendo—. Supongo que he reaccionado exageradamente. Siento haberte molestado. Y… siento… ya sabes.

Hizo una mueca.

—Hablaré contigo más tarde.

CAPÍTULO 12

La noche siguiente, me excusé de salir a cenar tarde con Kyle y Donna después de que se marcharan las últimas visitas, y me quedé ayudando a mi madre a cerrar el negocio. La encontré en el escritorio, contando el efectivo.

—Estoy preocupado por Eunice —dije.

—¿Ah, sí? —preguntó, sin levantar la vista.

Le conté mis razones (exceptuando la sexualidad de Eunice), y cuando terminé, se recostó sobre su asiento y se frotó los ojos con los talones de las manos. Por primera vez, noté los mechones grises de su pelo, los surcos de las líneas de risa alrededor de su boca. Había cumplido cincuenta y un años, pero hasta ese momento no había advertido que realmente estaba envejeciendo.

—Eunice siempre ha sido así —dijo—. Una pelea con su amiga podría intensificar las cosas, pero mientras esté tomando sus medicamentos, lo único que queda es esperar que pase. Mejorará cuando esté lista para hacerlo.

—Esta vez parece diferente —dije.

Alzó las cejas.

—¿En qué sentido?

¿Acaso podía ser tan ciega? ¿No había notado el cambio en Eunice cuando Brin había entrado en nuestras vidas? ¿No había sospechado nunca?

—¿De verdad no lo sabes? —pregunté.

Me dirigió una mirada fría, como retándome a seguir, a atravesar la frontera que nos separaba, a cruzar la tierra de nadie en que se había convertido la desaparición de Sydney y a empezar a admitir cosas. Cuando no lo hice, retomó el recuento de dinero.

—Entiendo que estés preocupado por tu hermana, pero te aseguro que estará bien.

Pero cuando llegué a casa, encontré una nota garabateada por Eunice en la encimera del baño de arriba:

Cuanto más se retraía del mundo que lo rodeaba, más maravillosos se volvían sus sueños; y habría sido completamente inútil intentar transcribirlos al papel. —H. P. Lovecraft, «Celephaïs»

No sé si tenía intención de que yo la viera o no.

CAPÍTULO 13

La semana pasó sin muchos incidentes. Mi Amigo aún no había reaparecido, así que pasé mis ratos libres leyendo y viendo la televisión con el volumen bajo, para poder prestar atención a los movimientos de Eunice. No se movió mucho... mayormente del dormitorio al baño o a la cocina. Su pelo estaba grasiento y revuelto, y sus ojos hinchados ya fuera por demasiado sueño o demasiado poco. Hice lo que me había dicho mi madre: le di su espacio.

Al lunes siguiente Kyle se quedó en casa enfermo, así que Donna y yo comimos juntos en la cafetería sin la presencia de nuestro mediador habitual, ambos en silencio mientras comíamos la pizza fría y gomosa servida por el colegio. Aun ofuscado por la preocupación que sentía por Eunice y Mi Amigo, me daba cuenta de que Donna estaba preparándose para decir algo.

—La otra noche, ¿recuerdas cuando Kyle me llevó en coche a casa después de irnos? —preguntó—. ¿La noche en que te quedaste atrás para ayudar a tu madre? Pasó algo, y tengo miedo de cómo te lo tomarás.

—¿Qué pasó? —pregunté.

—Nos dimos una especie de beso.

—¿Una especie? —Como si fueran dos palabras por las cuales valiera la pena discutir.

—No fue algo que planeáramos. —Por fin, me dirigió la mirada—. Lo invité a entrar para que viera la gentileza de ébano… que aún sigue viva, dicho sea de paso… y luego… —Su voz se fue acallando, y se encogió de hombros—. Me distraje, y cuando volví en mí, estábamos besándonos. Sé que parece mentira, pero por un minuto fue como si me hubiera olvidado de que tuviera un novio. De hecho, últimamente he estado olvidándome de muchas cosas.

No supe qué decir… o siquiera cómo sentirme. Me sentí echando mano de las herramientas que me habían entregado todas las escenas de ruptura y engaño de todos los programas de televisión o películas que jamás hubiera visto. Pero me contuve cuando me di cuenta de que sería algo vacío. La admisión de Donna solo me provocó un sentimiento de alivio. Acabaría y no sería mi culpa.

—No te preocupes —dije—. No pasa nada. —Clavé el tenedor en mi pizza; en realidad, no tenía hambre.

—¿Lo dices en serio?

—Claro. No pasa nada. Estamos bien. —Dejé el almuerzo sobre la mesa y salí de la cafetería. Mi mente ya estaba en otro sitio.

CAPÍTULO 14

Aquella noche me situé en el borde del tejado y grité hacia las sombras de la noche.

—Si estás ahí fuera, te necesito.

La llamada funcionó. Instantes después, el monstruo descendió a través del aire hasta quedar suspendido delante de mí.

—Gracias por venir —dije—. Entra.

Volví a entrar mi habitación, y la criatura me siguió. No ocupó su sitio habitual sobre la cama, sino que permaneció junto a la ventana, como listo para volver a despegar.

—Te he echado de menos las últimas dos semanas —dije. Algo en mis palabras ablandó su postura—. ¿Dónde has estado?

Levantó la libreta y el bolígrafo de mi escritorio y escribió: ¿NECESITAS ALGO?

Me di cuenta de que se resistía a contarme dónde había estado, pero decidí no seguir insistiendo en ello.

—No sé si te mantienes informado de las noticias —dije—, pero han desaparecido dos chicos en las últimas semanas. Todo el pueblo está bastante asustado por ello... y también mi familia. Pero hoy se me ha ocurrido que yo tengo un mejor amigo que puede volar y hacer magia. Así que he pensado que quizás puedas ayudarme, ya sabes, a encontrar a los chicos. Y traerlos de vuelta a casa.

La criatura se inclinó de nuevo hacia la libreta y garabateó una única palabra con trazos rápidos y decisivos:

NO.

—¿No? —pregunté. Mi Amigo jamás me había rechazado antes—. Esos chicos necesitan nuestra ayuda. Incluso si estás enfadado conmigo, ¿no te importan?

Subrayó ese NO tres veces. Luego escribió: PÍDELE AYUDA A DONNA.

—¿A Donna? —pregunté—. Donna y yo hemos terminado. Estoy pidiéndotelo a ti.

Mi Amigo me miró un instante, y por primera vez en años, me sentí incómodo bajo la intensidad de su mirada y el movimiento de sus hombros al respirar. Por fin suspiró y escribió: ¿QUÉ PUEDO HACER?

A petición mía, volamos al Winn-Dixie cerrado donde habían encontrado la bicicleta de Maria Davis. Tras dar vueltas al área por encima para asegurarnos de que no hubiera coches patrulla vigilando, aterrizamos en el aparcamiento. Tenía una hilera de farolas, pero estaban quemadas o habían sido apagadas por quienquiera que fuera el dueño de la propiedad. La única luz provenía de la calle, a unos veinte metros del escaparate de la tienda. Los ojos de la criatura lanzaban chispas en la luz vespertina mientras me dirigía una mirada inquisitiva.

—Echemos un vistazo —dije—. Llámame si encuentras algo.

Encendí mi linterna y me dirigí en una dirección mientras la criatura echaba a andar en la otra. El aparcamiento que alcancé a ver a la luz del amplio recorrido de mi linterna estaba casi sobrenaturalmente limpio, puesto que ya había sido revisado por un ejército de investigadores federales especialistas en escenas de crimen. Cuando llegué al borde del cemento, apagué mi luz y me giré para observar a Mi Amigo. Inclinado hacia delante, olisqueaba con la nariz a ras de la tierra.

Intenté imaginar lo que debió de haber pasado el día que habían raptado a Maria: el cielo parcialmente nublado, con el sol asomándose cada cierto rato entre los bancos de nubes; el cruce en bicicleta de un terreno vacío, una extensión de cemento toda para ella: algo que no terminaba de ser una prohibición pero de todos modos resultaba excitante; quizás una leve brisa agitándole el pelo cuando echaba a andar a toda prisa; la curiosidad cuando un coche aparcó en el terreno y condujo directo hacia ella. ¿Conocía al conductor? ¿O era un desconocido? ¿La convencieron para entrar en el coche o la metieron a la fuerza? Cuando el secuestrador se alejó, ¿pasó delante de la casa de Maria? ¿Llegó a echarle un último vistazo?

Al otro lado del terreno vacío, solo percibía el contorno oscuro y corpulento de la criatura, y una serie de olisqueos mientras recorría el terreno de un lado a otro. Pero luego los sonidos se detuvieron abruptamente. Mi Amigo hizo una pausa cerca del medio del aparcamiento, ahora mirando hacia mí.

—¿Qué pasa? —pregunté—. ¿Tienes algo?

Olisqueó un par de veces más el suelo. Luego me miró y sacudió la cabeza: *No*.

—¿No sientes nada raro? ¿No hay malas vibraciones en el aire?

La criatura inclinó la cabeza, y luego la volvió a sacudir... *No*... y supe lo que debería haber sabido... lo que al menos debí haber sospechado... semanas atrás. La criatura estaba mintiéndome.

—¿Conoces a mi madre? —pregunté.

No respondió, pero me pareció ver un indicio de sorpresa en el hundimiento de la curva de sus hombros, en el ligero retraimiento de la cabeza.

—Aquel dibujo de ti que realicé para el disfraz de mi trabajo —dije—. Cuando se lo mostré a mi madre, se comportó de modo extraño. Ya te ha visto antes, ¿verdad?

La criatura sacudió la cabeza.

—Justo después de enseñarle aquel dibujo, empezó a hablar de Maria Davis. ¿Por qué un dibujo de ti la haría empezar a pensar en niños desaparecidos? —pregunté—. Salvo que, de algún modo, ¿asocie el dibujo de ti con la desaparición de Sydney?

Un gruñido le subió desde la garganta y se apartó de mí. Lo más sensato habría sido olvidarlo, pero ahora me había enfadado. Era la primera vez en varias semanas que sentía algo *real*, y estaba preparado para sobrellevarlo. Me lancé hacia el monstruo y le di un empujón. Lo pillé por sorpresa, y de hecho se desplomó hacia delante sobre las rodillas.

—¡Puedes volar! —dije, corriendo para alcanzarlo—. ¡Haces magia! De algún modo sabes cómo encontrar juguetes de Batman, o qué ventana le pertenece a Donna en su casa. Desapareces cada vez que uno de esos chicos desaparece. *Tienes información.* Sé que sabes lo que les sucedió a Sydney, a Maria y a Brandon. ¡Así que deja de mentirme y dímelo! —Extendí el brazo para aferrar el hombro de la criatura, y me apartó de un manotazo. Esta vez fui yo quien se cayó de culo.

La criatura me enseñó los dientes y soltó un gruñido, lanzando destellos naranjas con sus ojos. Gotas de saliva chorreaban de entre sus dientes apretados. Cerré los ojos y alcé mis antebrazos, sabiendo que era una defensa penosa contra la carnicería y preguntándome por qué había tenido que llevar a la criatura hasta allí, tan lejos de casa, donde al menos podría haber pedido ayuda a gritos. Esperé para morir.

Y esperé.

Cuando abrí los ojos, la criatura había desaparecido, dejándome solo en un aparcamiento quién sabe dónde.

CAPÍTULO 15

Caminé hasta la gasolinera más cercana y llamé a casa desde una cabina telefónica. La cara de mi madre estaba lívida cuando entró en el aparcamiento media hora después, la mandíbula desencajada y los orificios nasales ensanchados a través del parabrisas del coche. Seguía llevando el pijama.

Corrí desde el escaparate de la tienda y me desplomé dentro del asiento del acompañante. Sentí que me taladraba con la mirada, pero miré hacia delante.

—No sé ni por dónde empezar —dijo.

—Lo siento —dije.

—¿Qué *narices* hacías aquí? ¿Solo?

—Me escabullí para dar una vuelta con algunos amigos y me han dejado plantado —respondí.

—¿Qué amigos? ¿Ha sido Kyle? —Resultaba raro que su inquietud maternal pareciera emerger solo cuando estaba enfadada conmigo. Me hubiera gustado decir que eso hacía que su furia fuera más agradable, pero hubiera sido una mentira. Seguía pareciéndome una mierda.

—No, mamá, no ha sido Kyle —dije—. Esta noche Kyle está con Donna. —No lo sabía a ciencia cierta, pero parecía una apuesta segura. Como estaba «enfermo», quizás le hubiera llevado caldo de gallina y le hubiera contado lo de mi permiso e indiferencia.

—¿Kyle con Donna? —preguntó, suavizando la voz. Crucé los brazos sobre el pecho y bajé la mirada a mi regazo. Dejaría que sacara sus propias conclusiones.

—Lo siento —dijo. Y luego, casi para sí—. Te has sentido herido, así que has salido y has hecho algo estúpido.

—Quería ver dónde había desaparecido Maria Davis —dije. Nunca estaba de más deslizar una dosis de verdad—. Creía que tal vez podía encontrar algo que se le hubiera escapado a la policía y… —mi voz se fue perdiendo y me encogí de hombros.

—Menuda estupidez —dijo, su voz recobró su tono de acero—. Cielo santo, ¿sabes la suerte que tienes de estar aquí, en *este* coche, en este momento, en lugar de estar en las noticias, como tu hermana y los otros dos?

—Sí —dije. Se me ocurrió que era aún más consciente que ella. Me arriesgué a mirarla a los ojos, y vi preocupación real mezclada con furia.

—Debería despedirte —dijo—. Hacer que te quedes en casa sin participar en el Laberinto del Terror durante el resto del año. Quizás sea lo único que te ayude a entender la gravedad de lo que has hecho esta noche. Y si Sydney no hubiera desaparecido justo después de renunciar al Laberinto en 1989, eso es exactamente lo que habría hecho. Pero prefiero que estés en un sitio donde pueda mantenerte vigilado. Así que así es como funcionará: quedas castigado de ahora en adelante. Vas al colegio, vas a trabajar, y vuelves a casa. Y esa será toda tu vida hasta que yo diga lo contario.

Después de la noche que acababa de pasar, me pareció que estaba librándome de una buena. Asentí e hice un esfuerzo por parecer contrito.

CAPÍTULO 16

Castigado, sin novia, temporalmente distanciado de mi mejor amigo y mortalmente aterrorizado del monstruo. Estaba mucho más tiempo en casa, pero apenas veía a Eunice. Se ocultaba en su dormitorio o se apropiaba del ordenador de la familia. Tecleaba a un ritmo vertiginoso durante horas, y rara vez parecía detenerse para pensar. Mi madre decía que teníamos que darle espacio, que Eunice atravesaría el territorio de la depresión a su propio ritmo, pero es difícil vivir con una persona deprimida. La depresión ocupa espacio físico, se desparrama y se filtra bajo puertas cerradas. Se cuela entre habitaciones como un gas letal, cubriendo la casa como un manto de neblina.

En un acto de supervivencia, decidí intentar alegrar a Eunice. El tercer día de mi castigo, llamé a la puerta de su habitación cuando llegué del colegio. No obtuve respuesta alguna, pero entré de todos modos. La encontré en la cama, enredada en un lío de sábanas. Había clavado una manta sobre la ventana, bloqueando la mayoría de la luz exterior, y la habitación olía a carne humana sin lavar. El suelo estaba abarrotado de ropa sucia; platos cubiertos de pegotes de comida seca estaban apilados sobre el escritorio.

La sacudí del hombro y se despertó con un sobresalto.

—No pasa nada —dije, con tono suave—. Soy yo.

La brusca inhalación de aire provocada por el temor emergió como un largo e irritado suspiro. Abrió y cerró la boca con un chasquido. Curvó sus labios en un mohín de disgusto ante lo que fuera que estaba probando.

—¿Qué hora es? —preguntó.

—Cerca de las cuatro.

Soltó un gemido, se estiró y le dio una patada a un libro que había sobre la cama. Aterrizó abierto sobre el suelo, boca abajo, con las hojas torcidas. *El ciclo del sueño, de H. P. Lovecraft: Sueños de terror y muerte.* Alzó la cabeza, pareció hallarlo demasiado difícil y lo volvió a dejar caer sobre la almohada.

—Tengo la noche libre —dije—. Estoy castigado, pero no creo que a mamá le importe que alquiles algunas películas para que veamos juntos.

—No me siento con ánimos —dijo.

—¿Y cenar? —intenté de nuevo—. Tengo dinero. Podríamos pedir una pizza.

—Invita a Donna.

—Hemos roto —dije.

Miró el techo.

—Noah, no seas tan obtuso. Quiero estar sola. No puedes esperar que de pronto sea tu mejor amiga porque te han dejado.

—No es así.

—Ya entiendo —dijo—. Mamá te ignoró cuando eras pequeño, así que fui yo quien tuve que ocuparme de alimentarte y quererte y felicitarte cuando sacabas una buena nota o venías con un proyecto de arte. Pero ya no eres un niño, ¿así que qué te parece si dejas de joderme y me das un poco de tiempo para mí?

—Esto no va únicamente de mí —dije, intentando no alterar el tono—. Me ha parecido que te vendría bien un poco de tiempo fuera de tu habitación… o incluso de tu propia cabeza.

—No tengo la suerte de poder abandonar esta habitación —dijo—. Tengo un cerebro tan grande como Saturno, pero voy a una universidad comunitaria por una alteración química. Estoy atrapada en un infierno de cemento conservador, descomponiéndome por dentro y justificándole mis decisiones a un narcisista con un 6 de promedio, que tiene problemas con su madre. Así que, por favor, escúchame bien antes de seguir soltando una sarta de tonterías sobre mi bienestar: si te vas a la mierda y me dejas sola, no me pasará una mierda.

—Eunice.

—Vete. A. La. Mierda.

Empecé a dirigirme hacia la puerta, pero estaba demasiado enfadado. Me volví y dije:

—No, vete tú a la mierda. Solo intentaba ayudar a que olvidaras a esa estúpida zorra religiosa, eres una… —Busqué algo para hacerle daño como ella me lo había hecho, y tomé la fruta más vil y rastrera—: Espero que Brin tenga razón y te pudras en el infierno.

Cerré la puerta de un golpe detrás de mí. Me temblaba todo el cuerpo. Podría haber matado a alguien en aquel momento. Quería matar a alguien. En cambio, bajé las escaleras como una tromba y arranqué las llaves de su coche del gancho de la puerta principal.

Robé el coche lo más silenciosamente que pude. No salí acelerando o con la radio a todo volumen. El acto de conducir, que seguía siendo nuevo y raro, me relajó los nervios. Me deslicé a través del pueblo sin rumbo. A medida que el sol descendía, disminuía el tráfico. Conduje de vuelta al Winn-Dixie clausurado, donde Mi Amigo y yo habíamos discutido agresivamente por última vez.

Aparqué mi coche en el terreno y miré fuera del parabrisas, intentando imaginar de nuevo lo que había sucedido: el monstruo, arrancando a Maria Davis de su bicicleta y llevándosela en secreto a… ¿a dónde? ¿Y a plena luz del día? Brandon Hawthorne había sido raptado de noche, pero no Maria. ¿Mi Amigo aparecía alguna vez en algún sitio a la luz del sol? Supongo que era una prueba de lo poco que lo conocía de verdad.

Una vez que el sol se puso y, a pesar de mi angustia interna, empecé a sentir hambre e inquietud. Encendí el coche y me dirigí a casa, conduciendo apenas por debajo del límite de velocidad. Intentaba pensar qué decirle a mi hermana, cómo retractarme de las palabras odiosas que le había lanzado. Estaba tan preocupado que alrededor de tres kilómetros de mi casa, al empezar un giro exclusivo hacia la izquierda, no vi al otro coche hasta que la luz inundó la ventanilla del lado del pasajero y el mundo se dio la vuelta, una ráfaga confusa de hormigón y farolas.

CAPÍTULO 17

El coche se detuvo con un chirrido, y me quedé sentado con las manos sobre el volante, respirando agitado. No me dolía nada, pero mi cuerpo lanzaba destellos como el agua al sol. Cristal. Estaba cubierto de cristal roto. A través del parabrisas resquebrajado vi el otro coche, una furgoneta VW, también detenida, orientada en dirección contraria, hacia el tráfico que venía en sentido opuesto. Uno de sus faros estaba roto, y la puerta corrediza colgaba abierta.

Me llevó tres intentos quitarme el cinturón de seguridad. Cuando abrí la puerta, caí sobre el hormigón, pero apenas lo sentí. Me puse de pie sobre las piernas tambaleantes y crucé trastabillando hacia la furgoneta. El conductor estaba desplomado sobre el volante. La cabeza me daba vueltas y retumbaba.

—¿Está bien? —pregunté.

La figura al volante gimió y se movió un poco. La puerta lateral estaba abierta y la luz interior estaba encendida, un resplandor amarillo tenue y tranquilizador. Me detuve en mitad de la calle, alegrado por su calidez reconfortante. Pero cuando un hedor putrefacto y dulzón me alcanzó de golpe tuve que taparme la boca y la nariz con las manos. Contuve el aliento y escudriñé el contenido de la furgoneta: latas de cerveza vacías, basura de comida rápida, un extintor tumbado en el suelo, y, en mitad de todo ello, un bulto negro brillante. Una bolsa de basura… no, varias bolsas de basura apiladas, con un cargamento deforme e irregular.

Una mano me aferró del antebrazo y me apartó de un tirón. Me encontré ante un hombre alto y sucio, con barba y pelo grasiento. Llevaba una variedad de prendas reusadas dispares, de las que se consiguen en una tienda de segunda mano. Olía terriblemente mal. Sangraba de un corte en la frente. Lo conocía de algún sitio.

—¿Qué hace? —pregunté—. ¿Está bien? Está sangrando.

—¿Por qué mirabas dentro de mi camioneta? —preguntó—. No es asunto tuyo.

—Y-yo no quería… lo siento —dije. Su hedor me hacía difícil pensar con claridad. No pude evitar echarle otro vistazo a la puerta abierta.

Su mano me apretó el brazo aún más fuerte.

—No es asunto tuyo —repitió.

Cuando empezaba a volver la vista, algo se movió en la parte trasera de la furgoneta. Una de las bolsas, impulsada por algún cambio minúsculo y oculto, rodó hacia delante, se inclinó fuera del automóvil y cayó golpeando la calle con un sonido fuerte y pesado. La bolsa estaba bien atada, así que no hubo nada que detuviera el objeto pálido cuando cayó fuera y quedó expuesto en marcado contraste con la bolsa negra y el pavimento gris: una única mano pequeña.

El hombre me vio advertirla. Tuve el tiempo suficiente para detectar otro brillo, esta vez, el de un cuchillo dentado, pero no el suficiente para poder reaccionar antes de que la hoja levantara el vuelo, trazando un arco lateral en el aire entre los dos, extrañamente bello. Me pregunté por qué tenía que ser tan bonito. Antes de que se me ocurriera una respuesta, un gran peso se estrelló contra mí, el mundo volvió a girar y caí derribado sobre el pavimento. Oí el cuchillo alejarse con un repiqueteo.

Me incorporé un poco, tanteando mi cuerpo para ver si tenía heridas, sin encontrar ninguna. Una figura encapuchada se agazapó entre mí y el otro hombre, impidiéndome ver. Se alzó alcanzando su altura total: Mi Amigo. Un gruñido grave brotó de su garganta. Su capa roja parecía ondear a su alrededor, libre del peso de la gravedad.

Mi agresor inclinó la cabeza al tiempo que la criatura se acercó, dirigiéndome una mirada de leve consideración. Abrió la boca, pero antes de que saliera una palabra, algo más cayó del cielo y aterrizó entre los dos. Se parecía a Mi Amigo, pero era diferente, con el pelo más gris que marrón. Una cicatriz le recorría el lateral de la cara. Llevaba una capa azul, en lugar de roja.

El mío no era el único. Allí había otro monstruo de aspecto más feroz. Emitió un rugido y exhibió los colmillos, protegiendo al hombre roñoso. Mi Amigo estiró los brazos y retrocedió un paso. El hombre gritó de nuevo: «¡No es asunto tuyo!», y la Bestia Gris se abalanzó con un bramido. Mi Amigo cayó al suelo y se cubrió la cabeza con las zarpas. La Bestia Gris tropezó y cayó encima de él, las piernas quedaron atascadas con las capas enredadas, y se estrelló contra la calle.

Mi Amigo se dio la vuelta y se quedó a cuatro patas al tiempo que la Bestia Gris hacía lo mismo. Ahora esta se puso de cuclillas entre Mi Amigo y yo. Ambas criaturas parecieron advertir el revés al mismo tiempo, aunque la Bestia Gris fue más veloz. Galopó hacia mí sobre las cuatro patas y abrió sus enormes fauces de dientes afilados. La boca pareció abrirse más y más, llenando un espacio que no debía ser posible, creando un firmamento estrellado de colmillos.

Gateé hacia atrás con un brazo en alto, desplazándome demasiado lentamente. Cerré los ojos. Un chorro de algo húmedo me golpeó la cara, y Mi

Amigo aulló como un perro herido. Abrí los ojos para ver su cara junto a la mía, irradiando un dolor y un temor reales. Había metido el antebrazo entre las fauces de la Bestia; me encontraba cubierto de una capa brillante de su sangre negra.

Golpeó a la Bestia Gris con el brazo libre, pero sus golpes eran débiles. Me desplacé detrás de la Bestia, poniéndome en pie, y me arrojé sobre su espalda. Envolví los brazos alrededor de su garganta como un luchador de la televisión. Era como intentar estrangular el tubo de una estufa. La Bestia soltó la zarpa con la que tenía atenazado mortalmente a Mi Amigo y se giró en círculo lanzándome un puñetazo. Procuré envolver las piernas alrededor de su cintura, pero no encontraba apoyo. Intentó lanzarme zarpazos, primero a la izquierda, luego a la derecha; no pude esquivar ambos brazos a la vez. Sus garras me dieron en el lado izquierdo de la cara y se clavaron en ella. Grité al sentir que la vista de mi ojo izquierdo se tornaba roja y luego gris.

Alguien me arrancó a la Bestia de la espalda, y quedé colgado en el aire. En seguida, Mi Amigo me pegó a su cuerpo, su brazo débil empapando mi camisa de sangre. La Bestia Gris volvió a abalanzarse hacia nosotros. Mi Amigo me dejó caer. Se plantó con las rodillas dobladas y la atrapó por las fauces abiertas. Aulló al sentir que los colmillos le perforaban las zarpas, pero no la soltó. La lengua larga y de color púrpura de la Bestia se meneó casi de modo cómico en el interior de la boca abierta a la fuerza, sacudiéndose contra las zarpas de Mi Amigo como si fuera capaz de desprenderlas.

Mi Amigo se inclinó hacia delante y se puso de pie, obligando a la bestia a ponerse de rodillas. Esta le dio una bofetada, sus golpes rebotando a medida que le abrían la boca más y más. En aquel momento debí apartar la mirada. Mi Amigo le desgarró la mandíbula, separando la parte inferior del cráneo del resto. Arrojó los trozos a ambos lados. La mandíbula se unió al cuchillo de mi agresor en la oscuridad. Finalmente, el cuerpo de la Bestia se derrumbó formando una pila, un revoltijo de tela y sangre negra. Sus ojos naranjas se habían extinguido.

Mi Amigo profirió un grito de dolor y triunfo iracundo. El cristal que aún permanecía en el coche de Eunice y en la furgoneta VW estalló, y las farolas de la calle quedaron destrozadas, dejando toda el área inmediata sumida en la oscuridad.

—Mierda. No es asunto tuyo. —Era el hombre mugriento: su tono, menguado y aterrorizado—. No tenía que salir así. Quiero hacerlo de nuevo. Empezar de nuevo.

Por fin reconocí a quien había estado a punto de matarme. Lo había visto solo una vez: el día en que el coche de mi madre se incendió en 1989. Había apagado las llamas. Mierda. Qué pequeño mundo de mierda.

Mi Amigo empezó a caminar hacia él, probablemente con la intención de acabar el trabajo. En algún sitio las sirenas aullaron. Se acercaban coches con luces destellantes, llenos de individuos a quienes les pagaban para que restauraran al menos la ilusión de orden del mundo terrenal.

—Detente —dije, y Mi Amigo obedeció—. Déjalo. —Que fuera ese hombre quien explicara el accidente del coche, la pelea de los monstruos y el bulto de bolsas de basura en su furgoneta. Se lo tenía merecido.

Mi Amigo se arrodilló para levantarme. Su cara se estremeció de dolor y me miró queriendo saber adónde íbamos.

—*Lejos* —dije—. No a casa.

CAPÍTULO 18

El viento nos azotaba y luego se calmó. El aire adquirió un olor sulfuroso. Intenté alzar la cabeza y mirar alrededor, pero Mi Amigo me volvió a empujar la cara con suavidad dentro del pecho. Estaba prácticamente dormido cuando aterrizamos en el pequeño claro de un denso bosque. Los árboles eran tan gruesos que solo alcanzaba a ver oscuridad entre ellos. La arboleda y el césped eran negros como la tinta, y, por encima, el cielo tenía un matiz verde sombrío que parecía de algún modo familiar. Un montículo bajo, amplio y cubierto de hierba se alzaba en el centro del claro con una puerta a un lado. La colina estaba rodeada por gentilezas de ébano como la que le había regalado a Donna.

—¿Dónde estamos? —pregunté.

Mi Amigo me llevó en brazos a través de la puerta y descendimos una escalinata breve y serpenteante. La puerta se cerró detrás de nosotros, y las velas parpadearon y cobraron vida, iluminando el camino hacia una única habitación grande con suelo y paredes de madera. La criatura me colocó sobre una cama grande cubierta de mantas gruesas y peludas, y se dirigió a lo que parecía una pequeña cocina. Las paredes estaban decoradas con pinturas, empezando con imágenes sencillas de coches, edificios y personas, y pasando a piezas más complejas y abstractas que representaban tramas de color y sombras de figuras desenfocadas. En un rincón había un caballete tosco y una banqueta, y una paleta manchada sobre un taburete, junto con un jarro lleno de pinceles. Una serie de lienzos se apilaban detrás del caballete. El que estaba encima representaba dos caras horriblemente desfiguradas; el hecho de que estuvieran superpuestas lo convertía en un cuadro de tres dimensiones.

—¿Vives aquí? —pregunté.

La criatura no respondió. Trabajó con rapidez, aplastando algo y revolviéndolo en un tazón con agua. Cuando se dio la vuelta para mirarme de nuevo, sostuvo dos tazones en una zarpa, acomodando el brazo herido contra el cuerpo. Cruzó la habitación y me ofreció el recipiente. Mi brazo tembló al extenderse para recibirlo.

La criatura apoyó los tazones sobre el suelo y me envolvió con una manta de la cama. Levantó uno de los tazones y lo llevó a mis labios. El contenido era seco y amargo como la tierra. Intenté apartar la cabeza, pero me topé con los ojos de Mi Amigo y advertí su furiosa determinación. Me obligué a tragar el té de tierra. Poco a poco, los temblores disminuyeron, y un calor agradable se esparció por mi cuerpo adormeciéndome.

Cuando acabé mi tazón, la criatura apuró el suyo. Extendió su brazo herido y levantó la manga. Seguía sin pelo, pero las heridas se habían desvanecido y ahora eran cicatrices de color rosa pálido. Mi propio dolor había desaparecido en su mayor parte, pero aún veía solo una mancha gris con el ojo izquierdo.

—Mi ojo —dije—. ¿Se pondrá bien?

Mi Amigo sacudió la cabeza.

Empecé a llorar… al principio a causa del ojo, pero luego por mi pelea con Eunice, los horribles insultos que le había lanzado, el accidente, el otro conductor, el bulto de bolsas pestilentes en su furgoneta, y el otro monstruo.

—Los de la furgoneta eran ellos, ¿verdad? ¿Los chicos desaparecidos?

La criatura asintió con la cabeza.

—Así que ambos están muertos —dije.

La criatura volvió a asentir.

—Ese hombre los mató. Quizás mató a Sydney. Y también quería matarme a mí. Y aunque yo te acusé a ti, tú me salvaste la vida.

La criatura me tocó la cara, girando mi barbilla para fijar sus ojos en los míos. En un lapso de pocos segundos, su cuerpo se estrechó y redujo su tamaño, los hombros fornidos se acortaron y descendieron hasta estar a mi altura, el hocico se retrajo. Los ojos pasaron de ser dos oquedades brillantes de color naranja a cobrar un suave tinte verdoso. El pelaje fue lo último en desaparecer, retrayéndose tras la carne rosa para revelar a una mujer pálida con pómulos afilados, un mentón firme y una boca pequeña y resuelta. El largo pelo rojo estaba sujeto hacia atrás en una coleta.

Carraspeó.

—Te quiero —dijo—, y jamás te haría daño. —Tenía la voz ronca, y un acento que no conseguí identificar.

Quizás fuera la conmoción de la noche o la sencilla declaración de amor tras nuestro distanciamiento, la alegría de volver a juntarnos tras una experiencia al borde de la muerte. Cualquiera que fuera el motivo, me incliné hacia delante y atrapé su boca con la mía. Su beso fue enérgico, firme; sus manos, frías y callosas al rodear mi cara. Me empujó de espaldas quitándome la manta para que pudiera moverme. Le tomé la cara, las caderas, los muslos, bajo la túnica que ahora resultaba demasiado grande. Mis manos estaban demasiado excitadas, demasiado ávidas para quedarse quietas. Se montó sobre mí a horcajadas, apretándose contra mi ingle. Mi cuerpo respondió a la presión, fácil y libre, colmado de un urgente deseo.

Se abrió la túnica y dejó que se deslizara sobre sus hombros, descubriendo su piel de alabastro, sus pechos turgentes y redondos, la mata de vello púbico de color rojizo. Se movió sobre mí, empujando contra mi erección con una sonrisa leve.

Me desabrochó el cinturón, hizo saltar el botón de mis vaqueros y me abrió la cremallera de un tirón. Levanté el trasero, y juntos tironeamos de mis pantalones hasta que descendieron alrededor de mis rodillas. Luego me sujetó en su mano, me oprimió y descendió sobre mí.

Como mi primer beso, la primera vez que tuve sexo acabó antes siquiera de empezar. Me sentí avergonzado, pero la mirada compasiva y amable jamás abandonó la cara de la mujer. Lo soportó, aliviando mi humillación sobre oleadas de placer. Cuando terminaron los espasmos y empecé a ablandarme y a deslizarme fuera de ella, colocó las manos sobre mi pecho y dijo: «De nuevo». Una luz dorada se esparció en mi visión mental, y me sentí listo. Lo inesperado de la erección fue como una estocada al deslizarme de nuevo dentro. Soltó un leve jadeo.

La segunda vez duró mucho más. Me cabalgó con intensidad, frotándose con la mano, los ojos cerrados, la cabeza echada hacia atrás. Mientras se corría, gritó palabras que no comprendí, repitiéndolas una y otra vez hasta que se desplomó contra mi pecho y me provocó un segundo orgasmo, casi doloroso.

Después, se quedó recostada a mi lado con un brazo y una pierna sobre mi cuerpo, y presionó la cara contra mi cuello.

—Puedes cambiar de forma —dije, acariciando el muslo lechoso encima de mi torso.

—Sí —dijo, haciéndome cosquillas en la oreja con sus labios.

—¿Puedes convertirte en cualquier cosa? ¿En cualquiera?

—No. Solo en esto.

—¿Por qué no me lo habías enseñado antes?

No respondió, pero me sujetó con fuerza, como temiendo que fuera a abandonarla. Estaba demasiado exhausto para moverme, y feliz de permanecer donde estaba, lejos de los problemas complicados del mundo real.

CAPÍTULO 19

No había ventanas en la pequeña casa, así que no tenía ni idea de si era de día o de noche cuando desperté y la encontré mirándome, acariciando mi cara.

—¿Cómo te sientes? —preguntó.

—Con hambre —dije—. ¿Tienes comida?

—Nada que pueda gustarte —respondió—. Pero puedo traerte lo que quieras.

—No te preocupes —dije—. Es probable que deba volver a casa. Voy a estar metido en graves problemas por estrellar el coche de Eunice. Además, necesito ir a ver a un médico. Y ropa limpia. —Con reticencia, salí de la cama y empecé a vestirme.

Ella se incorporó apoyándose contra la pared, despeinada y preciosa.

—No *tienes* que irte.

—Claro que sí.

—Puedes quedarte aquí todo lo que quieras.

—¿Qué? ¿Y abandonar mi vida entera?

Inclinó la cabeza.

—Puedo traerte lo que quieras o necesites.

—¿Dónde estamos exactamente? —pregunté.

Hizo como si no me hubiera escuchado, y me observó vestirme en silencio.

—Me gustas más desvestido —dijo.

—¿Me llevarás a casa?

Se puso de pie y cruzó la cabaña, arrodillándose ante uno de los armarios. Observar su cuerpo desnudo realizando esos gestos cotidianos empezó a excitarme de nuevo, y estuve a punto de estar listo una tercera vez cuando volvió con una pequeña piedra negra en las manos. Estaba sujeta a un delgado trozo de cuerda.

—Toma esto —dijo, deslizándola sobre la cabeza. La piedra reposó fría sobre mi pecho. La levanté para examinarla: era perfectamente lisa, sin defecto alguno.

—Cuando quieras venir a verme —dijo—, solo aprieta la piedra en el puño y piensa en mí. No importa dónde estés, la piedra te traerá directamente a mi puerta principal. Y cuando estés listo para volver, vuelve a apretarla y piensa a dónde quieres ir. Yo te llevaré allí.

—Gracias —dije.

Sonrió, pero había un atisbo de tristeza en su sonrisa.

—Me gustaría que no tuvieras que irte.

—A mí también.

—¿Prometes que volverás? —Agachó la cabeza y me miró con sus ojos verdes de párpados pesados.

—En cuanto pueda.

CAPÍTULO 20

Mi primer viaje haciendo uso de la piedra negra me depositó en el porche delantero de mi familia bajo un día de sol luminoso. Podía oír los ladridos de perros y las risas de unos chicos en algún lugar al final de la calle. Busqué mis llaves con torpeza antes de recordar que las había dejado en el coche de Eunice. Sin muchas esperanzas, intenté entrar por la puerta. Para mi sorpresa, se abrió.

Entré y llamé:

—¿Hola?

La palabra quedó suspendida en la entrada y murió en el aire silencioso. Caminé hacia el comedor y encontré un cuenco a medio comer de Cheerios sobre la mesa. Los cereales estaban blandos, como si el cuenco hubiera estado fuera desde hacía muchas horas. Encontré otras cosas fuera de lugar: un marco de fotos que generalmente colgaba al pie de las escaleras, sobre el suelo, con el cristal agrietado y roto; una única gota de sangre sobre la alfombra de color crema; el auricular del teléfono colocado de lado al pie del sofá.

Encontré una nota de Eunice a mitad de la escalera, donde mi madre probablemente la hubiera dejado caer al abalanzarse hacia la puerta cerrada del baño. Estaba derribada; el agua en la bañera de color rosa; la porcelana teñida de color rojo, encima de la línea de flotación; la navaja de afeitar caída de forma descuidada sobre la alfombra.

Me senté sobre el retrete. El ojo izquierdo me latía, y el mundo giraba a mi alrededor.

Abajo sonó el teléfono. Su trino agudo llenó la casa. Sonaba imposiblemente lejano, un grito de auxilio que jamás podría responder a tiempo.

La última carta de Eunice

Querido Noah:

Lo primero que quiero que hagas es que dejes esta carta a
un lado, y no la vuelvas a levantar hasta que me hayas
perdonado. Lo digo en serio. Hazlo.

Está bien. Quizás ya hayan pasado seis meses y estés
hecho un ovillo en tu cama, tomándote un descanso de los
deberes mientras mamá ve la televisión en la habitación de
al lado, o quizás hayan transcurrido años y años y estés
sentado en alguna mecedora del porche de un idílico hogar
de ancianos con ventanas altas y un extenso parque verde.
Tal vez tu pelo ya haya encanecido y tu piel tenga el
efecto moteado de la vejez. No lo sé; no puedo verlo, y ese
es el problema. No puedo verte. Ya no puedo ver nada, salvo
esto, ahora.

Es 28 de octubre, y estoy en la habitación del
ordenador con las luces apagadas. En el exterior la noche
está despejada, y un morboso dedo de luz verde se asoma a
través de las cortinas metálicas; riñe con la luz del
monitor sobre el suelo a mis espaldas, peleando por mi
sombra. He guardado todos mis libros, CD y ropa en cajas
etiquetadas. Solo queda la tarea final. Aunque había
algunas alternativas tentadoras, he elegido el método
anticuado. Quiero dejar algún pequeño desorden, aunque no
mucho. Cuando acaben todos los lamentos y rechinamientos
de dientes, puedes quitar el tapón, hacer correr un poco
de agua limpia, y usar las burbujas para limpiar la
porcelana.

He hecho esto porque te quiero.

Por favor no creas que esto es tu culpa. Siento lo que te dije, y no estoy enfadada porque te hayas llevado el coche. Es importante decir estas cosas porque solo hay una palabra que importa en estas situaciones: *¿Por qué?* Si no explicas tu respuesta (o respuestas) con precisión legalista, las personas que quedan se echan la culpa a ellas mismas. Para esas cosas, las personas son egoístas y egocéntricas.

Cuando me despierto por la mañana, me duele todo. Es como si tuviera gripe, pero sin la fiebre ni los vómitos. Solo un dolor aplastante y pena por haber sobrevivido otra noche más. Sé lo que estás pensando: *Eunice, hace años que sabemos lo de tu depresión. Por eso es importante que te tomes los medicamentos.* El problema es que los medicamentos han dejado de funcionar. Los tomo todos los días, y aun así sufro. Cuando me miro en el espejo, no veo mi cara. Veo a un ser que se desintegra poco a poco, con círculos oscuros bajo los ojos turbios y desenfocados, y labios agrietados que sangran cuando intentan sonreír. A veces, cuando las personas me hablan, no puedo oírlas, y cuando las oigo, no sé qué responderles. Suele ser algo desacertado, como ha quedado demostrado esta noche.

No tengo intención de ser así. He intentado mejorar, pero jamás seré una persona normal. Siempre tendré algún defecto. Por mucho que lo intente, por mucho que haga, siempre fallaré. No seré bonita ni deportista, y no gustaré a los chicos. Y lo peor: a mí no me gustarán los chicos. Noah, si alguna vez te cruzas con ella, y consigues decirlo de modo natural, dile a Brin que lamento no haber nacido chico. No es que quiera ser realmente un chico, pero cambiaría toda mi identidad si pudiera amarla de ese modo.

No dejo de hacer una pausa cada vez que oigo la puerta de un coche. Me levanto y voy a la ventana, pensando que eres tú, sereno y listo para intentar volver a hablar

conmigo. Imagino tus disculpas farfulladas, la
preocupación reflejada en tu cara sencilla y abierta, mi
coraje y decisión que vacilan al construir juntos el
incómodo puente que nos reconectará. Me veo cediendo a tu
necesidad de que todo esté bien, y arrastrándome un día,
o una semana, o un mes más. Quizás arrastrándome toda la
vida por ti. Pero luego miro fuera de la ventana y no eres
tú.

Probablemente, dentro de poco, cuando organicen mi
funeral, alguna persona con lágrimas en los ojos se ponga
de pie detrás de un púlpito junto a mi ataúd y hable
extensamente sobre mi egoísmo. ¿Cómo me atreví? ¿Qué
derecho tenía? A esa persona le digo (y espero que lo
transmitas): debería avergonzarse. Kierkegaard dijo (creo)
que la sociedad siempre ha considerado el suicidio como un
tabú porque, cuando una persona se mata, la gente que la
conoce empieza a preguntarse por el valor de su propia
vida, y eso los incomoda. Descúbrelo tú mismo: ¿por qué es
tan valiosa tu vida?

¿Por qué es tan valiosa mi vida? La curva de las caderas
de Brin. Su risa. Las caras que ponías tú cuando te solía
leer. Ver a papá hacer reír a mamá, y el cuerpo de ella
sacudiéndose. Ver a Sydney bailar, la forma en que el
movimiento parecía liberarla y convertirla en otra mujer.
La sensación de cuando tecleaba tan rápido que mi Commodore
64 apenas podía seguirme el ritmo. La boca de Brin
cubriendo la mía.

Estoy atrapada aquí, en el *home office* familiar, lejos
de todo aquello (salvo el tecleo, por supuesto). Atrapada
en este cuerpo, atascada en el tiempo lineal.

Hace poco tuve un sueño interesante. Por lo general
tengo sueños aburridos, como perder las llaves del coche
u olvidarme de estudiar para un examen, pero la otra
noche soñé que Brin aparecía en nuestra puerta principal
y me pedía que saliera a dar una vuelta con ella. Nos

metíamos en su coche y cruzábamos la noche, atravesando
un extraño territorio montañoso. El cuero sintético del
tapizado dañado del asiento me raspaba la nuca. El motor
avanzaba resoplando como el jubilado más simpático del
mundo, y todo el tiempo Brin tan solo miraba el camino
con la sonrisa extraña de una Madona. No nos detuvimos
para comer, ni para echar gasolina, ni para usar el baño.
No hacía falta.

Al final, nos detuvimos en un aparcamiento de gravilla
en la cima de una colina.

—Quédate donde estás —dijo—. Y mantén los ojos cerrados.

Hice lo que dijo. Dio la vuelta, abrió mi puerta, y me
ofreció la mano para ayudarme a salir. Me guio para que
saliera de la gravilla y pisara el césped.

—Ahora —dijo—. Abre los ojos.

Me quedé de pie en la cima de la colina. Las estrellas
brillaban como bombillas grandes allí arriba, y había una
luna creciente convertida en halo. A mí izquierda había un
tocón marrón. Extendí la mano para tocarlo, y me di cuenta
de que parecía un cuadro impresionista viviente: las
pinceladas de mi cuerpo vibraban y se movían, no de modo
equilibrado, pero de todos modos era grato en cuanto al
desapego por cosas tan simples y aburridas como la
uniformidad. Levanté la mirada al cielo y vi un precioso
jardín de estrellas, como dientes de león atrapados por un
viento visible que se desplegaba. Titilaban con cierto
orden, como comunicando un mensaje cifrado.

El viento visible se plegaba y se desplegaba. Se plegaba
y se desplegaba. Se plegaba, lo contenía, y lenta e
indulgente, se desplegaba. Se movía al ritmo de mis
pulmones. Le eché una mirada a Brin, que estaba detrás. Se
había quitado el disfraz punk. Llevaba un vestido negro y
verde que se adhería a su figura y empujaba sus pechos
hacia su barbilla. Llevaba el pelo desatado alrededor de la
cara, una confederación suelta de rizos oscuros insinuados

en grandes pinceladas que danzaban alrededor de su cabeza, cambiando su aspecto de un segundo a otro.

—Vamos —dijo, y señaló hacia un pequeño pueblo al pie de la colina—. Te enseñaré los alrededores.

La seguí colina abajo por el sendero. Los edificios enclavados en las laderas y la imponente torre de la iglesia aumentaron de tamaño a medida que me acerqué, y noté luces cálidas en las ventanas, figuras que iban y venían por las calles a pesar de lo tarde que era. Oí el zumbido de conversación, risa dispersa, música.

Me condujo calle arriba y nos internamos en la aldea, pasando puertas cerradas y ventanas esmeriladas con luces naranjas detrás de ellas. Una de las puertas se abrió, y una figura pequeña salió como una flecha: un niño, con una capa y una capucha negras. Corrió por el sendero delante de nosotros, el pelo revoloteando por detrás, y giró una esquina, desapareciendo.

—¿Qué ha sido eso? —pregunté, señalando al chico, segura de que lo reconocería.

—Vamos —dijo Brin, conduciéndome por el sendero—. Ya verás.

La calle serpenteante terminaba en una especie de plaza, amplia y adoquinada, con un pozo en el centro. La gente se apiñaba en torno a los vendedores ambulantes para comprar fruta y pescado y pan; los niños corrían, y un hombre tocaba el acordeón mientras parejas jóvenes bailaban. Las notas que tocaba eran tan visibles como el viento, una aurora boreal que subía lanzando destellos desde su instrumento. Reconocí al señor Ransom, corpulento y sonrojado, vendiendo pescado, y a Sydney bailando con un hombre apuesto que no reconocí. Su vestido de campesina volaba a su alrededor, atrapado en el viento. Empecé a reconocer también a otras personas: Merrin Price, mi antigua coguionista del Laberinto del Terror, vendiendo fruta; Hubert Sangalli, mi amigo del colegio primario, comprando un sombrero. Rick, el antiguo colega de mi padre del departamento de carreteras, construyendo un escenario. Mientras lo observaba colocar una pata en su sitio con el martillo, me di cuenta de que, a medida que el viento llevaba el compás de mi aliento, el mundo llevaba el compás de la melodía. El viento visible fluía junto con las notas del acordeón, ejecutando una especie de danza interpretativa. Y bajo la música, casi enterrado, el golpeteo de teclas de una vieja máquina de escribir manual que marcaba el ritmo de la canción.

—¿Dónde…? —pregunté, buscando indicios del mecanógrafo en la plaza. Pero antes de que pudiera terminar la pregunta, Brin pegó su cuerpo contra el mío, apoyando la mano derecha sobre mi cadera.

—Baila conmigo —dijo, haciéndome girar. El mundo dio vueltas a mi alrededor, al principio, de modo lento, y luego más veloz. Figuras discernibles, como personas, casas, el pozo, los puestos ambulantes, perdieron definición, y se convirtieron en un chorro de pintura exprimida de tubos, mezclándose como un remolino cargado de color. Lo único que retuvo su definición fue Brin, el centro de gravedad que me mantenía en órbita, haciéndome girar. De algún modo, conocía los pasos del baile; desapareció mi torpeza cotidiana, arrastrada por el torrente de color, el tecleo de mis pies sobre los adoquines. Mantuve los ojos fijos en Brin. A medida que la canción alcanzó su clímax, me atrajo hacia ella haciéndome girar y me besó. Me demoré sobre su boca mientras se alejaba; mi cara quedó suspendida en el espacio vacío. Parecía a punto de decir algo más cuando el niño con la capa volvió a cruzar la plaza a toda carrera. Tú, Noah, con seis años y obsesionado con Batman, zigzagueando entre la gente camino a las puertas de la iglesia de torre elevada. Aferraste la manilla de una de las puertas dobles y tiraste de ella. Al principio, no se movió, así que te inclinaste hacia atrás y apoyaste todo tu peso en ella. La puerta se abrió chirriando con evidente reticencia, derramando una luz blanca, pura y casi cegadora, sobre la plaza.

Solté a Brin y me lancé para alcanzarte cuando entraste en la iglesia. Pero me detuve en el umbral, confundida por lo que veía. Trata de imaginar dos o tres películas diferentes proyectadas simultáneamente sobre una pantalla, una confusión de imágenes que compiten entre sí, ninguna una iglesia. Vi a papá, empujándome sobre un columpio en un parque; a mamá, dándome una compresa de hielo después de golpearme la cabeza en el patio de recreo; a mí y a Merrin, escribiendo juntas en el Laberinto del Terror; a mí y a Brin en mi habitación oscura, las narices pegadas y cubiertas de sudor, enredadas entre las sábanas. Vi La Tumba y el Laberinto del Terror superpuestas, la primera, de algún modo, afianzando la segunda. Vi al monstruo arrastrando a las Katie y los Brad mientras me paraba a un lado en mi túnica blanca, observando. Y luego las imágenes que competían entre sí se desvanecieron, y vi lo que pareció una galería de arte, un espacio amplio y tenuemente iluminado, paredes blancas cubiertas de cuadros, y en el centro, una mujer pelirroja que jamás había visto, con un vestido rojo. Corriste hacia ella, te rodeó con un brazo, y la puerta se cerró de golpe. Avancé, intentando abrirla de un tirón, pero le habían echado la llave para que yo no entrara.

Me volví para ver a Brin a mi lado, las manos dobladas por delante.

—¿Qué lugar es este? —pregunté.

Brin abrió la boca como para responder, pero en ese momento me desperté.

He estado intentando volver a aquel sueño desde entonces, pero me es esquivo. En cambio, he vuelto a soñar con clases suspendidas y llaves de coche perdidas. No

puedo quitarme de la cabeza aquella aldea: llena de
personas que conozco, sonriendo y riendo, pintadas en su
mejor y más perfecta versión. Aquella iglesia-galería de
arte, contigo y la mujer pelirroja y toda la eternidad
tras sus puertas. La Brin del sueño, a punto de responder
a mi pregunta, la pregunta que podría responder a todas
las demás. Después de un sueño así, ¿cómo se supone que
tengo que vivir con la monotonía de estar atrapada en este
cuerpo feo que se pudre, yendo a mis clases de mierda y
moviéndome a cámara lenta a través del tiempo en la
dirección equivocada?

Sentada aquí, mientras escribo todo esto, creo que por
fin lo entiendo. Papá me dijo una vez que todo relato de
terror tiene un final feliz, pero estaba equivocado. Mira
cómo ha terminado mi vida. No hay tal cosa como un final
feliz, Noah. Las canciones, los libros y las películas con
«finales felices» se detienen en el momento de triunfo. No
cuentan toda la historia. Solo las viejas tragedias cuentan
la verdad. Beowulf vence a Grendel y a su madre, para caer
peleando contra un dragón. Gilgamesh pierde a su mejor
amigo. Aquiles también. Todo el mundo muere en *Hamlet*. Esa
es la pura verdad.

De todos modos, hay buenos sitios en los que parar.
Cometí el error de pasarme el mío, es todo. Soy como la
leche estropeada que queda olvidada dentro de una jarra.
Necesito que me viertan fuera y seguir adelante. Necesito
tener libertad para circular por la eternidad y la
infinidad, para pasar un siglo sobre el pecho de Brin,
escuchando los latidos de su corazón, y una eternidad
arropándote en la cama, tus ojos radiantes de amor y
confianza. Pasaré una década observando a Sydney bailar, a
papá haciendo reír a mamá. Tendré una eternidad con mis
éxitos más importantes. Eso es lo que debe haber dentro de
la iglesia. Esa tiene que ser la respuesta. Después de
cierto punto no podemos crear nueva felicidad, pero podemos

permanecer eternamente en la felicidad de tiempos anteriores, atrapados a la perfección por el ojo de quien nos recuerda.

Recuérdame, Noah, cuando te arropaba en la cama y te daba un beso de buenas noches. Recuerda las historias que te conté. Nos volveremos a ver.

Te quiere siempre.

Eunice.

Parte cinco

LA CIUDAD
SIN NOMBRE

CAPÍTULO 1

En otoño de 2002 me tomé una noche libre del Laberinto del Terror para visitar una casa demoníaca cristiana en Mansfield, Texas, llamada Inferno. Había querido ir con Kyle, pero se excusó en el último momento, aduciendo planes con Donna, así que aquella tarde conduje a la Iglesia Bíblica del Espíritu Santo, con un libro de bolsillo de Anne Rice. Terminó siendo buena idea, ya que la cola para entrar a Inferno empezaba en las puertas de la iglesia y se extendía a lo largo de todo un amplio prado. En cuanto llegué todos los que estaban en ella empezaron a mirarme.

Deberí haber estado acostumbrado a la atención. El parche del ojo era mucho más llamativo que un ojo de cristal, e incluso sin él me habrían reconocido de todos modos como el Hardy Boy de Vandergriff, el chico que sin querer había cerrado el caso del secuestrador de niños en 1999. Las miradas iban a ser una parte normal de la vida mientras viviera en Vandergriff o en sus alrededores, pero aún me sentía incómodo siendo escrutado. No me gustaba que me miraran, salvo que llevara puesto mi traje de monstruo en el trabajo.

A la luz menguante del ocaso leí e ignoré a la variedad de mirones hasta que llegué al comienzo de la cola. Allí, un empleado con una camiseta polo que decía INFERNO me sumó al grupo impar de jóvenes religiosos que tenía delante. La muchedumbre de adolescentes y sus acompañantes de unos treinta y tantos me dirigieron miradas incómodas mientras pasábamos juntos por las solapas de caucho de la entrada.

Una figura menuda envuelta en una túnica negra nos recibió dentro, con la cabeza agachada. Las luces a nuestro alrededor subieron poco a poco, y la figura alzó la cabeza, revelando una máscara flexible de calavera diabólica. Los ojos que había detrás estaban embadurnados de maquillaje negro y brillaban con una dicha malevolente.

—¡Bienvenidos! —dijo. Era una chica adolescente. Su voz deformada salió cascada al traspasar la máscara de látex—. Me alegra mucho que hayáis podido venir a esta pequeña jornada de puertas abiertas. ¡Espero que disfrutéis tanto que decidan hacer de esta casa su residencia permanente! Pero me estoy adelantando. ¿Por qué no echamos un vistazo?

La seguimos por un largo pasillo; por encima brillaban luces rojas, y abajo luces azules a través de un suelo de plástico transparente. Una neblina azul se arremolinaba bajo la superficie, hipnótica y serena, hasta que una mano atravesó las volutas y golpeó el plástico, rasgándolo con los dedos extendidos. Una de las chicas que estaba delante soltó un chillido y retrocedió de un salto. Más manos emergieron de la neblina, lanzando manotazos y golpes. Dispersaron la bruma y descubrieron caras de bocas abiertas que sollozaban pidiendo ayuda.

—No les hagáis caso —dijo la guía—. Son solo algunos de nuestros recién llegados. —Se carcajeó y siguió avanzando, pero yo me detuve, impresionado por la calidad del trabajo.

Cuando alcancé al grupo, habían llegado a un ambiente decorado como una fiesta hogareña. Un chico con una cara larga y cubierta de granos fingía ser el DJ, deslizando las manos entre dos tocadiscos vacíos. Luces de colores se derramaban formando dibujos caprichosos sobre un grupo de adolescentes tiesos que bailaban con torpeza. Dos chicas estaban paradas cerca del público, bebiendo de vasos de plástico rojo. Una tenía el pelo rubio largo y lacio, nariz gruesa y grandes ojos marrones. La otra tenía pelo verde y una cara más infantil.

—Os presento a Miranda y a Ashley —dijo la guía, señalando a cada chica por turno—. Miranda acaba de mudarse desde Connecticut. Separada de su antigua iglesia y sus amigos cristianos, ha empezado a andar con malas compañías. Ashley creció con padres ateos y lee Harry Potter para entretenerse. No ve que haya nada malo en ir a fiestas y beber un viernes por la noche.

—Miranda, ¿acaso no es divertido todo esto? —preguntó Ashley, la chica de pelo verde.

Miranda lanzó una mirada de desconfianza dentro de su taza y bebió un sorbo.

—Claro —dijo, haciendo una mueca—. Es todo muy nuevo, ¿sabes?

—¡Mira allí! —exclamó Ashley, interrumpiendo el discurso de la otra chica. Señaló al otro lado de la habitación, hacia un grupo de chicos que les lanzaban miradas lascivas y movían la cabeza al compás del ritmo—. Trent y Evan. Oh, cielos, vienen hacia aquí.

—¿Estáis divirtiéndoos, chicas? —preguntó uno de ellos.

—Y tanto —dijo Miranda.

—¿Sabéis cómo podríamos divertirnos aún más? —preguntó el otro—. Con esto. —Levantó una pequeña pastilla blanca, dejando que la viera el público—. Os hará sentir fenomenal.

—Yo ya me he tomado dos —dijo el primer chico.

—Suena genial —dijo Ashley. Aceptó la pastilla ofrecida y se la tragó con ayuda de su bebida.

—¿Y tú, guapa? —preguntó el segundo chico a Miranda.

—No sé —respondió. Miró a Ashley, torturada por la indecisión. Mientras tenía la cabeza apartada, el segundo chico dejó caer la pastilla en su vaso. Sin darse cuenta, Miranda se bebió el resto de su bebida.

Los chicos se acercaron todavía más a las chicas, y la Guía se interpuso delante de ellos, impidiendo que pudiéramos ver.

—Lo que Miranda no sabe es que acaba de tomar la droga de los violadores —dijo con el falso alarido de Guardiana de la Cripta—. Ahora se siente bien, pero en treinta minutos no sentirá absolutamente nada.

Las salas que siguieron relataban historias con moraleja similares: tiroteos en colegios, accidentes por conducir en estado de embriaguez, la violenta cultura de la compra y venta de drogas, la asistencia a misas negras, la lectura de novelas de fantasía no escritas por C. S. Lewis, la violencia doméstica, y más. Las escenas se volvieron más visceralmente perturbadoras a medida que avanzaron; la mayoría terminaba con el protagonista muriendo de algún modo horrible. Mi malestar fue en aumento, como se suponía que debía ser, hasta que entramos a lo que era obvio que debía ser el dormitorio de una chica adolescente. Miranda, la chica que había tomado la droga de la violación, entró dando tumbos, con el pelo revuelto y una expresión perdida, los brazos alrededor de ella misma como si no se sintiera bien.

—Recordáis a Miranda —dijo nuestra guía—, tan desesperada por hacer nuevos amigos que intentaba lo que fuera con quien fuera. Por supuesto, no recuerda qué probó o con quién lo hizo. ¿No es cierto, Miranda?

La joven se sentó en la cama, con la mirada fija en una distancia intermedia. Me pregunté cómo llevaban y traían a la actriz entre las salas sin alterar el flujo de visitantes. ¿Sería difícil arreglarse y desarreglarse el pelo y el maquillaje una y otra vez?

—¿Qué pasa, Miranda? —preguntó la Guía—. ¿Acaso no te has divertido?

—Cállate —respondió la chica, su voz baja y afligida.

—Es una pregunta sencilla —insistió la Guía—, salvo que ¿quizás no lo puedes recordar?

—Cállate —repitió, esta vez más fuerte, meciéndose a sí misma.

—¿Recuerdas ese día en tu antigua iglesia cuando firmaste un juramento de abstinencia? Estabas muy orgullosa. Te sentías muy segura de que Dios te protegería.

Miranda se desplomó al suelo. Abrió un cajón de la mesilla de noche y sacó un dibujo enmarcado de Jesús.

—¡Ahí está Él! —exclamó la Guía—. Oculto en un cajón, fuera de la vista. No ha sido demasiado útil allí dentro, ¿verdad?

—¿Cómo has podido dejar que sucediera esto? —preguntó Miranda a la imagen. La dejó caer y volvió a meter la mano en el cajón. Esta vez extrajo una pistola. La chica guardaba cosas extrañas en su mesita de noche.

—Ohh, ¿qué tienes ahí? —preguntó la Guía.

—Te odio —le dijo la joven a la imagen de Jesús. Presionó la pistola contra su frente, amartilló el arma y oprimió el gatillo. Sonó un fuerte estallido, y las luces cambiaron de color, pasando de un suave amarillo a un rojo turbio. La Guía se arrodilló a su lado y la atrapó al tiempo que la joven se desplomaba hacia delante.

—Buena chica —murmuró—. Buena chica.

Me sentí a punto de vomitar.

A continuación venía una sala de urgencias ficticia, donde una mujer cubierta de sangre por una «píldora abortiva» rogaba la gracia de Dios y su perdón en el momento en que moría. Solo seguí vagamente todo aquello, concentrado en no vomitar en mitad de la atracción. Justo cuando llegué a la siguiente sala conseguí recuperar el control de mí mismo. Estaba cubierta de papel de aluminio dorado, y una música etérea salía de los altavoces ocultos detrás de una cruz enorme. Los personajes de escenas anteriores entraron, sus caras resplandecían de asombro.

—Qué bonito —dijo la chica de la píldora abortiva—. No como ningún sueño que haya tenido jamás. —Estaba tan cerca que podía oler la pintura roja de sus pantalones.

—¿Esto es el Cielo? —preguntó Miranda.

—Así es, hija mía —resonó desde los altavoces—. Decidme, ¿obedecisteis mis mandamientos y acogisteis a mi Hijo en vuestros corazones? ¿Lo aceptasteis allí todos vuestros días y os arrepentisteis de vuestros pecados?

Miranda y los otros farfullaron excusas. Habían estado confundidos, engañados, inseguros. Hicieron silencio y se dividieron. La chica que había abortado se acercó a la cruz.

—Fui a la iglesia de niña —confesó—, pero dejé de hacerlo cuando mis padres dejaron de obligarme. Crecí fuera de tu gracia y amor, y me reí cuando personas buenas intentaron predicarme tu palabra. Pero luego tuve sexo sin protección con un desconocido, tomé una píldora para evitar quedarme embarazada, y todo salió mal. No podía dejar de sangrar, y el nombre de tu Hijo fue el único al que pude acudir para que me ayudara.

—Bienvenida a casa, hija —retumbó la grave voz. Una puerta se abrió bajo la cruz y pasó por ella. Pero cuando los demás intentaron seguirla, la puerta se cerró de golpe.

—¿Y el resto de nosotros? —preguntó Miranda.

—Vosotros me negasteis en vida —dijo la voz incorpórea—, y yo os negaré en la muerte. ¡Apartaos de mí! —La habitación quedó sumida en la oscuridad.

—¡Por fin! —se carcajeó la Guía desde algún sitio por detrás—. ¡El día de la retribución!

Una luz roja se elevó desde los zócalos. Los personajes a quienes se les había negado el Cielo daban la vuelta en círculos.

—¿Qué está sucediendo? —preguntó Miranda.

—Es hora de volver a casa, querida —dijo la Guía—. ¡Atrapadlos, chicos!

Una horda de figuras monstruosas salió a toda velocidad de detrás de los cortinajes. Los condenados forcejearon, pidiendo ayuda a gritos, mientras los sacaban a rastras. Miranda fue quien más peleó, se abalanzó hacia delante y perdió el equilibrio. Aterrizó sobre las manos y las rodillas delante de mí y su mirada se cruzó con la mía. El pánico y el temor desaparecieron de su cara, reemplazados por franca sorpresa. Me miró con la boca a medio abrir mientras los demonios le sujetaban los brazos y se la llevaban.

—Vaya, eso ha sido divertido —dijo la Guía—, pero aquí es donde os dejo. ¡Espero veros pronto! —graznó, mientras seguía a sus esbirros fuera de la sala. Otra puerta se abrió, y una mujer con vaqueros y camiseta apareció en la entrada, su silueta contorneada por una luz fluorescente.

—Por aquí, por favor —dijo, hablando con una voz cálida y amable. Resultó un alivio tras todo el griterío.

El grupo avanzó arrastrando los pies hacia una última sala con paneles de madera y una alfombra gris. Un hombre alto y sombrío estaba de pie entre dos puertas, en el otro extremo de la sala.

—¿Cómo estáis? —preguntó.

El grupo juvenil intercambió miradas furtivas y dejó escapar un murmullo de risas nerviosas.

El hombre sombrío nos dirigió una mirada seguramente pensada para parecer comprensiva.

—He estado viendo esa misma mirada toda la noche, y, creedme, ahora que habéis salido del fondo del Inferno, me gustaría ofreceros algún alivio. Lo que habéis visto esta noche es la absoluta verdad, eterna e imperecedera, del universo. Las cosas malas suceden todo el tiempo. Las personas se hacen daño. Las personas mueren. Y si mueren sin tener a Jesús en el corazón, quedan condenadas a un abismo de dolor y a sufrimientos inacabables. —Hizo una pausa, tomándose las manos y evaluando las caras—. Esta misma noche un conductor ebrio podría chocarse con vosotros de camino a casa. Un drogadicto podría entrar a robar en vuestras casas y asesinaros por lo que hay en vuestra hucha cerdito. Jesús podría volver mañana por la mañana y llevar a los fieles al Cielo antes de que vuestro despertador salte siquiera. No podéis saberlo. Lo que debéis preguntaros es, si alguna de estas cosas sucediera, ¿estaríais preparados? ¿Podríais mirar a Jesús a los ojos el día del juicio y decirle con sinceridad que habéis vivido y muerto en Su gracia? —De nuevo, hizo una pausa, dándonos tiempo para reflexionar sobre la pregunta—. Hay dos puertas a mi espalda. A través de la puerta a mi derecha, hay una habitación llena de personas buenas que esperan para rezar con vosotros, y esa habitación abrirá durante los siguientes sesenta segundos. —La mujer de voz amable que nos había llevado a aquella sala abrió la puerta a la sala de oración y entró, juntando las manos por delante.

Ya había tenido suficiente. Me aparté del grupo y caminé a través de la puerta que estaba a la izquierda del hombre. Se comunicaba con el frío aire nocturno y se cerró de golpe, librándome de la voz del individuo, una última réplica impactante que me dirigió y que no alcancé a oír. Había un carro de heno que esperaba para conducir a las personas de nuevo al aparcamiento, pero elegí caminar. Mantuve las manos en los bolsillos y los hombros encorvados mientras cruzaba el campo oscuro.

¿Por qué me había sometido a aquel sitio para empezar? Porque el Laberinto del Terror estaba en problemas. Las ventas de entradas habían estado disminuyendo los últimos dos años, y ahora resultaba excepcional que nuestro aparcamiento estuviera siquiera medio lleno un sábado por la noche. La mayoría de nuestros clientes eran familias con niños pequeños, y los pocos adolescentes y adultos que venían parecían aturdidos y apáticos, como un público drogado con Thorazine. Mi madre quería cerrarlo, e incluso había esquivado ofertas para vender el sitio, pero le pedí que me diera algunas noches para echarle una ojeada a la competencia. Quería ver quién estaba robándonos nuestro negocio, y qué podíamos hacer para recuperarlo.

Había acudido a tres atracciones de terror en la última semana: Baño de Sangre, un parque temático de horror en Dallas; La Casa de los Sustos, una colección de miniguaridas para toda la familia; y ahora Inferno, una casa demoníaca cristiana, dirigida por una megaiglesia en Mansfield, que pervertía las metáforas con fines religiosos. Debería haber sido capaz de desestimarlas todas, pero me sentía inquieto, perturbado. No podía olvidar la imagen de Miranda, la víctima de violación que se había suicidado, suplicándome mientras se la llevaban al Infierno.

CAPÍTULO 2

Mi madre ya estaba en la cama cuando llegué a casa. Subí a mi habitación, y en cuanto estuve dentro, tomé la piedra negra que colgaba de mi cuello. Cerré mi ojo y me concentré, y cuando lo volví a abrir me hallé en el claro del bosque oscuro. El aire estaba espeso y fétido, los árboles entintados y densos como las pinceladas de un impresionista.

La puerta se abrió antes de que pudiera llamar, y allí estaba, con la túnica abierta para exhibir una franja de carne que se extendía desde el hueco de su garganta hasta la mata de vello rojo sobre el pubis.

—*Leannon si* —dijo.

Leannon si. Pronunciado *lihanan shi*. Era un apodo, una broma interna que había tomado de un libro de cuentos de hadas celta: una hermosa hada que tomó a un hombre mortal como amante. Fui yo quien sugirió el nombre *Leannon* para llamarla de algún modo; para pensar en ella de otro modo que no fuera «el monstruo», «la criatura» o «Mi Amigo»; para reformular nuestra relación fuera de los límites de *Danny y el dinosaurio* o *E. T. Leannon si*, para que resultara menos raro cuando descendía acunándola en mis brazos sobre su cama. *Leannon si*, al depositarla sobre las mantas, ponerme de rodillas y separarle las piernas. *Leannon si*, deletreado con mi lengua mientras me tiraba del pelo. *Leannon si*, sus muslos apretándome la cabeza, mi nariz aplastada contra ella mientras su cuerpo se estrechaba, y soltaba un grito. *Leannon si* cuando me subía a la cama jadeando, luchaba por quitarme los pantalones y me deslizaba dentro de ella. *Leannon si*, con sus dientes en mi oreja, sus tobillos alrededor de la parte baja de mi espalda. *Leannon si*, abrazándome y susurrando, «Buen chico» al tiempo que el caleidoscopio dorado me fragmentaba en cientos de minúsculos brotes estelares. *Leannon si*.

Quedamos enlazados y sudorosos por la humedad. Hacía tres años que sucedía aquello. Tres años de visitar esa pequeña casa en ese pequeño claro situado en otro mundo, de permanecer con ella en esa cama. ¿Me parecía raro? No sentía un particular deseo por anunciarle nuestra relación a nadie, y ahora, un año después del instituto, había empezado a cuestionar la viabilidad a largo plazo del acuerdo, pero solo un poco. Más que nada, me había divertido, y mi pasión por Leannon seguía ardiendo, prolongándose de un modo que ninguna pasión humana parece prolongarse jamás.

Ahora recosté la cabeza sobre su pálido estómago y estudié el lienzo sobre su caballete. Representaba dos figuras sobre una colina bajo un cielo que combinaba amarillos, granates, azules y negros. Una luna creciente y una estrella deforme y alargada colgaban en el cielo, y una segunda estrella yacía sobre el suelo. No supe lo que significaban ambas figuras. La que estaba a la derecha parecía un animal, encorvada y envuelta en amarillo, su cabeza gris púrpura con forma de apóstrofe. Tenía un ojo alienígena, cubierto con un párpado solo en la parte inferior y mirando sin aparente expresión hacia el cielo. La figura de la izquierda parecía una flor con un tallo ancho y dos pedúnculos que culminaban en dos bulbos disparejos, uno con alas; el otro, una vulva púrpura. Detrás de la vulva, casi oculta en la pintura, estaba la figura de una mujer; sus caderas se elevaban hacia un par de pechos redondeados. Pensé en Miranda, en Inferno. También había tenido esas curvas.

—¿Qué te parece? —preguntó Leannon, provocándome un sobresalto.

Me incorporé, fingiendo querer mirarla mejor.

—No estoy seguro de comprenderla.

Ella también se enderezó y apoyó el mentón sobre mi hombro.

—No es un códice que haya que descifrar. Es una pintura. Está bien decir lo que te hace pensar y sentir.

—¿Qué sientes y piensas tú de ella? —pregunté.

Pareció reflexionar y no respondió en seguida.

—Pienso en ti —dijo. No parecía una mentira, pero no era toda la verdad. Era un equilibrio que había notado con frecuencia. La primera vez que la había escuchado hablar, había supuesto que los misterios que la rodeaban irían desapareciendo, pero no me sentía mucho más cerca del corazón de la verdad ahora que en 1999. Aún no conocía su verdadero nombre, la edad que tenía, o qué era siquiera. No sabía dónde estaba situada esa casa, o por qué la piedra que llevaba alrededor del cuello me ayudaba a atravesar la distancia de mi dormitorio hasta la puerta principal de Leannon.

Percibiendo que la conversación se desviaba en una dirección que no le gustaba, se levantó y cruzó a uno de los armarios de su cocina.

—¿Tienes hambre? —preguntó—. Tengo comida. —Sacó un cuenco de manzanas y las puso delante de mí.

Di un mordisco a una de las manzanas y me di cuenta de que tenía hambre... de hecho, estaba famélico. Devoré dos mientras me miraba. Cuando acabé, llevó los corazones y las manzanas restantes de nuevo al armario. No sabía lo que hacía con los residuos de comida. Siempre volvía a colocarlos de vuelta en la estantería, y para la siguiente vez que iba, habían desaparecido. Otro misterio para añadir a la lista.

Mientras guardaba los corazones de las manzanas, un rumor sordo sonó en algún lugar en la distancia. Leannon se puso rígida. Levantó su túnica del suelo y la sujetó alrededor de la cintura.

—¿Qué…? —empecé, pero hizo chasquear los dedos para acallarme. El ruido se volvió más y más fuerte. El suelo empezó a vibrar, y la casa a sacudirse. El caballete se meció de una pata a la otra, y la pintura se inclinó. El interior del cráneo me empezó a zumbar. Leannon saltó sobre la cama y me envolvió con sus brazos y piernas. Estaba febril y ardiente; sus extremidades eran como cables de metal. La vibración constante y enloquecedora siguió y siguió hasta que se sumó otro sonido: cuatro notas lentas, como un canto de ballena letárgico y somnoliento. El estruendo disminuyó y se detuvo. Llevó las manos a mis mejillas y me dejó apartar la cabeza de su garganta.

—¿Estás bien? —preguntó.

—Sí, eso creo.

Giró mi cara de un lado a otro, escudriñando mi ojo sano.

—¿Estás seguro? ¿No ha cambiado… nada? ¿No sientes nada roto?

—Estoy bien.

Me soltó y nos sentamos. La casa parecía haber sido dada la vuelta y sacudida. Los armarios tenían las puertas abiertas como testigos boquiabiertos, y el suelo estaba sepultado bajo una variedad de fragmentos de vajilla rota, trapos, raíces secas, bloques de arcilla, libretas y lápices. La pintura yacía junto a la cama, intacta pero abollada de un lado.

—Mierda —dije.

Suspiró pero sacudió una mano desestimándolo.

—No pasa nada.

—Por lo menos déjame ayudarte a limpiar. —Empecé a incorporarme, pero ella me aferró el brazo.

—No necesito ayuda, pero gracias por ofrecerte. —Permaneció sentada y me oprimió la mano de modo doloroso. Parecía disgustada. Aterrada.

—¿Qué acaba de pasar? —pregunté.

—No lo sé. —Esta vez no leí una verdad parcial en su voz. Esta vez detecté una mentira descarada.

CAPÍTULO 3

Dormí mal en mi propia cama. Un leviatán invisible me perseguía a través de un laberinto de pesadillas. Me desperté cuando el sol ya estaba alto en el cielo. Mi reloj despertador marcaba las once y media. Me maldije a mí mismo. Se suponía que debía reunirme con Eunice al mediodía para almorzar

Llegué al café diez minutos tarde y la encontré sentada en el patio, leyendo un libro de Tami Hoag y bebiendo una mimosa. Me miró enfurecida mientras yo tomaba asiento.

—Lo sé, lo sé —dije, alzando las manos en señal de rendición—. Me he quedado dormido.

—Dios no quiera que necesites alguna vez un empleo real de ocho a cinco —dijo. Apuró los restos de la mimosa—. De todos modos, gracias por venir.

—Claro —dije. Era la respuesta más positiva que se me ocurrió. No conseguía decir, *No me lo hubiera perdido* o *Me alegra haber venido*. Aunque nominalmente estábamos en buenos términos, las cosas habían estado tensas entre nosotros desde la noche en que había robado su coche y ella había intentado suicidarse. Tras dos meses en una institución psiquiátrica con una fuerte dosis de Prozac, había abandonado la universidad, había obtenido su certificado de asistente legal y se había marchado a trabajar para una firma en Fort Worth. Se había ido de casa y había conseguido un apartamento cerca de su empleo, y aunque venía de visita cada pocas semanas, nuestra conversación era siempre cordial, jamás cálida. Se quejaba mucho de su jefe arrogante y sabelotodo, y no dejaba de mirar su reloj, como si mi madre y yo fuéramos un trámite que había que terminar lo antes posible, como un empleo más. Siempre traía un postre con ella… un pastel, galletas, pastelillos… para regalar a mi madre, pero generalmente ella misma los acababa. Lo menciono no porque quiera juzgarla, sino porque empezó a comer en exceso al mismo tiempo que dejó de escribir. Durante sus visitas generalmente le preguntaba si estaba trabajando en algo y, si bien al principio puso excusas, al final solo decía «No» cada vez que lo mencionaba. Lo negaba como si la tuviera sin cuidado, como si le hubiera estado preguntando acerca del tiempo.

—Las voces han dejado de hablarme —dijo—. Estoy haciendo lo posible por seguir adelante.

Cerca de un año después del hospital, empezó a salir de nuevo. Habría estado encantado, salvo que empezó a salir con hombres y, tras unos meses, se concentró en un hombre en particular: Hubert Sangalli, un amigo perdido de sus días de primaria. Los presentaron en una cita a ciegas, y tras la sorpresa de reconocerse, habían iniciado un noviazgo acelerado, que incluyó un peregrinaje para conocer a mi madre y a mí tras solo dos semanas. Hubert era alto y delgado, con una calva mal tapada de color rubio y ojos azules acuosos. Parecía deformado, como si alguien lo hubiera empujado a través de una de aquellas máquinas que aplastan monedas para grabarles una imagen, salvo que la imagen de Hubert no había quedado impresa.

El día que lo conocí, hablaba en voz baja sobre la suerte y el destino. Eunice se sentó junto a él, dándole la mano. La mueca ligera con que lo miraba revelaba más tolerancia que aceptación. Seis meses después, se habían comprometido y ahora solo faltaba un mes para la boda.

Eunice y yo estábamos almorzando para discutir la despedida de soltero de Hubert, de la cual yo, el padrino de facto renuente, era responsable.

—¿Sabe Hubert que nos estamos reuniendo? —pregunté—. Normalmente, el novio y su padrino hacen esto sin la novia.

—No seas idiota —dijo Eunice—. Sabes que es tímido. Le gustas, pero es un poco intimidante estar contigo. —Sacudió la mano en el aire para llamar la atención del camarero.

—Qué estupidez —dije.

No me lo discutió. Nuestro camarero llegó, y de nuevo tuve la sensación de que un desconocido me reconocía y evaluaba. Si Eunice lo vio, no dijo nada. Pidió otra mimosa.

—¿Qué tiene Hubert en mente? —pregunté, queriendo decir: ¿Qué tienes tú en mente?

—No bebe, así que no será un problema que tú seas menor de edad —dijo. Dentro del restaurante, vi a nuestro camarero hablando con un colega. Ambos se volvieron para mirarme, y luego apartaron la vista cuando se dieron cuenta de que los estaba observando.

—¿Y el otro clásico de las despedidas de soltero? —pregunté, volviendo a centrar la atención—. ¿Un club de striptease? —Jamás había ido a uno y sentía curiosidad.

—Se pone nervioso cuando un desconocido le corta el pelo. No puedo imaginar cómo reaccionaría a un sitio lleno de mujeres desnudas intentando tocarlo.

—Es un razonamiento noble por tu parte —respondí.

—Vete a la mierda —dijo.

—Así que nada de alcohol o de strippers —dije—. ¿Qué es lo que *sí* quiere?

—Fun Mountain —dijo—. Minigolf, juegos, kartings, y una buena cena. Quizás una película si hay algo bueno en el cine.

—¿Quiere la fiesta de cumpleaños de un chico de diez años? —pregunté.

—Este hombre será tu hermano en un mes —dijo—. Por favor, solo hazlo feliz. E intenta no burlarte de él en su cara mientras lo haces. Sería muy importante para mí.

—Está bien —dije, aunque no era capaz de disculparme—. Lo haré.

—Genial —dijo. Me dio una lista de otros hombres que Hubert conocía... no necesariamente amigos... y a los que podría recurrir para ir a la fiesta. Habiendo concluido nuestro asunto principal, me preguntó acerca de mí y el Laberinto del Terror. Lo conté cómo estaba espiando a nuestra competencia en busca de ideas.

—¿Has encontrado algo que valga la pena robar? —preguntó.

—Aún no —admití—. Nosotros ya hacemos mejor lo que ellos están haciendo. La única ventaja que tienen estos sitios es que no son nosotros. Si vamos a innovar, tendremos que hacerlo solos.

—¿Alguna idea? —preguntó.

—Me gustaría crear una experiencia más inmersiva, algo que vaya más allá de sustos vulgares. Un sitio donde las personas puedan pasar la noche, como un bed-and-breakfast embrujado, o un motel donde siempre están pasando cosas raras. Y dependiendo del nivel de susto para el que te inscribas, obtienes una experiencia que va de «escalofriante» o «levemente inquietante» a una en la que «realmente temes por tu vida».

Eunice ladeó la cabeza. Era inescrutable tras sus gafas de sol.

—¿Qué? —pregunté.

—Nada. —Apretó los labios—. Papá tuvo una idea parecida justo antes de morir.

Hacía años que nadie mencionaba a mi padre en mi presencia.

—No sé cuánto la llegaron a desarrollar —dijo—. Era algo en lo que él y mamá trabajaban para pasar el rato, pero para entonces estaba muy mal. Mamá dijo que todo era simplemente una tontería de la que tomó nota para darle el gusto. Ideas de una persona loca.

CAPÍTULO 4

Me reuní con mi madre aquella tarde en el taller de disfraces del Laberinto del Terror. Ella trabajaba mientras yo hablaba; reparaba la última versión de mi disfraz de monstruo. Gruesos hilos negros y rojos mantenían unidas las tiras de pelo de varios tonos, desde casi negro a un marrón apagado rayando en amarillo. El pelo de mi madre tenía ahora gruesos mechones grises, y bajo sus ojos verdes colgaban bolsas permanentes. Tenía grabadas en la cara patas de gallo y arrugas alrededor de la boca. Ese año cumplía cincuenta y cuatro años, pero las gafas bifocales que tenía encaramadas en la nariz la hacían parecer aún más mayor.

Caminé de un lado a otro mientras presentaba mi informe, contándole lo que le había contado a Eunice, y mi teoría acerca de que nuestro mayor problema era la familiaridad.

—Tiene sentido —dijo—. Imagina manejar una sala de cine en la que solo se reproduce una película todos los días durante trece años. —Lanzó una mirada furibunda al disfraz—. El sitio está cayéndose a pedazos de todos modos. Te juro que los disfraces jamás habían parecido desgastarse tan rápido.

—Quizás podamos hacer algo completamente nuevo —dije. Apoyó el disfraz y se recostó hacia atrás sobre la silla—. Se me ha ocurrido la idea de un hotel embrujado, y Eunice ha dicho que tú y papá tuvisteis una idea parecida alrededor del momento en que nací, así que he pensado que, quizás, si me dejaras mirar sus notas viejas…

Empezó a sacudir la cabeza antes de que terminara la oración. Me preparé para una discusión, pero no para lo que mi madre terminó diciendo:

—Tiré todo eso a la basura hace años.

Dejé de caminar.

—¿Por qué hiciste algo así?

Se quitó las gafas y se frotó los ojos.

—Intenta imaginar una caja en tu casa que existe solo para recordarte el momento más doloroso y terrible de toda tu vida. ¿Crees que *tú* querrías conservarla?

—Podrías haberla escondido en el desván y habérsela entregado a Eunice cuando se mudó. Podrías habérmela dado a mí.

Volvió a ponerse las gafas.

—Hice lo que hice. No puedo deshacerlo.

—Ni siquiera he visto una foto de papá —dije. Con el tiempo vería una, pero no en los siguientes once años.

—Mírate en el espejo, y tendrás una idea general. E incluso si todavía conservara la caja, no cambiaría nada. Prometiste ideas para salvar este sitio, pero vuelves sugiriendo que levantemos algo completamente nuevo y diferente, algo que costaría una fortuna y quizás no sea legal. Pero aparte del dinero y las cuestiones legales, supones que estoy interesada en edificar algo nuevo. Me metí en este negocio en 1989 para salvar a nuestra familia de la ruina financiera. Terminó siendo una buena fuente de dinero durante un tiempo. Significó mucho para ti y para Eunice, y ha sido un bonito tributo a Sydney. Pero ahora ha dejado de dar dinero, y parece que no tienes ninguna idea sólida para remediarlo. Mi consejo para ti sería que disfrutes de tus últimas semanas aquí. Aprovéchalo y despídete de él.

CAPÍTULO 5

Abandoné mis actividades de espía industrial y volví a ser el monstruo. Seguía siendo un placer, pero ahora atemperado por la tristeza de que llegaba a su fin. Como con Leannon, traté de evitar pensar a largo plazo, pero en este caso era difícil porque me quedaba poco tiempo para cosechar gritos y aterrar a desconocidos.

Una noche, alrededor de una semana después de volver al trabajo, asomé la cabeza a través de una «escotilla» y vi a «Miranda» del Inferno entre un grupo de visitantes dentro de la biblioteca del Profesor. Los desconocidos se sobresaltaron y gritaron cuando aparecí. Miranda no. Se echó levemente hacia atrás y escudriñó, como intentando ver mejor. Su falta de asombro me sorprendió, y retrocedí, desapareciendo dentro de mi laberinto. Más tarde, cuando salí en el salón de baile, teniendo intención de llevarme a un Brad, me detuve a su lado. Olisqueé su codo y deslicé mi hocico a lo largo de su brazo, pasando su hombro y su cuello, hasta dejar la cara colgando justo delante de la suya. Su respiración se mantuvo tranquila y estable. No me tenía ningún miedo.

—¡Oye! —balbuceó el Brad. Parecía confundido, pero intentó permanecer en el personaje—. ¡Déjala en paz!

Su verdadero nombre era Jimmy, un chico delgado, sin mentón, a quien se le había dado un papel que no le iba. Apoyó una mano sobre mi hombro como queriendo apartarme, y nos enzarzamos en nuestro forcejeo coreografiado. Intentó lanzarme un puñetazo, y lo estrangulé hasta dejarlo inconsciente, tras lo cual hui con él de vuelta al laberinto.

—Creía que no podías acercarte tanto a los visitantes —dijo después de que nos quedáramos solos y lo ayudara a ponerse en pie.

Jamás hablaba cuando hacía mi papel de monstruo, y no lo hice ahora.

—Ha sido muy terrorífico, pero no sé si ha sido apropiado, ¿sabes?

Después, cuando terminó la noche y cerramos, lo encontré hablando con un par de chicas en la sala de descanso. Se detuvo cuando me vio. Ambas chicas me echaron un vistazo y luego apartaron la mirada. Me acordé del almuerzo con Eunice y de la espera en la cola de Inferno. En 1999 me habían llamado héroe, pero aquella novedad había desaparecido rápido, siendo reemplazada por esto. La incomodidad, las miradas esquivas, un profundo sentido de otredad, de estar apartado del grupo. Como si fuera un pararrayos que atrajera la tragedia y nadie quisiera estar demasiado cerca.

En aquel momento me pregunté si quizás no era el Laberinto del Terror el que estuviera fracasando. Si quizás era yo. Quizás estuviera boicoteándolo solo por trabajar aquí. Mi sola presencia estaba haciendo que la gente se sintiera incómoda, pero en el mal sentido.

Esperé a que los chicos se hubieran marchado a casa antes de abandonar el edificio. Me sorprendí al encontrar a Miranda de pie sola en el aparcamiento. Parecía nerviosa, cambiando el peso de una pierna a la otra.

—¿Noah Turner? —preguntó.

—Sí —respondí, pensando que estaba a punto de ganarme una reprimenda de una fanática religiosa y sabiendo que me lo tenía merecido. Solo después se me ocurrió que había estado llevando mi disfraz en el interior de la atracción, y que, en realidad, no había ningún motivo para que me conectara con el monstruo. Solo estaba inextricablemente unido con mi otra piel en mi propia mente.

En lugar de regañarme, me ofreció una mano.

—Megan Gaines.

Nos dimos la mano.

—¿En qué puedo ayudarla, señorita Gaines?

—Megan. Y… tengo que ser honesta: trabajo en otra atracción de terror en la zona…

—Inferno —dije—. Vi tu función la semana pasada.

—Cierto —dijo—. Me pareció ver una cara conocida. —No me cabía ninguna duda. ¿Cuántos clientes vería con un parche en el ojo? Además, parecía estar mintiendo, y que sabía que parecía estar mintiendo, y que yo también lo había notado. ¿Qué diablos estaba ocurriendo? No lo sabía, pero inmediatamente sentí el instinto de salvarla de su propio malestar y de sentirse a gusto.

—Tu actuación me conmovió —dije (cierto)—, y quedé impresionado con toda la atracción. —(No cierto)—. ¿Hay alguna posibilidad de que quieras tomar un café y hablemos del trabajo?

Deslizó los labios cerrados de un lado a otro sobre los dientes como alguien que se enjuaga la boca.

—No tomo café —dijo al fin—. Pero estoy famélica. ¿Te gustan los gofres?

CAPÍTULO 6

Fuimos a un restaurante pequeño, bien iluminado y terriblemente grasiento; pertenecía a una cadena que permanecía abierta toda la noche. Nos sentamos en una mesa cerca de una ventana que daba a una calle vacía. Megan pidió

una montaña de gofres con salchichas y zumo de naranja. Yo pedí un sándwich de huevo y café.

—¿Ha sido tu primera vez en el Laberinto del Terror? —pregunté.

Asintió.

—Mi madre nunca me dejaba celebrar Halloween cuando era pequeña
—dijo, cubriéndose la boca—. Siempre decía que era la fiesta del demonio.
Una celebración pagana del ocultismo de la que se apropiaron las corporacio-
nes norteamericanas y que bendijeron los especiales animados de televisión.
Decía que era una prueba de la influencia cada vez mayor de Satán en el
mundo.

—No sé si es tan terrible como lo cree tu madre —dije.

—Como lo creía. Murió hace un par de años.

—Oh, lo siento —dije.

Bajó la mirada a su comida.

—¿Puedo hacerte una pregunta personal?

—Claro.

—¿Por qué llevas un parche en el ojo?

Apoyé mi tazón de café.

—¿No lo sabes?

Sacudió la cabeza.

—¿Debería saberlo?

Esperé para ver si dejaba de fingir y admitía que me estaba engañando.
No sucedió.

—Es una larga historia —dije.

—¿Tienes algún otro sitio a dónde ir?

Así que le conté la versión oficial, la que había narrado tan a menudo y de
modo tan consecuente que, en líneas generales, se consideraba cierta: que Eunice y yo nos habíamos peleado; que le robé el coche para divertirme un poco;
que un hombre llamado James O'Neil me había embestido lateralmente en
una intersección; que perdí el ojo en el accidente; que encontré una bolsa de
residuos abultada en su furgoneta, con los restos humanos de Maria Davis y
Brandon Hawthorne en estado de descomposición; que James O'Neil intentó
matarme, y había escapado por poco; que me llevó toda la noche volver a mi
casa, en estado de shock. Omití algunos detalles: que la policía dejó pasar que
hubiera estado conduciendo sin seguro y huyendo de la escena del accidente

por haber resuelto, sin pretenderlo, el caso de los chicos desaparecidos y también por el intento de suicidio de mi hermana. Que, como la fiscalía pedía la pena de muerte, había tenido que ir a declarar. Que lo había hecho mirándome el regazo para no tener que mirar la cara de James O'Neil mientras declaraba; que la fiscalía argumentó que James O'Neil también había raptado y asesinado a Sydney, puesto que nos había visto el día que se incendió el coche de mi madre. Omití la presencia de furgonetas de noticias en nuestra calle durante algunas semanas, y la extrañeza con que me miraba la gente del pueblo. También que, aunque supuestamente fuera un héroe, a medida que pasaban los años la gente parecía sentirse incómoda cuando estaba cerca de mí, como si yo fuera el responsable de las desapariciones y las muertes.

Megan se inclinó hacia delante en su asiento, sin dejar de mirarme con sus brillantes ojos marrones durante todo el relato.

—Recuerdo —dijo cuando terminé— haber visto algo en las noticias acerca de ello hace un par de años. Es raro conocer a alguien a quien realmente le haya pasado algo. —Dirigió de nuevo la vista a su plato, y tuve la impresión de que había tenido intención de decir algo más pero que se arrepintió en el último momento.

—Dilo de una vez —dije, indicándole con la mano que se diera prisa.

Tomó un gran sorbo de su zumo antes de hablar.

—¿Viste algo… *raro* aquella noche?

—¿Más raro que un hombre loco que llevaba cadáveres en su furgoneta?

Dio un pequeño respingo, y lamenté mi tono de voz. Estaba decidiendo si me contaba algo o no.

—No lo sé —dijo finalmente—. Jamás he estado cerca de una persona loca. ¿Cómo fue? ¿Dijo o hizo algo raro? —De nuevo, no era lo que había querido decir. ¿Qué ocultaba?

—Fue como un sueño en el que todo parece normal, pero sabes que algo va mal. Como la sensación que hay en el aire momentos antes de que se desate una gran tormenta. Tenía algo raro, pero estaba actuando con bastante normalidad, en vista de las circunstancias, hasta que sacó el cuchillo.

Megan frunció el ceño levemente.

—Suena horrible —dijo, aunque no era lo que quería escuchar.

Después de eso se quedó callada. Llené el vacío con preguntas e hilvané una pequeña biografía: había crecido en los alrededores, y cuando su madre murió, la Iglesia del Espíritu Santo la ayudó con los gastos de mudanza para incorporarse al programa de teatro de la Universidad de Chicago. A cambio, volvía todos los años para colaborar con Inferno; obtenía un permiso especial de sus profesores, consiguiendo de algún modo justificar el viaje como una obligación religiosa y un proyecto propio. Le encantaba actuar, pero tenía pocas ilusiones respecto de ganarse la vida en el ámbito del arte. Más bien imaginaba que terminaría enseñando teatro en un instituto o en un centro de estudios superiores.

Cuando acabamos nuestra comida, pagué la cuenta y nos dirigimos al aparcamiento.

—Me he divertido —dije, porque quería que fuera verdad.

—Yo también —dijo.

Saqué una de mis tarjetas de negocios y se la di.

—Si te sobra un poco de tiempo antes de volver a Chicago, me gustaría volver a invitarte a comer gofres.

Estudió la tarjeta y sonrió con reticencia.

—Lo tendré en mente. —No tenía muchas esperanzas de que estuviera diciendo la verdad.

No se me ocurrió hasta después de llegar a casa que Megan no había preguntado nada sobre el Laberinto del Terror.

CAPÍTULO 7

Durante los días siguientes no podía dejar de pensar en la mirada brillante de Megan y en su comportamiento sereno. No me había dado cuenta de lo ávido que estaba de que alguien me mirara de un modo normal; de lo privado que estaba ni que fuera de aquella pizca de amabilidad. Revisé el contestador del Laberinto del Terror y mi propio correo electrónico, esperando que se pusiera en contacto conmigo, aunque sintiéndome también culpable por ello. Después de todo, estaba saliendo con Leannon (lo que fuera que eso significara). Mi única comida con Megan no era técnicamente un engaño, pero se le parecía lo bastante como para que me sintiera incómodo.

No supe nada más, así que hice lo posible por seguir adelante. Cambié la batería de la linterna en el Laberinto del Terror, renové las bombillas fluorescentes quemadas, sustituí los cables defectuosos de nuestro sistema de altavoces oculto... lo que fuera que ocupara mis manos y alejara mi mente del hecho de que estábamos a punto de quebrar. Empecé a pedir por correo formularios para inscribirme en diferentes universidades. Quizás si me iba a estudiar, podría empezar de nuevo en una ciudad nueva. También me puse en contacto con los hombres que integraban la lista de despedida de soltero de Hubert. Le supliqué a Kyle que me acompañara para que tuviera a alguien con quien hablar, y accedió. No habló demasiado del asunto, pero últimamente había estado ansioso por tener cualquier excusa para estar fuera de casa de sus padres. Cuando intentaba tocar el tema, sacudía la cabeza y decía: «No sé qué narices están haciendo».

Cuando finalmente volví a visitar a Leannon, tras una ausencia de casi una semana, abrió la puerta antes de que hubiera llamado siquiera.

—*Leannon si* —dijo—. Empezaba a preocuparme.

Entré en la casa detrás de ella, me quité los zapatos y me senté en la cama. Había llevado una bolsa de comida rápida y desenvolví una hamburguesa para darle un mordisco.

—No hace falta que esperes a que yo venga —dije—. Puedes venir a visitarme cuando quieras.

Se sentó a mi lado.

—Esta es la temporada en que más trabajo tienes.

—Antes eso jamás impedía que vinieras —dije, con la boca llena de hamburguesa.

—Eso fue antes que te enseñara a usar esto —dijo, tocando la piedra negra que tenía alrededor del cuello—. Además, yo también he estado ocupada. —Señaló hacia un nuevo cuadro sobre su caballete: la pareja que había estado pintando la última vez que había ido de visita. Representaba a varias figuras vestidas con túnicas contra un fondo sórdido de negros y amarillos. Las figuras se apiñaban bajo una luna creciente, con miradas temerosas y conspirativas.

—Es inquietante —dije.

Había arreglado la casa desde la última vez. Había tirado la vajilla rota, colgado de nuevo las raíces de sus ganchos en la cocina, y limpiado la pintura del suelo de madera. Solo el cuadro de la última vez mostraba señales del terremoto. Estaba apoyado en un rincón detrás del caballete; había una hendidura en la esquina superior izquierda, donde faltaba un pequeño trozo de pintura.

—Es una pena —dije, señalándola con el mentón.

—Hay cosas que ni siquiera yo puedo arreglar.

El ojo muerto me latía en su cuenca.

—¿Ha habido más temblores? —pregunté.

—No.

—¿Tienes idea de qué pudo haberlo causado?

Se paró frente al caballete y se inclinó hacia delante de modo que estuvo a punto de tocar la nariz con la tela.

—¿Cuál es la causa de un terremoto? Los movimientos de placas o algo así.

—¿Y los tonos musicales cuando acabó?

—Estoy tan desconcertada como tú. —Se quitó el cinto de la túnica y dejó que cayera al suelo. Me miró por encima de un pálido hombro—. ¿Querías tener sexo?

Esa noche me sentía extrañamente reticente.

—Leannon —dije—. ¿Nosotros qué relación tenemos?

—¿A qué te refieres?

—Me refiero a que ¿somos una pareja? ¿Estamos casados? ¿Cómo funciona esto a largo plazo?

—No sé si te entiendo —dijo.

—Quiero decir, ¿cómo será nuestra relación en diez años? ¿O en veinte?

Se dio la vuelta, y me distraje con los contornos de su cuerpo.

—¿Por qué debería ser diferente a ahora?

—Me refiero a que, con el tiempo, tendré que irme de casa de mi madre. La gente me mira de forma extraña en el pueblo. Se preguntarán por qué no tengo citas. Hablarán.

—¿Y eso por qué te importa? —preguntó.

—No es solo eso. Empezaré a envejecer. Quizás me quede calvo. Es posible que engorde. Lo quiera o no, la vida me sucederá.

Volvió a mirar la pintura y dejó caer la cabeza, como si examinara su propia desnudez.

—¿Es lo que quieres? —preguntó—. ¿Una vida ordinaria?

Ir allí había sido un error. En lugar de esclarecer mis sentimientos, los había confundido aún más. Arrojé la hamburguesa en la bolsa y me puse de pie.

—He herido tus sentimientos —dije—. Me iré.

Se puso la bata de nuevo de un tirón y me interceptó antes de que alcanzara las escaleras.

—No tienes que irte. Podemos estar juntos y *no* tener sexo.

—Lo sé —dije. Quise apartar su mano pero no lo hice—. No estoy de humor para estar con nadie.

Me soltó.

—Pero tú y yo… ¿estamos bien?

No tenía el valor para mirarla a los ojos.

—¿Por qué no íbamos a estarlo?

CAPÍTULO 8

A la mañana siguiente mi madre entró a mi habitación sin llamar e hizo una mueca de disgusto al ver el desorden.

—No tengo intención de interrumpir tus ensoñaciones —dijo—, pero tengo algunos encargos para que hagas y quiero darte esto antes de que me olvide. —Me entregó un trozo de papel doblado—. Un mensaje que te dejaron en la taquilla anoche.

—Gracias —dije a su figura en retroceso. Desdoblé la nota.

Noah,

Esta noche he vuelto para experimentar una vez más el Laberinto del Terror, pero me han dicho que era tu noche libre. Lamento no haberte visto. De todos modos, si quieres, deberías venir a una reunión conmigo y algunos amigos mañana por la noche. Me encantaría seguir hablando.

xoxo Megan

Rocé con el dedo las palabras de despedida, y mi corazón se aceleró levemente.

Aquella noche sustituí mi conjunto habitual de camiseta y sudadera
con capucha por una camisa y una chaqueta deportiva. Luego conduje a la
dirección que había indicado. Terminó siendo una de las infinitas urbani-
zaciones en los suburbios de Vandergriff; todas las casas eran todo lo genéricas y de clase media que podían ser. Megan estaba de pie en la entrada,
con vaqueros y una camisa con las mangas arremangadas y el cuello completamente abierto.

—¿Me estabas esperando a mí? —pregunté, saliendo del coche.

Metió las manos en los bolsillos.

—No quería que te perdieras.

—Estás guapa—dije.

—Gracias —dijo, apartándose un mechón de pelo detrás de una oreja.

Nos quedamos parados sobre la pendiente de la entrada; su posición la
hacía momentáneamente más alta que yo. Intenté pensar en algo que decir.

Movió los labios sobre los dientes como me gustaba.

—Serás amable, ¿verdad? ¿Eres una persona amable?

—Cuando no llevo el disfraz puesto.

No parecía completamente convencida, pero me condujo a la casa de
todos modos. Parecía un sitio en el que hubiera podido vivir una abuela:
muebles tapizados con diseños anticuados, mantas de croché tendidas sobre
el sofá y el sillón, tapetes que cubrían un sinnúmero de superficies. Un grupo
de adolescentes y adultos (y una anciana de pelo blanco que supuse que sería
la dueña) estaban colocando las sillas en un círculo, en la sala, y poniendo
bocadillos sobre la mesa de café. Todo el mundo se detuvo y nos miró cuando
entramos por la puerta.

—Hola a todos —dijo Megan. Su voz sonó fuerte en el abrupto silencio—. Os presento a Noah Turner. —Aferró mis hombros al pronunciar mi
nombre.

La alegre energía del sitio no se restauró, pero una mujer menuda con
pelo marrón ensortijado se tocó la zona bajo el ojo izquierdo, como si estuviera sintiendo un dolor fantasma por mí.

Un hombre fornido con barba rubia y un sombrero de camionero se
cruzó de brazos delante del pecho.

—Megan, conoces las reglas.

—Vamos, Josh —respondió ella—. Se trata de un caso especial.

El hombre se mesó la barba, y todo el mundo lo miró buscando su aprobación. Parecía ser la persona que estaba a cargo.

—A mí me gustaría que se quedara —dijo la anciana.

—Ellen —dijo Josh.

—Ya está aquí —dijo la mujer (Ellen)—, y por si no lo recuerdas, esta es *mi* casa. Así que salvo que quieras pasar la reunión de pie en la calle, ve y búscale una silla.

Sus hombros se hundieron un poco.

—Está bien. —Me apuntó con un dedo—. Pero no hablarás salvo que te dirijan la palabra, y no puedes decirle a nadie lo que veas o escuches aquí, ¿lo has entendido?

Megan resopló.

—Lo ha entendido, Josh. —Me guio a una silla vacía—. No le hagas caso —dijo, sentándose junto a mí—. Josh tiene una actitud protectora hacia el grupo. Quiere que todo el mundo se sienta seguro, incluido él mismo. Especialmente, él mismo.

—¿Qué grupo? —pregunté, pero nadie me respondió. Un pánico sordo empezó en la parte baja de mi abdomen. ¿A dónde diablos había ido?

Todo el mundo tomó asiento en el círculo. Conté ocho personas, incluido yo mismo. Todos dirigieron la mirada hacia Josh. Cerró los ojos y, cuando los volvió a abrir, parecía sobrio y sereno. Colocó una grabadora de microcasetes sobre la mesa de café y la puso a grabar.

—Bienvenidos a la división tejana de la Hermandad de Desaparecidos, un grupo de personas que se ayudan entre sí para lidiar con pérdidas misteriosas e inexplicables —dijo—. Esta suele ser una reunión cerrada, pero esta noche tenemos a un invitado. Noah, como no eres miembro, solicitamos que no hables durante la reunión salvo que te lo pidamos.

Lo miré levantando el pulgar. Vaya, que se fuera a la mierda.

—Ahora nos presentaremos solo por nuestro nombre. Hola, soy Josh, de Denton, y tuve una pérdida inexplicable.

—Hola, Josh —respondió la sala. Todo el resto se presentó de este modo: Ellen, de Fort Worth; Sarah, de Rusk (la mujer baja que había exclamado al ver mi ojo); Laura, de Athens (una mujer con una cara delgada y pelo lacio y largo); Hector, de Paris (un chico de mi edad aproximadamente); Eli, de Houston (un adolescente con pelo verde en punta); y Megan, de Mansfield. Cada uno alegó haber sufrido una pérdida inexplicable.

—La Hermandad de Desaparecidos es un grupo de hombres y mujeres que comparten sus experiencias, su fuerza y su esperanza, como todo un grupo de apoyo —dijo Josh—. Sin embargo, a diferencia de otros grupos de apoyo, que ayudan a las personas a aceptar pérdidas, adicciones o un diagnóstico médico, nosotros no enseñamos la catarsis a través de la discusión ni compartimos nuestras historias solo para crear sentimientos de solidaridad. Creemos que solo se puede conseguir la catarsis resolviendo la causa de la pérdida del individuo y afrontando el motivo. Compartimos nuestras historias para que nuestros compañeros puedan prestar atención a las pistas y los detalles que ayuden a resolver nuestro problema común de una vez por todas.

—En este punto me volvió a mirar—. Recuerda tu promesa de confidencialidad: lo que escuches aquí se queda aquí. Además, están prohibidos el cruce de opiniones o las interrupciones. —Consultó la tabla sujetapapeles que tenía en el regazo—. Sarah, veo que según el programa te toca a ti compartir esta noche.

Todo el mundo se giró para mirar a Sarah. Eli, el chico de pelo verde, le dirigió una sonrisa dulce de aliento.

—Todos conocéis la historia —dijo—, pero haré lo posible por contarla como si no la conocierais. —Se aclaró la garganta, un sonido infantil raro—. Mi hermano Stephen desapareció cuando yo estaba en noveno curso y él en el undécimo. Era un chico agradable... popular, muy querido. No hacía deporte, pero sí salía con animadoras. Era lector. Quería enseñar historia. —Mientras hablaba, todos los integrantes del círculo tomaban notas. Yo fui el único que escuché la historia sin distracciones, con las manos juntas en el regazo.

Stephen había salido con una chica llamada Daisy la noche de su desaparición. Había cogido prestado el coche de su padre, y había salido de casa a las seis. Sarah estaba viendo la televisión en su dormitorio cuando se fue, así que no se había despedido, y no había vuelto a pensar en su hermano hasta la mañana siguiente, cuando Daisy regresó en el coche del padre de Sarah, sola. El coche estaba en perfecto estado, pero Daisy parecía hecha un desastre. Tenía el pelo lleno de residuos forestales, el maquillaje corrido y surcado de lágrimas. Sus padres tuvieron que hacer varios intentos para conseguir que la chica dijera algo coherente; Sarah se quedó al pie de las escaleras, escuchando a escondidas mientras Daisy contaba su historia.

Stephen la había recogido aquella noche según lo previsto. Habían salido a cenar, pero se habían saltado el cine para liarse, en cambio, en el aparcamiento del parque. Tras alrededor de veinte minutos, Stephen empezó a parecer distraído. No dejaba de interrumpir los besos para preguntarle a Daisy si oía algo raro. Ella en ningún momento había oído nada. Una y otra vez Stephen se llevó las manos a las sienes haciendo una mueca de dolor. Describió el sonido como un puñal que le traspasaba la cabeza, y, a pesar de las objeciones de Daisy, salió del coche para investigar. Cruzó el aparcamiento dando tumbos y se adentró en la línea de árboles que separaba el parque, sujetando las manos con fuerza a los lados de la cabeza.

Daisy esperó cerca de una hora, pero finalmente salió y lo siguió. Deambuló por los senderos boscosos en la oscuridad, llamando a gritos a Stephen, sin oír respuesta. Aunque conocía bastante bien el parque, por algún motivo se perdió en la oscuridad, y le llevó hasta el amanecer encontrar la salida del bosque y volver al coche.

La siguiente parte del relato resultaba incómodamente conocida. Los padres de Sarah llamaron a la policía, y hubo una búsqueda, pero a pesar de recorrer el parque, no encontraron ni rastro del chico, ni siquiera de su paso por el bosque, aunque encontraron amplias pruebas de las enérgicas pisadas de Daisy. Una investigación a gran escala de la chica, la familia de Sarah, y los alrededores produjeron resultados igualmente decepcionantes. Stephen había desaparecido. Pero dos años después la historia tuvo un escalofriante epílogo: su cartera apareció en la caja de leche de un supermercado de barrio, en Topeka, Kansas. Seguía teniendo su carné de conducir, su carné escolar, el recibo de su cena con Daisy, veinte dólares en efectivo y un trozo de papel con una única palabra garabateada encima: *DUELE*.

Temí mirar a Megan, tenía miedo de lo que pudiera confirmarle aquello que viera en mi cara. ¿Por qué me habían invitado allí?

—Gracias, Sarah —murmuró Josh, mientras terminaba de escribir algo en su sujetapapeles—. ¿Lo que has dicho es, según lo que tú sabes, cierto?

—Sí —respondió ella.

—¿No has exagerado la historia ni has cambiado ningún detalle para intentar que la percibiéramos de un modo particular?

—No —dijo Sarah, tras una pausa.

Josh se recostó hacia atrás y señaló alrededor de la sala.

—Entonces haremos un turno de preguntas.

—¿Tenía tu hermano antecedentes de migrañas? —preguntó Hector.

—De niño, pero habían desaparecido en su mayor parte para cuando llegó al instituto —respondió Sarah.

—¿Y Topeka? —preguntó Laura—. ¿Alguna vez mencionó Topeka?

—Jamás —respondió Sarah, con más firmeza respecto de este punto.

Transcurrió un instante de silencio.

—¿Hay más preguntas? —preguntó Josh.

Sarah echó un vistazo esperanzado alrededor de la sala, como si alguien estuviera rumiando una pregunta cuya respuesta resolvería todo el misterio. Mi corazón se partió un poco ante la sinceridad de su gesto, lo dispuesta que aún estaba a conservar una mínima esperanza. Me obligué a mirar al suelo. Volví a temer lo que podía haber revelado, lo que esos desconocidos, excepcionalmente situados por la tragedia, serían capaces de sospechar de mí.

—Pensemos en esto —dijo Josh—, y si se os ocurre alguna idea o reflexión, compartidlas con todos. Siguiendo adelante, deberíamos pasar al invitado de Megan.

La mirada colectiva de la sala se posó en mí, como sabía que sucedería.

—¿Qué pasa conmigo? —pregunté.

Josh giró la grabadora hacia mí.

—En tus propias palabras, ¿por qué no empiezas por explicarnos la noche en que tu hermana desapareció, y luego pasas a la noche en que conociste a James O'Neil?

Intenté captar la atención de Megan, pero miraba su diario como si tuviera un texto vital y difícil de descifrar.

—Megan dice que eres un poco reticente a hablar sobre lo que sucedió esa noche —dijo Ellen—. Pero te garantizo que este es un lugar seguro.

—Dime —dijo Josh—. ¿Cómo consigues perder un ojo con una ventanilla hecha añicos?

Me puse de pie, abriéndome paso entre Eli y Hector a empujones, y salí corriendo por la puerta principal. Megan me alcanzó a medio camino a través del jardín y me sujetó del brazo.

—Por favor, no te vayas —dijo.

Me liberé de un tirón.

—Mi hermana no está desaparecida —dije—. La secuestró y asesinó James O'Neil. Así que no reúno los requisitos para ser miembro de tu pequeño club. —Me metí en el coche. Se quedó de pie en la acera mientras me alejaba.

CAPÍTULO 9

En cuanto llegué a casa fui a ver a Leannon, y tuvimos el tipo de sexo frenético en el que hay arañazos en la espalda y tirones de pelo. Intenté olvidar la vergüenza y la frustración follando, y ella pareció dispuesta a seguirme. Fue al encuentro de mis embestidas con una intensidad dolorosa y áspera. Cuando me llevó más allá del límite y me perdí a mí mismo, mi consciencia se desintegró como un papel de seda en el agua. Apoyó mi cabeza sobre su pecho, acariciándome el pelo.

A medida que se aquietó mi pulso y se apaciguó mi respiración, la apreté alrededor de la cintura, besándole la parte superior de un pecho. Ella emitió un sonido suave y feliz.

Ahora que tenía la cabeza despejada, me pregunté por qué había reaccionado como lo había hecho a las preguntas de la Hermandad de Desaparecidos. ¿Por qué me había enfadado tanto? En parte, era la actitud condescendiente de Josh, la forma en que me habían emboscado. En parte, la vergüenza por haber malinterpretado el tipo de interés que Megan sentía por mí. Pero ninguno de esos motivos explicaba el pánico que había sentido al inicio del interrogatorio, la alarma y el dolor que empezaron en cuanto habían mencionado la desaparición de Sydney. Como si me hubieran pillado haciendo algo malo. Como si de algún modo fuera responsable del dolor de sus vidas, y les debiera respuestas. Porque era cierto que yo sabía ciertas cosas: sabía que existía la especie de Leannon, y que uno de ellos había estado conectado de algún modo con James O'Neil. Pero, y lo digo sinceramente, jamás se me ocurrió preguntarle a Leannon qué tipo de vínculo era.

—¿En qué piensas? —me preguntó.

—¿Cuántos de vosotros hay? —pregunté—. Me refiero a tu gente.

—No lo sé —dijo.

—Si tuvieras que adivinar, ¿más de cien?

—Seguro.

—¿Más de cien millones?

—Cielos, no —dijo, con una carcajada suave.

—¿Tenéis un nombre?

—Tienes muchas preguntas esta noche —dijo.

—Quiero conocerte mejor.

—Conoces lo más importante. Dónde vivo, qué aspecto tienen mis dos caras, y que te quiero.

—Ni siquiera conozco tu nombre real.

—Fuiste tú quien me lo dio —dijo. Me apartó y se puso de pie, cruzando hacia su caballete. Sostenía el lienzo que había visto en mi última visita, las figuras que llevaban túnicas coloridas y se agazapaban bajo un cielo oscuro y una luna creciente, en posturas de súplica y casi terror místico.

Me incorporé contra la pared.

—He dicho algo que te ha molestado.

—No —respondió, pero siguió dándome la espalda—. No estoy ocultando nada importante, pero hay cuestiones que prefiero no discutir. —Por fin, me volvió a mirar—. Si no te cuento algo, es porque estoy protegiéndote. ¿Confías en mí?

—Disculpa —dije, y lo lamentaba de veras. Por raro que fuera, aquella era la única relación que funcionaba en mi vida—. Estoy muy ocupado con la boda de Eunice. Tengo que organizar una despedida de soltero para su estúpido novio, y fingir que me gusta, y que estoy feliz con todo este lío. —Quizás no fuera lo que más me preocupara en aquel momento, pero de todos modos me provocaba un grado apreciable de ansiedad.

Depuso la actitud crispada.

—¿Cómo está Eunice? Hace años que no la veo.

Y con la misma rapidez, la inquietud se volvió a apoderar de mí.

—No sabía que la hubieras conocido siquiera —dije.

—Durante diez años dormí casi todas las noches en tu cama. Por supuesto que la he conocido.

—Pero ella nunca te ha visto —dije—. O si te ha visto, jamás me ha dicho nada al respecto.

—No todo el mundo *puede* verme —dijo—. No salvo que yo quiera que me vean.

—Así que cuando te vi por primera vez, ¿fue porque tú quisiste que te viera?

Sonrió un poco.

—No. Tú me viste en seguida. Eres excepcional.

—Pero a Eunice… ¿nunca pasas a verla en secreto? ¿O a mí, o a mi madre?

—¿Por qué habría de hacerlo? —preguntó—. Tú sabes dónde vivo, y vienes lo bastante a menudo. Solo iría a verte si desaparecieras o si creyera que corres peligro.

Así que no tenía ni idea de lo de Megan. Era probable que fuera mejor así.

CAPÍTULO 10

Algunas noches después, Hubert estaba esperando en su porche delantero cuando Kyle y yo llegamos a recogerlo para la despedida de soltero. Sentado sobre el escalón, parecía un niño crecido. Llevaba pantalones caqui y una camisa. La camisa estaba cubierta de cuadrados diminutos como una hoja de papel milimetrada.

—Este es un hombre que nació para ser padre —dijo Kyle.

—Directo del departamento de casting —dije, dándole la razón.

El hombre del momento trajo consigo un CD mezclado especial, titulado *Jams de libertad para las despedidas*, que describió como una «especie de mezcla de conceptos»; trazaba el viaje sentimental de su romance con Eunice. Durante el viaje a Fun Mountain, escuchamos los atroces hits de rock suave, que culminaban con «Higher», de Creed. Kyle y yo evitamos mirarnos deliberadamente, sabiendo que si lo hacíamos estallaríamos en carcajadas que nos harían perder el juicio.

Algunos de los invitados se encontraron con nosotros en el vestíbulo de la sala de juegos de Fun Mountain, una cueva azul y púrpura llena de hombres que echaban fichas en las máquinas sin parar. Todos los tipos parecían mayores que Hubert, tíos con los vientres hinchados de cerveza y la afable cordialidad de hombres que se adaptan cómodamente a sus roles de padres, maridos y robots de oficina. Hombres con nombres mono y bisílabos, como Steve, Brian y Jack, que sabían cómo estrechar las manos con fuerza y tenían caras apenas distinguibles. Los conduje al campo del minigolf del fondo y llevé la puntuación mientras golpeaban la bola y decían idioteces. Kyle se deslizó dentro de la conversación sin aparente esfuerzo, y se me ocurrió que yo mismo había frecuentado muy poco a los hombres. Aunque compartía con ellos las mismas características básicas de la biología, parecían una raza extraña. Fanfarrones, bulliciosos, intensos, incluso esos hombres gordos entrados en años seguían mostrándose orgullosos y seguros de sí, como si fueran los dueños del mundo. ¿Dónde se originaba esa seguridad? ¿Y de dónde sacaban ese sentido innato de compañerismo?

Al cuarto hoyo, Hubert se retrasó para hablar conmigo.

—A veces son un poco pesados —dijo, al tiempo que Steve se inclinaba para colocar su bola sobre el tapete de caucho—. Pero son buenos tipos. Steve hace trabajo de voluntario con su iglesia para las personas sin hogar, y Jack adoptó a su hija en Rusia.

Me concentré en la tarjeta de puntuación chillona de colores naranja y púrpura.

—Son tus amigos, Hubert. No hace falta que me des sus credenciales.

Puso un brazo alrededor de mis hombros.

—Lo sé. Pero Eunice me dijo que no tienes muchos amigos hombres. Si les das una oportunidad, creo que este grupo te puede sorprender.

Mi piel se erizó bajo su mano.

—Estoy seguro de que tienes razón —dije.

Aun así, no me soltó.

—Para mí es importante que tú y yo seamos amigos. Tu hermana... lo es todo para mí. —Parpadeó, y sus ojos se llenaron de lágrimas tras las gafas. Se rio y se enjugó la mejilla—. Lo siento. Es una época sensible. Verás, creía...

estaba acostumbrándome a la idea de que estaría solo durante el resto de mi vida y, por eso, cuando apareció Eunice y lo cambió todo… pues… —Finalmente, se emocionó demasiado para continuar, y se limpió los ojos con el dorso de una mano. Quería sentirme asqueado, pero me sentí conmovido contra mi voluntad. Allí había un hombre que pensaba en planes a largo plazo. Comparado conmigo, que seguía viviendo en casa y tenía un monstruo con el que mantenía una relación de sexo sin compromiso y un empleo que desaparecería a final del mes, Hubert era un parangón de la vida adulta.

—¿Estáis a punto de besaros vosotros dos? —llamó Jack. Todo el mundo se rio, hasta Kyle y Hubert. Por fin me soltó el hombro y se dirigió al siguiente hoyo.

—¿Noah?

La voz me detuvo antes que pudiera unirme al grupo. Megan estaba a mi izquierda, blandiendo el palo de golf hacia atrás como si fuera un rifle, y con una bola roja ahuecada en la mano como una granada. Parecía alguien que intentaba causar una impresión, un poco avergonzada pero intentándolo de todos modos. Una actriz.

—¿Qué haces aquí? —pregunté.

—No me gustó cómo quedaron las cosas la otra anoche —dijo—. Cuando he llamado al número de tu tarjeta, hablé con tu madre y me ha dicho dónde estarías.

—¿Le ha dado mis datos a una desconocida? —pregunté.

—Le he dicho que era una emergencia—dijo—. *Quizás* crea que estoy embarazada. —Sus mejillas se tiñeron de rojo. Yo también sentí la cara un poco tibia.

—¿Así que has decidido colarte en una despedida de solteros? —pregunté.

—Quería pedirte disculpas —dijo—. Jamás debí emboscarte así.

—¿Has venido hasta aquí para pedirme disculpas? —pregunté—. ¿Y el palo de golf?

—La chica detrás del mostrador no me dejaba venir a buscarte salvo que pagara una ronda —dijo—. Hasta ahora estas disculpas me han costado seis dólares más la gasolina.

—¡Noah! —llamó Kyle, las manos ahuecadas alrededor de la boca—. ¡Te toca!

—Tengo que irme —le dije a Megan.

—¿De verdad te marcharás dejándome aquí? —preguntó.

—¡Noah! —gritó Kyle—. ¿Qué porras pasa, hombre?

Agité un pulgar hacia él.

—Está bien —dijo Megan, resoplando a través de sus fosas nasales ensancha-das—. Noah, por favor, no te vayas. O si lo haces, por lo menos dame el número de tu casa. Me falta poco para irme, y me gustaría... explicarte algunas cosas. Y me gustaría pasar un poco más de tiempo juntos. Para ir a comer gofres o lo que sea.

Esa chica. Desplegando todos sus encantos conmigo y sabiendo que es-taba funcionando.

—Espera aquí —dije, y corrí de vuelta al grupo.

—Ya era hora —dijo Steve.

—Una despedida de soltero no es el sitio para un idilio romántico —se-ñaló Jack.

—Los colegas antes que las zorras, Noah —dijo Hubert. Las palabras sonaban como si hubiera tomado prestado el cliché y estuviera probándoselo por primera vez. Un par de hombres se rieron.

—Kyle, lleva la puntuación un minuto —dije, pasándole la tarjeta—. Ya os alcanzo. —Rodeado de abucheos, tomé la mano de Megan y la conduje a mi coche. Cuando encendí el motor, «Sister Christian», de Night Ranger, empezó a sonar a todo volumen.

Cerró los ojos e hizo una mueca. Apagué la radio.

—No es mi música, por si te interesa saberlo —dije.

Conduciendo en piloto automático, la llevé al Laberinto del Terror. Es-taba cerrado por la noche, pero mi madre había olvidado cerrar el portón al aparcamiento. Acerqué el coche a la puerta principal, enmarcada con su cala-vera de poliestireno descascarillada y descolorida.

—Me subo a tu coche, me pongo a tu disposición, y de todos los lugares a los que podrías llevarme, ¿me traes aquí? —preguntó Megan.

Vacilé con la mano sobre la llave. No sabía si apagar el motor.

—Podemos ir a otro sitio —dije, aunque no tenía ni idea de a dónde. Pasaba todo mi tiempo allí, en casa o con Leannon. Trabajaba, follaba y dor-mía. No tenía sitios favoritos, nada en el mundo razonable que pudiera com-partir salvo mi trabajo. Hubert realmente era mejor que yo. Por lo menos tenía amigos y hobbies.

—No, has tenido una intuición —dijo—. Sigámosla.

Salimos del coche y entramos, atravesando la oficina polvorienta y sin muebles para entrar en el almacén mismo. En la sala de descanso tomamos agua y barritas de cereales y luego le di el tour. Cuando llegamos a la sala de baile, nos sentamos sobre el borde del escenario para comer nuestros tentempiés, meciendo los pies. Después de terminar su barrita, hizo girar la envoltura una y otra vez en las manos. El sonido susurrante llenó el espacio silencioso y vacío.

—Te he prometido una explicación —dijo.

—Así es —dije, aunque ahora tenía ganas de dejarlo, visto que se sentía incómoda, y queriendo preservar la tranquilidad entre ambos.

—Es difícil para mí hablar de esto —dijo—. Pero mereces saberlo. —Respiró profundamente—. Todos los que integran la Hermandad de Desaparecidos han perdido a alguien a quien quieren. Alguien a quien querían ha desaparecido de un modo que resulta inexplicable. Salvo yo. Yo sé exactamente dónde está mi persona. Está en la Unidad Polunsky de la prisión de West Livingston, en el corredor de la muerte. Se llama James O'Neil.

—¿Lo conoces?

—Es mi padre —dijo. Seguramente vio mi cara de preocupación porque me puso una mano sobre la rodilla—. No te preocupes, esto no se parece a *La hija de Drácula*. No estoy buscando venganza. Solo intento entenderlo, como el resto de mis amigos.

Levanté mi botella de agua para beber. Estaba vacía.

—Jamás fue un tipo normal —explicó Megan—. Siempre tuvo problemas mentales. Mi madre lo abandonó cuando yo era pequeña, así que no crecí con él. Enviaba tarjetas por mi cumpleaños, cuando lo recordaba, y vino de visita un par de veces. Siempre fue amable pero triste. Sabía que no era apto para ser un padre a tiempo completo, pero me echaba de menos, creo. Jamás pareció peligroso para nadie salvo para sí mismo. Así que cuando lo arrestaron hace un par de años, no tenía sentido, y cuando lo acusaron de cometer tres asesinatos y lo condenaron por dos, tuvo aún menos sentido. Fui a visitarlo a la prisión, pero no dejaba de decir que quería una segunda oportunidad.

—Es lo que me dijo a mí también —dije—. La noche que lo conocí. ¿Sería un brote psicótico?

—Es lo que creí —dijo—. Pero luego empezó a enviarme cartas. Cartas muy detalladas acerca de una fiera que había estado atormentándolo toda su vida, haciéndolo decir y hacer cosas que no quería decir o hacer. Insistió en que jamás había tocado a tu hermana, Noah, pero aquella fiera lo había hecho matar a Maria Davis y a Brandon Hawthorne. Me escribió que la fiera ya estaba muerta y que se sentía mucho mejor. A veces también me enviaba fotos de la fiera. —Sacó una hoja de papel del bolsillo y me la dio. La desdoblé y me encontré mirando un dibujo al carboncillo de la Bestia Gris, la fiera que me había atacado y destruido el ojo izquierdo. Intenté mantener una expresión de escepticismo (aunque compasiva a la vez).

—Al principio, creí que se trataba de una persona delirante que intentaba reconciliar el acto terrible que había cometido, y no respondí ninguna de sus cartas. Pero una noche, mientras mi madre se estaba muriendo, me levanté y empecé a curiosear en Internet. Fue cuando encontré la Hermandad. En sus tablones de anuncios tienen fotos muy parecidas a esta. Y las personas que acuden son personas reales. Puedes buscar a Sarah o a Josh y ver… que no están mintiendo. Realmente pasaron por aquellas cosas. Es de conocimiento público. Y sin embargo, a pesar de todo el tiempo que hemos pasado juntos, de lo que hemos hablado y teorizado, no tenemos ninguna prueba real de estas cosas. —Señaló el dibujo—. Ni tenemos ni idea de por qué hacen lo que hacen. Hace años que quiero hablar contigo, Noah. Mi madre me impidió asistir al juicio, y me hizo prometer que te dejaría en paz. Dijo que tú no querías escuchar las excusas o las mentiras de mi padre acerca de tu hermana. Pero yo guardé tu foto, y cuando te vi en Inferno… pareció haber una chispa, una conexión instantánea, y creí… —se interrumpió y parpadeó un par de veces. Con el tiempo conocería bien esa mirada. Era la cara que ponía cuando intentaba no llorar, y aquella primera vez que la vi me atravesó el corazón.

Le di la mano. Ella se sobresaltó pero no la alejó.

—No he sido completamente sincero contigo —dije—. ¿La noche que conocí a tu padre? Vi a este monstruo. —Asentí hacia el dibujo—. Vi a este y a otro exactamente igual. Estaban peleándose por… por tu padre, creo. Hui en mitad de todo ello porque estaba aterrado. Jamás se lo conté a nadie porque temí…

—Que la gente creyera que estabas loco —concluyó.

Eso pareció aflojar algo en su interior. Sus hombros se hundieron un poco, y luego empezó a llorar. No sé por qué elegí aquel momento para besarla, pero no me rechazó. Se inclinó hacia delante para devolverme el beso. Supo un poco dulce, como una barrita de cereales, y salada, como las lágrimas.

CAPÍTULO 11

Cuando volvimos, Fun Mountain estaba desierto. Esperaba encontrar la despedida de soltero fuera, todos los hombres con los brazos cruzados, desaprobando de modo paternal mi conducta, pero solo había un par de coches. Megan se inclinó para besarme antes de salir, y luego me quedé solo en el aparcamiento.

No volví a casa en seguida, sino que me quedé sentado en el coche con la luz del techo encendida, estudiando el dibujo que me había dado. Realmente, guardaba un parecido perfecto. ¿Por qué no había hecho ningún esfuerzo por investigar a Leannon y a los suyos? Hacía trece años que la conocía. ¿Por qué no había sentido más curiosidad? Claro, le había hecho preguntas, pero ella siempre cambiaba de tema o me distraía con comida o sexo, y después mis preguntas ya no parecían tan importantes. Sin duda, eso lo explicaba en parte. Pero también se daba la circunstancia de que yo había sospechado que ella había raptado y matado a Maria Davis y a Brandon Hawthorne en 1999, y había quedado demostrado que estaba equivocado. A modo de disculpas perpetuas, había aprendido a tomar lo que me dijera al pie de la letra. Me convencí a mí mismo de creer que James O'Neil y la Bestia Gris eran excepciones, no la regla. Pero ¿qué prueba tenía de ello? ¿Cómo sabía que James O'Neil y yo no estábamos en vías paralelas? Quizás O'Neil y la Bestia también habían empezado como amigos secretos. Quizás hubieran gobernado sus centros de placer, manipulándolo y haciéndolo participar en un proyecto mucho más sombrío. Pero ¿cuál podría ser ese proyecto? ¿Por qué la Bestia Gris lo haría raptar o matar niños? ¿Y si decía la verdad cuando insistió en que no había matado a Sydney? ¿Entonces qué? Si no la había matado, ¿a dónde había ido mi hermana? ¿Y se hallaba Leannon involucrada de algún modo?

La cabeza empezó a martillearme de nuevo. Dejé el dibujo a un lado sobre el asiento del pasajero para frotarme las sienes. ¿Cómo podía encontrarle la lógica a todo aquello?

Cuando llegué a casa, el sol se asomaba por encima del horizonte, tiñendo el cielo con pinceladas naranjas y rosas. El coche de Eunice estaba en la entrada, y cuando ingresé, metiéndome el dibujo en el bolsillo trasero, la encontré con mi madre, Kyle y Hubert en la sala, todos encarándome como si se tratara de una pequeña intervención.

—Hola, Noah —dijo Kyle, con un hilo de voz.

—¿Dónde narices has estado? —preguntó Eunice.

—Fuera. —Hundí las manos en los bolsillos traseros de mis vaqueros—. Surgió algo.

Hubert asintió.

—Lo entendemos, Noah. Nos alegra que estés bien.

Eunice apoyó una mano con fuerza sobre la delgada rodilla de su novio, los dedos blancos bajo el llamativo anillo de compromiso.

—Tras lo que has hecho, las únicas excusas aceptables son el secuestro o el asesinato. El único sitio donde debería ver tu cara es en un envase de leche o en las noticias, donde le dan a la gente un número para llamar…

Saqué de un tirón el dibujo de mi bolsillo trasero y lo desdoblé para que lo vieran.

—¿Alguno reconoce esto?

La diatriba de Eunice se detuvo abruptamente, y una mirada lejana y soñadora se adueñó de su cara. Mi madre se recostó sobre el sofá, con la boca ligeramente abierta. Kyle y Hubert solo parecían confundidos.

—Lo reconoces, ¿verdad? —pregunté mirando a mi madre.

—Claro —dijo, recomponiéndose—. Se parece a tu disfraz de monstruo.

—*Vamos* —dije—. ¿Cuánto tiempo vamos a jugar este juego? ¿Cuánto tiempo seguiremos mintiéndonos, fingiendo que todo está bien cuando no lo está? ¿Qué me estáis ocultando? ¿Qué sabéis?

Hubert dirigió a Eunice una mirada inquisitiva, y ella me miró con odio puro esculpido en la cara. Mi madre permaneció impasible, con expresión pétrea.

—No tengo ni idea de lo que hablas —dijo mi hermana—. Deja de ser dramático y de intentar cambiar de tema. Anoche abandonaste a tu cuñado y mejor amigo, y…

No me quedé para escuchar. Corrí saltando las escaleras a mi habitación, atranqué la puerta tras de mí, cerré el ojo y llevé ambas manos a la piedra negra alrededor del cuello. Cuando abrí el ojo, estaba de pie en el claro fuera de la casa de Leannon.

CAPÍTULO 12

El cielo también estaba clareando en aquel lugar, aunque permaneció de color oscuro y musgoso. No había ventanas en la casa, así que no tenía ni idea de si Leannon estaría despierta o no. Pensé en llamar a la puerta, pero vacilé. Lo que fuera que iba a descubrir, tenía que hacerlo solo, antes de que ella pudiera interferir o dar explicaciones para justificarse.

Me aparté de su casa y me abrí paso con dificultad hacia el bosque oscuro. Como no tenía un plan mejor, caminé en línea recta. Los árboles y los matorrales eran lo bastante escasos para permitir que avanzara, pero aquella negrura densa no se aclaró. Cada vez que intentaba mirar algo de cerca, el objeto retrocedía contorneándose hacia las tinieblas y era apenas una mera insinuación. Apresuré el paso, con los brazos extendidos por delante para no tropezar con nada. Esquivé árboles negros como el carbón y atravesé a patadas la enmarañada espesura hasta llegar a un espacio en la oscuridad por el que se colaba una débil luz verde a través de los árboles.

Crucé la línea de árboles para salir de nuevo del bosque al aire libre. El suelo frente a mí se detuvo ante un abrupto acantilado. Caminé hacia el borde y miré detenidamente el paisaje que tenía debajo. En lugar de más bosque, vi una vasta red de edificios y calles; hormigón, cristal y piedra negra brillante se extendían durante kilómetros y kilómetros. Los rascacielos hendían sus picos como dientes contra el horizonte y, en el centro, un pilar ciclópeo de piedra negra, tan elevado que llegaba casi hasta las nubes cubiertas de bruma. Con solo mirarlo me dolió la cabeza, como mirar a través de las gafas de otra persona.

Los edificios tenían un diseño moderno pero parecían antiguos, ruinosos y deteriorados. Se hallaban sumidos en un silencio inquietante, por lo que parecía, estaban vacíos. El suelo retumbó, al principio de modo suave, y luego con más vehemencia. Retrocedí y me aferré del árbol más cercano. Mis dedos se cerraron alrededor de la corteza gomosa. La Ciudad empezó a moverse, y tramos enteros de calles se desplazaron como los paneles de la imagen de un rompecabezas... no, eso no es totalmente cierto. La Ciudad se *deslizó*, y las calles adyacentes rechinaron unas contra otras en direcciones opuestas. Una cabeza de serpiente de pavimento emergió del suelo y se precipitó hacia mí a tal velocidad que no tuve tiempo de entrar en pánico ni de pensar. Se detuvo al borde del acantilado y se quedó completamente tumbada, salvando la distancia entre ambos con una floritura de cuatro notas lánguidas y aletargadas.

Esperé para ver si la calle arremetería y me golpearía, pero permaneció quieta. Se trataba de una invitación, no de una amenaza. Descendí por la acera de obsidiana inclinada y entré en la Ciudad, pasando a un desfiladero de piedra y cristal. Los edificios parecían estructuralmente sólidos, las ventanas estaban limpias y brillantes, la fluorescencia de detrás era amarilla verdosa. Además de la ausencia de tráfico y de la elección de materiales de construcción, podía haber pisado cualquier calle de cualquier distrito financiero importante de Norteamérica, salvo por la sensación de que aquí había algo que iba más allá de las apariencias y acechaba sin ser visto. De qué se trataba esa presencia, no lo sabía, pero parecía importante. Como una promesa que se extendía, una respuesta a alguna pregunta sin formular, a la vuelta de la siguiente esquina.

Al final de la calle, giré a la derecha, adentrándome aún más. Al empezar a caminar por la segunda manzana de edificios casi idénticos, el suelo se estremeció y tembló. Me detuve, extendiendo los brazos para no caerme al tiempo que las construcciones al final de la calle, delineando la parte superior de la intersección con forma de T, se alejaron deslizándose hacia la derecha y descubrieron una calle nueva y diferente, bordeada de farolas de hierro negro. Adoquines rojizos sustituyeron la obsidiana, y los edificios se volvieron más pequeños, de aspecto más antiguo. Los restaurantes y los cafés tenían mesitas fuera. Si antes había estado metido en el bosquejo de un distrito financiero, ahora había entrado en el del Barrio Francés. Un conjunto de jazz oculto tocaba en algún sitio cercano. Un letrero de sándwiches a mi izquierda prometía *beignets* reales y EL MEJOR CAFÉ CON LECHE DE LA CIUDAD. Al otro lado de la calle, hubo un movimiento tras una ventana de cristal oscura. Crucé para ver mejor, ahuecando mis manos alrededor del ojo para impedir el reflejo del brillo sobre el cristal.

El interior parecía una barbería anticuada, con enormes espejos y sillones afelpados de color rojo, y un suelo de mosaicos reluciente. Un hombre de grueso pelo plateado y el cuerpo con forma de pera se hallaba sentado en el sofá del medio, recostado hacia atrás como esperando a que lo afeitaran.

Di un golpecito en el cristal con los nudillos. Alzó la cabeza lentamente, como un hombre que se despierta de un sueño, los ojos adormilados y turbios.

—¿Está bien? —pregunté.

Antes de que pudiera responder, las superficies del sofá estallaron, y gruesos apéndices negros irrumpieron a través de la tela. Se alzaron temblando en el aire, como tentáculos armados con aguijones en los extremos, y luego descendieron como puñales perforándole los antebrazos y muslos. La sangre brotó de las heridas al tiempo que los tentáculos se hundían. El hombre inclinó la cabeza hacia atrás para gritar. Forcejeó contra la silla, pero el monstruo lo ciñó con firmeza.

—Dios —dije—. Oh, dios mío. —La silla lo mataría. Corrí a la puerta de la tienda y tiré de ella, pero no se movió. Miré alrededor en busca de algo para romper la ventana, pero mientras estaba de espaldas la calle había retirado sus cubos de basura y las mesas al aire libre. Solo pude golpear el escaparate y observar mientras el hombre se retorcía, gritaba... y empezaba a sufrir un cambio.

Comenzó con sus extremidades, donde la silla lo había tenido anclado. Sus brazos y piernas se estiraron y adelgazaron como la plastilina cuando se hace rodar entre las palmas, hasta que las manos y los pies se desprendieron y cayeron al suelo, desprovistos de huesos. Luego los tentáculos empezaron a latir, como si algo los estuviera recorriendo por dentro. Los miembros del hombre se abultaron e inflaron. Las mangas de su camisa y las piernas de sus pantalones se desgarraron. A medida que sus pies aumentaron de tamaño, sus zapatos explotaron. Las uñas de los dedos y los pies se hicieron más gruesas y se enroscaron, y mechones de pelo brotaron de su carne pálida y blanda, cubriéndolo de pelaje. El hombre golpeó la cabeza con fuerza hacia atrás, gritando más como un animal que como un ser humano. Su nariz y mentón se estiraron, alejándose de la cara hasta convertirse en un hocico. Cerró los ojos, y cuando los abrió, se habían vuelto de color naranja. Se había transformado en uno de ellos. En uno de la especie de Leannon.

La silla lo soltó, y cayó rodando al suelo como un montículo peludo. Retrocedí un paso y me di contra algo duro. Los vi reflejados en los espejos de la barbería: toda una hilera de monstruos vestidos con túnicas, de pie justo detrás de mí. Me volví y quedé cara a cara con aquel con el que me había chocado; enseñó los dientes y gruñó. Retrocedí otro paso más, esta vez dándome contra la vitrina. La fiera lobuna alzó una de sus garras, lista para propinarme un golpe.

Un áspero ladrido de algún sitio cercano interrumpió el momento. La criatura que me amenazaba dejó caer el brazo, y la hilera se abrió: al otro lado de la calle estaba Leannon, llevando su cara bestial por primera vez en años. Se cuadró firme y extendió las garras; un gruñido resonó en lo más profundo de su garganta. La horda de monstruos que tenía delante intercambió miradas y, por lo visto, decidió no luchar. Las criaturas se separaron. Leannon extendió una garra hacia mí. Caminé hacia ella. Tiró de mí para acercarme a su cuerpo, y echamos a volar.

Solo nos llevó unos segundos estar de vuelta en su claro; me dejó caer sobre el césped antes de aterrizar. Rodé hasta detenerme, y se posó delante de mí, habiendo recuperado su forma humana. Intenté ponerme de pie, pero me volvió a empujar al suelo, su cara pálida.

—¿Qué *porras* creías que hacías? —preguntó. Otra vez en pie, contuve las ganas de empujarla también.

—¿Qué narices acabo de ver?

—Se trata de una ceremonia privada y sagrada —dijo—. No tenías ningún derecho a andar husmeando.

—La Ciudad me invitó a pasar —señalé—. Quería que lo viera.

Me estudió un momento, su furia consumiéndose. Se llevó la palma a la frente.

—Te ha visto; ha olido tu rastro.

—¿Así nacen los de tu especie? ¿Así te convertiste en lo que eres?

No respondió.

—¿Eso es lo que hacen? ¿Raptan gente, la traen aquí y la transforman en monstruos? ¿Era eso lo que debía sucederle a James O'Neil? ¿Eso es lo que tenía intención de hacer con Maria Davis?

Y luego recordé a Josh en la reunión de la Hermandad, preguntándome por Sydney. Sydney, que había desaparecido en esta época del año hacía trece años.

—¿Qué pasó realmente con Sydney? —pregunté—. ¿Está muerta? ¿Está aquí? —Señalé de nuevo hacia la Ciudad, donde acababa de ver a un hombre sufrir la transformación—. ¿Fue eso lo que le sucedió? ¿Fuiste *tú* quien se lo hizo?

Leannon se acercó y extendió la mano hacia mí.

—Sé que tienes preguntas, pero en este momento tienes que confiar en mí, Noah. —Su modo de esquivar mis dudas me dijo todo lo que necesitaba saber. Era ella quien había raptado a Sydney en 1989 e intentaba distraerme, como siempre lo hacía.

—No me toques —dije, dando un paso atrás, horrorizado—. Déjame en paz. —Presioné la piedra y cerré el ojo. Leannon seguía protestando cuando llegué a mi propia habitación.

La casa se encontraba ahora en silencio; no tenía que sufrir la reprimenda de mi familia. Me recosté en la cama e intenté dominar mis temblores.

CAPÍTULO 13

Llamé a Megan y le pedí que se reuniera conmigo de nuevo en Fun Mountain aquella noche. Cuando llegó, sonriendo, me encontró sentado con las piernas cruzadas sobre el capó de mi coche. No debió de gustarle lo que vio porque al instante su alegría mutó a preocupación.

—¿Qué ha pasado? —preguntó.

—Necesito tu ayuda —respondí.

La secuencia Turner IV: Noah

La Ciudad ha visto a Noah: tiene su rastro. Así que, a
pesar de que sus visitas son esporádicas y suelen ser
breves, lo observa cuando está en el exterior. Su tortura
no es algo de lo que pueda despertarse empapado en un sudor
frío, algo que desaparezca con la caricia tranquilizadora
de una amante o con la televisión de madrugada. Es el rumbo
de su vida.

Empieza en 2002 mientras espera a Megan en el
aparcamiento de Fun Mountain. Se siente nervioso, a solas
con el hormigón y las lámparas de vapor de sodio que emiten
un brillo amarillo verdoso demasiado familiar. Una parte de
él quisiera haber entrado en la caverna tenuemente púrpura
de la sala de juegos. Pero por una vez está harto de la
oscuridad.

Así que espera, con las piernas cruzadas, sobre el capó
de su coche, y los dedos metidos en la hendidura donde se
tocan sus muslos. Espera parecer guapo y travieso, como un
Peter Pan del siglo veintiuno, cubierto con el parche de un
pirata, que ha venido para conducir a su Wendy a alegres
aventuras. No deja de llevarse la mano a la piedra
alrededor del cuello, como hace a veces cuando está
nervioso, sin dejar de sorprenderse de que ya no esté. La
ha dejado en un cajón del escritorio de su dormitorio,
donde si por él fuera, puede pudrirse. Solo desea que su
ausencia no lo haga sentir desnudo y expuesto.

Aquí llega Megan ahora, saliendo del coche, lista para
una noche activa salvando almas, el pelo sujeto hacia
arriba en una coleta. A Noah le parece la viva imagen de la

salud y la normalidad. Después del día que ha tenido, añora estar con ella.

¿Qué hay?, pregunta. Su sonrisa desaparece al ver su expresión.

Durante horas ha debatido acerca de qué decirle, pero decide contarle la verdad pura y dura. *Necesito tu ayuda*.

Le explica que hay más en esta historia de lo que le ha contado hasta ahora. Se sube a su coche, y le habla sobre la noche en que Sydney desapareció: el grito y el corte de luz simultáneos. Le cuenta lo de los sonidos raros ante la ventana de su dormitorio en las semanas previas a su desaparición, y lo de las desconcertantes reacciones de su madre y su hermana al dibujo que realizó James O'Neil de la criatura lobuna.

Sin embargo, no se lo cuenta todo. No le cuenta lo de su amistad con la criatura, ni el nombre que le dio, ni que, hasta hoy, son amantes. Desea que lo que Megan siente por él permanezca libre y sin complicaciones. Tiene que verlo como una víctima adorable que busca fuerza para decir lo que piensa por primera vez, no como el chico que creció para follarse a un monstruo.

Cuando termina su confesión parcial, Megan le toma de la mano, y una hora después ambos están en la sala de Ellen para una reunión de emergencia con la Hermandad de Desaparecidos. La sala parece mucho más desordenada que la última vez que Noah estuvo allí. Pasa que todos los miembros de la Hermandad han estado durmiendo en casa de Ellen las últimas semanas. En general, se comunican a través del tablón de anuncios de Internet, pero una vez por año se proponen reunirse para hablar de trabajo y estar juntos. Por los cuencos de palomitas de maíz y el fotograma paralizado de la televisión, Noah supone que ha interrumpido la noche de cine.

Repite su relato abreviado a los miembros reunidos. Durante todo ese rato Josh le echa una mirada asesina, pero no hace preguntas. Se sienta y escucha, e incluso toma notas.

Solo falta una semana antes de que Megan tenga que volver a la universidad en Chicago, y el resto de quienes integran esta sección de la Hermandad se disperse y vuelva a casa. Incapaz de obligarse a ir a casa de su madre, Noah permanece con la Hermandad en casa de Ellen, durmiendo sobre una tarima de mantas en el suelo de la sala. Él y el grupo se pasan los días y las noches repasando su historia una y otra vez, en busca de pistas. Noah no les proporciona más información, se adhiere a su versión de sucesos con tal rigidez que casi se la cree él mismo. La Hermandad se siente frustrada y entusiasmada a la vez. Noah no comparte su entusiasmo. No le interesa saber más acerca de las criaturas ni de la Ciudad. Lo único que quiere es alejarse de su vida y de este sitio. Cuando acaba la semana y Megan lo invita a que vuelva a Chicago con ella, accede al instante.

Le cuenta a su madre lo de la mudanza por teléfono. Ella maneja la situación con aplomo y sensatez, pero le advierte que no hay una sola persona que pueda resolverle todos los problemas para siempre.

A Eunice ni siquiera se lo cuenta. No han hablado desde el día siguiente a la despedida de soltero de Hubert.

Cuando Megan sale del pueblo en su coche, rumbo a Chicago, Noah va adelante, de copiloto, ambos intercambiando miradas nerviosas pero alentadoras. Solo ha traído una maleta llena de ropa y un ejemplar de *La llamada de Cthulhu y otros relatos* que le ha dado Eli, el miembro más joven de la Hermandad. Descansa sobre su regazo como un talismán mientras Vandergriff corre a toda velocidad al otro lado de la ventanilla, avanzando entre chirridos y traqueteos, bajo el golpeteo suave de la lluvia contra el techo.

Pero al subir a la carretera, el bullicio desaparece por completo, como si el mundo se hubiera quedado en silencio.

Noah se da la vuelta para mirar a Megan, para ver si también está oyendo esta anomalía, y advierte el lanzamiento en paracaídas de Fun Mountain a través de la ventanilla de su lado del conductor.

Un rayo de luz rasga el cielo gris, como un relámpago que golpea el parque. En ese instante, el lanzamiento en paracaídas adopta el aspecto de una torre colosal del color de la tinta negra, suave como el cristal volcánico, que alcanza los cielos temporalmente iluminados. Su superficie reluce como alquitrán fresco, pringoso y resbaladizo.

A medida que la imagen desaparece, el sonido vuelve. El mundo se sacude con el gruñido de algo enorme, una larga cresta resonante que estremece la tierra. Noah rechina sobre su borde, los dientes apretados, aterrado de caerse a un abismo, donde quedará a solas con… con…

Consigue mirar a Megan y ve que le está echando miradas preocupadas. Ha bajado la velocidad. Las vibraciones se desvanecen y los ruidos del mundo vuelven de inmediato, como si se hubiera girado la ruedecita del volumen demasiado rápido, demasiado alto.

¿Qué sucede?, pregunta ella. Los sonidos le raspan el cerebro. *¿Quieres que me detenga?*

Noah se da cuenta de que está pegado contra la puerta del pasajero, con los brazos contra el tablero y el reposacabezas.

Relaja la mandíbula con esfuerzo.

No, dice. *No te detengas. Sácame de aquí.*

En Chicago encuentra un apartamento diminuto de una habitación en el tercer piso de un viejo edificio lleno de corrientes de aire. Comparte un lavabo con todo el resto de la planta. Es terrible, pero es todo lo que le alcanza con sus ahorros mientras sale en busca de un empleo. Megan duerme en su residencia, pero lo visita casi todos los días y a veces pasa la noche. Noah encuentra un empleo en un Barnes & Nobles cerca de la universidad. Aunque al comienzo solo le dan veinte horas a la semana, también pasa allí sus días libres. Es un sitio tibio y bien iluminado, y le dan el cincuenta por ciento de descuento en el café, lo cual resulta preferible a su apartamento cada vez más helado. Lo mejor es que, aunque el parche sigue atrayendo las miradas de desconocidos, la gente no lo trata como algo digno de temer. Para la gente de Chicago, Noah es solo un vendedor de libros más.

Durante algunos meses, no sucede nada. A Noah le va bien en la tienda, le dan más horas, y llega a conocer a Megan fuera del amplio terreno compartido de dolor y pérdida. Es una persona amable, pero hay cierta dureza en su interior, la fuerza de alguien que ha tenido que lidiar con demasiado dolor, demasiado pronto en la vida. Es la fuerza que desea tener él mismo.

Cuando se acuestan por primera vez, es tierno y dulce. No termina en una profusión de luz dorada, una fractura de la consciencia o la trascendencia del tiempo y el espacio. En cambio, son una serie de agradables espasmos musculares hasta terminar desplomándose, revueltos y enredados.

Megan le toca la mejilla mientras Noah desciende rodando de ella, y siente sus lágrimas. *¿Qué pasa?*, pregunta.

Solo estoy realmente feliz, dice, porque quiere que sea cierto. Quiere sentir la ausencia de complicaciones respecto de lo que acaba de suceder, como si no acabara de cometer un acto de infidelidad. Intenta apartar a Leannon de su visión mental. Esa parte de su vida ha acabado. Por el bien de su cordura y de su alma, debe ser así.

Al día siguiente sucede algo cuando está caminando a casa de Barnes & Noble. Dobla a la izquierda en la esquina de Blevington y King, y en lugar de salir a una calle amplia y concurrida, se encuentra en un callejón entre dos edificios de ladrillo anónimos que no reconoce. Una puerta de metal se abre de golpe a su derecha, y un hombre barbudo y cubierto de tatuajes sale con dos bolsas de residuos.

Lleva vaqueros y una camiseta; se detiene para mirar el abrigo y la bufanda de Noah. De pronto, siente un calor excesivo con la ropa que lleva puesta.

¿Estás perdido?, pregunta el hombre.

Noah no responde. En cambio, se da la vuelta y vuelve caminando por donde ha venido. Cuando sale en el otro extremo del callejón, está en una ancha calle bordeada de edificios decrépitos de ladrillo que de algún modo parecen desaturados, como si alguien hubiera empleado una pajita para aspirar casi todo el color. Las ventanas están cubiertas de polvo y de telas de araña, y no hay más personas alrededor. Mira de nuevo hacia el callejón, pero ha desaparecido. Está de pie ante un muro blanco.

Se detiene bajo el letrero de una calle y alza la cabeza para leerlo. Está escrito en un lenguaje que no reconoce, y el cielo por encima es de un verde brumoso. Un sonido de sorpresa, casi una carcajada, escapa de su garganta. «Eh». El tipo de sonido que podría escucharse de un artesano sorprendido e impresionado por el trabajo de otro.

¿Hola?, llama. Si hay alguien escuchando, no responde. Y luego, con un cambio tan veloz que un parpadeo parece demasiado prolongado, Noah está de nuevo en la intersección de Blevington y King, rodeado de árboles desprovistos de hojas que se estremecen bajo el aire gélido, y ante una hilera de coches aparcados, uno tras otro, junto a la acera. El letrero ha vuelto a adquirir su imagen cotidiana, y la gente lo empuja de un lado a otro al pasar con prisa.

Se plantea contárselo a Megan, pero ¿de qué serviría? Le preocuparía, o peor, podría alejarla. Si lo supiera, ¿no lo abandonaría como un caso perdido?

Así que ese día no dice nada, y tampoco de las noches en que se despierta alrededor de las tres de la mañana, convencido de que puede oír a una mujer canturreándole al oído. Y se dice que no es feliz con estos sucesos, que no le intrigan estas insinuaciones místicas y anómalas.

En primavera, tras los exámenes trimestrales, Megan recibe una llamada del abogado de su padre. Han fijado por fin una fecha para la ejecución. Ella y Noah logran reunir el dinero suficiente para la gasolina para conducir a Texas.

Cuando llegan, la prisión le recuerda a Noah a su instituto: las mismas paredes pintadas de bloques de hormigón y luces fluorescentes, la misma sensación de indiferencia mecánica. Solo falta la vitrina de trofeos y las pancartas motivacionales.

Megan está en la lista aprobada de visitantes, y entra para hablar a solas con él. Cuando sale, tiene la cara hinchada y no dice nada. La dirigen junto a Noah a una sala pequeña con dos hileras de sillas que dan a una ventana de cristal. Se sientan en la hilera de adelante, y la encargada les explica que se trata de un espejo polarizado. Podrán ver lo de dentro, pero el condenado no podrá ver lo de fuera. El reportero de un periódico y los padres de Maria Davis llegan poco después. Nadie de la familia de Brandon Hawthorne. Noah siente al resto de la sala observándolo, y se le pone la carne de gallina. Se obliga a mirar el cristal y le da la mano a Megan. Yace flácida en la suya, algo frío y muerto.

James O'Neil entra empujado en una camilla, ataddo con correas. Su brazo derecho está sujeto a una extensión, separándolo de su cuerpo. Parece estar lánguidamente crucificado. Ahora está bien rasurado y calvo; tiene la cara cansada y cubierta de cicatrices. Su mirada es pensativa y sumisa, sin la energía frenética que Noah recuerda.

Cuando uno de los oficiales de la prisión detrás del cristal le pregunta si tiene unas últimas palabras, solo sacude la cabeza. La madre de Maria Davis empieza a llorar a la vez que un hombre encapuchado le administra la inyección. James O'Neil aparta al fin la mirada del techo y la dirige hacia el cristal. Parece ver más allá; de hecho, parece haber elegido a Noah para esta última mirada distante y triste.

A Noah le recuerda a cuando estaba en la Ciudad, mirando al hombre sujeto a la silla de la barbería. También en aquella ocasión miró a través de un cristal cuando la silla transformó a aquel hombre en algo inhumano. Ahora apenas siente a Megan retirando la mano cuando los labios de O'Neil se separan. Parece a punto de decirle algo, pero se detiene ante un sonido, uno que parece reconocer. Noah también lo reconoce: crich-crich-crich. Crich-crich-crich, como garras largas que arañan el cristal. Cuando se detiene, O'Neil cierra los ojos y sale empujado de la sala. Quizás aún no esté muerto, pero el espectáculo ha acabado.

Noah y Megan no se tocan ni hablan cuando vuelven caminando al coche. Ambos pasan varios minutos mirando fuera del parabrisas al edificio donde acaba de terminar la vida de un hombre con precisión clínica. Noah no puede quitarse de encima la mirada del viejo, y el ruido de arañazos se ha instalado en la base de su cráneo, provocándole escalofríos que lo recorren de arriba abajo. Sujeta el volante para evitar los temblores. A su lado, puede sentir el sufrimiento de Megan. Peor, puede sentir un vacío que se abre ante él, un hoyo en el que podría caer si no tiene cuidado. ¿Cuánto tiempo pasará hasta que sea él mismo quien esté tras el cristal, recibiendo la inyección letal?

Casémonos, dice.

A ella le lleva mucho tiempo girar la cabeza y aceptar lo que ha dicho.

¿En serio?

En serio.

¿Te refieres a ya mismo?

Lo antes posible.

Alargan su estancia en Texas lo bastante para organizar juntos una pequeña ceremonia en la Iglesia del Espíritu Santo, a la que asisten en su mayoría miembros de la congregación y la sección local de la Hermandad. Noah no invita a su familia, ni siquiera les avisa que está en la ciudad. Kyle acude para ser el padrino. Cuando Noah y Donna llegan a la iglesia, Donna parece tener un balón de baloncesto atado al vientre: en un par de semanas dará a luz. Por algún motivo, esta imagen, esta prueba irrefutable del paso del tiempo, hace que Noah eche de menos a Eunice. Se perdió su boda, y ahora ella está perdiéndose la suya.

Noah y Megan pasan la noche en un hotel cerca de los mataderos de Fort Worth, decorado con pinturas de cactus y cráneos de vacas. Después del sexo, Megan llora y deja de hablarle. Él decide darle su espacio y se queda dormido a un lado de la cama.

Se despierta alrededor de las tres, muerto de sed. Toma el cubo del hielo del lavabo y sale al pasillo bien iluminado. Busca un letrero que señale el camino hacia la máquina de hielo, pero solo ve puertas y pinturas caricaturescas del Sudeste que se extienden en ambas direcciones. ¿No había una ventana en un extremo del pasillo cuando entraron? Debe de haberlo olvidado.

Pasa una serie de puertas, escucha el murmullo de conversaciones, el zumbido monótono de los televisores, el tufillo a marihuana. Cuando dobla la esquina, se topa con una puerta que dice ESCALERAS. Quizás tenga más suerte en la planta de abajo.

Sus chancletas golpean los escalones alfombrados con un sonido sordo, pero no hay una puerta al final del primer tramo ni del segundo. Se detiene delante de las escaleras del quinto tramo inclinándose sobre la barandilla, intentando adivinar cuántas más quedan. Siente una bola dura, mezcla de temor y anticipación, en la boca del estómago. Advierte que esta sensación no es ajena a él. Es tan conocida que es casi como una manta cálida. Es lo que siente cuando por fin está llegando a la mejor parte de una historia de terror, o entrando por primera vez en una casa embrujada nueva. Es como se sintió la primera vez que entró en la Ciudad.

Con solo un ojo y sin percepción de profundidad, es difícil darse cuenta de cuántos tramos más le quedan. Levanta la mirada, pero siente otra vez que su maldita percepción de profundidad le está jugando una mala pasada. Este hotel solo tiene seis pisos de altura, pero parece haber decenas de tramos de escaleras encima, que se pierden más allá de la vista.

Algo se mueve allí arriba, una silueta negra contra un fondo gris. Recula. Atrás ha quedado la anticipación que sentía hacía apenas unos instantes, además de estar sobre terreno irregular. Agita los brazos para mantener el equilibrio, aleteando como un pájaro ridículo. En ese momento, se inclina y cae por las escaleras, cada golpe una explosión brillante de dolor. Aterriza en la parte inferior en un montículo, jadeando y esperando que se calme la agonía. Una serie de pisadas fuertes descienden reverberando desde arriba, así que no tiene la certeza de si son un par de pies o varios o muchos. *Ploft-ploft-ploft*, más y más fuerte. El sonido se eleva a un crescendo. Noah se tapa los oídos con las manos. Algo se cierra alrededor de su brazo.

¡No lo hagas!, grita. *¡Por favor!*

Tranquilo. Soy yo. Oye la voz como si viniera del interior de su cabeza. Leannon, dulce y apacible.

Levanta la vista y ve la expresión de dolor en su cara humana. Le ofrece una mano, pero vacila antes de ayudarlo a levantarse. Recorre con el pulgar su alianza reciente.

¿Por qué has hecho esto?, pregunta. Su tono permanece amable, pero el dolor se cuela por los resquicios.

¿Por qué no me dejas en paz?, le pregunta Noah.

Leannon aparta la mirada de la alianza con gran esfuerzo, y se pasa la lengua por los labios antes de hablar. *Así no funciona esto. Hay muchas cosas que no comprendes.* Extiende la mano para sostener su cara, pero él la aparta bruscamente.

Deja que te ayude a comprenderlo, dice Noah. *No quiero terminar como el padre de Megan. No quiero terminar como Sydney. No quiero hacerle daño a nadie, y no quiero volver a verte. Quiero olvidar que alguna vez te he conocido.*

Leannon si, dice ella.

¡Vete!, grita, y al hacerlo, Noah se encuentra delante de una puerta abierta, a través de la cual ve el vestíbulo del hotel. El empleado de la recepción se inclina hacia delante, mirándolo con extrañeza.

¿Se encuentra bien, señor?, pregunta.

Noah ve el cubo del hielo volcado, a algunos metros, aun envuelto en una capa de plástico delgado y chirriante. Lo recoge, saluda al recepcionista y cruza el vestíbulo hacia los ascensores. Vuelve al tercer piso y de inmediato encuentra el rincón de la máquina de hielo. Llena el cubo y regresa a su habitación. Se bebe el agua y vuelve a meterse en la cama. Yace despierto durante un largo rato, pensando en Leannon y en la Ciudad. Se esfuerza por convencerse de que hizo lo correcto desterrándola de su vida. Que no ha sido agradable volver a verla. Que no ha resultado excitante quedar en manos de la Ciudad por un instante, sin saber qué encontraría al pie de un tramo de escaleras o a la vuelta de una esquina.

Él y Megan van de luna de miel a Ashland, Oregon, sede del Festival de Shakespeare de Oregon. Se trata de un pueblo pequeño e idílico, como algo salido de una película, con amplias aceras y escaparates, tiendas que se llaman CD o No CD, y tres teatros diferentes. Parece el sitio ideal para levantarle el ánimo a una novia que es una apasionada del teatro. La primera noche en el pueblo ven una obra llamada *La vida es sueño*, de Pedro Calderón de la Barca, donde consiguen asientos de palco. Observar el desarrollo de la obra dramática es como fisgonear a unos vecinos pintorescos desde una ventana elevada. La historia sigue a Segismundo, el príncipe de Polonia, encarcelado por su padre, el rey Basilio, por una profecía del oráculo que indica que su hijo causará estragos en todo el país. Por supuesto, Segismundo consigue ser liberado y, presa de la furia, desata una oleada de violencia que obliga a Basilio a volver a encerrarlo y convencerlo de que su breve libertad fue, en realidad, un sueño.

Cuando Megan y Noah vuelven caminando al hotel más tarde, ella hojea la revista de espectáculos, animada por primera vez en muchas semanas, señalando los retratos de los actores y leyendo en voz alta la información de sus biografías. ¿Sabía Noah que uno de los guardias interpretó a Benedick en *Mucho ruido y pocas nueces*? Noah admite que no lo sabía. Le cuesta hablar. La obra le ha aplastado la mente como un pulgar aplasta un malvavisco; la siente abultada y lenta al recuperar su forma original.

¿Te sientes bien?, le pregunta ella, percibiendo su estado de ánimo.

Solo pensaba en la obra, dice.

Le toma el brazo y se apoya sobre él. *Yo te protegeré, apuesto príncipe. Estás atrapado a salvo en la torre de nuestro matrimonio.* Luego lo empuja, y por segunda vez esa semana, cae girando velozmente. Esta vez aterriza en un seto al borde de la acera.

Pero ¿quién te protegerá de mí?, grita, escapando entre risas.

El último día de la luna de miel, tras una semana de ver obras teatrales, de sexo libre de lágrimas y del encanto shakesperiano del pequeño pueblo, almuerzan en una imitación terrible de un pub inglés donde la comida sabe a

verdadera bazofia. Megan vuelve a parecer desanimada, y
Noah teme que el hechizo de las vacaciones se haya roto.

Tras hacer una mueca de disgusto con su quinto o sexto
bocado de pollo al arándano, le dice: *No tienes que*
terminarlo si no te gusta.

Megan apoya el tenedor y se da unos toques en los labios
con la servilleta. Se trata de un gesto remilgado,
crispado.

Quiero preguntarte algo, dice. *Algo que hace un tiempo*
he estado retrasando. Y necesito que me digas la verdad,
incluso si crees que es algo que no quiero saber.

Está bien, dice, preparándose para lo peor.

De niño oías arañazos en la ventana de tu dormitorio, y
luego tu hermana desapareció. Diez años después, viste a
esos monstruos pelearse por mi padre.

Así es.

Pero por lo que sé, eso es todo. No has mencionado
volver a encontrarte con ellos o haberlos visto o haber
sufrido algún episodio raro. Así que mi pregunta es la
siguiente: ¿Eso es realmente todo? ¿Ha habido algo más?
¿Algo que no me hayas contado?

Lleva escrita la angustia en la cara. Lo ha ocultado
bien los últimos días, pero ha vuelto y da la impresión de
que se quedará grabada allí para siempre. Noah intenta
alcanzar su mano, y por un instante le preocupa que lo
rechace. Si lo hace, sabe que se lo contará todo, todo de
una sola vez, cada segundo de las experiencias
sobrenaturales que ha vivido desde que salieron de Texas
juntos. Incluso confesará la tórrida relación con Leannon.

Megan no relaja la mano en la suya, pero tampoco la
retira.

Te juro que eso fue todo, dice. *Creo que fue una*
coincidencia rara, o el destino, o como quieras llamarlo.
Tal vez, intervención divina. Pero sabes todo lo que hay
que saber.

Al final acaba retirando la mano, pero no sin antes darle un pequeño apretón. Megan sacude ligeramente la cabeza y sonríe avergonzada, como cuando intenta no llorar. Sabe que no debe intentar impedir las lágrimas ni estimularlas. Ella siempre prefiere librar esta batalla sola. Noah se sienta y espera.

Cuando se recompone, ella dice: *Si no te importa, no quiero seguir participando en la Hermandad.*

¿Por qué no?

Porque siento que ya tengo todas las respuestas que voy a tener, dice. Traga con fuerza. *Y tendrá que ser suficiente. Es mi modo de pasar página. Quiero seguir adelante.*

Conmigo, espero, dice Noah.

Por supuesto que contigo, dice. *Eres mi marido.*

Ambos hacen una pausa. Es la primera vez que ella ha pronunciado la palabra en voz alta desde la ceremonia, y todavía conserva su poder de conjuro original. Le vuelve a sorprender haberse casado. Tiene una *esposa*. Independientemente de lo que haya sucedido antes, Noah ha elegido: Megan es su responsabilidad.

Lo soy, dice. *Y como tu marido, tengo una petición que hacerte.*

¿Qué quieres?

Después de que te gradúes, no quiero vivir más en Chicago, dice.

¿Dónde quieres vivir?

¿Por qué no aquí? Me refiero a que no exactamente aquí, en este restaurante…

Dios no lo permita, dice ella.

Pero aquí, en Ashland. Un pueblo de teatros. Podría encontrar trabajo en un taller de escenografía, y quizás tú puedas actuar en una obra de teatro o dos.

Este sitio parece en cierto modo hecho para nosotros, ¿no es cierto?, pregunta ella.

Ese mes de mayo Megan se gradúa, y se mudan al segundo piso de un apartamento encima de una tienda de velas de Ashland. Su nuevo hogar tiene un olor placenteramente delicioso a todas horas. Megan no consigue trabajar como actriz, pero sí encuentra un empleo enseñando teatro en el instituto local. Noah trabaja en el taller de escenografía del teatro Angus Bowmer, construyendo decorados. Por un tiempo, las cosas van bien. La confusión, el temor y la irrealidad constantes de su vida anterior se convierten en un sueño de colores suaves y aromas apetecibles. Se desvanece la sensación de ser observado, y su pasado parece menos algo que le ha sucedido que las escenas vívidas de un libro que una vez leyó, una pesadilla que tomó prestada. El amor y una vida sencilla. Esa es la magia real.

Pero los años pasan cada vez más rápido. Las hojas caen de los árboles solo para volver a aparecer encima de la noche a la mañana, verdes y renovadas, mientras Noah y Megan salen de la juventud y se encaminan al país tenebroso y ceniciento de la mediana edad. En algún momento de esta superposición de años, algo se les escabulle. Para cuando Noah cumple veintinueve, el esófago le arde cada vez que consume algo con salsa de tomate. La espalda y las rodillas le duelen todo el tiempo sin motivo alguno. Lleva consigo un paquete de antiácidos y una botella de Advil adondequiera que vaya. Cada vez que dobla una esquina, está exactamente donde espera encontrarse. La geografía no guarda sorpresas ni inconsistencias para él. Está todo el tiempo cansado, agotado por su trabajo. A veces se sorprende mirando el cielo, preguntándose cómo se vería Ashland desde arriba. ¿Hará frío allí arriba? ¿Necesitaría gafas para ver su edificio de apartamentos? Solía montar sobre los vientos de la noche. El cielo era suyo, y también lo era Leannon. O él era suyo. Sabe que está mal echar de menos a un monstruo. Y por eso se dice a sí mismo que no lo echa de menos.

Sería más fácil si todo siguiera yendo bien con Megan. No es que de por sí estén mal. No se pelean. Ni siquiera discuten. Pero ya no se ríen ni sonríen ni conversan demasiado. Al final de casi todos los días, pasan el tiempo estando juntos en lados opuestos del sofá, comiendo hamburguesas o pizza o anestesiándose con el consuelo miserable de las comedias con risas enlatadas. Jamás hablan del padre de Megan, ni de la Hermandad, ni del pasado de Noah, y rara vez se tocan a propósito.

A veces Noah mira a Megan, tan lejana en su lado del sofá, y se pregunta por qué parece tan infeliz. Cada cierto tiempo se lo pregunta, y ella siempre encoge los hombros y le repite la pregunta a él mismo.

¿Eres feliz?, le pregunta.

Noah se siente adormecido. No se siente él mismo, y no entiende por qué. Se salvó. ¿Por qué no le bastó su salvación? ¿Por qué está tan decepcionado cuando gira una esquina y se encuentra exactamente donde tiene que estar? ¿Por qué ha empezado a garabatear paisajes urbanos sobre trozos de papel?

Y luego, una noche, cuando tiene treinta años, se despierta en mitad de la noche con el sonido de arañazos sobre el cristal de su ventana: *crich-crich-crich*. Una parte de él ha estado esperándolo, lo había esperado antes. Se levanta, con el corazón acelerado, y cruza la habitación. Pero antes de que pueda abrir las cortinas de un tirón, su teléfono empieza a sonar. Vacila ante la ventana, con la mano sobre las cortinas, momentáneamente desorientado. Megan se mueve ligeramente, y Noah extiende la mano hacia el teléfono. Lo levanta de la mesilla y lee un número de Texas que no reconoce.

¿Hola?, pregunta.

¿Quién es?, pregunta Megan, con la voz espesa por el sueño.

La voz al otro lado se oye lejana, llena de estática, como una señal de radio que se apaga. No alcanza a entender nada excepto la última palabra, pronunciada con la respiración entrecortada, presa del pánico: *principito*.

¿Eunice?, pregunta. *¿Hola, Eunice?*

¿Noah? Ahora es la voz de un hombre, mucho más clara. Parece confundida.

¿Quién es?, pregunta Noah.

Camina hacia la ventana para apartar las cortinas, pero lo que sea que estuviera fuera ha desaparecido. Solo están él, Megan y la voz en el teléfono, que dice: *Noah, soy Hubert. Ha sucedido algo terrible.*

Parte seis

LA CASA MALDITA

CAPÍTULO 1

Volví a Vandergriff un domingo de marzo de 2013, viajando en clase turista cerca del ala de un vuelo de American Airlines. Se sumergió bajo el manto de nubes y entró en la húmeda, triste y gris realidad del aeropuerto de DFW. Complicaciones relacionadas con las condiciones meteorológicas nos mantuvieron sobre la pista casi una hora, y tuve que apretar mi Kindle para no gritar de frustración. Era solo lluvia, por todos los cielos. Los coches conducían todo el tiempo bajo la lluvia. ¿Qué mierda podía retrasar un avión *ya aterrizado*?

A mi lado, en el asiento junto a la ventanilla, Megan me puso una mano sobre el brazo.

—Cálmate un poco. Estás a punto de partir ese chisme por la mitad.

Apoyé el Kindle de nuevo sobre mi regazo y la miré, arrepentido. Ella me apretó el brazo. Había comprensión en su mirada, pero algo más. Volví la cabeza y la dirigí hacia la ventana.

Cuando finalmente desembarcamos, Kyle se reunió con nosotros en la recogida de equipaje. Nos habíamos mantenido en contacto a través de las redes sociales, pero no lo había visto en persona desde mi boda, así que su barriga cervecera y el pelo cano me pillaron por sorpresa.

—Me alegro de verte —dijo—, aunque el motivo sea una calamidad.

Le volví a presentar a Megan, y ella sonrió mientras se estrechaban las manos. Intenté recordar la última vez que la había visto sonreír por otra cosa que no fuera una telecomedia y no lo logré. Un revoltijo confuso de celos y nostalgia me inundó el pecho.

Kyle insistió en llevar el bolso de ella a su Prius y cargarlo atrás. Quería que ella también se sentara delante, pero sobre este punto Megan se mostró inflexible. Se estiró en el asiento trasero y yo me senté en el asiento del acompañante. El coche se deslizó fuera del aparcamiento, y entramos en el embotellamiento bajo una tormenta eléctrica que oscurecía la vista.

Señalé hacia las hileras interminables de coches a nuestro alrededor.

—Disculpa este desastre. Es probable que tuvieras mejores cosas que hacer hoy.

—¿Bromeas? —preguntó Kyle—. Si no estuviera aquí, estaría en casa lidiando con los chicos mientras Donna asiste a su club de lectura. En lugar de ello hoy están con mi madre. Hoy es como un día de spa para mí.

Megan resopló en el asiento trasero.

—¿Cómo está tu familia? —pregunté.

Kyle carraspeó.

—Mi madre echó a mi padre de casa. Esta vez para siempre.

—¿Por qué motivo? —pregunté. Traté de que no pareciera que tenía mis propias teorías. No tenía pruebas de que el señor Ransom hubiera seguido siendo un mujeriego después de que Sydney desapareciera, pero parecía probable que un hombre que podía enamorarse de una adolescente también siguiera conquistando a otras.

—No hay uno en particular —dijo—. Por lo menos, no que yo sepa. Mi madre parece mucho más contenta. Ha remodelado toda la casa. Ya ni siquiera parece el sitio donde crecí.

—¿Y tu padre? —pregunté.

—Vive en un parque de caravanas —dijo Kyle.

Siguió hablando un rato de su matrimonio, de sus tres hijos y, finalmente, del Laberinto del Terror, motivado por las preguntas que le hacíamos Megan y yo. Él y Donna le habían comprado el sitio a mi madre en 2003 y lo habían reconstruido sobre la estructura vieja, reconvirtiendo la atracción de un laberinto de horror en un safari a través del país de los muertos vivientes. Lo rebautizaron Mansión Zombi y abrió, sin que lo hubieran planeado, al mismo tiempo que arrancó la moda zombi con *28 días después* y *Zombies party (una noche... de muerte)*. Les fue bien un tiempo, pero, como había aprendido mi familia, en el negocio del terror, la familiaridad engendra indiferencia. La Mansión Zombi había acabado cerrando el año anterior. Kyle había aceptado un empleo en una compañía que vendía cajas y suministros de embalaje, y Donna respondía teléfonos en una oficina.

—Aún tenemos el almacén y todo lo que hay en él —dijo—. Estoy pensando en ideas para recuperarlo. —Las palabras sonaban huecas, como si ni siquiera él las creyera. Sería difícil abandonar la estabilidad de su empleo actual. Al final la edad adulta nos alcanza a todos.

Después de eso hubo silencio. Kyle encendió el parabrisas a toda velocidad. Hacía un ruido chirriante contra el cristal, y sentí que todos estábamos pensando en algo de qué hablar... lo que fuera... que no tuviera nada que ver con el motivo de nuestro regreso a Vandergriff.

Al final, Megan se arriesgó con una táctica.

—Así que, Kyle... ¿me han dicho que mi marido salía con tu mujer?

—Durante menos de un mes —dije, siguiéndole la corriente—. Y luego, Kyle, *mi mejor amigo*, me la robó.

—*Robar* es un modo un poco fuerte de decirlo —dijo Kyle.

—También lo es *mejor amigo* —dije. Todos nos reímos, y por un momento, me sentí feliz de estar en casa, en un coche con mi esposa y mi mejor amigo, viendo que ambos se llevaban bien, haciendo equipo para convertirme en blanco de sus bromas. Era un atisbo de la vida que creí que tendría cuando Megan y yo nos acabábamos de conocer, la que jamás llegó a materializarse del todo.

La sensación se desvaneció al entrar en el vecindario de Eunice y Hubert. Bueno, llamarlo vecindario era una exageración. La calle sobre la cual estaba la casa de Eunice era la primera y única hilera de casas terminadas de la urbanización. Estructuras esqueléticas y sin terminar y terrenos vacíos llenos de malezas bordeaban las calles más allá. Un letrero descolorido en la esquina de la calle prometía CASAS Y TERRENOS A PARTIR DE $30.000.

—El letrero parece viejo —dije mientras entrábamos.

—Ha estado ahí durante años —dijo Kyle—. La gente que financiaba el proyecto quebró y nadie vino a terminarlo. Solía haber montacargas y grúas allí fuera, pero supongo que alguien las compró y se las llevó. Ahora el resto se ha quedado ahí, en estado ruinoso.

Aparcó en la entrada de Eunice detrás de un coche familiar 4x4 que debía de ser de Hubert. El coche de Eunice, que figuraba en el periódico como un Toyota Camry 2009 negro, no estaba; probablemente seguía bajo custodia policial. Se trataba de una casa de ladrillo de dos pisos con amplias ventanas en la fachada, césped en pendiente y una vista del parque industrial al otro lado de la urbanización.

Kyle y yo nos bajamos del coche para buscar las maletas y subimos por la entrada para coches corriendo delante de Megan.

—Llamadme si necesitáis algo —dijo—. Podemos ir a tomar unas cervezas.

Volvió corriendo al coche, saludando a Megan con la mano en alto mientras esta subía la entrada con una revista abierta sobre el pelo a modo de paraguas lastimoso. Llamé al timbre, y Hubert abrió la puerta de par en par. Conservaba la delgadez y la tez pálida, pero tenía un aspecto macilento, el pelo desgreñado, y círculos oscuros bajo los ojos.

—Noah —dijo, y me atrajo hacia él para abrazarme con fuerza, a pesar de mi vestimenta empapada—. Gracias a Dios que has llegado.

CAPÍTULO 2

Como el exterior de la casa, todo el interior parecía calculado para comunicar un mensaje de normalidad suburbana: el comedor con la mesa de madera lustrosa y las sillas de respaldo recto; la consola para vajilla del mismo juego; los cuadros atractivos y olvidables de barcos y paisajes, junto a retratos familiares de Sears; la inmaculada alfombra de color crema y los muebles blancos de la sala. *Aquí todo va bien*, parecía decir la casa a través de dientes apretados. *Somos normales y felices, maldita sea.*

Dos niños se hallaban sentados en el suelo de la sala, jugando con ladrillos Lego: Caroline, de diez años, y su hermano, Dennis, de ocho. Ambos levantaron la mirada cuando entré. Dennis parecía una versión más pequeña y rolliza de su padre, y Caroline era increíblemente parecida a su madre, con el mismo pelo rojizo y complexión pálida, las mismas extremidades desgarbadas y barbilla poco pronunciada. Cuando Hubert nos presentó, Dennis me dirigió una mirada perdida, pero Caroline nos miró furiosa, como sospechando de antemano que yo había cometido alguna infamia. Hubert nos ofreció café, y nos sentamos en el rincón del desayuno a beberlo.

—¿Qué sabéis? —preguntó.

—¿Disculpa? —pregunté. Una descarga helada me recorrió el cuerpo como si me acabaran de acusar de algo. De nuevo sentí la mirada de Megan posándose en mí. No la miré, sino que, en cambio, me concentré en mi taza de café. El silencio se prolongó.

—Oh —dije, sin demasiada convicción, como si hubiera malinterpretado su pregunta original—. Solo lo que hemos leído en Internet.

Por turnos, Megan y yo repetimos la versión pública de la historia: el lunes anterior, Eunice había ido a trabajar, había pasado toda la mañana ante su escritorio y, según sus colegas, «parecía estar bien». Al mediodía, había salido a almorzar y jamás había vuelto. Hallaron su coche aparcado en la urbanización sin terminar que estaba a una calle de donde estábamos sentados en ese momento. Su bolso estaba en mitad de una de las casas sin terminar. Todo, hasta el efectivo, estaba intacto. Cuando la policía intentó hablar con mi madre para ver si sabía algo de Eunice, no pudieron comunicarse con ella por teléfono. Tampoco obtuvieron respuesta al llamar a la puerta de su casa. Una vez dentro, encontraron el televisor encendido y una cafetera quemándose en la cocina, pero la casa estaba vacía. Desde entonces, no se sabía nada de mi madre ni de Eunice.

—Muchas veces Eunice trabaja hasta tarde y a veces se olvida de comprobar el teléfono —dijo Hubert cuando terminamos—. No me preocupé hasta la mañana siguiente cuando me desperté y no estaba en casa. Perdí todo un día hasta que se me ocurrió que podría haber pasado algo.

—Hubert, lo siento —dije.

—No, soy yo quien lo lamenta —dijo, golpeando la mesa con el puño. Mi café se derramó por encima del borde del tazón, encharcando la madera—. Hice unos votos al casarme con tu hermana: se supone que debía cuidarla. —Le di una palmadita sobre el hombro y me atrajo de nuevo hacia su pecho para abrazarme con más fuerza aún. Dejé que me aplastara como un peluche.

Cuando me soltó, se enjugó la cara con el dorso de la mano.

—Hubo cosas que debí haber notado.

—¿Como cuáles? —preguntó Megan.

—Dejó de tomar su medicación. Encontré el equivalente a tres meses dentro de una caja de zapatos en su armario.

—¿Y no notaste ningún cambio en ella? —pregunté.

—Parecía… más animada —dijo—. Más energética. A veces se quedaba despierta toda la noche. Pero, Noah, te juro por Dios, creía que significaba que era feliz. Que quizás empezaría a escribir de nuevo.

Caroline y Dennis vinieron a la cocina en ese momento, y la conversación quedó interrumpida. El resto de la tarde transcurrió en silencio. Megan y yo hicimos el papel de los miembros preocupados de la familia que lo ignoran todo, mientras veíamos películas animadas, sentados en la sala. Los niños construyeron una casa de Legos en el suelo.

—Ha quedado bastante bien —dijo Megan, cuando terminaron las paredes principales y empezaron el techo.

—Es solo una estúpida casa —dijo Caroline.

—Cuando yo era pequeño, jamás me salía hacer nada con Legos —dije.

—¿Eras estúpido? —preguntó Dennis.

—¡Dennis! —exclamó Hubert, pero yo me reí.

—Sí, supongo que lo era.

Alrededor de las nueve, Hubert envió a los niños a la cama. Estaban durmiendo juntos en la habitación de Caroline para que Megan y yo pudiéramos dormir en la cama de Dennis. En cuanto entramos en la habitación, fue evidente que el chico era fan de los Lego. Un póster de Bionicle colgaba encima de su cama, y las estanterías empotradas en las paredes exhibían todos sus diseños terminados.

Una vez cerramos la puerta detrás de nosotros, Megan me encaró:

—Sigo creyendo que tenemos que ponernos en contacto con la Hermandad. —Había estado expresando ese mismo deseo varias veces al día desde que nos habíamos enterado de lo de mi madre y Eunice.

—Ya decidimos poner fin a los asuntos de la Hermandad —dije—. Hace años.

—Eso fue en 2003. Esto es ahora. Quizás puedan ayudarnos.

Me puse de pie y caminé de un lado a otro de la habitación. Fingí que estaba interesado en las estanterías de Dennis, repletas de coches de carrera, naves espaciales, guaridas de supervillanos, aeropuertos y casas, una galería de instrucciones seguidas con esmerado cuidado. Semejante pulcritud debía de haber sido heredada de su padre. Eunice y yo éramos ambos terriblemente desordenados.

—No estoy diciendo que no sea un asunto de la Hermandad —dije—, pero mi familia ha desaparecido y no quiero que un grupo de gente empiece a hurgar en las vidas de Hubert y los chicos. Y, sea como sea, supón que tienes razón. Supón que mi familia ha sido raptada por los monstruos. No hay *nada* que podamos hacer. Es lo que han sufrido todos los miembros de la Hermandad, y es lo que sufrió Sydney.

Aparté la mirada de los juguetes de Dennis para mirarla a la cara. Estaba sentada en la cama, con las rodillas pegadas al pecho.

—¿Por qué no querías que viniera a casa contigo? —preguntó, con un hilo de voz.

—*Claro* que quería que vinieras —dije, esforzándome por mirarla a los ojos.

Suspiró y extendió la mano hacia mí.

—Ven a la cama.

En vez de eso, saqué los artículos de aseo de mi maleta y fui a ducharme. Megan estaba durmiendo cuando volví, pero me había dejado encendida la lámpara de la mesilla. Me metí en la cama junto a ella y apagué la luz.

Era cierto que no había querido que viniera a Texas conmigo. Hacía mucho tiempo que las cosas estaban raras entre nosotros. Ella parecía infeliz, y cuando me miraba, siempre había una expresión inquisitiva en sus ojos. Me recordaba a cómo me miraba la gente en Vandergriff durante los años después de 1999... como si hubiera algo poco fiable en mí. Y en este caso, ella tenía razón. Parte de mi deseo de venir solo era querer tener tiempo y espacio para mí mismo para entender la desaparición de mi familia, sin sentir que estaba bajo un incesante escrutinio. Pero la otra parte tenía que ver con las circunstancias en torno a las desapariciones. Los arañazos en la ventana de mi habitación, la voz lejana en el teléfono. Cuando Megan y yo vivíamos en Chicago, la Ciudad solía llamarme cuando estaba solo. Sería mucho más difícil estar solo con Megan cerca, vigilándome constantemente.

Pero, por supuesto, no podía admitirle aquello a mi esposa sin otra serie de hechos que le había ocultado. Así que allí estábamos, en Texas, donde ella quería involucrar a la Hermandad, y sin acabar de entender por qué yo no. Ambos en la cama de mi sobrino, ella con sus sueños atormentados, yo completamente despierto.

Sabía que no me iría a dormir pronto. Salí de la cama, me vestí y encontré mi teléfono. Envié un mensaje a Kyle:

¿Qué te parece un tour nocturno de la Mansión Zombi?

Su respuesta llegó casi de inmediato: *Dame treinta minutos.*

CAPÍTULO 3

Esperé a Kyle en el jardín delantero. El aire nocturno estaba fresco y húmedo, el césped aún mojado. Me recordó a la perenne humedad del mundo de Leannon. No podía escapar a la sensación de estar siendo observado, como si la calle entera estuviera mirándome.

—¿Estás ahí fuera? —pregunté, sin saber a quién le dirigía la pregunta—. ¿Puedes verme?

La calle no dio respuestas, pero la sensación de ser vigilado no disminuyó. Cuando el Prius de Kyle se acercó, no perdí ni un instante en saltar dentro.

—¿Quieres hablar? —preguntó.

—No.

Encendió la radio, y cruzamos la ciudad hasta el viejo almacén de mi familia. Mi primer atisbo del edificio fue parcial, iluminado solo por las luces altas de Kyle: un monumental edificio cuyo anterior exterior de color gris había sido pintado por encima con un mural detallado. Zombis grises y azules deambulaban por un paisaje postapocalíptico infernal de edificios en ruinas cubiertos de humo, coches estrellados, la osamenta de parques infantiles, y un cielo naranja oscuro. Parecía el grafiti más recargado del mundo.

—Guau —exclamé.

—Donna lo odia —dijo—, pero yo quería provocar una primera impresión fuerte.

—Y lo has logrado.

Salimos del coche, y sacó un paquete de seis cervezas de Shiner Bock de la puerta trasera. Tomé una botella mientras quitaba el cerrojo al edificio. La calavera de poliestireno de los días del Laberinto del Terror había desaparecido, y la entrada de los visitantes se había trasladado al otro extremo del edificio. Entramos al almacén en sí, donde los talleres, las oficinas y la sala de descanso seguían más o menos iguales. Accionó la electricidad en la sala de control. El edificio se iluminó a nuestro alrededor, y experimenté una punzada de nostalgia. Finalmente, me sentía *en casa*.

Dejamos el resto del paquete de cervezas en el refrigerador de la sala de descanso y volvimos a salir para dirigirnos a la entrada de visitantes, una puerta negra en lo alto de la rampa. Bebimos cerveza mientras Kyle me guiaba por la atracción.

—La idea es que eres parte de un grupo de supervivientes que intenta abrirse paso en una ciudad llena de zombis —dijo, mientras caminábamos por un estrecho callejón entre dos cercas. Detrás de la alambrada metálica, a ambos lados, había viejos coches desguazados y torpes indicios de escaparates y edificios de oficinas—. Así que hay un grupo de «infectados» que deambulan a ambos lados, y parecen estar ocupándose de sus asuntos, cuando de pronto una mujer no infectada corre hacia vosotros desde la derecha y empieza a rogar que la ayudéis. Aquello llama la atención de los infectados, que acuden rápidamente a la alambrada. A partir de ese momento, las sirenas empiezan a aullar, y cualquier cosa puede pasar. No de verdad, pero ya sabes a lo que me refiero.

El resto de la atracción consistía en una serie de encuentros cada vez más arriesgados con los muertos vivientes. Los visitantes se arrastraban por tuberías, ascendían rampas empinadas, y tenían que ayudarse a cruzar amplios desfiladeros. Era más intenso que cualquier idea que hubiéramos considerado alguna vez mientras nosotros habíamos sido los dueños: un circuito de cuerdas infernal.

—Donna quería darle a la gente un motivo para hacer ejercicio —dijo Kyle, mientras atravesábamos a gatas un tubo rojo de plástico, intentando no derramar nuestras cervezas—. Algo así como un servicio de bien público—. Salimos del tubo en la base de una rampa amplia y empinada con cuerdas sujetas a la parte superior. Terminamos nuestras cervezas y empezamos la subida.

A medida que nos abrimos paso dentro de la atracción, los desafíos se volvieron más exigentes y dejamos de hablar. El corazón me latía con fuerza, y la camisa se pegaba a mi cuerpo. Seguía esperando aquella sensación familiar, la mezcla rara de inquietud y excitación que indicaba el inicio de un viaje a la Ciudad, pero no llegó jamás. Con cada nuevo desafío, cada nuevo recodo que doblaba, permanecí junto a Kyle. Nos mecimos entre plataformas elevadas, cruzamos puentes, y recorrimos lentamente vigas de equilibrio a alturas que parecían poco seguras. Para cuando salimos disparados por el tobogán que nos depositó en la salida, me ardían los pulmones y tenía una punzada en el costado. También, por primera vez en mucho tiempo, estaba completamente en la gloria. Me quedé recostado sobre la alfombra en el extremo inferior del tobogán, resollando. Sentía como si me hubieran vaciado la mente.

Cuando volví en mí, me levanté y seguí a Kyle de vuelta a la sala de descanso de los empleados, donde terminamos el paquete de cervezas.

—Gracias —le dije, al recobrar el aliento—. Lo necesitaba.

Chocó su botella contra la mía. En aquel silencio, liberado temporalmente de la ansiedad, se me ocurrió algo.

—Oye, ¿te ha quedado algo del Laberinto del Terror?

—Dejamos el viejo laberinto del monstruo en su sitio —dijo Kyle—. Nos resultó útil para trasladar a los zombis de un sitio a otro.

—¿Y los disfraces?

—Reconvertimos la mayoría en disfraces de zombis —respondió—. Recortamos la tela, le dimos un aspecto andrajoso y ensangrentado. —Se incorporó, y lo seguí al taller de disfraces. Señaló una pila de cajas de cartón en un rincón—. Lo que no pudimos usar está ahí.

Abrí la caja que estaba en lo más alto. Extraje una chaqueta de traje marrón arrugado, una blusa con volantes y hombreras, y un par de vaqueros cortados. Reconocí cada prenda, pequeños trozos de mi pasado, olvidados hacía mucho tiempo, pero no eran lo que buscaba. Seguí hurgando en más cajas.

—Si me dices lo que buscas… —dijo Kyle.

Pero lo encontré en la cuarta caja, metido dentro, solo: un pelaje moteado de color marrón de varios tonos que tenía un aspecto viejo y ordinario bajo las luces intensas, despojado de la oscura majestad que poseía en su hábitat natural. Mi segunda piel. Mi traje de monstruo.

—Debería haberlo adivinado —dijo Kyle.

Lo revisé.

—No le has hecho nada.

—Por supuesto que no. Es tuyo. Arruinarlo habría sido un error. De todos modos, ¿para qué necesitamos un disfraz de monstruo en una mansión de zombis?

En el viaje de vuelta, sostuve el disfraz sobre el regazo, deslizando los dedos a través de las guedejas revueltas y apelmazadas. Me sentía un poco más completo que una hora atrás.

—¿Te importa si paramos aquí? —preguntó Kyle, entrando al aparcamiento—. Le prometí a mi padre que le traería un medicamento para la lombriz intestinal.

Lo seguí dentro, donde encontró la medicina y nos unimos a una cola para pagar sorprendentemente larga. Tras cerca de dos minutos de escuchar a la mujer de delante de la cola debatiendo los términos de un cupón con la cajera, esta nos dirigió al mostrador de la farmacia, al fondo. Allí, una mujer con cara de aburrida, enfundada en una chaqueta blanca, registraba ventas en la caja. Tenía algo en la cara —el gesto de la boca, como si estuviera chupando un caramelo ácido— que me resultaba familiar, pero no recordaba de dónde la conocía. Lo dejé pasar y me entretuve con el móvil mientras avanzábamos a paso lento hacia la caja registradora.

—¿Noah? ¿Noah Turner?

Levanté la mirada. La mujer me miraba con una media sonrisa.

—¿Sí? —dije.

La sonrisa afloró.

—Cuánto tiempo —dijo. Tocó una mano sobre la placa de identificación que tenía en el pecho: HOLA, ME LLAMO BRIN. Brin. La primera y única novia de mi hermana. Brin, que le había roto el corazón a Eunice tan completamente que había quedado sumida en una depresión suicida. Maldita, puñetera, jodida Brin.

—Te recuerdo, Brin —dije.

Su alegría se atenuó.

—Me he enterado de lo que les pasó a Eunice y a tu madre. Si hay algo que pueda hacer…

—Puedes cobrarle a mi amigo —respondí—. Tenemos un poco de prisa.

Dirigió la mirada hacia abajo, y sentí una satisfacción brutal ante esa pequeña crueldad. Que se fuera a la mierda. Me di cuenta de que Kyle estaba intrigado, pero fingí estar enfrascado en mi móvil mientras sacaba su tarjeta de débito y pagaba.

—¿Qué ha pasado ahí? —preguntó mientras salíamos de la tienda.

—¿Te parece bien si no hablamos de ello? —pregunté.

—Tú mandas. —Abrió el coche, pero antes que pudiéramos montarnos, Brin salió trotando de la tienda, con el abrigo ondeando tras la espalda.

—¡Oye! —llamó.

—¿Quieres que me deshaga de ella? —preguntó Kyle.

—Deja que yo me encargue. Espera en el coche. —Me encontré con Brin a mitad de camino del aparcamiento—. ¿Qué quieres?

—Escucha, entiendo por qué no te apetece hablar conmigo —dijo—. Traté a Eunice de un modo inexcusable. Y lo que sucedió después... —Se frotó una mano sobre la cara—. Es lo que más lamento en mi vida. Puede ser duro salir de una religión, especialmente, cuando se trata de una religión rara, como la que yo practicaba. Puede convencerte de que te comportes de las formas más estúpidas y crueles. Puede hacer que tengas miedo de ti mismo. Pero en lugar de lidiar con todo ello, le endilgué la responsabilidad a Eunice. —Se volvió a tocar la cara—. Me llevó mucho tiempo aceptarme a mí misma. Siempre quise volver a contactar algún día con ella, pero luego me enteré de que se había casado y tenía hijos. No lo sé. Creía que aún tenía tiempo para corregir mis errores.

—Yo también —dije.

—Sea como sea, lo siento —dijo—. Si tú o tu familia necesitáis algo... pues toma, deja que te dé mi número de teléfono. —Sacó un bolígrafo y un trozo de papel del bolsillo de la solapa y lo apuntó. En cuanto lo acepté, se dio la vuelta para volver con rapidez dentro.

—¿Brin? —pregunté.

Hizo una pausa.

—Me gustaría ser valiente como tú —dije.

Me saludó con la mano en alto y volvió a desaparecer dentro de la tienda. Me metí en el coche.

—¿Todo bien? —preguntó Kyle.

—Sí —dije.

Condujimos al parque de caravanas donde estaba viviendo el padre de Kyle, una planta de hormigón plana y sin césped llamada Meadow Lake. Kyle me preguntó si quería acompañarlo a la puerta principal.

—Si mi padre supiera que estás en el pueblo, probablemente querría saludarte —dijo.

—No, gracias —dije, intentando no sonar grosero.

Observé desde el asiento del acompañante a Kyle subiendo los escalones de bloques de hormigón a la caja de metal corrugado que contenía a su padre. Cuando Daniel Ransom abrió la puerta, quedé momentáneamente desconcertado. Se había convertido en un hombre desorientado, enjuto, marchito, de pelo ralo y blanco, empequeñecido por un pijama que le quedaba demasiado grande. La vida no había sido amable con él y, por un instante, sentí algo parecido a la compasión. Pero luego pasó de largo.

Aparté la mirada, concentrándome en el trozo de papel que Brin me había dado. La cara me ardía de solo pensar en volver a casa de Eunice, dormir en la cama de su hijo y fingir estar tan desorientado como todos los demás.

CAPÍTULO 4

Megan seguía durmiendo cuando volví. Exhausto, me desplomé en la cama a su lado y finalmente caí rendido. Dormí sin despertarme hasta la tarde del día siguiente, cuando la luz que se colaba a través de la ventana del dormitorio de Dennis se volvió imposible de ignorar. Bajé y encontré a la familia en la cocina. Hubert estaba restregando platos en el fregadero y pasándoselos a Dennis para que los pusiera en el lavaplatos. Caroline y Megan estaban sentadas a la mesa de cocina, Megan bebiendo café y Caroline leyendo un grueso tomo de bolsillo. Su pelo rojizo ocultaba casi toda su cara. Se parecía tanto a Eunice que sentí una náusea ligera.

—Buenas tardes —dijo Hubert—. Hay café, si quieres.

—Claro —dije, dirigiéndome a la cafetera para servirme una taza.

—¿Mala noche? —preguntó Megan. Las palabras me golpearon como una bola de béisbol entre los omóplatos, y tuve que hacer un esfuerzo para no doblarme.

—Sí —dije—. Me costó dormir.

—A mí también —dijo Hubert—. No he dormido bien desde que sucedió.

Tomé asiento en la mesa con Megan y Caroline, ahuecando la taza entre las manos.

—¿Qué haremos hoy? —pregunté.

—Por ahora, no demasiado —dijo Hubert—. Solo tratábamos de decidir qué hacer con el resto de nuestra tarde y noche.

—Quiero ir al zoo —dijo Dennis.

Caroline levantó la mirada de su libro.

—¿Bromeas? ¿Por qué ibas a querer visitar una prisión de animales?

—¿Una prisión de animales? —preguntó Dennis. Por lo visto, jamás se le había ocurrido que quizás los animales no quisieran vivir en un zoo.

—No tenemos que ir a un zoo —dije—. Podemos ir a un parque. O a ver una película.

Caroline se puso de pie y cogió su libro. Salió por la puerta al jardín trasero y cerró de un portazo tras ella.

Hubert se inclinó contra la encimera y cruzó los brazos largos y esqueléticos.

—Lo está pasando mal —dijo—. Iré a hablar con ella.

—Dale espacio —dijo Megan, deslizándose en la silla vacante—. Bebe un poco de café conmigo. Desahógate.

Hubert cumplió, contento de obedecer. Dennis siguió cavilando acerca de la idea de una prisión para animales.

Alegué haber olvidado mi móvil y subí corriendo al dormitorio de Dennis, donde descorrí las cortinas y abrí las celosías justo a tiempo de ver a Caroline pasar a horcajadas por encima de la verja trasera y desaparecer por encima para entrar en la urbanización inconclusa que se extendía por detrás.

CAPÍTULO 5

Me escabullí por la puerta principal y elegí el camino más largo que rodeaba la manzana tras Caroline. La encontré sentada con las piernas cruzadas sobre los cimientos de hormigón de lo que probablemente había tenido intención de ser la primera versión de una sala o una cocina. En cuanto me oyó, se puso de pie y empezó a correr.

—Vengo en son de paz —dije, levantando ambas manos. Entré en la habitación y dejé el acceso libre, para que pudiera huir si quería hacerlo. Era un gesto simbólico: la habitación abierta quería decir que podía huir en la dirección que quisiera, pero resultó eficaz.

—¿Vienes aquí a menudo? —pregunté.

—A mi mamá y a mi papá no les gusta —respondió—. Les asusta que me haga daño.

—Eso no me habría detenido cuando tenía tu edad.

—Sobre todo, vengo para observar a Dennis jugar y asegurarme de que esté a salvo.

—Cuidas a Dennis —dije.

Asintió.

—Tu madre siempre me cuidaba cuando éramos pequeños. ¿Sabes que eres igual que ella?

No se relajó.

—¿Cómo sabías que estaba aquí?

—Ha sido suerte —dije—. Se me ha ocurrido mirar por la ventana de arriba y te vi trepando la cerca.

—No he hecho nada malo —dijo con una mirada desafiante. No le llevé la contraria, sino que esperé. La indignación desapareció poco a poco de su cara—. Por un tiempo, mamá parecía tan feliz... más feliz de lo que la había visto jamás... pero luego un día se volvió mala. Como si todo lo que hiciéramos estuviera mal. Y papá... lo maltrataba de una forma terrible. Lo llamaba débil y cobarde, y decía que jamás debió casarse con él. Lo hacía delante de mí y de Dennis, como si no le importara que lo escucháramos. Y papá encorvaba los hombros y lo toleraba hasta que ella terminaba.

Parpadeó un par de veces y tragó con fuerza, lo bastante fuerte como para oírla.

—Debería ser más amable con él —dijo.

—Yo también —dije.

—Luego se volvió aún peor. A veces me despertaba en mitad de la noche y la veía caminando de un lado a otro de su oficina, con los brazos cruzados y la cabeza gacha. Tenía la esperanza de que las cosas mejoraran. Empezó a emprender largas caminatas, sola, en mitad de la noche. A veces me escabullía a la habitación de Dennis para mirar fuera de la ventana, y la veía yendo y viniendo en este sitio, sacudiendo la cabeza. Y luego, un día, ella y la abuela desaparecieron.

Apartó la mirada para lo que dijo a continuación:

—A veces, cuando mamá estaba en su oficina, podía ver algo fuera de su ventana que la observaba.

—¿Qué clase de cosa? —pregunté.

Me miró enfadada.

—Un monstruo vestido con una túnica. Era como si el lobo malo hubiera salido con la capa de la Caperucita Roja. Mamá jamás pareció verlo, pero yo sí. —Me miró, vio algo en mi expresión, y luego dijo—: Tú lo has visto también, ¿verdad?

Pensé en negarlo. Pero sentía cierta afinidad con esa chica; me recordaba a Eunice, sí, pero también a mí. Inteligente, atemorizada e intentando entender las medias verdades y mentiras que su familia le había contado hasta el momento.

—Sí, lo he visto.

—¿Sabes dónde están mamá y la abuela? —pregunté.

Cerré mi ojo, temiendo estar a punto de vomitar. Todo aquello era culpa mía. Leannon me lo había advertido años atrás, la noche de mi boda. Me había dicho que pedir que me dejara solo no era «cómo funcionaban las cosas». Me dijo que había cosas que no entendía. Y ahora lo había demostrado. Se había llevado a toda mi familia.

Cuando volví a abrir mi ojo, vi a Caroline mirándome con gran preocupación.

—¿Puedes traerlas a casa? —preguntó.

—No sé ni siquiera por dónde empezaría —dije. Pero en cuanto lo dije, me di cuenta de que no era cierto. Sabía exactamente por dónde empezar. Yo no *tenía* que esperar a que la Ciudad me volviera a invitar a pasar. Quizás podría volver allí gracias a mi propio poder.

CAPÍTULO 6

Dejé a Caroline en la casa vacía y volví a dar la vuelta a la manzana para regresar. Cuando volví a entrar en casa de Eunice, todos estaban en la cocina, lo cual hizo fácil que pudiera sustraer las llaves del coche de Hubert del gancho en la parte interior de la puerta principal y salir de nuevo sin que me vieran. Conseguí atravesar la entrada y avanzar calle abajo sin que nadie saliera por la puerta. Crucé el pueblo con el teléfono en modo silencio, sin saber si tenía llamadas o mensajes perdidos.

Había caído el atardecer para cuando llegué a casa de mi madre al otro lado del pueblo. El sol se ocultaba detrás de gruesas nubes de tormenta, trayendo consigo una noche precoz. La casa se alzaba más grande de lo que la recordaba; parecía más elevada y amplia, como si hubiera estado creciendo como cualquier otro ser vivo, a base de una dieta ininterrumpida de lo que fuera que consumieran las casas. Sus ventanas reflejaban la luz de las farolas, como los ojos negros de un insecto.

No había coches patrulla en el camino de entrada ni en la calle, pero la puerta principal estaba precintada con cinta amarilla. Me agaché por debajo para probar mi llave; aún encajaba en la cerradura. Una vez que estuve dentro, dejé las luces apagadas. No quería que los vecinos vieran que había alguien allí. En lugar de ello, pasé deslizando con el dedo cualquier notificación de la pantalla de mi móvil y usé la linterna para echar una mirada alrededor.

Era evidente que habían inspeccionado la casa en busca de pruebas y que luego la habían abandonado. Habían arrancado los cojines del sofá, y todos los armarios de la cocina tenían las puertas abiertas, abandonando el contenido sobre las encimeras y el suelo. Me recordaba a la casa de Leannon después del terremoto.

Además del caos, muy poco había cambiado. Las mismas cortinas colgaban en las ventanas, y la misma mesa ocupaba el comedor. El interior olía mustio, el aire viciado, como si los habitantes hubieran pasado su fecha de caducidad. Subí a mi antigua habitación. Con la cama deshecha y la ropa sucia esparcida por todo el suelo, parecía como si el Noah de diecinueve años hubiera estado a punto de volver en cualquier momento. Los mismos pósteres colgaban de la pared, y había la misma pila de libros sobre la mesilla de noche: *La cámara sangrienta; Fantasmas; Ceremonias macabras; Memnoch, el diablo.*

Encontré un trozo de papel que había quedado sobre mi escritorio, acumulando polvo durante más de una década:

Noah:

Esta noche he vuelto para experimentar una vez más el Laberinto del Terror, pero me han dicho que era tu noche libre. Lamento no haberte visto. De todos modos, si quieres, deberías venir a una reunión conmigo y algunos amigos mañana por la noche. Me encantaría seguir hablando.

xoxo Megan

Sentí una punzada de remordimiento y empecé a abrir mi pantalla de notificaciones perdidas, pero me detuve. Antes de preocuparme por Megan, tenía que acometer lo que me había propuesto. Me puse de cuclillas delante del escritorio y abrí el último cajón. Estaba atestado de viejos proyectos escolares del instituto, cuadernos de espiral y libros de historietas. Metí la mano dentro de todos los papeles y tanteé hasta que cerré los dedos alrededor de lo que buscaba. Lo extraje y lo contemplé en el dormitorio oscuro: una pequeña piedra lisa y negra. Mi llave para entrar en el mundo de Leannon, abandonada allí once años atrás, todavía exactamente donde la había dejado.

La apreté dentro del puño, cerré mi ojo con fuerza, y me vi en la casa de Leannon en el bosque negro, el cielo miasmático, y el aire húmedo y espeso.

Abrí mi ojo, pero seguía agazapado en mi viejo dormitorio. No había funcionado. ¿Por qué? ¿Se le habría acabado la energía? ¿Se le habrían gastado las baterías tras años de falta de uso? Giré la piedra en mi mano. No se veía en absoluto distinta de lo que la recordaba.

Aquello ciertamente ponía fin a mi gran idea. De todos modos, no estaba listo para darme por vencido y regresar a Hubert, Megan y los chicos.

Dejé caer la piedra en mi bolsillo y terminé de revisar la habitación, pero no encontré nada útil. Lo mismo con el viejo dormitorio de Eunice y el *home office* al final del corredor, donde el retrato de Sydney de su época del instituto seguía posado sobre el archivador.

Bajé para examinar el primer piso; no había nada raro ni fuera de lugar en la cocina o la sala. Le habían quitado las sábanas y las mantas a la cama de la habitación de mi madre, y la ropa y los zapatos eran un lío sobre el suelo del armario. Estaba a punto de abandonar mi búsqueda cuando el haz de mi linterna pasó encima de algo pequeño y marrón, pegado contra la pared del fondo. Me arrodillé y vi una caja de cartón, tan vieja y desteñida que era casi amarilla. Separé las solapas superiores. Contenía una sola carpeta antigua de tres anillas, a rebosar con papel amarillo envejecido. Habían metido la portada dentro del plástico de la cubierta, escrita en lápiz descolorido, las letras con forma de bloques, como las de la cubierta de un viejo cómic de *Superman* o *X-Men*.

La ciudad anónima
de Harry y Margaret Turner

Parecía como algo que un chico podría dibujar en una sala de estudio, y me dijo mucho sobre mis padres: el padre que jamás conocería, y la versión de mi madre que había muerto con él. Personas divertidas. Personas alegres.

Habían pegado una foto con cinta adhesiva bajo el título, aquella descrita tantas páginas atrás: mis padres agachados junto al letrero de la CASA EMBRUJADA GRATUITA, sonriendo orgullosos de su creación. (Esta es y sigue siendo la única foto de mi padre que tengo, un objeto preciado que aún conservo en su funda de plástico).

Llevé la carpeta a la cama y la abrí. Tal como prometía la cubierta, contenía los planos que ambos habían delineado antes de la muerte de mi padre... aquellos a los que Sydney y yo quisimos echar mano. Mi madre aseguró que se había deshecho de ellos, pero allí estaban, los diseños para una inmensa atracción que giraba en torno a tres hoteles: el Gilman, basado en la ciudad costera de Innsmouth, de la novela de H. P. Lovecraft; el Glitz, un hotel elevado con una gran vista, provisto de un laberinto de setos y muebles de latón fijos; y Ma's, un bed-and-breakfast con una verja de hierro forjado negro y un cementerio en el jardín trasero.

Irradiando desde del núcleo de los hoteles había, por lo que pude ver, una ciudad real, con edificios de oficinas, tiendas y restaurantes, todos dibujados hasta el mínimo detalle. Pero de una página a la siguiente, el diseño de la ciudad cambiaba. Era imposible encontrar un punto de anclaje para realizar un plano fiable. Hojeé de un lado a otro, pero cuanto más buscaba más azaroso resultaba, igual que el plano de la Ciudad que yo mismo había experimentado.

No tuve demasiado tiempo para reflexionar sobre el nuevo descubrimiento y sobre su valor para ayudarme a cruzar al mundo de Leannon. Oí la puerta principal abrirse y el sonido de voces apagadas. Alguien había venido.

—¿Noah? —llamó Megan—. Puedes salir. Hemos llegado.

CAPÍTULO 7

Cuando pasé de la sala a la entrada, encontré a Megan junto con Josh, Eli, Hector, Laura y Sarah. A pesar de mi petición, había llamado a la Hermandad y los había llevado consigo. Habían encendido las luces.

—¿Cómo sabías dónde encontrarme? —pregunté.

—Solo había dos sitios adonde se me ocurrió qué podías ir —dijo—. He tenido suerte con el primero.

—Te dije que no necesitaba la ayuda de la Hermandad —dije.

—Quizás no —respondió con un tono de voz calmado y razonable, y también un poco apenado—. Pero yo necesito respuestas. —Advertí algo gélido y peligroso en ella. No tenía demasiado margen de maniobra.

—¿Por qué no vamos todos a la sala? —sugirió Sarah.

Todo el mundo tomó asiento sobre los sofás y las sillas, salvo Megan y yo. Nos quedamos de pie delante del televisor. A medida que el grupo me miraba, tuve la misma sensación de hormigueo que había sentido de adolescente, la sensación de estar expuesto, de ser considerado un sospechoso. Aquella experiencia de ser el otro, un intruso entre personas normales.

—¿Qué queréis saber? —pregunté.

—Finge que estamos en una reunión —dijo Sarah con dulzura—. Empieza por el comienzo de este último evento y cuéntanos qué pasó.

Reprimí la ira que sentía por haber sido acorralado de ese modo. Me lancé a contar la historia de la rara llamada telefónica y de los arañazos que oí en la ventana la noche que Eunice y mi madre desaparecieron. Les conté que Caroline me había revelado que había visto una de esas criaturas. Les conté que decidí ver si había algo que pudiera hacer respecto de las desapariciones, pero admitía que estaba atascado. Les mostré la carpeta de anillas que había encontrado en el armario de mi madre, aunque no la piedra negra. Eso me lo guardé para mí.

Cuando terminé, todo el mundo hizo silencio un instante.

—Es todo una estupidez.

—¿Una estupidez? —pregunté.

Nadie quería mirarme a los ojos. Hasta Megan, de pie junto a mí, se sintió de pronto interesada en la alfombra.

—Mi madre desapareció cuando yo tenía ocho años —dijo Josh—. Era una periodista autónoma en San Antonio. Investigaba la comunidad clandestina de vampiros, no los vampiros reales, ya sabéis, sino los adictos raros que leían a Anne Rice, jugaban a disfrazarse y bebían sangre. Estaba haciéndose famosa, forjándose un hueco en la profesión. ¿Sabéis lo que estaba investigando justo antes de desaparecer?

—No tengo ni idea —dije.

—Desapariciones no resueltas. —Hizo una pausa y me miró, como esperando que hiciera un comentario. Le hice un gesto para que continuara.

—Hay muchas desapariciones de las cuales se pueden extraer conclusiones razonables —siguió diciendo Josh—. A veces, hay un cónyuge o un ex con una historia de violencia, incluso si no hay pruebas suficientea para imputarlos o declararlos culpables. Otras veces la persona desaparecida tiene una historia de abuso de sustancias o enfermedad mental. Mi madre no estaba interesada en esos casos, sino en aquellos que resultaban inconcebibles. Como el chico que entró en un simulador de fuerzas de gravedad en Huntsville, Alabama, una sala cerrada con una sola puerta para entrar o salir, y que nunca volvió a salir. O el hombre de Maine que desapareció de su celda de prisión cerrada en mitad de la noche.

—¿Supongo que tendría una hipótesis de trabajo? —pregunté, sin poder impedir que se colara la irritación en mi voz.

—Si la tenía, no la conozco —dijo—. Justo estaba empezando, haciendo llamadas y siguiendo pistas. En aquella época teníamos el teléfono apagado, así que tenía que caminar hasta el teléfono público calle abajo cada vez que tenía que hacer una llamada. No era raro que tuviera que realizar ese trayecto dos o tres veces por noche cuando estaba trabajando. Solo que esa única vez, se marchó y no volvió nunca más. La policía buscó. Salió en las noticias. Programas sobre misterios no resueltos se ocuparon de la historia un par de veces. Pero todavía nadie tiene respuestas. Directamente, despareció. La mayoría de la gente cree que los falsos vampiros la atraparon, pero sé que no es así.

—¿Qué tiene esto que ver conmigo? —pregunté.

—Después de que el resto de tu familia desapareciera la semana pasada, tu nombre empezó a despertar algo en el fondo de mi mente. Tuve un presentimiento y empecé a hurgar en las notas que mi madre había tomado para aquel último trabajo sin terminar, ¿y sabes lo que encontré?

—No tengo ni idea —dije.

—Las notas de una mujer llamada Deborah Turner. ¿Te resulta conocido?

Sacudí la cabeza.

—Padecía esquizofrenia paranoide —dijo Josh—. Era viuda, habían matado a su marido en Corea. La encontraron caminando a un lado de la carretera una noche, en camisón. Intentó quitarse de encima a la policía cuando se acercaron, y no dejaba de hablar de una ciudad. Tenía un hijo llamado Harry. El nombre de tu padre, si no me equivoco.

Asentí.

—Murió justo antes de que yo naciera. Y su madre no mucho después. Mi madre jamás me habló de ninguno de los dos.

Josh se quitó el sombrero de camionero y se pasó una mano por el pelo rubio y escaso.

—Es raro que estas criaturas estén tan involucradas en la historia de tu familia. Todos los demás incidentes que la Hermandad ha estudiado parecen casos aislados. Nada hereditario.

—Eso es una novedad para mí —dije, y era al menos parcialmente cierto. ¿Mi abuela encontrada a la vera de la carretera? ¿Hablando de una Ciudad? ¿Significaba que la habían raptado y había conseguido de algún modo huir? ¿Significaba que podía hacerse a pesar de todo?

—Permitimos que entraras en nuestro grupo —dijo—. Compartimos nuestras historias. La mayoría fuimos a tu boda. Aceptamos tu relato sobre la noche en que desapareció tu hermana mayor. Aceptamos tu relato sobre lo que sucedió la noche que arrestaron al padre de Megan. Confiamos en tu veracidad porque estábamos desesperados por obtener cualquier tipo de información sobre lo que les sucedió a las personas que queremos. Pero resulta *raro* lo conectada que está tu familia con estas criaturas. Todos hemos tenido un mal presentimiento acerca de ti durante mucho tiempo, y ahora te escabulles en la noche y le mientes a Megan sobre lo que sabes, e intentas impedir que hable con nosotros. Así que ¿por qué no dejas ya de mentir y nos dices la maldita verdad de una vez por todas?

Metí las manos en los bolsillos e intenté pensar en alguna estrategia nueva, algún modo para que dejaran de mirarme. Los dedos de mi mano derecha jugueteaban con un trozo de papel, deslizándose alrededor de los bordes. Lo saqué del bolsillo. Era el teléfono de Brin. Lo miré, los engranajes de mi mente momentáneamente paralizados.

Aparté la vista del trozo de papel y los vi todavía esperando una respuesta.

—Y-yo… —empecé, y me detuve, carraspeando. Cerré mi ojo y vi la cara de Brin en el aparcamiento, surcada por años de dolor. Brin, que había sido valiente y sincera conmigo. Que había asumido su propia responsabilidad, y se había hecho cargo de lo que había hecho.

—Todo lo que os conté es cierto —dije, abriendo mi ojo para empezar de nuevo—. Pero tenéis razón, no es toda la verdad. La primera vez que vi a una de estas criaturas tenía seis años. Aparecía fuera de mi ventana todas las noches, arañando el cristal. Hasta que finalmente me enfrenté a ella.

—¿Entonces por qué no desapareciste? —preguntó Josh.

—No lo sé —respondí—. Pero durante los siguientes doce años, esta criatura fue mi amiga, mi protectora, y luego mi amante.

Sentí que el escepticismo del grupo se transformaba en repugnancia. Megan arrugó la nariz como si acabara de oler algo putrefacto.

—No sabía lo que eran estas criaturas ni lo que hacían —dije—. La criatura que conocía me ocultaba todo esto. Yo era un chico solitario con un mejor amigo mágico. Una vez que conocí a Megan, y a todos vosotros, mis sentimientos empezaron a cambiar. Acudí al mundo del monstruo empleando esta piedra. —Extraje la piedra negra del bolsillo izquierdo y se la mostré—. Y vi a una persona atrapada allí convirtiéndose en monstruo. Me enteré de cómo una de estas criaturas había sometido al padre de Megan llevándolo a la locura. No quería pasar por lo mismo. Desterré al monstruo de mi vida y empecé mi relación con Megan.

—Si este ser estaba preparándote, el sexo solo era un componente más —dijo Sarah, dulcemente—. Te manipularon. No fue tu culpa.

—¿Por qué no me lo contaste? —preguntó Megan. Tenía las manos cerradas formando puños, y la mirada dura y terrible.

—Por la expresión que tienes en este momento —dije—. Y además porque acababa de conocerte. ¿Realmente crees que la gente inicia una nueva relación hablando sobre todos sus ex? —Pero entonces una sensación de repugnancia me embargó al darme cuenta de que seguía mintiendo. Incluso ahora. Suspiré y apreté la piedra negra dentro del puño.

—Maldita sea, y eso no es todo —dije—. Sí, el monstruo y yo estuvimos juntos, y, sí, lo desterré. Y, sí, te lo oculté porque te quería y no quería ahuyentarte. Pero la pura verdad... toda la verdad —dije— es que, desde que te conozco, he tenido un pie dentro y otro pie fuera. Creía que estando contigo, contándote a ti y a tus amigos parte de la verdad... creía que me cambiaría. Creía que si ocultaba esta parte de mí mismo lo suficiente, desaparecería. Creí que me salvaría de terminar como tu padre. Pero a pesar de saber lo que es mi monstruo y lo que hace, la sigo echando de menos. A pesar del hecho de que me ha perseguido a mí y a mi familia durante aparentemente los últimos cincuenta años... que Dios me ayude... la sigo queriendo.

En cuanto pronuncié las palabras, el mundo se tornó gris. Oí por un instante las exclamaciones de sorpresa de la Hermandad, pero el sonido se desvaneció y me rodeó un aire espeso y húmedo, como una manta empapada. Por fin había cruzado.

CAPÍTULO 8

En el pasado, cuando había empleado la piedra negra, siempre había elegido mi destino. Pero esta vez ella lo eligió por mí. Cuando la neblina se aclaró y el mundo se volvió a consolidar, me encontré de pie en un calco de la sala de mi madre, oscura y vacía. Crucé el recinto para darle al interruptor, la niebla arremolinándose alrededor de mis pies. La lámpara del techo se encendió, pero la oscuridad siguió siendo una presencia física que consumía luz como el fuego consume oxígeno.

Caminé hacia la puerta trasera, la abrí y miré el prado de césped negro, atiborrado de gentilezas de ébano. Un bosque de árboles sombreados se alzaba a cierta distancia. Casi di un paso fuera, con la intención de abrirme paso hasta el bosque, hacia la cabaña de Leannon, pero un sonido me detuvo. Un gemido quedo y sordo, que provenía de una habitación que daba justo a la sala: el dormitorio de mi madre.

Entré de nuevo y abrí su puerta. Un tenue resplandor color rosa iluminaba la habitación. La cuna y la mecedora le daban el aspecto de una habitación infantil, pero las fotos enmarcadas que cubrían las paredes lo desmentían. El gemido volvió a oírse, esta vez detrás de mí. Me volví en el instante en que mi madre entró tambaleándose. Llevaba puesto un camisón y se la veía aturdida. Había perdido peso desde la última vez que la había visto, y parecía esquelética en su camisón ondulante, salvo el vientre protuberante y perfectamente redondeado. Estaba embarazada.

—Mamá —dije.

No respondió, sino que se aferró a la barandilla de la cuna agachándose hasta quedar de rodillas. Extrajo otra fotografía enmarcada de debajo de la cuna y se sentó para mirarla. Una gruesa capa de polvo se acumulaba sobre el cristal, pero de todos modos distinguí a mi madre y a mi padre en lo que debió de ser el día de su boda. Mi madre llevaba un vestido verde, y mi padre un traje que parecía quedarle demasiado grande.

Pasó la mano por el cristal del marco, dejando huellas sobre el polvo. Se masajeó el vientre hinchado y gimió.

Me arrodillé a su lado.

—¿Mamá? —Siguió sin responder. Apoyé una mano sobre su vientre; se desinfló como una bolsa de residuos llena de hojas, y luego tembló. Aparté la mano justo antes de que algo traspasara la tela con un desgarro, y saliera disparado del vientre: una presencia delgada, negra, que se movió velozmente. Me escabullí y me di contra la pared. Dos lianas negras habían brotado del vientre de mi madre. Se agitaban como las extremidades anteriores de una mantis religiosa, erguidas y acechantes. Cuando los tallos no encontraron nada para perforar o arrebatar, se retrajeron de nuevo bajo la tela desgarrada de su camisón.

Mi madre no manifestó reacción alguna a todo esto. Permaneció inclinada sobre la fotografía, realizando sonidos débiles y apenados desde el fondo de la garganta. Quise seguir intentando sacarla de su letargo, pero tuve miedo de que si las lianas negras volvían a emerger, quizás esta vez no consiguiera escapar. Me puse en pie y salí tambaleando de la habitación.

Subí las escaleras. El segundo piso de la casa también era el reverso de la real, un pasillo con una sucesión de puertas cerradas. La puerta al final del pasillo, la «oficina» de mi madre, que por lo general estaba vacía, se abrió con un chasquido. Me acerqué con lentitud hacia ella, intentando detectar algún sonido tras las otras puertas, queriendo estar preparado en caso de que alguna se abriera de golpe y arrojara horrores inconcebibles. Al acercarme, oí música saliendo de la puerta abierta: «Campanas tubulares», la banda sonora de *El exorcista*. Era uno de los temas de películas que solíamos poner por los altavoces en el exterior del Laberinto del Terror. Pasé por la puerta abierta.

La siguiente habitación era algo así como un concierto improvisado de aficionados o un escenario cambiante: una mujer realizaba un espectáculo sobre un pequeño tablado delante de un público con disfraces de Halloween. Una corriente de humo soplaba sobre el escenario, y una luz estroboscópica emitía destellos, confiriéndole a los movimientos de la mujer sobre el escenario un aspecto fantasmagórico y de algún modo irreal. Llevaba un tutú de color negro, un complemento perfecto de su piel fantasmal y pelo negro azabache. Entorné los ojos para poder verla mejor a la luz palpitante.

—Sydney —dije. Sydney, todavía prisionera pero todavía viva, aún *humana*, después de todos estos años. Apenas podía creerlo.

La persona a mi lado, un tipo con traje, capa y antifaz dominó con una nariz larga y puntiaguda, se dio la vuelta con un dedo sobre los labios.

—Shhh —dijo con aspereza. Su antifaz no tenía cordón alguno que lo sujetara a su cabeza. El material brillante y metálico parecía soldado a su cara en la zona alrededor de las sienes, emergiendo de bultos de cicatrices. Los ojos detrás del antifaz no estaban apagados como los de mi madre o Sydney; al contrario, eran brillantes y vidriosos, absortos en el espectáculo.

Sobre el escenario Sydney giraba y se estiraba, como un fantasma bajo la luz intermitente. Era difícil ver los detalles. ¿Tenía el pelo encanecido? ¿Arrugas en la cara antiguamente tersa? Había tenido diecisiete años cuando desapareció en 1989. Ahora tendría cuarenta y uno. ¿Habría estado bailando sin pausa todos esos años?

Gruesas vides negras se enroscaban alrededor de sus tobillos y muñecas, tensándose y aflojándose al compás de sus movimientos. Había algo fuera del escenario que tiraba de sus cuerdas.

—Volveré a por ti —dije, y salí de la habitación. El hombre con el antifaz soldado giró rápidamente para silenciarme una vez más.

En cuanto entré en el corredor, la puerta de la oficina se cerró y la de la habitación de Eunice se abrió de par en par.

—Está bien, ahora lo entiendo —dije, alzando la voz—. ¿Dónde estás? —Dejé atrás la habitación de Eunice y me dirigí a mi propia puerta. La manilla no giraba. Quise abrirla de un golpe con el brazo, pero fue como darme contra cemento. Me dirigí a las escaleras, pero al llegar, las encontré custodiadas por una verja de hierro de dos metros de alto. Por la experiencia con mi puerta, no tenía sentido intentar escalarla. En esta atracción no había atajos. Tendría que recorrerla tal como lo había dispuesto su creador. Entré en la habitación de Eunice.

Estaba tan desordenada y revuelta de cosas como la recordaba, atestada de libros, y con un escritorio de madera colocado bajo la ventana. Eunice se encontraba desplomada sobre la silla, golpeteando las teclas de una máquina de escribir negra y de aspecto aceitoso. El repiqueteo resultaba sonoro y rítmico en la quietud escalofriante, como si la máquina fuera un piano. Llevaba los restos de ropa de trabajo formal hechos jirones. Su pelo rojizo estaba enmarañado y apelmazado. Me acerqué a ella lentamente, con el pecho oprimido. Tallos largos y negros de múltiples coyunturas habían crecido de varios puntos de su escritorio, alojándose en sus brazos, piernas y estómago, e incluso su frente. Los tallos danzaban al ritmo de su tecleo. Parecía que la estaban preparando para la transfiguración.

Eunice extrajo una hoja de la máquina de escribir y la añadió a una pila a su derecha. Levanté las hojas, y dejó de teclear. Alzó la cabeza. Parecía más pálida de lo que la recordaba, con la mirada ausente. La piel de su cara languidecía por algo más que el cansancio. La sangre se escurría por su cara donde los tallos negros habían perforado su piel.

Encima del manuscrito había una portada:

La Secuencia Turner

Pasé la página a la siguiente y leí:

La Secuencia Turner I: Margaret

Cuando Margaret irrumpe despierta en el sueño fluido
de la Ciudad, aquella mezcla de recuerdo y pesadilla,
cree que está en el minúsculo apartamento que
compartía con Harry, en el sector más empobrecido de
Lubbock: aquel cuartucho ruinoso de una sola

habitación con la alfombra raída y las paredes
forradas de madera, aunque apenas puedan verse detrás
de las pilas de cajas que invaden la habitación,
cajas llenas de libros de bolsillo, comics y revistas
pulp.

Eunice resolló, y me sobresalté, retrocediendo un paso para alejarme de ella.

—De… vuél… velo —La voz provenía de su boca, pero no sonaba en absoluto como la suya—. Aún… no… lo he… acabado.

Apoyé las hojas sobre el escritorio y abandoné la habitación, sin lamentar oír el golpe seco de la puerta tras de mí. De nuevo en el pasillo, la puerta a mi habitación por fin se abrió.

En el instante en que entré, el suelo se desvaneció bajo mis pies. Caí con un chillido poco heroico, aterrizando sobre manos y rodillas en un duro suelo de madera. Una suave y cálida luz iluminaba la habitación a mi alrededor, y la oscuridad disminuyó un poco. Contra los muros se apoyaban lienzos, y plantas y raíces disecadas colgaban del techo. Había llegado a la cabaña de Leannon. Leannon, con su cara lobuna, yacía desplomada sobre una silla en mitad de la habitación, de espaldas a mí. Sus brazos peludos envolvían sus rodillas.

Me puse en pie.

—Estoy aquí —dije.

No respondió. Crucé la sala dando fuertes pisotones y le aferré el hombro.

—Oye —dije, y me detuve cuando levantó la mirada hacia mí, exhibiendo sus ojos de color naranja profundamente atormentados. Me aferró la mano, y apenas alcancé a leer lo que había garabateado sobre el suelo antes de que el mundo entero se volviera blanco:

AMIGO

AYUDA

EL SABUESO

En esta película casi muda, una mujer pálida, de pelo rojizo y con una capa roja, lleva una cesta de flores a través de un bosque de árboles altos y delgados. Se detiene al llegar a un claro con tres cruces sencillas clavadas en la tierra. Si fuera un día más bonito, los rayos del sol estarían iluminando este pequeño cementerio, pero hoy las nubes de tormenta oscurecen el cielo. La mujer coloca un lirio blanco sobre cada una de las lápidas; luego se sienta delante de ellas. Varias veces parece a punto de hablar, pero elige en cambio el silencio y el estruendo del cielo por encima.

Las nubes estallan. Entonces, se echa encima la capucha y vuelve con prisa por donde ha venido. Llega a una pequeña casa de madera al borde del bosque, en las afueras de una pequeña aldea de edificios de madera. Las carreteras están enlodadas y vacías, todas las puertas cerradas para protegerse de la tormenta.

La casa de la mujer es una única habitación con un suelo de tierra apelmazada, una cama, un fogón y una pequeña cocina. Se sienta en una silla ante el fuego, con una pila de hojas en el regazo, dibujando con un trozo de carbón. A medida que el mundo fuera de su ventana se oscurece, permanece sentada, dibujando las mismas tres caras una y otra vez: un hombre calvo con una barba oscura y dos niños de pelo oscuro. Con cada nuevo boceto, los dibujos van mejorando, como si la mujer estuviera centrándose con cada vez más precisión, apelando a las líneas de expresión, el brillo travieso de las miradas, las bocas melancólicas. Mientras dibuja no se mueve ni se acomoda para estar más confortable. Cada cierto tiempo cierra los ojos, pero jamás levanta la mirada y jamás cambia la expresión de su concentración atenta y ceñuda.

Dibuja hasta que se le acaba el papel, y luego da la vuelta las hojas y dibuja en los reversos. Cuando llega al final de esta segunda serie, se pone de pie y se estira. Coloca sus hojas sobre la cama y extrae un monedero de tela del interior de su vestido. Empieza a contar lo que hay dentro, pero suelta el dinero cuando empieza a oírse un arañazo fuera de su puerta.

La mujer suelta un jadeo y el monedero cae y golpea el suelo con un sonido metálico sordo. Los arañazos cesan. La mujer echa un vistazo al monedero como preguntándose si debe empezar a contar de nuevo, pero luego los arañazos se vuelven a iniciar, percibiéndose incluso por encima del tamborileo de la lluvia. La mujer pasa por encima de su monedero y abre la puerta principal. El umbral y las carreteras de la aldea parecen vacíos, aunque es difícil ver a través del martilleo de la lluvia.

Empieza a retroceder dentro de la casa, pero algo llama su atención más allá de la línea de árboles: un par de brillantes ojos de color naranja, de mirada límpida y despejada, incluso a través de la tormenta.

En lugar de sobresaltarse o replegarse, la mujer inclina la cabeza y frunce el ceño. Siente más curiosidad que temor.

Toma su capa y sale fuera. Con la capucha puesta, la cabeza gacha, avanza chapoteando entre el lodo hasta entrar en el bosque. Bajo el dosel de árboles, aparta la capucha hacia atrás y mira a su alrededor. Los ojos de color naranja aparecen de nuevo, justo delante de su cara. La mujer se queda inmóvil mientras la figura se estira, desde su posición en cuclillas, hasta alcanzar su altura máxima... al menos medio metro más alta que ella, enfundada en una larga capa amarilla. La mujer extiende los brazos en un gesto claro de rendición. Con delicadeza, casi con ternura, la criatura despliega sus largas extremidades y se impulsa hacia arriba, levantando el vuelo a través de los árboles y en dirección de la tormenta.

La lluvia acribilla la cara de la mujer, y los rayos relampaguean en la distancia, iluminando momentáneamente el cielo, y luego cambia de un púrpura-negro a un verde pantanoso. La aldea ha desaparecido. En su lugar hay una extensa concentración de torres y edificios negros que parecen templos y mausoleos, pero más colosales y de algún modo más terribles que cualquier cosa que haya sido erigida sobre la tierra alguna vez.

Después de esto, la película empieza a entrecortarse, y el relato se pierde por una serie de secuencias y sensaciones veloces: un tazón de algo espeso y penetrante; una somnolencia inexplicable, acompañada de un sonido como el de ramas secas que arañan un suelo de cemento; un dolor insoportable y agudo y una opresión en las muñecas y los tobillos; oscuridad, oscuridad, oscuridad.

Luego, otro tipo de dolor. Recuerda este momento con demasiada lucidez, lo sufre desde dentro. Sus ojos se abren en una habitación oscura al oír el sonido de carne troceada y sentir un dolor agudo en los brazos, las piernas, la cara y el pecho, la sensación de que le están quitando… *succionando*… algo del cuerpo, y de que otra cosa, algo espeso y viscoso, fluye dentro para sustituirlo. Su cuerpo se sacude y se tensa, y desea la muerte, desea cualquier cosa para detener este dolor. Luego, una picazón insoportable se extiende sobre la superficie de su cuerpo. Su carne se desprende, y mechones de pelo brotan de su piel. El mundo se vuelve de color naranja.

Cae derribada de la silla a la que estaba atada y aterriza sobre el suelo, temblando. Una hilera de monstruos con caras lobunas, vestidos con trajes de colores, entra en la sala y la rodean. Uno de ellos, un lobo gris de traje azul, se arrodilla y le ofrece una túnica roja. Se la pone de prisa con manos temblorosas, no, no son manos. Garras. Ahora tiene garras. Se pone de pie y el lobo vestido de azul descubre sus colmillos en una sonrisa salvaje.

Lo que sigue es una sucesión borrosa de años de color naranja, durante los cuales el lobo deja de ser alguien. Son pocos los impulsos que la guían: *nútrete de su dolor; apresa trabajadores; sirve a la Ciudad.* Caras diferentes van y vienen: lo único que no cambia es la tristeza, la depresión, el dolor, la enfermedad mental y el temor a todas ellas, cada una un cultivo para ser cosechado. A algunas personas solo prueba (una separación dura por aquí, la muerte de una mascota familiar por allá), y a otras cultiva como jardines: quienes padecen depresión profunda, los que sufren desconsuelo, los locos, los enfermos terminales. De algunos se nutre durante años, y a otros se los lleva para que trabajen fatigosamente y padezcan pesadillas en la Ciudad. A unos pocos elegidos, los más fuertes, los que sufren con más intensidad, los escoge para la ascensión, y se convierten ellos mismos en lobos.

Para la loba, sus caras son todas anónimas, fácilmente olvidables… hasta que conoce a los Turner. Empieza con Deborah, una mujer que está al borde del abismo. La loba la rapta, pero se arrepiente cuando ve al hijo de la mujer, Harry. Un pequeño de pelo oscuro, de pie en la habitación de su madre, en mitad de la noche, aterrado de quedarse solo. Algo en la cara del chico despierta un recuerdo profundo y oculto hacía mucho tiempo en su interior.

Otro pequeño asustado, cuya cara no consigue ubicar del todo. Por motivos que la loba no termina de entender, deja que Deborah vuelva a casa, y los deja en paz durante diez años.

La loba vuelve a Harry cuando ya ha crecido, con la intención de nutrirse de él; de su esposa, Margaret; y de sus hijas, Eunice y Sydney. Durante años apenas entra y sale de la periferia de sus vidas, dejando que vean atisbos y pistas de su presencia, contribuyendo a intensificar su sufrimiento y temor a medida que Harry se marchita y muere, disfrutando de la progresiva desunión de la familia. Pero su trabajo vuelve a quedar interrumpido cuando conoce a otro pequeño: Noah Turner, de seis años, el vivo retrato de su padre muerto. De pie detrás de la ventana de su dormitorio, la observa con abierta fascinación, sin ningún tipo de temor, capaz de verla, lo quiera o no lo quiera.

¿Cuánto tiempo hace que alguien no la contempla sin terror ni repugnancia? ¿Décadas? ¿Siglos? La curiosidad del pequeño y su cordialidad han liberado algo en su corazón. Vuelve a él una y otra vez. Pasa las noches en el patio fuera de la habitación del chico, copiando dibujos de sus libros de cuentos sobre el cemento con tiza. En el instante en que coloca la garra sobre su mano y lo guía para que realicen juntos su primer dibujo, se pierde por un instante en un destello de luz blanca y brillante, la sensación de una sincronización perfecta entre los dos.

Cuando acaba aquel momento, demasiado pronto, observa lo que han dibujado juntos: una imagen caricaturesca de la Ciudad. Pero lo más importante es que puede ver el dibujo, la acera y a Noah en colores. El tinte de color naranja ha desaparecido.

Es el chico. Estar cerca de él produce un efecto que devuelve los colores y sugiere otras realidades aún más importantes, que están fuera del alcance de su mente. La loba encuentra la forma de ser parte de su vida. Apresa a su hermana mayor para llevársela a la Ciudad, y aprovecha la confusión del niño para conseguir que lo invite a su habitación. Duerme en su cama, lo observa crecer, le enseña a volar. Durante el tiempo que pasan alejados, la loba se construye su pequeña casa en los bosques oscuros fuera de la Ciudad, un sitio parecido a la última morada humana que tuvo, y allí ensaya sus primeras pinturas, intentando conservar su visión a puro color.

Se dice a sí misma que Noah es solo una herramienta o una mascota para ella, pero los celos la consumen al observarlo entregarle una gentileza de ébano a Donna Hart y recibir su primer beso a cambio. Se da cuenta de que quizás los colores que Noah ha traído a su mundo son un efecto secundario de algo más profundo que ha ido acumulándose en silencio durante años.

Cuando salva a Noah de la Bestia Gris, se siente dominada por la ira y alcanza un nuevo nivel de claridad y color al redescubrir su forma humana, encontrar su voz humana y hacer el amor con Noah por primera vez. El amor la ha rescatado de la oscuridad, y por fin le ha dado un nombre: Leannon.

Durante años Leannon pinta y le hace el amor a Noah. Lo mantiene oculto de la Ciudad; esconde sus colores, su forma humana, su felicidad. Pero, por supuesto, este estado de dicha no puede durar para siempre. Es demasiada la información que le oculta a su joven amante, demasiadas las preguntas que ignora. El joven se vuelve curioso, desconfiado y encuentra la Ciudad por sí mismo. Cuando esta lo ve, exige su vida, como exige la vida de todos sus visitantes.

Leannon intenta proteger a Noah, incluso después de abandonarla. Rapta a muchos otros en su lugar para satisfacer a su amo, incluso mientras el color se escurre de su mundo y su mente se vuelve confusa. Se olvida de cómo manejar un pincel o estirar un lienzo. De cómo adoptar una cara humana o de sonreír. La Ciudad permanece inflexible, y le cuesta cada vez más resistirse a sus órdenes. En un intento final y confuso que podría estar destinado a salvar a Noah o a pedirle ayuda, rapta a Eunice y a Margaret Turner en una sola noche. Espera que Noah encuentre el camino hasta aquí y los rescate a todos, o que la Ciudad quede saciada al menos un poco más de tiempo, al obtener a dos esclavas más en su lugar.

Tras el rapto, se sienta en el suelo de su casa, con la cabeza entre las garras, intentando aferrarse a la imagen de su cara, las letras de su nombre. Todo se esfuma. *Ella* se esfuma.

Y Noah logra, por fin, encontrar un modo de volver a ella, empleando las palabras justas para abrir la puerta entre ambos mundos. Y cuando llega, cuando su mano se posa sobre su hombro, los secretos se acaban. Ella lo toma de la mano y por fin se lo muestra *todo*.

EL MORADOR DE LAS TINIEBLAS

CAPÍTULO 1

El torrente de fulgor blanco se atenuó. Había visto todo lo que necesitaba ver. Leannon empezó a soltarme la mano, pero me aferré a su garra. Me arrodillé a su lado y la envolví en mis brazos.

—Te he echado tanto de menos —dije.

Me devolvió el abrazo y emitió un gemido agudo desde el fondo de la garganta.

Acaricié su espalda y la rasqué detrás de las orejas.

—No te preocupes. Ahora estoy aquí.

CAPÍTULO 2

Después de hacer el trato, fui primero a ver a Sydney. El público había abandonado el pequeño teatro al final del pasillo de la planta de arriba, y la música había sido silenciada. Sydney bailaba sola, sin melodía ni público alguno. Cuando trepé arriba y le desaté las vides de alrededor de los brazos y las piernas, se desplomó encima de mí y casi nos caemos del escenario. Luché por mantener el equilibrio y la hice descender al suelo, apoyando su cabeza sobre mis rodillas dobladas. Sus párpados se agitaron.

—Sydney —dije, acariciando su pelo apelmazado—. Sydney, es hora de que te despiertes.

Sus ojos se abrieron bruscamente.

—¿Papá? —graznó.

Asentí. Así era más fácil.

—No lo entiendo —dijo. Se frotó los ojos con los puños cerrados, como una niña—, ¿es un sueño?

—Sí —respondí—. Y necesito que me ayudes para que ambos nos despertemos. ¿Crees que puedes caminar?

Rodeándonos mutuamente los hombros, bajamos con dificultad las escaleras a la sala. Me senté junto a ella sobre el sofá y le tomé las manos.

—En un instante más, te despertarás —dije—. Pero antes, necesito que bebas algo. —Me puse de pie, tomé una taza humeante de la barra del desayuno y se la entregué. La olisqueó y frunció el ceño.

—¿Qué es esto? —preguntó.

—Es medicina —dije—. Sé que huele raro, pero tienes que beberlo, ¿de acuerdo?

Respiró hondo, reunió fuerzas, y luego se detuvo al oír un golpe arriba, seguido por el sonido de voces.

—¿Qué ha sido eso? —preguntó.

—Otra parte del sueño. Tienes que beber.

Inclinó la taza hacia sus labios y apuró el contenido en unos pocos sorbos. Se llevó un puño a la boca, como intentando no vomitar. Tras un momento, pareció más despierta.

—¿Cómo puedes estar aquí? —preguntó—. Te vi morir.

—Es un sueño —le recordé—. Y en los sueños podemos vernos tantas veces como queramos.

CAPÍTULO 3

En segundo lugar, acudí a mi madre. Seguía sentada sobre el suelo de la habitación de niños de color rosa, con los ojos bien cerrados. Apretaba en el puño la foto del día de su boda y sollozaba. Las vides que habían estado personificando un embarazo yacían alrededor de ella como serpientes muertas.

—Mamá, ¿puedes oírme? —pregunté.

Levantó la mirada y parpadeó. Como Sydney, estaba aturdida.

—Ya podemos irnos —dije, ofreciéndole la mano.

Apretó la foto contra el pecho y se meció de delante hacia atrás.

—No puedo irme.

—¿Por qué?

—Lo he jodido todo —dijo—. Todo. Perdí a mi marido, a mi mejor amiga, y a mis hijos. Me dije que los estaba protegiendo, pero... —Sacudió la cabeza—... en realidad, los alejé. No merezco volver a casa.

Me puse en cuclillas junto a ella.

—Lo comprendo. Era más fácil dejar que nos alejáramos y fingir que todo estaba en orden, que no había nada fuera de lugar. Era más fácil que pelear y esperar y aguantar. Pero nos mantuviste unidos a través de la enfermedad, la pobreza, las desapariciones y los intentos de suicidio. Tú creaste el Laberinto del Terror, un sitio dentro de nuestro mundo que me enseñó a hacerme camino en el mundo. Es por ti que tengo la posibilidad de llevar a todos a casa. Y eso quiere decir que a ti también, mamá.

Entonces dejó que la abrazara, se apoyó contra mí y me rodeó con sus brazos.

—Os echo mucho de menos —dijo—. Echo de menos a tu padre.

—Lo sé —dije—. Pero la pesadilla está a punto de acabar y las luces están a punto de encenderse de nuevo. No puedo devolverte a papá, pero puedo darte a casi todo el resto. Solo necesito que salgas a la sala conmigo.

CAPÍTULO 4

En tercer lugar, acudí a Eunice. De todos los que liberé, ella fue la única con la que tuve que recurrir a Leannon para desenredar de las vides. Las vides negras la habían apuñalado, encadenándola al escritorio y ordenándole que escribiera hasta su transfiguración, y Leannon tuvo que sellar las heridas para que no se desangrara. Después de que esta le frotara su bálsamo especial y se marchara, Eunice se quedó sentada ante su escritorio, meciéndose levemente, con la mirada fija en una distancia intermedia.

Le toqué el brazo y soltó un chillido. Aparté la mano rápidamente.

—Lo siento —dije.

Siguió meneándose y escorándose como una boya en aguas turbulentas. Una lágrima se deslizó por una de sus mejillas.

—Tengo algo para ti —dije. Metí la mano en el bolsillo y extraje un papel escrito con el número de Brin. Lo aceptó casi mecánicamente, pero dejó de mirar a lo lejos y enfocó la mirada.

—Brin —dijo, con tono apagado.

—Está trabajando como farmacéutica en el pueblo —dije—. Siempre quiso ponerse en contacto y arreglar las cosas contigo, pero no sabía cómo hacerlo.

—Brin —repitió. Esta vez parecía haber recuperado su tono habitual de voz. Esbozó una pequeña sonrisa—. Siempre odiaste a Brin.

—Yo también quería arreglar las cosas contigo, y jamás supe cómo hacerlo. —Volví a tocarle el brazo, y esta vez lo permitió, me dejó sujetar su mano en la mía—. Llames o no a Brin —dije—, mereces ser feliz. —Apreté su mano—. Y Caroline y Dennis te echan de menos.

—Caroline. Dennis. —Esos nombres estaban cargados de poder, la ayudaron a caminar un poco más. Me dejó que la guiara a la sala y aceptó una taza de té, pero lo miró con desconfianza antes de bebérselo.

—¿Qué tiene?

—Es un extracto de una flor que solo crece en este mundo. Yo la llamo la gentileza de ébano. Puede hipnotizarte, intensificar tu capacidad de ser sugestionada e incluso alterar tus recuerdos.

Bebió más despacio.

—No recordaré nada de esto —dijo.

—Todo se esfumará como una pesadilla —dije.

—¿Por qué? ¿Por qué pedirme que beba esto?

—Es parte del trato que he hecho —dije—. Podéis ir a casa, pero el recuerdo se queda aquí. Una vez que termines el té, yo te ayudaré a olvidar.

—¿Y tú? —preguntó—. ¿Quién te hará olvidar?

Cuando no respondí, pareció comprender cabalmente la importancia de lo que yo callaba. Me sujetó la mano con tanta fuerza que me dolió.

—Oye —dije—, ¿a quién quiero yo más?

—Al principito —dijo. Apoyó la taza y me aferró también la otra mano—. Déjame disfrutar de este momento contigo —dijo—. Un momento más, por favor.

CAPÍTULO 5

El cielo de Vandergriff tenía los bordes teñidos color rosado cuando Eunice caminó calle arriba con paso tambaleante hacia su propia casa. Su ropa de trabajo estaba hecha jirones allí donde el escritorio la había perforado, cubierta de una costra de sangre seca y tierra. Tenía la cara pálida e inexpresiva con las primeras luces del amanecer, y aunque viviría, aún le faltaba casi toda su fuerza. Con cada pisada hacía un gesto de dolor, y siseaba a través de dientes apretados.

Caroline y Dennis debían de estar mirando por la ventana, en aquel estado de alerta que los niños a veces manifiestan, sabiendo algo antes de que sea posible saberlo, porque la puerta principal se abrió de golpe y salieron corriendo a través del césped, con la cara arrebolada. Chocaron tan fuerte con Eunice que perdió el equilibrio y se cayó dentro del jardín de un vecino, cuyo césped aún seguía húmedo por la lluvia del día anterior. Se aferraron a ella, hundiendo la cara contra su cuerpo, sus voces apagadas. Poco después salió Hubert. Se resbaló sobre el césped, cayó de rodillas y chocó contra su familia como una bola de bolos.

—No me lo puedo creer —repetía una y otra vez—. No me lo puedo creer. —Sostuvo la cara de Eunice entre las manos, besó sus mejillas, su frente, sus párpados. Ella tenía una expresión apenada y culpable, soportando más que disfrutando de la atención de su marido. La euforia de Hubert no duraría mucho: la Eunice que había vuelto a casa no era la misma que la que se había marchado.

CAPÍTULO 6

En las afueras de Vandergriff, el Prius de Kyle Ransom se detuvo en la entrada de la caravana de su padre. Avanzó al trote por el sendero, con prisa. Había prometido ir a ver cómo estaba antes del trabajo, pero ya iba tarde.

Golpeó la puerta rítmicamente y esperó. El anciano solía tardar un minuto en levantarse y acudir a la puerta. Kyle miró el reloj de su móvil. Cuando habían pasado treinta segundos sin respuesta ni sonido alguno del interior, volvió a llamar. Aún no hubo respuesta. Pensando que su padre estaría atascado en el retrete, Kyle extrajo las llaves del bolsillo y abrió la puerta, empujándola para entrar.

—¿Papá? —preguntó, mirando de un lado a otro de la oscura caravana—. ¿Te encuentras bien?

Había un olor extraño en el aire, algo espeso y acre. Parecía familiar, aunque no recordaba de dónde lo conocía. Sin duda, no era algo que hubiera olido antes allí dentro. Se quedó de pie en el silencio durante algunos instantes más, resollando en el aire húmedo, rastreando el olor por la madriguera de sus recuerdos. Por algún motivo le recordó a Donna, y al instituto, y a la culpa de besarla cuando seguía saliendo con Noah.

Sin saber aún de qué olor se trataba, se giró y salió de la caravana vacía, cerró la puerta con llave, se metió de nuevo en su coche y se alejó de allí. En los días siguientes, daría la voz de alarma sobre su desaparición y se iniciaría una investigación policial. Pero la policía no pondría demasiado empeño ni encontraría nada de valor, y nadie (ni siquiera Kyle) sería capaz de sentirse apenado por nada de ello.

CAPÍTULO 7

Al otro lado del pueblo, Sydney Turner se despertó en una habitación rara y bien dispuesta, con libros apilados sobre todas las superficies. Se enderezó y vislumbró su reflejo en el espejo situado detrás de la puerta: una mujer de mediana edad con mechones blancos en el pelo, y la piel que en un tiempo había sido tersa fruncida alrededor de la boca y los ojos. Se tocó la cara y vio las magulladuras rosados alrededor de los puños como brazaletes de dolor.

Se levantó tambaleándose y salió de la habitación cojeando. Caminó pasillo abajo, luego descendió algunos escalones, aferrándose a la barandilla para mantener el equilibrio.

—¿Hola? —llamó, con voz rasposa. Oyó un golpe en algún sitio de la planta baja y entró deprisa en la sala vacía. Volvió a llamar—: ¿Hola?

Una puerta se abrió quedamente, y una anciana salió a trompicones, con los ojos somnolientos. Su mirada se agudizó al posarse en Sydney. Las dos mujeres se miraron. Cada una trataba de situar a la otra. Sydney fue la primera en lograrlo.

—¿Mamá?

Margaret parpadeó un par de veces más.

—Oh, cielos, ¿Sydney?

Corrió hacia delante y la estrechó en un abrazo fuerte. Sydney intentó recordar la última vez que su madre la había abrazado. Debió de ser en algún momento cerca de la época del funeral de su padre. ¿Quién era esa desconocida de edad avanzada que la estrujaba y lloraba? Sin duda que no podía ser Margaret Turner. Quizás eso también fuera un sueño. Si así fuera, era un sueño bueno, en el que la ira pertinaz que la había acompañado toda su vida empezó a disolverse bajo el torrente de disculpas acongojadas de su madre. Sydney la abrazó. Tenía muchas preguntas: ¿Cuánto tiempo había estado ausente? ¿Qué año era? Pero por ahora, era suficiente con haber vuelto a casa, estar viva y llorando con su madre.

Casi podría terminar la historia aquí, en uno de los «buenos sitios en los que parar»: la familia reunida, a salvo, incluso si su futuro parecía un poco ambiguo. Y una parte de mí, tan feliz con la calidez y el alivio del momento, se siente tentada de escribir «fin» y dejarla. Pero aún tengo una pequeña historia que contar. Un poco más de felicidad, y un poco más de sufrimiento, algunas preguntas más que responder y cabos sueltos que atar. No sé si me llega para hacer un lazo, pero haré lo posible.

CAPÍTULO 8

Poco menos de un año después de que mi familia volviera a casa, me escabullí a una pequeña ceremonia en el salón de baile de un hotel de Fort Worth. No había muchos invitados, y la mayoría era gente que no reconocí, pero había algunos antiguos trabajadores que habían participado en el Laberinto del Terror agrupados cerca del fondo, junto con Sally White y su marido. La energía de todos los presentes era tan manifiestamente cálida y feliz que casi podía sentirme yo también parte de ella.

Un instante después de que una de las novias y el juez de paz ocuparan sus sitios ante el altar, el cuarteto de cuerdas cerca de la parte delantera de la sala empezó a tocar, las puertas del salón se abrieron y salieron las damas de honor. Sydney y Caroline avanzaron majestuosamente por el corredor, tan solemnes y preciosas como elfos de Tolkien en marcha hacia los Puertos Grises. Sydney llevaba un vestido de manga larga y una expresión vacía, y no parecía advertir nada al detenerse en su sitio designado y volver la cara hacia el público. Pero Caroline... cuando se giró hacia los invitados, su mirada se cruzó con la mía, al otro lado del salón. Podía verme. No debería haber podido hacerlo, pero me veía.

El cuarteto cambió la melodía, y apareció Eunice del brazo de mi madre. El camino hacia el altar fue una marcha lenta para mi madre, que tenía sesenta y seis años y aún cojeaba ligeramente tras haber morado en la Ciudad. Tuve el presentimiento de que seguiría cojeando un poco durante el resto de su vida. Se detuvo cerca de la última hilera para sonreírle a Sally. Sally, que no sabía qué pensar de esta nueva versión gregaria de Margaret Turner, le sonrió a su vez y le hizo un gesto para que siguiera adelante. *El espectáculo debe continuar.* La pausa me dio suficiente tiempo para estudiar a Eunice, despampanante, con un vestido sin tirantes de color verde, su pelo rojizo recogido encima de la cabeza. Estaba más saludable de lo que la había visto en años; el brillo suave de algún modo impedía que se vieran las cicatrices en los brazos y la cara. Deseé que hubiera un modo de detener el tiempo, y alargar el momento para siempre. En cuanto a momentos en los cuales quedar eternamente enredado, los había visto mucho peores.

Brin empezó a sorberse las lágrimas a medio camino de la procesión de Eunice. Dennis, junto a ella como padrino, le ofreció un paquete de pañuelos, que aceptó agradecida. Y luego, mucho antes de lo que yo lo habría dispuesto, Eunice llegó a la arcada, sonriéndole a su futura cónyuge.

CAPÍTULO 9

Durante la recepción, permanecí entre las sombras, pero Caroline no dejaba de dirigirme miradas extrañadas a lo largo de toda la noche. Fingí no advertirlas. En cambio, observé a Eunice y a Brin bailar, abrazándose en mitad del salón de baile. Observé el modo en que Brin acunaba la parte de atrás de la cabeza de mi hermana con una mano, y la mirada de amor desesperado que cruzó la cara de Eunice mientras lo hacía. Observé a Sydney bailar con Caroline y Dennis; sonrió cuando la miraron, pero frunció el ceño cuando la dejaron sola. Casi un año después y, aunque seguía en casa, aún no se había recuperado por completo. Me pregunté si alguna vez lo conseguiría.

Observé a Eunice y a Brin cortar y servir el pastel. Observé a mi madre sentada a la mesa con Sally White y su marido. Me di cuenta por el modo en que mi madre no dejaba de apretar el brazo de Sally de que cuando se fuera sería duro para ella. Había echado de menos a su mejor amiga y tenía una necesidad casi compulsiva de compensar todo el tiempo perdido.

Me hubiera gustado poder sumarme a mi familia en mitad del salón de baile. Me hubiera gustado contarles que sus días de ser perseguidos y acechados habían acabado. Pero creo que de todos modos lo entendieron; su noche estuvo llena de risas, bebida, música y baile. Los Turner habían vuelto a ser una familia. Mi familia. Y solo había tenido que darle un pequeño empujón para unirla de nuevo.

En lugar de interferir, me contenté con respirar la atmósfera desde la periferia del salón, y, a medida que la noche tocaba su fin y los invitados se dispersaban, y las recién casadas se retiraban a sus aposentos, intenté no sentirme demasiado decepcionado o temeroso. Pero no pude evitar estremecerme un poco cuando Leannon apareció sobre mi hombro, con su cara humana, y su túnica roja sustituida por un vestido de color rojo sangre.

—Ha sido una ceremonia preciosa —dijo.

—¿Crees que funcionará? —pregunté.

—¿Que funcionará qué?

—La boda. Mi familia. ¿Seguirán siendo felices tras esta noche?

—No lo sé —dijo—. Pero les has dado tiempo, y una segunda oportunidad. Es más de lo que recibe cualquiera. Tendrá que bastar.

Sabía que era cierto, aunque no me gustara.

—Es hora de irnos —dije.

—¡Espera!

Caroline debió de presentir que se su oportunidad se acababa porque cruzó el patio a toda velocidad, su vestido de dama de honor revoloteando a su alrededor.

Leannon y yo intercambiamos una mirada. Retrocedió un paso e hizo un gesto con una mano. *Si es necesario*. Caroline se detuvo justo delante de mí, resollando.

—Te conozco —dijo. Y luego, como dudando de lo que había dicho—: ¿No?

—¿Me conoces?

—Es como si tuviera la mente nublada —dijo—, pero recuerdo que mamá y la abuela habían desaparecido… —Se llevó una mano a las sienes y siseó—. Y recuerdo tu cara. Noah. —Continuó frotándose las sienes, como para sonsacar información de su cabeza—. El tío Noah. Tú estuviste allí. Luego mamá y la abuela volvieron. Y también la tía Sydney. Y desapareciste. Y a veces te recuerdo, pero luego es como si te olvidara de nuevo. —Entrecerró los ojos hasta cerrarlos y los volvió a abrir bien grandes—. Tú has hecho algo, ¿verdad? Nos salvaste.

Sus palabras me provocaron un sobresalto. Leannon y yo les habíamos administrado a todos los miembros de la familia una dosis de gentileza de ébano. No me borraba a mí por completo, pero debía hacer que fuera casi imposible que pudieran pensar en mí durante mucho tiempo.

—Intenta olvidar haberme conocido alguna vez —dije—. Te mantendrá a salvo.

—Pero ¿qué has hecho? —preguntó. Señaló a Leannon—. ¿Y quién es ella?

Seguía haciendo preguntas cuando tomé la mano de Leannon, pero las palabras se desvanecieron al cruzar al otro lado.

CAPÍTULO 10

He esperado hasta el final para contar esta parte porque, si he de perder tu buena opinión de mí, debe ser ahora. Quería que vieras el resto de las escenas con mi familia, para entender que tuve buenos motivos.

Antes de liberar a mi familia, regresé de la Ciudad a casa de mi madre solo. Megan y la Hermandad seguían reunidos en la sala, gritándose unos a otros en un estado de excitación febril. Me había ausentado durante más de una hora, pero, para mi alivio, habían esperado. En cuanto reaparecí, se callaron y me miraron como sobrecogidos. Me sentía como Moisés, descendiendo del Monte Sinaí. Bueno, al menos hasta que Megan me dio una bofetada en la mandíbula y me caí al suelo.

—Hijo de puta —dijo—. Maldito cabrón.

No me defendí. Tenía bien merecido cualquier tipo de improperio, verbal o físico, que quisiera soltarme.

—Es obvio que ha funcionado —dijo Eli. Sonaba un poco emocionado, y también un poco avergonzado de lo emocionado que se sentía—. ¿Has encontrado a tu familia?

—Sí —dije—. Pero no puedo liberarlos solo. Todavía voy a necesitar vuestra ayuda.

—¿Por qué porras íbamos a ayudarte? —preguntó Josh, jugueteando con el ala del sombrero.

Rodé hasta ponerme de rodillas, frotándome la mandíbula.

—Lamento si os he dado la impresión de que teníais opción en el asunto. —Señalé por encima del hombro mientras los monstruos iban apareciendo.

No hubo sangre, pero sí una gran cantidad de gritos. No lo describiré aquí, pero te recordaré la noche que vi por primera vez a Megan en Inferno. Imagina el momento al final de aquella primera atracción, cuando las fieras emergieron de las paredes y arrastraron a todos los pecadores desconsolados y suplicantes al infierno.

Cuando acabó, solo Megan, Leannon y yo permanecíamos allí. Megan había caído de rodillas y se cubría la cara con las manos. Quería ir a consolarla, pero aquel ya no era mi lugar. En cambio, esperé hasta que se recompuso de nuevo. Parpadeó un par de veces y pareció sorprenderse de verse aún en la sala de mi madre.

—¿Por qué sigo aquí? —preguntó.

—Hice un trato con ellos —dije, señalando a Leannon con el pulgar—. Mi familia por la Hermandad. Y tú también eres parte de mi familia.

Leannon emitió un ruido de impaciencia y avanzó un paso para ponerse junto a mí. Extendió una taza del té de gentileza de ébano. La tomé y se la pasé a Megan.

—Lo único que tienes que hacer es beber esto, y cuando despiertes mañana, estarás de vuelta en nuestro apartamento, y no recordarás nada de esto.

Megan miró con fijeza dentro de la taza y recorrió el borde con un pulgar.

—Lo recordaré y volveré a por ellos. Os detendré. Encontraré el modo de hacerlo.

—No lo harás —dije con la mayor dulzura posible.

Durante un momento creí que montaría una escena o empezaría a pelear. Que me arrojaría el té en la cara. En cambio, empezó a sollozar. En ese momento casi me derrumbé. Podría haberle dicho que lo lamentaba. Que de todas las personas que había conocido en mi vida, ella era la que menos merecía aquella atrocidad. Podría haberle dicho que aún la quería, porque era cierto. Es solo que quería más a mi familia, a Leannon y a la Ciudad.

—Te odio —dijo.

—Bébete el té —dije, sorprendido por la frialdad de mi propia voz.

Cuando se quedó dormida, Leannon la llevó de vuelta a nuestro apartamento en Oregon. En este punto Megan abandona mi relato, y espero que encuentre algo de paz alejada de mí, de mi familia y de la Ciudad. Espero, por el bien de ambos, que no pueda penetrar la niebla cerebral que le he concedido y que nuestros caminos no se vuelvan a cruzar.

En sus vidas, los miembros de la Hermandad solo se tenían unos a otros, y junto con el señor Ransom (un sacrificio extra que tuvo que hacerse para conseguir la libertad de Megan), siguen juntos ahora, inmovilizados en lechos de vides negras. Al final, obtuvieron las respuestas que deseaban y pagaron por ellas. Son esclavos de la Ciudad, y trabajan penosamente sumidos en un oscuro sopor, incapaces de despertar.

No rechazo las decisiones que he tomado ni el precio que he pagado por ellas. Supongo que no resulta tan sorprendente. Mi traje de monstruo siempre me quedó mejor que mi propia piel. Jamás fui un guardián ni un héroe, sino un creador y un cosechador de temores.

CAPÍTULO 11

Leannon y yo acabamos de volver de la boda y hemos subido a la habitación en la que encontré a Eunice el año pasado. El escritorio donde escribió sigue aquí, las vides negras bamboleándose desde su superficie como si las meciera un viento suave. Me han colgado encima durante los últimos meses mientras escribía esta crónica, mi versión excesivamente larga y poco elegante de las notas de suicidio de Eunice. Esta noche, ha llegado al fin su momento.

Me gustaría decirte que me he vuelto a sentar con una determinación férrea, listo para cumplir con mi parte del trato, pero la verdad es que al subir las escaleras mis piernas han flaqueado y Leannon ha tenido que llevarme arriba y sentarme en la silla.

—Ahora debes ser valiente, *Leannon si* —ha susurrado, y me ha besado el cuello—. Estaré aquí.

La Ciudad entera parece silenciosa salvo por el repiqueteo de mis teclas y mi respiración agitada y áspera. Se trata de la segunda parte del trato que hice, la condición final que debo cumplir. A cambio de la seguridad y el éxito de mi familia, me convertiré en un esclavo de la Ciudad. Ahora debo sentarme ante el escritorio destinado en su origen a Eunice, esperando ser transfigurado en algo salvaje y feroz. Espero para poder unirme a la faena de alimentar a la Ciudad y poblarla con soñadores.

Mi esperanza, al teclear con manos temblorosas, a medida que las vides negras empiezan a moverse más decididamente, emocionadas por iniciar su labor, es que Leannon, mi compañera de juegos, mi mejor amiga, y el amor de mi vida, sea capaz de devolverme a quien soy, como yo la he devuelto dos veces antes. Mi esperanza es deambular por las calles interminables y ocultas, los callejones y las oficinas de la Ciudad, explorar sus oquedades y examinar sus oscuros secretos. Mi esperanza es montar los vientos de la noche con Leannon para siempre.

Siempre existe la posibilidad de que no pueda volver a mí mismo como lo hizo ella. De quedarme atrapado como un animal con la mente vacía, que solo tiene pensamientos teñidos de color naranja. Si eso sucediera... pues que así sea. Siempre me he sentido cómodo en la oscuridad.

El escritorio está empezando su trabajo.

Oh, cielos.

Duele.

La Secuencia Turner V: Harry

Aunque Harry ve la Ciudad, jamás acude allí. Va a algún
otro sitio.

Empieza en su lecho de muerte en el Vandergriff Memorial
Hospital. Nadie lo llama así, por supuesto. *Lecho de muerte*
es uno de aquellos clichés que todo el mundo usa en las
conversaciones diarias, acerca de lo que recordarán, lo que
lamentarán, aquellas cosas de las que se retractarán. Pero
cuando aparece un lecho de muerte de verdad, el término
desaparece del léxico. Nadie pronuncia su nombre, porque
pronunciar su nombre acelera su terrible trabajo.

Harry siente tanto dolor ahora que no le importaría que
las cosas se aceleraran. Esta enfermedad ha sido
interminable. Al principio, para pasar el rato, hacía diseños
para una casa embrujada que sabe que no estará vivo para
construir. Fue divertido soñar a lo grande, darle voz a las
imágenes que han excitado sus pensamientos al despertar y al
acostarse desde que tenía diez años. Una Ciudad enorme y
extensa, sumida en un silencio inquietante y enigmáticamente
fascinante por razones que jamás ha sido capaz de expresar.
Siempre ha tenido miedo de hablar de ello, pero ahora, con la
excusa de un juego, ha sido capaz de mostrárselo a Margaret,
compartiéndolo por fin con alguien.

De todos modos, sus fuerzas han menguado, y está
demasiado débil para seguir dibujando. Esta noche, yace
solo en la oscuridad después que su familia volviera a casa
a descansar, sufriendo despierto unos dolores diáfanos y
constantes, y susurra el término para conferirle poder:
lecho de muerte, lecho de muerte, lecho de muerte.

Para lo que le sirve. El final parece imposiblemente lejano. La única ventaja de la distancia de la muerte es que su familia vuelve a casa de noche y lo deja en paz. Familia: una esposa, dos hijas y ahora un hijo. La gente que se supone que debe querer, pero cuyas caras le provocan ahora apatía, irritación, o (cuando se siente suficientemente provocado), ira. Desea que simplemente se queden en casa. Está harto de sus caras tristes y necesitadas.

Solía ser una persona cálida y reflexiva. Puede señalar momentos específicos de felicidad abrumadora con esas personas en su pasado: el primer beso con su esposa, Margaret, una noche cálida en Searcy en 1968; la carcajada aguda de Sydney cuando la columpiaba en el parque, mientras su pelo oscuro revoloteaba alrededor de su cabeza; Eunice al otro lado del cristal de un manatí en el World Aquarium de Dallas, comunicándose con la bestia blanca y rolliza mientras él la sostenía en alto. Lo recuerda todo, pero ya no siente nada de todo ello. Los médicos le dicen que esto es obra del tumor, que le distorsiona la personalidad y lo convierte en una versión deformada de sí mismo, pero él siente que este es el Harry real, el que acecha en las sombras, que al fin puede salir.

Ahora yace en la cama, mirando por la ventana, débil y dolorido, y repitiendo su mantra: *lecho de muerte, lecho de muerte, lecho de muerte. Lecho de muerte, lecho de muerte, lecho de muerte. Lecho de muerte, lecho de muerte, lecho...*

Al otro lado de la ventana, el cielo se ilumina, un brillante resplandor de color azul interrumpe el devenir de sus pensamientos. Al principio, cree que se trata de un relámpago, pero no hay lluvia ni truenos. Parpadea, la imagen residual resplandeciendo contra sus párpados. Quizás sea una alucinación. Pero vuelve a suceder: un estallido radiante de color azul que baña de luz el mundo entero.

Levanta el mando de la televisión de su cama y presiona el
botón de llamada. Nadie responde.

Cierra los ojos y presta atención a los sonidos que dan
cuenta de que hay gente fuera en el pasillo: el crujido de
papel, el rechinar de los zapatos sobre el suelo de
linóleo, las conversaciones susurradas, pero no oye nada.
Abre la boca para volver a llamar, pero la luz azul inunda
la habitación, más intensa que antes, y por algún motivo
esto confirma lo que ya sospecha: no hay nadie fuera.

Se desconecta los diferentes tubos y cables que lo
mantienen «cómodo». El esfuerzo lo agota, pero no tanto
como había creído. Presiona la palanca que hace descender
la barandilla de seguridad de la cama, y se desliza hacia
abajo, quedando tendido en el suelo. Le duele, pero de
nuevo, menos de lo que creía.

Se pone de pie y avanza arrastrando los pies hacia el
pasillo, pero en cambio sale a la habitación principal de
su casa al otro lado del pueblo. Al ver su reflejo, se
detiene: está más grueso, y aún tiene la cabeza llena de
pelo. Lleva vaqueros y una sudadera en lugar de su bata de
hospital. No se siente genial, pero sin duda se siente
mejor que hace un par de segundos. Una funda plástica
cuelga de la barra de la ducha a sus espaldas. Le abre la
cremallera y encuentra un traje blanco en el interior. El
disfraz de espectro que Margaret confeccionó para la Tumba.

Hay un golpe en la puerta, y Margaret la abre. Va
vestida de Sepulturera, con un bigote falso pegado a la
cara.

—¿Por qué no te has vestido todavía? —pregunta.

—He perdido la noción del… —Cierra los ojos para
despejar la cabeza.

—¿Te encuentras bien?

Asiente.

—Sí.

—Entonces, date prisa, despistado. Se hace tarde.

Margaret cierra la puerta. Harry se desviste y se pone el traje encima. Tras volver a fijarse en su reflejo, abandona el lavabo, pero en lugar de salir a su habitación, se encuentra en el minúsculo apartamento que compartía con su mujer durante su época universitaria: un piso de un dormitorio con una alfombra raída y las paredes forradas de madera. Cajas llenas de sus libros de bolsillo, cómics y revistas *pulp* invaden la habitación. Sus cosas están por todos lados. La mesa de la cocina está enterrada bajo su máquina de escribir y pilas de artículos del colegio.

Tun.

El sonido parece provenir de la habitación. Abandona la sala atestada de cosas para investigar. Se ve a sí mismo y a Margaret en la cama, ambos con veintipocos años, tan guapos y saludables como podrán estarlo. Es tarde, y el Harry en la cama está dormido con la máscara de dormir de ella para que pueda dejar la luz encendida y leer. A su lado, Margaret levanta la mirada de su ejemplar de *La maldición de Hill House*, y se inclina hacia Harry para besarlo en la mejilla. El Harry en la cama continúa roncando, sin darse cuenta. El Harry que observa se toca la mejilla; siente una punzada de añoranza en el corazón.

El estallido azul y blanco atraviesa la ventana de la habitación como una llamarada. Cuando recupera la vista, está en una habitación diferente, una noche diferente. Al principio, su entorno parece ominosamente grande: la cama, la mesilla de noche, el tocador. Luego se mira el cuerpo y advierte que no es la habitación la que se ha agrandado. Es él quien se ha empequeñecido.

Tiene diez años, y ha caminado dando tumbos hasta la habitación de su madre en mitad de la noche porque ha creído oírla gritar. Solo ha encontrado el cubrecama arrugado sobre la cama. En la historia que contará innumerables veces a lo largo de su vida, este es el momento en el que se da la vuelta y corre a la sala, hacia

el teléfono que usará para llamar pidiendo ayuda. Admitirá
que lo que creyó oír debió de ser una pesadilla, porque
cuando la policía encuentra a su madre, descalza, magullada
y mareada, está a casi veinte kilómetros de la casa. Si ha
caminado hasta tan lejos, debe de haberse ausentado durante
horas. Es imposible que la haya oído llamarlo.

Pero esto es lo que realmente sucede: Harry se dirige a
la cama de su madre y la encuentra tibia. Al pasar la mano
sobre las sábanas, roza algo frío y duro. Levanta el
objeto. Es una piedra negra perfectamente lisa, y reluce
incluso en la oscuridad. Cuando la encierra en el puño, un
hoyo se abre en el mundo ante él, suave y redondo como la
piedra misma. A través de él, ve algo que no olvidará
jamás: un revoltijo inmenso y ciclópeo de diferentes tipos
de arquitectura: castillos medievales que colisionan contra
edificios de oficinas y estadios deportivos bajo un cielo
negro verdoso. Una bandada de criaturas vuela a través de
los cielos, pequeñas figuras con forma de murciélagos que
se recortan contra la fetidez.

De nuevo lo oye: su madre llamándolo por su nombre,
gritándolo desde muy lejos: *¡Harry! ¡Harry! ¡Harry, por
favor!*

Alejándose del hoyo del mundo, sus pies se enredan y se
cae al suelo. La piedra sale volando de su mano al apoyar
las palmas para sostenerse, y el portal se cierra. Sale
atolondrado por la puerta hacia el teléfono, buscando
adultos que puedan resolverle el problema.

Pero al salir a toda prisa de la habitación, la luz de
color azul emite un destello ante sus ojos, y cuando
recupera la vista, se ve a sí mismo, calvo y huesudo en la
cama de hospital (*lecho de muerte*), durmiendo. Una Margaret
embarazada está sentada en la silla junto a él,
observándolo con una expresión difícil de descifrar. Aparta
la mirada del Harry que duerme y la dirige a la carpeta de
anillas que descansa en el regazo de él, llena de diseños

para una casa embrujada del tamaño de una ciudad. Una expresión de fascinación cruza los rasgos de Margaret, y él sabe, como solo se saben las cosas en los sueños, que de algún modo su visión de la Ciudad, la imagen que lo ha condenado y fascinado durante toda su vida, ha infectado a toda su familia. La obsesión no acabará con su muerte.

Por primera vez en meses, puede sentir los bordes del tumor, y encuentra a su verdadero ser, el que lloraba cuando nacieron sus hijas y deseaba a la chica bonita de pelo rojizo de la librería. Su verdadero ser está avergonzado. Avergonzado de no haber escuchado a Eunice cuando le dijo que había visto algo en la ventana de su habitación, de no haber escuchado a Margaret cuando le enseñó las marcas de garras en el ladrillo fuera de la casa. Avergonzado de no haber escuchado cuando las mujeres de su vida intentaron decirle que algo iba mal. Avergonzado de haber fingido que todo iba bien y era normal cuando no lo era en absoluto.

Está a punto de caminar hacia Margaret al otro lado de la habitación, pero al alcanzarla, el destello de luz azul emite un resplandor fuera de la ventana y la escena vuelve a cambiar. Sigue en la habitación del hospital, pero ahora es el Harry en la cama. El dolor es más acuciante que nunca, y siente la respiración agitada en sus propios oídos. Apenas es consciente de Sydney a su lado, sosteniéndole la mano. Se vuelve hacia ella, porque tiene que contárselo a alguien, tiene que advertirles de algún modo. Parece tan asustada, tan deseosa de complacerlo. Ordena sus pensamientos, pero le cuesta. Es como intentar recoger hojas con un rastrillo con un viento fuerte.

Eunice tenía razón, dice con dificultad.

¿Papi?, dice ella.

Margaret, dice él.

Sydney. Soy Sydney, papi.

Los dibujos. Los diseños. Está todo allí. Tienes que hacerlo, dice.

¿Tengo que hacer qué?, pregunta Sydney.

Nos ha visto. Tiene nuestro rastro.

Y luego la escena vuelve a cambiar. Sigue en la cama de hospital, pero Sydney está de pie al otro lado de la habitación, con expresión sombría, mientras Margaret le entrega a él un bebé recién nacido.

Noah. El bebé se llama Noah. El cuerpo de Harry está atormentado por el dolor, pero su mente está despejada, y le han dado una segunda oportunidad para conocer a su hijo. Libre de las distorsiones del tumor, hay tanto que quiere decirle al chico, pero lo más importante, tal vez, es esto: la vida convierte a todos en monstruos, pero siempre es posible volver. El dolor y la muerte son reales, pero también lo son el amor, y la familia, y el perdón. Pero las palabras no le salen. En cambio, se inclina hacia delante y besa la frente de Noah y espera que este diminuto bulto rosado que es una persona crezca para entenderlo.

El estallido emite un nuevo resplandor fuera de la ventana, ahora mucho más rápido, y cuando su visión se despeja, parece estar en el jardín trasero de la Casa Embrujada, recostado encima de Margaret sobre una alfombra. Es octubre de 1968, y ella lo mira con esos ojos verdes, intentando decidir algo, y él sabe que se trata de algo importante, algo genial, pero antes de que ella pueda hablar, la alfombra se desploma por debajo. No, no se desploma. Permanece donde está. Él y Margaret son quienes se mueven, elevándose a través del aire, a la deriva. Y tampoco son los únicos. Al mirar alrededor, ve a decenas de otros que se elevan flotando hacia arriba, entre coches, bolsas de residuos, contenedores de basura, hojas muertas, equipamiento deportivo, periódicos, coches, gatos y perros: lo que sea que no esté atornillado al suelo se eleva a través del espacio. El cielo emite destellos: azul-blanco-azul-blanco-azul-blanco.

Margaret envuelve los brazos y las piernas alrededor de él, sosteniéndolo con fuerza. Giran elevándose lentamente, como Superman y Lois Lane bailando en los cielos. Quisiera poder volver a ver a Sydney y a Eunice. Quisiera ver cómo terminarán las cosas para ellas, si ellas y su pequeño hermano han conseguido quitarse el yugo que les ha colocado sobre los hombros. Pero tendrá que conformarse con esto. Con este último momento con Margaret.

La besa, su esposa graciosa, irascible y atormentada, y cuando se detiene, la encuentra sollozando.

Oh, Harry, dice. Él lo entiende. Él también lo siente. El peso de los años, del dolor, de todo aquello que ambos han perdido, cosas que incluso la muerte de la gravedad no puede alejar.

Está bien, dice él. La besa una y otra vez, sus mejillas, sus sienes, su mentón, el pelo encendido color rojizo. *Está todo bien. Te quiero, Margaret. Hasta el final de los tiempos y lo que venga después...*

AGRADECIMIENTOS

Stephen King dijo una vez: «Nadie escribe una novela solo». Estoy de acuerdo con él, pero me gustaría añadir que «Nadie se convierte en un novelista solo». Tengo una larga lista de profesores, profesionales, parientes y amigos que me han ayudado, y me gustaría dar las gracias a algunos de ellos en este espacio:

A mis editores, Tim O'Connell y Anna Kaufman, por su entusiasmo inagotable, sus ideas increíbles y su determinación inquebrantable por conseguir que esta historia llena de laberintos y espinos quedara absolutamente perfecta. A todo el equipo de Pantheon Books por poner al servicio del manuscrito toda su profesionalidad para convertirlo en un libro real: Susan Brown, editora de textos; Kathleen Fridella, editora de producción; Abigail Endler, publicista; Julianne Clancy, de marketing; Michael Collica, interiorista; Kelly Blair, diseñadora de cubierta, y, por supuesto, al editor Dan Frank.

A mi increíble agente literario Kent Wolf, que vio algo en este híbrido literario raro, y apostó por él. Gracias también a mis coagentes de cine y televisión, Lucy Carson y Kim Yau, que siguen cuidándome mucho en el terreno de los medios.

A mis suegros, Jim y Melany Harrelson, que me ofrecieron un sitio tranquilo y bonito para terminar de trabajar en este libro y que siempre están encantados de saber cualquier novedad del mundo literario.

A mi esposa talentosa y resistente, Rebekah, por alentar y apoyar este proyecto, incluso mientras sufría una embolia pulmonar y el arduo proceso para diagnosticar un trastorno autoinmune. Sus pinturas me acompañaban junto a mi escritorio a lo largo de la composición de esta novela y fueron una fuente de inspiración infinita.

Al Iowa Writer's Workshop, tanto a quienes lo mantienen en marcha —Connie Brothers, Deb West y Jan Zenisek— como a mis profesores:

Ethan Canin, que me recordó que la buena ficción tiene que ver con las personas; Lan Samantha Chang, que leyó mis primeras páginas y me dijo que quería sentirse atemorizada; Ben Hale, que no escatimó el buen asesoramiento técnico; y Paul Harding, que siempre me animó a buscar lo que era humano, honesto y verdadero, incluso en un libro lleno de casas embrujadas y monstruos.

A mis amigos y colegas del Iowa, que leyeron los primeros pasajes de esta novela y proporcionaron críticas constructivas: Jake Andrews, Kris Bartkus, Noel Carver, Patrick Connelly, Susannah Davies, Mgbechi Eroundu, Sarah Frye, Jason Hinojosa, J. M. Holmes, Erin Kelleher, Maria Kuznetsova, Jennie Lin, Alex Madison, Magogodi Makhene, Kevin Smith, Lindsay Stern, Nyoul Lueth Tong, Monica West y, especialmente, a Joe Cassara y Sorrel Westbrook-Wilson, colegas escritores y cómplices en el crimen.

A mis profesores de escritura en Texas: Kristin vanNamen y Matthew Limpede, de la revista *Carve*, y a Tim Richardson, Tim Martin y Joanna Johnson, de la Universidad de Texas en Arlington. A otra profesora de UTA que merece un elogio particular: Laura Kopchick, que me puso en este camino y sigue ofreciéndome oportunidades cada vez que puede.

Al Barnes & Noble de Arlington, Texas, donde trabajé durante ocho años. Aprendí a pelear las noches de lanzamientos de Harry Potter, escribí mi primer cuento de verdad mientras hacía de cajero, descubrí innumerables autores nuevos y conocí a mi esposa. No tengo una familia grande, pero el personal de aquella tienda me hizo sentir que la tenía.

Y a mis padres, Rick y Patrice Hamill. Papá se inventaba para mí todas las noches historias personalizadas a la hora de ir a dormir, y mamá me enseñó a prestar atención a los personajes y la estructura narrativa. Ellos fueron quienes me iniciaron en el amor por contar cuentos, siempre alentándome a escribir, y nunca podré estarles lo bastante agradecido.

NOTA SOBRE EL AUTOR

Oriundo de Arlington, Texas, Shaun Hamill se crio con una dieta permanente basada en las ficciones de terror y las películas de monstruos. Tiene un título de grado de la Universidad de Texas en Arlington y un máster en escritura creativa del Iowa Writers' Workshop. Su ficción ha aparecido en *Carve* y en *Spilt Infinitive*. Si realmente quieres ponerlo en una situación incómoda, ve a ver los cortometrajes en su IMDb. *El relato del monstruo* es su primera novela.

ECOSISTEMA DIGITAL

NUESTRO PUNTO DE ENCUENTRO

www.edicionesurano.com

2 AMABOOK
Disfruta de tu rincón de lectura
y accede a todas nuestras **novedades**
en modo compra.
www.amabook.com

3 SUSCRIBOOKS
El limite lo pones tú,
lectura sin freno,
en modo suscripción.
www.suscribooks.com

DISFRUTA DE 1 MES DE LECTURA GRATIS

1 REDES SOCIALES:
Amplio abanico
de redes para que
participes activamente.

4 APPS Y DESCARGAS
Apps que te
permitirán leer e
**interactuar con
otros lectores.**